POLITICAL AND CIVIC ENGAGEMENT

Based upon a three-year multi-disciplinary international research project, *Political and Civic Engagement* examines the interplay of factors affecting civic and political engagement and participation across different generations, nations and ethnic groups, and the shifting variety of forms this participation can take.

The book draws upon an extensive body of data to answer the following key questions:

- Why do many citizens fail to vote in elections?
- Why are young people turning increasingly to street demonstrations, charitable activities, consumer activism and social media to express their political and civic views?
- What are the barriers that hinder political participation by women, ethnic minorities and migrants?
- How can greater levels of engagement with public issues be encouraged among all citizens?

Together, the chapters in this volume provide a comprehensive overview of current understandings of the factors and processes that influence citizens' patterns of political and civic engagement. They also present a set of evidence-based recommendations for policy, practice and intervention that can be used by political and civil society actors to enhance levels of engagement, particularly among youth, women, ethnic minorities and migrants.

Political and Civic Engagement is an invaluable resource for all those who are concerned with citizens' levels of engagement, including: researchers and academics across the social sciences; politicians and political institutions; media professionals; educational professionals and schools; youth workers and education NGOs; and leaders of ethnic minority and migrant organisations and communities.

Martyn Barrett is Emeritus Professor of Psychology at the University of Surrey, UK. He also works as an expert for the Council of Europe, is a Fellow of the British Psychological Society and a Fellow of the Academy of Social Sciences.

Bruna Zani is Professor of Social and Community Psychology at the University of Bologna, Italy, and is currently Head of the School of Psychology and Education. She is a member of the Executive Committee of the European Community Psychology Association.

POLITICAL AND CIVIC ENGAGEMENT

Multidisciplinary perspectives

Edited by Martyn Barrett and Bruna Zani

LONDON AND NEW YORK

First published 2015
by Routledge
27 Church Road, Hove, East Sussex BN3 2FA

and by Routledge
711 Third Avenue, New York, NY 10017

Routledge is an imprint of the Taylor & Francis Group, an informa business

© 2015 Martyn Barrett and Bruna Zani

The right of the editors to be identified as the authors of the editorial material, and of the authors for their individual chapters, has been asserted in accordance with sections 77 and 78 of the Copyright, Designs and Patents Act 1988.

All rights reserved. No part of this book may be reprinted or reproduced or utilised in any form or by any electronic, mechanical, or other means, now known or hereafter invented, including photocopying and recording, or in any information storage or retrieval system, without permission in writing from the publishers.

Trademark notice: Product or corporate names may be trademarks or registered trademarks, and are used only for identification and explanation without intent to infringe.

British Library Cataloguing in Publication Data
A catalogue record for this book is available from the British Library

Library of Congress Cataloging-in-Publication Data
Political and civic engagement : multidisciplinary perspectives / edited by Martyn Barrett, Bruna Zani.
pages cm
Includes bibliographical references and index.
1. Political participation. 2. Civics. 3. Citizenship. I. Barrett, Martyn D. II. Zani, Bruna.
JF799.P6366 2014
323'.042–dc23
2014021469

ISBN: 978-0-415-70467-0 (hbk)
ISBN: 978-0-415-70468-7 (pbk)
ISBN: 978-1-315-75814-5 (ebk)

Typeset in Bembo
by Cenveo Publisher Services

To all those who made it possible to realise the research reported in this volume, especially the young people, women, ethnic minorities and migrants whose voices should be heard.

CONTENTS

List of contributors xi
Preface xv
List of abbreviations xix

PART I
Introduction 1

1 Political and civic engagement: theoretical understandings, evidence and policies 3
  Martyn Barrett and Bruna Zani

PART II
Theoretical understandings 27

2 Individual political participation and macro contextual determinants 33
  Kateřina Vráblíková and Ondřej Císař

3 Influencing women's civic and political participation: contextual and individual determinants 54
  Yvonne Galligan

4 Participation and integration: the contextual factors influencing minority and migrant participation 71
  Victoria Montgomery

5 How context shapes individual-level determinants of political
   participation: the impact of multiple negative party
   identification on turnout in deeply divided Northern Ireland   85
   John Garry

6 Standby citizens: understanding non-participation in
   contemporary democracies   96
   Erik Amnå and Joakim Ekman

7 Democratic ownership and deliberative participation   109
   Cillian McBride

8 Social and psychological factors influencing political and civic
   participation: a psychosocial perspective   124
   Elvira Cicognani and Bruna Zani

9 Explaining political participation: integrating levels of analysis   146
   Nicholas P. Emler

10 An integrative model of political and civic participation:
   linking the macro, social and psychological levels of explanation   162
   Martyn Barrett

PART III
Evidence   189

11 Political and civic participation: findings from the modelling
   of existing survey data sets   195
   Ian Brunton-Smith and Martyn Barrett

12 Civic organizations and the Internet as the opportunities
   for minority youth civic participation: findings from the
   Czech Republic   213
   Jan Šerek, Zuzana Petrovičová and Petr Macek

13 Participation and engagement of young people in Germany:
   findings on adolescents and young adults of German and
   Turkish family background   232
   Peter Noack and Philipp Jugert

14 Civic engagement among migrant youths in Sweden:
do parental norms or immigration generation matter? 248
Yunhwan Kim and Erik Amnå

15 Predictors of civic and political participation among native and
migrant youth in Italy: the role of organizational membership,
sense of community, and perceived social well-being 268
*Cinzia Albanesi, Davide Mazzoni Elvira Cicognani
and Bruna Zani*

16 Participation among youth, women, and migrants: findings
from the Wallonia-Brussels Federation of Belgium 292
Claire Gavray, Michel Born and Bernard Fournier

17 Participation among youth, women, and migrants:
findings from Portugal 311
*Maria Fernandes-Jesus, Carla Malafaia, Norberto Ribeiro
and Isabel Menezes*

18 Participation among Turkish, Roma, and Bulgarian
resettler youth living in Turkey 334
Tülin Şener

19 The expectations and understandings of influential others
who can mobilise youth participation: findings from England 352
Dimitra Pachi and Martyn Barrett

PART IV
Policies **373**

20 Europeanisation of policy discourses on participation
and active citizenship 377
Cristiano Bee and Roberta Guerrina

21 The 'Europeanisation' of gender policies in Portugal:
transformations in women's access to civil, political,
and social rights 403
*Norberto Ribeiro, Pedro D. Ferreira, Carla Malafaia and
Isabel Menezes*

22 Government perspectives on civic and political participation of youth and women in Turkey: deriving insights from policy documents 420
Sümercan Bozkurt, Figen Çok and Tülin Şener

23 Active citizenship in Italy and the UK: comparing political discourse and practices of political participation, civic activism and engagement in policy processes 436
Cristiano Bee and Paola Villano

PART V
Reflections and extensions 457

24 Cross-national political and civic engagement research on European adolescents and young adults: considerations at the individual, context, and process levels 461
Judith Torney-Purta and Jo-Ann Amadeo

25 The Council of Europe's work on 'Education for Democratic Citizenship and Human Rights Education' and its links to the PIDOP project 480
Reinhild Otte

26 In search of political participation 499
Giovanni Moro

Appendices

A The focus group guide used in the PIDOP project 512
B The interview schedule used in the PIDOP project 516
C The questionnaire used in the PIDOP project 519
D The recommendations for policy, practice and intervention which emerged from the PIDOP project 535
Martyn Barrett and David Garbin

Name index *549*
Subject index *553*

LIST OF CONTRIBUTORS

Cinzia Albanesi, Department of Psychology, University of Bologna, Bologna, Italy.

Jo-Ann Amadeo, Department of Psychology, Marymount University, Arlington, Virginia, USA.

Erik Amnå, School of Humanities, Education and Social Sciences, Örebro University, Örebro, Sweden.

Martyn Barrett, School of Psychology, University of Surrey, Guildford, UK.

Cristiano Bee, European Institute – Jean Monnet Center of Excellence, İstanbul Bilgi University, Istanbul, Turkey.

Michel Born, Faculty of Psychology and Education, University of Liège, Liège, Belgium.

Sümercan Bozkurt, Department of Political Science and Public Administration, Middle East Technical University, Ankara, Turkey.

Ian Brunton-Smith, Department of Sociology, University of Surrey, Guildford, UK.

Elvira Cicognani, Department of Psychology, University of Bologna, Bologna, Italy.

Ondřej Císař, Department of Sociology, Faculty of Social Sciences, Charles University, Prague, Czech Republic.

Figen Çok, Department of Educational Sciences, Guidance and Psychological Counseling, TED University, Ankara, Turkey.

Joakim Ekman, School of Social Sciences, Södertörn University, Flemingsberg, Sweden.

Nicholas P. Emler, School of Psychology, University of Surrey, Guildford, UK.

Maria Fernandes-Jesus, Faculty of Psychology and Educational Sciences, University of Porto, Porto, Portugal.

Pedro D. Ferreira, Faculty of Psychology and Educational Sciences, University of Porto, Porto, Portugal.

Bernard Fournier, Department of Political Science, Vrije Universiteit Brussel, Brussels, Belgium.

Yvonne Galligan, School of Politics, International Studies and Philosophy, Queen's University Belfast, Belfast, UK.

David Garbin, School of Social Policy, Sociology and Social Research, University of Kent, Canterbury, UK.

John Garry, School of Politics, International Studies and Philosophy, Queen's University Belfast, Belfast, UK.

Claire Gavray, Faculty of Psychology and Education, University of Liège, Liège, Belgium.

Roberta Guerrina, School of Politics, University of Surrey, Guildford, UK.

Philipp Jugert, Department of Psychology, University of Leipzig, Leipzig, Germany.

Yunhwan Kim, School of Law, Psychology and Social Work, Örebro University, Örebro, Sweden.

Cillian McBride, School of Politics, International Studies and Philosophy, Queen's University Belfast, Belfast, UK.

Petr Macek, Institute for Research of Children, Youth and Family, Masaryk University, Brno, Czech Republic.

Carla Malafaia, Faculty of Psychology and Educational Sciences, University of Porto, Porto, Portugal.

Davide Mazzoni, Department of Psychology, University of Bologna, Bologna, Italy.

Isabel Menezes, Faculty of Psychology and Educational Sciences, University of Porto, Porto, Portugal.

Victoria Montgomery, School of Politics, International Studies and Philosophy, Queen's University Belfast, Belfast, UK.

Giovanni Moro, FONDACA – Active Citizenship Foundation, Rome, Italy, and Faculty of Education, Roma Tre University, Rome, Italy.

Peter Noack, Department of Psychology, Friedrich-Schiller-University, Jena, Germany.

Reinhild Otte, Education for Democratic Citizenship and Human Rights (EDC/HRE), Council of Europe, Strasbourg, France.

Dimitra Pachi, Department of Psychology, BPP University, London, UK.

Zuzana Petrovičová, Institute for Research of Children, Youth and Family, Masaryk University, Brno, Czech Republic.

Norberto Ribeiro, Faculty of Psychology and Educational Sciences, University of Porto, Porto, Portugal.

Tülin Şener, Department of Psychological Services in Education, Ankara University, Ankara, Turkey.

Jan Šerek, Institute for Research of Children, Youth and Family, Masaryk University, Brno, Czech Republic.

Judith Torney-Purta, Department of Human Development and Quantitative Methods, University of Maryland, College Park, Maryland, USA.

Paola Villano, Department of Education, University of Bologna, Bologna, Italy.

Kateřina Vráblíková, Chair of Political Science and International Comparative Social Research, University of Mannheim, Mannheim, Germany.

Bruna Zani, Department of Psychology, University of Bologna, Bologna, Italy.

PREFACE

This book represents the culmination of a major international research project on political and civic engagement entitled *Processes Influencing Democratic Ownership and Participation (PIDOP)*. The project was funded by the European Commission under the 7th Framework Programme (FP7-SSH-2007-1, Grant Agreement No.: 225282). The project was funded for a period of 36 months, with a start date of 1 May 2009 and an end date of 30 April 2012. The project website can be found at: http://www.fahs.surrey.ac.uk/pidop/.

Of course, work on the project began long before 2009, and the analysis of the data from the project will continue long after 2012. Work for the project actually began back in 2007, when Bruna Zani first convened a group of European researchers with interests in youth civic engagement to consider submitting a grant application to the 7th Framework Programme. The key individuals in this initial group were Martyn Barrett, Michel Born, Elvira Cicognani, Figen Çok, Nick Emler, Margaret Kerr,[1] Evanthia Lyons, Isabel Menezes, Petr Macek, Peter Noack, Tülin Şener, Håkan Stattin and Bruna Zani. Because of his previous experience in running European research projects, Martyn Barrett took on the formal role of coordinator for the group. A first meeting took place in February 2007 at the University of Surrey, UK, at which the (not inconsiderable) realities of submitting a grant application to the European Commission were considered and a decision was made to proceed with the application. The research teams in the consortium grew as the proposal was developed, in particular to bring on board expertise from a much wider variety of academic disciplines as the scope of the project expanded. The expertise in the project eventually spanned the disciplines of Psychology, Politics, Sociology, Social Policy and Education. The research proposal was developed and written over a period of ten months and was finally submitted to the European Commission in November 2007. It was not until December 2008 that news was received that the application had been successful and that the project would be funded. Contract negotiations between the research consortium and the Commission took place between January and April 2009, and the consortium held its first 'kick-off' meeting in May 2009 at the University of Surrey. The nine research teams that made up the PIDOP research consortium were based at the following universities: University of Liège, Belgium; Masaryk University, Czech Republic; University of Jena, Germany; University of Bologna, Italy; University of Porto, Portugal; Örebro University, Sweden; Ankara University, Turkey; Queen's University Belfast, UK; and University of Surrey, UK.

Over the course of its development and execution, numerous individuals provided invaluable support and guidance for the project, and we would like to acknowledge these individuals here. First and foremost, we must thank the three Project Officers from the European Commission, Brussels, Belgium, who provided the PIDOP consortium with a great deal of extremely helpful guidance throughout the lifetime of the project: Jean-François Dechamp, Andreas Obermaier and Sylvie Rohanova. Sylvie, in particular, became a real champion of the project as it neared completion, providing the consortium with a great deal of support in the formulation of the policy recommendations, helping the project in its dissemination activities and organising a Policymakers Briefing Meeting which was held at the European Commission in Brussels in April 2012.

We would also like to thank several key individuals at the University of Surrey, UK (the coordinating institution for the project) for their help with the project. They include: Sophie Stos, the University's EU research funding officer, who gave Martyn Barrett an immense amount of support during the writing of the proposal and the process of contract negotiation; Phil Lidiard, a member of the University's pre-awards research administration services, who assisted with the costings and who, on behalf of the consortium, submitted all of the financial information which was required for the grant application to the European Commission; Simon Peacock and Sarah Gillies, members of the University's post-awards research administration services, who managed the finances of the project, including the distribution of the grant from the Commission to the research partners, the collation of financial information from the partners for periodic and final reporting purposes, and the auditing of the project's accounts; and Andrew Barnes, a member of the technical support staff of the School of Psychology, who built and maintains the website for the project. To all of these individuals, a very big thank you.

During its lifetime, the project also benefited from the expertise of its International Advisory Board. The Board was composed of renowned academic figures from a number of different disciplines, as well as influential activists and policy-makers concerned with political and civic engagement. The members of the Board were: Robert Andersen, University of Toronto, Canada; Jorge Benedicto, Universidad Nacional de Educación a Distancia, Spain; Eugene Borgida, University of Minnesota, USA; Jan van Deth, University of Mannheim, Germany; Udo Enwereuzor, Co-operation for the Development of Emerging Countries (COSPE), Florence, Italy; Constance Flanagan, University of Wisconsin-Madison, USA; Anita Harris,

Monash University, Australia; Annette Lawson, National Alliance of Women's Organisations and The Judith Trust, London, UK; Giovanni Moro, FONDACA – Active Citizenship Foundation, Rome, Italy; Reinhild Otte, Education for Democratic Citizenship and Human Rights (EDC/HRE), Council of Europe, Strasbourg, France; Philip Pettit, Princeton University, USA; Marian Sawer, Australian National University, Australia; Sidney Tarrow, Cornell University, USA; and Judith Torney-Purta, University of Maryland at College Park, USA. Our very grateful thanks to all the members of the Board.

Many other individuals also assisted the project in various ways over the years. Here, we would specifically like to thank Alberto Bertocchi and Elena Consolini, who helped to organise the first PIDOP conference held in Bologna, Italy, in May 2011; Mirela Dumic, who helped to organise the final PIDOP conference held at the University of Surrey, UK, in April 2012; and Christopher Reynolds, Council of Europe, who chaired the PIDOP Policymakers Briefing Meeting held at the European Commission in April 2012.

Finally, we would like to thank Annette and Giorgio, our long-suffering partners, for their incredible patience, tolerance, support and understanding while this book was being compiled.

Martyn Barrett and Bruna Zani
March, 2014

Note

1 Very sadly, Margaret Kerr passed away on 18 November 2012. An outstanding and consummate researcher, she was a committed and dedicated member of the PIDOP consortium until shortly before her death.

LIST OF ABBREVIATIONS

AJP	Action for Justice and Peace (Portugal)
ALECSO	Arab League Educational, Cultural and Scientific Organization
APA	American Psychological Association
BES	Equitable and Sustainable Well-being (Italy)
CEDAW	Convention on the Elimination of Discrimination Against Women
CEOMW	Grand National Assembly Commission on Equality of Opportunity of Men and Women (Turkey)
CIFP	Country Indicators for Foreign Policy
CIVED	Civic Education Study (IEA)
CNAI	National Centres of Immigrant Support (Portugal)
CP	community psychology
CDA	critical discourse analysis
CINGO	Conference of International Non-Governmental Organisations (CoE)
CLRA	Congress of Local and Regional Authorities (CoE)
CoD	Community of Democracies
CoE	Council of Europe
COSPE	Co-operation for the Development of Emerging Countries (Italy)
DA	discourse analysis
DG EAC	[EU] Directorate-General for Education and Culture
DGSW	Directorate General on the Status of Women (Turkey)
DNP	discursive nodal point
DUP	Democratic Unionist Party (Northern Ireland)
ECHR	European Convention on Human Rights
EDC/HRE	Education for Democratic Citizenship and Human Rights Education
EIGE	European Institute of Gender Equality

ERRC	European Roma Rights Center
ESS	European Social Survey
EWC	European Wergeland Centre
EYF	European Youth Forum
GDYS	General Directorate of Youth and Sports (Turkey)
GEI	Gender Equality Index
GGI	Global Gender Gap Index
GNI	Gross National Income
GSEU	General Secretariat for European Union
GSS	General Social Survey (US)
HREA	Human Rights Education Associates
ICCS	International Civic and Citizenship Study
IDEA	Institute for Democracy and Electoral Assistance
IEA	International Association for the Evaluation of Educational Achievement
INE	National Institute of Statistics (Portugal)
ICRC	International Committee of the Red Cross
ISSP	International Social Survey Programme
ISTAT	Italian National Institute of Statistics
JDP	Justice and Development Party (Turkey)
MdM	Doctors of the World
MRNI	Market Research Northern Ireland
MYS	Ministry of Youth and Sports (Turkey)
NGO	non-governmental organisation
NILT	Northern Ireland Life and Times survey
NIMBY	'not in my back yard'
OAS	Organization of American States
ODIHR	Office for Democratic Institutions and Human Rights
OECD	Organisation for Economic Cooperation and Development
OHCHR	Office of the High Commissioner for Human Rights
OSCE	Organisation for Security and Cooperation in Europe
PACE	Parliamentary Assembly of the Council of Europe
PIDOP	Processes Influencing Democratic Ownership and Participation
PMHRP	Prime Ministry Human Rights Presidency (Turkey)
PNAI	National Action Plan for Inclusion 2006–2008 (Portugal)
POS	political opportunity structure
PSAI	Political Studies Association of Ireland
RPP	Republican People's Party (Turkey)
SDLP	Social Democratic and Labour Party (Northern Ireland)
SEF	Foreigners and Border Services (Portugal)
SES	socio-economic status
SIMM	Awareness and Integration of Migrant and Marginalised Women: On the Road to Equality (Portugal)
SIT	social identity theory

SoC	sense of community
SIMCA	Social Identity Model of Collective Action
SPO	State Planning Organization (Turkey)
TPB	Theory of Planned Behavior
TESEV	Turkish Economic and Social Studies Foundation
TSI	Turkish Statistical Institute
UMAR	Union of Women Alternative and Response (Portugal)
UNDP	United Nations Development Programme
UNESCO	United Nations Educational, Scientific and Cultural Organisation
UUP	Ulster Unionist Party (Northern Ireland)
VPM	volunteer process model
WP	work package
WVS	World Values Survey

PART I

Introduction

The chapter in this opening section by Martyn Barrett and Bruna Zani provides an introduction to and overview of the book. It discusses what is meant by the term 'political and civic engagement' in the context of this book, and offers some observations on why political and civic engagement is important for democratic societies. The chapter also provides an overview of the range of factors that are related to political and civic engagement and of the multiple levels at which these factors operate. It is argued that the complexity of these factors and levels means that a multidisciplinary approach is required for the investigation of political and civic engagement. Four specific groups of individuals that have traditionally been considered to be at risk of disengagement and which are the focus of many of the discussions in this book are introduced: youth, women, ethnic minorities and migrants. The chapter then provides an overview of the PIDOP project, which was an international research project through which much of the theoretical, empirical and policy work reported in this book was conducted. The chapter concludes by offering a general overview of the structure and contents of the book.

1
POLITICAL AND CIVIC ENGAGEMENT

Theoretical understandings, evidence and policies

Martyn Barrett and Bruna Zani

This book aims to provide a comprehensive overview of current understandings of the factors and processes which influence the political and civic engagement of citizens. The book draws on theoretical insights provided by a range of disciplines including Politics, Sociology, Social Policy, Psychology and Education, presents a wealth of new evidence on political and civic engagement that has recently been gathered from across Europe, and reports on the policy discourses which frame debates about citizen participation in Europe. It also offers a series of wide-ranging reflections on the nature of political and civic engagement and disengagement, and presents a set of evidence-based recommendations for policy, practice and intervention that can be used by political and civil society actors to enhance levels of political and civic engagement and participation, particularly among youth, women, ethnic minorities and migrants.

Much of the discussion in this book is based on work which was conducted as part of an international research project funded by the European Commission under the Seventh Framework Programme, Processes Influencing Democratic Ownership and Participation (PIDOP). This multidisciplinary research project collected data on political and civic engagement in nine European countries and has significantly advanced our understanding of the factors and processes that influence citizen engagement and participation.

What is political and civic engagement?

Before proceeding further, however, it will be helpful to clarify the meanings of some of the key terms which are used throughout this book. Unless specified to the contrary, the term *citizen* is used in this book to refer to all individuals affected by political and civic decision-making and who can engage with political and civic processes through one means or another. Not all of those who are citizens in this broad sense of the term are legal citizens. For example, first-generation migrants may not have legal citizenship of the country in which they reside; however, even if they are unable to vote in national elections, they are able to participate in political and civic processes through a variety of other means, including community organisations, trade union membership and union politics, and membership of pressure groups (e.g. anti-racist, human rights or environmental organisations). This book generally uses the term *citizen* with this broader meaning.

The term *political engagement* is used in the book to denote the engagement of an individual with political institutions, processes and decision-making. By contrast, *civic engagement* is used to denote the engagement of an individual with the interests, goals, concerns and common good of a community. Here, *community* may be understood as denoting either the people who live within a particular geographical area (such as a neighbourhood, a town, a country or a transnational unit like Europe or Africa – or indeed the world in the case of the 'global community'), a more geographically diffused social or cultural group (such as an ethnic group, a religious group, a recreational group, an occupational group, a sexual orientation group, etc.), or any other kind of social or cultural group which might be salient to an individual.

Engagement typically involves participatory behaviours which are directed towards either the polity (in the case of political engagement) or a community (in the case of civic engagement). However, not all engagement is behavioural. One can have an interest in, pay attention to and have knowledge, opinions or feelings about political or civic matters without necessarily participating in any overt actions towards either the polity or the community. In other words, individuals can be cognitively or affectively engaged without necessarily being behaviourally engaged. Psychological engagement can be indexed in many different ways, for example via levels of political or civic knowledge, the intensity of feelings about political or civic matters, levels of attention to media sources such as newspapers, television news or news on the Internet, and the extent to which an individual discusses politics or civic affairs with family or friends.

However, political and civic engagement more usually involves not only psychological states and processes but also active participatory behaviours. The term *political participation* is used in this book to denote those behaviours that have the intent or the effect of influencing political institutions, processes and decision-making at either the local, regional, national or supranational level. These behaviours may be aimed either directly at influencing the content or the implementation of specific public policies, or more indirectly at influencing the selection of the individuals who are responsible for making those policies (cf. Verba *et al.* 1995).

Political participation takes many forms. Some forms involve electoral processes. These so-called *conventional* forms of political participation include voting, election campaigning, donating money to a political party, standing for election, etc. Other forms of political participation take place outside the electoral arena. These *non-conventional* forms of political participation include signing petitions, participating in political demonstrations, protests and marches, writing political articles or blogs, daubing political graffiti on buildings, etc. Both conventional and non-conventional political participation can be undertaken either alone (e.g. voting, writing a political article) or collectively in cooperation with other people (e.g. election campaigning, marching for a cause).

By contrast, the term *civic participation* is used in this book to refer to activity which is focused either on helping others within a community, working on behalf of a community, solving a community problem or participating in the life of a community more generally (cf. Zukin *et al.* 2006). Once again, such activity can include work which is undertaken either alone (e.g. helping an elderly neighbour, boycotting a product on environmental grounds) or in cooperation with others (e.g. attending a community meeting about an issue of concern, helping to construct a children's playground).

Thus, political and civic engagement and participation can take a wide variety of different forms (see Table 1.1, adapted from Barrett and Brunton-Smith, 2014).

TABLE 1.1 Some of the different forms of conventional political participation, non-conventional political participation, civic participation and psychological engagement

Forms of conventional political participation
- Voting
- Membership of a political party
- Running for political election
- Working on political election campaigns for candidates or parties
- Donating money to political parties
- Trying to persuade others to vote

Forms of non-conventional political participation
- Protests, demonstrations, marches
- Signing petitions
- Writing letters/emails to politicians or public officials
- Writing letters/emails/phone calls with a political content to the media (both old and new media)
- Writing articles/blogs with a political content for the media (both old and new media)
- Using social networking sites on the Internet to join or like groups which have a political focus
- Using social networking sites on the Internet to distribute or share links which have a political content to friends and contacts
- Wearing or displaying a symbol or sign representing support for a political cause
- Distributing leaflets which express support for a political cause
- Participating in fund-raising events for a political cause
- Writing graffiti on walls which expresses support for a political cause
- Participating in other illegal actions (e.g. burning a national flag, throwing stones, rioting, etc.) in support of a political cause
- Membership of political lobbying and campaigning organisations/attending meetings of these organisations/expressing one's point of view at these meetings/participating in the activities of these organisations/holding an office in these organisations

(Continued)

TABLE 1.1 Some of the different forms of conventional political participation, non-conventional political participation, civic participation and psychological engagement *(Continued)*

Forms of civic participation
- Informally assisting the well-being of others in the community
- Community problem-solving through community organisations/membership of community organisations/attending meetings of these organisations/expressing one's point of view at these meetings/participating in the activities of these organisations/holding an office in these organisations
- Membership of other non-political organisations (e.g. religious institutions, sports clubs, etc.)/attending meetings of these organisations/expressing one's point of view at these meetings/participating in the activities of these organisations/holding an office in these organisations
- School-based community service
- Undertaking organised voluntary work
- Translation and form-filling assistance for non-native speakers
- Sending remittances to others living elsewhere
- Donations to charities
- Fund-raising activities for good causes
- Consumer activism: boycotting and buycotting (preferential buying)

Forms of psychological engagement
- Paying attention to or following political or civic events
- Having political or civic knowledge or beliefs
- Holding opinions about political or civic matters
- Having feelings about political or civic matters
- Having political or civic skills
- Understanding political or civic institutions
- Understanding or holding political or civic values

Adapted from Barrett and Brunton-Smith (2014).

In addition, a further distinction may be made between those who are engaged vs. those who are disengaged. *Disengagement* is displayed when an individual does not exhibit any of the characteristics of engagement (such as those shown in Table 1.1). Individuals can be disengaged for a variety of reasons. Some people may be passively and quietly *apolitical* while others may be actively and strongly *antipolitical*. In other words, some disengaged individuals might think that politics is uninteresting and boring and feel no desire or need to participate or to make their voices heard, while others might refuse to engage with or participate in politics by any means, perhaps because they think that politics is fundamentally objectionable, corrupt and dishonest (Ekman and Amnå 2012). A parallel conceptual distinction can be drawn between those who are *acivic* and those who are *anticivic*, that is, between those who simply keep themselves to themselves and do not feel any need to engage in activities with or on behalf of other people, and those who are more actively opposed to engaging with others, perhaps because they are suspicious and mistrustful of other people.

Why is political and civic engagement important in democratic societies?

Citizens' political and civic engagement is important in democratic societies for a variety of reasons. First, in a democracy, the political engagement of citizens through voting in elections is extremely important because, if too few citizens vote, it is unclear whether the government that is elected has the consent of the people to govern and whether there is sufficient popular support for the decisions and actions of that government. Such a government may be viewed as suffering from a democratic deficit (i.e. as failing to fulfil the basic principles of democracy) and, as a consequence, lacking in legitimacy.

Second, within healthy democracies, governments also need to be kept under scrutiny and actively monitored in order to ensure that citizens are protected against the arbitrary exercise of power and to ensure that decision-makers are not dishonest or corrupt. Democratic governments are, of course, held to account for their decisions and actions at periodic elections, but it is arguable that such governments should be required to account for their decisions and actions not only at elections but throughout their terms of office. In order to perform this monitoring function effectively, citizens need to be politically engaged.

Third, citizen participation is also required in a democracy to enable public authorities to make better-informed decisions. If citizens do not communicate their views to decision-makers, the latter may be deprived of vital information which is needed to reach informed outcomes, with the result that they may then make ill-informed decisions which have negative or deleterious consequences for citizens. This point is especially important in the case of disadvantaged and marginalised groups. The views of such groups often fail to achieve any formal representation at the political level due to the design of electoral systems. In such cases, if the politically excluded do not attempt to influence decision-making through non-electoral means, the decisions that are made on their behalf may well not respond to their concerns or meet their needs. For this reason, the perspectives, preferences, choices and opinions of such groups must be actively expressed by their members so that they can be taken into account when decisions affecting their lives are being made, and it is crucial that such expressions are attended to and heard by those in power (Phillips 1995; Young 2000).

Fourth, and extending the arguments beyond the political sphere to include the civic sphere as well, it has been argued by some authors that participation is an inherently beneficial and valuable activity in its own right for citizens (e.g. Pateman 1970; Putnam 2000; Smith 2009). This is because participation helps individual citizens build up a wide range of personal and social capacities, including a sense of personal efficacy, a sense of responsibility towards others, an appreciation of civic duty, social capital, trust, and civic and political skills. In other words, participation helps to enrich the lives of individuals – it leads to personal empowerment and the sense that one has the ability and the agency to make decisions and to influence change in one's own life and the lives of others, and it helps citizens to fulfil their own interests and to attain benefits for themselves and other people. There is also evidence that participation enhances people's sense of subjective well-being, life satisfaction and tolerance towards others (Morgan and Streb 2001; Putnam 2000; Stutzer and Frey 2006).

A fifth argument frequently made on behalf of participation is that citizens themselves are the most appropriate people to judge what is in their own best interests, and therefore political decisions need to be made with the active involvement of those whose lives are going to be affected and bound by those decisions. Without citizens' involvement in the deliberations leading to decision-making, any decisions that are made will lack democratic legitimacy. Given that most decisions are controversial, decision-making based on a process of public deliberation between citizens on the basis of equality is the most defensible justification that can be offered for provisionally settling these issues (Cohen 1989; Fishkin 1991; Gutmann 1996). Such a process of deliberation, which can aid the acceptance of controversial collective decisions and confer democratic legitimacy on them, requires the active engagement and participation of citizens.

However, this fifth argument is controversial. To participate actively in decision-making can require specialised capacities, and some have argued that citizens often lack the knowledge, competence and expertise needed to make well-informed and coherent judgments and decisions (Schumpeter 1976). Thus, while citizen initiatives and democratic innovations might work well for small-scale communities such as neighbourhoods, recreational associations and local communities, the challenges for political decision-making at city, regional, national or indeed supranational level usually exhibit a completely different order of complexity (Dahl 1998). Furthermore, if participation is made simple and undemanding to aid deliberation by citizens, then this may only encourage a lack of careful consideration of issues, a failure to give full and proper consideration to the views of others, the expression of poorly informed opinions and the promotion of self-interested actions which, if taken into account, could result in very poor decisions being made (Esaiasson 2010). Hence some political theorists have argued that increasing citizens' influence over decision-making at a large-scale political level is undesirable because it is likely to result in much poorer decisions being made than those that would be made through representative democratic procedures.

While the relative merits of representative vs. direct deliberative democracy are clearly open to debate, we would argue that citizen engagement and participation within democratic societies are crucial for: (1) conferring legitimacy on elected governments; (2) monitoring governments and holding them accountable for their actions; (3) giving voice and expression to the views of citizens so that their perspectives can be factored into public decision-making; and (4) enriching and empowering the lives of citizens. Thus encouraging and fostering citizens' political and civic engagement and participation is an important goal within any democratic society.

That said, there are some forms of citizen participation which should never be encouraged or fostered. These include forms aimed at undermining the very principles of democracy, human rights and the rule of law, and forms seeking to promote hatred and intolerance towards others. These limits on citizen participation have been expressed and defended most extensively and vigorously by the Council of Europe in its numerous publications and activities (see Council of Europe 2012, 2014).

The range of factors and processes related to political and civic engagement

However, in order to enhance citizen participation effectively, especially among disadvantaged and marginalised groups, it is necessary to understand the underlying factors and processes which facilitate and hinder political and civic engagement so that these can be harnessed or tackled through appropriate actions, policies or interventions. Previous research has revealed that political and civic engagement and participation are related to factors and processes operating at four main levels: the macro-contextual level, the demographic level, the social level and the psychological level.

At the *macro-contextual* level, citizens' patterns of engagement are related to factors such as the historical longevity of democracy in a country, the structure of political institutions and the opportunities for participation which these institutions make available to citizens, and the rules and design of the electoral system. For example, the importance which young people attribute to conventional political participation tends to be higher in countries in which democratic institutions have been strengthened in the previous 30 years (Torney-Purta et al. 2001); citizens who live in states with decentralised political institutions with a dispersed power structure and a large number of independent veto points in the system have higher levels of non-electoral participation than citizens who live in states with highly centralised institutions in which decision-making power is concentrated at the centre (Kriesi et al. 1995; Vráblíková 2014); and the turnout of citizens to vote in national elections is higher in countries where voting is compulsory, voter registration processes are simple and multiple elections are held concurrently (Geys 2006).

Patterns of political and civic engagement are also related to *demographic* factors such as socio-economic status (SES), gender and ethnicity. For example, people who have higher levels of education and income typically also have higher levels of political and civic engagement (Verba et al, 1995; Wolfinger and Rosenstone 1980); males and females often differ in their levels of political interest, participation in voluntary organisations and voter turnout (van Deth and Elff 2000; Inglehart and Norris 2003; Barnes and Kaase 1979); and there are differences in political and civic engagement as a function of ethnicity even after income and educational attainment have been taken into account (Diehl and Blohm 2001; Foster-Bey 2008).

Social factors such as parental attitudes and behaviours, educational practices, practices in the workplace and membership of associations are also related to patterns of engagement and participation. For example, parents' political interest, participation in protests and civic volunteering are commonly related to their offspring's patterns of political and civic engagement (Schulz et al. 2010; Zukin et al. 2006;

Jennings 2002); having an open classroom climate at school (i.e. the opportunity to discuss controversial social issues and to express and listen to differing opinions in the classroom) is related to people's political interest, trust, civic knowledge and likelihood of voting in the future (Hahn 1998; Torney-Purta et al. 2001); involvement in workplace decision-making is related to the likelihood of being involved in campaigning for a political party and being involved in the affairs of one's local community (Sobel 1993); and there is a strong relationship between membership of civic associations and political participation (Putnam 2000; Stolle 2007).

Finally, at the *psychological* level, patterns of political and civic participation are related to people's perceptions, beliefs, feelings and motivations. For example, overall levels of both civic and political participation are related to the extent to which an individual is politically attentive and knowledgeable, feels politically efficacious, identifies with a political party and is infused with a sense of civic duty (Zukin et al. 2006); the willingness to take part in collective protest is related to the perception of injustice, the strength of subjective identification with the group and the belief that the goals of the protest are achievable (van Zomeren et al. 2008); and the longevity of voluntary service is linked to the strength of the personal motivations underlying the volunteering and the satisfaction derived from volunteering (Omoto and Snyder 1995).

Given the fact that patterns of political and civic engagement are related to factors at all four levels, and the likelihood that the processes which drive citizens' engagement are a product of highly complex interactions between multiple factors both within and across these four levels, it is clear that any theoretical explanation of engagement which does not address factors at all four levels will, at best, only be a partial explanation. To obtain a comprehensive understanding of the processes that drive the engagement and participation of citizens in political and civic affairs, it is instead necessary to adopt a multidisciplinary perspective, in particular a perspective which spans the social science disciplines that have different levels of analysis as their primary foci. For this reason, the work which was conducted in the PIDOP project and which is reported in this book was based from the outset on a close collaboration between political scientists, sociologists and psychologists. This scientific work was used to generate a set of evidence-based recommendations concerning the actions which may be taken by a range of political and civil actors to enhance citizens' levels of engagement and participation, especially levels of engagement among disadvantaged or marginalised groups who might be judged to be at risk of disengagement.

Groups potentially at risk of disengagement

Traditionally, four specific groups of individuals have been considered to be at risk of disengagement: youth, women, ethnic minorities and migrants. In addition, individuals of lower SES typically exhibit lower levels of engagement and participation.

As far as *youth* are concerned, many researchers and observers have drawn attention to the historically low levels at which youth have been voting in elections in recent years, and this has given rise to the expression of concern about the future of democracy in countries in which youth appear to have become disengaged from conventional politics (International IDEA 2008; MacFarlane 2005; Putnam 2000). However, this trend in voting behaviour needs to be balanced against other evidence which suggests that a shift is currently taking place among younger generations, with non-conventional political and civic participation coming to be prioritised over more traditional forms of political participation (Forbrig 2005; Marsh et al. 2007; Zukin et al. 2006). As a result, issues that might have mobilised individuals into taking conventional political action in the past now often appear to be tackled instead by many young people through voluntary, community and charitable activities, consumer activism, and protests and demonstrations. Thus it is possible that while traditional forms of political participation such as voting are currently in decline in many European countries (International IDEA 2004), this trend may not be indicative of public disengagement per se but of a shift to a qualitatively different kind of public activism.

If this is the case then the prognosis that the process of generational replacement will inevitably result, over time, in a significant erosion of the public engagement of citizens may well be wrong. This is because civic participation in young people is actually a good predictor of political engagement and participation in later life (Sherrod et al. 2002; Verba et al. 1995) and promotes a sense of belonging to one's community as well as personal and social competencies for political action (Albanesi et al. 2007; de Piccoli et al. 2004; Hansen et al. 2005; Morgan and Streb 2001; Stewart and Weinstein 1997). However, the processes which are currently driving younger people away from conventional political participation towards other forms of participation are poorly understood.

Concerns have also been expressed about the low levels of participation that are sometimes exhibited by *women*, and indeed previous research has identified a wide range of factors that are responsible for gender differences in political participation (Barnes and Kaase 1979; Burns et al. 2001; Inglehart and Norris 2003). These factors can be grouped into three broad categories: cultural and societal (e.g. the religion of a country, the level of economic development of a country, the longevity of democratic traditions within a country), social (e.g. level of education, labour force participation, marriage, motherhood) and civic (e.g. degree of participation in informal politics, membership of voluntary civic organisations) (Galligan 2012). However, precisely how these various factors interact to generate the differences in patterns of participation between women and men is still not well understood.

Ethnic minorities and migrants have also been found to exhibit lower levels of political participation than those displayed by members of national majority groups, a pattern which is not surprising given the restrictive criteria and practices and the racism and discrimination that often prevent minority and migrant individuals from participating fully in the political life of the country in which they live (Ahmad and Pinnock 2007; Martiniello 2005; Penninx et al. 2004; Phillips 1995). Levels of participation among ethnic minorities and migrants have been found to be linked to a wide range of factors, including cultural and societal factors (e.g. the cultural heritage of the minority group, the political institutions and opportunities that are made available within the country of residence), demographic and social factors (e.g. migrant generational status, nationality, employment status, level of education, membership of community organisations, social capital) and individual and psychological factors (e.g. fluency in the language of the country of residence, political values, knowledge of civic and political institutions in the country of residence, sense of belonging). However, we currently have a poor understanding of how these various factors interact to generate patterns of participation by minority and migrant individuals.

Finally, there is also good evidence that individuals who are of lower SES often exhibit lower levels of political and civic engagement and participation: they tend to have poorer political and civic knowledge (Delli Carpini and Keeter 1996; Hart and Atkins 2002; Schulz et al. 2010) and participate civically and politically to a lesser extent (Bynner et al. 2003; Foster-Bey 2008; Zukin et al. 2006). For example, two of the main indices of SES, education and income, are both independently related to political knowledge (Delli Carpini and Keeter 1996); to interest in politics, voting and the absence of a cynical view of politics and politicians (Bynner et al. 2003); and to the likelihood of volunteering, attending community meetings and working on neighbourhood problems (Foster-Bey 2008). The likelihood is that education is the principal driver here. Education influences the civic skills that individuals come to exercise in their jobs and other organisations as well as their later social networks, and these civic skills and social networks are the more immediate influences on various aspects of psychological engagement (including political attentiveness, political interest and political knowledge) and various forms of political and civic participation (including voting, contacting public officials, donating campaign money, working on campaigns, protesting, working with others on community problems and attending meetings on a regular basis) (Brady et al. 1995; Nie et al. 1996; Verba et al. 1995).

All of these issues were at the core of the PIDOP project, which investigated political and civic engagement across Europe with the aim of explaining, and finding ways to enhance, levels of political and civic participation, particularly among youth, women, ethnic minorities and migrants.

The PIDOP project

It is clear that the political and civic engagement of citizens is a highly complex phenomenon which requires a multidisciplinary approach for its investigation. Furthermore, because macro-contextual factors affect the engagement of citizens, a cross-national comparative approach is also essential to enable analysis of the influence of these factors. For these reasons, a multidisciplinary cross-national comparative approach was adopted by the PIDOP project. The project examined the factors and processes that influence political and civic engagement and participation in nine European countries – Belgium, Czech Republic, England, Germany, Italy, Northern Ireland, Portugal, Sweden and Turkey. The project drew on the disciplines of Politics, Sociology, Social Policy, Psychology and Education, and it examined the macro-contextual factors (including political, institutional, electoral, economic and policy factors), demographic factors (including age, gender, ethnicity and SES), social factors (including family, educational and media factors) and psychological factors (including motivational, cognitive, affective, attitudinal and identity factors) which facilitate and/or inhibit political and civic engagement.

Because many of the chapters in this book are based on research that was conducted under the PIDOP project, additional background information about the project is provided here.

The PIDOP research teams and their locations

The locations of the nine research teams that participated in the PIDOP project were as follows:

- University of Liège, Belgium
- Masaryk University, Czech Republic
- University of Surrey, England
- University of Jena, Germany
- University of Bologna, Italy
- Queen's University Belfast, Northern Ireland
- University of Porto, Portugal
- Örebro University, Sweden
- Ankara University, Turkey[1]

These countries were chosen to ensure that the consortium as a whole contained countries which varied on a number of different features, including:

- countries where voter turnout has fallen since 1988 (e.g. Italy, Portugal, England) vs. countries where it has not fallen (e.g. Belgium, Sweden);
- countries where voting is compulsory (Belgium, Turkey) vs. countries where voting is voluntary (other countries);
- countries with different historical periods over which free elections have been held: throughout the lifetime of present-day voters (England), consistently since 1945 (Italy), for a quarter of a century (Portugal) and recently democratised (Czech Republic);
- countries which have joined the EU at different historical points in time, including founder members (Belgium, Germany, Italy), older members (UK, joined 1973), less old members (Portugal, 1986), newer members (Sweden, 1995), a recent accession member (Czech Republic, 2004), and a country currently outside the EU (Turkey);
- countries in which some third-country nationals are granted voting rights at the local, regional and/or national level (Portugal, Sweden, UK) vs. countries which do not allow foreign nationals to vote in elections at any level unless they are nationals of EU countries (Germany, Italy);

- countries with specific potentially relevant characteristics, including a post-communist state which is in the process of political and social transformation (Czech Republic), a state which has recently been reunified (Germany), a state in which Muslims are in the majority (Turkey) and a country which has experienced deep sectarian division and repeated reinstitutions/suspensions of a devolved assembly (Northern Ireland).

These characteristics of the specific countries which participated in the PIDOP project should be borne in mind when reading the chapters in this book, particularly the chapters in Parts III and IV.

The aims of the PIDOP project

The PIDOP project had five overarching aims. These were:

- To audit existing theory and research on political and civic engagement and participation in the disciplines of Politics, Sociology, Social Policy, Psychology and Education.
- To audit and analyse existing policies on political and civic engagement and participation within Europe.
- To identify empirically the factors and processes which are responsible for political and civic engagement and participation within Europe, particularly among youth, women, minorities and migrants (four groups which the European Commission had identified as being at risk of disengagement).
- To develop multilevel theoretical understandings of the factors and processes responsible for political and civic engagement and participation.
- To formulate, based on the findings of the project, new evidence-based recommendations for policy, practice and intervention, specifying the actions which may be taken by social and political actors to enhance levels of participation, particularly among youth, women, minorities and migrants.

The work package structure of the PIDOP project

In order to achieve these objectives, the work undertaken in the PIDOP project was broken up into a series of discrete work packages (WPs). There were six research WPs:

- Collation and analysis of current policies on participation (WP2)
- Development of political theories of participation (WP3)
- Development of psychological theories of participation (WP4)
- Modelling existing survey data on political and civic participation (WP5)
- Collection and analysis of new data on political and civic participation (WP6)
- Theoretical integration and the development of recommendations for policy and practice (WP7)

In addition there were two project management work packages:

- Consortium management and coordination activities (WP1)
- Dissemination activities (WP8)[2]

The work carried out under each of the six research WPs was as follows.

Collation and analysis of current policies on participation (WP2)

The primary aim of WP2 was to identify and describe the dominant policy discourses at EU, national and regional levels that are relevant to political and civic participation, with a particular focus on youth, women, minorities and migrants. WP2 explored similarities and differences in the ways in which these groups are considered at EU, national and regional levels, and investigated the extent to which there is coherence or tension between relevant policies at these levels. It also analysed the views of policy-makers and members of relevant policy networks. Thus the WP aimed to provide an understanding of the policy contexts within which the project would be collecting data on political and civic participation and within which the new policy recommendations would be formulated towards the end of the project.

Discourse analysis (Hajer 2002; Howart and Torfing 2005) was used to analyse the official documents of public institutions and NGOs (e.g. white papers, green papers, policy briefs, reports, position papers, etc.) in order to identify the key concepts underlying policies on participation and the metanarratives that are used to justify these concepts. In addition, semi-structured interviewing was used with policy-makers and activists in all of the participating countries. These interviews examined the various stages of the policy cycle, with a focus on agenda setting by different institutional and non-institutional policy actors, exploring the importance of the power relations existing between the various actors, and their attempts to shape the meanings of specific policy concepts.

A set of core policy concepts was uncovered in the course of the analyses, with different concepts being used by policy actors in different contexts and in different countries. These concepts included, inter alia, the need for greater levels of active citizenship and participation among citizens, the value of participatory democracy, respect for human rights, social inclusion, social justice, anti-discrimination and the integration of minorities.

Chapters 20 to 23 in Part IV of this book are based on work which was carried out under WP2.

Development of political theories of participation (WP3)

WP3 was responsible for: (1) auditing existing theory and research on political and civic engagement and participation, particularly in the disciplines of Politics, Sociology and Social Policy; (2) conducting an analysis of the macro-contextual factors which influence political and civic participation; and (3) generating new theoretical insights into engagement and participation from the perspectives of Politics, Sociology and Social Policy which could be used to inform the empirical work which was to be conducted by WP5 and WP6.

Macro-influences on participation were analysed at the institutional level (e.g. the roles played by political opportunity structure, structural inequalities, mobilising channels and civic education), the country level (e.g. the political history, economic development and religion of a country) and the supranational level (e.g. the political opportunity structure created by international institutions such as the EU). In addition, WP3 examined demographic, social and individual level factors, including group norms, roles within the family, and SES and the resources which are associated with this status. Conceptual and theoretical work was also conducted on the different forms that political and civic engagement and participation may take, the nature of political passivity, and the role of the civic sphere in enhancing and/or inhibiting participation.

Chapters 2 to 7 in Part II of this book are based on work which was conducted under WP3.

Development of psychological theories of participation (WP4)

Complementing WP3, WP4 was responsible for: (1) auditing previous research on political and civic engagement and participation in the disciplines of Psychology, Political Science and Education; (2) conducting an analysis of the social and psychological factors which influence political and civic participation; and (3) generating new theoretical insights into engagement and participation from the perspectives of Psychology, Political Science and Education which could be used to inform the empirical work which was to be conducted by WP5 and WP6.

The audit of existing research identified the wide range of social factors that can influence political and civic engagement and participation, which may be classified as stemming from seven main sources: the family, education, the peer group, the workplace, the mass media, non-political organisations and political institutions. WP4 also identified the numerous psychological factors that are related to political and civic participation, including cognitive factors (e.g. knowledge, beliefs, attitudes, opinions and social and cultural values), affective factors (both positive and negative emotions), feelings of efficacy, trust, social identifications, personal motivations and goals, and perceptions of opportunities for and barriers to participation. In addition to this audit of previous research, WP4 developed several new theoretical models of how the various psychological factors might relate to one another and of how the social factors might relate to psychological factors.

Chapters 8 to 10 in Part II of this book draw upon work which was conducted under WP4.

Modelling existing survey data on political and civic participation (WP5)

While WP3 and WP4 were concerned with generating theoretical ideas for empirical investigation, WP5 was responsible for analysing existing survey data. The aim here was to identify empirically the factors that are associated with political and civic participation within Europe. There were two main sub-goals here: (1) to describe patterns of political and civic participation across EU member states over time and across key demographic groupings; and (2) to identify the factors which are related to the variations in these patterns of political and civic participation across EU member states.

In order to achieve these goals, WP5 drew together data from a number of international surveys that contain questions relating to participation: the European Social Survey, Eurobarometer, the International Social Survey Programme, the Comparative Study of Electoral Systems and the World Values Survey. The analyses conducted on these datasets included: basic descriptive statistics; structural equation models examining the psychological and demographic factors that are related to participation (guided by the theoretical models developed in WP4); multilevel models linking these micro processes to broader macro-contextual factors (guided by the thinking developed in WP3); and latent class analysis to identify distinct 'classes' of political participation. Four types of participation were examined by WP5 in these analyses: voting, other forms of conventional political participation, non-conventional political participation and civic participation.

A summary of the main results which were obtained in WP5 are reported in Chapter 11 in Part III of this book.[3]

Collection and analysis of new data on political and civic participation (WP6)

While WP5 was responsible for the analysis of data from existing survey datasets, WP6 was responsible for collecting new data. WP6 was specifically designed to target variables which were not always present in the WP5 survey datasets but which WP3 and WP4 had revealed to be of theoretical importance. The overall aim of WP6 was to examine political and civic engagement among members of different age, gender, minority and migrant groups within each participating country, and to examine differences in the factors and processes which are related to engagement in these different demographic groups in the different national contexts.

For WP6, each team in the consortium collected data from their own local national group and two ethnic minority or migrant groups living in their country. The national and ethnic groups which were studied in each country were as follows:

- *Belgium*: Belgians, Turks, Moroccans
- *Czech Republic*: Czechs, Roma, Ukrainians

- *England*: English, Congolese, Bangladeshis
- *Germany*: Germans, German resettlers from Russia, Turks
- *Italy*: Italians, Albanians, Moroccans
- *Northern Ireland*: Northern Irish (both Catholics and Protestants), Chinese, Poles
- *Portugal*: Portuguese, Brazilians, Angolans
- *Sweden*: Swedes, Kurds of Turkish background, Iraqis
- *Turkey*: Turks, Roma, Turkish resettlers from Bulgaria

In all of these groups, data were collected from 16- to 26-year-olds, in order to capture possible differences in political and civic participation and engagement before vs. after achieving voting age. Both genders were represented in the samples, and the analyses explored interactions between gender and national, ethnic and migrant status. The data were collected in three phases, as follows.

Phase 1: Focus groups

In phase 1, focus groups were conducted with 16- to 26-year-olds from all 27 national and ethnic groups. In total, 117 focus groups involving 740 participants were conducted. The group discussions explored perceptions of citizenship and participation as these individuals viewed them across a wide range of different life contexts. Issues examined included: personal and group experiences of participation; perceptions of opportunities for, and barriers to, participation; sources of information about participation; influences on attitudes to participation; the relevance of participation for young people; perceptions of social exclusion; and proposals for inclusion.

The focus group guide which was used to structure the focus group discussions is given in Appendix A at the end of this book.

Phase 2: Individual interviews

In phase 2 of WP6, interviews were conducted with some of the individuals who had been identified during the focus groups as important sources of influence on the focus group participants. These interviews primarily involved parents, teachers and youth workers, as these were the most frequently cited sources of influence. The interviews examined the conceptions of citizenship which were held by these influential individuals, their perceptions of young people's patterns of participation, their perceptions of young people's motivations for participating, their perceptions of the barriers to young people's participation, the practical measures which they themselves take to try to enhance young people's participation, and their suggestions for promoting young people's inclusion and civic and political participation. A total number of 96 individual interviews were conducted.

The semi-structured interview schedule which was used for these interviews is given in Appendix B at the end of this book.

Phase 3: Quantitative survey

Phase 3 of WP6 consisted of a quantitative survey. On the basis of the theoretical models developed by WP3 and WP4, and the findings which had emerged from the focus groups and the interviews, a quantitative questionnaire was designed. This questionnaire was administered to 16- to 26-year-olds in all of the participating countries, with data being collected from both males and females from all 27 national and ethnic groups.[4] In total, data were collected from 8,197 participants. The variables that were measured in the survey included: political interest; political attentiveness; participation in the previous 12 months; perceived effectiveness of participation; future intentions for participation; participation and involvement in civic and political organisations; quality of participation; private citizenship; motivations for participation; perception of barriers to participation; internal efficacy; external efficacy; collective efficacy of youth; collective efficacy of own ethnic group; collective efficacy of own gender group; political knowledge; social norms for participation; trust in institutions; trust in government and forms of government; interpersonal trust; emotions in response to concrete issues; social well-being; sense of community; strength of identification with ethnic group, religious group, nationality, country of origin, gender, age and being European; religiosity; support for minority rights; personal experience of discrimination; and Left–Right political orientation. In addition, detailed demographic information about each participant was collected, including information about SES and family configuration.

A copy of the core questionnaire which was used for the survey is given in Appendix C at the end of this book.

Chapters 12 to 19 in Part III of this book report some of the findings obtained in WP6.

Theoretical integration and the development of recommendations for policy and practice (WP7)

The final research work package, WP7, had two main goals. The first was to produce a theoretical integration of the outputs from the preceding theoretical and empirical WPs. The second goal was to use the research findings from the project to formulate evidence-based recommendations for policy, practice and intervention which can be used to enhance civic and political engagement and participation, especially among youth, women, minorities and migrants.

The task of theoretical integration required a synthesis of the theoretical work conducted by WP3 and WP4 on macro, demographic, social and psychological factors, taking into account the findings from WP5 and WP6. A number of theoretical papers were produced addressing these issues. Chapters 6, 9 and 10 in the present book draw upon this body of work which was conducted in WP7.

Across WPs 3 to 6, the project identified a large range of factors which can promote political and civic participation as well as a large range of factors which can inhibit or hamper participation. In the light of the findings which emerged from

WP5 and WP6 in particular, WP7 developed a series of recommendations for policy, practice and intervention concerning the actions which may be taken by social and political actors and institutions to enhance political and civic participation among youth, women, migrants and minorities. These policy recommendations were broken down under the following four main headings:

- Recommendations for politicians and political institutions
- Recommendations for media producers and media organisations
- Recommendations for ministries of education, educational professionals and schools
- Recommendations for civil society actors, including youth workers, youth and leisure centres, youth and education NGOs and leaders of ethnic minority communities

The full set of recommendations for policy, practice and intervention which emerged from the PIDOP project is given in Appendix D at the end of this book.

Outputs from the PIDOP project

To date, papers reporting findings from the PIDOP project have been published in a variety of locations, including a special issue of the journal *Human Affairs* (Zani and Barrett 2012) and a special issue of the *Journal of Civil Society* (Bee and Guerrina 2014). A comprehensive and up-to-date listing of all the published outputs from the project, and of all the conference papers that have been based on the project, is available on the PIDOP project website at http://www.fahs.surrey.ac.uk/pidop/.

The structure and contents of the current book

The subsequent chapters in this book have been organised into four parts, as follows.

In Part II, theoretical approaches to and understandings of citizen engagement and participation are explored. This section of the book serves to re-emphasise the sheer number and variety of factors which can influence citizen engagement and participation at the macro, demographic, social and psychological levels. It is clear from these chapters that there are complex interactions between these various factors, both within levels and across levels. Numerous forms of engagement and participation are examined in these chapters, including voting, other forms of conventional political participation, non-conventional political participation, civic participation and psychological engagement. Attention is also devoted to the phenomenon of non-participation, and to how participation through deliberation can provide the conditions for creating a sense of democratic ownership. The final two chapters in this part of the book attempt to integrate theoretical explanations across the multiple levels of analysis.

The chapters in Part III of the book present new empirical evidence on political and civic engagement obtained in the various countries participating in the PIDOP project. The first chapter in this section provides an overview of the findings obtained through the secondary analysis of existing survey data sets, and demonstrates the complex interactions which occur between macro, demographic and psychological factors in influencing political and civic participation. For the remaining chapters in this part, each participating research team analysed a specific subset of the data which they collected for the project in their own country, highlighting aspects of civic and political participation which have particular relevance in their own social and political context. Each team chose minority or migrant groups which are salient within their own country, and used qualitative and/or quantitative methods to investigate the demographic, social and/or psychological factors that either facilitate or hamper engagement and participation in different populations within individual countries. The findings which are presented by these chapters provide an extremely rich and detailed account of the enormous variability in the factors and processes which influence engagement and participation depending on the particular aspect of engagement which is under scrutiny, the particular national/ethnic and demographic group which is involved, and the particular country in which that group is living.

Part IV of the book is devoted to policies on citizens' political and civic engagement, not only national policies but also EU policies that have been developed by the European Commission. National policies, in particular, form an important part of the institutional macro-context within which citizen engagement occurs. Although there is often an implementation gap between official government policy and actual practices on the ground, national policies are commonly used to frame debates and ways of thinking about political and civic engagement within individual countries. The chapters in this part provide analyses of policy texts at both national and EU level, and identify the key discourses which underlie these texts as well as the convergences and divergences between national and EU policies. In addition, they offer accounts of how civic activists working for non-governmental organisations regard national and EU policies. The analyses in this part of the book reveal that governance bodies can have varying approaches to the issue of active citizenship depending on the target group concerned (e.g. youth, women, ethnic minorities or migrants), that different policy approaches can be adopted towards the same target groups in different countries, and that the interpretation of policies by activists can vary significantly from one national context to another.

The final part of the book, Part V, consists of three chapters written by scholars external to the PIDOP project but who served on the project's International Advisory Board, providing feedback on the project's activities and outcomes. They offer a range of reflections and observations on the project and on the nature of political and civic engagement. In the first chapter, similarities and differences between PIDOP and the IEA 1999 Civic Education Study are illustrated and discussed. Particular attention is given to the implications of the two projects for understanding individual differences, contexts and processes, and to the adequacy of the findings of both projects for understanding the topic of civic and political engagement in adolescence and early adulthood. The second chapter focuses on the links between the PIDOP project and the Council of Europe's work on 'Education for Democratic Citizenship and Human Rights Education', discussing their differences, similarities and interconnections. The final chapter in this part provides reflections on the changing nature of citizenship and participation in the contemporary world, and the implications which these changes hold for social science research and the types of data which are required to investigate political and civic engagement. These three chapters together raise important questions and challenges that need to be addressed by future research in this field.

Conclusion

Political and civic engagement has become the focus of a great deal of attention from politicians, social commentators, the media and concerned citizens in recent years. This concern has arisen in part because of declining levels of conventional political participation, especially voting, in many countries. Such a trend, if continued into the future, poses a significant threat to the legitimacy of democratic governance. In addition, concerns are also often expressed about low rates of participation among youth, women, ethnic minorities and migrants.

Given these concerns about citizen engagement and participation, it is important to understand, from an informed social-scientific perspective, the underlying factors and processes which are responsible for these shifts in citizen behaviour. Such an understanding may then be used to help formulate effective policies and interventions to counter the changes in behaviour which are judged to be of concern, where this is deemed to be appropriate and beneficial. The hope is that the chapters in the current book will not only contribute to the formulation of an informed social-scientific understanding of political and civic engagement, but will also contribute to the identification of appropriate actions that can be taken by political and civil society actors to enhance citizen engagement and participation, thereby strengthening our democratic societies and enriching the lives of the citizens who live within them.

Notes

1 These research teams were led by the following individuals: Belgium – Michel Born; Czech Republic – Petr Macek; England – Martyn Barrett; Germany – Peter Noack; Italy – Bruna Zani; Northern Ireland – Evanthia Lyons; Portugal – Isabel Menezes; Sweden – Erik Amnå; Turkey – Tülin Şener. The project was coordinated by Martyn Barrett and the project manager was David Garbin.
2 Across the lifetime of the project, these eight work packages were led by the following individuals: WP1 – Martyn Barrett; WP2 – Roberta Guerrina, Rachel Brooks and Cristiano Bee; WP3 – Yvonne Galligan; WP4 – Nick Emler, Bruna Zani and Martyn Barrett; WP5 – Tereza Capelos and Ian Brunton-Smith; WP6 – Isabel Menezes and Evanthia Lyons; WP7 – Peter Noack and Martyn Barrett; WP8 – Martyn Barrett and Bruna Zani.

3 The full technical report of the findings of WP5 is available online from: http://epubs.surrey.ac.uk/739988/2/PIDOP_WP5_Report.pdf_revised.pdf.
4 In a few cases, teams collected data from a slightly broader age range, from 15 to 29 years overall.

References

Ahmad, N. and Pinnock, K. (2007) *Civic Participation: Potential Differences between Ethnic Groups*. London: Commission for Racial Equality.

Albanesi, C., Cicognani, E. and Zani, B. (2007) 'Sense of community, civic engagement and social well-being in Italian adolescents', *Journal of Community and Applied Social Psychology*, 17: 387–406.

Barnes, S. H. and Kaase, M. (1979) *Political Action: Mass Participation in Five Western Democracies*. Beverly Hills, CA: Sage.

Barrett, M. and Brunton-Smith, I. (2014) 'Political and civic engagement and participation: towards an integrative perspective', *Journal of Civil Society*, 10 (1): 5–28.

Bee, C. and Guerrina, R. (eds) (2014) 'Framing civic engagement, political participation and active citizenship in Europe', Special issue of *Journal of Civil Society*, Vol. 10 (1).

Brady, D., Verba, S. and Schlozman, K. L. (1995) 'Beyond SES: a resource model of political participation', *American Political Science Review*, 89: 271–94.

Burns, N., Schlozman, K. L. and Verba, S. (2001) *The Private Roots of Public Action: Gender, Equality, and Political Participation*. Cambridge, MA: Harvard University Press.

Bynner, J., Romney, D. and Emler, N. (2003) 'Political and related facets of identity in late adolescence', *Journal of Youth Studies*, 6: 319–35.

Cohen, J. (1989) 'Deliberative democracy and democratic legitimacy', in A. Hamlin and P. Pettit (eds), *The Good Polity: Normative Analysis of the State*. Oxford: Blackwell, pp. 17–34.

Council of Europe (2012) *The Council of Europe – 800 Million Europeans. Guardian of Human Rights, Democracy and the Rule of Law*. Strasbourg: Directorate of Communication, Council of Europe. Available from: https://www.coe.int/AboutCoe/media/interface/publications/800_millions_en.pdf (date accessed 8 January 2014).

Council of Europe (2014) Council of Europe home page at: http://hub.coe.int/ (date accessed 8 January 2014).

Dahl, R. (1998) *On Democracy*. New Haven, CT: Yale University Press.

de Piccoli, N., Colombo, M. and Mosso, C. (2004) 'Active participation as an expression of the sense of community', in A. Sánchez Vidal, A. Zambrano Constanzo and M. Palacín Lois (eds), *Psicologia Comunitaria Europea: Comunidad, Ética y Valores*. Barcelona: Publicacions Universitat de Barcelona, pp. 262–71.

Delli Carpini, M. and Keeter, S. (1996) *What Americans Know about Politics and Why It Matters*. New Haven, CT: Yale University Press.

Diehl, C. and Blohm, M. (2001) 'Apathy, adaptation or ethnic mobilisation? On the attitudes of a politically excluded group', *Journal of Ethnic and Migration Studies*, 27 (3): 401–20.

Ekman, J. and Amnå, E. (2012) 'Political participation and civic engagement: towards a new typology', *Human Affairs*, 22 (3): 283–300.

Esaiasson, P. (2010) 'Is citizen political involvement always a plus?', in E. Amnå (ed.), *New Forms of Citizen Participation: Normative Implications*. Baden-Baden: Nomos Verlagsgesellschaft, pp. 15–20.

Fishkin, J. S. (1991) *Democracy and Deliberation: New Directions for Democratic Reform*. New Haven, CT: Yale University Press.

Forbrig, J. (ed.) (2005) *Revisiting Youth Political Participation*. Strasbourg: Council of Europe.

Foster-Bey, J. (2008) *Do Race, Ethnicity, Citizenship and Socio-economic Status Determine Civic Engagement?* CIRCLE Working Paper No. 62. Medford, MA: Tufts University.

Galligan, Y. (2012) 'The Contextual and Individual Determinants of Women's Civic Engagement and Political Participation'. Unpublished paper, Work Package 3, PIDOP Project.

Geys, B. (2006) 'Explaining voter turnout: a review of aggregate-level research', *Electoral Studies*, 25: 637–63.

Guowei, J. and Jeffres, L. (2008) 'Spanning the boundaries of work: workplace participation, political efficacy, and political involvement', *Communication Studies*, 59: 35–50.

Gutmann, A. (1996) 'Democracy, philosophy, and justification', in S. Benhabib (ed.), *Democracy and Difference*. Princeton, NJ: Princeton University Press, pp. 340–7.

Hahn, C. (1998) *Becoming Political: Comparative Perspectives on Citizenship Education*. Albany, NY: State University of New York Press.

Hajer, M. A. (2002) 'Discourse analysis and the study of policy making', *European Political Science*, 2 (1): 61–5.

Hansen, D. M., Larson, R. W. and Dworkin, J. B. (2005) 'What adolescents learn in organized youth activities: a survey of self-reported developmental experiences', *Journal of Research on Adolescence*, 13: 25–55.

Hart, D. and Atkins, R. (2002) 'Civic development in urban youth', *Applied Developmental Science*, 6: 227–36.

Howart, D. and Torfing, J. (2005) *Discourse Theory in European Politics*. Basingstoke: Palgrave Macmillan.

Inglehart, R. and Norris, P. (2003) *Rising Tide: Gender Equality and Cultural Change Around the World*. Cambridge: Cambridge University Press.

International IDEA (Institute for Democracy and Electoral Assistance) (2004) *Voter Turnout in Western Europe since 1945: A Regional Report*. Stockholm: International IDEA.

International IDEA (Institute for Democracy and Electoral Assistance) (2008) *Youth Voter Participation: Involving Today's Young in Tomorrow's Democracy*. Stockholm: International IDEA.

Jennings, M. K. (2002) 'Generation units and the student protest movement in the United States: an intra- and intergenerational analysis', *Political Psychology*, 23: 303–24.

Kriesi, H., Koopmans, R., Duyvendak, J. W. and Giugni, M. G. (1995) *New Social Movements in Western Europe: A Comparative Analysis*. London: UCL Press.

MacFarlane, B. (2005) 'The disengaged academic: the retreat from citizenship', *Higher Education Quarterly*, 59: 296–312.

Marsh, S., O'Toole, T. and Jones, S. (2007) *Young People and Politics in the UK: Apathy or Alienation?* London: Palgrave.

Martiniello, M. (2005) 'Political participation, mobilisation and representation of immigrants and their offspring in Europe', *Willy Brandt Series of Working Papers in International Migration and Ethnic Relations*, 1/05. Malmö: Malmö University.

Morgan, W. and Streb, M. (2001) 'Building citizenship: how student voice in service-learning develops civic values', *Social Science Quarterly*, 82: 154–69.

Nie, N. H., Junn, J. and Stehlik-Barry, K. (1996) *Education and Democratic Citizenship in America*. Chicago: University of Chicago Press.

Omoto, A. M. and Snyder, M. (1995) 'Sustained helping without obligation: motivation, longevity of service, and perceived attitude change among AIDS volunteers', *Journal of Personality and Social Psychology*, 68: 671–86.

Pateman, C. (1970) *Participation and Democratic Theory*. Cambridge: Cambridge University Press.

Penninx, R., Martiniello, M. and Vertovec, S. (eds) (2004) *Citizenship in European Cities: Immigrants, Local Politics and Integration Policies*. London: Ashgate.

Phillips, A. (1995) *The Politics of Presence*. Oxford: Oxford University Press.

Putnam, R.D. (2000) *Bowling Alone: The Collapse and Revival of American Community*. New York: Simon & Schuster.

Schulz, W., Ainley, J., Fraillon, J., Kerr, D. and Losito, B. (2010) *Initial Findings from the IEA International Civic and Citizenship Education Study*. Amsterdam: IEA.

Schumpeter, J. (1976) *Capitalism, Socialism and Democracy*. London: Allen & Unwin.

Sherrod, L. R., Flanagan, C. and Youniss, J. (2002) 'Dimension of citizenship and opportunities for youth development: the what, why, when, where and who of citizenship development', *Applied Developmental Science*, 6: 26472.

Smith, G. (2009) *Democratic Innovations: Designing Institutions for Citizen Participation*. Cambridge: Cambridge University Press.

Sobel, R. (1993) 'From occupational involvement to political participation: an exploratory analysis', *Political Behavior*, 15: 339–53.

Stewart, E. and Weinstein, R. S. (1997) 'Volunteer participation in context: motivations and political efficacy within three AIDS organizations', *American Journal of Community Psychology*, 25: 809–37.

Stolle, D. (2007) 'Social capital', in R. J. Dalton and H. D. Klingemann (eds), *The Oxford Handbook of Political Behavior*. Oxford: Oxford University Press, pp. 655–75.

Stutzer, A. and Frey, B. S. (2006) 'Political participation and procedural utility: an empirical study', *European Journal of Political Research*, 45: 391418.

Torney-Purta, J., Lehmann, R., Oswald, H. and Schulz, W. (2001) *Citizenship and Education in Twenty-Eight Countries: Civic Knowledge and Engagement at Age Fourteen*. Amsterdam: IEA.

van Deth, J. and Elff, M. (2000) *Political Involvement and Apathy in Europe 1973–1998*, MZES Working Paper No. 33. Mannheim: MZES.

van Zomeren, M., Postmes, T. and Spears, R. (2008) 'Toward an integrative social identity model of collective action: a quantitative research synthesis of three socio-psychological perspectives', *Psychological Bulletin*, 134: 504–35.

Verba, S., Schlozman, K. L. and Brady, H. E. (1995) *Voice and Equality: Civic Volunteerism in American Politics*. Cambridge, MA: Harvard University Press.

Vráblíková, K. (2014) 'How context matters? Mobilization, political opportunity structures, and nonelectoral political participation in old and new democracies', *Comparative Political Studies*, 47 (2): 203–29.

Wolfinger, R. E. and Rosenstone, S. J. (1980) *Who Votes?* New Haven, CT: Yale University Press.

Young, I. M. (2000) *Justice and the Politics of Difference*. Princeton, NJ: Princeton University Press.

Zani, B. and Barrett, M. (eds) (2012) 'Engaged citizens? Political participation and social engagement among young people, women, minorities and migrants', Special Issue of *Human Affairs: Postdisciplinary Humanities and Social Sciences Quarterly*, Vol. 22, Part 3.

Zukin, C., Keeter, S., Andolina, M., Jenkins, K. and Delli Carpini, M. X. (2006) *A New Engagement? Political Participation, Civic Life, and the Changing American Citizen*. New York: Oxford University Press.

PART II
Theoretical understandings

In this part, a variety of theoretical views on the factors and processes which influence political and civic engagement are explored in detail. Between them, the chapters in this section highlight the sheer range of factors at the macro contextual, demographic, social and psychological levels that have been implicated in previous research, as well as the complexity of the interactions that occur across the factors operating at the different levels. These issues are discussed from several different disciplinary perspectives. All forms of engagement and participation are examined in this part of the book, including voting, other forms of conventional political participation, non-conventional political participation, civic participation and psychological engagement. The nature of non-participation and political passivity in contemporary democracies is also examined, as is the role of deliberation for providing the conditions under which a sense of democratic ownership may be established among citizens. The two final chapters in this part offer attempts at integrating theoretical explanations across levels of analysis.

In Chapter 2, **Kateřina Vráblíková and Ondřej Císař** begin the discussion by considering *macro contextual* influences on individual political participation, including both conventional and non-conventional forms of participation. They consider three main categories of macro influences: political institutions, socio-economic conditions and political culture. Drawing on the existing research literature, they demonstrate that these three categories of macro factors do not only have direct effects on the political participation of individuals, they also have indirect effects via their influence on individuals' social networks and mobilisation, attitudes and values, and socio-economic resources. The implication is that the effects of the macro context on individual citizens are not uniform: these effects vary, with different groups of citizens being affected in different ways, and factors operating across different levels interact with one another in complex ways. Vráblíková and Císař argue that theories of macro characteristics need to be specified much more precisely so that the various routes and interactions through which the macro context affects individual participation can be disentangled.

Chapter 3, by **Yvonne Galligan**, focuses on the contextual and individual determinants of *women's civic and political participation*. She considers not only the different structural opportunities which are available to women and men, but also how the gendered socio-political environment structures women's orientation to civic activities and politics differently from men's. She shows how many factors are responsible for women's patterns of participation, including educational levels, labour market participation, the lack of time for participation, the cues that are transmitted by institutions and organisations, opportunities to engage which differ for women and for men, and the cultural and social norms that shape the nature of the gender contract within society. Cultural and social norms in particular can predispose women to be uninterested in politics, and can contribute to women's lower sense of efficacy in relation to the political world, their lower levels of trust in political institutions, and a lower orientation to engage in acts of political participation.

Participation by *ethnic minority individuals and migrants* forms the focus of Chapter 4 by **Victoria Montgomery**. She discusses the factors which impact negatively on participation by minorities and migrants. These include macro contextual factors such as the use of language ability tests to disenfranchise minority individuals, the marginalisation of minority identities and values within the public sphere, and the use of an electoral system which systematically discriminates against minorities and migrants because it either requires the negotiation of bureaucratically complex registration procedures, permanent residence (which discriminates against nomadic minorities and migrants) and/or fails to deliver effective representation for minorities. Montgomery also describes the demographic and social factors which are linked to the exclusion and marginalisation of minorities and migrants from the public sphere, especially low socio-economic status, low levels of education and poor language skills. However, she also draws attention to the ways in which associational activity can enhance minority and migrant individuals' engagement through socialisation and education, equipping them with the resources which they need to participate in the public sphere. Montgomery argues that public institutions and political systems need to include the identities and concerns of minority communities to encourage them to participate fully in society, and that a multicultural approach which explicitly links participation to issues of identity and integration offers the best way forward. Such an approach requires both non-discrimination policies and policies to ensure that there is genuine equality in outcomes.

Chapter 5, by **John Garry**, further examines how both macro contextual and psychological factors influence individuals' political participation, focusing specifically on *voter turnout*. He notes that turnout is influenced by many macro factors, including population characteristics (e.g. population size, stability, concentration and homogeneity), political factors (e.g. the closeness of the electoral contest, campaign expenditure and political fragmentation), and institutional factors (e.g. compulsory vs. optional voting, holding concurrent elections, registration requirements, voting on a rest day vs. a working day, and the type of electoral system which is used). In addition, Garry outlines how psychological factors may impact on voter turnout (e.g. political efficacy, trust in parties and politicians, the perception that there is little choice on offer). He then explores in detail how identification with political parties is related to turnout, noting that identification may be either positive or negative and that citizens may identify with more than just a single party. Analysing data from Northern Ireland, he demonstrates how the Northern Irish macro context (in which the ethno-national question and conflict-related Northern Irish issues are prioritised) generates complex patterns of party identification which in turn are systematically related to voter turnout. Macro- and individual-level factors intertwine to influence individual behaviour.

In Chapter 6, **Erik Amnå and Joakim Ekman** change the focus of the discussion to the issue of *political passivity*. They argue for a more nuanced understanding of passivity which differentiates between, on the one hand, individuals who are completely disengaged from politics and therefore do not participate politically and show little interest in political matters and, on the other hand, individuals who have high levels of political interest but nevertheless do not participate. Those in the latter category engage in activities that reveal an involvement with society and an interest in current affairs (such as discussing politics with others and consuming political news in the media). They also show an awareness of political issues, have political knowledge and skills, and hold informed opinions about politics. However, they do not engage in participatory actions in relationship to the political world. Amnå and Ekman argue that individuals in this latter category display latent as opposed to manifest political participation, and should be construed as standby citizens who are not currently active, perhaps because they have high levels of trust in politicians and political institutions but are nevertheless prepared and ready to participate should they perceive a need to do so. They note that, in a recent study which they conducted with Swedish adolescents, the standby category formed the largest group of individuals in their sample, and they suggest that this may be a common orientation in contemporary democracies.

The role of *deliberation* in providing the conditions under which a sense of *democratic ownership* may be established among citizens is discussed in Chapter 7, by **Cillian McBride**. He suggests that, in a properly functioning democracy, citizens should be able to view the political decisions which affect their lives as being, in some way, the result of their collective will, and the institutions and procedures which have produced these decisions, as their own – in other words, they should feel that they have ownership of the decisions that are made. This is because, if they have a sense of ownership, they will then have reasons to respect and uphold those decisions, independently of any sanctions which may be applied. McBride argues that a deliberative democracy grounded upon fair procedures is essential for generating such a sense of ownership. Fair procedures are those that impose upon citizens who wish to advance a particular position a duty of justification to fellow citizens who are respected as equals. Fair procedures must also offer all citizens a genuine and equal opportunity to participate in the shaping of public opinion and thereby to have an influence on the decisions that are eventually made. While not all citizens may take up these opportunities, their existence will at least enable them to suppose that all relevant perspectives have been considered in the deliberation process from which political decisions emerge. The open availability of such opportunities to all is thus the minimal condition which must be met for citizens to feel a sense of democratic ownership over the decisions that affect their lives.

In Chapter 8, by **Elvira Cicognani and Bruna Zani**, the *social and psychological factors* which influence political and civic engagement take centre stage. This chapter reviews the research literature on the social psychology of collective action and protest, the social psychology of volunteers and volunteerism, and the community psychology of citizen participation. Drawing on these three bodies of research, Cicognani and Zani provide a detailed account of the numerous social and psychological factors that have been found to be related to people's patterns of political and civic participation. These include cognitive resources such as knowledge, beliefs and attitudes, personal motivations and goals, emotions, social identifications, and perceptions of barriers to, and opportunities for, participation. Summarising all of the psychosocial concepts which need to be taken into account in a unifying model of political and civic participation, Cicognani and Zani argue that such a model will need to incorporate all of the following elements: personal and demographic factors; individual and shared cognitions about the social world and participation; motivations and goals; emotions, both positive and negative; social and collective identities and the sense of belonging; the sense of perceived control, power and influence (both collective and individual); perceptions of opportunities for and barriers to participation; and actual engagement and participation experiences.

The final two chapters in this section of the book draw together many of the strands that have been covered in the preceding chapters in attempts to move the field towards a more *integrative approach* which incorporates reference to all four levels of factors and processes: the macro contextual, the demographic, the social and the psychological. Chapter 9, by **Nicholas Emler**, focuses specifically on political rather than civic participation and uses two lenses to frame the discussion: the variations that exist in political participation between individuals, and the declining rates of political participation over recent years. Starting with *psychological engagement*, he identifies a number of factors which determine individuals' capacity and inclination for participation: political interest, political attentiveness, political knowledge, political opinions, self-efficacy, ideological commitment and cost-benefit calculations. However, these psychological factors in turn are related to a host of *social factors*, including education (which, however, appears to operate to share out political resources differentially across citizens rather than increasing psychological resources per se), membership of organisations and associations (which provide contexts for political discussion and mobilisation), income, occupational prominence and social network centrality. In addition, Emler argues that these social factors, which of course all vary demographically, interact with aspects of the *macro political context*, especially institutional design, with the decentralisation of institutional structures and the horizontal separation of powers being implicated here in particular: thus, in states in which institutions are characterised by greater decentralisation, organisational membership and political discussion are more strongly associated with political participation. Emler concludes that the decline in participation in recent years is probably due to the decline in personal ties at the social level which have resulted from recent changes in occupational and recreational patterns and lifestyle.

Chapter 10, by **Martyn Barrett**, also attempts an integrative synthesis of the factors and processes at multiple levels which are related to political and civic engagement. He begins by providing a summary overview of all the numerous macro, social and psychological factors which are now known to be related to political and civic participation. *Macro factors* include the characteristics of the electoral, political and legal institutions and the historical, economic, cultural and population characteristics of countries; *social factors* include the factors that are associated with the family, education, the peer group, the workplace, the mass media, non-political organisations and political institutions; and *psychological factors* include cognitive resources such as knowledge, beliefs, attitudes, opinions and values, personal motivations and goals, negative and positive emotions, social identifications, and perceptions of barriers to, and opportunities for, participation. The review also notes how social and psychological factors are related to *demographic factors* such as family socio-economic status, family ethnicity and, in the case of migrants, generational status. Barrett goes on to provide an outline sketch of an integrative model of all these various factors, which attempts to articulate some of the causal pathways through which these factors might interact with one another and through which they might influence political and civic engagement and participation. The model focuses on voting, collective action and volunteering as three distinctive forms of conventional political, non-conventional political and civic participation, respectively.

The chapters in this part of the book reveal a great deal about the complexities of political and civic engagement and the sheer number of factors and processes that are involved. The chapters in the following third part of the book draw upon these theoretical formulations and report the findings of new studies which have advanced our understanding still further.

2

INDIVIDUAL POLITICAL PARTICIPATION AND MACRO CONTEXTUAL DETERMINANTS

Kateřina Vráblíková and Ondřej Císař[1]

Introduction

The macro-context, traditionally understood by the comparative politics literature as the nation state, obviously has an effect on individual political participation. The available studies have shown dramatic cross-country differences in how active citizens of various states are in politics; explanations of participation across these countries can differ, too. Until lately the lesson taken from these observations has been that social phenomena must be studied in their particular contexts, which in practice meant controlling for the country context in various ways. For instance, studies have analysed individual political participation separately in particular countries or geographical regions, such as the old Western democracies and the newer democracies of Central-Eastern Europe, or South America.

However, this 'context sensitivity' recognises the role of the macro-context only to a limited extent. As argued by the classical comparative social science literature decades ago, the macro-context should be seen as a research puzzle in itself, not just as an inconvenient element inserting error into the quasi-universalist laws governing human behaviour. The macro-context should be approached theoretically as a relevant explanation of its elements and the processes taking place within it. Specifically, even the macro-context of national states is characterised by attributes that systematically influence individual political participation and the processes that affect it within these contexts (see the chapter by Brunton-Smith and Barrett in this volume). Hence the crucial research question is obvious: What are the relevant characteristics of the macro-context, and how do they affect individual-level political participation?

Only recently has this question begun to be asked and more systematically examined by the literature on political participation. This holds especially for political participation beyond voting. While macro-contextual research on voter turnout has been a more or less well-established stream of research, only lately has the macro-contextual perspective on individual non-electoral political participation both in terms of theories and their empirical testing triggered much political participation research. The goal of this chapter is to review the available literature on the macro-contextual determinants of individual political participation, particularly non-electoral participation. Before doing that, we will first discuss the classical agenda of political participation theories, which have emphasised the individual predispositions of potential participants, and have also studied the 'meso-level' predictors such as mobilisation and social networks. Then we identify the three main categories of macro-contextual determinants of individual political participation heretofore recognised by the available studies: political institutions, socio-economic conditions and political culture. We first discuss the direct effect of these characteristics on individual political participation. Second, we focus on interaction effects, that is on the conditioning effect of contextual characteristics on the individual-level predictors of political participation. We conclude the review by identifying potential gaps and challenges in the available literature, formulating potential avenues for future research.

Theories of political participation

Micro-level theories

Political science research on political participation has been widely dominated by micro-level approaches which emphasise individual predispositions as determinants of political participation. In the first place, the most attention has been paid to individuals' socio-economic status, mainly due to the very influential research of Verba, Schlozman, Brady and Nie (Verba and Nie 1972; Verba et al. 1978; Verba et al. 1995; Schlozman et al. 2012). The main finding of this stream of research was that political participation is unequally distributed among citizens and skewed towards those who are privileged. The explanation of why higher socio-economic status (SES) leads to more political participation is that SES is most of the time interrelated with the individual resources that are necessary for participation in politics. Individual resources, such as time, skills and money, help overcome the costs of participation, and hence participation is easier for people who individually possess them. In addition to SES, the role of individual civic orientations and attitudes has been researched. Various studies have shown that people who are more interested in politics feel a civic duty to participate, have higher levels of social trust, have higher political efficacy and are more likely to participate in politics (Dalton 2008; Norris 2002; Armingeon 2007).

The micro-level approach favouring personal characteristics – SES and civic orientations – as the crucial determinants of individual political participation has several consequences for our understanding of participation and the policy decisions that are made. Firstly, putting the main emphasis on individual resources and motivations fails to explain the timing and geography of individual political participation

(Leighley 1995; Rosenstone and Hansen 2003). Although the micro-level approach can tell us what type of people usually tend to participate, predispositions can hardly answer when and where people participate. Political participation fluctuates dramatically over time and place; for instance, people sign petitions and contact politicians only on some occasions and at some locations. However, SES and most of the civic orientations which affect political participation are more or less stable characteristics which do not change that quickly and are unable to account for this cross-context fluctuation.

Secondly, this approach underestimates the social character of political participation (Knoke 1990; Leighley 1995; Rosenstone and Hansen 2003). The micro-level approach sees individuals as isolated units and implies that political participation is performed spontaneously by atomised individuals. However, people do not make their participatory choices in a vacuum but are sensitive to a number of influences coming from their socio-political surroundings. A number of researchers have argued that even seemingly individual types of political participation, such as voting, are still heavily social (Knoke 1990). Even in the case of activities that should be the most individualised and hence least dependent on individuals' social surroundings, such as boycotting and contacting public officials, comparative studies show that fewer than one-third describe their performance of these activities as exclusively the result of their own initiative without any help from others (Kaase 1990).

Thirdly, the focus on predispositions also has important normative and policy implications. Taking this perspective seriously, political participation would seem to originate from the non-political world. Rosenstone and Hansen have complained that micro-theories of political participation 'do not have much to say about politics' (Rosenstone and Hansen 2003: 3). Following the micro-level approach, individual political participation is not primarily related to what is going on in politics: it is not a response to actual political quarrels, not related to political parties or social movements and not affected by the design of institutions. On the contrary, political participation originates from who the people are. If participation is primarily a matter of social stratification and civic orientation, then the possibilities for effective short-term policy change are very limited. For instance, if we wanted to increase political participation, we would have to change people's individual resources and civic motivations, which are, however, difficult to manipulate.

A number of policy programmes drawing on the micro-level perspective are being implemented. These policy strategies include citizens' civic education programmes that try to increase public political and civic involvement by promoting civic skills, political awareness and civic values to individual citizens. The difficulty of these policy programmes in bringing about large-scale change is that because they are trying to manipulate rather stable characteristics, such as resources and civic orientations, they require long-term influences. Simultaneously, since their effect is attached to the education of every single individual, the potential range of effect of these usually small-scale projects focused on a few local communities is questionable.

Meso-level theories

Although the greatest attention has been paid to the micro-level explanations, particularly to the SES model, this does not mean that the political participation literature has entirely disregarded meso-level socio-political influences on participation. Here, attention has been focused on the effect of people's connections to their acquaintances, social groups and discussion networks, and recruitment by politicians and activists. However, this type of determinant, especially when tested on participatory activities other than voting, has been researched to a much lesser extent by the political science literature, or these influences have been interpreted through the perspective of micro-level explanations (for a review, see Abramson and Claggett 2001). For instance, although the study by Verba and colleagues specifies mobilisation as the third important component determining political participation, they still devote most of their attention to SES and individual resources (Verba *et al.* 1995). Also, when analysing recruitment they use very severe restrictions that make it very unlikely that they will find the effect of mobilisation, or do not study it at all as an independent variable of participation (Verba *et al.* 1995; Brady *et al.* 1999).

When studying membership in voluntary associations and groups, these authors also specify the mechanism of its influence through individual predispositions. For Verba and his colleagues, voluntary associations affect individual political participation by producing individual resources, particularly civic skills (Verba *et al.* 1995). Similarly, Putnam's social capital theory (2000) expects social networks among individuals established within these organisations to mainly affect civic orientation, specifically to produce trust and reciprocity, which subsequently leads to higher participation in politics. Hence, according to this perspective, the primary reason why the social surroundings of voluntary groups matter for political participation is the change in micro-predisposition (resources and civic orientations) and not the effects of recruitment, information flow or politics in general.

There is an important stream of the political participation literature and especially social movement literature which sees political participation primarily as a social activity heavily dependent on mobilisation and the informational aspect of individuals' socio-political surroundings. These authors point out that political participation must be organised, and emphasise mobilisation by politicians, activists, media, voluntary groups and personal discussion networks through the explicit recruitment of individuals or the transmission of politically relevant information (Abramson and Claggett 2001; Diani and McAdam 2003; Huckfeldt and Sprague 1992; Knoke 1990; Leighley 1996; McAdam 1988; McAdam *et al.* 1996; McAdam 1986; Norris 2002; Rosenstone and Hansen 2003; Shussman and Soule 2005; Teorell 2003; Uhlaner 1989; Verba *et al.* 1978; Verba *et al.* 1995; Wielhouwer and Lockerbie 1994).

Although this type of literature has been growing recently, especially on the effects of discussion networks (Mutz 2002, 2006; McClurg 2003, 2006), most mobilisation research into political participation deals with voting. Mobilisation and recruitment, which should be even more important for other types of participation, are not studied to any degree (Abramson and Claggett 2001). Clear evidence of this situation is the lack of indicators falling below the meso-level of explanation in standard political participation surveys. None of the most important comparative survey programmes focusing on political participation asks questions about recruitment into political participation other than voting.

Macro-level theories

Beyond one's immediate social surroundings, i.e. people's social networks and their recruitment by political elites, there is also a much wider macro-context that shapes incentives for political participation. This macro-context, such as political institutions and national culture, provides an arena in which the political participation and mobilising activity of social networks and political elites takes place. With the exception of voting, which has been well researched from this point of view (Dalton and Anderson 2011; Geys 2006; Powell 1986; Jackman 1987; Jackman and Miller 1995; Karp and Banducci 2008; Norris 2002; Blais 2006; Blais and Dobrzynska 1998), the role of the macro-context for other types of individual political participation has been seriously overlooked until recently (but see Verba *et al.* 1978; Inglehart and Welzel 2005).

This is not to say that comparative research on political participation does not exist – rather the opposite. However, most of the comparative studies have not taken the macro-context seriously as a research puzzle in itself. The vast majority of comparative studies instead control for the effect of national context, and test the micro- and meso-theories across contexts without trying to see how and why national context affects participation (Armingeon 2007; Teorell *et al.* 2007; Marien *et al.* 2010; Dalton 2008). Even the comparative political participation study by Verba *et al.* (1978), which has gone farthest from the main body of studies in this regard and theorised about the effect of political institutions and socio-economic cleavages on inequality in political participation, was not constructed to study the macro-context. On the contrary, the main purpose was to show that the 'individual-level law' of socio-economic resources holds across various types of national context. For this reason, the authors selected 'the maximum difference research design', which 'is strong if one is seeking for uniformities across nations.' For them 'cross-national heterogeneity ... is essentially an unspecified heterogeneity' (Verba *et al.* 1978: 24).

This lack of primarily macro-contextual analyses of political participation beyond voting comes as a surprise, because this very puzzle has been an essential focus of comparative politics since its very beginning (Przeworski and Teune 1970; Lazarsfeld and Melzel 1965; Almond and Verba 1963). Przeworski and Teune (1970: 7) explicitly acknowledge that 'identification of the social system in which a given phenomenon occurs is a part of its explanation'. Similarly, Almond and Verba (1963) point out that micropolitics (individual behaviour) can be explained by macropolitics (characteristics of political systems). Lazarsfeld and Melzel (1965) describe the same idea when referring to members and their collectives.

The main point emphasised by this literature is that individuals are embedded in different types of contexts that affect both their individual activities and the attitudes and processes that lead to these attitudes and activities. When studying these contexts, comparative social science research should go beyond the simple determination of these various contexts. Specifically, identifying that political participation is higher in the US and that SES plays a bigger role in the US than in Germany is not enough to study context effectively. In order to perform effective comparative analysis and study context seriously, researchers should move 'from cases to variables' (Przeworski and Teune 1970) and examine what contextual characteristics make the US and Germany different (see also Chapter 11 by Brunton-Smith and Barrett in this volume).

Compared to the political science literature dealing with the individual determinants of political participation, the social movement literature has, since the 1970s, been working intensively on the macro-structural theory of political opportunity structure (POS), which is understood to be one of the most crucial determinants of the mobilisation of social movements (Eisinger 1973; Tilly 1995; Meyer 2004; Kriesi 2004; Tarrow 1998; Kriesi et al. 1995). The POS is conceptualised as the various characteristics of the external environment, mostly the formal and informal aspects of state institutions and elite politics, that shape people's incentives for activism (Tarrow 1998: 76–8). However, until lately this theory has not been used for the macro-level explanation of individual-level political participation. It has been used to explain variations over time in the mobilisation of particular social movements (McAdam 1999; Meyer and Minkoff 2008), or in qualitative small-N studies comparing protest across a limited number of countries (Kriesi at al. 1995; Kitschelt 1986).

Only very recently have researchers started to study the macro-context of citizens' political behaviour beyond voting as the main research problem and in a more systematic way. The recent boom in these studies is to a large extent possible thanks to the availability of a large quantity of comparative survey data and new statistical techniques. Recently a large number of comparative surveys focused on political participation and related concepts have been made available, such as the World Value Survey, the European Social Survey, the International Social Survey Programme and the Comparative Study of Electoral Systems, which make possible systematic statistical large-N analyses of individual political participation across time and space. Also, a suitable statistical technique in the form of multilevel or hierarchical modelling (Gelman and Hill 2007; Hox 2010), which is able to effectively analyse the interplay between micro- and macro-determinants of individual political participation, has only recently became available and popular among a wider group of political participation researchers (for more see Chapter 11 by Brunton-Smith and Barrett in this volume and Brunton-Smith 2011). The following text will summarise this more or less new stream of literature, review the most important findings on how the characteristics of the macro-context affect individual political participation and explain the mechanisms through which they influence it. Since macro-contextual determinants of voter turnout have been well

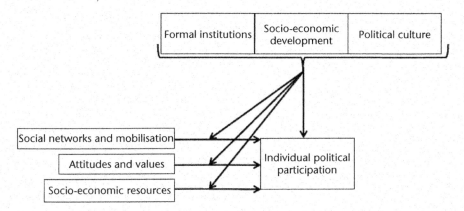

FIGURE 2.1 Direct and indirect macro-contextual effects on individual political participation

studied, the text will primarily focus on reviewing the more recent literature on forms of political participation other than voting.

What type of macro-context affects individual participation?

Recognising that macro-context matters is only the first step. The necessary follow-up question is what characteristics of the macro-context are, and why and how they matter for political participation. Generally, the available studies on the macro-contextual determinants of individual political participation have focused on three main types of contextual determinants: formal political institutions, economic development and political culture. Figure 2.1 summarises the findings – both direct and conditioning effects – available in the literature. The macro-context can affect political participation directly, which is displayed by the direct arrow from the macro-context to individual political participation. In addition to that, the macro-context can also affect the processes within particular contexts, i.e. it conditions the effect of the lower-level determinants of individual participation. Available studies have explored how various characteristics of the macro-level context interplay with the effects of the above-mentioned explanations of micro- (SES and attitudes and values) and meso-level factors (networks and mobilisation).

Direct effects of the macro-context

Formal political institutions

The micro-oriented research on political participation has tended to emphasise the similarities among individual types of political participation while using more or less the same micro-predictors, and points out the 'conventionalisation/normalisation' of protest, which is nowadays similar to other types of political participation activities (Dalton 2008; Norris 2002; Verba *et al.* 1995). However, when taking the macro-contextual perspective, electoral and non-electoral political participation is viewed as qualitatively different phenomena. This probably holds the truest in the case of macro-institutional determinants. For instance, while elections are held once every four years and are explicitly regulated by electoral laws, different macro-level mechanisms probably correspond to protest and contacting officials, which tend to take place between elections (Weldon and Dalton 2011: 16; Marien *et al.* 2010). Political institutions have been widely studied as the main source of cross-national variation in voter turnout (Dalton and Anderson 2011; Powell 1986; Jackman 1987; Jackman and Miller 1995; Karp and Banducci 2008; Norris 2002; Blais 2006; Blais and Dobrzynska 1998). The effect of institutional context on non-electoral participation has been researched to a much lesser extent (Dalton *et al.* 2009; van der Meer *et al.* 2009; van der Meer 2011; Weldon and Dalton 2010; Christensen 2011).

When theorising about the mechanism of how formal political institutions shape individual political participation, studies mostly rely on rational choice theory. The formal political institutions of the nation state should shape incentives for participation, affecting individuals' costs and benefits of participation. In the case of voting, authors usually expect that the macro-level context shapes individual incentives to take part in elections by determining electoral costs, the character of electoral choices offered and the chances of having an impact (Norris 2002; Dalton and Anderson 2011). In the case of electoral costs, the explanation is straightforward: when electoral costs are reduced, casting a ballot should be easier. The electoral choices play a role for voter turnout in several ways. A higher number of options should motivate people to vote because they have a greater chance of finding a party close to their views. The choices must also be distinguishable from one another and predictable in order to motivate individuals to vote. Also, situations that increase the chances of one vote having an impact should increase electoral participation (Dalton and Anderson 2011).

Similarly, the social movement literature has relied on rational choice theory in identifying the mechanism by which institutional political opportunities affect protest and non-electoral participation in general. They expect that people participate more when two mechanisms operate simultaneously: (1) when people's chances to have an impact are increased; and (2) when people have a higher number of access points for influencing politics (Koopmans and Kriesi 1995: 38–40; also Koopmans 1999: 97; for individual non-electoral participation, see Vráblíková 2014).

What institutions specifically affect political participation? Voter turnout research has mostly dealt with the characteristics of electoral and party systems. Among the factors that reduce the costs of casting a ballot, studies have found that automatic registration, holding the elections on weekends and voting by mail can increase voter turnout (Jackman 1987; Jackman and Miller 1995; Norris 2002; Blais 2006).

Many studies have found that a proportional electoral system increases voter turnout (Powell 1986; Jackman 1987; Karp and Banducci 2008). The exact theoretical mechanism of how it affects voters' incentives is not clear (Blais 2006; Dalton and Anderson 2011). Some explanations relate this effect to the higher number of political parties typical of proportional electoral systems. However, research has brought mixed results regarding the effect of multi-partyism (Geys 2006; Karp and Banducci 2008). For example, Jackman (1987) finds a negative effect for a higher effective number of parliamentary parties on aggregate voter turnout; he explains this by observing that voters do not decide the actual composition of the government. Others find a positive effect. Lijphart (1999) explains it in terms of the inclusiveness of the consensual and cooperative culture produced by institutional decentralisation in general. Other authors suggest that a higher number of parties inspires citizens to vote because they have more options from which to choose and the options offered better fit their needs, or because parties will be more active in the mobilisation of individuals (Geys 2006; Karp and Banducci 2008, 2011; Blais 2006). Analysing individual voting in a multilevel study, Karp and Banducci (2008) show that a proportional electoral system increases voter turnout because these systems better represent minorities, produce stronger party preferences and increase political efficacy, while a greater number of parties in the government, though common in proportional electoral system, decreases voter turnout by undermining efficacy due to the lower accountability and responsiveness of political elites.

In addition to electoral laws and party system characteristics, Lijphart (1999) also expects the general institutional design of the political system to affect people's willingness to cast a ballot. According to Lijphart, consensual democracies characterised by institutional decentralisation, such as horizontal and territorial power-dispersion, corporate interest mediation and multi-partyism, support higher voter turnout and participation in general, by increasing the inclusiveness of these consensual and cooperational settings. Recent studies testing this theory on individual voting in a multilevel setting do not find support for any of the indicators measuring Lijphart's two dimensions of consociationalism (van der Meer *et al.* 2009; Weldon and Dalton 2010). In contrast to the expectations, institutional decentralisation neither in the executive parties dimension nor in the federal–unitary dimension affects individual electoral participation.

In the case of non-electoral political participation, researchers have not researched electoral laws; instead, drawing on the political opportunity structure literature from social movements or the literature on comparative institutions, most have focused on the general institutional design of the state. Drawing on political opportunity structure theory, Dalton and his colleagues (2009) show that the level of democratic development measured as Rule of Law by the World Bank has a linear positive effect on individual protest. However, when Welzel and Deutsch (2012) retest this theory using a different measure of Voice and Accountability from the Freedom House and control for emancipative culture and socio-economic development, they find no effect of opportunities on individual protest. Christensen (2011) operationalises political opportunities as various types of institutional decentralisation, and expects it to increase political participation within the system, such as contacting officials or party membership, and decrease protest. The findings are rather mixed: some indicators of institutional decentralisation dampen individual non-electoral participation, some increase it and others do not show any effect, thus not following the expected different pattern between participation within and outside the system.

Van der Meer and colleagues (2009) and Weldon and Dalton (2010) also study institutional decentralisation, and explicitly aim at testing Lijphart's theory of consociationalism. They expect that a culture of inclusion, consensus and efficacy created by consociational systems should also increase non-electoral participation. In line with Lijphart and his predictions for electoral participation, this expectation relies on the voice mechanism, which expects decentralised systems to increase inclusiveness. Van der Meer and others (van der Meer *et al.* 2009; van der Meer 2011) also theorise a negative effect, because the opposite of consensual institutions – majoritarian institutions – increase accountability, which should motivate higher levels of non-electoral participation. The findings of the two studies do not consistently fit Lijphart's expectations. While consensualism measured by the executive-party dimension weakens most non-electoral political activities, the second federal-unitary dimension shows no effect or positive influence.

Drawing on a reconceptualised political opportunity structure theory, Vráblíková (2012, 2014) argues that only some types of institutional decentralisation increase non-electoral participation, and that the mechanisms by which they do so are not inclusiveness, cooperation and consensus as expected by Lijphart. She distinguishes between power-sharing and power-separation types of decentralisation and shows that only the latter enhances non-electoral participation. The reason is that power-separation, such as territorial and horizontal decentralisation, implies a competitive setting with a higher number of veto players in the political system, which provides participants with better access to the system and greater chances of being successful. In contrast, the power-sharing type of institutional decentralisation, such as multi-partyism or corporate interest representation, does not increase non-electoral participation. Although they are inclusive and hence provide access, these settings lack the element of competitive checks and balances that increases participants' chances of being successful.

Socio-economic conditions

Macro-contextual studies of individual political participation have also examined the effect of socio-economic development. There are several theories that explain the effect of socio-economic well-being on participation. In general, all of the theories more or less explicitly suggest two main mechanisms through which socio-economic macro-contextual determinants affect individual participation. First, macro socio-economic conditions contribute to the development of individual resources, which are more stable predispositions for participation by individual citizens. For instance, potential participants themselves are more educated or have more time and capacity to devote to politics when socialised in a more socio-economically developed context. Secondly, socio-economic macro-conditions also develop the societal resources for participation. They shape the immediate but external surroundings of individuals, such as the development of civil society and communication technologies.

The effect of socio-economic macro-conditions on individual electoral participation is usually studied from the standpoint of more or less explicitly formulated modernisation theory (Norris 2002; Blais 2006). As Norris summarises, processes such as mass education, urbanisation, the development of mass communication technologies, secularisation, urbanisation and the development of mobilising organisations such as political parties or trade unions should increase voter turnout. The reason is that these processes lead to a higher politicisation of individual citizens, who are therefore more politically informed and engaged (Blais 2006). This theory sees socio-economic conditions from the long-term developmental perspective, and is best suited to explain long-term variation in participation (Norris 2002).

Several studies have shown that various indicators of socio-economic development increase voter turnout (Blais 2006; Norris 2002). However, the trend is not linear and a ceiling effect is observed. The influence is strongest when less socio-economically developed societies are transforming into industrial ones. Here socio-economic conditions strongly boost voter turnout. However, when a certain point of socio-economic development is reached, the effect of socio-economic development on voter turnout decreases and disappears. In post-industrial countries we no longer find an effect of socio-economic conditions on voter turnout (Norris 2002; Blais and Dobrzynska 1998).

Socio-economic development is also positively related to non-electoral participation. There are a number of explanations available as to why this happens. Inglehart's modernisation theory identifies the effect with the change of values and culture resulting from the shift from industrial to post-industrial society (Inglehart 1990, 1997). The experience of existential security, autonomy in decision-making, the development of cognitive skills and creativity, and the diversification of interpersonal interactions in post-industrial societies should lead to a cultural value change by which more people have post-materialist/self-expressive values which correspond to more new forms of participation that are a post-materialist alternative to the passive activities associated with elite-led hierarchical organisations such as voting and party membership.

Dalton et al.'s study (2009) of the effect of socio-economic development on individual protest sees socio-economic development through the lens of resource mobilisation theory taken from social movement literature (McCarthy and Zald 1977). This approach focuses on mobilising organisations, such as social movements, voluntary groups and NGOs, which recruit individuals into protest. Socio-economic development should lead to a higher number of these actors, that is to a more developed civil society sector, and increase the resources available to them for mobilising individuals into protest participation, such as a skilled public interested in politics, communication technologies and independent media.

Although closely related, the two perspectives are slightly different. While the classical modernisation theory emphasises the development of post-materialist values and culture across national populations, the resource mobilisation theory of economic development stresses the role of intermediary actors and their capacity to mobilise individuals without reference to the value component present in classical modernisation theory. Contextual studies of non-electoral participation have not yet examined the mechanism of socio-economic development in greater depth to disentangle the two, and mostly use these modernisation-related indicators as control variables.

Political culture

While formal political institutions and socio-economic conditions have been well-researched in contextual studies of voter turnout and received some attention in analyses focused on other participatory activities, the contextual role of political culture on all types of individual participation has been heavily understudied. In fact, there are very few studies that have systematically examined the effect of national culture on individual political behaviour.

What is macro-political culture and how can it be expected to affect individual political participation? In general, the topic of political culture has received much attention in political science, and there are a number of available theories examining its effect on individual participation, such as theories of civic culture, social capital and post-materialism (Almond and Verba 1963; Putnam 1995, 2000; Inglehart 1990, 1997; Inglehart and Welzel 2005). The crucial point here is that political culture is a macro-contextual phenomenon characterising societies and political systems. Hence, although the measures used to indicate political culture are constructed as the aggregation of individual-level attitudes representing the countries' populations, they indicate a societal-level phenomenon which should be conceptually different from individual attitudes. In doing this, contextual studies of individual participation follow the classic conceptualisation of political culture as a 'particular distribution of patterns of orientation toward political objects among the members of the nation' (Almond and Verba 1963: 14–15). This is also related to the political culture's mechanism of influence. The political culture perspective implies that if political culture is to matter, then it should, in addition to affecting individual participation through individual attitudes, also (and more importantly) affect individual participation beyond the effect of individual predispositions.

Although contextual determinants of voting have been studied for decades, almost all of the studies analyse institutions and economic development. Only a few studies have looked at how national social capital affects voter turnout. Relying on bivariate relationships of aggregated data, Putnam (2000) shows that the decline over time in US voter turnout follows the decline of social capital. In contrast, van Deth's (2002) cross-country bivariate analysis of aggregate voter turnout does not find support for social capital theory. In a multilevel analysis of individual electoral participation, Whiteley *et al.* (2009) find a negative effect of aggregate social trust on individual voting, and no effect of aggregate group membership. A multilevel analysis by van Deth and Vráblíková (2013) shows the positive effect of an aggregated composite measure of social capital on individual voting. As they put it: 'The general availability of a dense and active civil society offers easy access to trustful relationships and all kinds of networks, lowering the opportunity costs for engagement and compliant behaviour for all citizens in this society' (van Deth and Vráblíková 2013: 8).

The contextual effect of social capital has also been studied in the case of other participatory activities. An analysis of aggregated protest by Benson and Rochon (2004) shows a positive effect of social trust. The multilevel analysis of Whiteley and his colleagues (2009) finds a positive effect of both aggregated social trust and group membership on individual non-electoral participation. However, they do not explain the mechanism by which the contextual effect works in greater detail, and treat the country-level social capital as the contextual parallel to the individual-level theory. Controlling for rival cultural explanations of self-expressive culture and economic and political development, Vráblíková (2012) finds no effect for the aggregated composite measure of social capital on individual non-electoral participation. She links social capital to the previously mentioned power-sharing institutions, explaining that both of these characteristics produce a mechanism of consensus and cooperation which, in contrast to competition and contestation, does not increase non-electoral participation.

As already mentioned, one version of the modernisation theory stresses the role of post-materialist/self-expressive culture, especially for 'elite-challenging' types of political participation. This expectation has been supported by several studies. Both fully aggregate-level analyses and multilevel studies analysing individual non-electoral participation, found a positive effect for self-expressive/post-materialist/emancipative culture on protesting or other non-electoral activities (Benson and Rochon 2004; Inglehart and Welzel 2005; Welzel and Deutsch 2012; Vráblíková 2012). Multilevel analyses have also shown that self-expressive culture as a macro-contextual phenomenon has its effect beyond individual-level attitudes, i.e. it is the prevalence of these values in a given society that matters. Welzel and Deutsch (2012) explain that political culture works as a 'mental climate' because people are more exposed to these types of political participation, and the process of social contagion spreads it across all groups so that not only people individually possessing self-expressive values perform these activities.

Indirect conditioning effects of context

Macro-context shapes individual political participation not only directly, but also indirectly by affecting the influence of its micro- and meso-level determinants. From a different perspective, this means that the influence of the macro-context on individual citizens is not even, but affects different groups of citizens differently. For instance, education can have a stronger effect on individual participation in some contexts than in others, which means that the inequality among participants is higher here. The question then asked by this type of analysis is: what contextual determinants are responsible for this cross-contextual variation in the effect of individual education on political participation? The available studies do not always provide well-specified theoretical expectations about interaction effects. Rather, they test a number of interactions in a more exploratory manner without a clear specification of what mechanisms are responsible for the observed findings.

The contextual effect on the relationship between SES and participation has already been examined by Verba et al. (1978). In their study of seven countries, they show that inequality in political participation is affected by the strength of mobilisation and cleavage structure of a particular country. Using the dichotomist measure of closed and open political systems, which combines a number of various types of institutional decentralisation, Christensen (2011) concludes that open systems tend to decrease inequality in individual non-electoral participation, and activate groups of citizens that are more politically passive in closed systems. In contrast, Dalton et al. (2009) and Marien et al. (2010) obtained the opposite results. More open opportunities (as indicated by the World Bank's Rule of Law indicator) and a higher level of democracy (as measured by the Freedom House Index) amplify the effect of education, indicating that participation is less equal in more democratic and politically open countries. Similarly, higher socio-economic development strengthens the effect of individual level resources (Dalton et al. 2009; Welzel and Deutsch 2012), which means that the socio-economic inequality in non-electoral participation is higher in wealthier countries.

Several studies have examined how the macro-level context affects the role of individual attitudes for individual-level political participation. Dalton et al. (2009) show that a more open political context, that is a higher score on the Rule of Law indicator, strengthens the effect of Left–Right attitudes and post-materialism on individual protest. Marien et al. (2010) show that a higher level of democracy increases the role of political interest for individual participation. Despite well-developed and strong theoretical expectations that consociational institutions should diminish the ideological polarisation of participants because ideological conflicts are less salient in these systems, van der Meer et al. (2009) do not find a significant conditioning effect of institutions and several measures of Left–Right attitudes on individual participation. However, some of the findings of Christensen (2011) suggest that institutional decentralisation decreases the effect of some pro-participatory attitudes. Only Dalton et al. (2009) look at how economic development conditions individual attitudes. They show that both Left vs. Right ideological orientation and post-materialism have a greater influence on individual protest in more economically developed countries.

Analysing the interplay between macro-level political culture and individual attitudes, Welzel and Deutsch (2012) show that emancipative culture strengthens the positive effect of individual emancipative values. They explain this effect in terms of the mechanism of social confirmation. People possessing emancipative values have more contacts in cultures with a high prevalence of these values, which should reinforce the impulse of personal values to take part. Similarly, Vráblíková

(2012) shows that self-expressive/emancipative culture amplifies the positive effect of a number of pro-participatory attitudes, such as political interest, political efficacy, social trust and norms of good citizenship. Her results also show that a national culture with a low prevalence of self-expressive/emancipative values deactivates the positive effect of pro-participatory attitudes on individual non-electoral participation.

In examining how the effect of the meso-level predictors of non-electoral participation is conditioned by the macro-level context, available studies have looked at the determinants of a diversified effect of voluntary groups and associational membership and political discussion on individual participation. Dalton et al. (2009) show that group membership has a higher effect on individual protest in countries with more open opportunities (i.e. with a higher score on the Rule of Law indicator) and in more economically developed countries. However, when Welzel and Deutsch (2012) use the Freedom House Voice and Accountability index as the indicator of open opportunities, they find no conditioning effect of group membership on protest. Using the two groups of open and closed opportunities combining various types of institutional decentralisation, Christensen (2011) shows that voluntary groups in closed systems are more likely to function as schools of democracy because they produce more non-electoral participation than in open systems. In contrast Vráblíková shows the opposite effect, with higher openness of political systems as indicated by higher institutional power-separation (indicating more veto players in the political system) increasing the role of group membership and political discussion for individual non-electoral participation (Vráblíková 2012, 2014). She explains that mobilising actors tend to activate social links for the mobilisation of individuals more in these institutional settings because they have simultaneously higher access to the political system and higher chances to be successful with their demands. This interpretation also means that more open opportunities do not work as an alternative to mobilisation by groups and acquaintances; rather, they amplify the participatory gap between mobilised and non-mobilised citizens.

Discussion

The previous sections have reviewed the findings of the available studies of the macro-contextual determinants of individual political participation. What are the weaknesses, potential gaps and challenges that should be dealt with in future studies? We identify three areas in which we think valuable contributions are possible for this stream of research: (1) theories; (2) technical solutions; and (3) new topics and approaches.

The first comment is related to the role of theory in macro-contextual studies of individual participation. Although a decade ago the biggest problem in studying the macro context of individual political participation still seemed to be mainly technical because of the lack of statistical techniques that could effectively disentangle the multilevel character of this research puzzle, paradoxically the problem seems to be the exact opposite now. With the development of multilevel modelling and its more-or-less easy application, researchers now have in their hands a very powerful statistical tool which allows them to model very complex tasks. However, this type of analysis is better suited for theory testing rather than for theory development. Without an effective and well-specified theory of how particular macro-contextual characteristics affect political participation and its determinants, one can easily end up with models that are too complex.

This problem crops up especially in the case of potential cross-level interactions. As we said before, most of the available studies tend to underestimate the role of theory when developing and testing particular cross-level hypotheses. Very few studies attempt to specify a theoretical mechanism of why and how a particular macro-contextual characteristic should condition the effect of a given individual-level predictor. More theoretical work could contribute by studying the direct effect of macro-context on political participation, particularly with regard to competing theories. The mechanism of how the contextual characteristics might influence individual level participation is not always precisely and clearly specified, which leaves room for very general theoretical interpretations, including at the end of the day almost every possible mechanism. Individual theories should be specified more precisely and in more detail to make it possible to disentangle potentially different mechanisms of how the macro context affects individual participation. For instance, the already identified difference between modernisation theory and resource mobilisation theory is worth further investigation.

One way to develop our theoretical thinking further would be through careful review of the results and discussions of existing studies. Increased communication across individual studies would also help to solve other issues related to the technical tasks of macro-contextual studies. The literature on non-electoral participation has not developed a standard portfolio of its predictors, which should be included in all analyses at least as controls. As it is, the available studies differ in which macro-contextual determinants they take into account in their models. Apart from the problem that some of these models are probably underspecified and do not provide reliable findings, another practical consequence is the difficulty of comparison across studies. Put bluntly, when a particular study reports that one macro-contextual characteristic is an important determinant of individual non-electoral participation, we cannot know whether this result is just a spurious correlation.

Another technical challenge for macro-contextual analyses is the relatively low number of countries that are usually used at the second level of the multilevel analysis. The problem is that when analysing a low number of cases, it is very likely that the findings result from a few highly influential cases rather than describing the general trend that holds for most countries (van der Meer *et al.* 2010). To avoid this, a number of tests for checking influential cases are available (van der Meer *et al.* 2010) and it should become a standard procedure in this type of analysis to perform these. More than half of the available studies do not check for influential cases.

As a third point, we want to outline several topics that have not been touched on by the macro-contextual literature. Most of the available studies have been limited to cross-sectional analyses of political participation among democracies.

This means that the role of time has not been explored for individual-level political participation. However, as shown mainly by the social movement literature, non-electoral participation varies heavily over time (Rucht 1998; McAdam 1999). Also, the context of non-democratic or semi-democratic regimes has not received much attention.

Another potential for new topics is that the notion of context need not be limited only to national countries, which are taken as the 'natural' units in the comparative social research and surveying industry. There are still unexplored puzzles and theories that better fit different levels of analyses. For instance, as already mentioned, not only the macro-context but also the meso-level context for individual non-electoral participation have yet to be studied more extensively. In this sense, a promising strategy may be found in complementing individual-level surveys with data on mobilising actors such as representatives of organisations and their members (Leighley 1996; Maloney and van Deth 2010) or the protestors and the mobilising actors organising demonstrations (Walgrave and Rucht 2010; van Stekelenburg et al. 2012).

Note

1 The authors gratefully acknowledge funding from the Czech Grant Agency (Grant 'Protestors in Context: An Integrated and Comparative Analysis of Democratic Citizenship in the Czech Republic', code GA13-29032S).

References

Abramson, P. R. and Claggett, W. (2001) 'Recruitment and political participation', *Political Research Quarterly*, 54 (4): 905–16.
Almond, G. A. and Verba, S. (1963) 'The civic culture', *Political Attitudes and Democracy in Five Nations*. Princeton, NJ: Princeton University Press.
Armingeon, K. (2007) 'Political participation and associational involvement', in J. W. van Deth, J. R. Montero and A. Westholm, A. (eds), *Citizenship and Involvement in European Democracies. A Comparative Analysis*. London and New York: Routledge, pp. 358–84.
Benson, M. and Rochon, T. R (2004) 'Interpersonal trust and the magnitude of protest: a micro and macro level approach', *Comparative Political Studies*, 37 (4): 435–57.
Blais, A. (2006) *To Vote or Not to Vote: The Merits and Limits of Rational Choice Theory*. Pittsburgh: University of Pittsburgh Press.
Blais, A. and Dobrzynska, A. (1998) 'Turnout in electoral democracies', *European Journal of Political Research*, 33 (2): 239–61.
Brady, H. E., Schlozman, K. L. and Verba, S. (1999) 'Prospecting for participants: rational expectations and the recruitment of political activists', *American Political Science Review*, 93 (1): 153–68.
Brunton-Smith, I. (2011) *Modelling Existing Survey Data: Full Technical Report of PIDOP Work Package 5*. Department of Sociology, University of Surrey. Available online from: http://epubs.surrey.ac.uk/739988/2/PIDOP_WP5_Report.pdf_revised.pdf.
Christensen, H. S. (2011) *Political Participation Beyond the Vote. How the Institutional Context Shapes Patterns of Political Participation in 18 Western European Democracies*. Abo: Abo Akademi University Press.

Dalton, R. J. (2008) *Citizen Politics: Public Opinion and Political Parties in Advanced Industrial Democracies*. Washington, DC: CQ Press.
Dalton, R. J. and Anderson, C. (eds) (2011) *Citizens, Context and Choice: How Context Shapes Citizens' Electoral Choices*. Oxford: Oxford University Press.
Dalton, R. J., van Sicle, A. and Weldon, S. (2009) 'The individual-institutional nexus of protest behaviour', *British Journal of Political Science*, 40 (1): 51–73.
Diani, M. and McAdam, D. (2003) *Social Movements and Networks. Relational Approaches to Collective Action*. New York: Oxford University Press.
Eisinger, P. K. (1973) 'The conditions of protest behavior in American cities', *American Political Science Review*, 67 (1): 11–28.
Gelman, A. and Hill, J. (2007) *Data Analysis Using Regression and Multilevel/Hierarchical Models*. New York: Cambridge University Press.
Geys, B. (2006) 'Explaining voter turnout: a review of aggregate-level research', *Electoral Studies*, 25: 637–63.
Hox, J. J. (2010) *Multilevel Analysis: Techniques and Applications*, 2nd edn. New York: Routledge.
Huckfeldt, R. and Sprague, J. (1992) 'Political parties and electoral mobilization: political structure, social structure, and the party canvass', *American Political Science Review*, 86 (1): 70–86.
Inglehart, R. F. (1990) *Culture Shift in Advanced Industrial Society*. Princeton, NJ: Princeton University Press.
Inglehart, R. (1997) *Modernization and Postmodernization: Cultural, Economic and Political Change in 43 Societies*. Princeton, NJ: Princeton University Press.
Inglehart, R. F. and Welzel, C. (2005) *Modernization, Cultural Change, and Democracy: The Human Development Sequence*. Cambridge: Cambridge University Press.
Jackman, R. and Miller, R. A. (1995) 'Voter turnout in the industrial democracies during the 1980s', *Comparative Political Studies*, 27 (4): 467–92.
Jackman, R. W. (1987) 'Political institutions and voter turnout in the industrial democracies', *American Political Science Review*, 81 (2): 405–24.
Kaase, M. (1990) 'Mass participation', in M. K. Jennings and J. W. van Deth (eds), *Continuities in Political Action: A Longitudinal Study of Political Participation in Three Western Democracies*. Berlin and New York: De Gruyter, pp. 23–64.
Karp, J. A. and Banducci, S. A. (2008) 'Political efficacy and participation in twenty-seven democracies: how electoral systems shape political behavior', *British Journal of Political Science*, 38 (2): 311–34.
Karp, J. A. and Banducci, S. A. (2011) 'The influence of party and electoral systems on campaign engagement', in R. Dalton and C. Anderson (eds), *Citizens, Context and Choice: How Context Shapes Citizens' Electoral Choices*. Oxford: Oxford University Press, pp. 55–78.
Kitschelt, H. P. (1986) 'Political opportunity structures and political protest: anti-nuclear movements in four democracies', *British Journal of Political Science*, 16 (1): 57–86.
Knoke, D. (1990) 'Networks of political action: toward theory construction', *Social Forces*, 68 (4): 1041–63.
Koopmans, R. (1999) 'Political opportunity structure. Some splitting to balance the lumping', *Sociological Forum*, 14 (1): 93–105.
Koopmans, R. and Kriesi, H. (1995) 'Institutional structures and prevailing strategies', in H. Kriesi, R. Koopmans, J. W. Duyvendak and M. Giugni (eds), *New Social Movements in Western Europe: A Comparative Analysis*. Minneapolis, MN: University of Minnesota Press, pp. 26–52.

Kriesi, H. (2004) 'Political context and opportunity', in D. Snow, S. Soule and H. Kriesi (eds), *The Blackwell Companion to Social Movements*. Malden: Blackwell, pp. 67–90.

Kriesi, H., Koopmans, R. and Duyvendak, J. W. (1995) *New Social Movements in Western Europe: A Comparative Analysis*. London: UCL Press.

Lazarsfeld, P. F. and Menzel, H. (1965) 'On the relation between individual and collective properties', in A. Etzioni (ed.), *Complex Organizations*. New York: Holt, Rinehart & Winston, pp. 422–40.

Leighley, J. E. (1990) 'Social interaction and contextual influences on political participation', *American Politics Quarterly*, 18 (4): 459–75.

Leighley, J. E. (1995) 'Attitudes, opportunities and incentives: a field essay on political participation', *Political Research Quarterly*, 48 (1): 181–209.

Leighley, J. E. (1996) 'Group membership and the mobilization of political participation', *Journal of Politics*, 58 (2): 447–63.

Lijphart, A. (1999) *Patterns of Democracy: Government Forms and Performance in Thirty-Six Countries*. New Haven, CT: Yale University Press.

McAdam, D. (1986) 'Recruitment to high-risk activism: the case of freedom summer', *American Journal of Sociology*, 92 (1): 64–90.

McAdam, D. (1988) 'Micromobilization contexts and recruitment to activism', *International Social Movement Research*, 1: 125–54.

McAdam, D. (1999) *Political Process and the Development of Black Insurgency, 1930–1970*, 2nd edn. Chicago: University of Chicago Press.

McAdam, D., McCarthy, J. and Zald, M. N. (1996) *Comparative Perspectives on Social Movements: Political Opportunities, Mobilizing Structures, and Cultural Framing*. Cambridge: Cambridge University Press.

McCarthy, J. and Zald, M. (1977) 'Resource mobilization and social movements', *American Journal of Sociology*, 82: 1212–41.

McClurg, S. (2003) 'Social networks and political participation: the role of social interactions in explaining political participation', *Political Research Quarterly*, 56 (4): 228–464.

McClurg, S. D. (2006) 'The electoral relevance of political talk: examining disagreement and expertise effects in social networks on political participations', *American Journal of Political Science*, 50 (3): 737–54.

Maloney, W. A. and van Deth, J. W. (2010) *Civil Society and Activism in Europe: Contextualizing Engagement and Political Orientations*. London: Routledge.

Marien, S., Hooghe, M. and Quintelier, E. (2010) 'Inequalities in non-institutionalised forms of political participation: a multi-level analysis of 25 countries', *Political Studies*, 58 (1): 187–213.

Meyer, D. (2004) 'Protest and political opportunities', *Annual Review of Sociology*, 30: 125–45.

Meyer, D. S. and Minkoff, D. C. (2008) 'Conceptualizing political opportunity', *Social Forces*, 82 (4): 1457–92.

Mutz, D. (2002) 'The consequences of cross-cutting networks for political participation', *American Journal of Political Science*, 46 (4): 838–55.

Mutz, D. (2006) *Hearing the Other Side: Deliberative Versus Participatory Democracy*. Cambridge: Cambridge University Press.

Norris, P. (2002) *Democratic Phoenix: Reinventing Political Activism*. New York: Cambridge University Press.

Powell, G. B. (1986) 'American voter turnout in comparative perspective', *American Political Science Review*, 80 (1): 17–43.

Przeworski, A. and Teune, H. (1970) *The Logic of Comparative Social Inquiry*. New York: John Wiley.

Putnam, R. D. (2000) *Bowling Alone: The Collapse and Revival of American Community*. New York: Simon & Schuster.
Rosenstone, S. J. and Hansen, J. M. (2003) *Mobilization, Participation, and Democracy in America*. New York: Longman.
Rucht, D. (1998) 'The structure and culture of collective protest in Germany since 1950', in D. Meyer and S. Tarrow (eds), *The Social Movement Society*. New York: Rowman & Littlefield, pp. 28–58.
Schlozman, K. L., Verba, S. and Brady, H. E. (2012) *The Unheavenly Chorus: Unequal Political Voice and the Broken Promise of American Democracy*. Princeton, NJ: Princeton University Press.
Shussman, A. and Soule, S. A. (2005) 'Process and protest: accounting for individual protest participation', *Social Forces*, 84 (2): 1083–108.
Tarrow, S. (1998) *Power in Movement: Social Movements and Contentious Politics*. Cambridge: Cambridge University Press.
Teorell, J. (2003) 'Linking social capital to political participation: voluntary associations and network of recruitment in Sweden', *Scandinavian Political Studies*, 26 (1): 49–66.
Teorell, J., Sum, P. and Tobiasen, M. (2007) 'Participation and political equality: an assessment of large-scale democracy', in J. W. van Deth, J. R. Montero and A. Westholm (eds), *Citizenship and Involvement in European Democracies. A Comparative Analysis*. London and New York: Routledge, pp. 384–414.
Tilly, C. (1995) *Popular Contention in Great Britain 1758–1834*. Cambridge, MA and London: Harvard University Press.
Uhlaner, C. J. (1989) 'Rational turnout: the neglected role of groups', *American Journal of Political Science*, 33 (2): 390–422.
van der Meer, T. (2011) *States of Freely Associating Citizens? Cross-National Studies into the Impact of State Institutions on Social, Civic, and Political Participation*. Nijmegen: Radboud University Nijmegen/ICS.
van der Meer, T., Grotenhuis, M. T. and Pelzer, B. (2010) 'Influential cases in multilevel modeling: a methodological comment', *American Sociological Review*, 75 (1): 173–8.
van der Meer, T., van Deth, J. W. and Scheepers, P. L. H. (2009) 'The politicized participant: ideology and political action in 20 democracies', *Comparative Political Studies*, 42 (11): 1426–57.
van Deth, J. W. (2002) 'The proof of the pudding: social capital, democracy and citizenship', in J. W. van Deth (ed.), *Social Capital in Democratic Politics*. Exeter: Rusel, pp. 7–55.
van Deth, J. W. and Vráblíková, K. (2013) *Does National Social Capital Make Individual Citizens Better Democrats?* Paper presented at the Annual Meeting of the Western Political Science Association, 28–30 March 2013, Hollywood, CA.
van Stekelenburg, J., Walgrave, S., Klandermans, B. and Verhulst, J. (2012) 'Contextualizing contestation: framework, design and data', *Mobilization*, 17 (3): 249–62.
Verba, S., Nie, N. H. and Kim, J. (1972) *Participation in America: Political Democracy and Social Equality*. Chicago: University of Chicago Press.
Verba, S. and Nie, N. H. (1978) *Participation and Political Equality: A Seven-Nation Comparison*. Cambridge: Cambridge University Press.
Verba, S., Schlozman, K. L. and Brady, H. (1995) *Voice and Equality: Civic Voluntarism in American Politics*. Cambridge, MA: Harvard University Press.
Vráblíková, K. (2012) 'Between Contestation and Consensus: How Context Matters for Non-electoral Political Participation in Western Democracies'. Dissertation manuscript.
Vráblíková, K. (2014) 'How context matters? Mobilization, political opportunity structures, and nonelectoral political participation in old and new democracies', *Comparative Political Studies*, 47 (2): 203–29.

Walgrave, S. and Rucht, D. (2010) *The World Says No to War: Demonstrations Against the War on Iraq*. Minneapolis, MN: University of Minnesota Press, pp. xiii–xxvi.

Weldon, S. and Dalton, R. J. (2010) *Democratic Structures and Democratic Participation: The Limits of Consociational Theory*. Paper presented at the conference 'Elections and Representative Democracy: Representation and Accountability', Twente University, The Netherlands, November.

Welzel, C. and Deutsch, F. (2012) 'Emancipative values and non-violent protest: the importance of "ecological" effects', *British Journal of Political Science*, 42: 465–79.

Whiteley, P., Stewart, M., Sanders, D. and Clarke, H. (2009) 'Do institutions really influence political participation? Contextual influences on turnout and participation in the world's democracies', *International Journal of Market Research*, 52 (1): 21–42.

Wielhouwer, P. W. and Lockerbie, B. (1994) 'Party contacting and political participation, 1952–1990', *American Journal of Political Science*, 38 (1): 211–29.

3

INFLUENCING WOMEN'S CIVIC AND POLITICAL PARTICIPATION

Contextual and individual determinants

Yvonne Galligan

Introduction

Why do women appear less interested in politics than men? This is a question that has puzzled social science for almost three generations, since Maurice Duverger investigated the political role of women for UNESCO in 1955. His findings – that there were few differences in the voting patterns of women and men, but women's participation in all other aspects of political life was much less than that of men – provided the first evidential basis for examining gender differences in civic engagement and political participation. He went on to explain these differences as emanating from 'the general structure of society, in the psychological and social environment':

> If the majority of women are little attracted to political careers, it is because everything tends to turn them away from them; if they allow politics to remain essentially a man's business, it is because everything conduces to this belief, tradition, family life, education, religion and literature.
>
> *(1955: 129)*

Sixty years on, the legal, social and economic environments, as well as individual opportunities and constraints, have been extensively explored in an effort to shed some light on the enduring gender differences in civic participation. This chapter reflects on this corpus of research, synthesising the findings of qualitative and quantitative investigations to see how far we have come in providing an answer to our opening question. It is an exploration of how far women feel that they have ownership of, and exercise influence over, the civic and political processes shaping twenty-first-century liberal democratic societies.

Addressing this research question calls for a clarification of what it is we mean by 'participation'. In general, the concept of participation invokes an expectation of active involvement in public life, be it in the civic or political sphere. Borrowing from Parry *et al.* (1992: 39), Ekman and Amnå (2012: 40) define participation broadly, as 'ways in which ordinary citizens try to influence the political decision-making process'. Thus activities grouped under the heading of political participation include voting, signing petitions, contacting politicians, campaigning and running for election. This dimension is the subject of extensive quantitative studies measuring the extent and intensity of political participation and the sex-based differences observed therein (for example, Burns *et al.* 2001; Van Deth and Elff 2000; Jelen *et al.* 1994).

The civic form of participation encompasses activities directed towards helping others (such as charity work, volunteering) or achieving a public good (attending meetings about issues of concern, using collective resources to improve the community). The disparate and diffuse nature of civic participation presents researchers with more challenges than the focused activities of political participation. Indeed, given the interaction of gender-role socialisation and a gendered distribution of social and economic resources (such as mobility, time and money), civic participation is often gender-differentiated. For instance, studies have repeatedly found that women are more likely than men to be involved in charity and religious-based organisation and activities (Taniguchi 2006; Djupe *et al.* 2007), and that younger women are more volunteer-oriented but less attentive to political affairs than their male peers (Jenkins 2005).[1] Understanding, at least in some part, why these gender differences appear is the focus of this chapter.

Determinants of public engagement

For participation in either civic or political arenas to take place, a number of pre-requisite conditions need to be present. These are generally seen as three-fold: the *structural opportunity* to participate (related to gender differences in opportunities to access and engage in organisational and associational life), the effects of this opportunity structure on the *orientation* of women and men towards public involvement, and the combination of macro and individual factors that shape the *predisposition* of individuals to use their time and talents in public engagement for the general good, be it civic volunteering, political action or both.

Structural opportunity

Gender differences in the structural opportunity to participate derive from the profile of gender power relations in a country, or a context within that country. These arrangements take place at the individual and societal level. They are inscribed in law, societal customs and practices, and in expectations of who rightfully occupies public roles. They are reinscribed (often unconsciously) on a daily basis, in the gendered performance of everyday life in private and in public (Chappell 2013: 614). This is the gender contract of a society, whose nature differs from one country to another. Drawing on feminist thought, the gender contract is summed up succinctly by the European Commission (2004) as

> A set of implicit and explicit rules governing gender relations which allocate different work and value, responsibilities and obligations to men and women and is maintained on three levels – cultural superstructure – the norms and values of society; institutions – family welfare, education and employment systems, etc.; and socialisation processes, notably in the family.

The form taken by a gender contract within a state influences the extent to which the empowerment of women and men differs. These gender empowerment differences derive from the different structural opportunities available to women and men, and interact with capacity and predisposition to influence citizens' involvement in general public life. Of course, the nature of the macro-political system matters too – a liberal democracy affords greater opportunities for the sustainability of an active civil society than an authoritarian regime, for example. In this chapter, though, we will take as given a macro-context of liberal democratic politics, in which the rule of law is respected, corruption is not endemic and civil society is fostered. In this macro-context, it is possible to delve more deeply into the opportunities for equal participation enjoyed by women and men. Identifying and measuring the nature of the gender contract is a complex matter, and has given rise to multiple indexes that seek to provide an insight into the relational social, economic and political empowerment of women and men (OECD 2007). Two sets of indices are particularly insightful – the World Economic Forum's Global Gender Gap Index (GGI) and the European Union's Gender Equality Index (GEI).

The World Economic Forum categorises countries according to a global gender gap index, measuring how countries divide their resources between women and men. Countries are benchmarked in terms of national gender gaps on economic, political, education and health criteria, with the intention of prompting the design of effective measures by governments and international organisations to eliminate gender inequality (Hausmann *et al.* 2012: 3). The countries in the PIDOP study were ranked in this index as shown in Table 3.1.

TABLE 3.1 Gender Gap Index (GGI) 2012 rankings

Country	Global rank	Global score	EU GGI rank
Sweden	4	0.8159	2
Belgium	12	0.7652	6
Germany	13	0.7629	7
UK	18	0.7433	10
Portugal	47	0.7071	15
Czech Republic	73	0.6767	23
Italy	80	0.6729	25
Turkey	124	0.6015	29

Source: Hausmann *et al.* (2012: 8–9); data is from 2011. A score of 1 indicates no gender gap.

Table 3.1 indicates that of the 135 countries included in the index, Sweden was among the most gender equal countries in the world, while Turkey was among those showing the greatest gender gaps in economic, educational, health and empowerment measures. In terms of income group (based on World Bank gross national income (GNI) per capita), all, with the exception of Turkey, were in the high-income category. Turkey was classified as being at the bottom of the upper-middle income group, bordering the lower-middle income classification. As with all measurement indices, the Global Gender Gap Index (GGI), the basis of the data informing the construction of the rankings, can be criticised. The GGI calls for complex data provision by participating states, not all of whom have available comprehensive national statistical data on gender, as well as on other measures. A second important drawback when gender relations are assessed is that the GGI (along with many other global indices) does not include a measurement of informal work, caring and unpaid labour or time-use data (OECD 2007: 6).

A newly constructed European gender equality index by the European Institute of Gender Equality (EIGE) addresses the lacunae above in determining gender gaps – the levels of achievement between women and men on six indicators – work, money, knowledge, time, power and health. Additionally, it incorporates two satellite domains: intersecting inequalities (immigrant status, older workers and lone parents/carers) and violence against women. It provides a comprehensive and nuanced view of how close each EU member state is in achieving gender equality. The overall results for the countries in the PIDOP study are, as one can see from Table 3.2, quite similar to that of the EU GGI ranking. The difference in country order between the two rankings can be explained by the more detailed and nuanced data measuring in the EIGE index.

For instance, the reversal of rank in the case of Portugal and the Czech Republic can be explained by important time-use differences. In Portugal, outside of work and education, 90 per cent of time spent on domestic work is provided by women, while 63 per cent of time engaged in this unpaid work is provided by Czech women. This means that Portugese women have little time for volunteering and spend only 4 per cent of their time on this activity. Their Czech counterparts can afford to spend more (8 per cent) of their time volunteering. While there are differences in non-work and non-educational time use between women, there are marked

TABLE 3.2 EIGE Gender Equality Index (GEI), 2013 rankings

Country	EIGE rank	EIGE score	EU Global GI rank
Sweden	1	74.3	2
UK	5	60.4	10
Belgium	6	59.6	6
Germany	12	51.6	7
Czech Republic	17	44.4	23
Portugal	23	41.3	15
Italy	25	40.9	25

Source: EIGE (2013); data is from 2010. A score of 1 indicates no gender gap.

TABLE 3.3 Ratification of the Optional Protocol to the Convention on the Elimination of Discrimination Against Women (year)

Country	Year
Italy	2000
Czech Republic	2001
Germany	2002
Portugal	2002
Sweden	2003
UK	2004
Belgium	2004

Source: http://www.un.org/womenwatch/daw/cedaw/protocol/text.htm

differences between women and men across all countries. Throughout the EU, women perform the vast bulk of caring activities, while men spend much less time on domestic activities and are more likely to participate in sporting and cultural activities and volunteering. This point about time use matters for the formation of a pre-political – and indeed political – orientation.

Although the macro-political environment in each of the EU countries above is based on broadly similar foundations (though each country has its own unique political history and cultural heritage), the nature of gender power relations show marked differences. In our sample of countries Sweden is the most egalitarian according to the EIGE index while Italy is the least. Were the gender equality indicators of Turkey to be measured in this way, one would expect to find a more pronounced version of the Italian trajectory. What these indices tell us, though, is that despite having legal gender equality, the equal right to vote and run for election, and the right to take international action to prevent violation of their human rights (through the CEDAW optional protocol procedure (Table 3.3), women do not enjoy equal status with men in our case countries. This gendered public and private context, with its unequal distribution of economic and social resources, plays an important role in shaping differences in women's and men's orientation to politics.

Orientation

Having established that the macro-context is gender-differentiated to the advantage of men, the next aspect to consider is how this gendered socio-political environment specifically structures women's orientation to politics, and civic activity more generally, differently to that of men.

The influences of education and labour force participation have long been identified as important determinants of gender differences in civic engagement and political participation. The main explanatory argument suggests that as men are likely to be more highly educated and have higher levels of employment than women, they are more disposed to acquire the necessary social capital to enable them be more socially engaged and politically active than women. Inglehart and Norris contend that 'people with higher socio-economic status – those possessing the advantages of more education, income and more secure careers – are usually more active in politics' (2003: 120). This point is reiterated by Randall (1982: 62) and Conway (1991: 34) and is a widely accepted analytical fact in this field of study. Burns *et al.* (2001: 42) note the gendered effects of workforce progression, with men acquiring more power, authority and financial and supportive resources as they progress in their careers. Women are observed not to acquire these advantages to the same extent as men.

Nonetheless, the emphasis on the salience of labour force participation as a precondition, or facilitator, of engagement and participation is contested. The point is made that labour force participation *in itself* does not contribute to enhanced political knowledge for either women or men. Instead, education and gender are seen as the two most important predictors of political interest, with better educated women more interested in politics than their less-educated sisters (van Deth and Elff 2000: 16). Indeed, the 2005–8 World Values Survey[2] reaffirms this point, with 63 per cent of university-educated women (73 per cent of men) indicating an interest in politics compared with 34 per cent of women (and 50 per cent of men) who had completed compulsory elementary education.[3] Yet, although higher education levels produce greater interest in politics among women, it alone is not sufficient to equalise the level of orientation between women and men. While it is beyond the remit of this chapter to explore the reasons behind the gender gap in career paths and employment, this discussion draws our attention to the systemic difficulties faced by women in becoming politically engaged as a consequence of their socially determined roles. This view puts an emphasis on the differentiated labour force participation profiles of women and men, with women more likely to occupy part-time, underpaid and non-permanent positions. The resulting economic insecurity (or their economic dependence on male partners), coupled with their caring responsibilities, has the effect of making women resource- and time-poor compared with men. As a result, they are less likely to take advantage of opportunities to be civically engaged and politically active.

Alongside this point, there is a related analysis that seeks to link women's caring roles and their oft-observed lesser interest in politics. When women primarily identify as mothers and home-makers, the argument goes, this construction of their identity contributes to women's lesser sense of 'internal' efficacy with regard to participating in political affairs, which in turn leads to a lesser interest in and involvement of women in political activities (Sapiro 1984: 90). Lovenduski (1986:130) observes that being resigned to the home and low-paying jobs has produced 'feelings of low efficacy amongst women, which impede an active interest in an area normally portrayed as male defined and clearly male occupied'. There is, nonetheless, scope to question this causal argument on the grounds that the adoption of a particular social role need not necessarily determine a woman's sense of political efficacy and interest. The resource of time and lack thereof and the capital-rich resource of educational attainment may have more explanatory power than motherhood (and caring responsibilities more generally) in determining the background conditions facilitating women's civic and political participation. In this sense, then, the extent of latency in women's propensity to engage in politics (discussed more generally by Ekman and Amnå 2012) is an aspect that needs more careful attention.

In keeping with this point, it is useful to note that some authors make an important distinction between motherhood and marriage, with the latter now appearing to have a positive effect on female political knowledge and interest, contrary to earlier assumptions that conflated marriage and motherhood. Claibourn and Sapiro (2001: 9) suggest that being married, or indeed partnered, has a positive effect on men's and women's political knowledge in Britain, Poland and the Netherlands, has no effect in the Czech Republic and Ukraine, and in Hungary has a positive impact on men's but not on women's levels of political knowledge. Their study leads them to conclude that 'in general, where marriage is related to political knowledge, it has positive effects, but much more often for women than for men' (2001: 9). However, this claim needs to be treated with some caution, as results from the 2005–8 World Values Study for the countries of special interest to this chapter show that women's interest in politics remains relatively steady, at about 42 per cent, irrespective of their marital status. Being widowed is the only circumstance that slightly raises women's interest in politics (45 per cent). In contrast, being married or partnered enhances men's political interest (over 60 per cent) and, presumably, their political knowledge.

Interest in political affairs, leading to the acquisition of knowledge in this area, has long been considered a reliable indicator of orientation or attention to public decision-making. Moreover, the more interested a person is, the more likely they are to understand institutions, the electoral system and politics more generally. These higher levels of political awareness facilitate participation. Along with efficacy – the sense that one can wield influence or believe that one's voice matters – these two variables provide strong predictors of a citizen's readiness to participate. Van Deth and Elff (2000: 17) sum up the overwhelming finding of surveys and studies on the gendered nature of political interest by observing that while the effect of gender on levels of political interest or apathy varies among European countries, the effect is 'significant in all countries and all point to the same conventional direction: females are less interested in politics than males'. Other studies, focused on political knowledge, support the direction of this finding, with Claibourn and Sapiro (2001:13) observing that 'women, all other things equal, were less knowledgeable than men in all the countries under consideration'.

Figure 3.1 shows that in five countries relevant to this discussion, more men than women declare that they are interested in politics,[4] and country-specific variations are strong. The proportion of men and women indicating that they are 'very interested' in politics is more equal in Sweden and Germany, and least equal in Italy and Turkey, where men outnumber women by a factor of three in this category.

At the other end of the spectrum, we find the reverse pattern occurring – women outnumber men in being 'not at all interested', and overall this response category

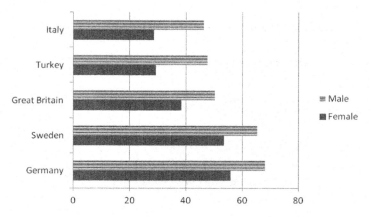

FIGURE 3.1 Interest in politics by sex (%)
Source: Values Surveys Databank.

constitutes one-fifth (20.9 per cent) of the population. What is striking is the persistence of this gender gap in political interest, even after controlling for differences in resources (Verba *et al.* 1997; Banducci and Semetko 2002: 17–18).

The gender gap in political interest has a relevant impact on women's and men's trust in government institutions. Trust, or confidence, in public institutions is often taken as an indicator of political efficacy. Coffé and Bolzendahl (2010: 3) recently noted that 'Women, on average, feel significantly less politically efficacious and have substantially less trust in government and interest in politics than men.' However, our country cases seem not to bear out this observation on two counts. Firstly, there is very little difference in women's and men's expressed confidence in parliament. Indeed, in Turkey, a majority of both women and men have confidence in their parliament, and more women (64 per cent) than men (59 per cent) hold this view (Figure 3.2).

Secondly, it is true that men with an interest in politics (either very or somewhat interested) are more likely to have confidence or trust in parliament than women of the same disposition, but the only substantial gender difference is among the small group of those very interested in politics, who account for less than 15 per cent of respondents overall. Among this select group of dedicated politics-watchers, 22 per cent of men and only 9 per cent of women indicate a 'great deal' of confidence in parliament. In contrast, women expressing no interest in politics indicated considerable confidence in parliament (39 per cent), suggesting that they were willing to leave decisions on issues of governance and public policy in the hands of elected representatives. They did not indicate feeling less politically efficacious. Indeed, the explanation for gender differences in orientation may have as much to do with the nature of the democratic institutions, especially the electoral system (Caul Kittilson and Schwindt-Bayer 2010; Karp and Banducci 2008). The significance of this institutional variable has to do with the type of cue it sends to

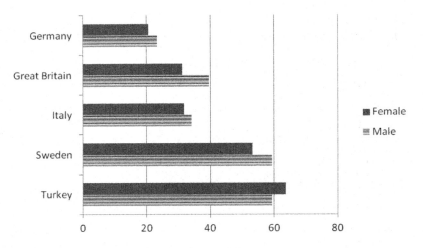

FIGURE 3.2 Confidence in parliament, by sex (%)
Source: World Values Survey Databank.

citizens. Proportional electoral systems send out a message of inclusiveness, thereby encouraging all citizens – and especially women – to take an interest in public affairs. This point brings to our attention the importance of cues in promoting civic and political engagement, and the different responses of women and men to these cues (Djupe *et al.* 2007).

Thus it is not sufficient to rely on individual-level factors alone in explaining orientation to civic and political life. The institutional setting, and the signals of inclusion (or otherwise) sent out by political institutions – especially electoral systems – has a stronger impact on women's propensity to engage than that of men, although it remains important for both genders. This is a very under-researched aspect of orientation, and its further investigation could greatly improve our understanding of why it is that women and men have different inclinations towards politics and public life.

The focus on gender differences in political interest, knowledge and confidence in institutions is relevant to the broader study in which we are engaged, as they constitute an indicator of the extent of women's and men's latent predisposition for political participation. Generalised factors, such as education levels, employment patterns and the social culture, operate on a society-wide scale as potential facilitators, or otherwise to political participation. And, as we have seen, political institutions also signal participatory cues. But for these general factors to take effect requires the action, or otherwise, of individuals in pursuing opportunities for engagement. In this regard, men's and women's experiences of their society differ: women's feelings of attachment to the wider society are conditioned by these experiences, and by the nature of the gender contract sustained within that society. Understanding the manner in which the predisposition to engage is different, as well as similar, for women and men can shed light on their subsequent involvement in civic and political action.

Predisposition

A long-standing theme in the literature on gendered patterns of political participation is that women are more likely to participate in informal politics than in formal political spheres. However, informal politics as a concept covers a very wide spectrum of political behaviour, ranging from relatively simple, individualised and time-efficient activities such as signing a petition and making decisions on product purchases according to a principled position (e.g. Fair Trade coffee) to mass action protest politics such as striking and demonstrating. As discussed in the typology by Ekman and Amnå (2012), informal activity also includes civic engagement – an aspect that is generally ignored in the treatment of gender gaps in political behaviour. While civic engagement itself is not 'political', it does imply a move from being a passive citizen to being an active one, and thus possibly more predisposed to being interested and participative in political affairs. Although in the standard literature on political action, civic engagement-type activities (such as volunteering in the community, charity) based on personal interest in specific issues is treated as a dimension of informal politics, the Ekman and Amnå study breaks that link and treats civic engagement as a separate category of observable citizen behaviour. Where both strands of thinking come together is in agreeing that volunteering is predominantly an individualised expression of interest in, and attachment to, one's society.

It has long been held that women use their 'free' time to engage in volunteering activities and that their socialisation experiences lead them on this path of public activity compared with men, who are more socialised towards politically focused pursuits. Data from the time-use section of the EIGE gender equality index provide valuable information on the pattern of women's and men's participation in volunteering activities (Figure 3.3). Across the EU, women and men spend much the same amount of time in this way (14.4 per cent and 14.7 per cent respectively). There are interesting country variations contained within this average. Women in Sweden (23.3 per cent) and Germany (22.6 per cent) spend over one-fith of their time in charity and volunteering work. In Sweden, however, men spend even more time (30.5 per cent) than women in this activity. Both genders are surpassed by women and men in the Netherlands, who spend over one-third (33.8 per cent and 37.5 per cent respectively) of their time in this way, making them the leading volunteers in the European Union. German men give slightly more of their time than their female peers to this activity. In the remaining countries of our study, women spend more time on volunteering than men. The time period given to volunteering varies considerably too – Portugese women and men are the least likely to spend time volunteering, while in our study Swedish women and men are the most likely to do so. The variation in time use needs further investigation, but it is possible that the role of religion in shaping a political culture – and indeed a sense of civic-mindedness – has a part to play.

64 Yvonne Galligan

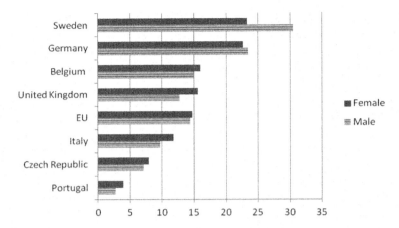

FIGURE 3.3 Time spent on volunteering and charitable activities, by sex (%)
Source: EIGE Gender Equality Index.

Indeed, the role religion plays in orienting women and men to public life in different degrees is a matter of extensive debate in the participation literature. Inglehart and Norris (2003), for example, illustrate that in countries with predominantly Catholic traditions, women are less likely to exhibit interest in, and knowledge of, politics, and are less likely to be involved in non-party political activity and participate generally in political life. In countries with a predominantly Protestant tradition, they hold that women are more likely to be civically and politically engaged. This general analysis is backed, at least in part, by the time-use gender gap in volunteering, indicated in Figure 3.3. It is a finding also broadly indicated by Inglehart (1981, quoted in Banducci and Semetko 2002), who suggest that in countries in which Catholicism is dominant on the whole 'men have a greater store of political knowledge, are more interested in politics, and feel more efficacious than women.' This general statement is contradicted by Claibourn and Sapiro, who contend that although in Catholic and Orthodox societies female political participation is lower than in Protestant societies, overall levels of female political knowledge are seemingly unaffected by the predominance of Catholicism or Orthodox Christianity (2001: 19). Yet there seems to be sufficient evidence to suggest a link between the religious tradition of a society and the nature of its gender contract, the latter an indicator of the scope for women to be socialised into public affairs. In this regard, one can say that Protestant countries have a stronger tradition of egalitarianism, individual responsibility and support for women's rights, which creates an environment that is more supportive of women's (and men's) participation in the civic and public sphere than that created by Catholicism. However, one must be mindful too of the degree to which civil society is developed, and volunteering is a part of the civic culture. Spending time on volunteering and charitable activities was not extensive in many former East European countries, hence the low result for the Czech Republic in our study.

Deriving robust generalisations from levels of civic participation, such as volunteering, is a complex matter as the above discussion reveals. Individual predisposition to partake in civic-minded activities is modulated by the macro-level environment, such as the health of civil society, the cultural imprint of religion, as well as the time women and men necessarily spend on making a living and caring for families and other dependants. Nonetheless, the extent of time spent in volunteering gives an indication of the attentiveness of women and men to matters in the civic and public sphere, and hence their likelihood of extending volunteering and charity work into more politically directed activities.

For some individuals, the move from civic engagement to political participation is a seamless transition flowing from their interest and engagement in activities that lead in the direction of political life. In many cases, this move either never takes place, or only happens sporadically, for example at election time. Nonetheless, this is an important transition point in terms of our typology, for it marks the bridge between latent and manifest political participation, and opens up the possibility of individual socialisation to political life. It also is the point at which the engagement choices entered into by women and men can influence the nature and form of their subsequent political participation and activism. Not surprisingly, it has been found that although women and men's voting turnout is similar in advanced democracies, they differ in their choice of site in which they engage in manifest political participation – as distinct from the latent form indicated by volunteering.

When women and men engage in activities that suggest they are politically attentive citizens, these activities often take place in different arenas. Trade union activity is a case in point. Trade union involvement has a complex gendered connection with labour-force participation and sex-role socialisation. While there are not significant gender differences in trade union membership, men are twice as likely as women to be active, and therefore in a better position to take advantage of leadership opportunities. Given the close association between trade union activism and political party membership (especially left party membership), this particular form of activity can introduce an individual into networks of a political nature. Many women trade union activists, as men, have entered conventional party politics and gone on to develop political careers. Other sites of manifest political participation include business and employer associations, with a similar close affiliation to formal politics. When elected women are asked about their routes into politics, they often mention their leadership of civic and issue organisations with an orientation to public decision-making as a catalyst to further political participation. For men, civic leadership is less of a route to conventional politics than is activism in the peak labour and employer organisations.

Recent theory points to the importance of the link between political participation and 'pre-political' activities that have the potential to lead to involvement in political matters. It also highlights the non-linear and fragmented nature of political engagement, an aspect of participation that has not been given sufficient attention in empirical studies to date. Ekman and Amnå (2012, and Chapter 6 by Amnå and Ekman in this volume) in particular explore these participatory nuances through their development of the concept of 'stand-by' citizen, characterised by high-capacity and predisposed individuals who are already socially active in the interests of a common good and are ready to be mobilised, in an episodic manner, when the right issue activates participation. They describe this orientation to engagement as 'latent' participation, involving two dimensions of activism – social involvement and civic engagement – along with a degree of attention to public affairs. Ekman and Amnå's broadening of the participatory concept to include 'standby', or likelihood of participating, captures a wider spread of people than the conventional understanding of participation.

One of the first studies to adopt this conceptual broadening of participation was the Hansard Audit of Political Engagement 2013. It found that while only 8 per cent of respondents in their survey claimed to have contacted a local elected representative in 2012, the likelihood of doing so increased five-fold if respondents felt strongly about an issue (Hansard 2013: 71). Indeed 39 per cent of respondents to this study were found to fall into the 'standby' category, while only 22 per cent could be classed as having taken part in a political activity over the previous 12 months (Hansard 2013: 73–4). Thus the Hansard study bore out empirically the theoretical hypothesis of Ekman and Amnå – that there is an underlying potential for participation among the general public that does not usually show up in conventional surveys on civic and political engagement.

Gender differences in political participation, and propensity to participate, were evident in the Hansard study: while almost one-quarter (23.3 per cent) of men engaged in at least one form of political activity in 2012, only one-fifth (20.8) of female respondents did so. Almost one half (45.8 per cent) of all men were in the 'standby' segment, compared to one-third (33.4 per cent) of all women. In contrast, one-quarter of women (25 per cent) did not define their participatory status, compared with only one in eight men (12.7 per cent). Finally, there was less of a gender difference in non-participants – 20.8 per cent of women declared in this group and 18.2 per cent of men. If one combines manifest and standby categories of citizenship, almost 7 out of 10 men (69.1 per cent) are potential or active engagers, compared with just over one half of women (54.2 per cent). Given that there is little or no difference in the views of manifest and standby citizens about the political system and involvement in politics (Hansard 2013: 78–82), it can be deduced that the gender differences in orientation to and participation in politics carry over into opinions about politics.

The 2005–8 World Values Survey reveals that women outnumber men in engaging in the most basic of participatory acts, signing a petition. Irrespective of education level, this is so: 44 per cent of women with no formal education in the countries of our study indicated that they had recently signed a petition, compared with 36 per cent of men with no formal education. At the other end of the educational scale, a significant 79 per cent of women with a higher education/university qualification had recently put their names to a petition compared with 68 per cent of their male peers. This pattern was persistent across four of the five countries in our WVS study – only in Turkey did women's petition-signing rate fall below that of men, yet over half of women (55 per cent, 64 per cent for men) still engaged in this activity. This fact points to the intersection of time, gender and political interest – time-poor women, of whatever educational background, will engage in a political act once it makes minimal demands on their personal resources, although higher educated women are more likely to do so. It does, however, indicate that if similar time-related resources were available to women as to men their predisposition to engage actively would increase.

Voting is one of the most common forms of citizen-oriented political participation. It requires some personal initiative and political awareness yet, unlike other conventional forms of political participation, it makes fairly minimal demands on time, knowledge and effort. Evidence from studies of electoral behaviour indicates that gender differences in voting have become insignificant since the 1980s in both Europe and the United States. This was the case in 2010: according to the European Social Survey, 67.6 per cent of men and 69 per cent of women reported voting in the last election. The WVS replicates this pattern, showing that younger men and women were less likely to vote than their older counterparts, and while there is a very slight gender difference in their participation (61.7 per cent of men aged 15–29 voted in a recent parliamentary election, compared with 59.9 per cent of women of this age), the overall pattern shows negligible gender differences in turnout (79.2 per cent for men, 78.5 per cent for women). Analysis of the 2004 ISSP data for 18 advanced Western democracies, conducted by Coffé and Bolzendahl (2010) confirmed the absence of differences in the voting rate of women and men. However, they offer a nuance of that general finding that takes account of the fact that women and men do not start from the same place in terms of their orientation to politics. They prove that when political attitudes are taken into account (political interest, political efficacy, trust in government) women were *more* likely than men to vote (Corsi *et al.* 2013). In other words, when the handicaps women experience in terms of their orientation to politics are allowed for, statistically women are more likely to vote than men – and in practice it is this more intense commitment of women to voting that drives the gender-equal voting pattern. As Coffé and Bolzendahl (2010) conclude: 'If women were to develop an interest in politics and feelings of political efficacy equal to that of men, women would vote more than men.'

Civic engagement does not always lead to formal or conventional political participation. Indeed, given that in any society only about 5 per cent of the population are active in formal politics, it is through extra-parliamentary participation (other than voting) that the majority of citizens express their political views and attachments. Indeed, this form of manifest political participation can be sporadic and carries less of an opportunity cost than formal and conventional participation. The gendered nature of extra-parliamentary activism, legal and illegal, has been recorded since the foundational Barnes and Kaase political action study (1979). Women have been found to prefer to engage in individual, discrete political acts – signing a petition, boycotting – that require less investment of time, money and energy than formal politics, yet are informed by an awareness of political issues. Men have been found to be more likely than women to engage in illegal extra-parliamentary activity – sit-ins, strikes and other protest actions. Both women and men, though, have been found to be involved in social movements and other loosely organised activities oriented to political ends – an aspect of extra-parliamentary activism that has been extensively treated in social movement research but not fully considered in the participation literature.

Turning to the more formal, or 'manifest', type of political participation, the evidence shows that there are strong gender differences. Men are more likely to donate to, contact and campaign for a political party than women. This pattern can be explained to some extent by the more scarce resources of time and money at the disposal of many women. Given that women are more open to being influenced by contextual cues, the male-dominated and often conflictual nature of these activities can play a role in deterring women from taking part. In addition, men's sites of latent participation, such as in formal organisations, sporting associations and other high-profile networks, may indicate their more general orientation to politics, as discussed above. Men are also more likely to become party members, though it is questionable if party membership actually indicates anything more than a sufficiently crystallised interest in political affairs to be amenable to declaring political partisanship. Furthermore, drawing conclusions on women's political participation based on their party membership must also to be treated with care, as their membership may be more formal than active.

Conclusion

The focus of this chapter is to lay out the broad differences in political participation between men and women, and seek to understand why this is so. In doing so, what emerges is the importance of the two dimensions of latent political participation – social involvement and civic engagement – in predisposing an individual to make the move into overt political activity or manifest participation. It is in this category of latent participation that the gender differences in predisposition to become politically active are visible, and which shape the gendered pattern of manifest political action in all its forms.

From the range of social characteristics discussed above, it appears that age, educational levels and labour market participation have a bearing on women's sense of political belonging in a more salient manner than that of men. An important factor in influencing the extent to which women are socially involved and engaged is that of time: and indeed the lack of time resources constrains women's involvement leading to their habitual disengagement from the many forms of political participation. And the third major dimension to come through is the psychological cues delivered by institutions and organisations that play a role in determining gendered patterns of inclusion or exclusion.

In considering gender differences in participation at both individual and collective levels, one must also take account of the facilitating factors that underpin action – the cultural and social norms, including religion, that shape the nature of the gender contract in a society. In addition, one must take account of the opportunities to engage that may be distinctively different for women and men, especially in ethnic minority conditions (Chapter 4 by Montgomery, this volume). Equally important is their influence on latent forms of participation, the forerunners of conventional and unconventional political action. The cultural and social norms can predispose women to be uninterested in the goings-on in the public sphere, and can contribute to women's observed lesser sense of efficacy in relation to the political world, their lower levels of trust in political institutions and their consequent lower orientation to engage in manifest forms of political action. At the end of the day, Duverger's succinct summary of the conditions that shape women's propensity to be active political citizens still holds.

Notes

1 Unfortunately, an important 2010 European Commission report, *Volunteering in the European Union*, pays little attention to gender-based patterns of engagement in this form of civic participation.
2 The 2005–8 wave of the World Values Survey (WVS) covered 59 countries, five of which are of particular interest in this chapter – Germany, Belgium, Italy, Turkey and Great Britain – as they are among the countries closely studied in the PIDOP project.
3 This combines 'very interested' and 'somewhat interested'.
4 This combines 'very interested' and 'somewhat interested'.

References

Banducci, Susan and Semetko, Holli A. (2002) 'Gender and context: influences on political interest in Europe', *Democratic Participation and Political Communication in Systems of Multi-level Governance*. Draft paper 5th Framework Research Programme.

Barnes, Samuel H. and Kaase, Max (1979) *Political Action: Mass Participation in Five Western Democracies*. Beverley Hills, CA: Sage.

Burns, Nancy, Schlozman, Kay Lehman and Verba, Sidney (2001) *The Private Roots of Public Action: Gender, Equality and Political Participation*. Cambridge, MA: Harvard University Press.

Caul Kittilson, Miki and Schwindt-Bayer, Leslie (2010) 'Engaging citizens: the role of power-sharing institutions', *Journal of Politics*, 72 (4): 990–1002.

Chappell, Louise (2013) 'The state and governance', in Georgina Waylen, Karen Celis, Johanna Kantola and S. Laurel Weldon (eds), *The Oxford Handbook of Gender and Politics*. Oxford: Oxford University Press, pp. 603–53.

Claibourn, Michelle and Sapiro, Virginia (2001) *Gender Differences in Citizen-level Democratic Citizenship: Evidence from the Comparative Study of Electoral Systems*. Paper presented at the Mid-West Political Science Convention, Chicago, April.

Coffé, Hilde and Bolzendahl, Catherine (2010) 'Same game, different rules? Gender differences in political participation', *Sex Roles*, 62: 318–33.

Conway, M. Margaret (1991) *Political Participation in the United States*. Thousand Oaks, CA: CQ Press.

Corsi, Marcella, Galligan, Yvonne and Ruiz-Ben, Esther (2013) 'EU Citizenship: A Gendered Perspective'. Brussels: Fondazione Giacomo Brodolini (FGB) and Istituto per la Ricerca Sociale (IRS), unpublished report.

Djupe, Paul A., Sokhey, Anand E. and Gilbert, Christopher E. (2007) 'Present but not accounted for? Gender differences in civic resource acquisition', *American Journal of Political Science*, 51 (4): 906–20.

Duverger, Maurice (1955) *The Political Role of Women*. Paris: UNESCO.

Ekman, Joakim and Amnå, Erik (2012) 'Political participation and civic engagement: towards a new typology', *Human Affairs*, 22 (3): 283–300.

European Commission (2004) Toolkit on mainstreaming gender equality in EC development cooperation, available at: http://ec.europa.eu/europeaid/sp/gender-toolkit/index.htm (accessed 9 September 2013).

Hansard Society (2013) *Audit of Political Engagement 10: The 2013 Report*. London: Hansard Society.

Hausmann, Ricardo, Tyson, Laura D., Bekhouche, Yasmina and Zahidi, Saadia (2012) 'The Global Gender Gap Index 2012', in Ricardo Hausmann, Laura D. Tyson and Saadia Zahidi, *The Global Gender Gap Report 2012*. Geneva: World Economic Forum.

Inglehart, Margaret L. (1981) 'Political interest in West European women', *Comparative Political Studies*, 14: 299–336.

Inglehart, Ronald and Norris, Pippa (2003) *Rising Tide: Gender Equality and Cultural Change Around the World*. New York: Cambridge University Press.

Jelen, Ted G., Thomas, Sue and Wilcox, Clyde (1994) 'The gender gap in comparative perspective', *European Journal of Political Research*, 25: 171–86.

Jenkins, Krista (2004) *Gender and Civic Engagement: Secondary Analysis of Survey Data*, Circle Working Paper 41. Baltimore, MD: CIRCLE, University of Maryland School of Public Policy.

Karp, Jeffrey A. and Banducci, Susan A. (2008) 'Political efficacy and participation in twenty-seven democracies: how electoral systems shape political behavior', *British Journal of Political Studies*, 38 (2): 311–34.

Lovenduski, Joni (1986) *Women and European Politics: Contemporary Feminism and Public Policy*. Amherst, MA: University of Massachusetts Press.

OECD (2007) Gender Indicators: What, Why and How. Available at: http://www.oecd.org/dac/gender-development/43041409.pdf (accessed 6 September 2013).

Parry, Geraint, Moyser, George and Day, Neil (1992) *Political Participation and Democracy in Britain*. Cambridge: Cambridge University Press.

Randall, Vicki (1982) *Women and Politics: An International Perspective*. London: Macmillan.

Sapiro, Virginia (1984) *The Political Integration of Women: Roles, Socialization and Politics*. Champaign, IL: University of Illinois Press.

Taniguchi, Hiromi (2006) 'Men's and women's volunteering: gender differences in the effects of employment and family characteristics', *Nonprofit and Voluntary Sector Quarterly*, 35 (1): 83–101.

van Deth, Jan and Elff, M. (2000) *Political Involvement and Apathy in Europe 1973–1998*, MZES Working Paper No. 33. Mannheim: MZES.

Verba, Sidney, Burns, Nancy, and Schlozman, Kay Lehman (1997) 'Knowing and caring about politics: gender and political engagement', *Journal of Politics*, 59: 1051–72.

4

PARTICIPATION AND INTEGRATION

The contextual factors influencing minority and migrant participation

Victoria Montgomery

Introduction

Political participation is a classical question in political scientific research and an indicator of the health of a democracy, the legitimacy of a political system and the level of engagement of its citizens. Indeed, it is not valued simply as a means to test issues such as those mentioned above; for some it is a value in and of itself, creating links of loyalty within society and between citizens (de Varennes 1998), thus furthering societal cohesion.

However, in recent years the nature of political life, and thus the context in which questions of political participation are considered, has changed substantially. Social and economic transformations wrought by globalisation, particularly with regard to migration (Bauman 2004) and the impact of new technologies (Castells 1996), has had significant impact on the makeup and organisation of society. Political participation must be reconsidered in light of this. Of increasing interest, therefore, is the question of political participation and migrant and minority communities. This is to a large extent a question of their integration since discrimination may be considered as a contextual impact on participation, and integration policies or frameworks are part of, and impact on, political structures and institutions. Undoubtedly, participation in society can facilitate integration by giving minorities a voice and by reducing prejudice against them through intercultural dialogue. Indeed, participation is now seen as part of the protection remit of minorities (Ghai 2003: 3). The exercise of minority rights and prevention of discrimination cannot be ensured without minority participation (Bieber 2003: 1).

This chapter then will consider the relationship between migrant and minority communities and political participation, paying attention to the link between participation and integration and focusing particularly on contextual issues. The chapter asks who migrants and minorities are and considers how definitions of participation relate to these communities. It discusses the relationship between identity, integration and participation, considering sources of marginalisation and relating models of integration to questions of participation. This is then taken forward to consider the practice of participation with particular emphasis on the intersection of institutional and community level factors.

Migrants vs. minorities: political inequality vs. participatory inequality

The former OSCE High Commissioner on National Minorities, Max van der Stoel, jokingly remarked, 'Even though I may not have a definition of what constitutes a minority, I would dare to say that I know a minority when I see one' (cited in Palermo and Woelk 2003: 227). And certainly it is the case that defining minority communities is a difficult and contested task. What is clear is that they are defined by real differences to the majority population or culture (Wheatley 2002: 4), or more specifically as

> numerically inferior to the rest of the population of a state, in a non-dominant position, whose members – being nationals of the state – possess ethnic, religious or linguistic characteristics differing from those of the rest of the population and show, if only implicitly, a sense of solidarity directed towards preserving their culture, traditions, religion or language.
> *(Capotorti 1976: 14)*

Thus minorities may be defined by ethnicity, religion, nationality, language or culture, and most likely a mixture of these. However, when considering participation it is necessary to note that this umbrella term contains two categories: those with citizenship (minorities) and those without (migrants). Those with citizenship have full political equality but often suffer from participatory inequality on account of discrimination, less identification with political institutions, different levels of access to participation due to poor language skills or a lower socio-economic status (Diehl and Blohm 2001). While it is important to make this distinction, it is clear that there are problems associated with either treating migrants and minorities as separate categories or in fact lumping them together. A lack of citizenship does not always mean a complete lack of political rights; it is all a question of status. While the situation varies across Europe, the last couple of decades have seen rights extended to non-citizens, which is an acceptance of the changing situation in societies, or what Ghai refers to a 'fact of migration' (Ghai 2003: 10). EU citizens and those from former colonies are often given voting rights at least in local elections, as are persons who have been resident for a minimum length of time. Moreover, to consider participation solely in terms of political rights or none not only obscures this issue of status, but also ignores the fact that migrants do participate in the public sphere, be this in a political or civil sense. Indeed, as Ugba (2005) has pointed out in relation to Ireland, large numbers of asylum-seekers who are prevented from working or enrolling in college often get involved in various types of activism.

And yet it is also important to consider how migrants may be members of wider minority communities, which again creates a certain fuzziness in the boundaries between these categories. While not all minority identities are underpinned by migration, it is certainly the case that significant proportions are what could be termed transnational or diaspora communities which may influence their patterns of participation.[1] Traditionally, considering diaspora as part of identity is acknowledging that '"the old country" – a notion often buried deep in language, religion, custom or folklore – always has some claim on loyalty and emotions' (Cohen 1997: ix). This does not just affect solely the first generation; subsequent generations also demonstrate an acceptance of an inescapable link with their ancestors' past migration history (McLeod 2000: 207). 'To be blunt, migrancy has effects which last long after the act of migrating has finished' (McLeod 2000: 207). As such, many transnational communities maintain political ties with their homeland, such as voting and engaging in debate. Yet this does not necessarily negate a sense of being part of the society in which a person lives or is born. Rather, it is when a sense of home becomes jeopardised by accusations or feelings of difference that a diaspora identity can become a more central focus in a person's life. Discrimination, low external political efficacy and a low socio-economic status can create a sense of marginalisation and alienation where the only meaningful political engagement is to be found elsewhere. Indeed, Messina (2004) has shown how lower voter turnouts among immigrant communities is linked to continuing politics with country of origin. Moreover, when political marginalisation takes on a collective understanding, disengagement can develop into a cultural norm, which can become a determining factor in the participation levels of minority communities (Uhlaner *et al.* 1989).

The terms 'migrants' and 'minorities' are individual categories but they are not entirely distinct and, unless the research is a case study of an indigenous minority for example, these two categories cannot be considered in isolation. Both may face similar sources of participatory inequality which in the case of migrants will frame their future participation when granted full political rights. Indeed, as previously stated, participation is not exclusive to those with citizenship; it is a question of defining participation, which is the focus of the next section. Therefore, while still accepting that there are differences, this chapter will consider migrant and minority communities under the heading of minorities, unless explicitly stated otherwise.

Political participation from a minority perspective

One consistent finding in many studies is that advantaged groups have higher levels of participation (Dalton 2002; Verba *et al.* 1978). Systematic inequalities in political participation can bias the process in favour of the advantaged by creating a vicious circle where political and social inequalities reinforce each other (Verba 2003). This suggests that minorities are disengaged from politics, which is not entirely the case. Such generalisations tend to relate to conventional political participation, more specifically voting. Indeed, it is almost entirely in electoral participation that this discrepancy between minorities and majority community participation exists (Sandovici and Listhaug 2006; Gallego 2007: 14). So although it is important that majority communities are benefiting disproportionately from the formal decision-making process, and as such have greater access to sources of power, a narrow definition of political participation such as this does not further our understanding of minority participation. This narrow conception of political participation obscures unconventional forms of political participation, various sources of civil engagement and the recourse to utilise new technologies in participation and engagement. And this applies to both minority and majority communities. For example, in the case of Britain, voting is in decline at all levels of the population with a decline in voter turnout of over 15 per cent between 1992 and 2005 (Dean 2007). Perhaps then, it would be more useful to consider the changing character of participation. New technologies are opening up new ways of participating, what is termed e-democracy. Online campaigns, blogs, e-petitions and the use of YouTube, for example, are activities that are increasing, although as Fossato points out, it must be questioned whether this leads to any tangible results 'offline' unless such activities are supported by informal ties to decision-makers (Fossato 2009). There are also growing trends towards newer forms of participation such as political consumerism. Although studies suggest that education facilitates participation in this activity (Gallego 2007: 11), it clearly does not preclude minority involvement. For example, Muslims in Cork stage a monthly protest outside shops selling Israeli goods in the city. Furthermore, the unconventional is becoming more conventional. As Norris *et al.* (2005) point out, demonstrators are more representative of the general population than they once were.

Therefore a definition is required that goes beyond electoral politics to represent all forms of migrant and minority participation. The definition put forward by Verba *et al.* does not discriminate between citizens and non-citizens and is wide enough to include almost any form of political participation. They describe it as 'activity that is intended to or has the consequence of affecting either directly or indirectly government action' (1995: 9). The key here is not so much the type of activity as its intention. Participation is about influencing outcome, be it selection of government personnel, agendas or values (Morales 2009: 24) and thus is action oriented with a will to make a difference. Political participation then requires both an interest in and an action or an attitude and behaviour. This is what distinguishes it from engagement. Ben Berger's (2009) ideas are useful in this regard. He argues that engagement can involve action without interest, an activity that is in a sense going through the motions (Berger 2009: 340), so voting out of habit for example, or buying Fair Trade products as a socially acceptable act without any real support for what it represents. It can also refer to an interest without an action, what he refers to as being engaged by (ibid.). Thus, we can consider participation as being a manifest form of engagement. While it may be a sign of full integration and a healthy democracy for all members of society to be in constant participative mode, the act of being engaged by a political issue is also beneficial and may be the precursor to participation. Indeed, for minorities, it is important to go beyond the purely political and consider the patterns and benefits of civil[2] participation and engagement. Indeed, this is absolutely necessary for a full understanding of minority participation. This of course relates to activities such as associations which will be discussed later in the chapter.

One final issue in relation to the definition of political participation is that for minorities it is of central importance that participation is 'effective'. Indeed, this is enshrined in international law. Article 15 of the Council of Europe Framework Convention for the Protection of National Minorities (1998) states, 'Parties shall create the conditions necessary for the effective participation of persons belonging to national minorities in cultural, social and economic life and in public affairs, in particular those affecting them.' Thus for minorities effective participation is when interests are heard, recognised and respected (de Varennes 1998) and thus effectiveness speaks not just to the process but also to the outcome. This highlights how participation is more than simply a good in itself; participation has to deliver relevant outcomes to be valuable. So for minorities, where participation is not effective in this manner, a sense of marginalisation and alienation from the political process can develop which may lead to informal participation or indeed complete disengagement. As Jedwab (2002: 82) points out: 'Very often non-electoral forms of political participation are a supplement or substitute for participation in partisan politics connected to a perceived inability to effect change within the formal political process.' Thus there is a clear link between identity, integration and participation.

The relationship between identity, integration and participation

Identity is a relational concept within society that not only says something about us, but also socially marks out sameness and difference through processes of inclusion and exclusion (Woodward 1997: 9). Collective identities produce and are products of boundaries in national states (Wiener 1999: 197). These boundaries are natural; difference is implicit in identity but in many states it is clear that collective identities are becoming politically relevant and boundaries oppositional. Any theory of participation therefore must consider the place and treatment of minority identities in the public sphere. After all if social groups provide the context in which our identities are shaped then the way those identities are treated will have a bearing on members (Kelly 2002: 7). This is central to understanding political marginalisation.

There are of course cases of overt discrimination even where there are, at least in theory, full political rights. Examples are where ethnic, religious or racial parties are banned such as in Bulgaria (Palermo and Woelk 2003: 237), or where there is disenfranchisement via language ability tests.[3] As de Varennes points out, this goes against the very essence of participation (de Varennes 1998: 3). However, there is also a form of discrimination and exclusion which is more subtle in nature and this involves marginalising minority identities and values from the public sphere, thereby making it more difficult for minorities to affect change or identify with public institutions. This marginalisation is underpinned by the myth of a neutral public sphere. Far from being neutral, the public sphere can in fact act to exclude certain voices and marginalise others (Chandhoke 2005), so while it has the potential to be the embodiment of citizen deliberation, if it is merely embodying the majority group it will effectively exclude minorities (Modood 2002: 117). Indeed, as Habermas points out, the majority culture often abuses its historically acquired influence and definitional power to decide according to its own standards what shall be considered the norms and values of the shared political culture (Habermas 2004: 14). As an example, Northern Ireland illustrates how institutions are not above partial concerns, but rather can reflect or be perceived to reflect particularity. This will serve to undermine their legitimacy in minority communities. This process of marginalisation can also be considered in terms of discourse. There are clearly negative discourses in operation in Europe to do with anti-immigration sentiment and terrorism that is framing minority participation as a threat. Discourse can also set the boundaries more generally of level of acceptable difference. Consider, for example, the impact of key European leaders such as Silvio Berlusconi, Angela Merkel and the Pope all suggesting that Europe needs to reconstitute itself on the basis of Christian roots. As Sinha points out, if aspects of our identity are not reflected in society then we do not belong (2002: 124). This demonstrates how citizenship does not overcome all forms of political inequality since certain collective groups of citizens are de facto at a structural disadvantage, with consequent marginalisation and alienation. An inclusive public sphere then cannot be one that is based on cultural homogeneity and historical continuity; public institutions and political systems must include the identity and concerns of minority communities to encourage them to identify with and participate fully in society.

In terms of identity and integration, the above discussion implies that an integration framework based on the traditional liberal model of a strict public/private sphere divide and equality of opportunity would not effectively address issues of discrimination and marginalisation. Rather, a multicultural model which values minority identities and aims at their public inclusion would be more beneficial. While it is beyond the scope of this chapter to discuss the full complexities of the integration debate, it may be useful to consider how these two frameworks of integration relate to the question of participation. Palermo and Woelk argue that normative models of participation range from one extreme of guaranteed representation to the other of merely non-discrimination applied to all citizens (Palermo and Woelk 2003: 240) and these would appear to at least broadly fit in with a liberal approach versus a multicultural one. While anti-discrimination is vital, it may not be enough to encourage minority participation. As Marko (1995: 475) remarks: 'If the equality principle is only interpreted in its strictest sense, i.e. as a prohibition of any differentiation in order to guarantee the equality of chances for all voters, the democratic principle is understood in merely quantitative terms … with the consequent political exclusion of structural minorities.' In contrast a multicultural model of participation, which links identity and integration, will make recognition the basis for increasing minority participation. Undoubtedly there are problems with this. Not only is it breaking up the idea of a common people by introducing categories, but is also challenging the link between democracy and the majority principle (Palermo and Woelk 2003: 226). Moreover, with respect to issues of participation, making recognition central to integrating minorities into the political process may invite calls for recognition of separate tribal and religious laws, thus paradoxically taking them out of the common political process. This may be progressive in tackling the disengagement of people who for moral reasons purposively do not participate in a system which they determine cannot be legitimised. It is certainly not a unique idea. In Israel all major religions have their own personal laws and in European countries such as Britain it is already taking place in a limited way under Arbitration Acts, which effectively allow people to settle some legal disputes outside the mainstream system according to their own customs. However, this is surely a challenge facing states which seek to increase participation and integration via an identity-based model, but still wish to maintain common laws and a common sense of identity. Is this merely furthering participation at the expense of societal cohesion, or are common laws for a common identity simply a continuation of majority dominance in the public sphere and thus a form of oppression (Ghai 2003: 25)? This highly politicised issue certainly demonstrates the variety of, and occasionally contradictory, ways in which identity, integration and participation impact on one another, and the importance for any theory of participation to give this relationship careful consideration.

Obstacles and opportunities: the intersection of institutional and community-level factors

Ghai argues that there are certain preconditions for effective participation, which can be considered in terms of obstacles and opportunities. Physical and emotional security, financial resources and education are factors which are necessary to facilitate participation (Ghai 2003: 10), and indeed their absence acts as an obstacle to minorities trying to access and affect the process of decision-making. Even where such obstacles are removed, there must be real opportunities to participate. This involves opening up avenues for participation by ensuring a public sphere and electoral system that are hospitable to difference. Such an endeavour requires both a negative idea of integration (non-discrimination policies) and a positive one (ensuring that there is equality of outcome and not just opportunity). This section then will consider the issue of obstacles and opportunities and in doing so will highlight the intersection between the institutional and community levels.

Different access to participation

Physical and emotional security may be considered in terms of political confidence, that which is necessary to encourage minorities to act and integrate into the political process. There are several factors which may impact on political confidence for minorities. The first is a question of demographics. Smaller minority populations may feel more wary about getting involved in a system that is at times alien and unwelcoming. Higher levels of social capital facilitated by increasing numbers often remove a fear of political visibility. Indeed, Taspinar (2003) points to such a process taking place among Muslim communities in France and Germany, where vocal foreign policy lobbies have emerged, and also crucially a potential to impact on elections. However, he does make clear that it is not just a question of numbers in this regard but rather numbers coupled with enfranchisement (Taspinar 2003). This highlights how factors relating to participation can interact with one another to promote or preclude greater participation. Indeed, a contradictory process is in evidence among the Chinese community in Ireland. The Chinese are the largest ethnic minority community in Ireland with quite high levels of enfranchisement and yet they tend to be politically invisible and almost entirely absent from anti-racism associations (Ugba 2005). In this case other factors must be militating against their participation.

A lower socio-economic profile has also been shown to reduce levels of participation (Gallego 2007: 5; Foster-Bey 2009: 4). While it is important to recognise that many minority communities have comparable socio-economic profiles to the majority community, there is at least a general trend of minorities being some of the most disadvantaged in society. Poverty, poor language skills and under-education are clearly barriers to both integration and participation, a situation that is felt very acutely by minority youth. Existing literature shows that young citizens who are reared in communities or have regular contact with social settings that maintain an unequal distribution of power with society at large are less likely to engage and feel alienated from civic and political institutions (Scholzman *et al.* 1999; Flanagan *et al.* 1998). Thus neither integration nor participation can be dissociated from the wider economic and political structures in society, requiring that a successful politics of recognition be linked to a politics of social justice (Parekh 2000: 2).

Obstacles and opportunities in the electoral system

The first factor which requires little elaboration is that there must be a political right of participation for this to occur. Therefore a political theory of participation must consider differing processes of naturalisation and the impact these have for the wider participation of minority communities. Other issues in relation to the electoral system require further comment. The electoral system is of central importance to effective participation. It is the most direct route to sources of power, and it is only through electoral participation that meaningful representation can be achieved. Representation is vital to minorities as it is an 'emphatic recognition of a positive right of the minority – to take part in the state political processes and to influence state policies' (Ghai 2003:12–13). Thus the rules and practical arrangements within the electoral systems are sources of opportunity to engender greater participation. Practical issues such as a need for registration and the day of voting can be obstacles to minority participation. Registration processes requiring time, knowledge of public codes of conduct, language and interaction with bureaucracy can act as a barrier to involvement. Indeed, this registration requirement is particularly problematic for nomadic minorities as it often requires a permanent residence. Moreover, if voting takes place on only one day which happens to be a religious holiday, then this essentially precludes participation by religious persons and sends out a message of indifference to that whole community, religious or secular.

The specific type of electoral system is also crucial to decreasing minority marginalisation and increasing perceptions of external efficacy. As the discussion on the definition of political participation highlighted, effective participation for minorities is not just about the act of participation, but is a matter of outcomes: minority interests need to be heard. Theorists such as Pitkin (1972) start from the premise that representation means to make present that which is absent and this can be considered in terms of making minority voices heard and also having a minority presence physically represented. For both cases the problem with majority rule systems such as first past the post is that minority votes get so diluted as to become invisible and their voice and interests lost. Majority rule therefore can often enshrine majority interest (de Varennes 1998). This problem was recognised in the Lund Recommendations on Effective Participation of National Minorities in Public Life (1999), which stated:

> Participation of national minorities in public life is an essential component of a peaceful and democratic society. Experience in Europe and elsewhere has shown that in order to promote such participation, governments often need to establish specific arrangements for national minorities.
>
> *(Cited in Wheatley 2002: 5)*

Such positive action measures, which it should be remarked upon fit into a more multicultural model of participation and integration, will necessarily be context specific. Depending on type or concentration of minority community, federal sub-units may be useful to guarantee their interests; such is the case in Belgium. Other tools which are in use in Europe are guaranteed seats (Romania) or a type of minority veto (Northern Ireland). Generally, it would appear that a form of proportional representation offers the best chance for minority representation. However, for smaller minority communities even this will be of little consequence and thus other forms of representation might be considered. Advisory councils, for example, work well where minorities tend to be small in number and can also represent those that are disenfranchised such as migrants (Ghai 2003: 13). One final tool that might be considered is compulsory voting. This of course is not so much about facilitating as forcing participation. Certainly it would make the polity more legitimate and bring minorities into mainstream politics (albeit under duress), but Dean (2007) argues that it would not address disengagement from parties or the political system. He says: 'A full turnout would be no more than a smokescreen for disengagement' (Dean 2007). While this could end up as a process of perfunctory engagement (activity without interest), it may be worthwhile assessing the impact of compulsory voting on wider patterns of political and civil participation.

Opportunities for participation do not stop at the systemic level. They can be created through minority mobilisation and political stimulation measures. For example, research by IMES in Rotterdam found that stimulation measures increased minority turnout. Indeed Foster-Bey argues that, whether in political or civil spheres, a lack of participation is often a matter of simply not being asked (Foster-Bey 2009: 9). Thus minority mobilisation may involve the state providing programmes to encourage political engagement but can also be considered at the level of party politics. Throughout Europe traditional parties have not been successful in mobilising minorities in the way that left-wing parties have been able to exert mobilisation on the working class (Verba et al. 1978). Often this is due to a lack of interest. Fanning et al. (2007), in their study of the main Irish parties, found almost an absence of outreach strategies for minorities. Thus minority identities must be included and considered not only in institutions and the electoral system, but by political parties also.

Opportunities and obstacles in the civil sphere

Up to now this chapter has dealt almost entirely with participation in the political sphere. However, participation and engagement in the civil sphere does have benefits for political participation, particularly for migrants who may find this their main or only outlet for participation. Indeed, as Berger points out, democracy can flourish with average levels of political participation but not without rich social and moral engagement (2009: 336). Associations may not have any specific political purpose, yet they should be considered a political resource. Studies by Putnam (1993, 2000) and Fennema and Tillie (1999) have found that higher levels of political participation by minorities are linked to greater associational life. Associations socialise and educate individuals and provide public codes of conduct (Van Londen et al. 2007: 1202). Thus, by providing such skills and resources, associational engagement serves as socialisation for political participation (Putnam 1993, 2000). Indeed, they can help to counter common obstacles to minority participation such as socio-economic inequalities (Gallego 2007: 3). Moreover, many such groups do have direct political consequences by encouraging minorities to use their vote (Ugba 2005) and by acting as a consultation body on minority issues, thereby facilitating contact and dialogue between state and minorities (Ghai 2003: 12). Furthermore, many associations tend to be concerned with issues of social justice, which of course crosses into the political sphere and requires engagement with the state, even if it is in oppositional terms. As Briggs notes, 'Activism and dissent can be a pathway into engagement in other forms of civic and political participation and it is only by surfacing and working through difference that we will achieve meaningful and lasting cohesion' (Briggs 2007). Thus associations may be considered a political resource for minorities and a stepping stone to greater political participation and engagement. Research on this subject should recognise associations as building blocks in wider minority participation.

Conclusions

This chapter has set out a relationship between minority identity, integration and participation that puts recognition at the heart of stimulating further participation. However, participation cannot be conceived of within the narrow political confines of voting. Political participation for migrant and minority communities is a process that incorporates both the civil and political, attitude and behaviour. It also includes the issue of power and social justice to break down obstacles and increase opportunities. Explicit throughout the chapter has been the importance of recognising and including pluralism within institutions, the electoral system, political parties and the political entity as a whole. Indeed, the European Court of Human Rights has established a bottom line that there cannot be democracy without pluralism (Palermo and Woelk 2003: 238).

> Therefore, the political participation of immigrants and minorities should continue to be high on a comparative European research agenda; their incorporation in national politics and civil societies will be a critical touchstone of the democratic legitimacy of our political institutions.
> *(Van Londen et al. 2007: 1223)*

Notes

1 Who are considered diasporas has become more flexible in recent years. Diaspora no longer solely applies to traumatic exile as in the Jewish case; it is now being used in a variety of contexts, including for ethnic and racial minorities (Cohen 1997: 21). It is about having a collective identity in their place of settlement but also a co-ethnic identity with members in other countries (Cohen 1997: 25). Cohen also expresses the importance of the retention of group ties within diasporas, which he sets out as norms, culture, endogamy, language and religion (Cohen 1997: 58).
2 I am employing Berger's use of civil as opposed to civic engagement and participation. While Berger argues that the concept civic has been overstretched so that it no longer clarifies anything (Berger 2009: 335), it is of equal if not greater importance to discussing migrant participation to avoid terms such as 'civic' that pertain to the citizen.
3 Palermo and Woelk (2003: 237) provide examples of where language ability has been used to disenfranchise.

References

Bauman, Z. (2004) *Wasted Lives: Modernity and Its Outcasts*. Cambridge: Polity Press.
Berger, B. (2009) 'Political theory, political science and the end of civic engagement', *Perspectives on Politics*, 7 (2): 335–50.
Bernhagen, P. and Marsh, M. (2007) 'Voting and protesting: explaining citizen participation in old and new European democracies', *Democratization*, 14 (1) : 44–72.

Bieber, F. (2003) 'Balancing political participation and minority rights: the experience of the former Yugoslavia', *Central European University*, online at: http://www.policy.hu/document/200808/Bieber.pdf&letoltes=1 (accessed 5 May 2009).

Blohm, M. and Diehl, C. (2001) 'Apathy, adaptation or ethnic mobilisation? On the attitudes of a politically excluded group', *Journal of Ethnic and Migration Studies*, 27 (3): 401–20.

Briggs, R. (2007) 'Who's afraid of the Respect Party? Dissent and cohesion in modern Britain', *Demos*, online at: http://www.demos.co.uk/files/Briggs.Respect.Renewal.20071.pdf (accessed 8 October 2009).

Capotorti, F. (1976) 'The protection of minorities under multilateral agreements on human rights', *Italian Yearbook of International Law*, 2: 14.

Castells, M. (1996) *The Rise of the Network Society*. Cambridge: Blackwell.

Chandhoke, N. (2005) 'What the hell is civil society?', *Open Democracy*, online at: http://www.opendemocracy.net/democracy-open_politics/article_2375.jsp (accessed 5 August 2009).

Cohen, R. (1997) *Global Diasporas: An Introduction*. London: UCL Press.

Council of Europe (1998) *Framework Convention for the Protection of National Minorities*, online at: http://conventions.coe.int/Treaty/en/Treaties/Html/157.htm (accessed 5 September 2009).

Crowley, J. (2001) 'The political participation of ethnic minorities', *International Political Science Review*, 22 (1): 99–121.

Dalton, R. J. (2002) *Citizen Politics: Public Opinion and Political Parties in Advanced Industrial Democracies*. London: Chatham House.

de Varennes, F. (1998) 'Towards effective political participation and representation of minorities', *UN Economic and Social Council*, online at: http://www.unhchr.ch/Huridocda/Huridoca.nsf/0/9bc6715374fa0079c125696d00445b1e?OpenDocument (accessed 10 July 2009).

Dean, S. (2007) 'Compulsory voting: the case against', *Open Democracy*, online: http://www.opendemocracy.net/article/compulsory_voting_the_case_against (accessed 5 September 2009).

Diehl, C. and Blohm, M. (2001) 'Apathy, adaptation or ethnic mobilisation? On the attitudes of a politically excluded group', *Journal of Ethnic and Migration Studies*, 27 (3): 401–20.

European Social Survey [online] http://www.europeansocialsurvey.org/ (accessed June 2010).

Fanning, B., Shaw, F., O'Connell, J. and William, M. (2007) *Irish Political Parties, Immigration and Integration in 2007*. Dublin: Migration and Citizenship Research Initiative.

Fennema, M. and Tillie, J. (1999) 'Political participation and political trust in Amsterdam: civic communities and ethnic networks', *Journal of Ethnic and Migration Studies*, 25 (4): 703–72.

Flanagan, C. *et al.* (1998) 'Ties that bind: correlates of adolescents' civic commitments in seven countries', *Journal of Social Issues*, 54 (3): 457.

Fossato, F. (2009) 'Russian cyberspace: reflecting not changing reality', *Open Democracy*, online at: http://www.opendemocracy.net/russia/article/Russian-cyberspace-reflecting-not-changing-reality (accessed 5 September 2009).

Foster-Bey, J. (2009) 'Do race, ethnicity, citizenship and socio-economic status determine civic engagement?', *Civic Engagement*, online at: http://www.civicengagementworks.org/print/117 (accessed 15 October 2009).

Gallego, A. (2007) 'Inequality in political participation: contemporary patterns in European countries', *Centre for the Study of Democracy*, online at: http://escholarship.org/uc/item/3545w14v (accessed 10 July 2009).

Ghai, Y. (2003) *Public Participation and Minorities*. London: Minority Rights Group International.

Habermas, J. (2004) 'Religious tolerance: the pacemaker for cultural rights', *Philosophy*, 79: 5–18.
Inglehart, R. (1988) 'The renaissance of political culture', *American Political Science Review*, 82 (4): 1203–30.
Jacobs, D. and Tillie, J. (2004) 'Social capital and political integration of migrants', *Journal of Ethnic and Migration Studies*, 30 (3): 419–27.
Jedwab, J. (2002) 'Representing identity: non-formal political participation and the role of the state in Canada', *Metropolis*, online at: http://canada.metropolis.net/events/Political%20 Participation/AGENDA_e.htm (accessed 10 October 2009).
Kelly, P. (2002) 'Between culture and equality', in P. Kelly (ed.), *Multiculturalism Reconsidered*. Cambridge: Polity Press, pp. 1–17.
McLeod, J. (2000) *Beginning Postcolonialism*. Manchester: Manchester University Press.
Marko, J. (1995) *Autonomie und Integration*. Vienna: Böhlau.
Messina, A. M. (2004) *The Political Incorporation of Immigrants in Europe: Trends and Implications*. Paper presented at the Conference on Immigration, Bourglinster, Luxembourg, online at: http://www.lisproject.org/immigration/papers/Messina.pdf.
Modood, T. (2002) 'The place of Muslims in British secular multiculturalism', in N. Alsayyad and M. Castells (eds), *Muslim Europe or Euro Islam: Citizenship in the Age of Globalization*. Oxford: Lexington, pp. 113–30.
Morales, L. (2009) *Joining Political Organisations: Institutions, Mobilisation and Participation in Western Democracies*. Colchester: ECPR Press.
Navarria, G. (2009) 'Mob rule', *CSD Bulletin*, 16 (1): 24–6.
Norris, P., Walgrave, S. and Van Aelst, P. (2005) 'Who demonstrates? Antistate rebels, conventional participants or everyone?', *Comparative Politics*, 37 (2): 189–205.
Palermo, F. and Woelk, J. (2003) 'No representation without recognition: the right to political participation of (national) minorities', *European Integration*, 25 (3): 225–48.
Parekh, B. (2000) *Rethinking Multiculturalism: Cultural Diversity and Political Theory*. Basingstoke: Palgrave.
Pitkin, H. (1972) *The Concept of Representation*. Cambridge: Cambridge University Press.
Pollack, J. et al. (2009) 'On political representation: myths and challenges', *RECON*, online at: http://www.reconproject.eu/main.php/RECON_wp_0903.pdf?fileitem=16662583 (accessed 10 November 2009).
Putnam, R. D. (1993) *Making Democracy Work: Civic Traditions in Modern Italy*. Princeton, NJ: Princeton University Press.
Putnam, R. D. (2000) *Bowling Alone: The Collapse and Revival of American Community*. New York: Simon & Schuster.
Rosenstone, S. J. (1982) 'Economic adversity and voter turnout', *American Journal of Political Science*, 26 (1): 25–46.
Sandovici, M. E. and Listhaung, O. (2006) *Ethnic Minorities and Political Participation*. Paper prepared for the Annual Meeting of the American Political Science Association, Philadelphia, 31 August – 3 September.
Scholzman, K. L, Verba, S. and Brady, H. E. (1999) 'Civic participation and the equality problem', in T. Skocpol and P. F. Morris (eds), *Civic Engagement in American Democracy*. Washington, DC: Brookings, pp. 427–59.
Sinha, S. (2002) 'Generating awareness for the experiences of women of colour', in R. Lentin and R. McVeigh (eds), *Racism and Anti-Racism in Ireland*. Belfast: BTP Publications, pp. 121–4.
Taspinar, O. (2003) 'Europe's Muslim Street', in *Brookings*, online at: http://www.brookings.edu/opinions/2003/03middleeast_taspinar.aspx (accessed 5 January 2009).

Ugba, A. (2005) 'Active civic participation of immigrants in Ireland: country report prepared for POLITIS', *POLITIS*, online at: http://www.politis-europe.uni-oldenburg.de/download/Ireland.pdf (accessed 5 January 2009).
Uhlaner, C. et al. (1989) 'Political participation of ethnic minorities in the 1980s', *Political Behavior*, 11 (3): 195–231.
Van Londen, M., Phalet, K. and Hagendoorn, L. (2007) 'Civic engagement and voter participation among Turkish and Moroccan minorities in Rotterdam', *Journal of Ethnic and Migration Studies*, 33 (8): 1201–26.
Verba, S. (2003) 'Would the dream of political equality turn out to be a nightmare?', *Perspectives on Politics*, 1 (4): 663–79.
Verba, S., Nie, N. H. and Kim, J. (1978) *Participation and Political Equality: A Seven Nation Comparison*. Cambridge: Cambridge University Press.
Verba, S., Scholzman, K. L. and Brady, H. E. (1995) *Voice and Equality: Civic Voluntarism in American Politics*. Cambridge, MA: Harvard University Press.
Wheatley, S. (2002) *Non-Discrimination and Equality in the Right of Political Participation for Minorities*, UN Office of the High Commissioner for Human Rights, online at: http://www2.ohchr.org/english/bodies/hrcouncil/minority/docs/Non_Discrimination_Equality.pdf (accessed 15 February 2009).
Wiener, A. (1999) 'From special to specialized rights: the politics of citizenship and identity in the European Union', in M. Hanagan and C. Tilly (eds), *Extending Citizenship, Reconfiguring States*. Oxford: Rowman & Littlefield, pp. 195–227.
Woodward, K. (1997) 'Concepts of identity and difference', in K. Woodward (ed.), *Identity and Difference*. London: Sage, pp. 1–50.

5

HOW CONTEXT SHAPES INDIVIDUAL-LEVEL DETERMINANTS OF POLITICAL PARTICIPATION

The impact of multiple negative party identification on turnout in deeply divided Northern Ireland[1]

John Garry

Introduction

This chapter investigates the influence of macro-contextual factors on an individual's decision to vote at election time. Specifically, I focus on the role played by political context (namely the deeply divided context of Northern Ireland) in conditioning the manner in which party identification (psychological attachment to political parties) drives citizens' electoral participation. I argue that the deeply divided context necessitates a particular conceptualisation and operationalisation of party identification theory (highlighting the importance of *multiple negative* party identities rather than *single positive* party identity) which aids our understanding of abstention in this particular context. I argue that in the deeply divided context abstention is likely to be driven by affective antipathy towards the range of parties representing one's particular community.

I begin with an overview of research on the contextual determinants of electoral participation. I then focus on one influential individual-level predictor of participation (party identification) and describe how the party identification approach may most usefully be used to explain participation in the context of a deeply divided society. I then briefly describe the Northern Ireland case, describe the data used in the analysis and empirically test the hypothesis that multiple negative party identification drives abstention in the deeply divided Northern Ireland case. I conclude with a discussion of the implications of the analysis for our understanding of participation in Northern Ireland and, more broadly, how macro-context shapes individual level explanations of citizens' political participation.

Macro-context and turnout

In a comprehensive analysis of aggregate-level predictors of citizens' political participation at election time, Geys (2006) identifies three sets of contextual characteristics that may influence turnout levels: demographic factors, political factors and institutional factors. Regarding the demographic factors, 'population size' may influence turnout by driving the probability that the vote of any given citizen would be decisive. This line of thinking is derived from rational choice theory (Downs 1957) which suggests that voters conduct a cost-benefit calculation when deciding whether or not to vote. Accordingly, the greater the size of the population the less chance that one's vote will determine the election result and hence the less incentive there is to participate. Also, 'population stability' may be associated with turnout as knowledge of local issues and candidates is likely to be higher for people who reside for a long time in a particular place, hence decreasing information costs and making participation 'more rational'.[2] Two other aspects of population may influence turnout because of their role in affecting social norms and associated 'social pressure' to turn out to vote. 'Population concentration' may have an impact on turnout levels because the more concentrated the population the more urbanised the environment is likely to be, with associated low levels of interpersonal bonds and 'social pressure' to participate. Similarly, 'population homogeneity' may enhance social solidarity and pressure to adhere to the 'norm' of voting.[3]

Turning now to the political context factors that may influence turnout, the closeness of the electoral contest is likely to boost participation as closeness raises the likelihood of one's vote actually affecting the outcome of the election, hence increasing the utility to be derived from participating. Also, high campaign expenditures by the political parties may increase turnout, although more so for positive than for negative campaigning. There may also be an expectation that political fragmentation (a large number of competing parties) may increase turnout as the choice for voters is enhanced. However, this may be offset by the fact that having a large number of parties is likely to lead to a coalition government which means voters may feel very distant from executive formation and this may decrease turnout (Brokington 2004).

Finally, regarding the institutional context, compulsory voting may be strongly expected to be linked to high turnout levels as abstention is disincentivised. Concurrent elections may also enhance participation; more than one election is likely to lead to more media attention and more campaign expenditure, and also should lower the cost of voting (as the cost incurred in attending the voting booth to vote at two elections is not twice the cost of attending to vote at one election). Registration requirements are also likely to have an effect, with tighter registration procedures likely to depress turnout. Also the particular day of the week that the election occurs on may influence turnout, with Sundays facilitating increased turnout, and having the election over a number of days is also likely to aid turnout (Franklin 1996). The electoral system is seen by some people as driving turnout: proportional representation systems may enhance participation as they are seen as 'fair' and also lead to more competitive campaigning. This may, however, be offset by the fact that PR systems lead to coalition governments which may discourage participation as it complicates the link between voting and government formation (Karp and Banducci 2008).

How these kinds of contextual factors are linked to individual-level explanations of electoral participation is analysed by Marsh *et al.* (2008). The authors begin by arguing that in order to understand how contextual level and individual level traits are related one must begin by conceptualising *two distinct types* of abstention. First, 'circumstantial abstention' relates to voters who would have liked to have voted but circumstances on the day of the election prevented them from doing so. Such circumstances may relate to being away from home or having pressing work or family commitments or being ill on the day of the election. In contrast, 'voluntary abstention' relates to the attitudes a citizen has which lead them not to vote. For example, low levels of political efficacy – a lack of interest in politics, a lack of trust in parties and politicians, a perception that there is little choice on offer or a sense one will have little influence on the election – are likely to be related to abstention (Almond and Verba 1963; Gabriel 1995). Also, the psychological relationship a voter has with the political parties in the system may determine the likelihood of participating (Marsh *et al.* 2008: 205; Franklin 1996), with people who feel close to a particular party likely to turn out to vote and those who do not feel close to a party likely to abstain (as noted earlier, the role of party identification is discussed and analysed in detail below).

The problem of circumstantial abstention may be addressed by generating a context which makes the act of voting as easy as possible. For instance, having voting on a Sunday or over two days may help individuals whose work or family commitments may otherwise prevent them from voting. The problem of voluntary abstention may be addressed by generating a context in which citizens are mobilised and persuaded to turn out to vote. For instance, a very close election in which intense campaigning increases people's interest may raise turnout. Figure 5.1 seeks to link the contextual and individual-level drivers of turnout by offering a typology of the factors which affect participation, distinguishing the role of mobilisation and facilitation.

I now focus on individual mobilisation rather than facilitation as this is arguably the greater challenge for analysts who wish to see high levels of participation and turnout. The following section highlights the importance of one particular attitudinal factor driving (or constraining) participation – namely psychological attachment to parties – and suggests that the manner in which psychological attachment relates to participation may be conditioned by political context.

Party identification theory, the deeply divided context and turnout

In their seminal analysis of voting behaviour in the US, Campbell *et al.* (1960) sought to explain the long-term stability of party support using the concept of

| | Location of the factor ||
Type of influence	Contextual level	Individual level
Facilitation	Contextual facilitation	Individual facilitation
	contextual factors encouraging voting (e.g. population homogeneity, voting on a Sunday)	factors relating to an individual's circumstances that make it easy to vote (e.g. not being ill on election day, having flexible working hours)
Mobilisation	Contextual mobilisation	Individual mobilisation
	contextual factors making people want to vote (e.g. close contest, intense campaigning and canvassing)	attitudinal traits of individuals that make them want to vote (e.g. interest in politics, having a positive psychological attachment to a particular party)

FIGURE 5.1 A typology of factors driving participation (derived from Marsh *et al*. 2008)

'party identification' which refers to citizens' general and enduring psychological orientations towards the political parties in the system. The authors defined the concept as follows:

> In characterizing the relation of individual to party as a psychological identification we invoke a concept that has played an important if somewhat varied role in psychological theories of the relation of individual to individual or of individual to group. We use the concept here to characterize the individual's affective orientation to an important group-object in his environment. Both reference group theory and small-group studies of influence have converged upon the attracting or repelling quality of the group as the generalized dimension most critical in defining the individual–group relationship, and it is this dimension that we will call identification … the political party serves as the group towards which the individual may develop an identification, positive or negative, of some degree of intensity.
>
> *(1960: 121–2)*

Thus party identification relates to a psychological rather than behavioural relationship between a citizen and the parties; it is subjective and based on self-definition rather than a result of voting for the party. Crucially, for present purposes, this definition suggests that party identification may be negative or positive (with certain parties perceived as either attractive or repellent) *and* citizens may identify with more than one party. However, this contrasts with the usual way in which party identification is usually operationalised, which facilitates only a *positive* attachment to a particular party and prohibits *multiple* attachments. Accordingly, Campbell *et al.* (1960) use the following measure:

Generally speaking, do you usually think of yourself as a Republican, a Democrat, an Independent, or what? Respondents identifying with one of the two parties are then asked: 'Would you call yourself a strong Democrat (or Republican) or a not very strong Democrat (or Republican)?' Respondents who identify as Independents in the initial question are asked: Do you think of yourself as closer to the Republican or Democratic Party?

This measure is criticised by Maggiotto and Pierson (1977) who argue in favour of 'the addition of partisan hostility, an equally stable, long-term affect' (p. 765). Similarly, Richardson (1991: 759) highlights the theoretical and explanatory value of negative as well as positive identity: 'Hostility to parties other than favoured ones may be as important behaviorally as positive ties to liked parties.' In a recent analysis, Medeiros and Noel (2014) emphasise the important 'autonomous' role played by negative partisanship (which they characterise as 'the forgotten side of partisanship') in driving electoral behaviour.

Furthermore, several analysts have emphasised that many citizens may have *multiple* identifications. Weisberg (1999: 727) notes that analyses of party identification in the US based on the Campbell *et al.* (1960) measure 'have assumed that people are Republicans or Democrats or Independents, but not more than one of the above', and such analyses represent a quite limited operationalisation of their general concept of party identification as it does not facilitate the holding of multiple identities by individuals. In a similar vein, van der Eijk and Niemoller (1983) argue that 'the assumption that voters identify with only one party (if they do so at all) turns out to be false when subjected to an empirical test in the Netherlands' (p. 338). Also, Schmitt (2002) states that 'multiple party identifications are indeed a relevant aspect of partisanship. Noteworthy proportions of national electorates identify with more than one political party' (p. 19).[4]

Conceptualising party identification in terms of positive and negative identification and in terms of multiple identification is likely to be particularly useful in the context of analysing participation in a deeply divided place. Such a context is typically characterised as comprising a number of party systems – one for each of the rival communities – and party competition occurs within each community bloc (Evans and Duffy 1997).

In the Northern Ireland case, party competition is typically seen as occurring within two distinct blocs: in the 'Catholic/Nationalist' bloc (between Sinn Fein and the Social Democratic and Labour Party (SDLP)); and in the 'Protestant/Unionist' bloc between the Democratic Unionist Party (DUP) and the Ulster Unionist Party (UUP)). Multiple party identities may well be plausible in such a setting. In the same way that Weisberg (1999: 727) notes that Dutch citizens who identify with one of the Dutch Calvinist parties may also identify with the other Dutch Calvinist party, one might expect that some Catholics may positively identify with both of the 'Catholic' parties. It may also be the case that at least some Catholics would *negatively* identify with both of the Catholic parties.

90 John Garry

This may be because they do not view politics through the prism of the ethno-national distinction. They do not, in Bar-Tal et al.'s (2009) terms, have an 'ethos of conflict' and may be repelled by the 'necessary' association of 'Catholic parties' with Catholics. The same may well be true, at least to some extent, on the Protestant side. At least some Protestants may negatively identify with both of the main 'Protestant parties'.

The argument that some members of each community may be repelled by both of the parties in their community is consistent with the argument of some 'integrationist' analysts who see the 'problem' of Northern Ireland as being driven by the very fact that Northern Ireland is seen as unique and hence deserving of its own unique party system. Roberts (1990) and Aughey (1989) argue that one of the main reasons that Northern Ireland electoral politics has been dominated by the ethno-national question is because the main British political parties have not organised and electorally competed in Northern Ireland. Hence political competition in Northern Ireland has been dominated by Northern Ireland parties, which have prioritised conflict-related Northern Ireland issues, rather than UK-wide parties which prioritise socio-economic issues relating to economic management and resource distribution. 'Integrationists' such as Roberts and Aughey have argued that the Northern Ireland 'problem' is a result of the fact that British parties do not compete in Northern Ireland. The salience of ethno-national issues would reduce and the potency of social class and economic-related political issues would increase if mainland British Conservative and Labour parties energetically competed for votes in Northern Ireland. One implication is that, for those citizens who do not wish for a party system which is ethno-nationally driven, a distancing from 'their' community parties may result. Such citizens with multiple negative identifications may simply abstain from voting at election time.

The Northern Ireland case is particularly important to focus on given the widely perceived problem of low turnout at recent Assembly elections. As illustrated in Figure 5.2, the most recent Assembly election witnessed a considerable fall in participation, with a turnout rate of 55 per cent. This compares with the high turnout level (70 per cent) in the 1998 Assembly election which

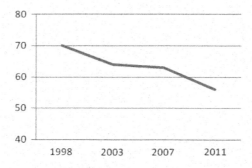

FIGURE 5.2 Turnout at Northern Ireland Assembly elections, 1998–2011

occurred in the direct aftermath of the Good Friday/ Belfast Agreement which established devolution and consociational power-sharing structures in Northern Ireland.

The next section focuses on the 2011 Northern Ireland Assembly election and describes the way in which I use data from the NI 2011 Election Study Survey to operationalise party identification and test the hypothesis that multiple negative party identification drives the decision to abstain.

Methods

I construct a measure of affective party identification for the deeply divided Northern Ireland context that facilitates multiple identification and positive and negative identification. The battery of survey items is:

> Some people feel close to a particular political party while other people feel distant from it. Taking each party in turn, do you feel very close to the party, fairly close, neither close nor distant, fairly distant from the party or very distant from it?
>
> *(All parties asked in turn)*

The survey items were asked in the 2011 Northern Ireland Assembly Election study, conducted by the author. This involved a post-election telephone survey (n = 1,200) which was conducted by Market Research Northern Ireland (MRNI) with quotas set for age, gender and religion within each of the 18 electoral areas. Respondents were also asked whether or not they had voted in the election. Fieldwork was carried out between 18 May and 17 June 2011. The survey was co-funded by the Political Studies Association of Ireland (PSAI) and Queen's University Belfast. The representativeness of the survey can be assessed by comparing the first preference votes (and turnout) from the real-world 2011 election with those from the survey; the relationship is very strong.[5]

Analysis and results

The responses to each party identification question are recoded into three categories: positive identification (very close or fairly close to), neutral identification (neither close to nor distant from) and negative identification (fairly or very distant from). Each community (Catholics and Protestants) was then analysed in turn. First, the manner in which citizens identify with the two parties in their community was assessed. Then the percentage turnout for each party identification category was investigated in order to assess the extent to which multiple negative identification drives abstention. In Table 5.1 we see that 16 per cent of Catholics hold multiple positive identifications: they feel close to both of their community parties (Sinn Fein and the SDLP). The same percentage hold multiple negative identifications:

92 John Garry

TABLE 5.1 Catholics' psychological attachment to Sinn Fein and the SDLP

		Sinn Fein		
		Close to	Neither	Distant from
SDLP	Close to	16.3	10.8	13.5
	Neither	7.5	26.5	2.1
	Distant from	6.3	1.0	16.1

Note: Figures in the table are percentages and all percentages sum to 100; total n = 480.

regarding both parties as repellent. The largest category, slightly over a quarter of Catholics, are neutral towards both parties.

In Table 5.2 the percentage of citizens in each cell who participated in the 2011 Assembly election is reported. Citizens who are close to at least one party (and who may be close to, distant from or neutral regarding the other party) have turnout rates of at least 70 per cent. A slightly lower rate (63 per cent) is indicated in relation to those who are neutral regarding both parties. However, the stark finding in Table 5.2 relates to the very low (37.7 per cent) turnout rate of those citizens who negatively identify with both parties.

Table 5.3 reports the distribution of Protestant voters regarding their psychological relationship with the two main parties in the 'unionist' bloc. The distribution is somewhat similar to the Catholic case (Table 5.1). Just over a fifth of Protestants have multiple positive identities with the parties, just over a fifth have multiple negative identities and just over a quarter have a neutral identification with the parties.

Table 5.4 reports the turnout percentage in each cell. The pattern that emerges is similar to, but less stark than, the Catholic case. The highest turnout percentages (between 57 and 71 per cent) are for those Protestants who positively identify with at least one party. The lowest turnout is for those with multiple negative identities (45.5 per cent) but the percentage is very similar to that for those who have neutral identities with both (47.0 per cent).

TABLE 5.2 Catholic turnout by Catholics' psychological attachment to Sinn Fein and the SDLP

		Sinn Fein		
		Close to	Neither	Distant from
SDLP	Close to	74.4	75.0	70.1
	Neither	75.8	63.0	**
	Distant from	83.3	**	37.7

Note: The figure in each cell is the percentage turnout; ** indicates too few cases, in all other cells the minimum n = 30.

TABLE 5.3 Protestants' psychological attachment to the UUP and the DUP

		UUP		
		Close to	Neither	Distant from
DUP	Close to	21.6	7.8	8.1
	Neither	4.2	27.0	1.5
	Distant from	6.6	1.9	21.3

Note: Figures in the table are percentages and all percentages sum to 100; total n = 670.

TABLE 5.4 Protestant turnout by Protestant psychological attachment to the UUP and the DUP

		UUP		
		Close to	Neither	Distant from
DUP	Close to	66.9	57.7	61.6
	Neither	71.4	47.0	**
	Distant from	56.8	**	45.5

Note: The figure in each cell is the percentage turnout; ** indicates too few cases, in all other cells the minimum n = 28.

Discussion

The aim of this chapter was to provide an overview of the contextual influences on turnout and to elaborate an example of how political context shapes the manner in which individual-level explanations of turnout should be operationalised. A wide range of contextual influences were described, ranging from characteristics of the population, traits of the particular electoral contest and rules of the voting game. How exactly these contextual-level factors link to individual-level explanations was discussed in the context of a distinction between two types of non-participation – namely abstention due to circumstances and deliberate abstention due to attitudes towards politics.

In order to discuss an example of how context shapes analysis of individual-level explanations of abstention I focused on the role of party identification theory. Psychological interpretations of political behaviour have been dominated by the party identification approach, although recent work has highlighted the important role of distinct emotions (Redlawsk 2006). Despite the dominance of party identification theory in accounts of political behaviour the theory has typically been operationalised in a surprisingly narrow way, merely facilitating positive and single-party identification. I suggest that the particular context of the deeply divided society necessitates a more appropriate conceptualisation and measurement – namely to facilitate, in line with the initial theorising of party identification, positive, negative and multiple identifications.

The empirical analysis finds support for the proposition that multiple negative party identification in the deeply divided context is related to abstention and the findings are particularly strong in the Catholic/Nationalist bloc.

Notes

1. The author would like to thank the PIDOP project, and particularly Martyn Barrett, for support in writing this chapter. The author would also like to thank the British Academy for very generously funding the author's position as 'British Academy Mid-Career Research Fellow 2012–2013'.
2. For an overview of the rational choice interpretation of abstention see, for example, Aldrich (1993) and Blais (2000).
3. A very common reason given by citizens who do vote is that it is their 'duty' to do so. See discussion in Jones and Hudson (2000) and Bowler and Donovan (2013).
4. See Garry (2007) for further discussion of the limitations of the conventional measure of party identification.
5. The election result (and survey estimate of that result) for each party is: DUP 30.0 (30.1 per cent), Sinn Fein 26.9 (26.1 per cent), UUP 13.2 (15.0 per cent), SDLP 14.2 (14.4 per cent), Alliance 7.7 (9.0 per cent), other 8.0 (5.4 per cent). Also, the turnout rate in the survey was 57.3 per cent, very close to the reality of 55.7 per cent. Gschwend (2005: 88) argues that in order to demonstrate the validity of using a quota-based sample (rather than a random selection-based sample) 'scholars should gather as much external evidence as possible to argue that their achieved sample represents the population on as many dimensions as possible. The more evidence they are able to compile, the more confidence there is that their estimation results are robust even based on quota sample data.' Distributions on ethno-national variables in this study have very similar distributions to questions asked on the 2010 Northern Ireland Life and Times (NILT) survey based on random sampling (the most recently available NILT). For example, the percentage in favour of a united Ireland was 17 per cent in the election study and 16 per cent in NILT, the percentage opting for a 'Northern Irish' identity was 31 per cent in the election survey and 28 per cent in NILT (see http://www.ark.ac.uk/nilt/2010/). The survey analysed in this chapter, while based on quota sampling, replicates well real-world voting behaviour and independently generated frequencies on important ethno-national issues derived from a random sampling based survey.

References

Aldrich, J. H. (1993) 'Rational choice and turnout', *American Journal of Political Science*, 37 (1): 246–78.

Almond, G. and Verba, S. (1963) *The Civic Culture: Political Attitudes and Democracy in Five Nations*. Boston: Little, Brown.

Aughey, A. (1989) *Under Siege: Ulster Unionism and the Anglo-Irish Agreement*. Belfast: Blackstaff.

Bar-Tal, D., Raviv, A. and Dgani-Hirsh, A. (2009) 'The influence of the ethos of conflict on Israeli Jews' interpretation of Jewish-Palestinian encounters', *Journal of Conflict Resolution*, 53 (1): 94–118.

Blais, A. (2000) *To Vote or Not to Vote? The Merits and Limits of Rational Choice Theory*. Pittsburgh, PA: University of Pittsburg Press.

Blondel, J., Sinnott, R. and Svensson, P., (1998) *People and Parliament in the European Union: Participation, Democracy and Legitimacy*. Oxford: Clarendon Press.

Bowler, S. and Donovan, T. (2013) 'Civic duty and turnout in the UK referendum on AV: what shapes the duty to vote?', *Electoral Studies*, 32 (2): 265.

Brokington, D. (2004) 'The paradox of proportional representation: the effect of party systems and coalitions on individuals' electoral participation', *Political Studies*, 52 (3): 469–90.

Campbell, A., Converse, P., Miller, W. and Stokes, D. (1960) *The American Voter*. New York: John Wiley.

Downs, A. (1957) *An Economic Theory of Democracy*. New York: Harper & Row.

Evans, G. and Duffy, M. (1997) 'Beyond the sectarian divide: the social bases and political consequences of nationalist and unionist party competition in Northern Ireland', *British Journal of Political Science*, 27: 47–81.

Franklin, M. (1996) 'Electoral participation', in L. LeDuc, R. G. Niemi and P. Norris (eds), *Comparing Democracies: Elections and Voting in Global Perspective*. London: Sage.

Gabriel, O. W. (1995) 'Political efficacy and trust', in J. W. van Deth and E. Scarborough (eds), *The Impact of Values*. Oxford: Oxford University Press.

Garry, J. (2007) 'Making party identification more versatile: operationalising the concept in the multi-party context', *Electoral Studies*, 26 (2): 346–58.

Geys, B. (2006) 'Explaining voter turnout: a review of aggregate level research', *Electoral Studies*, 25 (4): 637–63.

Jones, P. and Hudson, J. (2000) 'Civic duty and expressive voting: is virtue its own reward?', *Kyklos*, 53 (1): 3–16.

Karp, J. and Banducci, S. (2008) 'Political efficacy and participation in 27 democracies: how electoral systems shape political behaviour', *British Journal of Political Science*, 38 (2): 311–34.

Maggiotto, M. and Pierson, J. (1977) 'Partisan identification and electoral choice: the hostility hypothesis', *American Journal of Political Science*, 21 (4): 745–67.

Marsh, M., Sinnott, R., Garry, J. and Kennedy, F. (2008) *The Irish Voter*. Manchester: Manchester University Press.

Medeiros, M. and Noel, A. (forthcoming) 'The forgotten side of partisanship: negative party identification in four Anglo-American democracies', *Comparative Political Studies*.

Redlawsk, D. (2006) *Feeling Politics: Emotion in Political Information Processing*. New York: Macmillan.

Richardson, B. (1991) 'European party loyalties revisited', *American Political Science Review*, 85 (3): 751–75.

Roberts, H. (1990) 'Sound stupidity: the British party system and the Northern Ireland question', in J. McGarry and B. O'Leary (eds), *The Future of Northern Ireland*. Oxford: Clarendon.

Schmitt, H. (2002) *Multiple Party Identifications*. Paper prepared for the Conference of the Comparative Study of Electoral Systems (CSES) at the WZB in Berlin, 21–24 February.

van der Eijk, C. and Niemoller, C. (1983) *Electoral Change in the Netherlands*. Amsterdam: CT Press.

Weisberg, H. (1999) 'Political partisanship', in J. Robinson, P. Shaver and L. Wrightsman (eds), *Measures of Political Attitudes*. San Diego, CA: Academic Press, pp. 681–729.

6

STANDBY CITIZENS

Understanding non-participation in contemporary democracies

Erik Amnå and Joakim Ekman

Introduction

Drawing on recent developments in research on political participation and civic engagement, the present chapter offers a discussion about different ways of understanding political passivity. The text starts with a brief overview of current interpretations of what political passivity entails, highlighting in particular optimistic and pessimistic accounts of the state of affairs of contemporary democracies. Subsequently, we critically examine how 'civic engagement' and 'political participation' have been conceptualised in previous research, thereby demonstrating the need for considering a 'latent' aspect of participation and engagement. In the third section, we introduce the notion of 'standby citizens' representing a political orientation that transcends the conventional active/passive dichotomy. The chapter concludes with a discussion about the implications of our findings for party-based democracies.

Political participation and civic engagement in decline?

Research on political participation in contemporary democracies has for a number of years been concerned with declining levels of civic engagement and party membership, low electoral turnout and eroding public confidence in the institutions of representative democracy, among young as well as middle-aged and older citizens. In the post-industrial societies, it would seem, citizens have become increasingly disengaged from the conventional channels of political participation. Political passivity, or perhaps quite simply the lack of conventional forms of participation, has generally been considered to be a problem for democracy (Skocpol and Fiorina 1999; Dalton 1998, 2006; Putnam 2000).

At the same time, there are different notions of political passivity in the literature (cf. Norris 2002: 5–7; Stolle and Hooghe 2005; Berger 2009). Some scholars seem to believe that passivity (non-activity) is harmful, while others seem to be quite relaxed about it. Such notions have not only to do with actual observations of citizen behaviour; it is also a matter of different normative approaches. This becomes evident when looking at the normative aspects associated with the three conventional models of democracy typically found in political science textbooks. The Weber/Schumpeter-based *minimalist model of democracy* accepts passivity; indeed, it even embraces it. Democracy is not about mass participation; rather, non-qualified (and even qualified) citizens should keep out of politics in between elections. A radically different position is found among the advocates of *participatory democracy*. Here, within an overall more ethical Aristotelian tradition (McBride 2012), political passivity is unequivocally understood as a bad thing; it constitutes a threat to democracy. As many people as possible *ought* to get involved in politics on a regular basis, since it facilitates good decision-making and fosters responsible citizens. The *representative model of democracy* represents an intermediate position in this respect. Here, as suggested by Almond and Verba in a seminal work on political culture (1963), a sense of civic duty should ideally be combined with some level of passivity, in the sense that the incumbents should be left to decide on most political issues on their own, in order to facilitate effective government.

In addition to these normative questions about the best way of organising a democratic political system, the issue of political passivity has of course been a standing feature in the contemporary discussion on the quality of democracy. This literature encompasses both *optimistic* and *pessimistic* interpretations of current developments. The pessimistic interpretations include Putnam's analysis of the state of democracy in the US (2000), and similar concerned voices have resonated in a number of other democracies worldwide, e.g. in Western Europe, Scandinavia and South East Asia, where scholars have pointed to an ever-widening gap between citizens and politicians, declining political support and general feelings of disaffection (Kaase and Newton 1995; Norris 1999; Pharr and Putnam 2000).

On a more optimistic note, it has been argued that such fears are exaggerated; the development of 'critical citizens' is not the same thing as the erosion of democracy, and the assumption of the decline and fall of civic engagement is, at best, premature (e.g. Norris 1999, 2002; Berger 2009). In the more recent literature, we thus find some interpretations of current political developments where passivity – in the form of declining levels of conventional political participation and civic engagement – is not necessarily considered to be a threat in itself to democracy. Rather, we are told, this is more or less what we should expect from postmodern citizens. They avoid traditional forms of political participation, but they also develop new forms of political behaviour and stay interested in societal affairs.

The notion of 'monitorial citizens' (Schudson 1996, 1999) constitutes one of the most optimistic interpretations of citizens' political behaviour in contemporary democracies. Schudson claims that citizens today are not politically passive, even if they do not formally participate in politics; rather, they are politically involved as 'monitorial citizens', which is 'a critical and observational form of citizenship, avoiding any routine-based or institutionalized forms of political participation' (Hooghe and Dejaeghere 2007: 250–1). Thus the decline in conventional forms of participation does not entail a crisis of democracy; rather, 'monitorial citizens' supposedly stay interested in and informed about politics and display sufficiently high levels of political trust. The low level of formal political participation reflects rational decision-making. Only when there is a felt need to intervene will the 'monitorial citizen' act – but, up until then, she or he stays out of politics.

The academic debate about the state of Western democracies has been particularly animated when it comes to young people's political involvement. Some scholars have pointed to the alarmingly low levels of young people's engagement in politics, like membership in parties, voting in elections and activities in associational life (Marsh et al. 2007; Dalton 2008). Others have argued that, even if young people undoubtedly are less engaged in politics than middle-aged citizens, increasingly more young people have become involved 'in emerging forms of civic engagement that take place outside the institutionalized sphere of politics' (Stolle and Hooghe 2011; cf. Flanagan 2013). Also, the literature has covered *new styles of citizenship*, manifested, for example, in activity on the Internet, through political consumption (Micheletti 2003; Stolle et al. 2005; Micheletti and Stolle 2009) or in highly diversified reportoires of engagement (Hustinx et al. 2012).

Civic engagement and political participation

The discussion between optimists and pessimists has some important implications. For one thing, the different notions of what political passivity entails demonstrate some conceptual confusion surrounding the notion of 'civic engagement' and 'political participation'. Moreover, this is directly linked to the tendency in the literature to focus on manifest activities and neglect the 'latent' forms of political participation. We turn next to a brief examination of these conceptual issues, focusing on how civic enagagement and political participation have been understood in previous research.

Civic engagement

Somewhat provocatively, it has been argued that 'civic engagement' as a concept is ready for the dustbin. In recent years, it has been used as a buzzword, to cover everything from voting in elections to giving money to charity, or from bowling in leagues to participating in political rallies and marches (Berger 2009: 335). Putnam has been identified as the one that popularised the concept, and for him, it was a matter of pointing out the importance of 'social capital' for a vital democratic society. In a manner of speaking, his focus was more on 'engagement' than on the 'civic' or the 'political': when analysing citizens' levels of engagement, Putnam covered just about everything from reading newspapers, political participation, social networks and interpersonal trust to associational involvement. All of this was labelled civic engagement and the point was greatly simplified that such civic engagement tended to correlate with a functioning democracy and market economy (Putnam 1993). In a few articles and a larger study, Putnam expanded his thesis, and argued that civic engagement was on the decline in the US. American democracy was supposedly eroding from the inside (Putnam 1995, 1997, 2000). This sparked a global debate about the future of the established democracies. But again, Putnam was somewhat unclear about just what it was that was actually declining, since 'civic engagement' was a bit of everything (Berger 2009: 336).

Other scholars too have noted the lack of consensus on what constitutes civic engagement. Reviewing existing definitions of the term, Adler and Goggin (2005) conclude that there is no single agreed-upon meaning of civic engagement. That does not mean that all definitions are broad and all-encompassing. As Adler and Goggin point out, there are a number of more confined definitions that restrict civic engagement to apply to very specific action, such as community service, collective action and even political involvement (Adler and Goggin 2005: 238–40).

The definitions that limit civic engagement to mean community service stress voluntary work in the local community as something close to a *duty* for all citizens. Definitions of civic engagement as collective action assumes that such engagement most often comes in the form of collaboration or joint action to improve conditions in the civil sphere. Other definitions emphasise the political aspect of 'civic', and consequently equate civic engagement with 'activities that are not only collective but that are specifically political (i.e., that involve government action)' (Adler and Goggin 2005: 238).

Others have chosen to conceptualise civic engagement in more expansive ways, to include a number of activities. Adler and Goggin (2005) point out that Putnam (2000) in fact avoids any explicit definition of civic engagement. Rather – as Berger (2009) has also noted – all sorts of informal social activities alongside associational involvement and political participation are included in Putnam's analysis of what fosters 'social capital'. Also, Adler and Goggin (2005) point to Michael Delli Carpini as someone who defines civic engagement to include activities ranging from voluntary work and organisational involvement to electoral participation (cf. Zukin *et al.* 2006). Adler and Goggin thus demonstrate the wide variety of activities that are actually included in different notions of 'civic engagement' in the literature.

To sum up, one could perhaps think about the term as a continuum, spanning from the *private* sphere to the formal or *public* sphere. The former covers *individual* action like helping one's neighbours or simply discussing politics with one's friends. The latter encompasses *collective* action, like activity within a party, an organisation or interest group. Adler and Goggin also propose their own definition of civic engagement; it has basically to do with 'how an active citizen participates in the life of a community in order to improve conditions for others or to help shape the community's future' (Adler and Goggin 2005: 241).

Political participation

We certainly like to applaud Adler and Goggin's attempt to conceptualise civic engagement and bring order in the rich flora of definitions of the term. However, we also feel that Berger (2009) has a point when criticising such broad definitions. It is hard not to agree that a term covering everything from helping a neighbour to voting in elections or running for public office in fact entails conceptual stretching (cf. Sartori 1970).

Let us proceed by contrasting the image depicted by Berger (2009) and Adler and Goggin (2005) with another description of a field of research, focusing more specifically on 'political participation'.

Political science research on citizens' engagement in politics has conventionally focused on *electoral* participation (cf. Brady 1999; van Deth 2001). For a long time, voting was perceived as the primary way for a citizen to make his or her voice heard in the political system, and voting turnout has been described as the most commonly used measure of citizen participation in the US. When postwar American political scientists thought about political participation, they quite simply thought about acts intentionally aimed at influencing governmental decisions (Verba and Nie 1972; Easton 1953: 134). A frequently cited definition by Verba and his associates, from the 1970s, testifies to the focus on the election of political leaders and the approval of their policies:

> By political participation we refer to those legal acts by private citizens that are more or less directly aimed at influencing the selection of governmental personnel and/or the actions that they take.
>
> *(Verba et al. 1978: 1)*

Other often-cited definitions from the same era are quite similar: political participation was understood as the 'actions of private citizens by which they seek to influence or support government and politics' or as 'all voluntary activities by individual citizens intended to influence either directly or indirectly political choices at various levels of the political system' (Milbrath and Goel 1977: 2; Kaase and Marsh 1979: 42).

At the same time, Verba and others admitted that all allocations of values in society are not determined by *political* elites alone – private and civil society actors could also fulfil this function. Still, most political scientists at the time were not really interested in civic engagement in the wider sense or in how citizens acted in relation to social elites outside of the political domain; rather, it was a matter of pointing out that citizens could *also*, in addition to voting, participate in politics *between* elections (Verba *et al.* 1978: 47).

This way of thinking about political participation at least implicitly opened up analyses of activities that included not only voting behaviour, but also, for example, demonstrations, strikes, boycotts and other forms of protest behaviour. This line of thought was also quite early on followed by Barnes and Kaase in their seminal work on *Political Action* (Barnes and Kaase *et al.* 1979; Kaase and Marsh 1979; cf. Verba and Nie 1972; Verba *et al.* 1995; Montero *et al.* 2007: 434). Consequently, actions directed against all political, societal, media or economic actors (or elites) could be analysed as 'political participation' (Teorell *et al.* 2007: 335–6; Norris 2002: 193).

More recent definitions of political participation have thus tended to be wider in scope. Brady, for example, defines political participation as 'action by ordinary citizens directed toward influencing some political outcomes' (Brady 1999: 737; cf. Teorell *et al.* 2007: 336). Brady emphasises that we should think about political participation firstly as manifest and observable actions or activities that people voluntarily take part in. Secondly, 'people' means ordinary citizens, not political elites or civil servants. Thirdly, the concept refers to deliberate attempts to influence the people in power, to make a difference. To be interested in politics and societal issues, or even to discuss politics frequently, is not enough, Brady tells us. Political participation refers to attempts to influence *others* – any powerful actors, groups or business enterprises in society – and their decisions that concern societal issues. Brady thus offers us a wider definition of political participation. At the same time, one could argue that Brady too tends to place more weight on actions directed at *political* elites than on actions directed at other elites. This has in fact been a typical feature of the research field; even if scholars have suggested ever broader definitions of political participation, focus has remained on a more confined set of citizen activities. To give but one example, Parry *et al.* (1992) define political participation as 'action by citizens which is aimed at influencing decisions which are, in most cases, ultimately taken by public representatives and officials' (Parry *et al.* 1992: 16; cf. Brady 1999: 738).

Drawing on Verba and Nie as well as Brady, Teorell *et al.* have more recently developed what is perhaps the most comprehensive definition of political participation to date, encompassing actions or activities by ordinary citizens that in some way are directed toward influencing political outcomes in society. In line with this, Teorell *et al.* have introduced a wider typology than found in previous research (Teorell *et al.* 2007: 336–7).

Verba and Nie used four dimensions of participation in their often-cited typology: *voting*; *campaign activity* (including membership in or work for political parties and organisations as well as donating money to such parties or groups); *contacting* public officials; and *cooperative* or *communal activities*, basically understood by Verba and associates as all forms of engagement that focus on issues in the local community (Verba and Nie 1972: 56–63).

Teorell *et al.* (2007) suggest a more extensive typology, encompassing five dimensions. *Electoral participation* is the first of these. *Consumer participation* covers donating money to charity, boycotting and political consumption, as well as signing petitions. In a manner of speaking, it taps the role of citizens as critical consumers. The third dimension is *party activity*: to be a member of, active within, do voluntary work for or donate money to a political party. *Protest activity* is the fourth dimension, which covers acts like taking part in demonstrations, strikes and other protest activities. Contacting organisations, politicians or civil servants constitutes the fifth dimension, *contact activity*.

Latent forms of participation

The strength of the typology suggested by Teorell et al. is the explicit focus on manifest political participation in a more narrow sense – i.e. activities intended to influence actual political outcomes by targeting relevant political or societal elites (cf. Brady 1999). At the same time, the typology is wide enough to cover a lot more than just participation in elections. Moreover, the typology is based on previous studies that have demonstrated empirically that different forms of participation seem to be related: citizens involved in one mode or dimension of political behaviour tend to be involved in other forms of political behaviour within the same dimension, but not necessarily involved in political activities in other dimensions. For example, citizens involved in *illegal* demonstrations *also* tend to get involved in legal demonstrations, but not necessarily in conventional party activity.

However, we would nevertheless like to argue that the typology suggested by Teorell et al. is not optimal. For one thing, it is not obvious that all 'protest behaviour' could be tapped with measures like participation in demonstrations, strikes and illegal political action. Certain forms of voting – e.g. blank voting – could be described as a protest as well. Or, for that matter, non-voting, the signing of petitions and political consumption. In the typology suggested by Teorell et al., the two latter forms of participation are called 'consumer participation', a label that may in fact obscure the protest character of the specific action.

More importantly, the typology does not take into account *latent* forms of political participation, the kind of engagement that may be regarded 'pre-political', 'monitorial' or 'on standby'. This notion of latency is based on the simple observation that citizens actually do a lot of things that may not be directly or unequivocally classified as 'political participation', but at the same time could be of great significance for future political activities of a more conventional type. If we are interested in declining levels of political participation, we must not overlook such *potentially* political forms of engagement. People of all ages and from all walks of life engage socially in a number of ways, formally outside of the political domain, but nevertheless in ways that may have political consequences.

Even the relatively extensive typology developed by Teorell et al. ultimately fails to take such 'pre-political' actions or orientations into account. What do we miss, employing such a theoretical framework? A bit pointedly, only the rest of the iceberg. A lot of citizen engagement in the contemporary democracies seems to be formally non-political or semi-political on the surface, that is activities not directly aimed at influencing the people in power, but nevertheless activities that entail involvement in society and current affairs. People in general discuss politics, consume political news in papers and on TV or on the Internet, or talk about societal issues. People are aware of global problems, like environmental issues and the poverty or HIV situation in different parts of the world. People have political knowledge and skills, and hold informed opinions about politics. Some people write to editors in local papers, debating local community affairs. Others express their opinions online.

All of this is excluded from the typology suggested by Teorell *et al*. Although this is perfectly reasonable, we still feel that it is a shortcoming, since all these things may be important for us to accurately analyse and understand the conditions for political participation in different countries. What is more, if we are interested in *explaining* different forms of engagement in political affairs among different groups in society, e.g. youth, women or immigrants, we certainly cannot afford to overlook these aspects of 'pre-political' orientations.

The closest thing to the notion of 'latent participation' we find in the works of Schudson (1996, 1999) and his notion of 'monitorial citizens' (see above). Schudson's optimistic claim is that citizens today are not uninterested or uninformed about politics, or lack political efficacy; they just take a deliberate anticipative stand in which they seek out information about politics and stay interested. And (only) when they feel that it is really imperative, they will intervene or act politically. They thus avoid conventional channels of political participation, but it is not correct to say that they are not politically involved – they are, as 'monitorial citizens'. This notion is close to various ideas about 'postmodern' orientations among citizens today (cf. Hooghe and Dejaeghere 2007: 250–1; Inglehart 1990, 1997).

It may also be noted that Hibbing and Theiss-Morse (2002) have suggested an alternative logic for being on a standby mode. It supposedly has less to do with feeling confident about leaving politics to others, while at the same time staying alert and interested in politics. Rather, in this take on the monitorial citizen, deliberative non-involvement is rooted in *distrust* in politicians; even if people desire to stay out of politics altogether, they still feel that they have an obligation to intervene from time to time in order to prevent the worst forms of political corruption. This would essentially add up to a pessimistic interpretation (see above), since the core argument is that people are not really interested in politics or political participation (cf. Amnå and Ekman 2014).

Varieties of passivity and standby citizens

As we have demonstrated so far, 'civic engagement' has arguably become something of a catch-all concept in recent years, less than ideal for precise empirical analyses of the conditions for citizens' involvement in society. Furthermore, the literature on 'political participation' stands out as too narrow in scope, in some respects. Important aspects of citizens' political (or pre-political) engagement are systematically overlooked, using the standard definitions of political participation. Here, the idea is thus to enhance our understanding of the much-debated declining levels of political engagement, low electoral turnout and eroding public confidence in the institutions of representative democracy by suggesting a new way of analysing citizens' political *and* 'non-participatory' behaviour.

TABLE 6.1 Variable-centred approach vs. person-oriented approach

Variable-centred approach	Active	—	Passive
Focus on manifest activity: • Electoral participation • Consumer participation • Party activity • Protest activity • Contact activity • Civic engagement • Interest in politics	High frequency	Intermediate position	Low frequency
Person-oriented approach	Active	Standby citizen	Unengaged/disillusioned
Focus on specific combinations of orientations among individuals: • Level of activity • Level of interest • Citizenship competencies	Combination of activity (high) and interest (high)	Combination of activity (low to intermediate) and interest (high)	Combination of activity (low) and interest (low) Combination of activity (low) and hostility towards politics

Research on political participation (and civic engagement) has generally followed a variable-centred approach (cf. Ekman and Amnå 2012). From the postwar decades up until today, increasingly more items have been included in the social science opinion surveys in order to understand what citizens actually do when they engage in politics and society. Basically, more and more aspects have been covered – everything from electoral participation, protest behaviour and civic engagement to political consumption and online activity. Indeed, the study of political participation has become a 'theory of everything' (van Deth 2001).

The focus has thus been on different forms of *activity*. Passivity, on the other hand, has largely been left unexplored. However, in a recent study (Amnå and Ekman 2014), we have tested the notion of a 'monitoral' approach among young people, trying to understand different varieties of non-participation. Drawing on unique data on Swedish adolescents collected within a research programme on political socialisation at Örebro University (Amnå et al. 2009), we demonstrate empirically that what is sometimes dismissed as 'passivity' (i.e. the lack of manifest activity) actually consists of distinctly different orientations. In order to facilitate the analysis, we first constructed a simple framework that distinguished between – on the one hand – those interested in politics and societal affairs and those uninterested, and – on the other hand – active youths and passive youths. In contrast to a conventional variable-centred approach, this entailed a person-oriented approach (see Table 6.1). Subsequently, we included a number of questions about skills and competencies typically associated with the notion of political citizenship (like political knowledge, interest and media consumption) into the analysis.

Our research clearly demonstrated that the 'monitorial' or — which is the label we prefer — the 'standby' category actually exists (Amnå and Ekman 2014). In fact, we may identify four distinct groups when it comes to citizenship orientations: *active* youths (who score high on both our measures of political interest and political participation); those on *standby* (scoring high on interest but only average on participation); the *unengaged* (scoring low on both interest and participation); and the *disillusioned* (scoring low on participation and lowest of all groups on interest). Interestingly, just like in a recent study on young people in Belgium and the Netherlands (Hustinx et al. 2012), the 'standby' category is the largest group in the Swedish sample, suggesting that being on standby/a monitorial citizen is a common orientation in contemporary democracies.

Furthermore, the standby group stands out in meaningful ways when analysing how the four distinct citizenship orientations differ on a number of measures designed to tap political competencies among young people, such as efficacy, political ambition, feelings about politics, news consumption, attempts at influencing parents and friends, and the habit of bringing up political and societal issues during class. In short, being on 'standby' is actually something rather close — but not identical — to an 'active' orientation, and at the same time something distinctly different from a passive/alienated orientation to politics and societal affairs. This means, then, that if research on political participation should be able to contribute to our understanding of the dynamics of contemporary democracies, the analysis has to go beyond the simplistic passive/active dichotomy.

Concluding remarks

In this chapter, we have argued for the need to include 'latent' forms of participation when analysing citizens' levels of engagement in contemporary democracies. In particular, we have highlighted the notion of a 'standby' orientation, transcending the active/passive dichotomy. This notion ties in well with 'optimistic' interpretations of the state of affairs in Western democracies, such as Schudson's (1996) 'monitorial citizen'. At the same time, the presence of 'standby citizens' may also be regarded as a challenge to the organisation of political life in a democratic society.

Political elites frequently call for active citizens. Political passivity — e.g. not taking part in elections or in civil society organisations — is famed as a problem for democracy. At the same time, and not the least in the well-functioning Scandinavian democracies, it is precisely the political elites themselves that have prepared the ground for such a development. Members in parties and organisations have been made redundant, and ordinary citizens have been assigned the role of an audience rather than part of the input process in the political system. The political parties have become increasingly 'professional' and very little dependent upon members for their actual organisation or economic base — state grants take care of that. This development has apparently not gone unnoticed by — in this case — young people in Sweden. A little pointedly, the message coming from the parties and the political organisations is loud and clear: 'We want you as (passive) supporters, and as voters on Election Day, but please do not bother to get involved in our daily activities.'

In that sense, standby citizens are a product of 'too well' functioning democracies. Political participation has been rationalised away. But standby citizens may also exist in 'too poorly' functioning democracies, where people feel that they are waiting for a good reason to get involved – i.e. when things get too bad, or when people feel that they simply *have* to get involved. This is closer to Hibbing and Theiss-Morse's (2002) and more recent (Hansard Society 2013) warnings of political action as an expression of *distrust*. In any case, this is an issue that the conventional political parties are well advised to concern themselves with.

References

Adler, R. P. and Goggin, J. (2005) 'What do we mean by "civic engagement"?', *Journal of Transformative Education*, 3 (3): 236–53.
Almond, G. A. and Verba, S. (1963) *The Civic Culture: Political Attitudes and Democracy in Five Nations*. Princeton, NJ: Princeton University Press.
Amnå, E. and Ekman, J. (2014) 'Standby citizens: faces of political passivity', *European Political Science Review*, 6 (2): 261–81.
Amnå, E. et al. (2009) 'Political socialization and human agency. The development of civic engagement from adolescence to adulthood', *Statsvetenskaplig Tidskrift*, 111 (1): 27–40.
Barnes, S. and Kaase, M. et al. (1979) *Political Action: Mass Participation in Five Western Democracies*. London and Beverly Hills, CA: Sage.
Berger, B. (2009) 'Political theory, political science, and the end of civic engagement', *Perspectives on Politics*, 7 (2): 335–50.
Brady, H. (1999) 'Political participation', in J. P. Robinson, P. R. Shaver and L. S. Wrightsman (eds), *Measures of Political Attitudes*. San Diego, CA: Academic Press.
Dalton, R. J. (1998) *Citizen Politics in Western Democracies*. Chatham, NJ: Chatham House.
Dalton, R. J. (2006) *Citizen Politics: Public Opinion and Political Parties in Advanced Industrial Democracies*. Washington, DC: CQ Press.
Dalton, R. J. (2008). *The Good Citizen: How a Younger Generation is Reshaping American Politics*. Washington, DC: CQ Press.
Easton, D. (1953) *The Political System: An Inquiry into the State of Political Science*. New York: Alfred A. Knopf.
Ekman, J. and Amnå, E. (2012) 'Political participation and civic engagement: towards a new typology', *Human Affairs: Postdisciplinary Humanities & Social Science Quarterly*, 22 (3): 283–300.
Flanagan, C. A. (2013) *Teenage Citizens: The Political Theories of the Young*. Cambridge, MA: Harvard University Press.
Hansard Society (2013) *Audit of Political Engagement 10. The 2013 Report*, retrieved 23 May 2013 from: http://hansardsociety.org.uk/blogs/parliament_and_government/archive/2013/05/15/audit-of-political-engagement-10.aspx.
Hibbing, J. R. and Theiss-Morse, E. (2002) *Stealth Democracy: Americans' Beliefs about How Government Should Work*. Cambridge: Cambridge University Press.
Hooghe, M. and Dejaeghere, Y. (2007) 'Does the "monitorial citizen" exist? An empirical investigation into the occurrence of postmodern forms of citizenship in the Nordic countries', *Scandinavian Political Studies*, 30 (2): 249–71.

Hustinx, L. et al. (2012) 'Monitorial citizens or civic omnivores? Repertoires of civic participation among university students', *Youth and Society*, 44 (1): 95–117.
Inglehart, R. (1990) *Culture Shift in Advanced Industrial Society*. Princeton, NJ: Princeton University Press.
Inglehart, R. (1997) *Modernization and Postmodernization. Cultural, Economic, and Political Change in 43 Societies*. Princeton, NJ: Princeton University Press.
Kaase, M. and Marsh, A. (1979) 'Political action. A theoretical perspective', in S. Barnes and M. Kaase et al. (eds), *Political Action: Mass Participation in Five Western Democracies*. London and Beverly Hills, CA: Sage.
Kaase, M. and Newton, K. (eds) (1995) *Beliefs in Government*. Oxford: Oxford University Press.
McBride, C. (2012) 'Democratic participation, engagement and freedom', *British Journal of Politics and International Relations*, 15 (4): 493–508.
Marsh, D., O'Toole, T. and Jones, S. (2007) *Young People and Politics in the UK. Apathy or Alienation?* Basingstoke: Palgrave.
Micheletti, M. (2003) *Political Virtue and Shopping: Individuals, Consumerism, and Collective Action*. Basingstoke: Palgrave Macmillan.
Micheletti, M. and Stolle, D. (2009) 'Vegetarianism as life style politics', in M. Micheletti and A. McFarland (eds), *Creative Participation: Responsibility-taking in the Political World*. Boulder, CO: Paradigm.
Milbrath, L. W. and La Goel, M. (1977) *Political Participation. How and Why People Get Involved in Politics*. Chicago: RandMcNally.
Montero, J. R., Westholm, A. and van Deth, J. W. (2007) 'The realisation of democratic citizenship in Europe', in J. W. van Deth, J. R. Montero and A. Westholm (eds), *Citizenship and Involvement in European Democracies: A Comparative Analysis*. London and New York: Routledge.
Norris, P. (ed.) (1999) *Critical Citizens. Global Support for Democratic Governance*. Oxford: Oxford University Press.
Norris, P. (2002) *Democratic Phoenix: Reinventing Political Activism*. Cambridge: Cambridge University Press.
Parry, G., Moyser, G. and Day, N. (1992) *Political Participation and Democracy in Britain*. Cambridge: Cambridge University Press.
Pharr, S. J. and Putnam, R. D. (eds) (2000) *Disaffected Democracies: What's Troubling the Trilateral Countries?* Princeton, NJ: Princeton University Press.
Putnam, R. D. (1995) 'Bowling alone: America's declining social capital', *Journal of Democracy*, 6 (1): 65–78.
Putnam, R. D. (1997) 'Bowling alone: democracy in America at century's end', in A. Hadenius (ed.), *Democracy's Victory and Crises*. Cambridge: Cambridge University Press.
Putnam, R. D. (2000) *Bowling Alone: The Collapse and Revival of American Community*. New York: Simon & Schuster.
Putnam, R. D. with Leonardi, R. and Nanetti, R. (1993) *Making Democracy Work. Civic Traditions in Modern Italy*. Princeton, NJ: Princeton University Press.
Sartori, G. (1970) 'Concept misformation in comparative politics', *American Political Science Review*, 64 (4): 1033–53.
Schudson, M. (1996) 'What if civic life didn't die?', *American Prospect*, 25: 17–20.
Schudson, M. (1999) *Good Citizens and Bad History: Today's Political Ideals in Historical Perspective*. Paper presented at a conference on the Transformation of Civic Life, Middle Tennessee State University, 12–13 November.
Skocpol, T. and Fiorina, M. P. (eds) (1999) *Civic Engagement in American Democracy*. Washington, DC: Brooking.

Stolle, D. and Hooghe, M. (2005) 'Inaccurate, exceptional, one-sided or irrelevant? The debate about the alleged decline of social capital and civic engagement in Western societies', *British Journal of Political Science*, 35: 149–67.

Stolle, D. and Hooghe, M. (2011) 'Shifting inequalities. Patterns of exclusion and inclusion in emerging forms of political participation', *European Societies*, 13 (1): 119–42.

Stolle, D., Hooghe, M. and Micheletti, M. (2005) 'Politics in the super-market – political consumerism as a form of political participation', *International Political Science Review*, 26 (3): 245–69.

Teorell, J., Torcal, M. and Montero, J. R. (2007) 'Political participation: mapping the terrain', in J. W. van Deth, J. R. Montero and A. Westholm (eds), *Citizenship and Involvement in European Democracies: A Comparative Analysis*. London and New York: Routledge.

van Deth, J. W. (2001) *Studying Political Participation: Towards a Theory of Everything?* Paper presented at the Joint Sessions of Workshops of the European Consortium for Political Research, Grenoble, 6–11 April.

Verba, S. and Nie, N. H. (1972) *Participation in America: Political Democracy and Social Equality*. New York: Harper & Row.

Verba, S., Nie, N. H. and Kim, J.-O. (1978) *Participation and Political Equality: A Seven-Nation Comparison*. Chicago: Chicago University Press.

Verba, S., Schlozman, K. L. and Brady, H. E. (1995) *Voice and Equality. Civic Voluntarism in American Politics*. Cambridge, MA: Harvard University Press.

Zukin, C., Keeter, S., Andolina, M., Jenkins, K. and Delli Carpini, M. X. (2006) *A New Engagement? Political Participation, Civic Life, and the Changing American Citizen*. New York: Oxford University Press.

7

DEMOCRATIC OWNERSHIP AND DELIBERATIVE PARTICIPATION

Cillian McBride

What is 'democratic ownership' and how is it related to political participation? I will argue that democratic ownership requires us to think of ourselves as participating in a form of collective agency and that a proceduralist account of political legitimacy is better suited to explaining this collective political agency than an instrumental, purely outcome-oriented, account of legitimacy. While direct participation has traditionally been viewed as essential to the exercise of collective agency, I will offer reasons to think that it is the specifically *deliberative* quality of democratic procedures that does the real work of producing collective agency out of individual engagement, and not the *directness* of the participation involved. To stand in a relationship of ownership to democratic outcomes it is not enough that we benefit from these outcomes or find them desirable: we must also have had a share in producing them through an appropriate political procedure.

Democratic ownership can be directly contrasted with political *alienation*, and another way to express my argument would be to say that we have reason to think that inclusive deliberative democratic procedures will be less alienating than more minimalist accounts of democracy. Instrumental accounts of political legitimacy offer relatively weak defences against alienation precisely because they are not centrally concerned with the question of collective agency in the way proceduralist accounts are. Political alienation is clearly a direct threat to political *freedom*. When citizens are politically alienated they regard the political process and the decisions that are produced by it as 'alien', i.e. as disconnected from their own lives and goals. Political decisions appear to them as alien impositions interfering with their lives. In a well-ordered democracy citizens should be able to view political decisions as, in some way, the product of their collective will and the institutions and procedures which produced those decisions as their own and not as alien forces in their lives. We should hope, then, that citizens of democratic states should be in a position to *recognise* themselves in their political institutions and to regard collective decisions as consistent with their freedom rather than as potential threats to it.

Citizens who regard themselves as standing in a relationship of ownership to political decisions have reasons to respect and uphold these decisions, independently of any consideration of possible sanctions for not doing so. Citizens who enjoy democratic ownership will regard themselves as responsible for political decisions, in contrast to alienated citizens who are motivated primarily by the prospect of sanctions for non-compliance and who will not regard themselves as bound to or responsible for decisions made in their name.

To the extent that democratic government purports to be an exercise of freedom and claims authority over us on this basis, democrats should be worried about the prospect of political alienation. This is different, however, from the worry that contemporary citizens are apathetic, and unwilling to participate in politics (Sandel 1996: 6; Putnam 2001: 349). This moralising complaint focuses on the alleged lack of civic virtue exhibited by insufficiently altruistic modern individuals (Cohen 1999; McBride 2012). The threat of political alienation as presented here, however, is a worry about our *institutions* rather than about the *virtues* of our citizens. Specifically, it prompts us to consider whether or not the current configuration of our democratic institutions gives citizens *reasons* to view them as consistent with democratic ownership.

Citizens may, however, regard themselves as standing in a relationship of ownership to their political institutions *without* good reason. This may be adequate for producing a measure of political *stability*, but these cases should be just as worrying to the democrat as cases of political alienation. In each case, democratic institutions may be, *in reality*, alien impositions upon their citizens. Deliberative democratic procedures, however, make possible a form of collective agency which allows citizens to reasonably see themselves as sharing in ownership of the political institutions which shape the context of their lives.

The minimalist challenge

Even today, talk of democratic participation conjures up images of ancient Athenian direct democracy, and discussions of contemporary democratic politics are dogged by the nagging suspicion that large-scale representative democracy is, somehow, just a pale shadow of authentic, direct, democracy (Barber 1984: 145). There is, however, a tradition of sceptical thought about democratic politics which contests the primacy of this model. Schumpeter provides a classic statement of this 'minimalist' view, arguing that the key virtue of democratic rule is that it simply provides a peaceful means to exchange one political elite for another through periodic elections (Schumpeter 1965: 273). Schumpeter regards popular participation as, at best, unnecessary and, at worst, a recipe for ill-informed and irresponsible government, as the ordinary citizen knows little of and cares less about affairs beyond their immediate experience (1965: 258–9). Given general ignorance and civic irresponsibility, the 'minimalist' democrat may conclude that we have good reason to limit popular participation and that consequently we should view evidence of falling electoral turnouts with equanimity. If democratic politics is a marketplace, and the voter simply a consumer (Christiano 1996: 133) shopping around for the best deal, then perhaps low turnout simply reflects broad civic satisfaction with governments that do not sharply differ in terms of the deals that they are offering their customers.

Even if one is not swayed by these arguments, there are, in addition, significant moral reasons to question the classical model (Cohen 1997: 80). The Athenian model is not simply a blueprint for direct democratic institutions but an *ethical* vision of the best way for human beings to live. Man being a political animal, according to Aristotle, the *good* life is that of the active citizen, for only this sort of life will engage and perfect man's true nature (Aristotle 1946: 5–7). Liberals tend to be sceptical about this line of argument: this way of thinking about citizenship and democracy focuses on the 'sectarian' assumption that the life of the active citizen is of pre-eminent value, a view which is incompatible with ethical pluralism, i.e. the view that there are many good ways to live (Cohen 1997). For liberals there is something disturbingly authoritarian about the Aristotelian commitment to active citizenship. Instead of lamenting a lost world of tight-knit, active community, we should instead embrace the ethical possibilities which modern society affords its members, who may wish to be free *from* politics as much as free to engage in it when they choose. Liberals, however, need not regard the commitments of citizenship as on a par with lifestyle choice but may argue that everyone has a basic interest in political autonomy, even if we have reason not to choose to devote our entire lives to active political participation. The argument from value pluralism, then, suggests that there are reasons to reject aspects of the classical model, even if technology now holds out the prospect of making direct democracy feasible for modern states through electronic voting and web-based virtual publics etc. (Fishkin 1991: 21; Sunstein 2007: 34).

Instrumentalism and legitimacy

In the Aristotelian account, the reason why we should favour direct political participation is that any other form of political organisation is simply *unnatural*. This view was challenged first in the seventeenth century by Hobbes' (1996) contractarian account of political legitimacy. Hobbes makes two important moves: firstly, in presenting political society as a product of human will, he focuses our attention squarely on the problem of political legitimacy: the reasons we have for obeying the law. Secondly, he offers an essentially instrumental account of legitimacy of the sort relied on by minimalist democrats today. Hobbes' instrumental account of legitimacy assumes that liberty is essentially individual, and negative. I am free, on this view, only to the extent that I am not subject to deliberate external interference with my wishes (Hobbes 1996: 152; Berlin 1969: 122). The law of the land is clearly a threat to my liberty, as more law means less freedom. However, Hobbes argues that the absence of political rule poses an even greater threat to my welfare and, ultimately, to my life itself. Consequently, contracting into political society is a *good deal*. The cost to my liberty is more than made up for by the gain in security.

We see this line of argument developed further by Hume, who suggests that we can drop all this talk about social contracts and focus directly on the benefits which government produces for us, chiefly the protection of private property (Hume 1963: 463). The precise configuration of political institutions is of little consequence on this view, provided government delivers the desired outcomes. Defences of technocratic government today follow this pattern: it is rational to downplay the significance of political participation in favour of governments which possess technical expertise and a measure of independence from the grubby world of politics, provided these governments can deliver the sort of outcomes which the voters favour: stability and prosperity.

Richard Arneson's defence of an instrumental account of political legitimacy hinges on a similar trade-off, although his preferred outcome is characterised in terms of the defence of fundamental rights rather than in terms of peace or the protection of property (2003: 129). He argues that the legitimacy of a set of political institutions has nothing to do with the fairness of its procedures, of the opportunities for popular participation, but everything to do with the sort of consequences the system delivers for citizens (Arneson 2003: 122). Arneson acknowledges that his 'purely instrumental' view is controversial in view of the widely held assumption that democratic legitimacy is a product both of the fairness of the procedures for making collective decisions and of the beneficial consequences of the decisions taken. He insists, however, that it is this latter feature of democratic institutions that is fundamental (Arneson 2003: 136).

This poses a significant challenge to the claim that political participation has intrinsic value. There is nothing special about political participation as a method for producing political decisions and effective public policy. Romantic 'agonist' (Arendt 1958; Mouffe 2000) ideas about democratic participation which tend to focus on their value for participants can reasonably be said to have mistaken the point of democratic politics (Elster 1997: 25). Even if direct participation might make us better people it needs more argument to show that it delivers better public healthcare provision or the effective conduct of foreign affairs. Arneson suggests that the view that democratic procedures are distinguished by the way that they 'express' a public commitment to equality is misconceived (2003: 131). Democratic institutions themselves need not be especially participatory, particularly if a case can be made that less participatory institutional forms, such as judicial review, are more efficient at delivering the protection of fundamental rights.

Proceduralism and legitimacy

The instrumental argument suggests that we should be relatively unconcerned by hierarchical, exclusive, political institutions provided they work together to produce the appropriate outcomes. This is a theory of legitimacy which essentially dispenses with the idea of democratic ownership and its requirement that citizens can recognise themselves as agents producing political outcomes. While they may endorse the outcomes and judge that these are worth paying for in terms of the necessary reduction of personal liberty which government entails, they are not required to play a significant role in *producing* these outcomes. Citizens in this sort of minimalist democracy may enjoy a measure of individual freedom, some of which they have traded for a system which provides other benefits, but they cannot be said to be participating in the exercise of collective, political autonomy. Arguably, even their individual freedom may not be secure under such arrangements (Pettit 1996).

Our long-standing and deeply rooted understanding of democracy, however, is that it is the institution that makes a form of collective agency possible. Democracy does not simply protect individual freedom, it also makes possible a form of collective agency in which citizens share as participants in democratic co-authorship. In the *Social Contract* Rousseau (1997b) outlines a form of government which, if it cannot permit us total independence from one another, can perhaps ensure our equal freedom. The central feature of this form of rule is direct democracy which, Rousseau suggests, will enable the citizen to obey the law, while 'each, uniting with all, [will] nevertheless obey only himself and remain as free as before' (1997b: 49–50). Through sharing in the General Will, the Rousseauan citizen can recognise himself in the laws of the land as they are the product of his agency (Rousseau 1997b:49). Where Aristotelian accounts are focused more generally on the relationship between participation in a political community and human flourishing (*eudaimonia*), Rousseau's argument is specifically concerned with the relationship between individual and collective freedom.

Rousseau goes on, unfortunately, to suggest that individuals can be 'forced to be free' (1997b: 53) in obeying this General Will, giving rise to the suspicion that talk of collective agency must lead directly to totalitarianism (Berlin 1969). It is worth noting that while notions of collective freedom will make little sense to those who understand freedom to be essentially negative, Rousseau's account of political legitimacy is an important milestone in the development of the contemporary liberal theories of deliberative democracy on account of the way that the notion of the general will functions as an early version of the ideal of public reason (Cohen 2010). The task for contemporary democrats is to envision a model of collective agency that can generate the appropriate level of collective agency in citizens to allow them to stand in a relationship of democratic ownership to political outcomes without adopting the overly unified understanding of collective agency embodied in Rousseau's model (Pettit 2013: 15). We will need a model of collective agency that is consistent with respecting reasonable pluralism and political dissent, without surrendering the ideal of collective self-determination through democratic institutions.

The reason we should aim for an agency-centred account of political legitimacy is that it is more sensitive to the problem of political alienation than any instrumental account and it can, consequently, provide us with a more robust account of political legitimacy. Far from threatening to dismiss the problem of pluralism, the particular sort of procedural account of collective agency developed here is better suited to accommodating dissent than rival accounts of political legitimacy, thereby minimising the dangers of political alienation. It has greater potential to generate reasons to comply with political decisions in particular than the outcome-focused, instrumental view.

Collective decisions must be taken in the face of significant disagreement (Gutmann and Thompson 1995, 1996; Waldron 1999). But this in turn gives rise to the problem that while those on the winning side of a vote have a clear reason to uphold the outcome, i.e. their substantive agreement with the decision, it is less clear what reason those on the losing side must have, at least in a narrowly instrumental account of legitimacy. Citizens on the losing side have, on the contrary, a substantive reason to resist this outcome: their belief that this is simply the wrong outcome. The appeal to generalised outcomes such as 'peace', 'stability', 'overall welfare' or, as in Arneson's case, the protection of 'fundamental rights' is supposed to supply the missing reason for compliance, but it is not hard to see why this strategy is unsatisfactory.

Firstly, this relies on characterising outcomes with a high degree of generality in order to bolster the sense that they can supply reasons to all citizens. However, generalisation does not eliminate disagreement about what counts as a desirable outcome. It is clear that there is significant moral disagreement even about the content of basic rights, as disputes about the permissibility of abortion or gay marriage indicate. If what counts as an appropriate outcome can become the subject of significant dispute (and any significant account of basic resources, capabilities or welfare will typically be controversial), then the appeal to outcomes may not supply the legitimising reasons necessary to produce compliance. Secondly, we might also be concerned that outcome-oriented legitimacy might in effect be relying heavily on the wrong sorts of reasons for compliance. That is to say, faced with bad decisions producing the wrong sorts of outcomes, citizens may nonetheless comply simply because the costs of resisting are simply too high to risk dissent. This is unsatisfactory even where a regime can exert enough control to tip the costs in its favour, for citizens can only regard political decisions as alien impositions under such conditions.

Democratic states aspire to a higher standard of legitimacy than this: they aspire to recognition of their *authority* and not merely weary, conditional, compliance. But how can we understand compliance with laws one disagrees with as consistent with one's freedom rather simply a majoritarian imposition? The answer must lie in a proceduralist model of legitimacy. This model directs attention away from substantive judgments about particular courses of action and onto the reason-generating power of the procedures by which the decisions were made.

Richard Wollheim (1962) argued that the apparently paradoxical nature of democratic citizenship could be resolved in this way. When I vote for option A but am outvoted, I find myself in the apparently paradoxical position that I must now believe that both A and B – the option preferred by the majority – ought to be done (Wollheim 1962: 78–9). Given the fact of political disagreement this is not an uncommon situation. The solution, Wollheim argued, lies in stratifying the reasons for action involved here, i.e. distinguishing between the substantive reasons for preferring option A over option B, and the procedural reasons for acting on B rather than A (Wollheim 1962: 85). By assigning them to different levels, such that procedural reasons can, at least in the right conditions, override substantive reasons, we can see how one might have reasons for compliance despite substantive disagreement.

One of the most problematic features of Rousseau's particular account is that he has a strongly epistemic account of democratic procedures, i.e. he regards them as an extremely reliable way to track truth. The general will, he assures us, can never be wrong, with the alarming result that anyone on the wrong side of a vote must regard themselves as having made a mistake of some sort. In Rousseau's account, the procedural reason defeats the citizen's substantive judgment and *replaces* it with the collective judgment. While there are, contra Schumpeter, often good epistemic reasons to favour collective decision-making over elite decision-making, no one would want to go as far as Rousseau who effectively claims that dissent from the general will is always mistaken (Goodin 2003: 145). Recognising democratic authority is not a matter of *replacing* one's own judgment with that of the majority, but of accepting that one has reasons to comply in the face of one's dissent (Friedman 1990). On Wollheim's account, the right sort of procedure can offer reasons which override the citizen's substantive reasons without defeating them. That is to say, one can consistently, on this view, believe that one has a reason to accept a vote as authoritative, while at the same time viewing it as mistaken and working to reverse this decision (as opposed to merely resisting it as an individual). This sort of procedural account, unlike Rousseau's, does not simply dissolve the individual into the collective, but respects them as autonomous agents in their own right who may have reasons to participate in the exercise of collective agency notwithstanding their dissent from some of the decisions taken as a result.

The idea that is doing the work here is that of a *fair* procedure: an unfair procedure will obviously fail to generate the right sorts of reasons for action. A fair procedure will generate reasons for me to accept an outcome even where I disagree with it. These reasons allow me to identify with the outcome, even if this identification is limited by my substantive dissent, and where such identification is possible I can regard that decision as one I have a share in, i.e. one that I own. As such, even where I have reason to seek to have this decision overturned, this collective decision ought not to be automatically viewed as an obstacle to my self-determination. Without this sort of procedural account, only majorities on a given issue would be genuinely obliged to uphold that decision while minorities are merely corralled by the threat of sanctions. To avoid the charge of majority tyranny, democratic authority must be produced by procedures through which citizens can recognise themselves as the authors of collective actions, not merely enjoying the benefits of government, but contributing to the production of these benefits themselves.

What counts as a fair procedure?

In this account, one's reasons to comply are generated by one's underlying commitment to the particular procedure for arriving at collective decisions. Fair procedures may take a wide variety of forms, however, all the way from the simple coin toss or 'king for a day' (Estlund 1997) to complex democratic procedures involving majority and qualified majority decision rules of various sorts, as well as elections and, occasionally, referendums. What sorts of procedure are best suited to generating these sorts of reasons? Representative democracy relies, centrally, on participation in elections, the outcomes of which are determined by aggregating votes in various ways. This relatively 'thin' procedure relies on the idea that every citizen has a formally equal opportunity to influence the outcome of collective decision-making through the exercise of their vote.

One obvious problem with this account is that of the mismatch between formally equal opportunities provided by the distribution of votes and the unequal distribution of political influence within societies, which can be traced back to underlying inequalities in the distribution of economic, social and cultural capital in those societies. Against the backdrop of these inequalities, the claim of a simple vote-aggregating procedure to be sufficiently fair as to permit citizens to reasonably identify with political decisions may seem rather weak. While everyone may enjoy one vote, voting is only one of the ways in which the political agenda is shaped and substantive opportunities to shape that agenda are not distributed equally. The problem of the relationship between political equality and wider social equality and the ways in which the latter diminishes the worth of the former is a complex one which cannot be solved by attention to political procedures alone (Phillips 1999). We can say, however, that some political procedures offer stronger reasons to regard them as fair than others.

Is direct participation uniquely important in this respect? One might suppose that direct participation might go some way to evening out political influence by doing away with the distinction between representatives and ordinary voters. If nothing else, it would impose higher costs on social elites seeking to exert influence on decision-makers simply by increasing the numbers of decision-makers and, on the assumption of universal suffrage, increasing the social diversity of those decision-makers. In the ancient Greek version of direct democracy, democracy was not confined to direct participation through voting, but also included the distribution of political office by lottery and rotation, such that each citizen would have an equal opportunity of being selected to occupy public office (Manin 1997: 28). When Aristotle characterised democracy in terms of each citizen having an equal share in self-government, he meant this quite literally: citizens would take turns in ruling as well as having the opportunity to participate directly in decision-making (Aristotle 1946: 112).

This model, despite its iconic significance, fails to connect participation to political outcomes in a sufficiently robust way. Firstly, it is difficult to see taking turns in public office as sufficient to permit citizens to recognise collective decisions as their own. In effect, I am simply obeying others while I am waiting for my turn to rule. In practice the ratio of citizens to offices is likely to mean that even in very small political communities my number is unlikely ever to come up (Manin 1997: 29). On its own, taking turns in ruling is not, in any event, really a mechanism for producing collective agency; it only purports to make rule by others more palatable by holding out the prospect that, someday, each will get to exercise individual agency over others for a limited time.

Much more important than occupying executive positions is the way in which collective decisions are made and here, deliberative democrats have argued, there is little virtue to direct forms of participation over indirect. I may be consistently outvoted by self-interested majorities advancing their own interests at my expense in both direct and indirect representative forms of democracy. In each case, the claim to legitimacy relies on the formal equality offered by the equal distribution of votes, and in each case I may have good reason to regard the resulting decisions as alien impositions visited upon me by majorities to whom I am, at best, no more than a minor impediment to their projects. Indeed, as Fishkin notes, this problem may be accentuated in direct democratic polities where the small numbers may make democratic decision-making more vulnerable to populism (Fishkin 1991).

Deliberative democrats argue that the contrast between direct and indirect participation is less significant than that between purely aggregative procedures and those which include both deliberative and aggregative elements. As we noted above, the minimalist account of democracy as a procedure for exchanging political elites by means of popular elections relies on the assumption that voters are essentially consumers whose only concern is to make a rational choice between the benefits attached offered by different candidates. A purely aggregative procedure places no restriction on the reasoning involved in political choice or on the formation of majorities whose only concern may be to advance their own interests at the expense of others. In this respect there is no difference between direct and indirect political participation. Citizens in the minorities under both direct and indirect participatory systems may reasonably judge that political decisions are not *binding* upon them.

Against this, deliberative democrats argue that including a deliberative component in democratic procedures can constrain majorities and thereby strengthen the reasons of minorities to accept the resulting decisions (Gutmann and Thompson 1996). There are other advantages to replacing the aggregation of 'raw preferences' with considered judgments. By offering citizens opportunities to discuss their political preferences with others they may correct false assumptions and thereby contribute to the making of better informed political decisions. They may discover that some of their preferences are the product of processes of adaptation to inequality, which have lowered their ambitions and distorted their understandings of their own interests (Cohen 1997: 78) and in this way public deliberation may enhance their autonomy to the extent that their actions are more likely to reflect their considered interests.

Perhaps the most pertinent feature of deliberative democracy, however, relates to the link between public justification and equal respect. Any decision we make raises questions about the impacts of our actions upon others. These impacts may be positive or negative, and many political disputes centre on the problem of determining where to draw the line between which negative effects are permissible and which call for state interventions of various sorts. There is no clear-cut distinction between public and private, and even simple consumer decisions about what food to buy or what mode of transport to adopt may turn out to have significant impacts on the lives of others, posing pressing questions of distributive justice. Whatever the status of the choices we make as private citizens it is clear that the choices we make regarding collective decisions will not only have an *impact* on the lives of others, but also involve a further claim to *authority* over these lives. If I vote for a party promising me tax cuts in return for more limited public services, my choice will not only have an effect on my fellow citizens, I am committed to requiring them to uphold this decision should it win the vote. A purely aggregative model wrongly assumes that such choices are essentially private, despite the way that my choices not only affect others but also claim authority over them.

Deliberative democrats argue that these sorts of choices and claims impose upon citizens a duty of justification (Rawls 1996) and argue that to fail to offer appropriate justifications for one's attempts to direct our common coercive force essentially violates the basic moral requirement to respect our fellow citizens as equals. To respect others as equals is not necessarily to refrain from imposing costs upon them (we may punish others consistent with respecting them as persons) but it is to regard them as distinct persons with their own interests and projects which must be taken into consideration when we formulate our own political projects. The duty of justification also entails that we respect them as persons capable of responding to reasons, thereby ruling out the paternalist view that we may deliberate *about* the interests of others without deliberating *with* them. Finally, it recognises that others have the power to call us to account for our choices, i.e. to place us under this duty of justification. This broadly Kantian account of equal respect between democratic citizens presents us with an account of democratic procedures as embodying a key form of social recognition: that of our equal moral standing as citizens, and it assumes that recognition of our equal status imposes constraints on how decisions may legitimately be made about the sorts of reasons which may count as appropriate public justifications (Rawls 1996: 217).

This 'expressive' dimension is not incidental to democratic institutions as Arneson suggests. Given the 'burdens of judgement' (Rawls 1993: 56–7) it should be clear that public deliberation is not a device for producing deep consensus on political questions and it will not eliminate the need for voting once deliberation has taken place. Even if we recognise our duty as citizens to consider the interests of our fellow citizens and to offer public justifications for our political preferences which we judge they could not reasonably reject, we are still likely to disagree in our political judgments. Consequently, majority voting will still be necessary to move from deliberation to decision and action. However, while I may have little reason to regard myself as bound to uphold decisions produced by a purely aggregative procedure my reasons to accept decisions taken through aggregation which has been preceded by deliberation are considerably stronger. This is because public deliberation itself manifests recognition of my equal status in a more demanding fashion than the distribution of equal votes, and furthermore it gives me reasons to suppose that my interests have received some consideration by others which may be entirely absent on purely aggregative procedures (Gutmann and Thompson 1996: 72). As such I can reasonably regard myself as having shared in producing this decision, even where I reject the substance of that decision. In this way, a deliberative procedure can strengthen my reasons for judging that democratic outcomes are the product of collective agency in which I have participated and to which I stand in a relationship of democratic ownership.

The importance of political agency

The virtue of the proceduralist account of democratic authority is that it provides an account of the centrality of the idea of freedom, i.e. of self-determination, to democratic citizenship. It would be a mistake to view the normative claims of proceduralism as merely expressive, as Arneson does, for they are concerned rather with setting out the conditions whereby an individual agent can come to identify themselves as the co-author of collective actions, i.e. through participation in the right sort of procedure for taking collective decisions about how to use collective coercive power. The consequentialist is right to point to the fact that democratic politics is about successfully intervening in the world, but a pure consequentialism does not account for the difference between desirable outcomes and outcomes that are brought about through the exercise of collective agency. While the former, in its pure form, risks treating beneficial outcomes like good weather – a welcome occurrence over which we have no control – the latter aims at deliberate intervention in the world, which depends on the appropriate connection between deliberative inputs and real-world outcomes (Pettit and List 2011).

To be concerned with consequences without caring how these are to be produced is to take a curiously disconnected view of collective action, such that we should welcome desirable outcomes of such action without being concerned to take steps to ensure that we secure such outcomes and that we can, in consequence, have some confidence in our ability to intervene in the world over time. While a legitimate government must be one that delivers desirable outcomes with some measure of regularity, the degree to which we can reliably count on producing such outcomes must be closely related to the sorts of procedures in place for taking collective decisions and translating them into action. Otherwise, beneficial consequences would appear to fall like manna from heaven in an arbitrary fashion unrelated to the actions of citizens. It is plausible to suppose that we have an interest not only in receiving benefits from the actions of the state, as the instrumental account would have it, but also that we have an interest in participating in producing those benefits, i.e. an interest in self-determination, that explains our concern with the problems of political alienation and democratic ownership.

I have concentrated here on the problem of outlining the conditions under which individual citizens can reasonably regard themselves as participating in an exercise of collective agency through democratic participation. It is worth noting, however, that collective agency and democratic ownership are not exclusively concerned with the ways in which beneficial consequences can be produced through collective action. Focusing on the reason-generating powers of desirable outcomes in the way that instrumental accounts of legitimacy do has another important defect: it diverts us from the problem of collective responsibility for our collective actions, problems which must loom large if our shared institutions serve to produce bad consequences, whether for ourselves or for others. To the extent that we participate, individually, in institutional arrangements that threaten to unjustly distribute burdens to others, we appear to share in responsibility for these injustices (Pogge 2007: 30). We should, accordingly, be concerned, not only about our freedom to act together to intervene in the world, but also about our responsibility for the actions thereby produced. It is, then, a strength of the agency-centred account of political legitimacy that it focuses our attention on the connection between our actions and their outcomes, reminding us that democratic ownership is not simply a matter of enjoying the benefits of collective action, but also of taking responsibility for them.

This proceduralist account of collective agency focuses on our *reasons* for endorsing or identifying with political decisions. I have argued that public deliberation offers us reasons to identify ourselves as owners of political decisions, even when we would prefer that some other decision had been taken. I have stressed the question of whether or not we have reason to identify in this way with political outcomes in order to distinguish my procedural account from other ways in which people may come to identify with political outcomes. Instrumental democracy offers one very limited set of reasons to identify with outcomes: they benefit us in some way. Identity-based accounts offer different reasons, which rely on some alleged identity between citizens and decision-makers. What I have in mind here are nationalist or populist accounts of democracy, in which we share in self-government provided we are ruled by people with whom we share an identity (Habermas 1998). As long as the political elite is drawn from the relevant nation, then fellow nationals may come to identify with their decisions as 'ours'. While shared identity may provide reasons to suppose that one's representatives may share our interests and incentivise them to act as 'fiery advocates' for these interests (Phillips 1995), there is also a risk that shared social identities may produce unreasoned identification, i.e. that we will identify with political outcomes even though our institutions offer us little reason to suppose that decision-making is really affording us the sorts of opportunities for participation which sustain *genuine* political agency.

A second problem relating to the idea of reasons to identify with/endorse political decisions is that it is possible that identification/endorsement may come apart from any causal role in the production of these outcomes. One might say that arguments for direct participation focus almost exclusively on the causal inputs provided by individual preferences, but fail to explain how these are transformed into genuinely collective decisions which offer all citizens reasons to regard themselves as bound to those decisions. There is also a risk that we might have good reasons to endorse decisions which we have not had any role in producing. We might capture this contrast in the following ways. Firstly, as a direct democrat I may be personally present at a meeting in which the 'public deliberation' involves little more than grandstanding and barracking followed by a vote – a process that offers, at best, very limited reasons for compliance. Secondly, I may follow the progress of healthcare reform proposals through the legislature from the comfort of my armchair in which I browse the relevant websites and read the relevant newspaper reports, forming an informed view of the options and ultimately judging that I have reason to endorse the outcome, whether substantively or procedurally, but without my contributing to this outcome in any way.

If our current institutions offer limited opportunities for direct participation, we may be content with the idea that modern media make the decision-making process sufficiently transparent to make it possible that we could reasonably endorse decisions and processes without any involvement in their production. This is problematic, however, from the point of view of political agency: there must at the very least be genuine opportunities for citizens to actively shape public opinion and thereby to have some causal influence on the production of political decisions. Even if citizens do not often take up these opportunities, their existence would provide them with some reason to suppose that the relevant perspectives were being included and considered in the streams of public deliberation from which decisions flow. In the absence of such opportunities, however, we should have little reason to suppose that our deliberative procedures were working well and operating fairly. The existence of such concrete opportunities and their equal distribution might be thought of as providing the minimal conditions for judging that our political institutions genuinely afford us the possibility of democratic ownership. It is not clear that, in practice, we should be especially confident that our actually existing democracies meet these conditions.

Conclusion

The consequentialist account focuses on the consequences of what is done, without attending to how we might go about producing the desired consequences, while a purely proceduralist account might aim to take decisions fairly, regardless of the quality of those decisions. However, it is evident that as agents we care about making the right decisions in order to intervene in the world in the right ways, and in order to do so we must care about *how* we go about making such decisions – both inputs and outputs matter to the business of acting successfully. So too, in the case of collective action, we must care about the processes by which decisions are taken if we want to get the answers right more often than not.

Deliberative proceduralism has the resources to close the gap between what a citizen thinks ought to be done and what the demos has decided to do, whenever these come apart, as they must from time to time. In so doing, deliberative political procedures allow citizens to view themselves as sharing in collective political agency and as enjoying democratic ownership over the decisions which shape their lives.

References

Arendt, H. (1958) *The Human Condition*. Chicago: University of Chicago Press.
Aristotle (1946) *The Politics of Aristotle*. Oxford: Oxford University Press.
Arneson, R. (2003) 'Defending the purely instrumental account of democratic legitimacy', *Journal of Political Philosophy*, 11 (1): 122–32.
Barber, B. (1984) *Strong Democracy*. Berkeley, CA: University of California Press.
Berlin, I. (1969) *Two Concepts of Liberty. Four Essays on Liberty*. Oxford: Oxford University Press, pp. 118–72.
Christiano, T. (1996) *The Rule of the Many*. Boulder, CO: Westview Press.
Cohen, Jean (1999) 'Trust, voluntary association and workable democracy: the contemporary American discourse of civil society', in M. Warren (ed.), *Democracy and Trust*. Cambridge: Cambridge University Press, pp. 208–48.
Cohen, Joshua (1997) 'Deliberation and democratic legitimacy', in J. Bohman and W. Rehg (eds), *Deliberative Democracy*. Cambridge, MA: MIT Press, pp. 67–92.
Cohen, Joshua (2010) *Rousseau: A Free Community of Equals*. Oxford: Oxford University Press.
Elster, J. (1997) 'The market and the forum: three varieties of political theory', in J. Bohman and W. Rehg (eds), *Deliberative Democracy*. Cambridge, MA: MIT Press, pp. 3–34.
Estlund, D. (1997) 'Beyond fairness and deliberation: the epistemic dimension of democratic authority', in J. Bohman and W. Rehg (eds), *Deliberative Democracy*. Cambridge: MA: MIT Press, pp. 173–204.
Fishkin, J. (1991) *Democracy and Deliberation*. New Haven, CT: Yale University Press.
Friedman, R. B. (1990) 'On the concept of authority in political philosophy', in J. Raz (ed.), *Authority*. Oxford: Blackwell, pp. 56–91.
Goodin, R. E. (2003) *Reflective Democracy*. Oxford: Oxford University Press.
Gutmann, A. and Thompson, D. F. (1995) 'Moral disagreement in a democracy', *Social Philosophy and Policy*, 12 (1): 87–110.
Gutmann, A. and Thompson, D. F. (1996) *Democracy and Disagreement*. Cambridge, MA: Belknap Press.
Habermas, J. (1998) *On the Relation Between the Nation, the Rule of Law, and Democracy: The Inclusion of the Other*, eds C. Cronin and P. D. Greiff. Cambridge, MA: MIT Press, pp. 129–53.
Hobbes, T. (1996) *Leviathan*. Cambridge: Cambridge University Press.
Hume, D. (1963) *Essays: Moral, Political and Literary*. Oxford: Oxford University Press.
McBride, C. (2013) 'Democratic participation, engagement and freedom', *British Journal of Politics and International Relations*, 15 (4): 493–508.
Manin, B. (1997) *The Principles of Representative Government*. Cambridge: Cambridge University Press.
Mouffe, C. (2000) *The Democratic Paradox*. New York: Verso.
Pettit, P. (1996) 'Freedom as antipower', *Ethics*, 106: 576–604.
Pettit, P. (2013) *On the People's Terms*. Cambridge: Cambridge University Press.

Pettit, P. and List, C. (2011) *Group Agency*. Oxford: Oxford University Press.
Phillips, A. (1995) *The Politics of Presence*. Oxford: Oxford University Press.
Phillips, A. (1999) *Which Equalities Matter?* Cambridge: Polity Press.
Pogge, T. (2007) *Severe Poverty as a Human Rights Violation: Freedom From Poverty as a Human Right*. Oxford: UNESCO/Oxford University Press, pp. 11–53.
Putnam, R. D. (2001) *Bowling Alone*. New York: Simon & Schuster.
Rawls, J. (1996) *Political Liberalism*, 2nd edn. New York: Columbia University Press.
Rousseau, J. J. (1997a) *The Discourses and Other Early Political Writings*. Cambridge: Cambridge University Press.
Rousseau, J. J. (1997b) *The Social Contract and Other Later Political Writings*. Cambridge: Cambridge University Press.
Sandel, M. (1996) *Democracy's Discontent*. Cambridge, MA: Belknap Press.
Schumpeter, J. A. (1965) *Capitalism, Socialism and Democracy*. London: Allen & Unwin.
Sunstein, C. (2007) *Republic.com 2.0*. Princeton, NJ: Princeton University Press.
Waldron, J. (1999) *Law and Disagreement*. Oxford: Oxford University Press.
Wollheim, R. (1962) *A Paradox in the Theory of Democracy: Philosophy, Politics and Society*. Oxford: Blackwell, pp. 71–87.

8
SOCIAL AND PSYCHOLOGICAL FACTORS INFLUENCING POLITICAL AND CIVIC PARTICIPATION

A psychosocial perspective

Elvira Cicognani and Bruna Zani

This chapter presents a review of theoretical perspectives on civic and political participation based on the disciplines of social psychology and community psychology. The aim is not to provide an exhaustive overview of the literature, but to focus on some theoretical models that we think can provide useful contributions to the investigation of antecedents and psychosocial processes influencing individual and collective engagement and participation.

The analysis is articulated in four main parts. We first discuss the models that specify the predictors of collective action in the area of protest, suggesting explanations both at the group level and at individual level. Secondly, the area of prosocial action is considered and some well-known models are presented that try to understand volunteerism, its motives, determinants and processes at different levels of analysis. Then, attention is devoted to the contributions offered in the framework of community psychology, where particular importance is given to the concept of sense of community (SoC): recent studies illustrating the relationships of SoC with adolescent social and political participation are discussed. To conclude, some key concepts derived from the review of this literature are underlined with the view of integrating other more individualistic conceptualisations, and some considerations are advanced for developing a broader and unifying model of civic and political participation.

Contributions from social psychology on collective action and protest

Introduction

Efforts to explain why people participate in collective action and protest have generated many different answers by the academic community in the last three decades (see van Zomeren *et al.* 2008a and van Stekelenburg and Klandermans 2013 for meta-analytical overviews). According to Wright *et al.* (1990), collective action refers to the behaviours enacted by an individual as a representative of the group that are directed at improving the conditions of the entire group. Such actions may conform to the norms of the existing social system (e.g. normative actions like petitioning and taking part in a demonstration) or violate existing social rules (e.g. illegal protests and civil disobedience).

Current perspectives acknowledge the role of three basic factors in influencing the decision to participate in collective action: perceived grievances arising from relative deprivation or perceived injustice; self-efficacy and perceived effectiveness or instrumentality of participation; and social identity (collective identification with the group) (Klandermans 1997, 2002). More recently, researchers have included the role of emotions in collective action (van Zomeren *et al.* 2004).

Relative deprivation and perceived injustice

The concept of relative deprivation was introduced into the literature when it seemed clear that objective deprivation was not sufficient to predict the perception of injustice. Feelings of relative deprivation result when comparison of one's situation with a standard leads to the conclusion that one is not receiving what one deserves. Two types of relative deprivation have been distinguished (Runciman 1966): deprivation based on personal comparisons (egoistic deprivation), and deprivation based on group comparisons (fraternalistic deprivation). Research findings indicate that people who experience both personal deprivation *and* group deprivation are the most strongly motivated to engage in collective action and protest. Moreover, according to van Zomeren and colleagues (2008a), the affective component of group-based deprivation (e.g. feelings such as dissatisfaction, indignation and discontent about these outcomes) is a more powerful motivator for collective action than the cognitive component (e.g. the observation that one receives less than the standard of comparison).

Contributions from social justice theories (Tyler and Smith 1998) have examined the role of distributive and procedural justice judgments in collective action. Distributive justice refers to the fairness of outcomes. Procedural justice refers to the fairness of decision-making procedures and the relational aspects of the social process. According to Tyler and Smith procedural justice might be a more powerful predictor of social movement participation than distributive justice.

Following van Stekelenburg and Klandermans (2013), both theoretical perspectives (relative deprivation and social justice) describe people's experience of illegitimate inequality which can lead to protest. Depending on whether illegitimate inequality refers to perceived violations of material interests vs. violations of principles, people can take instrumental routes to encourage changes or use other means to express their feelings of indignation.

Perceived efficacy

Perceived injustice is not sufficient to explain collective action: an additional precondition is individuals' expectations that they are able, as a group, to modify the situation (collective efficacy), together with the belief that the context is receptive to such actions (external efficacy) (Klandermans 1992). The relevance of perceived efficacy has been emphasised both by resource mobilisation theory and instrumental-oriented approaches. The main assumption of resource mobilisation theory is that, in order to collectively solve problems (e.g. face perceived injustice), people need to be able to acquire resources and to perceive that they have the ability to solve group-related problems as a group. Instrumental-oriented approaches emphasise evaluations of the costs and benefits of collective action in order to reduce collective disadvantage. The role of collective efficacy beliefs in explaining collective action has been confirmed in the literature (Kelloway et al. 2007; van Zomeren et al. 2008a): the more people feel that collective action is effective, the more they become involved. However, the mechanisms through which this effect takes place are not always clear.

Social identification

Identity processes have been increasingly recognised as a significant predictor of collective action and social protest, in addition to perceived injustice and collective efficacy (van Zomeren et al. 2008b); in fact, several studies found that the more individuals identify with a group, the more they are willing to act on behalf of the group. Research and theory in this domain are indebted to social identity theory (SIT) and its developments. Tajfel (1978) defined social identity as 'that part of an individual's self-concept which derives from his knowledge of his membership of a social group (or groups), together with the value and emotional significance attached to that membership' (p. 63). According to SIT, when individuals define themselves as members of a group, they will think, feel and act as members of their group, transforming individual into collective behaviour (Turner 1999). Within this perspective people generally strive for and benefit from positive social identities associated with their groups. Such identity needs are managed differently depending on whether the boundaries of the group are perceived as *permeable* or not (e.g. if joining a higher status group is not possible, they may develop commitment to lower-status groups), or as *stable* vs. unstable (e.g. if status positions are perceived as variable, protest will be considered a possible method to heighten group status, especially when the low group status is perceived as *illegitimate*).

Studies of collective action from the perspective of SIT have generally considered members of low-status groups challenging the actions of high-status groups (or majority groups). However, it is also possible that members of high-status groups develop a form of political solidarity with low-status groups leading them to embrace the low-status members' cause as their own and to become willing to collectively challenge authority (van Stekelenburg and Klandermans 2013).

Identification with a group increases perceived similarity and shared fate with other members, feelings of efficacy, perceived obligation to support the group's cause, and motivation to participate in collective action. According to Simon and Klandermans (2001), in order to motivate collective action, collective identities should politicise, by identifying an external enemy as responsible for the perceived injustice and claiming for compensation. Politicised group members are more likely to engage in collective action directed at the government or the general public (van Zomeren et al. 2008b).

The role of emotions

The idea that negative emotions encourage collective action is so rooted in this research area as to be considered obvious: it has received sizeable empirical support (Smith et al. 2008). However, only more recently has the study of emotions in the context of collective action and protest gained popularity, being considered as *accelerators or amplifiers* of action (van Stekelenburg and Klandermans 2007). The guiding theoretical perspective is appraisal theories of emotion. Based on this perspective, Smith (1993) developed a theory of intergroup emotions according to which, when a social identity is salient, situations are appraised in terms of their consequences for the in-group, eliciting specific intergroup emotions and behavioural intentions. Individuals experience emotions on behalf of their group when the social category is salient *and* they identify with the group at stake.

The most typical protest emotion is anger. According to van Zomeren and colleagues (2004), group-based anger is an important motivator of protest participation of disadvantaged groups. Leach et al. (2006), in a study on political action among advantaged Australians to oppose government plans to redress disadvantaged aborigines, found that symbolic racism and relative deprivation generated group-based anger which in turn promoted willingness for political action. Advantaged group members can also perceive the in-group advantage as unfair and feel guilt and anger about it. Anger related to in-group advantage, and to a lesser degree guilt, appears to be a potent predictor for protest

Van Zomeren et al. (2008b) focused their attention on group-based anger among members of disadvantaged groups. They proposed that such an emotion would be stronger among highly identified disadvantaged group members because of their higher group concerns (that facilitate the emergence of anger) that in turn promote collective action tendencies. Among less identified people, involvement is motivated by the recognition that collective action could be effective and could produce positive outcomes; this suggests that identity and efficacy are key elements of two distinct coping processes: emotion and problem focused coping (cf. also van Zomeren et al. 2004). Their data support the distinction between individual and group-based relative deprivation consistent with intergroup emotion theory (Mackie et al. 2008) and confirm the emotional significance of perceived injustice as a relevant predictor of social outcomes.

Not all the findings on the role of anger are consistent, however. Mallett *et al.* (2008) examined the role of perspective-taking and emotions in collective action and found that taking the perspective of a disadvantaged group was associated with willingness to participate and with active participation in defence and on behalf of victims of hate crimes (e.g. attendance of rallies, conference lectures), both directly and through the mediation of feelings of (group-based) guilt. However, anger-based feelings (against the administration which was partially considered responsible) were not associated with perspective-taking. In order to fully understand the role of emotions and perspective-taking as predictors of collective action, the authors suggested that it would be worth distinguishing the motives of collective actions (e.g. helping other people vs. rising up against injustice).

Moreover, the importance of considering also other types of (negative) emotions has been stressed. Miller *et al.* (2009) suggest that feelings of fear, in particular when people perceive that they are being treated unfairly, can inhibit collective action and suppress the role of anger. They found that, when both anger and fear associated with taking action (in terms of negative consequence) are considered, the role of efficacy (ability to produce the desired outcome) is reduced. In general, anger moves people to adopt a more challenging relationship with authorities than subordinate emotions such as shame and despair or fear. Considering the types of actions available, two emotional routes to protest can be identified: an anger route based on efficacy leading to normative action, and a contempt route when legitimate channels are closed (Wright *et al.* 1990) and the situation is seen as hopeless, invoking a 'nothing to lose' strategy leading to non-normative protest (Kamans *et al.* 2011).

Integrative models of collective action and protest

Even though the distinct factors so far discussed (perceived injustice, efficacy, identification, emotions) have all proven to be necessary for explaining why people protest, there is also agreement on the need to move toward broader integrated explanatory models. Several examples have been proposed: Klandermans' model (1997) (which includes perceived injustice, efficacy and identification); Simon *et al.*'s (1998) dual path model of protest participation (which distinguishes between an instrumental pathway, guided by calculative reasoning that concentrates on the costs and benefits of participation, and an identity pathway, guided by processes of identification); van Zomeren and colleagues' (2004) dual path model (including an efficacy and emotion path); van Stekelenburg and Klandermans' (2007; van Stekelenburg *et al.* 2010) model integrating grievances, identity and emotion; and the Social Identity Model of Collective Action (SIMCA) proposed by van Zomeren and colleagues (2008) (see Figure 8.1).

Among the challenges that these models still need to face, according to van Stekelenburg and Klandermans (2013), is the 'paradox' of persistent participation. Explaining why people continue to participate despite its apparent ineffectiveness requires, according to the authors, the adoption of a more dynamic conceptualisation of the process, examining the antecedents of collective action also as potential

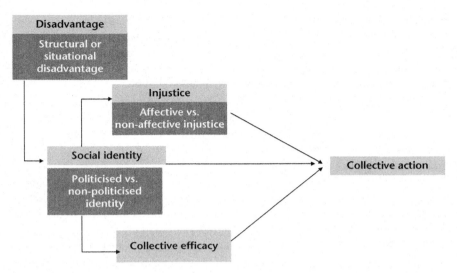

FIGURE 8.1 SIMCA – social identity model of collective action (van Zomeren *et al.* 2008a)

outcomes, for example considering also the consequences of participation for the individual in terms of empowerment outcomes (individual and collective).

A further aspect is the importance of including in the analysis the role of social interactions among people and social capital (Putnam 2000) (social embeddedness, or belonging to civic society organisations: see van Stekelenburg and Klandermans 2013). In fact, the decisions to become involved in collective action and protest occur within a social context where people collectively construct a common understanding and mobilise resources for action. Social capital and the social and organisational resources that it can mobilise are also important to explain continuity of action. Moreover, the role of positive emotions (e.g. satisfaction, sense of purpose) in explaining persistence of participation has not been considered by these theories. This aspect bridges the literature on collective action with community psychology perspectives on participation, emphasising, for example, the role of sense of community within the processes of social construction of a collective 'oppositional' identity vis-à-vis the dominant group (Mazzoni and Cicognani 2013).

Contributions from social psychology on volunteers and volunteerism

Introduction

Within social psychology there is a long history of interest in when and why individuals act prosocially (Penner 2002), and in more recent times the attention has been devoted to the explanation of sustained prosocial action or volunteerism. The concept of volunteerism is related to (and sometimes confused with) other concepts like altruism, solidarity, charity, active engagement. It is considered a prosocial action that can take different forms in terms of helping behaviours; it differs from spontaneous and occasional helping behaviour because it entails frequent interactions with other people and takes place within an organisational context or association ('long term, planned, prosocial behaviours that benefit strangers and occurs within an organizational setting' – Penner 2002: 448).

The literature review by Cnaan *et al.* (1996) covering over 300 articles on volunteerism identified 11 definitions and four factors that can be considered defining characteristics of the phenomenon: freedom to choose it; being free of charge for the receiver and the community; the existence of a formal organisational context; and an orientation of solidarity toward the receiver.

Further characteristics of volunteerism are the following: (1) it provides opportunities to help other people, enhance other people's well-being and fulfil their needs (i.e. positive, non-instrumental purposes); (2) it allows the freedom to choose the amount of time to devote to it and the types of volunteer activities; (3) it provides opportunities for investment and commitment, even if reciprocity or remuneration is not expected/provided; (4) it plays a mediating function between individuals and institutions by affirming values and promoting social change (Omoto and Snyder 1995; Snyder *et al.* 2000; Snyder and Omoto 2001). Penner (2002) similarly discusses the following four attributes of volunteerism: longevity (volunteering is usually a long-term behaviour), planfulness (volunteerism is typically a thoughtful and planned action), non-obligatory helping (volunteer actions are not motivated by a sense of personal obligation to a particular recipient) and the presence of an organisational context (most volunteers act as part of an organisation).

Volunteerism is typically considered as a prototypic form of civic participation; however, even if not all types of volunteerism have political implications, it can be argued that any group or collective entity that takes decisions and works actively within the community to solve problems of community members is involved in a political action. This becomes clearer when we examine the phenomenon not only from the perspective of the individual member of a volunteer association, but also from an organisational perspective, where a volunteer association may engage in a political (e.g. advocacy) action toward local administration and institutions on behalf of its target population (e.g. chronically ill patients, caregivers of the elderly with dementia).

Psychosocial correlates of volunteerism

Twenty years ago, Smith (1994) reviewed the American social science literature from the period 1975–92 on the predictors of individuals' participation in voluntary associations and volunteer work for non-profit organisations and found the following sets of relevant variables:

- *context* – this refers to the environment and includes the size of the community of residence and nature of the voluntary organisation or group;
- *social background* – which refers to social status and roles such as education and gender;

- *personality* – general and enduring personal response tendencies such as extraversion and assertiveness;
- *attitudes* – these refer to more situation-specific response tendencies, such as liking volunteer work or a specific voluntary association;
- *situation* – factors in one's immediate situation, such as the invitation to join a group or programme and the individual's definition of the situation.

More recently, Penner (2002) distinguished antecedents of volunteerism in dispositional and organisational factors. The former include the enduring attitudes of individuals such as beliefs, values, personality traits and motives, as well as socio-demographic factors. The latter include individual members' perceptions and feelings about how they are treated by the organisation and the organisational reputation. Moreover, Omoto and Snyder (2002) further classified the antecedents of volunteerism based on the level of analysis (agency, individual volunteers, social system) and stages of the volunteer process (antecedents, experiences and consequences).

Given that volunteerism is a multi-determined phenomenon including psychological (e.g. dispositional), situational and contextual (structural, organisational) factors, and having a temporal and dynamic component, several integrated theoretical models have also been proposed. In this context, we will consider the two most well-known: the volunteer process model (Omoto and Snyder 1995) and the role identity model (Callero *et al.* 1987).

The volunteer process model

The volunteer process model (VPM) (Snyder 1993; Omoto and Snyder 1995; Clary *et al.* 1998; Penner 2002) is based on the assumption that people volunteer in order to satisfy one or more needs, and such needs can change over time. Moreover, they may differ across members of the same organisation. The model describes a sequential process involving three interactive stages of the volunteer process: antecedents, experiences and consequences. Moreover, three levels of analysis are considered: individual, organisational and social.

The *antecedents* of volunteer behaviour include the factors that lead people to become volunteers (e.g. disposition to be helpful, motivations, social support and social norms among family, friends and other volunteers, community culture, cultural context). The dispositional variables play a more important role in this phase because there are few situational restrictions in the initial decision to become a volunteer. In this sense, the model places special emphasis on motives and needs. Volunteerism *experience* refers to the experiences that may promote or deter continuing involvement. At this stage, situations and experiences that enhance enduring engagement are important. Of particular relevance are the relationships that volunteers develop among themselves and with the helpees and the way they are perceived.

The *consequences* stage refers to the outcomes of volunteerism for the volunteers, the receivers, the organisation and the society (i.e. consequences for volunteers – knowledge, attitudes and behaviour change; positive outcomes for the people who have been helped; social and organisational change). Among these, empirical studies have focused on outcomes such as length of service as a volunteer and attitude change towards the target population of the intervention.

The VPM acknowledges the importance of individual motives in the decision to become a volunteer. On this point, the functional approach identifies six different motives or functions: the *values* function (concern for the welfare of others, and contributions to society); the *knowledge* function (volunteerism offers an opportunity to learn, understand, practise skills and abilities); the *career* function (volunteerism may serve to elaborate more on one's job prospects and enhance one's career); the *social* function (an individual volunteers due to strong normative or social pressure); the *protective* function (when volunteering activity reduces feelings of guilt about being more fortunate than others, or helps to cope with problems) and the *self-esteem or enhancement* function (volunteerism serves to enhance self-esteem, self-confidence and self-improvement).

The role identity model

Whereas the VPM is based on dispositional factors, another well-known theoretical model, more focused on situational factors, is the role identity model developed by Piliavin and colleagues (Callero *et al.* 1987; Grube and Piliavin 2000).

The role identity model emphasises the concept of role identity in explaining the continuity of volunteerism; this refers to the extent to which a particular role (being a volunteer) becomes part of the person's personal identity. Another relevant construct is perceived expectations, referring to the beliefs of significant others about volunteer behaviour. The model posits that experiences and behaviours associated with volunteering activity facilitate the development of a volunteer role identity, which is the immediate precursor of sustained volunteering. In other words, sustained volunteerism is thought be a consequence of the individual's relationships with the organisation and with volunteers.

In the attempt to integrate the functional and the role identity models, Penner (2002) proposed that motives are important antecedents of the decision to begin volunteering. According to Finkelstein and Penner (2004), each person's experience during the initial phase of volunteering determines his or her volunteer role identity. The more one volunteers, and the more involving is the activity, the stronger the identity. This self-concept becomes the proximal cause of sustained activities.

Contributions from community psychology on citizens' participation

Introduction

The study of participative phenomena among social groups and communities occupies a central place within community psychology (CP). Community participation is defined as 'a process in which individuals take part in decision making in the institutions, programs, and environments that affect them' (Heller et al. 2000). The community psychology perspective moves from the assumption that participation takes place within a community context, conceptualised as an ecological setting or system (Bronfenbrenner 1979). Forms of participation are determined by issues and needs arising within a (local) community, a place, and include its culture, norms, values and institutions (Cicognani and Zani 2009).

Within this discipline, theoretical perspectives on participation have focused not only on the explanation of what moves citizens' participation but also on the impact of participatory phenomena on individuals, groups and communities. In view of such applied interest, community participation is also conceptualised and intentionally adopted as an intervention strategy (e.g. participatory action research) to improve the social, economic, political and environmental conditions of the community, strengthen social bonds and cohesion, and enhance the well-being, health and quality of life of its members. In particular, it is bottom-up participation by citizens that is considered the most important form of action to improve well-being by changing the material circumstances of people's lives (Kagan 2007). At least two forms of bottom-up participation have been distinguished: (1) *social action*, more oriented toward conflict than consensus and focusing on direct action, aiming at organising a disadvantaged or aggrieved group to take action on their behalf (e.g. Civil Rights Movement); and (b) *locality development*, meaning a slower process of creating a network of continuing relationships allowing people to get together, share their supportive resources and experience a sense of belonging to their community (e.g. developing a sense of community for recent immigrants). Both forms require developing an organisational framework and learning the skills to maintain the group and take action. Among the several examples of social action groups, an issue of particular interest is understanding how such organisations that began in response to specific local issues have expanded to become organisations with broader goals (e.g. in Italy, the Movement for Public Water: Mazzoni and Cicognani 2013).

Another important contribution of the theoretical perspectives of CP is their greater attention toward socio-constructivist approaches, which offer a more dynamic vision of the processes involved than previous models (Zani 2012).

An example is provided by Campbell and Jovchelovitch's (2000) model, which defines community participation as 'the process by which the community is actualised, negotiated and eventually, modified' (p. 264). The authors distinguish three interdependent dimensions or preconditions for participation: the presence of shared social representations among community members; a shared social identity; and sharing the conditions and constraints of access to power in terms of both material resources and symbolic recognition (empowerment).

a. Shared social representations

We can conceive of the presence of a group, a community, an organised social entity, only if individuals share a set of social representations which organise the worldviews, values, culture, interpretations of reality and everyday practices. Such representations differ depending on social insertions of individuals and groups (related to socio-demographic variables); they change and modify, and may generate conflict. Social representations organise and guide the relationship that groups and communities have among themselves and with others (Moscovici 1982). The process of participation forms the ongoing arena that allows social representations to be expressed, reaffirmed and, if necessary, renegotiated; this occurs, for example, through exposure to different points of view, or interpersonal deliberation within the social networks in which people are embedded. The study of participation phenomena therefore provides the opportunity to verify how the different social groups in the community (including different ethnic and cultural groups, or organised groups pursuing different and even opposing goals) may express, negotiate and modify their shared worldviews and values, including conceptions about behaviours which characterise the 'good citizen' or citizenship (e.g. Sherrod 2008).

b. Shared social identity

The concept of social identity plays a central role in ongoing debates about how to define a community. According to Campbell and Jovchelovitch (2000), participation as members of a social group or a community can be seen as a process that depends upon and in turn helps to construct identities: 'Participation is an action organically linked to the awareness a social group possesses of who it is, what it wants, and how it projects itself in a future time horizon in which its identity can be perpetuated, renegotiated, and, if desired, changed' (p. 265). In this context, it is important to articulate, in the study of forms of participation, different levels of belonging and identification which may be significant for the individual with dynamics of the processes of inclusion and exclusion within group relationships, particularly in multicultural contexts.

c. Sharing the conditions and constraints of access to power in terms of both material resources and symbolic recognition

This dimension may be related to aspects such as *empowerment*, competences and sense of individual and collective efficacy. The issue of power calls attention to the role of objective conditions, influencing actual possibilities of participation; among these, of particular importance are socio-economic status and ethnic origins, such as immigrant status. Unequal conditions of access to power and resources among individuals impact on life choices and opportunities. Power can be described also as a space of possible action, where individuals and groups may negotiate and reach opportunities of influence depending on the contingencies of the various contexts in which power is exercised and develop feelings of individual and collective efficacy which in turn motivate action (e.g. the concept of 'symmetrical power': Montero 2011).

Antecedents of community participation: the role of sense of community

In their review of antecedents, processes and effects of participation in community organisations, Wandersman and Florin (2000) pointed to the role of individual or family characteristics (e.g. home ownership, length of residence in the area, having children, ethnicity) and attitudes toward the community (e.g. intentions to remain in the area, feelings of belonging, contact with neighbours). Perkins *et al.* (1990) also emphasised the need for both 'catalyst' factors (e.g. poorly maintained property) and 'enabling' factors (e.g. good relationships between community members). Considering the factors that enhance the stability of community organisations, the evidence indicated the importance of clearly defined tasks, democratic decision-making procedures, a positive and cohesive atmosphere, a clear leadership, greater structure, involvement in more activities and better capacities to establish linkages with other organisations (social capital).

Among the psychosocial factors involved in community participation, a central role has been given to sense of community (McMillan and Chavis 1986), referring to people's perceptions and subjective experience of community. Indeed, in this literature there is an assumption about the existence of a positive association between community participation and sense of community.

The concept of sense of community (SoC) was introduced by Sarason in 1974, who defined it as 'the perception of similarity with others, a recognised interdependence, a willingness to maintain such interdependence offering or making for others what is expected from us, the feeling to belong to a totally stable and reliable structure' (p. 174). In current theorising and empirical research, SoC conveys the belief that healthy communities exhibit an extra-individual quality of emotional interconnectedness of individuals played out in their collective lives.

SoC is used to describe feelings of belonging to different kinds of communities. These include formal and informal social organisations bounded by a physical or geographical location, such as the local community, the town or city, the nation, supranational entities such as the EU, the neighbourhood and the school. It has also been used when referring to social entities based on common interests, goals or needs, for instance sport groups, political groups and volunteering groups (Cicognani and Zani, 2009).

McMillan and Chavis (1986) proposed a four-dimensional model of SoC including the following components:

1. *Membership* – the feeling of being part of a territorial or relational community. It includes perception of shared boundaries, a common history and symbols, and feelings of emotional safety and personal investment in the community.
2. *Influence* – the opportunity of individuals to participate in community life, giving their own contribution in a reciprocal relationship. This dimension corresponds to the perceived influence that a person has over the decisions and actions of the community and is more directly related to actual participation.

3. *Integration and fulfilment of needs* – the benefits that people derive from their membership of a community. It refers to a positive relation between individuals and community, where they can satisfy some needs as a group or as community members.
4. *Shared emotional connection* – defined as the sharing of a common history, significant events and the quality of social ties.

Drawing from social identity theory, Obst et al. (2002) added a fifth orthogonal dimension of SoC: *strength of community identification*. SoC is stronger when individuals feel that belonging to a community is a central component of one's self-identity and when they highly identify with it.

Studies on participation carried out within CP have stressed the role of SoC in enhancing social and civic participation (Chavis and Wandersman 1990). Evidence of the connection between SoC, neighbouring and participation has been generally consistent across countries and cultures (Perkins et al. 1996; Brodsky et al. 1999; Prezza et al. 2001). Similar evidence on the role of attachment and sense of belonging to the territorial community in enhancing participation is provided by studies on NIMBY ('not in my backyard') phenomena (Devine-Wright 2009).

There is also evidence on the role of SoC in enhancing political participation (Davidson and Cotter 1989). For example, moving from the assumption that individuals' perceptions about their importance in a given community can have meaningful effects on the way in which communities influence politics, Anderson (2009) recently examined the role of SoC in explaining political participation within a community. On a sample of over 800 participants the author found that SoC has significant and positive effects on both political discussion and local voting even after controlling for other demographic, political and personal factors. Anderson concludes that, also by focusing on random (and de-contextualised) samples of the population to test models of political participation, previous research has failed to address two critical points: (1) the multiple contexts in which individuals interact; and (2) the variation of connectedness within any given context. By examining individuals' perceptions in multiple contexts, it is possible to gain a deeper understanding of how SoC works (e.g. through social interaction) to influence different types of political behaviours and attitudes.

The association between SoC and community participation has also been assessed among adolescents. Results of studies conducted using the SoC-A scale for adolescents (e.g. Chiessi et al. 2010) indicated that even though young people perceive that they have limited influence over their community, they would be interested in having more opportunities for having a voice. This result is consistent with Evans (2007: 704): 'SoC for these teens is incomplete without the experience of power [...] power comes from developing capacity, experiencing voice and resonance, and having opportunities to play meaningful roles in the context of caring adult support and challenge' (p. 695). Moreover, for adolescents the dimension *Support and emotional connection with peers* scores higher than *Support and emotional connection in the community*, confirming that at this age, the peer group is a more significant context for social interaction (a "nested community" within the territorial community).

In general, research findings indicate that SoC is higher among adolescents who belong to community organisations than among those who do not belong to any group. Moreover, SoC has positive correlations with both protest-oriented and prosocial-oriented civic engagement (Albanesi *et al.* 2007): the evidence shows that adolescents and young people who participate more in local community life have higher SoC compared to less involved youth and that enhancing participation can increase adolescents' SoC (Pretty 2002; Evans 2007). Other studies (Flanagan *et al.* 2007) have shown that 'sense of community connectedness' is a significant predictor of civic commitment and that it reinforces individuals' willingness to engage for the benefit of their neighbourhoods. Overall, these studies emphasise that during adolescence, SoC can play a significant role in the development of attitudes toward politics and in individuals' willingness to be involved in political processes.

A still open research question concerns the direction of the association between *participation and SoC*. According to Chavis and Wandersman (1990), SoC should be considered a catalyst for social participation (cf. also Simon *et al.* 1998). Hughey *et al.* (1999) suggest that participation itself might enhance SoC. If we examine SoC as an ongoing process, the bidirectional and reciprocal relationship becomes clear: a sense of personal connection and influence/control over the social environment is necessary to decide to engage (Perkins *et al.* 1996); at the same time, being involved in social and collective action allows individuals to develop a greater sense of competence and control, to increase self-esteem and self-efficacy, and to modify their social identity, strengthening their sense of belonging to their community and social well-being (Itzhaky and York 2000).

If we consider the role of *well-being* in participation, it is possible to think of it both as an outcome of participatory processes and as a motivator (e.g. if individuals feel good when participating, they will be more likely to continue). From this perspective it is worth considering the role of social well-being (Keyes 2008). As conceptualised by Keyes, social well-being (composed of the dimensions of social integration, social contribution, social acceptance, social coherence and social actualisation) can be considered a subjective indicator of how the individual conceives of the larger society in which he/she is embedded and his/her perceived social relationship with it. As such, it can be considered a potential contributor to participation. Individuals reporting higher social well-being will think of themselves as more integrated in their community, feel that their contribution is valued and that people can be trusted, and think that social organisation makes sense and that society is moving toward a positive direction. Such beliefs can both be an outcome of civic and political participation and an antecedent. There is evidence on the role of social well-being as outcome (e.g. Albanesi *et al.* 2007; Cicognani *et al.* 2008) and as antecedent/mediator (cf. Chapter 15 by Albanesi *et al.* this volume).

Some considerations and key concepts for a unifying psychosocial theory

In this section, we summarise some concepts to be considered in a unifying model of participation (see Figure 8.2), based on the factors reviewed in the previous sections and on which the empirical research of the PIDOP study was based.

All theoretical and empirical traditions we have reviewed underline the role of *socio-demographic* characteristics (like gender, age, status as immigrant, education, language, socio-economic situation, religiosity) likely to moderate the impact of the different explanatory factors (Box 1). For example, it is commonly reported that political participation is higher among men vs. women. A different approach would be to attempt to understand political participation from a woman's vs. a man's perspective (or from a majority vs. a migrant youth's).

In order to elaborate a social construction of participation, *individual and shared cognitions* about the social world and participation have to be taken into account (Box 2). The role of individual factors (e.g. traits, cognitions) has been widely acknowledged in the literature. Important cognitive variables are (political) knowledge and sophistication (integration of knowledge into a coherent belief system, socio-political awareness). Among cognitive variables (beliefs/attitudes), we include political trust (trust in politics and politicians), system responsiveness (belief that

FIGURE 8.2 Elements for a psychosocial model of participation

political institutions are responsive to the actions of citizens), social trust (trust in people), general worldviews (e.g. belief in a just world), social norms about citizenship (concept of citizenship), and values.

Besides individual cognitive variables, it is important to include in the model the social processes through which such cognitions are formed and modified, which include communication and social exchange processes in different contexts. A useful theoretical perspective is social representation theory (Moscovici 1982) that describes how group/community members come to agree on a shared reality through communication and negotiation processes in everyday social encounters (Campbell and Jovchelovitch 2000).

Traditional models of political participation have underscored the role of *motives and goals* for participation (Box 3). The notion of *individual motives* has also been considered in the literature on volunteering (e.g. functional models of volunteering processes, according to which people volunteer to satisfy some individual needs) (Omoto and Snyder 2002). Penner (2002) distinguished among prosocial values, organisational concern and impression management. The role of motives and goals has also been emphasised in the collective action literature, where other possible motives for participation have been pointed out (e.g. expressing one's values, influencing public opinion, identification motives, aspiring to a collective identity or identity affirmation, gaining power and control, altruistic motives, etc.). The theoretical literature on collective action suggests the usefulness of distinguishing among different levels of goals: personal goals, collective goals and personal and social values. Moreover, besides these classifications, qualitative data collected on young people's perceived motives of different forms of participation (political, civic, non-conventional, school) confirmed that different types of motives are present (Zani *et al.* 2011).

According to this literature, personal and collective goals and motivations seem relevant in order to define perceived efficacy and identity concerns. More attention should be devoted to the analysis of the relationship between personal motives to participate, collective goals and personal and societal values.

The role of *emotions* in participation (Box 4) has been considered in the literature on collective action. Usually, attention has been given to negative emotions as precursors of participation (e.g. anger, resentment, fear, dissatisfaction), associated with perceived injustice and relative personal and group deprivation. However, as the literature on volunteerism and community participation indicates, positive emotions (e.g. satisfaction, sense of purpose, feelings of emotional connection) might also be relevant for explaining participation.

The role of *(social and collective) identity* is central and has been widely recognised in the literature on different forms of participation (Box 5). Dominant theoretical perspectives are Social identity theory (SIT) and its subsequent developments (Tajfel and Turner 1986). Social identification with one's group or community has a central role in the explanation of collective action and community participation. Associated with social identification is sense of belonging, capturing the emotional quality of the relationships with the group. This leads to the concept of sense of community, which has been used to refer not only to relational communities (e.g. social groups) but also to communities arising from sharing a common geographical location or place. The inclusion of sense of community may thus help to better contextualise the notion of identity, by also including its place-related component (e.g. identity as resident of a specific location). Among both adults and young people, sense of community and social identification with the community have been found to be associated with civic and political participation (Albanesi *et al.* 2007).

Perceived control/efficacy, power and competences (Box 6) also play a role. In the social movement studies, power is conceived in terms of a struggle between social groups and as a societal or intergroup issue. Power is also a personal and an interpersonal phenomenon: people decide to engage in participatory behaviours in the context of groups if they perceive that they can have an influence and be taken into consideration inside the groups.

In order to participate, individuals need to feel capable and competent (as individuals and as collectives). Both individual and collective efficacy beliefs are relevant in explaining political and civic participation. At an individual level, personal efficacy, political efficacy (including the belief in one's competence at performing political actions) and locus of control are important. On a group level, collective efficacy (a person's belief in his/her capacity to perform effective collective political action together with other people (Bandura 1999)) is an important predictor of participation in collective movements. Empowerment is a further construct that has been discussed in community psychology as an antecedent (but also an outcome) of community participation. Competences for participatory actions include civic competences as well as social skills.

Perceived opportunities and barriers (Box 7) are also involved. The role of structural and organisational opportunities vs. barriers within the different participatory contexts (e.g. family, peer group, school, community, media) has been considered from sociological and political perspectives. From a psychological perspective, perception of opportunities and barriers to participation is a potentially relevant factor. Participatory contexts influence participation by providing opportunities or constraints and acting as sources of social norms and influence (cf. facilitating and enabling factors). For example, perceiving that the context allows opportunities for participation (existence of associations, groups, school service), as well as being members of associations (organisational membership), are important contributors to participation.

Among opportunities and barriers, time, the existence of a social network and social integration can be included (social capital) (e.g. Putnam 2000). Opportunities/barriers are also specific to the different contexts. For example, in the school context, these include aspects such as teaching methods, classroom climate, whether they enhance active participation and discussion, and opportunities to play significant roles. As regards family and peer groups, variables of interest include family education, family support (parenting style, family discussions) and socialisation (political socialisation), peer integration and peer political influence.

Actual/past participation should be considered a learning experience (Box 8) and its effects feed back dynamically into its precursors. This means that participation should be analysed as a dynamic, circular process, where the consequences of participation may impact on precursors by modifying initial conditions. Moreover, this requires distinguishing the factors promoting initial participation from factors explaining sustained participation over time (or decisions to cease participation after some actual experience). The role of past experience has been considered in the explanation of political participation (voting) and several models have looked at individual changes (e.g. identity, empowerment) as an effect of past participation.

Conclusion

Throughout the theoretical and empirical literature we have reviewed in this chapter on collective action, volunteerism and community participation, we found converging information on the multiple factors that enhance participation, this notwithstanding the fact that each approach focuses on partly different forms of participation (e.g. 'oppositional' forms of action vs. prosocial actions or consensual forms of action within the community), which also require specific explanatory factors. The three lines of theorising also differ in their focus on different phases of the process of participation (e.g. explaining the initial decision to become involved as in models of collective action vs. explaining also the continuity of individuals' involvement and its outcomes as in the volunteerism and community psychology perspectives), pointing to the need to include in the analysis a temporal dimension and to distinguish different phases, which can be characterised by specific explanatory factors. A further difference, related to different epistemological backgrounds, lies in the more 'static' perspective of collective action approaches vs. dynamic and socio-constructivist approaches more widespread within community psychology. The latter are also characterised by the explicit inclusion in the analysis of the ecological context (vs. collective action models' greater interest in normative, a-contextualised psychological and psychosocial processes). As we have noticed, some limitations of each model are being acknowledged (e.g. the recent call for a greater consideration of the role of social embeddedness and for a more dynamic approach in the collective action literature), suggesting the usefulness of cross-fertilisation among theoretical and empirical traditions. Moreover, a limitation of all perspective is the lack of a developmental focus.

References

Albanesi, C., Cicognani, E. and Zani, B. (2007) 'Sense of community, civic engagement and social well-being in Italian adolescents', *Journal of Community and Applied Social Psychology*, 17: 387–406.

Anderson, M. R. (2009) 'Beyond membership: a sense of community and political behavior', *Political Behavior*, 31 (4): 603–27.

Bandura, A. (1999) 'Self-efficacy: toward a unifying theory of behavioral change', in R. F. Baumeister (ed.), *The Self in Social Psychology. Key Readings in Social Psychology*. Philadelphia: Psychology Press/Taylor & Francis.

Brodsky, A. E., O'Campo, J. and Aronson, R. E. (1999) 'PSOC in community context: multi-level correlates of a measure of psychological sense of community in low-income, urban neighbourhoods', *Journal of Community Psychology*, 27: 659–80.

Bronfenbrenner, U. (1979) *The Ecology of Human Development: Experiments by Nature and Design*. Cambridge, MA: Harvard University Press.

Callero, P. L., Howard, J. A. and Piliavin, J. A. (1987) 'Helping behavior as role behavior: disclosing social structure and history in the analysis of prosocial action', *Social Psychology Quarterly*, 50: 247–56.

Campbell, C. and Jovchelovitch, S. (2000) 'Health, community and development: towards a social psychology of participation', *Journal of Community and Applied Social Psychology*, 10: 255–70.

Chavis, D. M. and Wandersman, A. (1990) 'Sense of community in the urban environment: a catalyst for participation and community development', *American Journal of Community Psychology*, 18: 55–82.

Chiessi, M., Cicognani, E. and Sonn, C. (2010) 'Assessing sense of community on adolescents: validating the brief scale of sense of community in adolescents (SOCA)', *Journal of Community Psychology*, 38: 276–92.

Cicognani, E. and Zani, B. (2009) 'Sense of community and social participation among adolescents and young adults living in Italy', in D. E. Dolejšiová and M. A. García López (eds), *Challenges for Citizenship: Citizenship Education and Democratic Practice in Europe*. Strasbourg: Council of Europe Publishing.

Cicognani, E., Albanesi, C. and Zani, B. (2008) 'The impact of residential context on adolescents' and young adults' well being', *Journal of Community and Applied Social Psychology*, 18: 558–75.

Clary, E. G., Snyder, M., Ridge, R. D., Copeland, J. T., Stukas, A. A., Haugen, J. A. and Miene, K. (1998) 'Understanding and assessing the motivations of volunteers: a functional approach', *Journal of Personality and Social Psychology*, 74: 1516–30.

Cnaan, R., Handy, F. and Wadsworth, M. (1996) 'Defining who is a volunteer: conceptual and empirical considerations', *Nonprofit and Voluntary Sector Quarterly*, 25 (3): 364–83.

Davidson, W. B. and Cotter, P. R. (1989) 'Sense of community and political participation', *Journal of Community Psychology*, 17: 119–25.

Devine-Wright, P. (2009) 'Rethinking NIMBYism: the role of place attachment and place identity in explaining place-protective action', *Journal of Community and Applied Social Psychology*, 19: 426–41.

Evans, S. D. (2007) 'Youth sense of community: voice and power in community contexts', *Journal of Community Psychology*, 35 (6): 693.

Finkelstein, A. M. and Penner, L. A. (2004) 'Predicting organizational citizenship behavior: integrating the functional and role identity approaches', *Social Behavior and Personality*, 32 (4): 383–98.

Flanagan, C., Cumsille, P., Gill, S. and Gallay, L. (2007) 'School and community climates and civic commitments: patterns for ethnic minority and majority students', *Journal of Educational Psychology*, 99: 421–31.

Grube, J. A. and Piliavin, J. A. (2000) 'Role identity, organizational experiences, and volunteer performance', *Personality and Social Psychology Bulletin*, 26: 1108–19.

Heller, K., Price, R. H., Reinhartz, S., Riger, S., Wandersman, A. and D'Aunno, T. A. (1984) *Psychology and Community Change: Challenges of the Future*. Monterey, CA: Brooks/Cole.

Hughey, J., Speer, P. W. and Peterson, N. A. (1999) 'Sense of community in community organizations: structure and evidence of validity', *Journal of Community Psychology*, 27 (1): 97–113.

Itzhaky, H. and York, A. S. (2000) 'Empowerment and community participation: does gender make a difference?', *Social Work Research*, 24 (4): 225–34.

Kagan, C. (2007) *Pillars of Support for Wellbeing in the Community: The Role of the Public Sector*. Paper presented at the Wellbeing and Sustainable Living Seminar, Manchester (UK).

Kamans, E., Otten, S. and Gordijn, E. H. (2011) 'Threat and power in intergroup conflict: how threat determines emotional and behavioral reactions in powerless groups', *Group Processes and Intergroup Relations*, 14: 293–310.

Kelloway, E. K., Francis, L., Catano, V. M. and Teed, M. (2007) 'Predicting protest', *Basic and Applied Social Psychology*, 29: 13–22.

Keyes, C. L. M. (1998) 'Social well-being', *Social Psychological Quarterly*, 2: 121–40.

Klandermans, B. (1992) 'The social construction of protest and multiorganizational fields', in A. D. Morris and C. M. Mueller (eds), *Frontiers in Social Movement Theory*. New Haven, CT: Yale University Press, pp. 77–103.

Klandermans, B. (1997) *The Social Psychology of Protest*. Oxford: Blackwell.

Klandermans, B. (2002) 'How group identity helps to overcome the dilemma of collective action', *American Behavioral Scientist*, 45: 887–900.

Leach, C. W., Iyer, A. and Pedersen, A. (2006) 'Anger and guilt about in-group advantage explain the willingness for political action', *Personality and Social Psychology Bulletin*, 32: 1232–45.

Mackie, D. M., Smith, E. R. and Ray, D. G. (2008) 'Intergroup emotions and intergroup relations', *Personality and Social Psychology Compass*, 2: 1866–80.

McMillan, W. D. and Chavis, M. D. (1986) 'Sense of community: a definition and a theory', *Journal of Community Psychology*, 14 (1): 6–22.

Mallett, R., Huntsinger, J. R., Sinclair, S. and Swim, J. (2008) 'Seeing through their eyes: when majority group members take collective action on behalf of an outgroup', *Group Processes and Intergroup Relations*, 11: 451–70.

Mazzoni, D. and Cicognani, E. (2013) 'Water as commons. An exploratory study on the motives for collective action among Italian Water Movement activists', *Journal of Community and Applied Social Psychology*, 23 (4): 271–361.

Miller, D. A., Cronin, T., Garcia, A. L. and Branscombe, N. R. (2009) 'The relative impact of anger and efficacy on collective action is affected by feelings of fear', *Group Processes and Intergroup Relations*, 12: 445–62.

Montero, M. (2011) 'From complexity and social justice to consciousness: ideas that have built a community psychology', in E. Almeida Acosta (ed.), *International Community Psychology: Community Approaches to Contemporary Social Problems*. Puebla, Mexico: Universidad Iberoamericana Puebla, pp. 51–71.

Moscovici, S. (1982) 'The coming era of social representations', in J. P. Codol and J. P. Leyens (eds), *Cognitive Analysis of Social Behaviour*. The Hague: Nijhoff.

Obst, P., Smith, S. and Zinkiewicz, L. (2002) 'An exploration of sense of community. Part 3: Dimensions and predictors of psychosocial sense of community in geographical communities', *Journal of Community Psychology*, 30 (1): 119–33.

Omoto, A. M. and Snyder, M. (1995) 'Sustained helping without obligation: motivation, longevity of service, and perceived attitude change among AIDS volunteers', *Journal of Personality and Social Psychology*, 68: 671–86.

Omoto, A. M. and Snyder, M. (2002) 'Considerations of community: the context and process of volunteerism', *American Behavioral Scientist*, 45: 846–67.

Penner, L. A. (2002) 'Dispositional and organizational influences on sustained volunteerism: an interactionist perspective', *Journal of Social Issues*, 58: 447–67.

Perkins, D. D., Brown, B. B. and Taylor, R. B. (1996) 'The ecology of empowerment: predicting participation in community organizations', *Journal of Social Issues*, 52: 85–110.

Perkins, D., Florin, P., Rich, R., Wandersman, A. and Chavis, D. (1990) 'Participation and the social and physical environment of residential blocks: crime and community context', *American Journal of Community Psychology*, 18: 83–115.

Pretty, G. M. H. (2002) 'Young people's development of the community-minded self: considering community identity, community attachment and sense of community', in T. Fisher and C. C. Sonn (eds), *Psychological Sense of Community: Research, Applications, and Implications*. New York: Kluwer Academic/Plenum, pp. 183–203.

Prezza, M., Amici, M., Roberti, T. and Tedeschi, G. (2001) 'Sense of community referred to the whole town: its relations with neighbouring, loneliness, life satisfaction and area of residence', *Journal of Community Psychology*, 29 (1): 29–52.

Putnam, R. D. (2000) *Bowling Alone. The Collapse and Revival of American Community*. New York: Simon & Schuster.

Runciman, W. G. (1966) *Relative Deprivation and Social Justice*. London: Routledge.

Sarason, S. B. (1974) *The Psychological Sense of Community: Prospects for a Community Psychology*. Cambridge, MA: Brookline Books.

Sherrod, L. R. (2008) 'Youths' perceptions of citizenship', *Journal of Social Issues*, 64 (4): 771–90.

Simon, B. and Klandermans, B. (2001) 'Towards a social psychological analysis of politicized collective identity: conceptualization, antecedents, and consequences', *American Psychologist*, 56: 319–31.

Simon, B., Loewy, M., Sturmer, S., Weber, U., Freytag, P., Habig, C., Kampmeier, C. and Spahlinger, P. (1998) 'Collective identification and social movement participation', *Journal of Personality and Social Psychology*, 74: 646–58.

Smith, D. N. (1994) 'Determinants of voluntary association participation and volunteering: a literature review', *Nonprofit and Voluntary Sector Quarterly*, 23: 243–63.

Smith, E. R. (1993) 'Social identity and social emotions: toward new conceptualizations of prejudice', in D. M. Mackie and D. L. Hamilton (eds), *Affect, Cognition, and Stereotyping: Interactive Processes in Group Perception*. San Diego, CA: Academic Press, pp. 297–315.

Smith, H. J., Cronin, T. and Kessler, T. (2008) 'Anger, fear, or sadness: faculty members' emotional reactions to collective pay disadvantage', *Political Psychology*, 29: 221–46.

Snyder, M. (1993) 'Basic research and practice problems: the promise of a "functional" personality and social psychology', *Personality and Social Psychology Bulletin*, 19: 251–64.

Snyder, M., and Omoto, A. M. (2001) 'Basic research and practical problems: volunteerism and the psychology of individual and collective action', in W. Wosinska, R. B. Cialdini, D. W. Barrett and J. Reykowski (eds), *The Practice of Social Influence in Multiple Cultures*. Mahwah, NJ: Lawrence Erlbaum Associates, pp. 287–307.

Snyder, M., Clary, E. G. and Stukas, A. A. (2000) 'The functional approach to volunteerism', in R. Maio and J. M. Olson (eds), *Why We Evaluate: Functions of Attitudes*. Mahwah, NJ: Erlbaum, pp. 365–93.

Tajfel, H. (1978) 'The achievement of intergroup differentiation', in H. Tajfel (ed.), *Differentiation Between Social Groups*. London: Academic Press, pp. 77–100.

Tajfel, H. and Turner, J. (1986) 'The social identity theory of intergroup behaviour', in S. Worchel and W. G. Austin (eds), *Psychology of Intergroup Relations*. Chicago: Nelson, pp. 33–57.

Turner, J. C. (1999) 'Some current themes in research on social identity and self-categorization theories', in N. Ellemers, R. Spears and B. Doosje (eds), *Social Identity: Context, Commitment, Content*. Oxford: Blackwell, pp. 6–34.

Tyler, T. R. and Smith, H. J. (1998) 'Social justice and social movements', in D. Gilbert, S. T. Fiske and G. Lindzey (eds), *Handbook of Social Psychology*. New York: McGraw-Hill, pp. 595–629.

van Stekelenburg, J. and Klandermans, B. (2007) 'Individuals in movements: a social psychology of contention', in C. M. Roggeband and B. Klandermans (eds), *The Handbook of Social Movements Across Disciplines*. New York: Springer, pp. 157–204.

van Stekelenburg, J. and Klandermans, B. (2013) 'The social psychology of protest', *Current Sociology*, 61 (5–6): 886–905.

van Stekelenburg, J., Oegema, D. and Klandermans, B. (2010) 'No radicalization without identification: dynamics of radicalization and polarization within and between two opposing web forums', in A. Azzi, X. Chryssochoou and B. Klandermans (eds), *Identity and Participation in Culturally Diverse Societies: A Multidisciplinary Perspective*. Oxford: Blackwell Wiley.

van Zomeren, M., Postmes, T. and Spears, R. (2008a) 'Toward an integrative social identity model of collective action: a quantitative research synthesis of three socio-psychological perspectives', *Psychological Bulletin*, 134: 504–35.

van Zomeren, M., Spears, R. and Leach, C. W. (2008b) 'Exploring psychological mechanisms of collective action: does relevance of group identity influence how people cope with collective disadvantage?', *British Journal of Social Psychology*, 47: 353–72.

van Zomeren, M., Spears, R., Fischer, A. and Leach, C. W. (2004) 'Put your money where your mouth is! Explaining collective action tendencies through group-based anger and group efficacy', *Journal of Personality and Social Psychology*, 87: 649–64.

Wandersman, A. and Florin, P. (2000) 'Citizen participation and community organizations', in J. Rappaport and E. Seidman (eds), *Handbook of Community Psychology*. New York: Kluwer Academic/Plenum, pp. 247–72.

Wright, S. C., Taylor, D. M. and Moghaddam, F. M. (1990) 'Responding to membership in a disadvantaged group: from acceptance to collective protest', *Journal of Personality and Social Psychology*, 58: 994–1003.

Zani, B. (ed.) (2012) *Psicologia di comunità. Prospettive, idee, metodi* [*Community Psychology. Perspectives, Ideas, Methods*]. Rome: Carocci.

Zani, B., Cicognani, E. and Albanesi, C. (2011) *La partecipazione civica e politica dei giovani*. [*Civic and Political Participation Among Youth*]. Bologna: CLUEB.

9

EXPLAINING POLITICAL PARTICIPATION

Integrating levels of analysis

Nicholas P. Emler

Introduction

In this chapter I begin by considering the psychological underpinnings of political participation. I then seek to integrate this level of theoretical analysis with ideas from other levels, notably the more macro-level of analyis that considers the role of societal structures and institutions. Finally, I turn to a social psychological analysis to provide a bridge between individual psychology and societal context.

A theoretical integration of this kind has an ambitous agenda. It offers to account not only for variations between individuals in levels of political participation, but also forms and levels of participation across populations and across time. Moreover, it cannot readily avoid normative questions, about how much participation and of what kind is a good thing.

The phenomenon

To set some manageable limits around the task, this chapter is concerned with political participation in Western parliamentary democracies. It is not concerned with civic participation (except insofar as this proves to be necessary to understand political participation). The focus is upon political engagement in European nation states but the relevant and informative data are derived from a much wider base. The key feature of this political context is that political control is by national governments granted a time-limited mandate by national electorates. Given this context the crucial form of political participation by the individual citizen is generally taken to be voting in these periodic national elections. However, there are reasons to take a considerably broader view of the focal concept.

First the European Union has introduced a new dimension to the political participation of citizens in member states through the creation of a directly elected parliament. It is likely, nonetheless, that its electorate understands rather less about its functions and powers than each national group does about those of its own government, this despite the European Parliament having been described as one of the most powerful legislatures in the world.

Second, there is growing awareness among electorates of global issues, including the interdependence of national economies, cross-national variations in extent of political rights and the global environmental impact of national policies, and these are increasingly a focus for pan-national protest movements. This global context thus constitutes a further arena for political participation.

Third, democratic institutions, whether local, national or super-national, require not just electorates; they also require that people put themselves forward for election to public office. Although one might expect the number doing so to be a tiny fraction of the eligible populations, the density of such opportunities a political system offers proves to be a non-trivial factor in wider political participation.

Fourth, if the principal opportunity the citizen has to influence political decision-making is via a vote cast in a national election, there are other avenues of influence open to citizens both in the intervals between elections and in election campaigns themselves. Consider, for example, the list included in the ISSP (2004) survey (cf. Vráblíková 2010): signed a petition, boycotted or deliberately bought certain products for political, ethical or environmental reasons, took part in demonstration, attended a political meeting or rally, contacted, or attempted to contact, a political or civil servant to express your views, donated money or raised funds for a social or political activity, contacted or appeared in the media to express views, joined an Internet political forum or discussion group, belonged to a political party. Most research into political participation that is not concerned exclusively with voting has examined this sphere of activities.

Fifth, somewhat less often acknowledged as levers of influence operated by the individual citizen but of growing importance, are expressions of views in opinion surveys. On the one hand, policies, parliaments and politicians and their programmes are now regularly evaluated though public opinion surveys. And it is clear that the results of such surveys have an impact on the actions of politicians, not to mention their treatment by electorates on polling day. In other words, they do represent a route through which citizens exercise political influence. Moreover, people are influenced by what they believe to be the opinions of others. On the other hand, citizens in this case are reactive, not proactive; whether this form of influence is available to any one person is largely a matter of chance. But theoretically what is of interest is the basis on which the citizen responds to the opportunity. This motivates much of the attention that political scientists have given to the cognitive sophistication of electorates, the extent of their political knowledge (e.g. Delli Carpini and Keeter 1996), and more generally to the roots and determinants of mass public opinion (Kinder 1998).

Sixth, in Western parliamentary democracies, people do from time to time step outside the conventional framework and seek to influence political decisions in other ways. These alternative, 'non-conventional' forms of action can also directly question the legitimacy of this framework. Moreover, acts of protest proscribed by current laws, including acts of terrorism, do nonetheless constitute forms of political participation. For these reasons, what the citizen understands, believes and accepts about the rules according to which politics is conducted is of interest and relevance in understanding contemporary political participation.

Taking the still rather broad delineation of political participation sketched above, the following points about the shape of the phenomenon indicate what a theory of political engagement might seek to explain.

Electoral participation remains, of all potential forms of participation, the most important because it is the most common, and also because it provides the principal claim to legitimacy of democratic systems. There are three particular features of electoral turnout that we might expect a theory of political engagement to illuminate. First, exercise of the right to vote is far from universal, and this reflects a mix of consistent voters, more or less occasional voters and consistent non-voters. In the US 1990 Citizen Participation Study (Nie *et al.* 1996), for example, the respective percentages were 47.4 per cent, 39.5 per cent and 12.1 per cent for presidential elections (with barely 21 per cent voting in all local elections). Second, there is the well documented secular decline in voting, albeit with short-term fluctuations. The decline has been in evidence for the longest in the older democracies. It has also characterised turnouts in European Parliament elections; turnouts have declined in every successive election so far held. Third, there are quite substantial cross-national differences in voter turnout. CSES data (see Brunton-Smith 2011), for example, includes figures of 83.1 per cent for Denmark (1998) and 81.4 per cent for Sweden (1998) while, in contrast, 59.4 per cent for Great Britain (1997) and 48.8 per cent for Poland (1997). Data for the subsequent elections in each country were comparable (though in Denmark turnout rose while in Poland it declined).[1] In addition to these three major patterns, there are also quite striking age differences in turnout with younger voters having been consistently less likely to vote, though the extent of this difference varies across countries. In contrast gender differences are small.

Turning to other conventional forms of participation, for example those in the ISSP list, a similar pattern of progressive secular decline and striking cross-national differences is apparent. Despite these similarities, there is virtue in treating these forms of participation as distinct from voting. The case of Switzerland illustrates this well: in the CSES data set it had the lowest voter turnout of all countries covered – 43.4 per cent in 1999 – but in the ISSP survey it had the highest participation rate of all countries surveyed, and ten times higher than the rate in Bulgaria. Also, in contrast to electoral turnout patterns, those for conventional participation do display gender difference (Brunton-Smith 2011); males are consistently more involved, though the degree of difference varies across countries and is often reversed for 'non-conventional' activities.

Explaining political participation: psychological engagement

Explanations of political participation typically invoke some combination of capacity, inclination and opportunity (e.g. Luskin 1990). While this is a reasonable summary of the likely determinants, in reality it is little more than a starting point and crucially it leaves to be understood and explained how these three classes of determinants interact with and influence each other. Moreover, the first two classes of determinant, focusing on the characteristics of individuals, introduce further causal questions: what are the determinants of capacity and what shapes inclination? In this section, I will briefly consider the psychology of political engagement (for a more extensive discussion, see Emler 2011), mainly to underline how far a focus on individual psychology can take us and how much more it leaves unexplained.

If politics can be regarded as a contest between differing objectives and priorities then participation in this contest presupposes: (1) a view as to the rules according to which the contest is conducted; (2) a point of view or objective to be advanced in the contest; and (3) tools for engagement in the contest (cf. Emler 2001).

As regards the actor's understanding of the rules of the political game, its relevance has thus far largely been seen in terms of tolerance of minority and dissenting positions and political rights associated with these. Education plays a significant role in variations in what might be called 'political tolerance'. And though there are several possible explanations for the basis of this role, the best supported empirically is that formal education has direct effects on cognitive sophistication and, linked to this, on capacity to reason about rights and justice (Emler 2011).

Potentially also relevant, but thus far not extensively investigated, is how people's views concerning the rules of the political game relate to their readiness to take part in or endorse alternative and particularly extra-legal and illegal means to secure political ends.

As regards the second element, the ends to which the role of political actor are directed, this is open to various interpretations. One has been to interpret it in terms of party preference or party loyalty, and then to ask what is the source of an individual's preference for one political party rather than another. This interpretation rests upon various assumptions about the manner in which citizens participate in the political life of their societies. These include the idea that views and attitudes on a wide range of issues are organised into coherent bundles; the coherence derives from the relatively small number of values that underlie opinions on specific issues. Put another way, any individual's position on diverse issues can be summarised by a relatively discrete position in ideological space. Depending on the structure of that space – and research has broadly endorsed the conclusion that it is a simple structure that can be described as a left–right dimension (Emler 2002) – individuals can be grouped together according to the position they occupy on this dimension. And political parties reflect – and indeed represent – the shared interests and outlook of these different groupings. Thus citizens participate in political life primarily through their ideological alignment with and consequently electoral and other kinds of support for particular political parties.

Insofar as this is a reasonable representation of how societies conduct politics it has been seen as an attractive solution to some significant problems. For the individual citizen, it simplifies participation to the point at which it becomes manageable. Without the convenient heuristic of a unique party preference, political choices would threaten to become too complex (Campbell *et al.* 1960). And for the conduct of politics at the level of national parliaments it allows considerable stability and consistency; politics becomes a contest between a small number of groups each with wide support and a broad policy agenda given coherence by a few underlying principles.

This interpretation has also been challenged, however. One significant challenge is to the idea that party identification is a 'durable attachment, not readily disturbed by passing events and personalities' (Campbell *et al.* 1960: 151). A more tenable position is that the support individuals give to parties is much more labile, even if many people do display considerable inertia in their party leanings.

A more significant challenge is to the idea that individuals always and everywhere have clear and coherent ideologically founded positions from which their preferences for one party or another naturally flow. It is this challenge, articulated by Converse (1964) in his influential analysis of the belief systems of mass publics, that shifted the focus from the origins of different political convictions to the origins of political conviction of any kind. And this in turn has led to questions about the third element of engagement.

This third element – and the one of most relevance here – encompasses the psychological 'tools' individuals might need to play a part in the political life of their societies. A key question concerns the extent to which the attributes of individuals that make up engagement constitute requirements or preconditions for participation versus the extent to which they develop as a *consequence* of participation.

One strategy in seeking an explanation for political participation has been to search for explanations in the psychological make-up of individual political actors. If they are psychologically more engaged, whether this is taken to mean being more keenly interested in politics, more attentive to political affairs, more knowledgeable about the political domain, in possession of stronger convictions on political questions, more confident in their ability to shape political outcomes, then they will *as a result* participate more extensively in politics.

If we accept this kind of causal interpretation – and we should be cautious about doing so without considerable qualification – then it is still not the end of the story; it leads only to further casual questions. What are the roots of differences in interest, attentiveness, knowledge, convictions or self-efficacy? It turns out they are all linked to education (Bynner *et al.* 2003; Delli Carpini and Keeter 1996; Nie *et al.* 1996) and quite plausibly mediate some of the effects of education on electoral and conventional participation. People with more years of education are more likely to vote in elections of all kinds and to participate in other ways. It is therefore tempting to conclude that these things are so because education develops interest in politics, supports attention to politics, fosters skills of media literacy, encourages stronger internal efficacy, perhaps through developing a capacity to understand politics, and helps individuals to clarify their opinions and articulate political identities. This line of thinking seems in its turn to lead in a straightforward way to the additional conclusion that raising population levels of education will increase population levels of participation. There are, however, reasons to treat this conclusion with great caution. The same reasons cast doubt on the simple engagement-leads-to-participation conclusion.

Nie *et al.* (1996) offer a powerful argument for this caution. Partly it rests on a simple empirical observation. Since the end of the Second World War, educational levels have increased steadily across successive generations in Western democracies. Over the same period levels of participation in politics have in these same countries progressively declined. Level of educational attainment may account for differences in level of participation within populations, but clearly it cannot account for differences in absolute levels of participation across time. Two questions therefore arise: what does account for the absolute amount of participation that characterises a population, and what accounts for apparent declines in this absolute amount? To answer these – and to appreciate the remainder of Nie *et al.*'s argument – we need to change to a different level of analysis. By way of introduction, we also need to look again at the central concept, political participation, this time in terms of a cost-benefit analysis from the perspective of the individual political actor.

Political participation as a zero-sum game

At some level – and although it may not routinely be articulated or even consciously recognised – people seek and expect benefits in return for their participation in political life. And at some level and with the same provisos they calculate the value of the benefits in terms of the costs they incur to achieve these. One fairly straightforward reason why rates of involvement in every other form of political action apart from electoral participation are so much lower is that the costs are comparatively so much higher. They require considerably more time, more attention, more psychological resources of all kinds and more money, and sometimes involve much greater personal risk. This has clear implications for the identity of those more and those less likely to participate.

It may be tempting to regard voting as cost-insensitive, but it is closer to the truth that voting in European states *currently* has few obvious costs. This not to say it is entirely without costs, and these will bear more heavily on some citizens than others. Moreover, the low cost position in Europe is not always and everywhere the case. In the United States, historically, there have been considerable obstacles to voter registration, many devised to disenfranchise the black population. Media coverage of elections in emerging and new democracies often reveals another kind of cost: the time taken queueing for the opportunity to cast a vote. Occasionally, other costs also appear in the media spotlight, including intimidation and harassment of voters. At a more benign level, the simple matter of the physical proximity of voting stations can create differential costs, one – but not the only – reason why campaigners often organise transport for voters. Likewise, weather on voting day has a documented and again differentiated impact on voter turnout.

Voting also looks different to other forms of participation in the matter of benefits. The benefit to any individual of the single vote he or she casts would be virtually undetectable. For this reason, it has been argued that an instrumental, cost-benefit view of voting is inappropriate. Instead, some scholars (e.g. Knack 1992; Meehl 1977) have argued it should be regarded as a form of altruism. If altruism is involved, then nonetheless it may be stronger among some of the electorate than others; Knack (1994) found that those who regarded voting as a duty were unaffected by voting-day weather, in contrast to those not feeling this civic obligation.

Whatever the case may be for voting, with respect to other forms of political participation cost-benefit considerations are more apparent, and altruistic or purely duty-driven motives are correspondingly less likely to be in play. People writing to elected officials, participating in strikes or demonstrations, taking part in leafleting campaigns, organising protest meetings or running for election to some public office expect to achieve a more specific and tangible result. But this is also where the zero-sum character of political participation is rather more obvious.

I referred earlier to politics as a contest and it is in the nature of a contest that there are winners and losers. Democracy offers the comforting impression that everyone can be a winner, so long as they take turns. And it often seeks to simplify the calculus by persuading citizens to align themselves with one of a small number of groupings, at the extreme only two, as in most US presidential elections. But the impression is illusory. The full range of individual interests can never fully be summarised in the agendas of national political parties, even in a multi-party state. There is therefore inevitably resort to political action outside of periodic national elections. But at the same time, however responsive a political establishment seeks to be, it can only respond to a portion, and quite a small portion, of the appeals addressed to it. The number of opportunities to influence policy is limited and always much smaller than the number seeking influence. So what determines who is most successful in the contest for these opportunities and who loses?

Nie *et al.*'s (1996) answer to this question is 'education', albeit indirectly. Success is a matter of the resources available to the individual actor and the actor's willingness to deploy these in pursuit of political objectives. If the winners are those with access to the most resources, then relative educational attainment plays a strong albeit not completely determining part in who, relatively speaking, has more of those resources. In Nie *et al.*'s analysis, access to one key resource is itself competitive given that the resource in question is finite; this is social network centrality operationalised as the number of opinion formers (journalists) and politicians at various levels an individual is known to. And access to this resource is won through three other things to which relative educational attainment influences access, namely income, organisational membership and, most important, occupational prominence. This last is interesting because the manner of its operationalisation probably means it reflects the possession of politically relevant skills, namely communication skills, leadership-supervisory skills and group decision-making skills. This is also consistent with much other research pointing to the importance of 'civic' skills as resources for political participation (e.g. Verba *et al.* 1995). Once again, however, it would appear that what matters is not having more of these skills or resources in an absolute sense but having more of them than one's competitors.

What I have identified as aspects of psychological engagement, in particular interest in and attention to politics, are identified in Nie *et al.*'s analysis not as among the determinants of levels of participation but as associated or correlated features of participation. Nie and colleagues do not posit a reciprocal relation between psychological engagement and participation in political activities but this is one possible interpretation of their conclusions (another is that these two aspects – the behavioural and the motivational – are indissociable). Instead, they treat the psychological syndrome of engagement as outcome, not cause, but more interestingly they treat it as a fixed resource allocated competitively. That is to say, the amount of political interest in a polity is shared out among competitors such that one individual can only have more if another has less. One of the analyses Nie *et al.*'s report appears to show that, as they put it, 'the total amount of political attentiveness is at a more or less fixed equilibrium in all democratic societies' (Nie *et al.* 1996: 182). Thus, although educational attainment influences attentiveness, it does so in the same way that it influences other aspects of participation, by acting as a sorting mechanism to decide who has more of it and who has less.

This might seem an odd conclusion. Interest and attention are after all properties of individual psychology, not goods or resources that exist outside of and independently of individuals as fixed quantities they seek or acquire greater or lesser shares of. Perhaps a more appropriate way to think about interest, attention and for that matter sense of self-efficacy, is as responses that are more or less encouraged and reinforced by the political environment. And it is the amount of encouragement or reinforcement available that is fixed and finite. But if encouragement/reinforcement is a fixed and finite resource, shared out competitively among citizens, what determines the extent of this resource? And is it fixed in some absolute sense?

The role of the political context

The short answer to the above questions is that the extent of this resource is a function of the national political context (I leave aside the degree to which pan-national political structures such as the EU alter the equation) and to this extent it is not absolutely fixed. At the same time it is not infinitely variable; there are practical upper limits. If one thinks, for example, of this resource as the encouragement that an elected official gives to the individual members of his or her electorate by responding positively to appeals received from them, then there is still an upper limit to the number of appeals that can be given such encouragement.

The extent to which a political system encourages the political participation of its citizens is now usually discussed in terms of opportunity structure. Political systems, it is recognised, differ in the density of meaningful opportunities available to citizens to exercise any kind of political role. McAdam (1996) offered a view of opportunity structure as defined by four elements: (1) the relative openness of political institutions; (2) the stability of elite alignments; (3) the presence of allies among elites; and (4) state capacity and propensity for repression. More recently, Tarrow (1996: 76–7) has defined opportunity structure as the 'consistent – but not necessarily formal or permanent – dimensions of the political environment that provide incentives for people to undertake collective action by affecting their expectations for success or failure'. Significant in this definition is the emphasis on the provision of *incentives* for action and the effect on expectations for success. However, this moves beyond the ratio of opportunities to actors, considering also the impact of this ratio on the motivations of actors.

Vráblíková (2010, 2014) considers various ways in which the ratio is influenced. She examines the impact of four aspects of context on conventional political participation (voting is not a part of her analyses). These include two aspects of institutional design: (1) territorial centralisation/decentralisation (operationalised as specifically fiscal decentralisation); and (2) horizontal separation of powers (number of independent veto points in the system as reflected in separation of powers between and within parliament, the executive and the judiciary); and two other factors identified as: (3) separation within powers (the number of political parties – more political parties should in principle correspond to more points of access to participation for citizens); and (4) corporateness or the prevailing strategies employed by political elites to deal with opposition (here, the extent to which social life is based on organised groups and collectives founded on such phenomena as class and occupation).

Vráblíková's analyses show that of these four contextual features, the two institutional design factors, horizontal separation of powers and, in particular, fiscal decentralisation, are associated with higher levels of political participation. In other words, the more opportunities there are within a state to influence policy the more participation there is. Thus some of the cross-national variation in rates of political participation can be attributed to these two kinds of cross-national difference in opportunity structure. Additionally, two social behavioural variables, group membership and political discussion, interact with fiscal decentralisation, as does the latter with horizontal separation of powers. Thus, where there is more decentralisation, group membership and political discussion are more strongly associated with political participation. And when there is more horizontal separation, political discussion has a stronger association with political participation.

Changing political context – why participation has declined

We are now in a better position to suggest reasons for the decline in electoral and other forms of political participation in Western democracies. One such reason may be the tendency for power holders to centralise power and control and thus reduce the range of meaningful opportunities for participation available to citizens. While there is little systematic documentation of such trends across nations, some analysts have noted clear movements towards greater centralisation in particular cases. For example, in the United Kingdom Simon Jenkins, a political journalist with conservative ideological sympathies, documents the progressive and systematic neutralisation of alternative sources of power by the conservative administrations of Thatcher and Major (Jenkins 1995). Others, however, point out that the centralising tendencies of political elites can vary with ideological orientation. This is particularly characteristic of American political life where this ideological divide is especially marked (Huntington 1981); those on the political right, ideologically speaking, are more suspicious of and inclined to oppose 'big' government. It may be that this affinity between conservatism and restraint of central government power was at the root of the dismay expressed by Jenkins; successive conservative governments appeared to be acting contrary to the basic creed of conservatism.

Whether or not there is creep towards the centralisation of powers irrespective of the ideological colour of current power-holders, societies also contain pressures in the opposite direction and in this respect the absolute level of education of the populace probably does matter. More educated citizens will be more informed about the political landscape, more aware of the connections between their own interests and political decisions and in possession of more of the skills needed to exert political influence. Again, however, this appears inconsistent with evidence of declining participation in parallel with rising levels of education. Some resolution of this apparent contradiction may be found in the recognition that engagement with politics is essentially a matter of social and not individual behaviour. Individuals engage with political life largely to the extent that they come together to influence one another, clarify their opinions, encourage and support one another and act in a collective and organised fashion.

Vráblíková (2010, 2014) provides indirect evidence for the role of social behaviour in political participation. Her analyses include two measures, defined there as reflecting channels for mobilisation, which each proved to have an independent impact on the extent of political participation (as noted above, these additionally interact with contextual factors). One assesses membership of different kinds of association or group and distinguishes more versus less active membership. The other assesses frequency of political discussions with others[2] together with attempts to persuade others of a political viewpoint.

Other research has documented the strong link between membership of different kinds of association or group and political participation but without entirely settling the reasons for this link. It seems likely that organisational membership has a number of correlated effects. One such does relate directly to processes of mobilisation. Mobilisation efforts, initiated by candidates, parties and campaign groups (Rosenstone and Hansen 1993), do increase the participation rates of their targets. But mobilisation efforts of these kinds will often, as Kinder (1998) puts it, take advantage of the social organisation of everyday life; people who already belong to identifiable social groups are easier and less costly to reach.

Remaining for a moment with mobilisation, there is evidence that declining electoral and conventional political participation reflects in part reduced efforts on the part of national political parties to mobilise citizens through direct contact, resources instead being diverted to indirect influence via media advertising campaigns (Rosenstone and Hansen, 1993). There is a certain irony to this given the long-established evidence that indirect influence is far less effective than direct and personal influence (Katz and Lazarsfeld 1955).

Organisational membership is also of relevance as a reflection of direct involvement in collective political action, given the overtly political purpose of some of the organisations that individuals may join. This gives a further clue to declining participation rates. Membership of political parties has been falling steadily in OECD nations since the 1950s; church and trade union membership have shown similar declines (Dalton and Wattenberg 2000; Putnam 2002).

This brings me to a further shift in level of analysis, to the level that stands between national context and individual psychology – that of the relations between individuals.

The personal underlies the political

We have already encountered two signficant hints as to the importance of the personal in the political. One is the role that social network centrality, defined as personal connection to politicians and opinion brokers (journalists), plays in political engagement (cf. Nie *et al.* 1996). The other is the regular appearance of 'political discussion' as a predictor of political participation (cf. Brunton-Smith 2011; Vráblíková 2010).

My assumption is that, at its root, political engagement is social behaviour, and the basic form of such behaviour is discussion of politics between acquainted individuals. The occurrence of such discussions is significant for a number of reasons. They are the means through which individuals clarify their opinions and views, share information, acquire knowledge and develop their understanding of politics. Such conversations are the vehicle for normative processes through which individuals decide and agree on what is appropriate, just, realistic and legitimate. They are the instruments through which individuals influence, persuade and are persuaded. In this way they are likewise the means through which individuals communicate to one another their own political identities and leanings. And they are also the tools with which people arrange, coordinate and organise political action. Political discussion thus nourishes political interest, builds political sophistication and fosters personal political efficacy. We should not be surprised that this social activity proves to be so intimately linked to these more internal psychological dimensions of engagement.

To say that *political* conversation between people presupposes *conversation* between people would seem to advance our understanding of political participation very little, except for two things. First, we now know a great deal about conversations in general, including between whom they are most likely to occur and how often (Emler and McNamara 1996). Second, we can extrapolate from this knowledge to conversations with specifically political content. Thus people with higher rates of conversational interaction also have more frequent conversations about politics (Emler and Palmer-Canton 2001). The correlation is by no means perfect, indicating that additional conditions are relevant, such the presence of a shared interest in political matters between those in conversation. Conversations with political content, like conversations more generally, occur almost entirely between people who know one another and are most likely to occur between people who describe one another as close friends (Emler and Palmer-Canton 2001), though this should not be taken to diminish the significance of such conversations between people less intimately connected.

The reason for this last qualification lies in the political significance of low-density networks and weak ties. Granovetter (1973) has shown that when people are embedded only within densely connected networks of personal ties they are less able to organise effectively for political action. They are also less easily reached through campaigns of mobilisation. Political participation would seem to benefit from access to a wider range of people through geographically dispersed ties and low-density networks. Ekman and Amnå's (2010) 'standby citizen' can more readily be aroused to effective action if connected to the wider society through such ties and networks.

The PIDOP project, and particularly the work of Vráblíková (2010, 2014), has confirmed once again the importance of another feature of social behaviour for political participation, namely regular involvement in various kinds of social organisation. Although involvement in groups with an overt political purpose – political parties, trade unions, for example – is often seen to be key here, Nie and colleagues (1996) show that membership of organisations without any explicit political agenda also underlies political engagement, both directly and indirectly through its impact on social network centrality. One reason for the significance of organisational membership of any kind for political participation is a reason already given: people who belong to organisations are easier to reach through campaigns of mobilisation. And underpinning organisational memberships are personal ties; people who have more frequent contact with a wider range of others are more likely to be drawn into organisations (see also McPherson 1983).

Finally, a link can be made between personal ties and the previously noted secular decline in political participation. Although the industrial revolution did not have the impact on personal lives that social theorists anticipated (e.g. Wirth 1938), more recent changes in the way people use time appear to have done so. There are various indications that rates of social contact have declined in recent decades in Western democracies. Putnam (2000) reported that average daily time spent on informal socialising by adult Americans had declined from 80–85 minutes to 57 minutes a day over a 30-year period to 1995. Over this period the percentage of days in which any kind of informal socialising occurred fell from 65 to 39. The data come from diary records covering a day in the life of their recorders. Putnam noted that the picture of decline here is consistent with other diary data. Based on sampling one day's activities at 30-minute intervals, the NPD Group (1999) study showed a 20 per cent decline in time spent visiting friends over a mere eight-year span to 1999. Evidence of a different but complementary kind, presented by McPherson et al. (2006), paints a similar picture. Their data come from two sweeps of the US General Social Survey (GSS) in respectively 1985 and 2004. In that 19-year interval the proportion of respondents reporting that there was no one with whom they discussed important issues grew from 10 per cent to almost

25 per cent. Especially marked was also a narrowing of the range of social contacts, a shrinkage of personal worlds. Additionally, this growing isolation was occurring at all levels of education, but was most marked among those with least education. As McPherson and colleagues (2006) note in their conclusions: 'The general image is one of an already densely connected, close, homogenous set of ties slowly closing in on itself, becoming smaller, more tightly interconnected, more focussed on the very strong bonds of the nuclear family' (p. 371). Thus the personal ties that underlie political engagement and participation are progressively disappearing.

What is the cause of these trends? In *Bowling Alone*, Putnam (2000) considers various possible factors and elaborates on these in a later publication (Putnam 2002). His conclusions are largely endorsed by McPherson *et al.* (2006). The most indispensable ingredient for building and sustaining personal ties is time; shifts in work, geographic and recreational patterns have progressively eroded the time available. As more women have entered the labour market, families have added 10 to 29 hours per week to time spent working outside the home (e.g. Jacobs and Gerson 2001). This is not necessarily by itself a source of reduction in social contact rates. The workplace is one of the most important settings for social contacts (Emler 2000), reflected also in the fact that the unemployed have dramatically lower rates of social participation. Jacobs and Gerson's point, however, is primarily about the impact on the time budgets of families with children. Of perhaps greater importance is urban sprawl making for longer commutes to and from work (Hochshild 1997); time spent commuting is social dead-time. Finally, recreational patterns have shown a trend towards progressive privatisation of leisure, reflected for example in time spent watching television or on the Internet.

With respect to this last, and the availability of other new communication technologies, optimism is regularly expressed that these can make up for the deficit in face-to-face contact, offering more efficient means for sustaining personal ties. This optimism has yet to be underpinned with any firm data. Indeed, some of the evidence available does not support it (e.g. Gershuny 2003).

Finally, therefore, if people have less social contact and fewer conversations then they will have fewer conversations about politics. And if they have fewer conversations about politics they will be less engaged in political life, less likely to vote and less likely to participate in any other way.

Conclusions

On normative grounds two features of political participation in contemporary democracies attract our attention. One relates to the marked inequalities in levels of participation within societies. The other is the secular decline in participation. As citizens our instinct is that neither is good for the health of democracy. Each of these features has its own explanation and thus distinct implications for remediation.

With respect to inequalities of participation the following points should be made. First, inequality is inevitable and unavoidable given that the responsiveness of political systems to citizens is finite and limited. The question therefore becomes one of how much inequality we should tolerate. On the one hand, governments can and do take actions that influence the opportunity structure, and to this extent the scope for remedial action lies squarely at the door of professional politicians. On the other hand, people differ in their propensity for engagement and some of this is a matter of predisposition. We have seen that interest, for example, is not entirely a predisposition in the sense of pre-dating any contact with the political environment. It is not immune to political context; it is not unresponsive to experience of participation or its consequences. On the other hand, it is also shaped by qualities more intrinsic to the individual. One such candidate quality is the personality trait of openness (cf. Caprara *et al.* 2006). Likewise, we have seen that educational attainment is a strong predictor of political participation. Differences in educational attainment are linked to another attribute of individuals, intellectual ability. It is unrealistic to expect the impact of such individual differences to be eliminated, yet they will influence relative success in the competition to exert political influence.

Of perhaps greater concern is the extent to which inequalities in political participation align with other inequalities, most obviously those of wealth. And we are rightly concerned that such inequalities should also be associated with gender, minority or migrant status. Again, however, given the underlying causes of these associations, it is no simple matter to eliminate or even reduce their impact. If the argument has merit that effective political participation is underpinned by the ways in which people are linked together through personal connections, then this has clear implications for the position of particular social categories. Women have in the past century come into political life through their evolving participation in the employment system and the nature of the social contacts this has afforded. At the same time some forms of employment are socially isolating, though not as isolating as unemployment. The social ties of migrants and minorities are more often characterised by high density and limited range. These constitute significant obstacles to their effective participation in political life.

Turning to the secular trend towards declining participation, some responsibility can be laid at the door of governments, for example through their centralisation of decision-making control, and of political parties through their withdrawal from direct mobilisation efforts. However, of similar importance are the changing patterns of individual behaviour, producing a diminishing pool of time available to invest in personal ties with one another, with knock-on effects for political discussion and for participation in various kinds of voluntary associations and organisations. These trends in individual time use may be reversible but policies that address them can only succeed if founded on good evidence as to their underlying causes. Evidence of this kind is now an urgent need.

Notes

1 Note, however, that different sources of evidence on voter turnout report different results, though the relative differences between countries remain.

2 It may be recalled that in the analyses reported by Brunton-Smith (2011), political discussion was not distinguishable from interest and self-efficacy and was included in a composite measure of engagement.

References

Abelson, R. P. (1995) *Statistics as Principled Arguments*. Hillsdale, NJ: Erlbaum.

Barrett, M. (2012) 'An Integrative Theory of Political and Civic Engagement and Participation'. Unpublished paper for WP7, PIDOP Project.

Brunton-Smith, I. (2011) *Full Technical Report of PIDOP Work Package 5: Modelling Existing Survey Data*. Available from: http://epubs.surrey.ac.uk/739988/2/PIDOP_WP5_Report.pdf_revised.pdf (accessed 6 January 2013).

Bynner, J., Romney, D. and Emler, N. (2003) 'Dimensions of political and related facets of identity in late adolescence', *Journal of Youth Studies*, 6: 319–35.

Campbell, A., Converse, P. E., Miller, W. E. and Stokes, D. E. (1960) *The American Voter*. New York: Wiley.

Caprara, G. V., Schwartz, S., Capanna, C.,Vecchione, M. and Barbaranelli, C. (2006) 'Personality and politics: values, trait and political choice', *Political Psychology*, 28: 609–32.

Converse, P. (1964) 'The nature of belief systems in mass publics', in D. Apter (ed.), *Ideology and Discontent*. New York: Free Press.

Dalton, R. J. and Wattenberg, P. (2000) *Parties Without Partisans: Political Change in Advanced Industrial Democracies*. New York: Oxford University Press.

Delli Carpini, M. X. and Keeter, S. (1996) *What Americans Know About Politics and Why It Matters*. New Haven, CT: Yale University Press.

Ekman, J. and Amnå, E. (2010) 'Political Participation and Civic Engagement: Towards A New Typology, Work Package 3'. Unpublished paper, PIDOP Project.

Emler, N. (1990) 'A social psychology of reputation', *European Review of Social Psychology*, 1: 171–93.

Emler, N. (2000) 'Social structures and individual lives: effects of participation in the social institutions of family, education and work', in J. Bynner and R. K. Silbereisen (eds), *Adversity and Challenge in the Life Course in England and the New Germany*. London: Macmillan, pp. 62–84.

Emler, N. (2001) 'Gossiping', in H. Giles and W. P. Robinson (eds), *Handbook of Language and Social Psychology*, 2nd edn. Chichester: Wiley, pp. 317–38.

Emler, N. (2002) 'Morality and political orientations: an analysis of their relationship', *European Review of Social Psychology*, 13: 259–91.

Emler, N. (2011) 'What does it take to be a political actor in a multi-cultural society?', in M. Barrett, C. Flood and J. Eade (eds), *Nationalism, Ethnicity, Citizenship: Multidisciplinary Perspectives*. Cambridge: Cambridge Scholars Press.

Emler, N. and McNamara, S. (1996) 'The social contact patterns of young people: effects of participation in the social institutions of family, education and work', in H. Helve and J. Bynner (eds), *Youth and Life Management: Research Perspectives*. Helsinki: Helsinki University Press, pp. 121–39.

Emler, N. and Palmer-Canton, E. (2001) 'Talking Politics: Who, Where, How Much'. Unpublished manuscript. London School of Economics.

Gershuny, J. (2003) 'Web-use and net nerds: a neofunctionalist analysis of the impact of information technology in the home', *Social Forces*, 82: 141–68.

Granovetter, M. (1973) 'The strength of weak ties', *American Journal of Sociology*, 78: 1360–80.

Hochschild, A. (1997) *The Time Bind*. New York: Metropolitan Books.

Huntington, S. P. (1981) *American Politics: The Promise of Disharmony*. Cambridge, MA: Belknap Press.

Jacobs, J. A. and Gerson, K. (2001) 'Overworked individuals or overworked families', *Work and Occupations*, 28: 40–63.

Jenkins, S. (1995) *Accountable to None: Tory Nationalization of Britain*. London: Hamilton.

Katz, E. and Lazarsfeld, P. F. (1955) *Personal Influence: The Part Played by People in the Flow of Mass Communications*. New York: Free Press.

Kinder, D. (1998) 'Opinion and action in the realm of politics', in G. T. Gilbert, S. T. Fiske and G. Lindey (eds), *Handbook of Social Psychology*, 4th edn, vol. 2. New York: McGraw-Hill.

Knack, S. (1992) 'Civic norms, social sanctions and voter turnout', *Rationality and Society*, 4: 133–56.

Knack, S. (1994) 'Does rain help the Republicans? Theory and evidence on turnout and the vote', *Public Choice*, 79: 187–209.

Luskin, R. (1990) 'Explaining political sophistication', *Political Behavior*, 12: 331–61.

McAdam, D. (1996) 'Conceptual origins, current problems, future directions', in D. McAdam, J. D. McCarthy and M.N. Zald (eds), *Comparative Perspectives on Social Movements*. Cambridge: Cambridge University Press.

McPherson, M. (1993) 'An ecology of affiliation', *American Sociological Review*, 52: 519–32.

McPherson, M., Smith-Lovin, L. and Brashears, M. E. (2006) 'Social isolation in America: changes in core discussion networks over two decades', *American Sociological Review*, 71: 353–75.

Meehl, P. E. (1977) 'The selfish voter and the throw-away vote argument', *American Political Science Review*, 71: 11–30.

Neubauer, D. E. (1967) 'Some conditions of democracy', *American Political Science Review*, 61: 1002–9.

Nie, N. H., Junn, J. and Stehlik-Barry, K. (1996) *Education and Democratic Citizenship in America*. Chicago: University of Chicago Press.

NPD Group (1999) *Time Lines: How Americans Spent Their Time During the '90s*, NPD Group Special Report. New York: Port Washington.

Putnam, R. (2000) *Bowling Alone: The Collapse and Revival of American Community*. New York: Simon & Schuster.

Putnam, R. (2002) *Democracies in Flux: The Evolution of Social Capital in Contemporary Society*. Oxford: Oxford University Press.

Rosenstone, S. J. and Hansen, J. M. (1993) *Mobilization, Participation, and Democracy in America*. New York: Macmillan.

Tarrow, S. (1996) 'States and opportunities: the political structuring of social movements', in D. McAdam, J. D. McCarthy and N. M. Zald (eds), *Comparative Perspectives on Social Movements. Political Opportunities, Mobilizing Structures, and Cultural Framings*. Cambridge: Cambridge University Press.

Verba, S., Sholzman, K. L. and Brady, H. E. (1985) *Voice and Equality: Civic Voluntarism in American Politics*. Cambridge, MA: Harvard University Press.

Vráblíková, K. (2010) 'Contextual Determinants of Political Participation in Democratic Countries. Unpublished paper for WP3, PIDOP Project.

Vráblíková, K. (2014) 'How context matters? Mobilization, political opportunity structures, and nonelectoral political participation in old and new democracies', *Comparative Political Studies*, 47 (2): 203–29.

Wirth, L. (1938) 'Urbanism as a way of life', *American Journal of Sociology*, 44: 1–24.

Zani, B., Cicognani, E. and Albanesi, C. (2012) 'The Perspective of Social and Community Psychology for a Model of Political and Civic Participation: Integrating Contextual and Individual Variables'. Unpublished paper for WP7, PIDOP Project.

10

AN INTEGRATIVE MODEL OF POLITICAL AND CIVIC PARTICIPATION

Linking the macro, social and psychological levels of explanation

Martyn Barrett

This chapter has two main goals. First, it aims to provide a broad overview of the numerous macro, social and psychological factors which have been found to be related to political and civic participation. Second, it aims to provide an outline sketch of an integrative model of these various factors, with a particular focus on collective action, voting and volunteering as three distinct forms of participation.

A conceptual distinction is drawn in this chapter between political and civic participation. The term 'political participation' is used to refer to behaviours which have the intent or the effect of influencing governance, whether this be through conventional means involving electoral processes (e.g. voting, election campaigning, etc.) or through non-conventional means which occur outside electoral processes (e.g. signing petitions, demonstrating, etc.). The term 'civic participation' is used to refer to behaviours which are focused either on helping others within a community, working on behalf of a community, solving a community problem or participating in the life of a community more generally (e.g. raising money for charity, volunteering, helping neighbours, participating in community associations, etc.).

For the purposes of this chapter, 'participation' is construed as behavioural and refers to participatory behaviours. By contrast, 'engagement' is construed in psychological rather than behavioural terms and is used to denote having an interest in, paying attention to, or having knowledge, beliefs, opinions, attitudes or feelings about either political or civic matters. In other words, 'engagement' is used in this chapter as a shorthand term for 'psychological engagement'.

This chapter falls into three main sections. The first section reviews the *macro* factors that are linked to political and civic engagement and participation, the second section reviews the *social* factors linked to engagement and participation, while the third section reviews the *psychological* factors linked to participation (i.e. the relationship between psychological engagement and behavioural participation).

In the course of the discussion, two interlocking integrative models will be outlined, one covering macro and social factors and the other covering psychological factors.

Macro factors linked to engagement and participation

The macro factors that are related to political and civic engagement and participation can be categorised into two main types: (1) those that concern the specific characteristics of the electoral, political and legal institutions in the country in which an individual lives; and (2) those that concern the broader historical, economic, cultural and population characteristics of the country. These two classes of macro factors will be discussed in turn.

Characteristics of electoral, political and legal institutions

The electoral system

Various aspects of the electoral system have been found to be related to the likelihood that people will vote in an election (Geys 2006; see also Chapter 5 by Garry in this volume). For example, voter turnout varies according to whether a *proportional representation or first-past-the-post system* is used, with voter turnout being higher under proportional representation (Jackman 1987). In addition, when *voting is compulsory rather than optional*, voter turnout is boosted significantly (Smith 1999). Similarly, *voter registration processes*, especially when registration is simple rather than cumbersome and is automatic rather than voluntary, increases voter turnout (Powell 1986). A further factor is whether *voting takes place on a working day or on a Sunday*, with turnout being higher under the latter arrangement (Mattila 2003). There is also evidence that *holding multiple elections concurrently* on the same day increases voter turnout (Smith 1999).

Political institutions

It has also been found that the design of the political-institutional system which is used to govern a country is related to citizens' patterns of participation. For example, citizens living in countries in which the state is relatively weak in the sense that there are a large number of *access points for non-state actors to exert an influence on policy* (e.g. Switzerland) display different patterns of participation from citizens living in countries in which centralised state authority is strong and where there are few opportunities for non-state actors such as social movement organisations to influence policy (e.g. France): in weaker states, there are higher levels of more moderate forms of action (e.g. signing petitions and participating in campaigns), while in stronger states, there are higher levels of more extreme forms of action (e.g. demonstrations and strikes) (Kriesi *et al.* 1995).

The extent to which *the state is decentralised* in its fiscal, administrative and political structure, and the extent to which there is a *horizontal separation of powers* through having independent veto points in the institutional system that are able to exercise real power, are also linked to participation. For example, Vráblíková (2014; see Chapter 2 by Vráblíková and Císař in this volume) found that higher levels of non-electoral participation occur in countries which are fiscally decentralised and in countries which have a high number of independent veto points.

In addition, Brunton-Smith (2011; see Chapter 11 by Brunton-Smith and Barrett in this volume) found two political-institutional factors to be systematically and strongly related to levels of participation by citizens: *government accountability* (i.e. the extent to which corruption is controlled, financial contributions to political parties are disclosed, freedom of the press is ensured, etc.) and *government and economic efficiency* (based on GDP, economic growth, whether taxes are paid, etc.). He found that levels of all forms of participation other than voting are higher in countries which are high on these two factors.

Legal and human rights institutions

Brunton-Smith (2011) also examined three aspects of the legal and human rights institutions within countries. These were: *rule of law* (i.e. the presence of an independent judiciary, impartial courts, legal protection for minorities, etc.), *human rights record* (i.e. women's and minority rights, extrajudicial killings, disappearances, use of torture, etc.) and *civil liberties* (i.e. freedom of expression and protest, freedom to form professional organisations and trade unions, religious tolerance, etc.). Brunton-Smith found that people are more likely to participate through conventional political and civic means in countries which are high on the rule of law and human rights record, and are more likely to participate through non-conventional means in countries which are high on civil liberties.

Historical, economic, cultural and population characteristics of countries

While the first class of macro factors concerns the specific political and institutional arrangements that apply within any given country, the second class concerns the broader characteristics of countries including their historical, economic, cultural and population characteristics.

Historical characteristics

There are now several findings reported in the literature which show that patterns of participation among citizens are related to the recent *history of a country*. For example, citizens in Eastern Europe tend to have lower levels of participation than those in Western Europe; however, in those countries where popular action contributed to the downfall of communist regimes, participation levels are higher (Bernhagen and Marsh 2007).

That said, the influence of recent history may differ for older and younger people. This appears to be particularly the case for psychological engagement. For example, the CIVED study (Torney-Purta et al. 2001) revealed that the importance which young people attribute to conventional citizenship (i.e. voting, joining a political party, etc.) varies across countries, and actually tends to be higher rather than lower in *countries in which conventional political institutions and forms of participation have been strengthened in the previous 30 years* and lower in *countries in which there are long-standing democratic traditions*. The CIVED study also found systematic differences in levels of trust in political and legal institutions among young people according to whether their country had *more or less than 40 years of continuous democracy*: higher levels of trust were found among young people living in countries with long-standing democratic traditions.

Economic characteristics

Another important set of macro factors stems from the *economy of a country*. As Brady et al. (1995) note, one of the reasons why people may not participate politically is because they lack the financial resources to do so. Participation may therefore be lower in countries that have a poorly performing economy because more people in such countries suffer from economic disadvantage. And indeed, there is evidence which shows that those who are poor and those who are unemployed are less likely to vote (Rosenstone 1982; Wolfinger and Rosenstone 1980). Additional confirmation that the economy of a country is related to patterns of participation emerged from Brunton-Smith's (2011) analyses: recall that he found higher levels of all forms of participation other than voting in countries characterised by higher rather than lower levels of *government and economic efficiency*.

The level of economic development of a country is likely to be related to women's participation in particular. This is because there is an especially close link between economic development and women's educational level and entry into the labour force, with both of these latter two factors being related to a range of different psychological and behavioural characteristics, including levels of political interest, political knowledge, voting in elections and civic participation; thus women in more economically developed countries are more politically engaged and participate to a greater extent than those in less well developed countries (Galligan 2012; Inglehart and Norris 2003).

Cultural characteristics of the country

The cultural characteristics of countries are also linked to patterns of political and civic engagement and participation. First, the *religion* of a country is linked to these patterns. For example, in countries which have predominantly Catholic traditions, women in particular have lower levels of political interest, political knowledge and political participation than women in countries which have predominantly Protestant traditions (Galligan 2012; Inglehart and Norris 2003).

Another cultural factor known to be related to patterns of engagement and participation is *the availability of associations, organisations and social networks* within a country. Associational and organisational involvement provides a context in which individuals can acquire the skills and resources which are needed for political participation (Putnam 2000). However, belonging to associations, organisations and networks might not only be important for the acquisition of civic skills. Voluntary group and network affiliations can also provide individuals with the opportunity to engage in political discussions, which in turn helps to generate political interest; they also provide opportunities to become civically and politically active (Verba 1978).

Finally, there are indications in the literature that there may be differences in patterns of civic and political participation and engagement between countries with *individualistic vs. collectivistic value orientations*, countries with *strong vs. weak religious traditions*, countries with *strong vs. weak ethics of social responsibility* and countries with a *welfare orientation vs. an opportunity orientation* (e.g. Berry et al. 2002; Flanagan et al. 1998; Flanagan and Campbell 2003). Further research is required to explore these factors.

Population characteristics

A final set of macro factors stems from features of the population that lives within a country. Geys (2006) has shown that three population features in particular are related to patterns of voter turnout in elections. First, the *size of the population* is related to voter turnout: the larger the electorate, the lower the electoral turnout. This pattern is probably due to voters' judgment that the greater the size of a community, the less likely it is that a single vote will have any effect on the outcome, a judgment which then reduces the incentive to vote (Mueller 2003). Second, *population stability* is also related to voter turnout: the more stable the population, the higher the level of voting. Possible explanations of this finding are that living in a location for a long time increases identification and solidarity with the community, improves knowledge of relevant issues and candidates, and increases social pressures towards voting. Third, Geys' work shows that voter turnout is also related to the size of the *minority share of the total population*: the higher the minority share, the lower the voter turnout. This finding is not a result of minority individuals being less likely to vote than majority individuals, because it has also been found that minority individuals are as likely to vote in elections as majority individuals once demographic differences are controlled (Bobo and Gilliam 1990). Instead, the explanation seems to be that as the proportion of minority individuals in a population increases, minority voting also increases while majority voting decreases, thereby reducing voter turnout overall (Oberholzer-Gee and Waldfogel 2001).

Macro factors related to participation by minorities and migrants

In addition to the preceding macro factors, there are several further factors which are related specifically to patterns of participation by members of minority and migrant groups. First, such participation depends on the political opportunity structures which are made available to them by the electoral, political and legal institutions in their country of residence, including whether or not they are *granted or denied voting rights*, the *rules for granting nationality and citizenship* to foreign nationals in a country and the extent which there are *formal consultative bodies or channels* for liaising with minority and migrant groups (Martiniello 2005).

A further macro factor related to participation by minorities and migrants is the extent of the *institutional discrimination* which they face in their country of residence (Montgomery 2012). For example, in some countries (e.g. Bulgaria), ethnic, racial and religious political parties are banned. Institutional discrimination can also occur in more subtle forms through characteristics of the electoral system. For example, *voter registration processes* that require skills to negotiate complex bureaucratic systems or language ability tests can discriminate against minorities and migrants. The *day on which voting occurs* can also be a further obstacle if this falls on a day of worship for a particular minority group.

Members of minority and migrant groups do usually have access to opportunities for participation through *minority community organisations, trade unions* (if they are in employment) and *pressure groups* (e.g. anti-racist, human rights or environmental organisations), even if they do not have full citizenship of their country of residence. Because access to these kinds of organisations is not subject to the same kinds of legal restrictions as access to the political arena, these alternative arenas may be much more accessible and open for participation by members of minority and migrant groups than those associated with conventional politics. Participation by minority individuals in minority community organisations and associations has been found to be related to higher levels of political participation (Fennema and Tillie 1999). This link is probably due to the role of these organisations in facilitating minority and migrant people's integration into society through the provision of practical advice and information, the creation of institutional and social trust, and the encouragement of greater interaction with the majority society. However, the availability of these civic organisations and associations varies across countries; the more extensive and the more organised that such organisations are, the higher the levels of civic and political participation by minority individuals (Fennema and Tillie 1999; Putnam 2000).

Conclusions

The macro factors that are related to political and civic participation and engagement can be viewed as falling into two main types: the institutional factors that together create the political opportunity structures for citizens, and the broader historical, economic, cultural and population characteristics of a country. Clearly, these two sets of macro factors are not independent of each other. The historical, economic and cultural characteristics of a country provide the context within which formal state institutions are constructed and developed by political elites. Furthermore, the operation of state institutions in turn influences the history of a country and its economy and culture. In other words, the two sets of macro factors are not independent but instead mutually influence one another.

Social factors linked to participation and engagement

Turning now to social factors, research has revealed that factors associated with the family, education, the peer group, the workplace, the mass media, non-political organisations and political institutions are all related to political and civic participation and engagement.

The family

Numerous aspects of the *family* have been found to be linked to political and civic participation and engagement. For example, it has been found that:

- literacy and educational resources in the family home predict levels of civic knowledge (Torney-Purta *et al.* 2001);
- adolescents whose parents are interested in political and social issues have higher levels of interest in these issues themselves and higher levels of civic knowledge (Schulz *et al.* 2010);
- a family ethic of social responsibility predicts levels of civic commitment in young people (Flanagan *et al.* 1998);
- individuals whose parents engage in civic volunteering have higher levels of civic and political participation, are more attentive to news about politics and government, and are more likely to engage in consumer activism, while individuals who have frequent political discussions with family members are more likely to volunteer and to vote (Zukin *et al.* 2006);
- parents who engage in protests are more likely to have offspring who also engage in protests (Jennings 2002);
- adolescents' political alienation is related to their perceptions of their parents' political alienation, and an authoritarian parenting style predicts adolescents' political alienation (Gniewosz *et al.* 2009); and
- family climate (measured in terms of cohesion/expressivity, organisation/control, and cultural/intellectual orientation) predicts young people's civic knowledge, political literacy, internal efficacy and trust in institutions (Azevedo and Menezes 2007).

Thus family discourses and practices with regard to political and civic participation are strongly related to young people's patterns of political and civic participation and engagement.

Participation and engagement also vary according to *family SES*. Individuals from families with higher SES have more political and civic knowledge (Delli Carpini and Keeter 1996; Niemi and Junn 1998; Schulz *et al.* 2010) and higher levels of participation (Hart *et al.* 1998; Zukin *et al.* 2006). However, it has been argued that what really matters as far as SES is concerned are the correlations between SES and educational attainment and between SES and the skills that are exercised in organisations and in jobs, with the latter factors being the determining predictors of engagement and participation (Verba *et al.* 1995).

Family ethnicity is also important (Jensen 2010). For example, ethnic minorities and majorities participate in different kinds of volunteer activities, with the former participating more in activities relating to their own ethnic community and to other minorities (Stepick *et al.* 2008). Perhaps not unexpectedly, minority individuals also have more positive attitudes towards minority rights (Torney-Purta *et al.* 2007). In addition, some minority youth are less likely than majority youth to have political and civic knowledge (Hart and Atkins 2002; Torney-Purta *et al.* 2007). They may also be less likely than majority youth to express their political opinions (e.g. by contacting officials, expressing opinions to the media, taking part in protests and petitions, etc.) (Zukin *et al.* 2006).

The *generational status* of migrant and minority individuals is also linked to their levels of participation (Seif 2010). For example, the first generation is less likely to be registered to vote than later generations and is also less participative in terms of actual voting, volunteering and boycotting when compared with majority group individuals; by contrast, the second generation is often more civically and politically participative than majority group individuals (Lopez and Marcelo 2008; Stepick and Stepick 2002).

The relationships between ethnicity and political and civic participation and engagement are complex, involving multiple interactions between the specific ethnicity of the individual, gender and levels of community and school participation (Bogard and Sherrod 2008). Furthermore, some of the findings involving ethnicity may well be due to the reduced opportunities for participation linked to low SES, lower educational attainment and differential religious affiliations rather than to ethnicity per se.

Education

Education is also related to patterns of political and civic engagement and participation (Delli Carpini and Keeter 1996; Nie *et al.* 1996; Verba *et al.* 1995). Some of the links here stem from the enhancement of the specific knowledge, skills or motivations that are targeted by the educational system. For example, political knowledge can be increased through civic education if an appropriate pedagogical approach is adopted (Niemi and Junn 1998) and the emphasis placed upon elections and voting in school classes is a significant predictor of young people's intentions to vote in the future (Torney-Purta *et al.* 2001). The contents of school textbooks are also related to young people's political knowledge and attitudes (Barrett 2007).

However, the relationship between education and participation and engagement is much more wide-ranging than just the specific knowledge, skills, motivations or attitudes targeted by the curriculum or by textbooks; educational influences appear to generalise to a wide range of participatory behaviours and aspects of engagement. For example, Zukin *et al.* (2006) report that students who attend schools which provide civic training in skills (e.g. in letter writing and debating) are more likely to be involved in organisations outside school, to sign petitions, to participate in boycotts, to follow political news, to engage in charitable fund-raising and to attend community meetings, and that students who participate in classroom discussions about volunteering are more likely to volunteer regularly, to work on community problems, to participate in charity fund-raising, and to try and influence other people's voting. These findings fit with those of Feldman *et al.* (2007) and Pasek *et al.* (2008) who found that a civic education intervention increased not only knowledge of politics and current affairs but also internal efficacy, interest in politics, attention to politics and subsequent voting.

Classroom climate is one of the major educational factors identified by the CIVED study, with open classroom climate (i.e. the opportunity to discuss controversial social issues and to express and listen to differing opinions in the classroom) predicting young people's levels of civic knowledge and likelihood of voting in the future (Torney-Purta *et al.*, 2001). Hahn (1998) also found that an open classroom climate predicts levels of political interest and trust, while Azevedo and Menezes (2007) found that classroom climate predicts civic knowledge, the interpretation of political messages, interest in politics, dispositions for future political activity, internal efficacy and political trust. Furthermore, perceptions that teachers practise a democratic ethic within the classroom predict the belief that one lives in a just society and levels of civic commitment (Flanagan *et al.* 2007).

The CIVED study also found that participation in school councils predicts both civic knowledge and the likelihood of voting in the future (Torney-Purta *et al.* 2001). Thus the influence of education appears to go well beyond the enhancement of the specific knowledge, skills and motivations targeted by the educational system. It is also important to bear in mind that education may actually have its most profound effects not through the enhancement of the individual's personal capacities, but through the effects which education has upon an individual's employment opportunities, social networks and positions of influence in later life (Nie *et al.* 1996).

Peer groups

Links have also been found between engagement and participation and the *peer group*. For example, civic participation is related to having positive relationships with peers (Wentzel and McNamara 1999; Yates and Youniss 1998), and there is evidence that when youth feel a sense of solidarity with peers and believe that most students in their school display institutional pride in the school, they are more likely to commit to civic and political goals and values (Flanagan *et al.* 1998). In addition, when youth believe that school, church and college are important in their friends' lives and that they can discuss issues and problems with their friends, they are more likely to be civically engaged in later life (Zaff *et al.* 2008). However, the CIVED study found that the amount of time spent in the evenings outside the home with friends is inversely related to civic knowledge in countries where peer group culture devalues education (Torney-Purta et al. 2001).

The workplace

Another important context is the workplace, with workplace arrangements that encourage democratic decision-making and the taking of responsibility being linked to wider political participation. For example, having the authority to tell others what to do in the workplace and involvement in workplace decision-making predict the likelihood of voting, being involved in campaigning for a political party or candidate, and being involved in the affairs of one's local community (Sobel 1993). However, Greenberg (2008) argues that 'spillover' effects from the workplace to broader participation are most pronounced when workplace decision-making is closest to what may be called 'direct democracy', where decisions about immediate everyday issues and long-term planning are made in face-to-face meetings, with full information being made available to employees. When decision-making is more distant and indirect (e.g. only involving voting for directors), there may not be any relationship at all with broader political participation.

The mass media

The *mass media* have also been found to be linked to participation and engagement. For example, the extent to which individuals attend to news reports on the television and in newspapers is related to levels of political and civic knowledge and to the likelihood of voting in the future (Hahn 1998; Torney-Purta et al. 2001). In addition, people appear to make decisions about whether to engage in consumer activism in response to information received from the news media and the Internet (Zukin et al. 2006).

Non-political organisations

Research has also identified links between membership of *non-political organisations* and political and civic engagement and participation, for example:

- involvement in formal groups (e.g. religious groups, sports groups, etc.) in which the individual is able to take on active and specific roles is related to prosocial-oriented civic participation (Albanesi et al. 2007);
- young people who belong to a club or team are much more likely to be involved in community service two years later (Hart et al. 1998);
- people who have high levels of religious attendance and religious activity are more likely to be civically and politically active (Crystal and DeBell 2002; Verba et al. 1995); and

- young people who participate in community-based organisations and in extra-curricular activities are more likely to be both civically engaged and politically active in later life (Glanville 1999; Youniss *et al.* 1997; Zaff *et al.* 2003).

Political institutions

Finally, the activities of *political institutions* themselves are related to levels of political activity. For example, being contacted and asked personally to participate in a political process is a powerful predictor of later political participation (Green and Gerber 2004; Zukin *et al.* 2006).

Additional observations

Three observations need to be made concerning these various social factors. First, it is important to recognise that individuals do not passively absorb influences from their social environment. Instead, people are agentic social actors who actively select the information to which they attend, scan contexts for information relevant to their own motivations, needs, preferences and goals, ignore or resist information which is irrelevant to their own concerns, and actively draw their own inferences from information in their environment (Bandura 1986).

Second, individuals themselves also have effects on how other people in their environment behave towards them. For example, young people may initiate political discussions with their parents and by so doing become more aware of (and possibly influence) their parents' political orientations, which in turn then influence their own attitudes (Kiousis *et al.* 2005; McDevitt 2006). Individuals actively construct their own representations, beliefs, attitudes and practices through interactions which take place within a variety of different contexts, and the causality which takes place within these contexts is often inherently bidirectional.

Third, the various macro and social factors do not operate in isolation from each other. The perspective of Bronfenbrenner's (1979) ecological theory of human development is useful here. He drew distinctions between microsystems, mesosystems, exosystems and macrosystems. Microsystems are the immediate settings within which the individual lives and which directly influence the experience of that developing individual. The family is a microsystem, the school (in the case of a young person) and workplace (in the case of a working adult) are others, and friendship groups are another. The mesosystem is the system of links between different microsystems through which experiences in one microsystem or setting influence or impact on experiences in another microsystem. For example, experiences within the family may impact on social relationships at school or in the workplace (and vice versa). Exosystems are settings in which the individual concerned does not directly participate but which nevertheless affect the functioning of the microsystems. For example, an adult's experience in the workplace may impact on their family life and hence influence what is experienced by another person within their family. The macrosystem is the wider set of institutions, ideologies, values, norms, etc., that characterise the society in which the individual lives, and which therefore constrain and shape exosystems, mesosystems and microsystems. These conceptual distinctions are useful for the purposes of articulating an integrative model of political and civic participation, as they help to emphasise the different levels of factors and the possible interrelationships which may exist between them.

An integrative model of macro and social factors

A diagrammatic attempt at representing the numerous pathways through which macro and social factors might either promote or inhibit political and civic participation and engagement is shown in Figure 10.1. This is a speculative model which attempts to integrate all of the macro and social factors which have been discussed above into a unified framework. The model is speculative in the sense that the causal relationships which are posited by the model go beyond the empirical evidence which is currently available; however, it should be noted that these relationships are consistent with the existing evidence.

On the left-hand side of Figure 10.1, depicted within the two large ellipses, the macro factors are parcelled up into two main types: (1) the specific characteristics of the electoral, political and legal institutions and processes in the country in which an individual lives and which therefore create the political opportunity structures for the people who live within that country; and (2) the broader characteristics of the country, including the historical, economic, cultural and population characteristics.

The proximal social factors which are posited to influence political and civic engagement and participation are depicted in the centre of the diagram. It is hypothesised that the beliefs, attitudes, values, norms, discourses and practices of many different social actors impact on an individual's patterns of participation and engagement, including those of parents and other family members, teachers, those who determine the content of educational curricula and textbooks, employers and colleagues in the workplace, peers beyond the family and the workplace, those who determine representational content in the mass media, and those who are responsible for the functioning and operation of political and non-political institutions and organisations in the society in which the individual lives.

The pathways through which these various social actors might influence an individual's patterns of engagement and participation are depicted by arrows in Figure 10.1. Mutual arrows of influence have been inserted between the two sets of macro factors because they impact on each other. Mutual arrows of influence have also been inserted between both sets of macro factors and the beliefs, attitudes, values, norms, discourses and practices of societal members. This is because the macro factors provide the background against which individuals within a society position themselves ideologically, politically and socially, and also because these individuals can bring about changes to the macro-context of their society through their own political, civic and social actions.

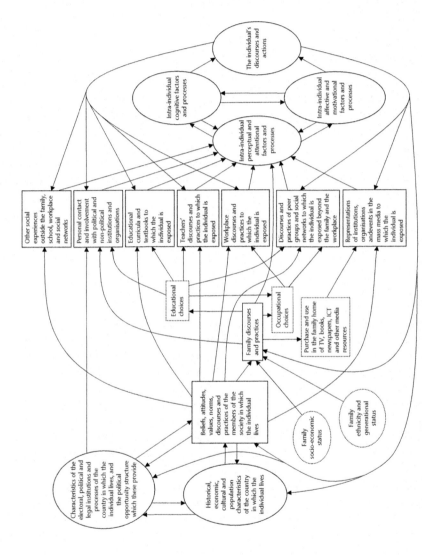

FIGURE 10.1 An integrative model of the macro and social factors that are linked to political and civic engagement and participation

The unidirectional arrows in the centre of the diagram represent the hypothesised patterns of influence which potentially operate within the more proximal social field. The family is postulated to play a central role here. First, the family exerts *direct* effects on the individuals within it through the discourses and practices which operate and circulate within the family context. Second, the family also exerts *indirect* effects via the educational choices which are made by parents for their children (which in turn influence the educational curricula, range of teachers and peer group to which their children are exposed), via the occupational choices made by family members (which are partially dependent on prior educational choices, and which in turn then influence the range of discourses and practices to which an individual is exposed in the workplace beyond the family and the school), and via the purchase and use within the family home of TV, books, newspapers, ICT and other media resources (which influence the range of representations of institutions, organisations and political and civic events in the mass media to which the individual is exposed). Family discourses and practices themselves are, of course, heavily constrained and influenced both by family socio-economic status and by family ethnicity and generational status.

The model depicted in Figure 10.1 therefore proposes that all of the following social factors may potentially impact on political and civic participation and engagement:

- family discourses and practices;
- educational curricula and textbooks;
- teachers' discourses and practices;
- workplace discourses and practices;
- discourses and practices of peer groups and social networks beyond the family and the workplace;
- other social experiences outside the family, the school, the workplace and social networks;
- personal contact and involvement with political and non-political institutions and organisations; and
- representations of institutions, organisations and political and civic events in the mass media.

Hence, this model accommodates much of the evidence which has been outlined above on these various factors.

However, this model proposes these are all only *potential* sources of influence. As noted above, the proximal social influences which actually exert effects on any individual are partially determined by intra-individual psychological factors. These psychological factors are depicted within ellipses on the right-hand side of Figure 10.1, where they are parcelled up into three main types: (1) perceptual and attentional factors and processes; (2) cognitive factors and processes; and (3) affective and motivational factors and processes. More detailed comments on these psychological factors are offered in the following section of this chapter.

The model in Figure 10.1 also incorporates the influences which stem from the individual's own discourses and actions on the various social and macro factors. As noted earlier, individuals have effects on how other people in their environment behave towards them, and the causality which operates within any social context (whether this be the family, the school, the workplace, the peer group, or indeed the accessing and appropriation of information from media sources) is often bidirectional. Similarly, in cases where individuals rise to positions of influence and power within a society, their discourses and actions can also have an impact on the macro characteristics of that society. This reciprocal influence from the individual onto the various social and macro factors is captured in Figure 10.1 by the arrows flowing backwards from right to left from the individual's discourses and actions.

The primary purpose of the model depicted in Figure 10.1 is to articulate and render explicit some of the interconnections which might exist between the different pathways operating at the macro and social levels, and to link these up into a single coherent integrative framework. However, for the sake of clarity, Figure 10.1 omits all of the arrows which depict possible mesosystem effects (i.e. the system of causal links between the different social microsystems depicted in the centre of the diagram). Nevertheless, the possibility of complex webs of interdependence between different microsystems should not be overlooked.

Pursuing the implications of Figure 10.1 further, it is likely that the balance of influence between the different social factors varies from one societal setting to another, depending on the specific configuration of macro and social factors which prevails. In other words, different factors may be the primary drivers of political and civic engagement and participation in different populations and in different settings, with the relative weightings assigned to the various arrows in Figure 10.1 varying from one setting to another and from one population to another. This model therefore predicts considerable variability both across and within populations in the macro and social factors which are operative, depending on the particular population involved and the specific societal and social settings within which they live.

Psychological factors linked to participatory behaviours

Turning now to the psychological factors that are linked to participatory behaviours, previous research has identified a large number of such factors. These psychological factors are reviewed in detail in Chapter 8 by Cicognani and Zani in this volume. Drawing on their review, it is clear that all of the following factors are potentially related to participation:

- Cognitive resources such as *knowledge*, *beliefs*, *attitudes*, *opinions* and *values*. Several specific cognitions that have been found to be particularly important are *political interest*, *political attentiveness*, *internal efficacy* (i.e. the belief that one understands civic and political affairs and has the competence to participate in those affairs), *external efficacy* (i.e. the belief that politicians and political institutions are responsive to citizens' views), *collective efficacy* (i.e. the belief that the

problems of a group can be solved through collective activity), *social trust* (i.e. the belief that other people will generally behave in ways that are beneficial rather than detrimental to oneself), *institutional trust* (i.e. the belief that societal and political institutions will generally operate in ways that are beneficial rather than detrimental to people) and *beliefs about good citizenship*.
- Personal motivations and goals, including *a disposition for participation, a prosocial orientation* and *specific motivations for participation* (e.g. the desire to learn, to develop the self, to be involved in a cause, to enhance self-esteem, etc.).
- Emotions, including both *negative emotions* (e.g. anger about a perceived social injustice, feelings of discrimination, dissatisfaction with the status quo, anxiety or fear about the consequences of action, etc.) and *positive emotions* (e.g. happiness, satisfaction with the consequences of past participation, institutional pride, etc.).
- *Social identifications*, which involve the subjective experience of a sense of belonging to social groups (e.g. a community, a social or political movement, an ethnic group, a national group, etc.).
- *Perceptions of barriers to, and opportunities for, participation*. Perceived barriers may take a number of forms (e.g. perceiving that one lacks the time, the financial resources or the energy to participate). The perception that the available structures for participation (e.g. political institutions, civic associations, social networks, etc.) are closed to outsiders can form a significant psychological impediment to participation: participation requires individuals to perceive that at least some opportunities to participate are open and accessible to them.

Most relevant to the present chapter's aim of constructing an integrative model, several studies that have explored psychological factors have used path analysis to identify the relationships that exist between subsets of these factors and specific forms of participation and/or engagement. Table 10.1 summarises nine such studies. Between them, these studies have explored a number of the factors that are related to collective action (such as demonstrations, strikes, etc.), voting and volunteering. It is noteworthy that there are several common factors across these studies, including perceived injustice, collective efficacy and social identification in the case of collective action, and political knowledge and political attentiveness in the case of voting. There are, in fact, sufficient common factors to enable the path models generated by these studies to be linked together to form larger integrated psychological models of collective action and voting, respectively.

Figure 10.2 shows these larger integrated models, together with a third model of the factors that are related to volunteering (based on Omoto and Snyder 1995). It should be noted that the nine studies listed in Table 10.1 provide clear empirical evidence for every pathway which is included in Figure 10.2. It should also be noted that there are no incompatibilities between the pathways identified by the nine studies.

Although Figure 10.2 is complex, it omits several further important psychological factors which have been identified in other research. One omitted factor is the

TABLE 10.1 Studies which have used path analysis to identify the relationships between the social and psychological factors linked to specific forms of participation or engagement

Study	Factors	Forms of participation or engagement predicted by the factors
Klandermans (2002)	Perceived injustice Collective efficacy Social identification Preparedness to take collective action	Collective action
Kelloway et al. (2007)	Perceived fairness of outcomes Collective efficacy Willingness to take action Intent to participate in collective action Affective commitment to group	Collective action
van Zomeren et al. (2008)	Disadvantage Perceived injustice Social identification Collective efficacy	Collective action
van Zomeren et al. (2004)	Perceived social opinion support Perceived social action support Procedural unfairness Group-based anger Collective efficacy	Collective action tendencies
Simon et al. (1998)	Social context Social identification Politicised social movement identification Calculation of costs and benefits of participation	Willingness to participate in collective action
Livingstone et al. (2009)	Identity threat Perceived injustice Group-based anger	Support for legal collective action Support for illegal direct action
Nie et al. (1996)	Educational exposure Verbal proficiency Organisational membership Occupational prominence Social network centrality Political knowledge Political attentiveness	Voting
Pasek et al. (2008)	Educational exposure Internal efficacy Political knowledge Political attentiveness	Voting
Omoto and Snyder (1995)	Helping disposition Motivations to volunteer Perceived social support Satisfaction from volunteering	Volunteering

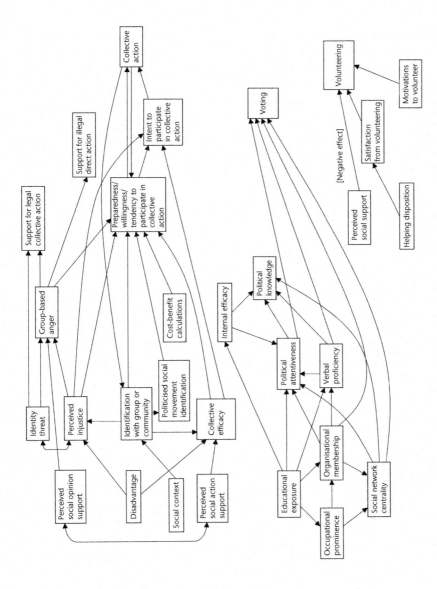

FIGURE 10.2 The integrative models of collective action, voting and volunteering which result from linking up the path models generated by the studies shown in Table 10.1

extent to which the individual internalises the norms of the social groups to which he or she belongs. Such internalisation is a core aspect of identification with a group or community. Research has revealed that when an identity based on a social group membership becomes salient to an individual, attitudinal, affective and behavioural group norms are constructed and internalised, and these norms then become prescriptive for that individual; however, the extent to which this occurs is dependent on the initial strength of identification with the group (Jetten et al. 1997; Terry and Hogg 1996). Furthermore, when group identification and the perception of strong group norms are measured as two distinct factors, it is the combination of these two factors (rather than just identification on its own) which best predicts behavioural intentions, which in turn predict actual behaviour (Terry and Hogg 1996). Thus a case may be made for including not only the strength of group identification but also the *internalisation of group norms* as two distinct factors in an integrative model.

Another factor missing from Figure 10.2 is *institutional trust*. This omission is significant given the role which institutional trust undoubtedly plays in this domain (Dalton 2008; Norris 1999). Torney-Purta et al. (2004) found that institutional trust predicts voting, volunteering, joining a political party and writing letters to a newspaper about social or political concerns. They also found that institutional trust itself is sometimes predicted by reading articles in newspapers about current affairs (an index of political attentiveness).

A further factor not included in Figure 10.2 is *external efficacy*. External efficacy needs to be distinguished from internal efficacy because these two factors are conceptually distinct and have different patterns of relationships to other variables. For example, internal but not external efficacy is related to political knowledge (Delli Carpini and Keeter 1996); relationships between internal efficacy and participation are stronger and more consistent than relationships between external efficacy and participation (Craig et al. 1990); and levels of attentiveness to political news are related to internal efficacy (Semetko and Valkenburg 1998) whereas political participation (in the form of voting and campaigning) is related to external efficacy (Finkel 1985). That said, both forms of efficacy are related to *political interest* (Craig et al. 1990) as well as to institutional trust (Acock and Clarke 1990), while internal efficacy is sometimes a predictor of institutional trust (Torney-Purta et al. 2004).

Finally, one further relevant psychological factor is *beliefs about good citizenship*, which have also been found to be related to voting, other forms of conventional participation, contacting officials, and various forms of collective and individual action (Theiss-Morse 1993). Hence, it is arguable that this factor also needs to be included within an integrative model of civic and political participation.

These additional factors (internalisation of group norms, institutional trust, external efficacy, political interest and beliefs about good citizenship) have therefore been included in the model shown in Figure 10.3, together with their relationships to other psychological factors as indicated by the above findings. In this figure, double-headed arrows represent relationships which have been identified through bivariate correlations, while single-headed arrows represent paths which have been identified through regression analyses or structural equation modelling.

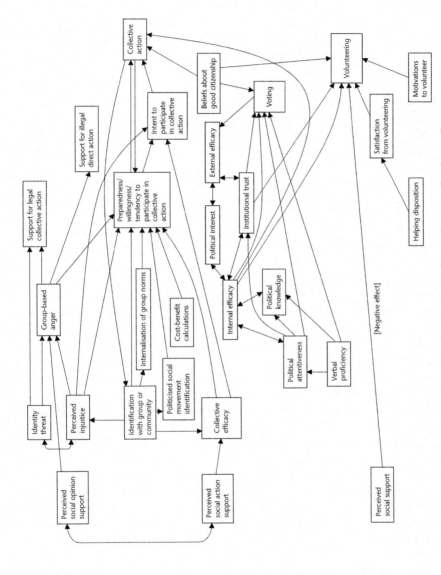

FIGURE 10.3 An integrative model of the psychological factors that are related to collective action, voting and volunteering

The external social factors which were included in Figure 10.2 have been deleted in Figure 10.3 as the focus of interest here is in constructing an integrated model of psychological rather than social factors. The deletion of these social factors also avoids Figure 10.3 conveying the (as yet untested) implication that the social factors in Figure 10.2 have a privileged relationship with only some psychological factors and not with others, when their connection with these other factors has not yet been examined empirically. However, the three different aspects of social support have been retained in Figure 10.3 because they represent *perceived* social support and are therefore psychological in nature.

It is interesting to note that the model depicted in Figure 10.3 represents a single integrated psychological model of participation, with there being shared factors across collective action, voting and volunteering, in particular internal efficacy. The centrality of internal efficacy in the model is notable insofar as Brunton-Smith (2011; see Chapter 11 by Brunton-Smith and Barrett in this volume) has confirmed that this particular psychological factor is indeed one of the most consistent and pervasive predictors of all forms of political and civic participation.

The integrative psychological model shown in Figure 10.3 therefore provides a detailed specification of the perceptual, attentional, cognitive, affective and motivational factors which are linked to three different forms of civic and political participation: collective action (a form of non-conventional political participation), voting (a form of conventional political participation) and volunteering (a form of civic participation).

However, despite its obvious complexity, this psychological model is still not complete. For example, the analyses of Brunton-Smith (2011) further revealed that there are two additional psychological factors which are missing from Figure 10.3. These are *opinionation* and *ideological identity*. Brunton-Smith found that these two factors sometimes act as mediators of the effects of all of the following factors on participation: political interest, political attentiveness, internal efficacy, external efficacy, institutional trust and identity threat. He further found that this mediating effect occurred in relationship to voting, other forms of conventional participation, non-conventional participation and civic participation. For the sake of clarity, Figure 10.3 omits opinionation and ideological identity and their associated arrows. However, the possibility of opinionation and ideological identity being mediators of effects of all six factors on different forms of participation should not be overlooked. Hence, the integrative psychological model shown in Figure 10.3 should not be regarded as a definitive or final model.

Importantly, Brunton-Smith's (2011) analyses also revealed that the psychological factors which are linked to the different forms of political and civic participation vary according to the specific form of participation involved, the specific demographic group involved (as defined in terms of age, gender and minority/majority status) and the specific pattern of prevailing macro factors. In other words, all of the qualifications which were made earlier in relationship to the model of macro and social factors (Figure 10.1) also apply to this second model of psychological factors (Figure 10.3). That is, the factors and pathways which are included in this model only denote *possible* factors and pathways. In practice, different subsets of factors and pathways may be the primary drivers of political and civic participation for different participatory behaviours among different demographic subgroups and in different macro settings. Thus there is considerable variability both across and within populations in the specific psychological factors and pathways which are actually operative, depending on the particular participatory behaviour, the particular demographic subgroup and the particular macro-societal setting in which that subgroup is living.

This second integrative model covering the psychological factors which is shown in Figure 10.3 may be viewed as an unpacking and much more detailed specification of the perceptual, attentional, cognitive, affective and motivational components contained in the macro-social integrative model presented in Figure 10.1. As such, this second integrative model locks directly onto that first model. Furthermore, connecting the two models together in this way produces a comprehensive integrative model of collective action, voting and volunteering covering all three levels of factors: macro, social and psychological.

Finally, it should be noted that this model of psychological factors is, just like the model of macro and social factors, a speculative model. The model attempts to integrate into a unified framework many of the psychological factors and their interrelationships that have been identified by previous research. It is speculative in the sense that the causal relationships which are posited by the model go beyond the empirical evidence which is currently available. Although these hypothesised causal relationships are consistent with this existing evidence, it is for future research to determine the extent to which this interpretation is warranted.

Conclusion

The complexity of Figures 10.1 and 10.3 is daunting from the perspective of translating these models into empirical research. However, the phenomena which have been reviewed in this chapter, namely political and civic engagement and participation, do indeed exhibit this level of complexity. The hope is that the formulations contained in Figures 10.1 and 10.3 will provide useful theoretical perspectives for selecting factors and pathways for future empirical investigations, and that they will also provide a useful basis for future theoretical elaborations.

References

Acock, A. C. and Clarke, H. D. (1990) 'Alternative measures of political efficacy: models and means', *Quality and Quantity*, 24: 87–105.
Albanesi, C., Cicognani, E. and Zani, B. (2007) 'Sense of community, civic engagement and social well-being in Italian adolescents', *Journal of Community and Applied Social Psychology*, 17: 387–406.
Azevedo, C. N. and Menezes, I. (2007) 'Learning politics beyond cognition: the role of experience and participation in political development', in N. Kryger and B. Ravn (eds), *Learning Beyond Cognition*. Copenhagen: Danish University of Education, pp. 95–104.

Bandura, A. (1986) *Social Foundations of Thought and Action*. Englewood Cliffs, NJ: Prentice-Hall.
Barrett, M. (2007) *Children's Knowledge, Beliefs and Feelings about Nations and National Groups*. Hove: Psychology Press.
Bernhagen, P. and Marsh, M. (2007) 'Voting and protesting: explaining citizen participation in old and new European democracies', *Democratization*, 14: 44–72.
Berry, J. W., Portinga, Y. H., Segall, M. H. and Dasen, P. R. (2002) *Cross-Cultural Psychology: Research and Appplications*, 2nd edn. Cambridge: Cambridge University Press.
Bobo, L. and Gilliam, F. D. (1990) 'Race, sociopolitical participation and black empowerment', *American Political Science Review*, 84: 377–93.
Bogard, K. L. and Sherrod, L. R. (2008) 'Citizenship attitudes and allegiances in diverse youth', *Cultural Diversity and Ethnic Minority Psychology*, 14: 286–96.
Brady, D., Verba, S. and Schlozman, K. L. (1995) 'Beyond SES: a resource model of political participation', *American Political Science Review*, 89: 271–94.
Bronfenbrenner, U. (1979) *The Ecology of Human Development: Experiments by Nature and Design*. Cambridge, MA: Harvard University Press.
Brunton-Smith, I. (2011) 'Full Technical Report of PIDOP Work Package 5: Modelling Existing Survey Data'. Unpublished paper, PIDOP Project.
Craig, S. C., Niemi, R. G. and Silver, G. E. (1990) 'Political efficacy and trust: a report on the NES pilot study items', *Political Behaviour*, 12: 289–314.
Crystal, D. S. and DeBell, M. (2002) 'Sources of civic orientation among American youth: trust, religious valuation, and attributions of responsibility', *Political Psychology*, 23: 113–32.
Dalton, R. J. (2008) *The Good Citizen: How a Younger Generation is Reshaping American Politics*. Washington, DC: CQ Press.
Delli Carpini, M. X. and Keeter, S. (1996) *What Americans Know about Politics and Why It Matters*. New Haven, CT: Yale University Press.
Feldman, L., Pasek, J., Romer, D. and Jamieson, K. H. (2007) 'Identifying best practices in civic education: lessons from the Student Voices program', *American Journal of Education*, 114: 75–100.
Fennema, M. and Tillie, J. (1999) 'Political participation and political trust in Amsterdam: civic communities and ethnic networks', *Journal of Ethnic and Migration Studies*, 25: 703–26.
Finkel, S. E. (1985) 'Reciprocal effects of participation and political efficacy: a panel analysis', *American Journal of Political Science*, 29: 891–913.
Flanagan, C. A. and Campbell, B. with Botcheva, L., Bowes, J., Csapo, B., Macek, P. and Sheblanova, E. (2003) 'Social class and adolescents' beliefs about justice in different social orders', *Journal of Social Issues*, 59: 711–32.
Flanagan, C., Cumsille, P., Gill, S. and Gallay, L. (2007) 'School and community climates and civic commitments: patterns for ethnic minority and majority students', *Journal of Educational Psychology*, 99: 421–31.
Flanagan, C. A., Bowes, J. M., Jonsson, B., Csapo, B. and Sheblanova, E. (1998) 'Ties that bind: correlates of adolescents' civic commitments in seven countries', *Journal of Social Issues*, 54: 457–75.
Galligan, Y. (2012) 'The Contextual and Individual Determinants of Women's Civic Engagement and Political Participation'. Unpublished paper, PIDOP Project.
Geys, B. (2006) 'Explaining voter turnout: a review of aggregate-level research', *Electoral Studies*, 25: 637–63.
Glanville, J. L. (1999) 'Political socialization or selection? Adolescent extracurricular participation and political activity in early adulthood', *Social Science Quarterly*, 80: 279–90.

Gniewosz, B., Noack, P. and Buhl, M. (2009) 'Political alienation in adolescence: associations with parental role models, parenting styles and classroom climate', *International Journal of Behavioral Development*, 33: 337–46.
Green, D. P. and Gerber, A. S. (2004) *Get Out the Vote! How to Increase Voter Turnout*. Washington, DC: Brookings Institution Press.
Greenberg, E. S. (2008) 'Spillovers from cooperative and democratic workplaces: have the benefits been oversold?', in B. A. Sullivan, M. Snyder and J. L. Sullivan (eds), *Cooperation: The Political Psychology of Effective Human Interaction*. Malden, MA: Blackwell, pp. 219–39.
Hahn, C. (1998) *Becoming Political: Comparative Perspectives on Citizenship Education*. Albany, NY: State University of New York Press.
Hart, D. and Atkins, R. (2002) 'Civic development in urban youth', *Applied Developmental Science*, 6: 227–36.
Hart, D., Atkins, R. and Ford, D. (1998) 'Urban America as a context for the development of moral identity in adolescence', *Journal of Social Issues*, 54: 513–30.
Inglehart, R. and Norris, P. (2003) *Rising Tide: Gender Equality and Cultural Change around the World*. New York: Cambridge University Press.
Jackman, R. W. (1987) 'Political institutions and voter turnout in the industrial democracies', *American Political Science Review*, 81: 405–23.
Jennings, M. K. (2002) 'Generation units and the student protest movement in the United States: an intra- and intergenerational analysis', *Political Psychology*, 23: 303–24.
Jensen, L. A. (2010) 'Immigrant youth in the United States: coming of age in diverse cultures', in L. R. Sherrod, J. Torney-Purta and C. A. Flanagan (eds), *Handbook of Research on Civic Engagement in Youth*. Hoboken, NJ: John Wiley & Sons, pp. 425–43.
Jetten, J., Spears, R. and Manstead, A. S. R. (1997) 'Strength of identification and intergroup differentiation: the influence of group norms', *European Journal of Social Psychology*, 27: 603–9.
Kelloway, E. K., Francis, L., Catano, V. M. and Teed, M. (2007) 'Predicting protest', *Basic and Applied Social Psychology*, 29: 13–22.
Kiousis, S., McDevitt, M. and Wu, X. (2005) 'The genesis of civic awareness: agenda-setting in political socialization', *Journal of Communication*, 55: 756–74.
Klandermans, B. (2002) 'How group identity helps to overcome the dilemma of collective action', *American Behavioral Scientist*, 45: 887–900.
Kriesi, H., Koopmans, R., Duyvendak, J. W. and Giugni, M. G. (1995) *New Social Movements in Western Europe: A Comparative Analysis*. London: UCL Press.
Livingstone, A. G., Spears, R., and Manstead, A. S. R. (2009) 'Illegitimacy and identity threat in (inter)action: predicting intergroup orientations among minority group members', *British Journal of Social Psychology*, 48: 755–75.
Lopez, M. H. and Marcelo, K. B. (2008) 'The civic engagement of immigrant youth: new evidence from the 2006 Civic and Political Health of the Nation Survey', *Applied Developmental Science*, 12: 66–73.
McDevitt, M. (2006) 'The partisan child: developmental provocation as a model of political socialization', *International Journal of Public Opinion Research*, 18: 67–88.
Martiniello, M. (2005) *Political Participation, Mobilisation and Representation of Immigrants and Their Offspring in Europe*, Willy Brandt Series of Working Papers in International Migration and Ethnic Relations, 1/05. Malmö, Sweden: Malmö University.
Mattila, M. (2003) 'Why bother? Determinants of turnout in the European elections', *Electoral Studies*, 22: 449–68.
Montgomery, V. (2012) 'Political Participation as a Process: Migrant and Minority Communities'. Unpublished paper, PIDOP Project.
Mueller, D. C. (2003) *Public Choice III*. Cambridge: Cambridge University Press.

Nie, N. H., Junn, J. and Stehlik-Barry, K. (1996) *Education and Democratic Citizenship in America*. Chicago: University of Chicago Press.
Niemi, R. and Junn, J. (1998) *Civic Education: What Makes Students Learn?* New Haven, CT: Yale University Press.
Norris, P. (ed.) (1999) *Critical Citizens: Global Support for Democratic Governance*. Oxford: Oxford University Press.
Oberholzer-Gee, F. and Waldfogel, J. (2001) *Electoral Acceleration: The Effect of Minority Population on Minority Voter Turnout*, NBER Working Paper 8252. Cambridge, MA: National Bureau of Economic Research.
Omoto, A. M. and Snyder, M. (1995) 'Sustained helping without obligation: motivation, longevity of service, and perceived attitude change among AIDS volunteers', *Journal of Personality and Social Psychology*, 68: 671–86.
Pasek, J., Feldman, L., Romer, D. and Jamieson, K. H. (2008) 'Schools as incubators of democratic participation: building long-term political efficacy with civic education', *Applied Developmental Science*, 12: 26–37.
Powell, G. B. (1986) 'American voter turnout in comparative perspective', *American Political Science Review*, 80: 17–43.
Putnam, R. (2000) *Bowling Alone: The Collapse and Revival of American Community*. New York: Simon & Schuster.
Rosenstone, S. J. (1982) 'Economic adversity and voter turnout', *American Journal of Political Science*, 26: 25–46.
Rosenstone, S. J. and Hansen, J. M. (2003) *Mobilization, Participation, and Democracy in America*. New York: Longman.
Schulz, W., Ainley, J., Fraillon, J., Kerr, D. and Losito, B. (2010) *Initial Findings from the IEA International Civic and Citizenship Education Study*. Amsterdam: IEA.
Seif, H. (2010) 'The civic life of Latina/o immigrant youth: challenging boundaries and creating safe spaces', in L. R. Sherrod, J. Torney-Purta and C. A. Flanagan (eds), *Handbook of Research on Civic Engagement in Youth*. Hoboken, NJ: John Wiley & Sons, pp. 445–70.
Semetko, H. A. and Valkenburg, P. M. (1998) 'The impact of attentiveness on political efficacy: evidence from a three-year German panel study', *International Journal of Public Opinion Research*, 10: 195–210.
Simon, B., Loewy, M., Sturmer, S., Weber, U., Freytag, P., Habig, C., Kampmeier, C. and Spahlinger, P. (1998) 'Collective identification and social movement participation', *Journal of Personality and Social Psychology*, 74: 646–58.
Smith, J. (1999) *Europe's Elected Parliament*. Sheffield: Sheffield Academic Press.
Sobel, R. (1993) 'From occupational involvement to political participation: an exploratory analysis', *Political Behavior*, 15: 339–53.
Stepick, A. and Stepick, C. D. (2002) 'Becoming American, constructing ethnicity: immigrant youth and civic engagement', *Applied Developmental Science*, 6: 246–57.
Stepick, A., Stepick, C. D. and Labissiere, Y. (2008) 'South Florida's immigrant youth and civic engagement: major engagement: minor differences', *Applied Developmental Science*, 12: 57–65.
Terry, D. J. and Hogg, M. A. (1996) 'Group norms and the attitude-behavior relationship: a role for group identification', *Personality and Social Psychology Bulletin*, 22: 776–93.
Theiss-Morse, E. (1993) 'Conceptualizations of good citizenship and political participation', *Political Behavior*, 15: 355–80.
Torney-Purta, J., Barber, C. H. and Richardson, W. K. (2004) 'Trust in government-related institutions and political engagement among adolescents in six countries', *Acta Politica*, 39: 380–406.

Torney-Purta, J., Barber, C. H. and Wilkenfeld, B. (2007) 'Latino adolescents' civic development in the United States: research results from the IEA Civic Education Study', *Journal of Youth and Adolescence*, 36: 111–25.

Torney-Purta, J., Lehmann, R., Oswald, H. and Schulz, W. (2001) *Citizenship and Education in Twenty-Eight Countries: Civic Knowledge and Engagement at Age Fourteen*. Amsterdam: IEA.

van Zomeren, M., Postmes, T. and Spears, R. (2008) 'Toward an integrative social identity model of collective action: a quantitative research synthesis of three socio-psychological perspectives', *Psychological Bulletin*, 134: 504–35.

van Zomeren, M., Spears, R., Fischer, A. and Leach, C. W. (2004) 'Put your money where your mouth is! Explaining collective action tendencies through group-based anger and group efficacy', *Journal of Personality and Social Psychology*, 87: 649–64.

Verba, S. (1978) *Participation and Political Equality*. Cambridge: Cambridge University Press.

Verba, S., Schlozman, K. L. and Brady, H. E. (1995) *Voice and Equality: Civic Volunteerism in American Politics*. Cambridge, MA: Harvard University Press.

Vráblíková, K. (2014) 'How context matters? Mobilization, political opportunity structures, and nonelectoral political participation in old and new democracies', *Comparative Political Studies*, 47 (2): 203–29.

Wentzel, K. R. and McNamara, C. C. (1999) 'Interpersonal relationships, emotional distress and prosocial behaviour in middle school', *Journal of Early Adolescence*, 19: 114–25.

Wolfinger, R. E. and Rosenstone, S. J. (1980) *Who Votes?* New Haven, CT: Yale University Press.

Wray-Lake, L., Syvertsen, A. K. and Flanagan, C. A. (2008) 'Contested citizenship and social exclusion: adolescent Arab American immigrants' views of the social contract', *Applied Developmental Science*, 12: 84–92.

Yates, M. and Youniss, J. (1998) 'Community service and political identity development in adolescence', *Journal of Social Issues*, 54: 495–512.

Youniss, J., McLellan, J. A. and Yates, M. (1997) 'What we know about engendering civic identity', *American Behavioral Scientist*, 40: 620–31.

Zaff, J. F., Malanchuk, O. and Eccles, J. S. (2008) 'Predicting positive citizenship from adolescence to young adulthood: the effects of a civic context', *Applied Developmental Science*, 12: 38–53.

Zaff, J. F., Moore, K. A., Papillo, A. R. and Williams, S. (2003) 'Implications of extracurricular activity participation during adolescence on positive outcomes', *Journal of Adolescent Research*, 18: 599–630.

Zukin, C., Keeter, S., Andolina, M., Jenkins, K. and Delli Carpini, M. X. (2006) *A New Engagement? Political Participation, Civic Life, and the Changing American Citizen*. New York: Oxford University Press.

PART III
Evidence

This part of the book consists of nine chapters that present new empirical evidence on political and civic engagement that was obtained in the PIDOP project. Details of the overall approach and the research methods which were used in the project have already been presented in Chapter 1. The first chapter in this third part provides an overview of the findings which were obtained through the secondary analysis of existing survey datasets. For the remaining chapters, each participating research team analysed a specific subset of the data which they collected for the project in their own country, highlighting aspects of civic and political participation which have particular importance in their own social and political context.

Chapter 11 by **Ian Brunton-Smith and Martyn Barrett** provides an overview of the analyses that were conducted on data from the European Social Survey, Eurobarometer, the Comparative Study of Electoral Systems, the International Social Survey Programme and the World Values Survey. These analyses revealed considerable variability across Europe in the levels of all types of political and civic participation and engagement. *Political interest* and *internal efficacy* were found to be the most consistent psychological predictors of all forms of participation, but other psychological factors sometimes had different relationships with different forms of participation (e.g. a postive relationship to one form of participation but a negative relationship to other forms). The analyses also revealed how the relationship between psychological and demographic factors and participatory behaviours depends in part on the macro characteristics of countries, underlining the complex interactions which occur between factors operating at different levels. Finally, an empirical classification of participants was produced, ranging from the inactive to the highly active: many people only tend to vote, but a similar sized group is highly active and participates in a range of different ways. Comparatively few people have no involvement at all. The demographic composition of these groups is markedly different from one another, with the highly active people tending to be older, male and from the majority ethnic group. The implications of the existence of different groups of participants are discussed.

The following seven chapters in this part focus on new data which were collected in the PIDOP project from adolescents and young people drawn from the national majority group and from two minority or migrant groups within each participating country. Each team chose minority and migrant groups which were particularly important in their own country. The data were either qualitative or quantitative, and were collected using either focus groups or a survey questionnaire (see Chapter 1). The analyses aimed to investigate the factors that either facilitate or hamper engagement and participation.

In Chapter 12, **Jan Šerek, Zuzana Petrovičová and Petr Macek** describe data collected in the Czech Republic, focusing on factors that can facilitate political and civic participation by young people belonging to two ethnic minority groups – the Roma as the largest non-immigrant minority group in the Czech Republic, and Ukrainians as the largest immigrant minority group. The analyses are based on qualitative and quantitative data collected from respondents aged from 15 to 28 years of age. Young people who are not involved in political and civic participation were compared to those who do spend some of their time engaging in such activities. Two factors emerged as being of special importance: *civic organisations* and the *Internet*. On the grounds of these findings, the authors give two recommendations on how to support ethnic minority youth in their political and civic participation: first, to support the foundation and functioning of civic organisations that are open to people of various ethnic backgrounds, and second, to guarantee easy access to the Internet for all social groups. However, the questions of whether online participation on the Internet can be seen as a facilitator for the establishment of ethnic identity and collective efficacy and whether it has the potential to motivate political and civic participation in the real world are still issues that deserve further research attention.

Young people of Turkish background, which is the largest minority group in Germany, are the main focus of Chapter 13 by **Peter Noack and Phillipp Jugert**: they try to shed light on possible differences between German and Turkish youth. Drawing on the observation that minority group members often show activities of engagement and participation within their own minority community, the question addressed was whether adolescents and young adults of Turkish background are mainly engaged in minority-specific cultural or religious groups, or whether such patterns of participation go together with a relationship to German majority culture. Based on comprehensive quantitative questionnaire assessments as well as on analyses of more in-depth focus group discussions, it was found that young people from the Turkish minority group that is, on average, more poorly integrated than most other minority groups in Germany, are as active as their German age-mates, if not more active. Those who are very active in the *cultural and religious groups* of their community are active youth in general, including activities beyond the boundaries set by their culture and religion, and there are no indications of segregation. Thus the traditional view of immigrants as passive citizens does not seem to be valid anymore, which raises the question of why this is the case.

Chapter 14 by **Yunhwan Kim and Erik Amnå**, which compares Iraqi and Kurdish immigrant youth in Sweden with native Swedish youth, also reveals that immigrant youth are not passive as far as their political and civic engagement is concerned. In most cases, levels of political and civic competence among Kurdish youth are significantly higher than those among native Swedish youth: thus immigrant youth seem to be a potential for Swedish democracy rather than a threat. The study also suggests that the engagement of immigrant youth reflects the civic culture and orientation of their country of origin, reflected in the youths' perception of *parental norms* for political and civic engagement: this is a reason for the higher political and civic competence of Kurdish youth compared to Iraqi youth. Another interesting point concerns the differences between first- and second-generation immigrant youth: the gaps in behavioural activity levels between the two immigrant youth groups tend to diminish with *generation*. This finding deserves more systematic examination in future studies.

The predictors of civic and political participation among native Italian and migrant youth in Italy are the focus of Chapter 15, in which **Cinzia Albanesi, Davide Mazzoni, Elvira Cicognani and Bruna Zani** investigate the explanatory role of *organisational membership* and *the quality of participation* in such organisations, testing two mediating factors of the association between organisational membership and civic and political participation drawn from theoretical perspectives in community psychology: *sense of community* and *social well-being*. The findings support the role of organisational membership among both majority and migrant youth in Italy. They also confirm that the nature and quality of participatory activities and their potential for learning and building competences are crucial factors, especially for migrants. For them, satisfactory participatory experiences within organisations have the potential to create a more positive overview and feelings of social integration. The role of sense of community in participation was confirmed, indicating that perceptions of having opportunities for influence over the community are important in explaining both civic and political participation. Interestingly, migrant youth reported higher social well-being than majority youth: among migrants, social well-being mediates the relationship between the active role played within the organisation and civic and political participation.

In some chapters, particular attention is given to the *gender gap* in participation. In Chapter 16, **Claire Gavray, Michel Born and Bernard Fournier** suggest that, in the Wallonia-Brussels Federation in Belgium, even if gendered socialisation continues to have an impact on the distribution of roles and motivations (e.g. the defence of prosocial or pro-traditional values for girls), young women are also determined to distance themselves with regard to gender-stereotyped choices. This is especially true for migrant youth: Turkish and Moroccan girls want to distance themselves from tradition and religion, and they consider gender equality to be very important, even if they are aware that it has not yet been realised. They want to benefit from the historical opportunities offered by Belgian society and they invest in the web to talk and obtain information (the private sphere being more legitimised for girls). Although differences clearly do exist between the two minority groups, it is important not to overlook interpersonal and intragroup diversity while focusing on intergroup diversity. This issue is particularly important for the females within each ethnic group.

In Chapter 17, **Maria Fernandes-Jesus, Carla Malafaia, Norberto Ribeiro and Isabel Menezes** report on an investigation conducted in Portugal into *discrimination based on age* among three groups of young people of Portuguese, Angolan and Brazilian origin. In line with a notion of citizenship based on an adulthood standard, all three groups stressed that young people are usually perceived as having no credibility in the public sphere, which leads to a feeling of having no opportunities to participate. The effect of age seems to be influenced by other factors, such as the economic and educational resources that each individual and her/his family have. The findings show different levels of civic and political participation – and also political interest and attentiveness – among non-migrants and migrants in Portugal. These disparities do not represent a clear disadvantage for migrants, but instead reveal that patterns of involvement change across groups. Interestingly, and although some studies stress the double disadvantage of women of immigrant background, these analyses show a decrease in gender gaps. In fact, women of all groups showed higher levels of social participation and similar levels of political interest and attentiveness to men. In addition, immigrant women reported higher levels of activism than men of immigrant origin, suggesting that non-institutionalised forms of participation reduce or even reverse gender inequalities.

In Chapter 18, **Tülin Şener** examines participation in Turkey among minority Turkish resettler youth whose families have returned to Turkey from Bulgaria, minority Roma youth and majority Turkish youth. Her data reveal that Bulgarian resettler youth have the highest levels of participation, followed by Roma youth, with Turkish youth having the lowest levels overall (cf. the findings in Chapters 13 and 14). However, psychological factors were distributed differently and variably across the three groups. The patterns of correlations between psychological factors also differed across the three groups. Furthermore, although the *perceived quality of action in previous participation experiences* was the main psychological predictor of participation in all three groups, other predictors of participation varied across the three groups: for Turks, *political interest* and low *external efficacy*; for Roma, the *perceived quality of reflection in previous participation experiences* and the strength of the *negative emotions* which were felt about issues; and for the Bulgarian resettlers, *institutional trust*. The finding that low external efficacy predicts high levels of participation in Turkish youth helps to explain why Turkish youth suddenly engaged in mass protests in the summer of 2013, when the Turkish government appeared to be totally unresponsive to citizens' views. More generally, this chapter serves to strongly underline the conclusion that different psychological factors drive participation in different ethnic groups.

Introduction to Part III **193**

The final chapter in this part of the book, Chapter 19 by **Dimitra Pachi and Martyn Barrett**, describes the findings of a study conducted in England which used in-depth qualitative interviews to explore the expectations and understandings held by significant others who are in a position to influence young people's political and civic participation. In a preceding focus group study, low levels of participation had been reported by English, Congolese and Bangladeshi youth, and these same youth also reported that they had been influenced in their attitudes and behaviours by their *parents, teachers, youth workers* and *church youth leaders* as well as by the *lyrics of international hip hop musicians*. Consequently, the study reported in this chapter examined the attitudes that are held by these influential individuals and also examined the views expressed in the lyrics of popular hip hop songs. The aim was to explore how these influential others view young people's political and civic participation, the levels and kinds of participation which these individuals expect from youth, the strategies which they employ in order to encourage youth to participate, and the barriers which they perceive to youth participation. The findings revealed that, in general, low expectations were held of youth, and that young people are embedded in a network of social influences which does little to disconfirm, or which (in the case of the hip hop lyrics) explicitly reinforces, the view that political and civic participation does not produce any real change in the world, effectively discouraging young people from both political and civic participation.

Taken together, the chapters in this part of the book provide a wealth of new data on the nature of political and civic engagement, especially on the specific social and psychological factors which influence participation in a wide range of different populations. These chapters also richly illustrate how political and civic engagement varies in different demographic subgroups within individual countries, while the first chapter also illustrates how the macro context of a country interacts with demographic and psychological factors to influence citizens' political and civic engagement.

11

POLITICAL AND CIVIC PARTICIPATION

Findings from the modelling of existing survey data sets

Ian Brunton-Smith and Martyn Barrett

Introduction

In this chapter, we examine four broad categories of political and civic participation:

- voting;
- other forms of conventional political activity, such as contacting a politician, being a member of/working for a political party, donating money to a political organisation, wearing a political party campaign badge, etc.;
- non-conventional political activity, such as participating in lawful demonstrations and illegal protests, buying/boycotting certain products, signing petitions, etc.;
- civic engagement, such as being involved in a social club, education or teaching group, religious or church organisation, cultural or hobby group, sports or outdoor activity club, environmental or humanitarian organisation, business or professional group, or a trade union.

While these various forms of participation are often examined through the collection of new data, they can also be investigated using existing survey data sets. Indeed, the European Union and its constituent national governments have invested considerable resources in the collection of survey data relating to the extent and nature of political and civic participation among its citizens (e.g. the European Social Survey, the International Social Survey Programme, Eurobarometer and the World Values Survey). This has provided researchers with a formidable resource for the empirical examination of the complex range of political, social and psychological factors that influence people's tendency to vote, participate in other forms of conventional and non-conventional political activity and be civically engaged citizens.

Using these existing data sets has a number of distinct advantages over collecting new data. The data sets are based on representative samples from different countries, which means that: the differences which emerge from cross-national comparisons cannot be attributed to sampling biases within countries; the large number of participants who have contributed the data means that powerful statistical techniques can be used to analyse the data; the large number of participants also facilitates fine-grained analysis across key demographic sub-groups of interest; and the secondary analysis of existing data, in comparison to the collection and analysis of new data, is a highly cost-efficient research strategy.

Using these data sets also enables us to address more complex research questions than might otherwise be possible. For example, while there is now a considerable evidence base detailing the macro-political, social and micro-psychological factors that influence participation (for reviews, see Part II of the present volume), there is far less evidence about the ways in which these three levels of factors *interact* to enhance or inhibit different forms and patterns of participation. The volume of data in these survey data sets is sufficient to allow analyses to be conducted to identify these interactions.

In addition, previous research in this field has tended to treat different forms of participation as empirically distinct from one another. However, some forms of participation may 'go together'. For example, having a belief that public and political officials are responsive to citizen requests (external efficacy) may increase someone's likelihood of voting and lead to greater involvement in other forms of conventional political activity (like belonging to a political party, wearing a campaign badge, etc.), while simultaneously reducing their inclination to be involved in non-conventional forms of participation; in contrast, it may be that some people are just particularly engaged, with high levels of involvement in all forms of participation, while other types of people are much less engaged citizens overall. The survey data sets allow us to examine how the different forms of participation are linked together.

In this chapter, we present a summary of some of the main empirical findings concerning political and civic participation that have emerged from the secondary analysis of survey data sets that was undertaken as part of the PIDOP project. Here we focus on the results from two studies; further information about both of these studies, together with the results of additional analyses, are reported in full in Brunton-Smith (2011). The first study summarised here used multilevel models to explore the macro socio-political influences on citizens' levels of participation and engagement. Here we demonstrate the ways that the socio-political structure of countries may be linked directly to the individual social and psychological processes that drive citizens' decisions whether or not to engage in conventional and non-conventional forms of political activity and in civic activity. The second study used latent class analysis to explore the patterns of participation across European citizens, identifying a number of distinct *types* of 'participant', defined by the combination of forms of participation that they engage in.

Before reporting on these two studies, however, we offer some preliminary comments based on the existing research literature and report some relevant findings from other analyses that were conducted concerning patterns and levels of participation across and within countries.

Political and civic participation across and within countries

There has been considerable previous research directed at the broader macro-contextual characteristics of countries that can either enhance or inhibit the level of participation of their citizens. Studies have identified a number of different contextual factors that shape levels of participation, including the structure and design of the political institutions within a country, as well as its broader historic, economic and cultural characteristics (see Chapters 2 to 4 in the present volume for detailed reviews). Other studies have focused attention on different features of the electoral system that are important, or placed emphasis on characteristics of the population within each country including the population size, stability and minority share of the population (see Chapter 5).

For example, studies focusing on the design and structure of political institutions have shown that in decentralised countries (where power is distributed more widely across society) there tend to be higher levels of moderate political action. In contrast, countries with a stronger centralised state (with power concentrated among a political minority) are characterised by higher levels of more extreme political action like strikes and demonstrations (Císař and Vráblíková 2012; Kriesi et al. 1995). Studies have also shown that in more decentralised states which have a high number of independent veto points in the institutional system, there are higher overall levels of non-electoral forms of political participation (Vráblíková 2010, 2014). Political participation has also been tied to the deeper historical, economic and cultural characteristics of countries, with lower levels of participation in Eastern European countries (but higher levels of participation in countries which have a history of collective popular action) (Montgomery 2012). There is also evidence that women are more likely to participate or be civically engaged in more economically developed (and predominantly Protestant) countries (Galligan 2012).

Perhaps unsurprisingly, voter turnout is also directly related to the characteristics of the electoral system within the country, with research identifying higher levels of voting in countries that employ compulsory voting (Geys 2006; Jackman 1987; Mattila 2003; Smith 1999), have simple registration procedures (Powell 1986; Caldeira et al. 1985; Highton and Wolfinger 1998) or employ a proportional representation system (Geys 2006; Jackman and Miller, 1995). Voter turnout has also been linked to population stability, the size of the resident population and the proportion of minorities within the population (Geys 2006).

Our analysis of the available survey data (from the European Social Survey, Eurobarometer, the Comparative Study of Electoral Systems and the International Social Survey Programme) confirms that there is considerable variability across Europe in the levels of all types of political participation and engagement (the analyses are reported in full in Brunton-Smith 2011). For example, voter turnout in the last election ranges from less than 50 per cent of the eligible population in

Switzerland and Poland to over 90 per cent in Belgium. There is also evidence of a clear disconnect between people's *intentions* to vote and their actual voting *behaviour* (whether measured using self-report data or looking at actual voter turnout), with more than 80 per cent of the population in each country reporting that they intended to vote in the next election. Involvement in conventional and non-conventional forms of political activity is notably lower than voting levels, with 24 per cent involved in conventional activities across Europe (primarily contacting politicians) and 45 per cent involved in non-conventional activities (most often signing petitions or buying certain products for political reasons). This also varies considerably across Europe (17 per cent in Portugal to 45 per cent in Norway when considering conventional participation, and 15 per cent in Portugal and Hungary to 70 per cent in Sweden when looking at non-conventional participation). Levels of civic engagement are also lower than voting levels but higher than other forms of participation (64 per cent across Europe), with as few as 24 per cent involved in Greece to a high of 94 per cent in Denmark.

However, overlaid on these differences between countries, we found evidence of a degree of consistency, with younger people (aged under 25) and minority groups less likely to vote in all countries. Younger people and women were also less likely to be involved in other conventional forms of political participation across all countries in Europe. What is also evident is the similarity in the pattern of differences in involvement across countries, with Portugal and Poland identified in the bottom five countries for all forms of participation and Denmark, Sweden, Norway and Finland consistently reporting the highest levels of involvement.

There is of course variability in participation not only across countries but also within countries. Previous research has identified many social and psychological factors that influence the levels of political and civic participation of citizens within countries (for detailed reviews, see Chapters 8 to 10 in the present volume).

For example, sociological drivers of participation highlight the importance of elements of human and social capital – including levels of education, socio-economic status (SES) and social trust – in informing levels of individual involvement in political activities (Delli Carpini and Keeter 1996; Emler and Frazer 1999; Hart and Atkins 2002; Nie *et al.* 1996; Verba *et al.* 1995). Education has been consistently linked with political participation and studies have emphasised the importance of both classroom climate (Azevedo and Menezes 2007; Hahn 1998; Torney-Purta *et al.* 2001) and teachers' practices (Flanagan *et al.* 2007; Gniewosz *et al.* 2009; Ichilov 1991). Differences in education have been used to explain the link between individual SES and levels of participation that has often been identified in existing studies (Hart *et al.* 1998; Lopez and Marcelo 2008; Zukin *et al.* 2006), with those from higher SES backgrounds also having access to greater levels of education.

Other studies have highlighted the importance of family and peer group relations in shaping and nurturing levels of engagement and participation (Flanagan *et al.* 1998; Schulz *et al.* 2010; Torney-Purta *et al.*, 2001). Research has also emphasised the role of involvement in non-political organisations, including religious groups, sports groups and sport group organisations, which are all associated with prosocial civic participation (Albanesi et al. 2007; Crystal and DeBell 2002; Zaff et al. 2008).

Differences in the nature and extent of participation among young people and minorities have also regularly been identified by existing research (Hart and Atkins 2002; Wray-Lake et al. 2008; Zukin et al. 2006), which shows that young people and minorities are less likely to participate in conventional political activities (including voting), with an increased level of involvement in non-conventional activities and civic engagement (Stepick et al. 2008). Minorities are also more likely to be involved in activities that relate to their own ethnic group (Jensen 2010).

Many of the micro-psychological factors shaping levels of participation have been combined under the label of 'political capital' (Zukin et al. 2006). This refers to the broad set of interlinked political resources that are available to individuals, including their levels of political knowledge, attentiveness to political issues in the media and internal efficacy (the belief that an individual understands civic and political affairs and has the confidence to participate). Those people who are more knowledgeable about politics are typically also more attentive to political issues and may also have a stronger sense of belief in their own potential contribution, which in turn results in higher levels of political and civic participation (Caprara et al. 2006; Jennings 1996; Torney-Purta and Amadeo 2003; Zukin et al. 2006).

External efficacy (the belief that public and political officials and institutions are responsive to citizen's needs, actions, requests and demands) and people's levels of trust in institutions including politicians, parliament, the police and the criminal justice system have also been closely linked to political participation as well as to an increased level of interest in politics (Abramson and Aldrich 1982; Craig et al. 1990; Schulz 2005). Psychological research has also pointed to the importance of a strong sense of identification with, and belonging to, particular social groups (e.g. a community or a social or political movement) for raising levels of participation (Deaux et al. 2006; Simon et al. 1998; van Zomeren et al. 2008). This is thought to be because of the adoption and transmission of group norms concerning participation among members, and also reflects the development of in-group models for participatory behaviours and a sense of social support for one's opinions and actions. Finally, other psychological factors linked to higher levels of political and civic participation include personal motivations and goals (Omoto and Snyder 1995, 2002), as well as individual emotions – both positive and negative (Flanagan et al. 1998; Leach et al. 2006; van Zomeren et al. 2004).

Using data from the European Social Survey, we explored more closely the ways that social and psychological factors are related to people's political participation and engagement. In these analyses, we focused in particular on the following factors:

- attentiveness to political issues and affairs, for example on television, on the radio and in newspapers;
- interest in politics;

- internal efficacy – the belief that one is able to understand politics and has the competence to participate in politics;
- external efficacy – the belief that public and political officials and institutions are responsive to citizens' views;
- institutional trust – how much one trusts institutions such as the police, the legal system, parliament, etc.;
- social capital – how much one trusts other people in general, and how often one meets with friends, relatives or colleagues;
- ideological identity – whether one holds an extreme position on either the right or the left of the political spectrum or whether one holds a more moderate centrist position;
- opinionation – holding opinions about civic and political matters;
- perceived discrimination – the perception that one is discriminated against because of the group to which one belongs.

Using structural equation modelling to explore the relationships between these factors and each of the four categories of participatory activity listed at the beginning of this chapter, we found consistently higher levels of participation among those who had high levels of interest in politics and high internal efficacy. These people were also more likely to hold stronger opinions about political issues, which in turn further increased their levels of participation (specifically in non-conventional political activities and civic engagement). Political interest and internal efficacy were in fact highly correlated with each other, so much so that they effectively formed a single factor predicting levels of participation. However, while higher attentiveness to political issues and affairs was similarly linked to a greater tendency to vote and to be civically engaged, higher attentiveness was also linked to *lower* levels of non-conventional participation.

We also found that people with higher levels of external efficacy were more likely to participate in conventional and non-conventional political activities, although interestingly they were not any more likely to vote than people with lower levels. Those with higher levels of institutional trust were more likely to vote, but were less likely to participate in other ways. In contrast, those who experienced high levels of perceived discrimination had a greater tendency to be involved in non-conventional forms of participation but typically chose not to vote (for full details see Brunton-Smith 2011).

Study 1: Cross-national variations in political and civic participation

To explore these variations further, in our first study we used multilevel models to examine between-country differences in levels of political and civic participation, as well as the link between the macro-structural characteristics of countries and the social and psychological drivers of participation. Data from three different surveys were used in this study: the European Social Survey (ESS, round 1, 2002); the

World Values Survey (WVS, round 2, 2000); and the International Social Survey Programme (ISSP, citizenship module, 2004). None of these surveys is ideally suited to an examination of cross-national variations in political and civic participation, but taken together their relative weaknesses are partially mitigated. Table 11.1 provides details of the scope of each of the surveys used in these analyses. The comparatively small number of countries in the ESS is offset by the methodologically rigorous sample design and the availability of individual data essential for linking macro and micro processes. The WVS is restricted to citizen participation in voting, but includes data on more than twice as many countries as the ESS (including many from outside Europe), enabling a more thorough examination of the contextual processes that are influential for participation. The ISSP also includes a larger number of countries than the ESS, along with data on conventional participation, non-conventional participation and civic engagement, but has only limited information on individual citizens.

Differences in the socio-political structure of different countries were captured using the 'Country Indicators for Foreign Policy' dataset (CIFP 2011), which classifies countries based on six dimensions of governance and democracy:

- the extent to which the political structure is democratic (including party dominance, legislature fractionalisation, proportion of female parliamentarians, proportion of minorities in public service, minority voting rights);
- government and economic efficiency (including growth and debt, economic freedom, unemployment and tax rates);
- accountability (including the extent to which corruption is controlled, the financing of political parties is disclosed and freedom of the press is ensured);
- human rights (including freedom of speech, women's political rights, civil liberties and the level of access to education);
- political stability and violence (including years since a regime change, size of the black market and political fragmentation); and
- rule of law (including an independent judiciary, impartial courts and legal protection for minorities).

Analytic strategy

Multilevel models (Goldstein 2010) were used to explore how the socio-political context of different countries shapes levels of political and civic participation. These are an extension to standard regression models which allow for the simultaneous examination of micro and macro processes relating to political participation and engagement, as well as the link *between* macro and micro processes. Separate models were estimated for voting, conventional political participation, non-conventional participation and civic engagement.[1]

For each form of participation and engagement, we began by identifying whether any systematic differences in participation were evident across countries, once differences in the overall composition of each country had been accounted for

TABLE 11.1 Available data sources

Survey	Year	Countries	Sample size range	Topics covered
European Social Survey	2002	Austria, Belgium, Germany, Denmark, Spain, Finland, France, United Kingdom, Greece, Hungary, Ireland, Israel, Italy, Luxembourg, Netherlands, Norway, Poland, Portugal, Sweden, Slovenia	1,207–2,919	Participation, political engagement, political attentiveness, external efficacy, institutional trust, social trust, ideological identity, political opinionation
International Social Survey Programme	2004	Australia, Germany, Great Britain, United States, Austria, Hungary, Ireland, Netherlands, Norway, Sweden, Czech Republic, Slovenia, Poland, Bulgaria, Russia, New Zealand, Canada, Philippines, Israel, Japan, Spain, Latvia, Slovak Republic, France, Cyprus, Portugal, Chile, Denmark, Switzerland, Flanders, Brazil, Venezuela, Finland, Mexico, Taiwan, South Africa, South Korea, Uruguay	833–2,784	Participation, political engagement, political attentiveness, external efficacy, institutional trust, social trust
World Values Survey	2000	Spain, USA, Canada, Mexico, South Africa, Sweden, Argentina, South Korea, Puerto Rico, Nigeria, Chile, India, Pakistan, China, Turkey, Peru, Venezuela, Zimbabwe, Philippines, Israel, Tanzania, Moldova, Saudi Arabia, Bangladesh, Indonesia, Vietnam, Albania, Uganda, Singapore, Serbia, Montenegro, Macedonia, Egypt, Morocco, Iran, Jordan, Bosnia, Algeria, Iraq, Kyrgyzstan	720–3,401	Participation, political interest, social trust, ideological identity

(the random intercept model). Next, all individual relationships with participation were allowed to vary across countries (the random coefficients model). This provides an indication of whether socio-political differences between countries may also have a role in modifying individual drivers of participation. Then, to further explore country differences, the six dimensions of governance and democracy were included. The comparatively small number of countries available for each analysis (20 countries in the ESS, 39 in the ISSP and 42 in the WVS) limits the extent to which we can specify complex macro-level models to explain any observed systematic variability in participation and engagement between countries (Garry 2010). Therefore each dimension of the political and economic structure of each country was examined separately. Finally, cross-level interactions were used to identify the ways in which the broader socio-political context can moderate individual relationships with participation. This directly links the macro-structural characteristics back to the social and psychological drivers of participation.

Results

A detailed discussion of all analyses and associated results is included in Brunton-Smith (2011). Here we simply provide an overall summary of the main findings from across the four types of participation (see Table 11.2). The top part of Table 11.2 (labelled *Country effect*) indicates how big the between-country differences are in each form of political participation. We find that there are significant between-country differences in all forms of political participation, with greater variability evident when the scope is extended to countries beyond Europe (using data from the ISSP and WVS). Between-country differences are largest when considering civic engagement, where they account for just over one quarter (26 per cent[2] using the ISSP and 25 per cent with the ESS) of all of the differences in engagement. Between-country differences also account for a considerable proportion of the total variability in voting (19 per cent using the WVS, falling to 7 per cent when using data from the ESS) and in non-conventional forms of political participation (22 per cent using the ISSP and 17 per cent with ESS data). There is considerably less variability between countries in levels of conventional participation (11 per cent), falling to 3 per cent of the variability between countries when the focus is restricted to Europe.

With the exception of voting, these differences between countries in average levels of participation can be partially accounted for by turning to differences in their macro socio-political context. This can be seen in the middle part of Table 11.2 (labelled *Macro*), which summarises the results from a series of multilevel contextual models. Here, a + represents a positive relationship between the country attribute (e.g. their democratic structures score) and whether or not people participate, a – sign represents a negative relationship and NS indicates that there was no link between the contextual measure and participation. With the exception of voting – where no significant relationships are found – all the country attributes are shown to be positively related to participation. The full results (reported in Brunton-Smith 2011) show that the magnitude of these relationships

TABLE 11.2 Multilevel results

	Vote	Conventional participation	Non-conventional participation	Civic engagement
Country effect				
ESS	7%	3%	17%	25%
ISSP		11%	22%	26%
WVS	19%			
Macro				
Democratic structures	NS	NS	+	+
Government efficiency	NS	+	+	+
Accountability	NS	+	+	+
Human rights	NS	+	+	+
Political stability	NS	+	+	+
Rule of law	NS	+	+	+
Macro → micro				
Democratic structures	NS	NS	Gender[+], Age[+], Interest and efficacy[-]	Social trust[+]
Government efficiency	NS	Gender[+], Age[+], Interest and efficacy[-]	Gender[+], Interest and efficacy[-]	Social trust[+]
Accountability	NS	Gender[+], Interest and efficacy[-]	Gender[+]	Social trust[+]
Human rights	NS	Gender[+]	NS	Social trust[+]
Political stability	NS	Interest and efficacy[-]	Interest and efficacy[-]	Social trust[+]
Rule of law	NS	Gender[+], Interest and efficacy[-]	Gender[+]	Social trust[+]

NS Non-significant; + higher score more likely to participate; − higher score less likely to participate; [+] stronger effect; [−] weaker effect

varies considerably, with some of the contextual measures being more closely related to the different forms of participation than others. In particular, the extent to which the government within a country is described as accountable and efficient and a country's record in relation to issues of the rule of law are both identified as strongly linked to participation rates (inclusion of these measures in the model accounts for well over half of the differences between countries). In each case, participation levels are higher in countries identified as performing well on these measures. The other socio-political characteristics of the country can also be linked to participation rates, although these are generally associated with smaller reductions in the variations attributable to between-country differences.

We also examined the extent that differences in participation levels *within* countries (between different types of people) are universal across different country contexts, or whether they are linked directly to a country's socio-political character. Initial exploratory models (not reported here) reveal significant differences across countries in the magnitude of many of the individual associations with each form of political participation. In extreme instances, this has the effect of reversing the direction of a relationship in some countries. For example, while on average across countries younger people are identified as more likely to be involved in non-conventional forms of political activity than older residents, in some countries they are the least likely to be involved. Similarly, while men are typically more likely to vote and be civically engaged across countries, women's participation rates are found to be higher in certain socio-political climates. These models also show that in countries with higher voter turnout there will generally be fewer differences in voter turnout between men and women, and a smaller positive effect of higher political interest on trust.

The bottom part of Table 11.2 (labelled *Macro → Micro*) summarises how these differences in participation *within* countries are related to the socio-political characteristics of the country. This shows that the magnitude of differences in participation levels based on gender, levels of political interest and internal efficacy (which are strongly correlated with one another), and to a lesser extent age and social trust, are partially shaped by the broader socio-political context in which the individuals are situated. For example, in countries that are rated more favourably in terms of governmental efficiency, the gender difference in levels of conventional and non-conventional participation is bigger than average (as represented by Gender[+]). In countries that do poorly in terms of governmental efficiency, the gender gap in these forms of participation is smaller than average. The magnitude of gender differences in conventional and non-conventional forms of participation is also linked to the extent that a country is accountable and has a good record on the rule of law in the same way. In contrast, differences in conventional and non-conventional participation based on political interest and internal efficacy are generally diminished in countries identified as more accountable, efficient and with a better record on the rule of law. We also find that the positive role of social trust in shaping levels of civic engagement is marginally more pronounced in countries scoring more favourably on all socio-political measures.

Discussion

We find considerable differences between countries in all forms of political and civic participation. We also find that the associations between some of the commonly identified social and psychological drivers of participation are not uniform across countries. Instead, for many of these factors, the specific nature of their relationship with participation is dependent on the broader socio-political structure of the country. This means that for governments to maximise the involvement of its citizens in the political process it is essential to adopt strategies that are sensitive to the socio-political climate of the country.

With the exception of voting, these differences can (in part) be explained with reference to measurable differences between the countries under study. Differences in participation rates between countries were most closely related to the degree of government accountability and efficiency, as well as their record on rule of law. This suggests that governments could achieve higher participation rates by ensuring that their mode of operation is transparent, accountable and efficient – including effectively controlling corruption, accurately disclosing the financing of political parties and ensuring the freedom of the press. Gains could also be made by ensuring that the country has a good record in relation to the rule of law – for example by guaranteeing the independence of the judiciary, ensuring impartiality of the courts and providing adequate legal protection to minorities.

Study 2: Identifying distinct types of participant

In Study 1, each category of participation (voting, conventional participation, non-conventional participation, civic engagement) was treated as an independent activity that individuals choose to be involved in. However, it is perhaps more reasonable to expect that the processes governing participation in different activities are interlinked, and that consequently there are distinct patterns of participation and engagement across these four categories of activity. This means that people may be clustered into distinct 'types' of citizen based on the combination of participation activities in which they are involved. Understanding these different patterns of participation may in turn highlight ways that we can enhance levels of involvement in political and civic processes. In our second study we used data from the European Social Survey to directly examine this possibility.

Analysis strategy

To see whether distinct groups of people can be identified based on their patterns of political and civic participation, we used latent class analysis (LCA). LCA allows us to identify distinct sub-populations (latent classes) in our data who share similar participation patterns, and then explore which *types* of people are likely to belong to specific classes of participant. This is an exploratory process, with the number of latent classes determined by examining the overall fit of LCA models with different numbers of classes, with the best fit indicating the optimal number of classes. Once this optimal model has been established, descriptive labels can be assigned to each group based on the estimated parameters within each class. An additional appealing feature of LCA is that, once the latent classes have been derived, regressions can be run between the latent class variable and other independent variables, allowing us to identify the types of people that are members of each class (Allua *et al.* 2008; Lubke and Muthén 2005).

Having determined the optimal number of classes, the relative membership of each class can be examined, as well as the multinomial regression coefficients from this model. Class membership is interesting in and of itself, as it enables us to classify people depending on their overall participation profile. Supplementing this with an examination of the multinomial regression coefficients affords us an alternative picture of the ways that different demographic groups engage politically and civically in society.

Results

Initial exploratory analyses led to the identification of four distinct classes of political participant that adequately summarised the varied patterns of participation behaviour in the data (Table 11.3). Based on the relative probabilities of membership in each of the four classes, descriptive labels have been applied to each group to produce a taxonomy of participants.

We define the first group as the *highly active*. Accounting for approximately 38 per cent of the sample, this group is highly likely to participate in all four ways. Not only do they vote in elections, they also have a high probability of taking part in conventional and non-conventional forms of political activity and are also likely to be members of different civic groups. Compared to the other three groups, members of the highly active group tend to be older, male and from the majority ethnic group.

The second group is described as *inactive*. This group is considerably smaller than the highly active group, with just under 13 per cent of the sample classified in this group. These people have a low tendency of participating in any form of political activity, whether conventional or non-conventional, and are also relatively low on civic engagement. Compared to the highly active group, this group is more likely to be younger, female and from a minority ethnic group.

TABLE 11.3 Types of participant

	Group share	*Probability of membership*
Highly active	38%	Vote (0.98), Conventional (0.52), Non-conventional (0.82), Civic engagement (0.92)
Inactive	13%	Vote (0.19), Conventional (0.05), Non-conventional (0.09), Civic engagement (0.36)
Non-conventional and civic activity	9%	Vote (0.51), Conventional (0.40), Non-conventional (0.84), Civic engagement (0.82)
Voting only	41%	Vote (0.95), Conventional (0.09), Non-conventional (0.11), Civic engagement (0.43)

The third group consists of *non-conventional and civic participants*. Members of this group have relatively low involvement in conventional political activities and are also quite unlikely to vote. However, they are highly likely to be involved in non-conventional activities and to be members of clubs and organisations. As such, they are generally politically and socially active, but seem to be disillusioned by the more traditional pathways that are typically open to people to have an influence on political issues, so instead opt to participate by non-conventional and civic means. This group is comparatively small, with less than 10 per cent of the sample. Members of this group tend to be younger, although the difference between this group and the inactive group is small. People from minorities are also more likely to be in this group than the highly active group, although they are less likely to be in this group than in the inactive group.

The remaining 41 per cent of people are those who engage in *voting only*. Despite their high tendency to vote, members of this group do not look for other ways in which they can participate in political and civic processes. This group is quite similar in demographic make-up to the highly active group but is more likely to be female.

Discussion

This analysis has identified four distinct groups in the population based on their patterns of political participation – ranging from the inactive to the highly active. That different groups participate in different ways is perhaps not altogether surprising, with existing evidence already suggesting that younger people tend to be involved in non-conventional forms of political activity but are under-represented in more conventional activities. However, this study has added to the existing evidence base by producing an empirical classification of participants. This has shown that many people only tend to vote and do not look to other avenues for participation in political and civic processes. A similar sized group is highly active, participating in a range of different ways. Comparatively few people have no involvement at all. It was also demonstrated that the demographic composition of these groups is markedly different from one another, with the most active people tending to be older, male and from the majority ethnic group. The existence of different groups of participants suggests that any interventions designed to promote participation need to be shaped in a way that recognises these differences, rather than attempting to adopt a 'one size fits all' approach. It also confirms that the biggest gains are to be had by focusing attention on younger citizens, women and those from minority groups, as these tend to be the least politically active members of society (at least when considering conventional means).

Final thoughts

Within the confines of this chapter, it has only been possible to provide a very cursory overview of some of the main findings from two parts of the secondary analysis work undertaken as part of the PIDOP project. Additional details on this research can be found in Brunton-Smith (2011), which includes a comprehensive examination of the complex pathways through which political, social and psychological factors shape levels of political and civic participation across Europe. This research has identified a number of ways that governments can work to enhance the levels of participation of their citizens, in particular among young people and minority groups and those who typically have lower levels of engagement in conventional political processes. Running throughout all of this work has been an emphasis on acknowledging the differences in the drivers of participation between groups, as well as the generalities that run across groups. Yet there are limits to the insights that can be gained from existing survey data, which is restricted in its scope for exploring the experiences of particular minority populations within countries, and there is a need to further define the specific mechanisms through which these factors influence levels of participation. Much of this work has been advanced through other parts of the PIDOP project, which is discussed in detail in the other chapters of this book.

Notes

1   All dependent variables are binary, therefore the logistic extension to the standard multilevel model was used. All models were estimated in Mlwin using second-order PQL.
2   These estimates are adjusted for differences in the socio-demographic composition of each country, ensuring differences are not simply the reflection of uneven participation rates between demographic groups across different countries.

References

Abramson, P. R. and Aldrich, J. H. (1982) 'The decline of electoral participation in America', *American Political Science Review*, 76: 502–21.
Albanesi, C., Cicognani, E. and Zani, B. (2007) 'Sense of community, civic engagement and social well-being in Italian adolescents', *Journal of Community and Applied Social Psychology*, 17: 387–406.
Allua, S., Stapleton, L. and Beretvas, S. (2008) 'Testing latent mean differences between observed and unobserved groups using multilevel factor mixture models', *Educational and Psychological Measurement*, 68 (3): 357–78.
Azevedo, C. N. and Menezes, I. (2007) 'Learning politics beyond cognition: the role of experience and participation in political development', in N. Krygerand and B. Ravn (eds), *Learning Beyond Cognition*. Copenhagen: Danish University of Education, pp. 95–114.
Brunton-Smith, I. (2011) *Modelling Existing Survey Data: Full Technical Report of PIDOP Work Package 5*. Department of Sociology, University of Surrey. Available online from: http://epubs.surrey.ac.uk/739988/2/PIDOP_WP5_Report.pdf_revised.pdf.
Caldeira, G. A., Patterson, S. C. and Markko, G. A. (1985) 'The mobilisation of voters in congressional elections', *Journal of Politics*, 48: 490–509.
Caprara, G. V., Schwartz, S., Capanna, C., Vecchione, M. and Barbaranelli, C. (2006) 'Personality and politics: values, trait and political choice', *Political Psychology*, 28: 609–32.
CIFP (2011) *Country Indicators for Foreign Policy: Governance and Democracy Processes*. Ottawa: Carleton University.

Císař, O. and Vráblíková, K. (2012) 'Contextual Determinants of Political Participation'. Unpublished paper, Work Package 3, PIDOP Project.

Craig, S. C., Niemi, R. G. and Silver, G. E. (1990) 'Political efficacy and trust: a report on the NES pilot study items', *Political Behaviour*, 12: 289–314.

Crystal, D. S. and DeBell, M. (2002) 'Sources of civic orientation among American youth: trust, religious valuation, and attributions of responsibility', *Political Psychology*, 23: 113–32.

Deaux, K., Reid, A., Martin, D. and Bikmen, N. (2006) 'Ideologies of diversity and inequality: predicting collective action in groups varying in ethnicity and immigrant status', *Political Psychology*, 27: 123–46.

Delli Carpini, M. and Keeter, S. (1996) *What Americans Know About Politics and Why It Matters*. New Haven, CT: Yale University Press.

Emler, N. and Frazer, E. (1999) 'Politics: the education effect', *Oxford Review of Education*, 25: 251–74.

Flanagan, C., Cumsille, P., Gill, S. and Gallay, L. (2007) 'School and community climates and civic commitments: patterns for ethnic minority and majority students', *Journal of Educational Psychology*, 99: 421–31.

Flanagan, C. A., Bowes, J. M., Jonsson, B., Csapo, B. and Sheblanova, E. (1998) 'Ties that bind: correlates of adolescents' civic commitments in seven countries', *Journal of Social Issues*, 54: 457–75.

Galligan, Y. (2012) 'The Contextual and Individual Determinants of Women's Civic Engagement and Political Participation'. Unpublished paper, PIDOP Project.

Garry, J. (2010) 'Studying formal participation in Europe: an assessment of the role of context and the individual – the empirical challenges', *Written Report on Workshop 2 by WP3, The PIDOP Project*. Belfast: Queen's University Belfast.

Geys, B. (2006) 'Explaining voter turnout: a review of aggregate-level research', *Electoral Studies*, 25: 637–63.

Gniewosz, B., Noack, P. and Buhl, M. (2009) 'Political alienation in adolescence: associations with parental role models, parenting styles and classroom climate', *International Journal of Behavioral Development*, 3: 337–46.

Goldstein, H. (2010) *Multilevel Statistical Models*, 4th edn. Chichester: Wiley.

Hahn, C. (1998) *Becoming Political: Comparative Perspectives on Citizenship Education*. Albany, NY: State University of New York Press.

Hart, D. and Atkins, R. (2002) 'Civic development in urban youth', *Applied Developmental Science*, 6: 227–36.

Hart, D., Atkins, R. and Ford, D. (1998) 'Urban America as a context for the development of moral identity in adolescence', *Journal of Social Issues*, 54: 513–30.

Highton, B. and Wolfinger, R. E. (1998) 'Estimating the effects of the National Voter Registration Act of 1993', *Political Behavior*, 20: 79–104.

Ichilov, O. (1991) 'Political socialization and schooling effects among Israeli adolescents', *Comparative Education Review*, 35: 430–47.

Jackman, R. W. (1987) 'Political institutions and voter turnout in the industrial democracies', *American Political Science Review*, 81: 405–23.

Jackman, R. and Miller, R. A. (1995) 'Voter turnout in the industrial democracies during the 1980s', *Comparative Political Studies*, 27: 467–92.

Jennings, M. K. (1996) 'Political knowledge over time and across generations', *Political Opinion Quarterly*, 60: 228–52.

Jensen, L. A. (2010) 'Immigrant youth in the United States: coming of age in diverse cultures', in L. R. Sherrod, J. Torney-Purta and C. A. Flanagan (eds), *Handbook of Research on Civic Engagement in Youth*. Hoboken, NJ: John Wiley & Sons, pp. 425–43.

Kriesi, H., Koopmans, R., Duyvendak, J. W. and Giugni, M. G. (1995) *New Social Movements in Western Europe: A Comparative Analysis*. London: UCL Press.

Leach, C. W., Iyer, A. and Pedersen, A. (2006) 'Anger and guilt about ingroup advantage explain the willingness for political action', *Personality and Social Psychology Bulletin*, 32: 1232–45.

Lopez, M. H. and Marcelo, K. B. (2008) 'The civic engagement of immigrant youth: new evidence from the 2006 Civic and Political Health of the Nation Survey', *Applied Developmental Science*, 12: 66–73.

Lubke, G. H. and Muthén, B. (2005) 'Investigating population heterogeneity with factor mixture models', *Psychological Methods*, 10: 21–39.

Mattila, M. (2003) 'Why bother? Determinants of turnout in the European elections', *Electoral Studies*, 22: 449–68.

Montgomery, V. (2012) 'Full Technical Report of the Political Theory of Civic and Political Participation Developed by WP3: Summary and Discussion'. Unpublished paper, PIDOP Project.

Nie, N. H., Junn, J. and Stehlik-Barry, K. (1996) *Education and Democratic Citizenship in America*. Chicago: University of Chicago Press.

Omoto, A. M. and Snyder, M. (1995) 'Sustained helping without obligation: motivation, longevity of service, and perceived attitude change among AIDS volunteers', *Journal of Personality and Social Psychology*, 68: 671–86.

Omoto, A. M. and Snyder, M. (2002) 'Considerations of community: the context and process of volunteerism', *American Behavioral Scientist*, 45: 846–67.

Powell, G. B. (1986) 'American voter turnout in comparative perspective', *American Political Science Review*, 80: 17–43.

Schulz, W. (2005) *Political Efficacy and Expected Participation Among Lower and Upper Secondary Students. A Comparative Analysis with Data from the IEA Civic Education Study*. Paper presented at the ECPR General Conference, Budapest, 8–10 September 2005.

Schulz, W., Ainley, J., Fraillon, J., Kerr, D. and Losito, B. (2010) *Initial Findings from the IEA International Civic and Citizenship Education Study*. Amsterdam: IEA.

Simon, B., Loewy, M., Sturmer, S., Weber, U., Freytag, P., Habig, C., Kampmeier, C. and Spahlinger, P. (1998) 'Collective identification and social movement participation', *Journal of Personality and Social Psychology*, 74: 646–58.

Smith, E. S. (1999) 'The effects of investments in the social capital of youth on political and civic behaviour in young adulthood: a longitudinal analysis', *Political Psychology*, 20: 553–80.

Stepick, A., Stepick, C. D. and Labissiere, Y. (2008) 'South Florida's immigrant youth and civic engagement: major engagement: minor differences', *Applied Developmental Science*, 12: 57–65.

Torney-Purta, J. and Amadeo, J.-A. (2003) 'A cross-national analysis of political and civic involvement among adolescents', *PS: Political Science and Politics*, 36: 269–74.

Torney-Purta, J., Lehmann, R., Oswald, H. and Schulz, W. (2001) *Citizenship and Education in Twenty-Eight Countries: Civic Knowledge and Engagement at Age Fourteen*. Amsterdam: IEA.

van Zomeren, M., Postmes, T. and Spears, R. (2008) 'Toward an integrative social identity model of collective action: a quantitative research synthesis of three socio-psychological perspectives', *Psychological Bulletin*, 134: 504–35.

van Zomeren, M., Spears, R., Fischer, A. and Leach, C. W. (2004) 'Put your money where your mouth is! Explaining collective action tendencies through group-based anger and group efficacy', *Journal of Personality and Social Psychology*, 87: 649–64.

Verba, S., Schlozman, K. L. and Brady, H. E. (1995) *Voice and Equality: Civic Volunteerism in American Politics*. Cambridge, MA: Harvard University Press.

Vráblíková, K. (2010) 'Contextual Determinants of Political Participation in Democratic Countries'. Unpublished paper, Work Package 3, PIDOP Project.

Vráblíková, K. (2014) 'How context matters? Mobilization, political opportunity structures, and nonelectoral political participation in old and new democracies', *Comparative Political Studies*, 47 (2): 203–29.

Wray-Lake, L., Syvertsen, A. K. and Flanagan, C. A. (2008) 'Contested citizenship and social exclusion: adolescent Arab American immigrants' views of the social contract', *Applied Developmental Science*, 12: 84–92.

Zaff, J. F., Malanchuk, O. and Eccles, J. S. (2008) 'Predicting positive citizenship from adolescence to young adulthood: the effects of a civic context', *Applied Developmental Science*, 12: 38–53.

Zukin, C., Keeter, S., Andolina, M., Jenkins, K. and Delli Carpini, M. X. (2006) *A New Engagement? Political Participation, Civic Life, and the Changing American Citizen*. New York: Oxford University Press.

12
CIVIC ORGANIZATIONS AND THE INTERNET AS THE OPPORTUNITIES FOR MINORITY YOUTH CIVIC PARTICIPATION

Findings from the Czech Republic[1]

Jan Šerek, Zuzana Petrovičová and Petr Macek

Introduction

An important task of a democratic society is to make sure that all its members have enough opportunities to participate in public life and make their voice heard. Civic participation is essential especially in the case of ethnic minority members who face rejection by the majority. The civic participation of these people is restricted not only by objective obstacles, such as the language barrier, but by psychological obstacles as well. Participation in public life can be very difficult if people do not feel good in the greater society and feel that the majority society does not accept them. However, if members of ethnic minorities are not involved in political decision-making and do not assert their interests, it is possible that decisions which are made only reduce their status. The growing civic passivity of ethnic minorities and their worsening status in society can easily result in a vicious circle which leads to a feeling of frustration and mutual alienation between the social groups. Therefore supporting civic participation of minority members, especially the disadvantaged, is not only a realization of an abstract democratic ideal, but also an essential step to providing more long-term social stability.

The aim of this chapter is to describe factors that can facilitate civic participation for young people from ethnic minorities. It is based on the analysis of qualitative and quantitative data collected in the Czech Republic within the PIDOP project from respondents aged from 15 to 28 years of age (Šerek et al. 2012; Šerek et al. 2011). As will be described in the next section, due to its ethnic homogeneity and the relative novelty of the phenomenon of immigration, the Czech Republic represents an interesting field for researching the civic participation of minorities. We will concentrate on two ethnic groups – the Roma as the largest non-immigrant minority and Ukrainians as the largest immigrant minority. In order to place these minorities in a broader context, the majority group will be included as well in all the analyses. Factors facilitating civic participation will be described on the basis of comparing young people who are not involved in civic participation with those who do spend some of their time engaging in civic activities. According to our findings, the following two factors are of special importance: civic organizations and the Internet.

The situation of ethnic minorities in the Czech Republic

In the second half of the twentieth century, the Czech Republic (or the Czech part of the former Czechoslovakia) was characterized by considerable ethnic and cultural homogeneity. It was caused mainly by the holocaust of the Jews and Roma in World War II and the postwar deportation of Germans, as well as the authoritarian communist regime that restricted the arrival of foreigners on Czech territory. More crucial changes in the ethnic composition of inhabitants occurred relatively recently in connection with the opening of borders after 1989 and the accession to the European Union in 2004, which allows foreigners from other member countries of the Union to settle freely on Czech territory and find a job there. The growth in temporary and permanent immigration presents a challenge for the social majority of how to cope with this previously unknown situation and how to involve the members of ethnic minorities in the functioning of society (Wallace 2002).

The attitude of the majority society to the ever-growing ethnic minorities can be referred to as ambivalent. On the one hand, the inhabitants of the Czech Republic tend to believe that discrimination against ethnic minorities is gradually declining (European Commission 2008), which corresponds with a growing tolerance of the majority of some ethnic minorities (Drbohlav et al. 2009). However, on the other hand, it is not possible to claim that all ethnic minorities in Czech society are fully accepted. Even though open xenophobia appears relatively rarely in Czech society, a substantial part of the majority has rather intolerant attitudes to some minorities. Increased intolerance is displayed especially towards the Roma, Ukrainians and immigrants from the Balkans. The relationship of the majority to these minorities is very much affected by stereotypes of their members (Leontiyeva and Novotný 2010). Within the European Union, the Czech Republic is one of the countries where inhabitants are the most afraid that their neighbor or main political representative will be a person from a different ethnic group (European Commission 2008). Hence it is no surprise that a number of members of the majority are in favor of preserving the ethnic homogeneity of Czech society. For instance, this attitude is evident in refusing to allow a more intensive inflow of immigrants into the Czech Republic (Rabušic and Burjanek 2003) and the belief that the state invests too much money in helping foreigners (Leontiyeva and Novotný 2010). Therefore, although there is no prevailing general grudge against minorities in Czech society, some minorities are exposed to great intolerance and there are clear tendencies to keep the society ethnically homogeneous.

It is especially attitudes towards the two most significant ethnic minorities in the Czech Republic – Roma and Ukrainians – that are loaded with little tolerance and negative stereotypes. As for the Roma, their status in society goes hand in hand with complicated historical developments. During World War II, a majority of the original Czech Roma were deported and murdered, as they represented an inferior ethnic group according to Nazi ideology (Horváthová 2002). After the end of World War II, encouraged by the government, the Slovak Roma came to the Czech territory and settled mostly in the border areas and big cities. Up until the fall of communism in 1989, the Roma had faced a policy of forced assimilation which, on the one hand, led to an increased standard of living for the Roma population but, on the other hand, resulted in the breakup of the traditional Roma joint families, the decline of Roma culture and the suppression of the Roma ethnic identity. It is mainly the arrival of the culturally distinct Slovak Roma and indifferent government policy towards this group that are identified as the main causes of the problematic status of the Roma in Czech society (Pečínka 2004). There are more people with low education among the Roma than in the majority population. Due to their low qualifications, many Roma struggle with unemployment or work as unskilled blue-collar workers. This is also related to a higher degree of poverty and social exclusion if the Roma and the majority population are compared (Horváthová 2002; Navrátil et al. 2003). Despite some partial progress, the legal system is still not able to efficiently prevent some cases of biased behavior or discrimination, and hence the Roma often feel that they are victims of non-violent and violent discrimination. The discrimination often concerns access to education and the labor market, the distribution of flats by authorities and treatment in public places such as restaurants (Černý et al. 2006; Kašparová et al. 2008; Zhřívalová and Kocourek, 2002). Moreover, a number of Roma do not consider it worthwhile defending themselves against discrimination legally, as they consider state institutions to be incapable of justly punishing offenders (Zhřívalová and Kocourek 2002).

As opposed to the Roma, Ukrainians represent an immigrant minority with a clearly identified country of origin. Although Ukrainian immigration has had a long tradition on Czech territory, its substantial increase started only twenty years ago. The reasons for immigration are principally economic, as the Czech Republic offers a relatively high number of jobs for unskilled workers (Novotná 2005). The economic motivation is usually accompanied by an effort to achieve more stable social security and a better quality of life (Leontiyeva and Nečasová, 2009). Another distinct group of migrants is represented by university graduates coming to the Czech Republic as entrepreneurs and academic workers (Leontiyeva 2006). The involvement of Ukrainians in Czech society is closely connected to the purpose of their stay in the Czech Republic. The most intensive involvement is evident in people who have a Czech partner and regard the Czech Republic as their new home (Novotná 2005). Crucial factors affecting integration into society are language skills, familiarity with Czech culture and a circle of friends in the new country (Leontiyeva and Nečasová 2009). However, the involvement of Ukrainian immigrants in Czech society is often complicated by a lack of trust and prejudice on the part of the majority. The relationship of the majority to Ukrainian immigration often reflects the fears of seasonal unskilled workers, which is a stereotype often associated with this minority (Leontiyeva and Novotný 2010; Novotná 2005). Other fears are of cheap competition in the labor market and historical reminiscences of the former Soviet Union. Similarly to the Roma, a number of Ukrainians exhibit dissatisfaction with the unsupportive approach of Czech institutions and discrimination in the labor market (Horáková 2001; Novotná 2005).

Due to the aforementioned problems, it may be difficult for the members of both ethnic minorities to assert themselves in public life. For many of them, civic participation means overcoming objective barriers provided by the complicated socio-economic situation, language or absence of some political rights. For instance, to have the right to vote or to become members of political parties, Ukrainian immigrants need to obtain Czech citizenship, which is possible only after a five-year permanent stay in the Czech Republic. Moreover, frequent encounters with stereotypes and discrimination undermine the relationship of ethnic minority members to majority society and reduce their motivation to participate actively in its functioning.

Types and modes of civic participation

In order to examine the factors promoting the civic participation of ethnic minority youth, first we identified what forms of civic participation occur among them. We drew on survey data from 203 Roma, 167 Ukrainian and 825 majority participants (aged 15–28) who completed self-report questionnaires on their civic behaviors, attitudes and socio-demographic characteristics. Recruitment of participants was performed through contacting elementary schools, secondary schools, universities, non-governmental organizations and social workers. Among other questionnaire items, participants were presented with a list of civic activities (e.g. donating money to a social or political cause/organization) and asked whether they had done these activities during the last 12 months. A five-point response scale, ranging from *never* to *very often*, was offered (see Appendix C for the full list).

Using exploratory factor analysis and subsequent multi-group confirmatory factor analysis, we found that in the case of both ethnic minorities as well as the majority, civic participation can be divided into three types of activities. The first type comprises activities undertaken *personally in the real world*, such as voluntary work, wearing symbols, donating money or participating in a charity event. It is a common category of civic participation that has a long-established tradition and is typically viewed by society as desirable. In addition, there is a second type containing activities taking place on the *Internet*, that is forwarding links, Internet discussions, browsing political web pages, participating in an online petition or joining a social network group. The distinctive features of Internet participation are greater anonymity and convenience, while simultaneously posing greater demands on a certain type of skill (computer literacy). Civic participation on the Internet is a relatively new type of civic activism representing an alternative to participation in the real world (Bennett 2008; Bennett et al. 2010). Yet at the same time, participating in the Internet can easily turn into real-world participation and vice versa.

For instance, discussion in an online social network (e.g. Facebook) can serve as a basis for a real-life demonstration just as boycotting goods made by a certain company can be extended to boycotting their web pages (Rojas and Puig-i-Abril 2009). Finally, the last type of civic activity to be found is *radical* activity including writing political graffiti and participating in illegal events. As opposed to the previous two types, radical activities differ by their non-normativity, that is by being beyond the limits of what the majority society approves and regards as acceptable (Wright et al. 1990). The tendency towards this type of civic participation is usually motivated by very different reasons from participating in socially acceptable normative activities (Tausch et al. 2011).[2]

In both ethnic minorities and the majority, it was personal participation and participation on the Internet that occurred most frequently, while radical participation was very rare. To understand the relative unpopularity of radical participation, we reanalyzed transcripts of 14 focus group discussions, organized separately with young Roma, Ukrainians, and Czechs. Participants were recruited via schools, online advertisements, non-governmental organizations, and snowballing in order to capture young people with different levels of civic involvement. In each focus group, four to eight young participants and two trained moderators were present. The moderators introduced discussion topics such as general beliefs on or personal experiences with civic participation, and they stimulated participants to express their ideas, to share their experiences, to react to each other, and to bring in their own new topics. Transcripts of the focus groups were coded and qualitatively analyzed using thematic analysis (Braun and Clarke 2006).

We discovered that young people report two general reasons for why they prefer normative activities to non-normative ones. First, they believe that non-normative activism leads to unnecessary damage and that it imposes a heavy burden for the people affected and society. The second reason is doubts about the effectiveness of non-normative activities accompanied by fears that these activities can be counterproductive under certain conditions. This is no surprise, as in today's Czech Republic radical activism more usually represents a marginal activity attracting only a limited number of people (Císař et al. 2011). The low importance of radical activities is also evident through looking at Czech history which has no tradition of radical civic protests. Therefore in further research we focused exclusively on normative activities representing the prevailing form of civic participation in the Czech environment.

Many young people are involved not only in one kind of civic activity but in a combination of activities. Therefore, in the next step, we used the survey data to find out what overall modes of civic participation are currently present among young people. Three types of participation (personal, Internet, and radical) were entered into hierarchical (Ward method) and k-means cluster analysis. Eventually, three basic modes of civic participation were found. The first mode was represented by people who were not active in civic participation at all or very seldom, either personally in the real world or on the Internet. Hence we labeled this approach *low participation*. The second mode was composed of people who participated only on

TABLE 12.1 Frequency of the three modes of civic participation

	Roma	Ukrainians	Majority
Low participation	109 (67%)	71 (57%)	310 (44%)
Only online participation	20 (12%)	28 (23%)	207 (29%)
Multiple participation	33 (20%)	25 (20%)	191 (27%)
Total	162 (100%)	124 (100%)	708 (100%)

the Internet, but not personally in the real world. This mode of participation can be referred to as *only online participation*. The last mode was characteristic of civic participation in both environments, that is both personal in the real world and on the Internet. As these people used for their participation many available means at once, we labeled their approach *multiple participation*. The exact numbers of persons in our sample representing these individual modes of civic participation can be found in Table 12.1. It is worth noting that there were only a few people participating personally in the real world and simultaneously not participating on the Internet. This shows the major role played by the Internet in civic participation among today's youth. Furthermore, radical participation was very scarce in all three modes of civic participation.

Organizations and other social contexts

I think it's really all about meeting the right people. Because for example me, if I hadn't found myself in [the organization], I wouldn't be taking up the opportunities. Like I care about school and I care about having a job, and then I care about having a family. And if I just have an opportunity to take part in an activity, then I go for it. But that I'd be voluntarily surfing the Internet and looking for some fundraisers to be able to take part in them, it just doesn't work that way. If I'm told by a friend of mine or somebody, come on, let's go and see it, then I do.

(Roma woman)

When I'm here in the Czech Republic, I hardly participate in anything, since I don't have people like that, or I don't have possibilities how to take part in anything. But it's a huge difference because I was quite an active person in Ukraine and I was in social organizations – I was in such an organization at university. We did some debates and conferences all the time.

(Ukrainian woman)

Well, I am happy to have actually found somebody who'd introduce me to something I'd enjoy. And they were people who had known me since I was a child and they knew what I could be good or bad at. Well, and if it hadn't been for them, then we could see each other in the pub.

(Roma woman)

The quotes above come from focus groups we conducted with the participants of our research. These and a number of other responses illustrate that civic participation is closely related to one's social environment. As current studies suggest, one's experiences from civic organizations are of specific importance: young people who have been members of civic organizations take part in a wide range of civic activities in their future lives more frequently than people who have never participated in such organizations (Beck and Jennings 1982; Kahne and Sporte 2008; McFarland and Thomas 2006; Smith 1999). There are two possible explanations for this. Organizations provide young people with the necessary information and material background, and an opportunity to develop their civic competences such as debating or public speaking (Andolina et al. 2003; McFarland and Thomas 2006). At the same time, in many organizations there is a very strong participatory norm; in other words, in these environments it is regarded as natural or even desirable to take part in civic activities. The feeling that others appreciate and approve one's civic activities considerably increases motivation to continue with these activities (Ajzen 1991; Glasford 2008). Moreover, in an environment with a strong participatory norm there is a greater chance that one will be asked to participate or will meet with positive role models of civic participation (Verba et al. 1995).

The link between participating in civic organizations and higher civic participation has also been found in young people from ethnic minority groups (Seif 2010). In addition to providing young people with supportive background and participatory norms, civic organizations give minority youth an opportunity to become more familiar with the majority society and to overcome potential cultural, linguistic, or information barriers (Youniss et al. 2002). Trust in social institutions and identification with the broader society (which does not contradict but complements one's sense of ethnic identity) create favorable conditions motivating minority members into civic participation (Chryssochoou and Lyons 2011; Jensen 2008; Simon and Grabow 2010). Furthermore, for the young who feel discriminated against or even threatened by the majority society, civic organizations can represent a safe place where they do not need to be afraid to share their feelings and opinions about society (Seif 2010).

In order to verify whether the link between organizations and participation also applies among Roma and Ukrainians in the Czech Republic, we divided the survey participants according to whether they had or had not collaborated with a civic organization. By civic organization we meant trade union, student, political, youth, human rights, or ecological associations. It was found that even a short-term collaboration with an organization was related to greater civic participation. Among people participating in civic activities (both 'only online' and 'multiple'), there was always a great prevalence of those who had collaborated with an organization at least once in their lives. By contrast, among people with low participation, contacts

TABLE 12.2 Relation between civic participation and organizational involvement

	Collaborated with some civic organizations					
	Roma[a]		Ukrainians[b]		Majority[c]	
Participation	No	Yes	No	Yes	No	Yes
Low	66%	34%	41%	59%	54%	46%
Only online	15%	85%	25%	75%	32%	68%
Multiple	41%	59%	16%	84%	16%	84%

[a]Cramer's V = 0.37; χ^2_2 = 21.15; p < 0.01.
[b]Cramer's V = 0.23; χ^2_2 = 6.18; p < 0.05.
[c]Cramer's V = 0.33; χ^2_2 = 76.07; p < 0.05.

with organizations were less frequent. The link between cooperation with organizations and civic participation was manifested in all three ethnic groups (both minorities and majority). This correlation was the strongest among the Roma while for the Ukrainians, the correlation between civic participation and organizations was the weakest yet still quite distinct (Table 12.2).

Further analyses also revealed that civic participation does not depend so much on the intensity of collaboration, but rather on whether the person cooperates with more organizations having various orientations. Among the young Roma and Ukrainians who had very intensively (for over six months) cooperated with a civic organization, low participation occurred just as frequently (44 percent in Roma; 53 percent in Ukrainians) as in those who had worked with organizations only occasionally (53 percent in Roma; 51 percent in Ukrainians). On the other hand, in young people who had collaborated with more varied organizations in the past (three organization types and more), low participation occurred significantly less frequently (26 percent in Roma; 24 percent in Ukrainians) than in those who had collaborated only with organizations of one type (67 percent both in Roma and Ukrainians).

These findings confirm that organizations represent an important arena for the civic participation of ethnic minority youth. Simultaneously, even occasional contact with more varied organizations appears to be more beneficial for the development of civic participation than intensive collaboration with a single, narrowly focused organization. It can be ascribed to the fact that collaboration with multiple organizations increases the likelihood that somebody will ask a person to participate (Teorell 2003). In addition, membership in organizations seems to encourage people to get involved in society only if they encounter openness to various opinions, plurality of approaches and people from various ethnic and social groups. On the other hand, taking part in a limited circle of organizations in which one only meets similar people and where there is strong accord of opinions and thematic bias does not contribute much to the development of civic participation (Stolle 1998; Stolle and

Rochon 1998). The aforementioned discovery is also in line with more general developmental findings. According to these, adaptive psychosocial development of youth from ethnically diverse and poor neighborhoods is best if they engage in and develop their competences in more varied areas (Pedersen et al. 2005).

Nevertheless, civic organizations do not represent the only social environment that can influence the civic participation of the young. A strong participatory norm can also be established in the circle of family and friends. By participatory norm, we mean the degree of parents' and friends' approval of participation, their positive appreciation of participation, and their actual level of participation. If young people grow up in families in which civic participation is regarded as important and where some members participate, it stimulates their own interest to take part in such activities. Likewise, in the environment of friends and peers with a strong participatory norm, it is more likely that one will participate as well (Beck and Jennings 1991; Duke et al. 2009; Zukin et al. 2006). Similar to the case of civic organizations, the following aspects play a role: development of civic skills, a greater likelihood that one will be asked to participate, presence of positive examples, and the motivating effect of the belief that one's behavior is approved by others.

Looking at the participants in our survey, the correlation between civic participation and the participatory norm[3] of the surrounding environment was evident especially among the Roma. The young Roma who took part in civic activities (both only online and multiple participation) perceived a much stronger participatory norm in their parents and friends than those with low participation. A very similar pattern was found also in the majority and partially also in the Ukrainians. However, in their case a stronger participatory norm was found only when comparing people with low and online participation, but not when comparing people with low and multiple participation[4] (Table 12.3).

TABLE 12.3 Relation between modes of civic participation and participatory norms

	Strength of participatory norm					
	Roma		Ukrainians		Majority	
Participation	Parents[a]	Friends[b]	Parents[c]	Friends[d]	Parents[e]	Friends[f]
Low	2.22	2.12	2.27	2.27	2.31	2.61
Only online	2.62	3.37	2.68	2.79	2.71	3.03
Multiple	2.81	2.84	1.85	2.38	2.84	3.23

[a]$F(2,157) = 4.71$, $p < 0.05$; $\eta^2 = 0.06$.
[b]$F(2,156) = 19.95$, $p < 0.01$; $\eta^2 = 0.20$.
[c]$F(2,105) = 5.18$, $p < 0.01$; $\eta^2 = 0.09$.
[d]$F(2,105) = 2.75$, $p = 0.07$; $\eta^2 = 0.05$.
[e]$F(2,600) = 22.95$, $p < 0.01$; $\eta^2 = 0.07$.
[f]$F(2,599) = 31.10$, $p < 0.01$; $\eta^2 = 0.09$.
Note: Higher numbers refer to stronger norms. Values could theoretically range from 1 to 5.

Hence whether we speak of formal environments such as civic organizations, or informal environments such as family and friends, it is evident that civic participation is usually not a matter of solitary activists. On the contrary, civic participation flourishes if one can rely on people of similar opinions in one's environment (Zukin et al. 2006). This, however, brings up the question of causality. Undeniably, an environment with a strong norm of civic participation has a great impact on people and their behavior. On the other hand, young people interested in civic participation are likely to actively look for organizations and circles of people with a similar interest, and to actively persuade their friends and parents to participate. Moreover, children's influence on parental civic attitudes and behavior can be particularly strong in immigrant families if parents' contact with the majority society is mediated by their children (Bloemraad and Trost 2008; Wong and Tseng 2008). In our opinion, both processes mutually complement each other. At the beginning, one's general interest in the surrounding society can lead to openness to meeting people or organizations that are civically active. In such an environment, one can encounter incentives that will help to specify an originally vague interest in society more closely. For instance, these incentives can involve engaging in discussions, observing role models, or getting practical advice and background in order to initiate civic participation. Consequently, through their own participation, young people meet others who can further shape their civic participation.

Participation on the Internet

Up to this point, we have approached civic participation as generally desirable and positive. However, civic participation does not necessarily bring only positive experiences to people, especially if they belong to a minority group with a complicated position in society. Although we stressed the importance of civic organizations in the previous section, people from ethnic minorities need not necessarily encounter only positive reactions in civic organizations, but also stereotypes, prejudice and non-acceptance (Seif 2010). Furthermore, the civic participation of minority youth is often aimed at helping other members of their community and at breaking down the stereotypes about their ethnic group (Stepick and Stepick 2002; Jensen 2010), which may result in direct confrontations with persons holding negative attitudes towards their ethnic group. One can expect that, in the long-term perspective, this kind of experience will evoke in some people negative feelings towards the majority society and doubts about the purpose of their own participation.

The presence of negative emotions in minority members who actively participate in society is evident from the analysis of our focus groups. Frustration and disillusion from the permanent struggle with negative stereotypes and prejudice was apparent especially in the Roma who were highly active in civic life. Some of them described their situation as 'somewhere in between' their own ethnic group and the majority. They did not feel trusted either by other Roma, who perceived them as being too similar to the majority, or by the majority, who viewed them on the basis of negative stereotypes about the Roma:

The Roma involved in civic organizations who go for it a hundred percent will burn themselves out twice as quickly as you [the majority]. Because they always battle with two sides. So it's demanding and I myself am not into always defending the Whites against the Roma and the Roma against the Whites every day, to be in the middle and keep fighting for something all the time.

(Roma woman)

Moreover, although some Roma respondents felt that they were regarded as non-stereotypical Roma by majority members, they still perceived their position as rather problematic. They viewed as especially bothersome the majority's expectations that as civically active Roma, they represented the entire Roma community and were responsible for all of its members. One young woman described it as annoying when she was not viewed by others as a person but only as a positive example of a non-stereotypical Roma:

I am engaged in the way that suits me, and I can absolutely imagine that I probably wouldn't want to represent and take up that post when I am here acting for the Roma minority and being responsible for everyone. Because that's the way it is. An engaged Roma holding high posts is considered to be representing everybody and that often deprives him of the possibility to be just on his own.

(Roma woman)

Regarding these findings, the question arises of whether there are means available to young people from ethnic minorities that allow them to be active in civic life without facing such negative experiences. Currently, there is a growing importance of civic participation on the Internet, which provides young citizens with new opportunities to share information, join various online groups, and coordinate civic activities (Bennett *et al.* 2010). Civic participation on the Internet seems to be an attractive tool not only for majority members, but also for minority youth (Bloemraad and Trost 2008). While it may be difficult for these young people to address a wider audience via personal communication or traditional media, the Internet provides them with a wide and easily accessible space to share their own experience, promote important issues, and create alternatives to the mainstream image of their minority group. Moreover, thanks to the possibility of partially concealing their own identity, Internet participation allows minority people who feel threatened in society in some way to express their ideas more freely (Seif 2011).

Thus we decided to take a closer look at whether there are negative feelings among ethnic minority youth and how people participating in the real world and on the Internet differ in this respect. According to previous research, civic participation tends to be accompanied by positive social orientations such as higher levels of trust in social institutions (e.g. government) and a positive view of society and its future development (Keyes 1998; Putnam 2000; Torney-Purta *et al.* 2004).

At the same time, civic participation often goes together with a personal concern for social problems, for example anger over perceived social injustice (Klandermans et al. 2008; Tausch et al. 2011). Hence we examined in what combinations these characteristics had occurred in the survey respondents with various modes of civic participation. Four orientations were captured. First, we measured participants' general *evaluation of society*, which was their overall evaluation of society's functioning and direction, understood as a combination of three sub-dimensions of social well-being (social coherence, actualization, and acceptance: Keyes 1998).[5] Second, participants' *trust in institutions* was measured as a mean of their trust in six important authorities of Czech society (national government, European Union, local governments, courts, police, and political parties).[6] Finally, the level of participants' *anger* over minority discrimination in Czech society and their *hope* that this discrimination can be eliminated were measured.[7]

There were differences both between the ethnic groups and between people with different modes of participation. In Ukrainians and the majority, there was the anticipated trend according to which people with multiple civic modes of participation trusted the institutions, had a more optimistic view of the functioning of society and a greater hope for the possibility of eliminating discrimination, but at the same time they felt more anger over discrimination than people with low participation. Moreover, it is no surprise that the more means a person used to participate (only online vs. multiple), the stronger the trend that was manifested. However, looking at young Roma with multiple participation, we also found greater trust in institutions and stronger anger over discrimination than in their non-participating peers, yet they showed only a weak belief that discrimination could be eliminated and that society functioned in a desirable way. We assume that this finding presents further evidence of the frustration and disillusion among civically active young Roma, evident also in the aforementioned responses. Even though these young people held at least basic trust in social institutions, without which participation would be nearly impossible, they exhibited much less optimism regarding the future development of society. Nevertheless, we regard it as crucial that this trend occurred only among the Roma who participated simultaneously on the Internet and in the real world. On the contrary, the Roma who participated only on the Internet evaluated society in the most positive way and held the highest hopes that discrimination could be eliminated (Figure 12.1).

Our findings lead to two conclusions. First, it is confirmed that civic participation can be associated with negative feelings, yet not necessarily in all ethnic minorities. Participating Roma are likely to frequently encounter stereotypes and prejudice from the surrounding society. Moreover, even if they manage to persuade others that they personally do not fit the stereotype, they still feel that they are more likely to be perceived as representatives of their ethnic group than as unique persons, or they also feel that they are expected to play a role as a positive example in contrast to other, stereotypically perceived, members of their minority (Šerek et al. 2011). Hence it is not surprising that they feel frustrated after some time and form a more negative view of society. On the other hand, participating

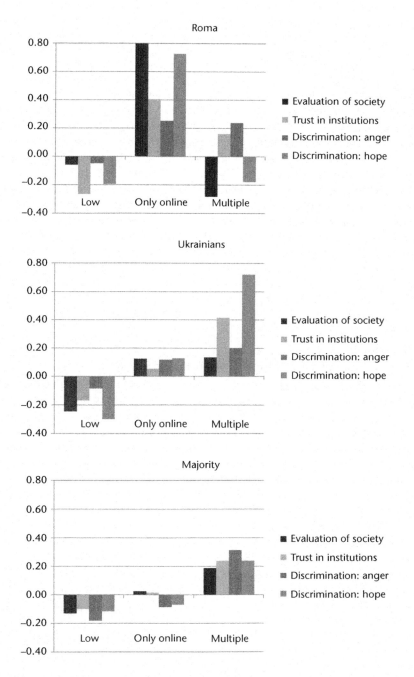

FIGURE 12.1 Relationships between civic participation and evaluation of society, trust in institutions, anger, and hope regarding discrimination

Note: Variables are standardized for each ethnic group separately.

Ukrainians probably do not have as many negative reactions in Czech society as young Roma. As described above, the stereotypes and prejudice towards Ukrainians in the Czech Republic are closely connected to the image of unskilled workers, fear of a cheap workforce and reminiscences of the Soviet Union. However, young people participating in society do not fit into all these categories at first sight and they may possibly encounter more favorable acceptance than older members of this minority. As a result, the absence of distinct negative experience enables young Ukrainians to keep a more positive view of Czech society. Therefore civic participation seems to be associated with completely different experiences, depending on how one is accepted by others (cf. Chryssochoou and Lyons 2011).

Second, it turns out that negative feelings are associated only with participation in the real world, not participation in the online environment. This may be explained by the fact that the Internet represents a safe environment for civic participation. The young participating Roma object in particular to the need to compare themselves, in the eyes of the majority, with the stereotypes of their group. However, thanks to its partial anonymity, the Internet environment might allow them to conceal their identity at times and be for others a 'person', not a 'Roma'. In addition, anonymous participation enables them to avoid some of the personal attacks that they would have to face in the real world. Furthermore, even if one does not try to hide one's identity, it is still easier in the online space than in face-to-face contact to check what environments one finds oneself in and with which people one is communicating. As opposed to that, civic participation in the real world means being exposed to a series of situations in which minority members experience dismissive reactions from various sides. For example, voluntary work, the most frequent civic activity among the Roma, is mostly based on direct personal contact with others, during which one can come up against a number of stereotypes and prejudice. Therefore, in comparison with participating in the real world, pure online participation can enhance an optimistic opinion that society is developing in a desirable direction and that it is possible to successfully fight social injustice.

Concluding remarks

In this chapter, we have described, on the basis of findings from the Czech Republic, two factors that can help young people from ethnic minorities facilitate their civic participation. The first factor is their social environment, in particular civic organizations, which provide young people with an opportunity to join civic activities. The second factor is the Internet, which can represent an alternative for young people from minorities who have a complicated position in the majority society of how to avoid the frustration and disillusion that they would face if they participated in the real world. On the grounds of these findings, it is theoretically possible to give two recommendations of how to support ethnic minority youth in their civic participation: first, it is desirable to support the foundation and functioning of civic organizations open to people of various ethnic background, and second, it is advisable to guarantee easy access to the Internet for all social groups.

However, both recommendations must be placed in a wider context. Based on previous findings and our own results, contact with civic organizations seems to have a positive effect only when one encounters, via organizations, a plurality of approaches, opinions, and issues. In contrast, it can be assumed that contact with a small circle of ideologically and socially homogeneous organizations can make a person shut themselves off into their own ideological or ethnic community (Theiss-Morse and Hibbing 2005). Therefore we see it as highly desirable to go one step further than simply supporting the founding of civic organizations focused on ethnic minority youth, and to deliberately create the conditions that will give young people from ethnic minorities an opportunity to engage with organizations of various types.

Similarly, concerning online civic participation, one cannot claim that it is a guaranteed method for supporting ethnic minority youth in their involvement in society. Online civic participation is such a new phenomenon that it cannot be clearly determined what consequences it may bring. On the one hand, we can regard online civic participation as a continuation of traditional offline participation by different means and appreciate that the young generation has found a way of their own to express themselves about social issues. On the other hand, however, there are voices saying that the environment of the Internet in fact does not allow real civic participation and the turn of the young to the Internet is only an expression of, or even a contribution to, the decline of the debate on politics and social problems (for the definition of both paradigms, see Bennett 2008). Moreover, if we are not sure of the consequences to which the online civic life of young people may lead in general, we know even less about its consequences for members of ethnic minorities. The Internet may represent a safe environment for many of them where they can express their opinions about issues related to their ethnic minority and wider society. Yet we still do not know whether and how online civic participation has an impact on the establishment of their ethnic identity, collective efficacy, and whether it has potential to motivate civic participation in the real world. Therefore online participation on the Internet is one of the main issues that deserves further research attention in the field of civic development rather than ultimate practical recommendations.

Notes

1 Work on this chapter was supported by the Program of 'Employment of Newly Graduated Doctors of Science for Scientific Excellence' (grant number CZ.1.07/2.3.00/30.0009) co-financed from the European Social Fund and the state budget of the Czech Republic.
2 Voting in elections, attending a public meeting, distributing leaflets, and boycotting/buying products are not present in this classification because they had different meanings in the different ethnic groups according to the factor analysis.
3 Participatory norm of parents was measured by three items: 'My parents would approve it if I engaged politically,' 'My parents are involved in political actions (e.g. by wearing a badge, taking part in a public demonstration, boycotting certain products, signing petitions, etc.),' 'My parents would agree that the only way to change anything in society is to get involved.' Participatory norms of peers were measured by the same three items but referring to 'my friends.' Total scores could range from 1 to 5.

4   In Ukrainians, participation in the real world was strongly correlated with the experience that they had in using the Czech language and how integrated they were into Czech society. Therefore it is possible that in the case of this type of participation, all other factors, including participatory norms, are overshadowed.
5   Evaluation of society was measured by three items: 'In the last month, how much time did you spend feeling that our society is becoming a better place?' '... people are basically good?' '... the way our society works makes sense to you?' Total score could range from 1 to 5.
6   Participants were asked: 'How much trust do you have in the following institutions?' Total score could range from 1 to 5.
7   Participants were asked: 'To what extent do you feel each of the following emotions when you think of instances of discrimination against minority groups where you live?' Then, emotions such as 'anger' and 'hope' were offered to them. Scores could range from 1 to 5.

References

Ajzen, I. (1991) 'The theory of planned behavior,' *Organizational Behavior and Human Decision Processes*, 50: 179–211.
Andolina, M. W., Jenkins, K., Zukin, C., and Keeter, S. (2003) 'Habits from home, lessons from school: influences on youth civic engagement,' *PS: Political Science and Politics*, 36: 275–80.
Beck, P. A. and Jennings, M. K. (1982) 'Pathways to participation,' *American Political Science Review*, 76: 94–108.
Beck, P. A. and Jennings, M. K. (1991) 'Family traditions, political periods, and the development of partisan orientations,' *Journal of Politics*, 53: 742–63.
Bennett, W. L. (2008) 'Changing citizenship in the digital age,' in W. L. Bennett (ed.), *Civic Life Online: Learning How Digital Media Can Engage Youth*. Cambridge, MA: MIT Press, pp. 1–24.
Bennett, W. L., Freelon, D., and Wells, C. (2010) 'Changing citizen identity and the rise of a participatory media culture,' in L. R. Sherrod, J. Torney-Purta, and C. A. Flanagan (eds), *Handbook of Research on Civic Engagement in Youth*. Hoboken, NJ: Wiley, pp. 393–424.
Bloemraad, I. and Trost, C. (2008) 'It's a family affair. Intergenerational mobilization in the spring 2006 protests,' *American Behavioral Scientist*, 52: 507–32.
Braun, V. and Clarke, V. (2006) 'Using thematic analysis in psychology,' *Qualitative Research in Psychology*, 3: 77–101.
Černý, J., Dvořák, M., Hrubý, M., Michal, J., and Růžička, M. (2006) *Sociální diskriminace pod lupou* [*Social Discrimination Under the Spotlight*]. Praha: Otevřená společnost.
Chryssochoou, X. and Lyons, E. (2011) 'Perceptions of (in)compatibility between identities and participation in the national polity of people belonging to ethnic minorities,' in A. Azzi, X. Chryssochoou, B. Klandermans, and B. Simon (eds), *Identity and Participation in Culturally Diverse Societies*. Chichester: Wiley-Blackwell, pp. 69–88.
Císař, O., Navrátil, J., and Vráblíková, K. (2011) 'Staří, noví, radikální: politický aktivismus v České republice očima teorie sociálních hnutí' ['Old, new, radical: political activism in the Czech Republic from perspective of social movement theory],' *Sociologický časopis*, 47: 137–67.
Drbohlav, D., Lachmanová-Medová, L., Čermák, Z., Janská, E., Čermáková, D., and Dzúrová, D. (2009) *The Czech Republic: On Its Way from Emigration to Immigration Country*, IDEA Working Paper No. 11. Retrieved from: http://www.idea6fp.uw.edu.pl/pliki/WP11_Czech_Republic.pdf.
Duke, N. N., Skay, C. L., Pettingell, S. L., and Borowsky, I. W. (2009) 'From adolescent connections to social capital: predictors of civic engagement in young adulthood,' *Journal of Adolescent Health*, 44: 161–8.

European Commission (2008) *Discrimination in the European Union: Perceptions, Experiences and Attitudes*, Special *Eurobarometer*, 296. Retrieved from: http://ec.europa.eu/public_opinion/archives/ebs/ebs_296_en.pdf.

Glasford, D. (2008) 'Predicting voting behavior of young adults: the importance of information, motivation, and behavioral skills,' *Journal of Applied Social Psychology*, 38: 2648–72.

Horáková, M. (2001) *Zaměstnávání cizinců v ČR. – Část 1. Integrace na trhu práce [Employment of Foreigners in the Czech Republic. Part I. Integration of Foreigners into the Labour Market]*. Praha: VÚPS.

Horváthová, J. (2002) *Kapitoly z dějin Romů [Chapters from the History of Roma]*. Praha: Lidové noviny.

Jensen, L. A. (2008) 'Immigrants' cultural identities as sources of civic engagement,' *Applied Developmental Science*, 12: 74–83.

Jensen, L. A. (2010) 'Immigrant youth in the United States: coming of age among diverse civic cultures', in L. R. Sherrod, J. Torney-Purta, and C. A. Flanagan (eds), *Handbook of Research on Civic Engagement in Youth*. Hoboken, NJ: Wiley, pp. 425–43.

Kahne, J. E. and Sporte, S. E. (2008) 'Developing citizens: the impact of civic learning opportunities on students' commitment to civic participation,' *American Educational Research Journal*, 45: 738–66.

Kašparová, I., Ripka, Š., and Sidiropulu Janků, K. (2008) *Dlouhodobý monitoring situace romských komunit v České republice. Moravské lokality [A Long-term Monitoring of the Situation in Roma Communities in the Czech Republic. Moravian Localities]*. Retrieved from: http://evropskyrok.vlada.cz/assets/ppov/zalezitosti-romske-komunity/dokumenty/monitoring_morava.pdf.

Keyes, C. L. M. (1998) 'Social well-being,' *Social Psychology Quarterly*, 61: 121–40.

Klandermans, B., van der Toorn, J., and van Stekelenburg, J. (2008) 'Embeddedness and identity: how immigrants turn grievances into action,' *American Sociological Review*, 73: 992–1012.

Leontiyeva, Y. (2006) 'Ukrajinská menšina a migranti v ČR' ['Ukrainian minority and migrants in the Czech Republic],' in Y. Leontiyeva (ed.), *Menšinová problematika v ČR: komunitní život a reprezentace kolektivních zájmů [The Issue of Minorities in the Czech Republic: Community Life and the Representation of Collective Interests]*. Praha: Sociologický ústav AV ČR, pp. 32–45.

Leontiyeva, Y. and Nečasová, M. (2009) 'Kulturně blízcí? Integrace přistěhovalců ze zemí bývalého Sovětského svazu' ['Cultural nearness? Integration of the immigrants from the countries of the former Soviet Union],' in M. Rákoczyová and M. Trbola (eds), *Sociální integrace přistěhovalců v České republice [Social Integration of Immigrants in the Czech Republic]*. Praha: SLON, pp. 117–60.

Leontiyeva, Y. and Novotný, L. (2010) 'Je česká společnost tolerantní? Postoje vůči národnostním menšinám a cizincům' ['Is Czech society tolerant? Attitudes towards national minorities and foreigners],' in T. Kostelecký, M. Škodová, T. Lebeda, and H. Maříková (eds), *Jaká je naše společnost? Otázky, které si často klademe [What Is Our Society Like? Frequently Asked Questions]*. Praha: SLON, pp. 116–30.

McFarland, D. A. and Thomas, R. J. (2006) 'Bowling young: how youth voluntary associations influence adult political participation,' *American Sociological Review*, 71: 401–25.

Navrátil, P. et al. (2003) *Romové v české společnosti [Roma in Czech Society]*. Praha: Portál.

Novotná, H. (2005) 'Imigrace z Ukrajiny v České republice po roce 1990' ['Immigration from Ukraine in the Czech Republic after 1990'], in D. Bittnerová and M. Moravcová (eds), *Kdo jsem a kam patřím? Identita národnostních menšin a etnických komunit na území České republiky [Who Am I and Where Do I Belong? Identity of National Minorities and Ethnic Communities in the Czech Republic]*. Praha: SOFIS, pp. 347–62.

Pečínka, P. (2004) 'Romská menšina v politice českých stran' ['Roma minority in the policies of Czech parties'], in M. Mareš, L. Kopeček, P. Pečínka, and V. Stýskalíková (eds), *Etnické menšiny a česká politika: Analýza stranických přístupů k etnické a imigrační politice po roce 1989* [*Ethnic Minorities and Czech Politics. Analysis of Party Approach to the Ethnic and Immigration Politics After 1989*]. Brno: Centrum pro studium demokracie a kultury, pp. 46–75.

Pedersen, S., Seidman, E., Yoshikawa, H., Rivera, A. C., Allen, L., and Aber, J. L. (2005) 'Context competence: multiple manifestations among urban adolescents,' *American Journal of Community Psychology*, 35: 65–82.

Putnam, R. D. (2000) *Bowling Alone: The Collapse and Revival of American Community*. New York: Simon & Schuster.

Rabušic, L. and Burjanek, A. (2003) *Imigrace a imigrační politika jako prvek řešení české demografické situace?* [*Immigration and Immigration Policy as an Element of the Czech Demographic Situation Solution?*] Brno: VÚPSV.

Rojas, H. and Puig-i-Abril, E. (2009) 'Mobilizers mobilized: information, expression, mobilization and participation in the digital age', *Journal of Computer-Mediated Communication*, 14: 902–27.

Seif, H. (2010) 'The civic life of Latina/o immigrant youth: challenging boundaries and creating safe spaces,' in L. R. Sherrod, J. Torney-Purta, and C. A. Flanagan (eds), *Handbook of Research on Civic Engagement in Youth*. Hoboken, NJ: Wiley, pp. 445–70.

Seif, H. (2011) '"Unapologetic and unafraid": immigrant youth come out from the shadows,' in C. A. Flanagan and B. D. Christens (eds), 'Youth civic development: work at the cutting edge,' *New Directions for Child and Adolescent Development*, 134: 59–75.

Šerek, J., Petrovičová, Z., and Macek, P. (2011) 'The civic life of young Czech Roma: perceived resources, barriers, and opportunities,' in M. Rašticová et al. (eds), *Diversity Is Reality: Effective Leadership of Diverse Teams in a Global Environment*. Brno: CERM, pp. 143–52.

Šerek, J., Petrovičová, Z., and Porubanová-Norquist, M. (2012) *Mladí a nevšední* [*The Young and the Uncommon*]. Brno: Munipress.

Simon, B. and Grabow, O. (2010) 'The politicization of migrants: further evidence that politicized collective identity is a dual identity', *Political Psychology*, 31: 717–38.

Smith, E. S. (1999) 'The effects of investment in the social capital of youth on political and civic behavior in young adulthood: a longitudinal analysis,' *Political Psychology*, 20: 553–80.

Stepick, A. and Stepick, C. D. (2002) 'Becoming American, constructing ethnicity: immigrant youth and civic engagement', *Applied Developmental Science*, 6: 246–57.

Stolle, D. (1998) 'Bowling together, bowling alone: the development of generalized trust in voluntary associations,' *Political Psychology*, 19: 497–525.

Stolle, D. and Rochon, T. R. (1998) 'Are all associations alike? Member diversity, associational type, and the creation of social capital,' *American Behavioral Scientist*, 42: 47–65.

Tausch, N., Becker, J. C., Spears, R., Christ, O., Saab, R., Singh, P., and Siddiqui, R. N. (2011) 'Explaining radical group behavior: developing emotion and efficacy routes to normative and nonnormative collective action,' *Journal of Personality and Social Psychology*, 101: 129–48.

Teorell, J. (2003) 'Linking social capital to political participation: voluntary associations and networks of recruitment in Sweden,' *Scandinavian Political Studies*, 26: 49–66.

Theiss-Morse, E. and Hibbing, J. R. (2005) 'Citizenship and civic engagement,' *Annual Review of Political Science*, 8: 227–49.

Torney-Purta, J., Barber, C. H., and Richardson, W. K. (2004) 'Trust in government-related institutions and political engagement among adolescents in six countries,' *Acta Politica*, 39: 380–406.

Verba, S., Schlozman, K. L., and Brady, H. E. (1995) *Voice and Equality: Civic Voluntarism in American Politics*. Cambridge, MA: Harvard University Press.

Wallace, C. (2002) Opening and closing borders: Migration and mobility in East-Central Europe. *Journal of Ethnic and Migration Studies*, 28: 603–25.

Wong, J. and Tseng, V. (2008) 'Political socialisation in immigrant families: challenging top-down parental socialisation models,' *Journal of Ethnic and Migration Studies*, 34: 151–68.

Wright, S. C., Taylor, D. M., and Moghaddam, F. M. (1990) 'Responding to membership in a disadvantaged group: from acceptance to collective protest', *Journal of Personality and Social Psychology*, 58: 994–1003.

Youniss, J., Bales, S., Christmas-Best, V., Diversi, M., McLaughlin, M. W., and Silbereisen, R. (2002) 'Youth civic engagement in the twenty-first century', *Journal of Research on Adolescence*, 12: 121–48.

Zhřívalová, P. and Kocourek, J. (2002) *Situace romské menšiny podle výzkumů* [*The Situation of Roma Minority According to Research*]. Retrieved from: http://www.helcom.cz/view.php?cisloclanku=2003061804.

Zukin, C., Keeter, S., Andolina, M., Jenkins, K., and Delli Carpini, M. (2006) *A New Engagement? Political Participation, Civic Life, and the Changing American Citizen*. Oxford: Oxford University Press.

13

PARTICIPATION AND ENGAGEMENT OF YOUNG PEOPLE IN GERMANY

Findings on adolescents and young adults of German and Turkish family background

Peter Noack and Philipp Jugert

Civic and political participation is vital for the survival and development of a democratic society (Putnam 2000). Consequently, political alienation and low levels of interest in participation among the young, which is often referred to in public discourse, is a source of concern as these adolescents and young adults are the future citizens on whose support and engagement the society will have to build. Indeed, engagement early in life, be it social or political, has been identified as an important precursor of later participation (e.g. Stallmann *et al*. 2008).

Concern about actual or alleged political apathy among young people does not only result from expectations with regard to the future of democratic countries but also from the crucial role that is commonly attributed to adolescence as a formative phase in the course of the political development of the individual (Sears and Levy 2003). Legally, most democratic countries allow voting at age 18 which is meant to mark the transition into political maturity. Likewise, scholars of developmental science consider political maturity including engagement and participation as a developmental task of adolescence (Sherrod *et al*. 2002).

A lot of the available information points to growing political alienation and declining participation among youth (Torney-Purta *et al*. 2001; Shell 2006). If true, this deplorable situation might be considered even more alarming in countries that look back on a comparatively short democratic tradition such as Germany. As elaborated in the following, however, a closer look at the evidence reveals a more differentiated picture. It should be noted that our existing knowledge based on quantitative survey research (Torney-Purta *et al*. 2010) provides a more superficial image than is true of research on many other domains of individual development. Moreover, what we know is by and large confined to ethnic majority youth. Besides the fact that young people with minority backgrounds form quantitatively substantial subgroups in their cohorts in most European countries, the social and political participation of minority members also seems to be of particular importance as it is considered to be a reliable indicator of integration (Glatzer 2004; Haug 2007).

In this chapter, we examine participation and engagement of adolescents and young adults in Germany. Our particular focus is on young people of Turkish background who are the largest minority group in the country. After a brief review of existing literatures on population statistics and survey data, we report on findings from our own studies conducted in Germany as part of the joint PIDOP project. In a first step, we will try to give a differentiated picture of actual and intended participation of young Germans and Turkish minority youth, distinguishing different forms of activities and enquiring into reasons for engagement or the abstinence thereof. Then, we examine the workings of factors suggested by the literature to be predictive of young people's participation. Our major interest is to shed light on possible differences between German and Turkish youth. Drawing on the observation that minority members often show activities of engagement and participation within their own minority community, we finally address the question whether adolescents and young adults of Turkish background are mainly engaged in minority-specific cultural or religious groups, as well as whether such patterns of participation go together with a more distant relationship to the German majority culture.

Our findings are based on comprehensive quantitative questionnaire assessments as well as on analyses of more in-depth focus group discussions. Information on the samples, methods of data collection, and analyses are provided to the extent necessary to understand and interpret the findings (for more details see Jugert *et al.* 2011; Jugert *et al.* 2013; Jugert and Noack 2013).

Civic and political participation of young people in Germany

Well aware of the difficulties of a precise and unambiguous definition of civic and political participation, we want to suggest building on a broad understanding that includes activities towards political goals in a narrow sense (cf. Verba *et al.* 1995) as well as engagement in the service of issues of public concern such as volunteering (APA 2012). We consider a comprehensive understanding as particularly instructive when it comes to young people, as the answers to the question as to how much youth do participate with regard to social and political issues are quite different depending on the form of participation in focus. Moreover, there is some evidence suggesting a developmental continuity between different forms of participation, with engagement during the adolescent years making adult political participation more likely (e.g. Hart *et al.* 2007; Oesterle *et al.* 2004).

Drawing on a broad definition, the Shell youth studies (e.g. Shell 2006, 2010) report on high levels of participation among young Germans. In this sense, more than two-thirds of the young respondents claim to be active at least from time to time while half of those active indicate frequent social or political engagement. It is important to note, however, that in their responses they often refer to activities in schools, universities, or organized leisure groups, while participation in political parties or organizations occurs far less frequently. By the same token, a survey addressing adolescents' engagement on the local level (Bertelsmann-Stiftung 2005) identifies a share of over-two thirds who have shown at least some engagement. Most of this, however, seems to take place in the service of people in need or in the realm of leisure pursuits. When it comes to political activities in a more narrow sense, signing petitions or participating in political rallies are the most widespread forms of participation.

The pattern observed concerning activities among Germans in the second and third decade of their life parallels findings concerning their orientations. The willingness to participate is high as is a stated interest in politics (DJI 2011). While the political interest of young Germans has somewhat declined since German unification, it still remains on higher levels than could be observed during the decades before 1990. It should be added that the level of interest among the young is lower than among Germans above age 30. Moreover, these orientations go along with low levels of trust in representatives of organized politics such as political parties and politicians.

Although the swift expansion of Internet availability and use has given rise to the assumption that, particularly among the young, online participation might displace or uniquely add to other (offline) forms of engagement and participation (cf. Zukin et al. 2006), the evidence rather suggests that there are generally more active youth and generally less active (or inactive) youth, with the more active youth using offline as well as online modes of participation (e.g. Chadwick 2006; Livingston et al. 2005). Paralleling this observation, the extensive German Youth Institute survey (DJI 2011) portrays Internet participation as just an extension of the opportunities for participation among those who are already active.

Besides macro-social factors such as a country's wealth, its political history, and the electoral system (Kriesi 2004), various individual factors have been identified as predictive of participation. Among these factors, education plays a major role, with the more educated young being more active (DJI 2011). Concerning gender, findings are mixed and less straightforward. The most important insight probably is systematic variation depending on the forms of participation and the issues at stake (e.g. Kuhn 2010; Oswald and Schmid 1998). For example, male adolescents seem to show a stronger inclination towards conventional forms of political activities than girls do who, in turn, are more attracted by non-conventional civic activities. Moreover, levels of engagement are affected by social contexts such as the family, peers, and school (Jugert et al. 2011).

Youth of Turkish background in Germany

Despite millions of people who have migrated to Germany, it has taken quite a while for the country to see itself as an immigration country. The largest minority group by far comprises people of Turkish background as shown by population statistics (Statistisches Bundesamt 2012). Following waves of migrants from Turkey who came into Germany starting in the early 1960s, about 1.6 million Turkish citizens live in Germany today. Despite a small decline during the last decade (1999: 2.1 million), the number of Turkish citizens in Germany is more than three times the second largest minority group. Turkish citizens in Germany and inhabitants of Turkish background who do not hold a Turkish passport (mostly German citizens) together form a group of nearly 3 million people in the country, representing almost 4 percent of the overall population.

The vast majority of Turkish people coming to Germany were so-called migrant workers (in earlier times referred to as 'guest workers') and to some extent family members often came into the country by way of active recruitment strategies during a time when the German economy was in need of a larger labor force. Five decades later, almost all young people of Turkish background in Germany were born in the country. Nevertheless, the Turkish minority is one of the worst integrated minority groups in Germany. Cases in point are unemployment rates, educational success, figures on health status as well as experiences of discrimination (BMI 2009). For instance, over two-thirds of students from a Turkish background leave German schools without having graduated or having graduated at the lowest level.

While the body of evidence is limited, previous studies suggest that minority group members show lower levels of civic and political engagement than members of the respective majority groups (e.g. Fridkin 2006; Torney-Purta et al. 2001). Interpreting this observation, it has been pointed out that minority status is often accompanied by a low socio-economic status that, in turn, is predictive of lower levels of participation (Hart and Atkins 2002; Verba et al. 2005). Even though low SES and, in particular, low levels of education strongly contribute to differences in participation between majority and minority members, this seems only to be part of the story. Further factors seem to also play an important role. For example, voting in elections in Germany, as in many other countries, is restricted to citizens. Thus more than half of the members of the Turkish minority in Germany is not allowed to vote. In general, the political organization of the country seems to be experienced as not open to minority members and their interests (Halm and Sauer 2005).

As mentioned earlier in this chapter, members of minority groups seem to be more attracted to engagement and participation within their community than in activities beyond their own group (Stepick et al. 2008). It seems plausible to assume that this is true of minority youth as well as of adults. Participation activities within the minority community might be a valuable experience, making future participation within and beyond their own community more likely. At the same time, however, doubts are voiced that point to the potential risk of this type of participation that could even increase the distance from the majority culture and its organizations. There are concerns about the emergence or expansion of 'parallel societies' accommodating the separate lives of majority and minority members (Leibold et al. 2006). So far, we do not have sufficient evidence to address this important issue.

Our empirical work

Our own findings on the engagement and participation of German and Turkish youth in Germany are based on analyses of focus group discussions and of data collected by way of questionnaire assessments. Altogether, 17 focus group discussions were conducted. Four to eight young people participated in each group. The groups were organized according to age, namely 16- to 18-year-old adolescents vs. 20- to 26-year-old young adults, and cultural background, distinguishing between group discussions of young Germans, youth of Turkish background, and young people from German resettler families (originating from the former Soviet Union). Only discussions of the former two groups are discussed in the current report.

Initiating the discussion with a set of photos showing young people in different situations of political participation, several questions were devised to make sure that different aspects of participation were touched upon during the 30 to 60 minutes of discussion. The recorded discussions were then transcribed, coded, and analyzed (cf. Braun and Clarke 2006).

Our questionnaire assessments included a total of 915 adolescents and young adults between the ages of 15 and 27. In the following discussion, we refer to data from 448 participants of German majority background and 192 youth of Turkish minority background. Participants were students in secondary schools, apprentices, or university students. While the sample is clearly not a representative one, it covers a wide variation of socio-economic backgrounds and circumstances of life.

Questionnaires were administered in a paper-and-pencil or online format. In addition to attitudes and activities concerning a broad range of forms of participation, questionnaire items addressed a variety of other aspects relevant to political development.

Engagement in different forms of participation

Starting with what we would consider our major finding based on the quantitative data, we have little evidence for lower levels of engagement and participation among our Turkish compared to our German respondents. If anything, the opposite is true. Summarizing various forms of offline engagement (e.g. volunteer work, donating money for a political cause, buying/boycotting) vs. online engagement (e.g. online-based petition, link online content to own contacts), we identified low to medium levels of activities on average, with participants of Turkish background scoring higher in offline as well as in online engagement than the young Germans. The finding held among adolescents as well as among young adults. In both groups, young adults were more active than were adolescents. All findings were controlled for educational attainment, parental education, books at home, and mode of data collection. Figure 13.1 shows the means according to group, age, and form of engagement.

The young people were also asked in which organizations they had participated in their lives. Eight different types of organizations were presented to them ranging from leisure groups (e.g. sports, music) to political parties. It may not come as a surprise that leisure group participation clearly ranked highest followed by volunteering/welfare groups, youth organizations, and religious groups. Participation in environmental groups, trade unions, and political parties or their youth organizations was far less frequent.

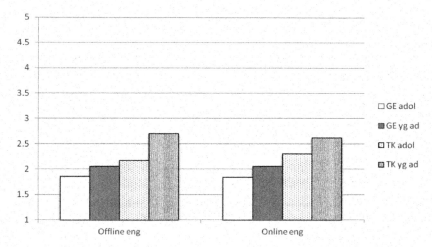

FIGURE 13.1 Offline and online engagement of adolescents (adol) and young adults (yg ad) of German (GE) and Turkish (TK) background

Again, Turkish respondents more often reported on participation experiences than did their German age-mates concerning six of the eight types of organization. Only when it came to leisure groups and environmental groups did more young Germans (GE) than Turkish (TK) youth indicate engagement (leisure groups: TK 64.9 percent vs. GE 75.9 percent; environmental groups: TK 17.6 percent vs. GE 21.3 percent). Differences in favor of respondents from the Turkish subsample were small but systematic in four cases (trade union, political party, volunteering organization, youth organization). Actual experiences with participation in religious groups and human rights groups were far more widespread among youth of Turkish background (religious groups: TK 54.6 percent vs. GE 23.2 percent; human rights groups: TK 34.1 percent vs. GE 14.1 percent). Thus, even with this stricter criterion of actual participation, Turkish youth reported higher levels of engagement.

While the size and composition of the sample of the focus group discussions, which served a different purpose from the questionnaire assessments, does not allow a direct comparison, three findings deserve attention. First, the overall level of participation reported by the participants in the discussions was quite low. Second, the group discussions also did not suggest more extensive patterns of engagement among the young Germans. Third, religious and cultural groups seem to play a major role in the engagement of youth of Turkish background as could also be seen in the analyses of the questionnaire data.

In the course of the discussions, it became obvious that abstinence from engagement is often explained with reference to politicians' lack of interest in the concerns of young people. Many of the participants stated a low opinion of politicians and expected little from them. By the same token, looking at the representatives of conventional politics, our young participants did not see much to identify themselves with. This lack of identification was particularly pronounced among youth from a minority background.

Issues that were addressed in the discussions by Turkish youth in particular were often related to experiences of discrimination. A case in point are German citizenship laws which are quite restrictive concerning dual citizenship[1] while at the same time a (solely) Turkish citizen in Germany lacks major rights of participation, for example the right to vote in political elections. Religious freedom, as well as pressure towards assimilation, were further points of concern raised.

Motivation for participation

Following analyses of mean level differences in participation and engagement of German and Turkish youth in Germany, we examined possible variations in processes leading to participation. More specifically, we set out to elucidate similarities and differences between these two groups concerning the prediction of the motivation for participation. Drawing on the Theory of Planned Behavior framework (TPB) (Ajzen 1991; Fishbein and Ajzen 1975), we focused on motivation for engagement as a proxy of young people's orientations towards engagement, social norms (namely perceived parental and peer approval), and political efficacy, and tested their effects on reported offline and online participation (Jugert et al. 2013).

Measures of offline and online engagement were the same as reported above. Motivation for engagement was captured by six items (e.g. 'I would participate in a political cause if I felt strongly about an issue') adapted from Collom (2011). The four-item measure of parental and peer norms (e.g. 'My friends/parents would approve if I engaged politically') was adapted from Pattie et al. (2003) while six items adapted from Yeich and Levine (1994) served to assess collective political efficacy (e.g. 'I think by working together young people/people from my own ethnic group/people of my own gender can change things for the better/are able to influence decisions which are made by government'). The analyses were conducted using structural equation modeling.

Multi-group analyses revealed that ethnic background moderated the associations between predictors and youth's offline engagement. While among young people of German as well as of Turkish background, collective efficacy proved to be a significant predictor of offline engagement, motivation for engagement only contributed to the explanation of variance in young Germans' offline engagement. In contrast, parental and peer norms only predicted offline engagement of Turkish youth, while it turned out as being of little importance for the engagement of young Germans. The findings are shown in Figure 13.2.

In our parallel analyses addressing online engagement as outcome, no group-specific variations were identified. Among young people of German as well as of Turkish background, motivation for engagement as well as collective efficacy contributed to the prediction of engagement while parental and peer norms were not a significant predictor.

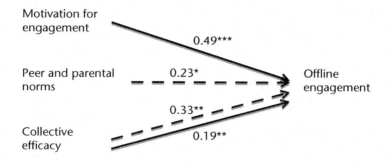

FIGURE 13.2 Predictors of offline engagement of young people of German (↑) and Turkish (↑̂) background
Note: * $p < 0.05$; ** $p < 0.01$; *** $p < 0.001$

Considering the nature of engagement activities pursued online it seems plausible to assume that views on engagement held among parents and peers do not systematically affect behavior. Parents and peers are typically not present when young people are on the Internet. Moreover, much of the engagement on the Internet can be done in an anonymous way. Thus there is little supervision that might result in consequences when young people do not act in line with the attitudes and expectations of both parents and peers.

Why might the ethnic groups differ concerning the prediction of their offline engagement? It is important to note that correlations between all three predictors, on the one hand, and offline engagement, on the other hand, were positive and significant in both groups (see Table 13.1). Moreover, intercorrelations between the predictors were also positive and significant. Thus what calls for an explanation is the relative importance of effects rather than their presence or absence, respectively. A possible explanation could refer to the collectivistic culture from which Turkish youth come (cf. Verkuyten and Masson 1996). In a cultural context characterized by collectivism, approval in close social relationships and, in particular, on the part of parents could be assumed to have stronger effects on young people than is the case in contexts that are less collectivistic. Our interpretation is quite speculative at this point and clearly calls for a more detailed examination of the possible moderating role of collectivism in future studies on civic and political engagement.

While reference to collectivism offers a plausible explanation of parental and peer influences on participation among Turkish youth, it has to be pointed out that the TPB focuses on significant others, i.e. important individuals in proximal contexts as holding social norms the perception of which are expected to affect intentions. It could well be that German adolescents and young adults are affected by norms prevalent in the social groups they identify with themselves and are relevant for their inclinations towards social and political engagement. These groups, which may differ from peers and parents, do not necessarily need to be face-to-face groups.

TABLE 13.1 Bivariate latent intercorrelations between model predictors and offline engagement for German and Turkish participants

Measure	1	2	3	4
1. Motivation for civic engagement	–			
2. Peer and parental norms	0.72***/0.68***	–		
3. Collective efficacy	0.61***/0.57***	0.64***/0.44***	–	
4. Civic engagement	0.74***/0.55***	0.61***/0.56***	0.61***/0.57***	–

***$p < 0.001$

Neither the theory nor our analyses have addressed this possibility. Proponents of the social identity approach (e.g. Smith and Louis 2009; Terry and Hogg 1996) have pointed out that the weak effects of subjective norms on people's intentions (see Armitage and Conner 2001) reflect a problem with the way norms are conceptualized in the TPB. From a social identity perspective, it is not (external) subjective norms but (internal) *group* norms that should affect intentions.

Engagement of Turkish youth in religious and cultural organizations

Previous research as well as our own findings show that engagement and participation of young people in Germany increase with age. A general criticism concerning low levels of engagement in absolute terms seems to be misleading. Indeed, there is a great deal of skepticism if not alienation among adolescents and young adults concerning conventional politics. As a mirror image of these views, participation in traditional political organizations is low. At the same time, young people seem to be willing to become active. However, their interest is rather focused on social engagement and activities in their more proximal contexts of life. Against this backdrop, engagement and participation of Turkish minority youth in Germany in cultural and religious groups and organizations of their community could be seen as paralleling the preferred types of engagement shown by German youth. Interestingly, according to our data, the engagement of adolescents and young adults of Turkish background does not lag behind the level of participation of their German age-mates. If anything, they even seem to be somewhat more active.

Taking a developmental perspective, the engagement of minority youth in their cultural organizations could be a double-edged sword. On the one hand, the general assumption that experiences of participation, in particular if these experiences are positive, foster future engagement might also hold concerning the consequences of engagement in minority organizations. Then the participation pattern of Turkish youth could be a precursor of future active citizenship. On the other hand, activities that strengthen young people's bonds within the minority community might also put them on a track that leads away from the majority culture. Concerns voiced in public discourse refer, in particular, to the risk of ideological influence Turkish youth might experience in the context of religious groups.

Our findings reported so far point to higher levels of engagement of Turkish youth not only in cultural and religious groups of their community but also in other types of groups and organizations. While it is difficult to tell whether volunteer groups, human rights groups, or youth organizations in which young people of Turkish background participate represent the majority culture or the Turkish community, Turkish youth also get engaged in trade unions and political parties more often than our young German respondents. These latter groups and organizations are not likely to mainly represent the Turkish minority.

Going beyond the examination of mean level differences, we examined associations between the engagement of Turkish youth in the different types of groups (Jugert and Noack 2013). The result is straightforward (see Table 13.2): all correlations were positive and significant. Thus those adolescents and young adults of Turkish background who were more active in their religious organizations also showed higher levels of engagement concerning other groups such as unions, political parties and environmental organizations. At least with regard to these groups, the segregation hypothesis would have predicted negative associations.

Likewise, we analyzed whether participation of Turkish youth in religious groups is related to other indicators of political interest and activity. Again, the pattern of correlations was quite clear (see Table 13.3). Those young people who showed

TABLE 13.2 Bivariate correlations between participation in religious organizations and participation in other kinds of organizations among immigrant youth of Turkish origin

Participation in ...	*Religious participation*
Trade unions or student associations	0.38**
Political parties or party youth groups	0.20**
Volunteering and charity groups	0.46**
Youth associations or groups	0.64**
Associations for the protection of human rights	0.46**
Environmental associations or animal rights groups	0.17*
Leisure or recreational associations or groups	0.21**

*$p < 0.05$; **$p < 0.01$

TABLE 13.3 Bivariate correlations between participation in religious organizations and indicators of civic competence among immigrant youth of Turkish origin

	Religious participation
Political interest	0.42**
Political attentiveness	0.32**
Intention for future civic engagement	0.49**
Political knowledge	0.26**
Internal political efficacy	0.29**
External political efficacy	−0.16*
Social well-being	0.32**

*$p < 0.05$; **$p < 0.01$

higher levels of religious participation reported more political knowledge, more political interest, stronger internal political efficacy, and stronger intentions to become civically engaged in the future than Turkish youth who participated in religious groups to a lesser extent. Taken together, these findings suggest differences between the more interested and active compared to less active Turkish youth. The former, more active youth also showed more engagement in religious groups than they did concerning other social and political activities.

If this is true, the religiously active should not necessarily be more distant from the majority culture. To address this issue we drew on Berry's (1997) acculturation model that specifies two crucial dimensions that he combines to form different acculturation strategies, namely cultural maintenance, on the one hand, and contact and participation, on the other. Cultural maintenance represents the closeness to minority members' culture of origin whereas the contact and participation dimension refers to the relationship with the majority culture. In this framework, for example, a constellation of openness and engagement (concerning the majority culture) and a high level of culture (of origin) maintenance forms the acculturation strategy of integration. High maintenance combined with low levels of contact and participation (in the majority culture) defines a separation strategy.

In our data, the level of Turkish youth's participation in religious groups was positively associated with cultural maintenance ($r = 0.25$, $p < 0.01$) as well as with the contact and participation dimension ($r = 0.14$, $p < 0.10$). In a follow-up analysis we compared the extent of participation in religious organizations across the four integration strategies suggested by Berry. We found a significant difference in terms of participation levels, $F(3,134) = 5.904$, $p = 0.001$, $\eta^2_p = 0.12$. Bonferroni-corrected post-hoc comparisons revealed that Turkish migrants with an integration strategy showed the highest level of religious participation ($M = 3.15$, $SD = 1.18$), which was significantly higher than persons with an assimilation ($M = 2.32$, $SD = 1.34$) or marginalization ($M = 1.89$, $SD = 1.18$) strategy. Persons with a separation strategy showed lower religious engagement ($M = 2.39$, $SD = 1.32$) but did not differ significantly from persons with an integration strategy. It should be noted that the correlations were low and the measures employed were not optimal to address our specific research question. Nevertheless, our finding certainly does not support the assumption that religiously active Turkish youth are characterized by a strong detachment from German mainstream culture. Rather than segregation, this pattern is suggestive of Berry's integration strategy which would mean that these young people have chosen a successful path of acculturation.

Where are we now and where do we have to go from here?

In this chapter, we wanted to give a short overview of social and political engagement of young people in Germany and, in particular, to shed light on the engagement of youth representing the largest minority in the country, namely people of Turkish origin. Even though it is a matter of norms and expectations to interpret absolute levels of engagement and participation, our data as well as the findings of others certainly point to a certain distance of the young people in the country from traditional politics and their representatives while, at the same time, adolescents and young adults seem to be willing to become active in the service of others beyond their immediate family and friendship contexts as well as of causes they can identify themselves with. Interestingly, young people who belong to the Turkish minority that on average is more poorly integrated than most other minority groups in Germany are as active as their German age-mates if not more so. While the engagement and participation of Turkish youth include quite a variety of different activities pursued in various kinds of groups and organizations, cultural and religious groups play an important role in this respect.

Given all uncertainties due to our limited database, our findings suggest that adolescents and young adults of Turkish background who are very active in cultural and religious groups of their community are active youth in general, including activities beyond the boundaries set by their culture and religion. We do not find indications for extensive engagement within the Turkish community to be a route towards segregation.

What, then, about the reports of young minority members indoctrinated in minority organizations and madrasahs (extra-curricular afternoon schools where children and adolescents are taught the Koran) who become increasingly militant and fanatic? Again, there is doubtlessly the need for confirmation of our observations by future studies based on representative data. Still, we would like to suggest a change to the question to some extent, in order to address the conditions under which engagement within the minority community is either a way into active and responsible citizenship or a way to drive young people away from the society they live in. Part of the answer might be found in societal conditions. Our own research gives us a view on minority youth in a given country at a certain point in time. For example, things might turn out differently in the future depending on the development of relationships between the German majority and the Turkish and other Muslim minorities in the country (cf. Leibold *et al.* 2006). By the same token, comparisons of young minority members in different European countries could be instructive. The PIDOP data sets include information on young members of Turkish minorities in Germany and Belgium as well as of Turkish majority youth (in Turkey) and are the subject of ongoing analyses (Eckstein et al. in preparation). The results reveal that overall – and contrary to expectations – in all three countries immigrant youth are more engaged than majority youth. Yet the results also reveal similar barriers to participation among immigrant and majority youth, which are in line with the assumptions of the civic voluntarism model (Verba et al. 1995).

At the same time, it could be worthwhile to consider individual characteristics and experiences as possible moderators of the effects of young people's engagement and participation. A lack of education, low levels of political efficacy, group-based emotions, or experiences of violence are but a handful of candidates that might make a difference when it comes to integration versus radicalization as a consequence of minority members' engagement in cultural and religious groups. Then more general psychological processes would be in operation. It would be a matter of immediate circumstances, namely the opportunity landscape in the proximal environment, and to some extent even a matter of chance which (ideological) direction a radicalization might take.

At this point, we can only raise questions instead of providing answers. Still, we consider the line of study pursued so far and our findings as quite encouraging and helpful to delineate directions for future research on an issue of scholarly as well as societal relevance.

Note

1 Only citizens from other EU countries are allowed to keep their native citizenship when applying for German citizenship. Since 2000, German law requires children from non EU-immigrants who were born in Germany to take a decision on one citizenship (e.g. German or Turkish) between the ages of 18 and 23. This is the legal situation relevant for our respondents, while the German government has recently decided on a law offering more liberal regulations.

References

Ajzen, I. (1991) 'The theory of planned behavior,' *Organizational Behavior and Human Decision Processes*, 50: 179–211.

American Psychological Association (APA) (2012) *Civic Engagement*. Retrieved from: http://www.apa.org/education/undergrad/civic-engagement.aspx.

Armitage, C. J. and Conner, M. (2001) 'Efficacy of the theory of planned behavior: a meta-analytic review,' *British Journal of Social Psychology*, 40: 471–99.

Berry, J. W. (1997) 'Immigration, acculturation, and adaptation,' *Applied Psychology: An International Review*, 46: 5–68.

Bertelsmann-Stiftung (ed.) (2005) 'Kinder- und Jugendpartizipation in Deutschland' ['Child and adolescent participation in Germany']. Retrieved from: http://www.bertelsmann-stiftung.de/bst/de/media/xcms_bst_dms_17946_17947_2.pdf.

Braun, V. and Clarke, V. (2006) 'Using thematic analysis in psychology,' *Qualitative Research in Psychology*, 3: 77–101.

Bundesministerium des Inneren (BMI) (2009) *Migrationsbericht des Bundesamtes für Migration und Flüchtlinge im Auftrag der Bundesregierung: Migrationsbericht 2007* [*Migration Report of the Federal Office for Migrants and Refugees in the Order of the Federal Government: Migration Report 2007*]. Nürnberg: Bundesamt für Migranten und Flüchtlinge.

Chadwick, A. (2006) *Internet Politics. States, Citizens, and New Communication Technologies.* New York: Oxford University Press.

Collom, E. (2011) 'Motivations and differential participation in a community currency system: The dynamics within a local social movement organization,' *Sociological Forum*, 26: 144–68.

Deutsches Jugendinstitut (DJI) (2011) 'Skepsis, Aufbruchsstimmung oder alles wie gehabt?' ['Skepticism, atmosphere of departure or everything as usual?'],' *DJI online*, 2011/08. Retrieved from: http://www.dji.de/cgi-bin/projekte/output.php?projekt=1109.

Eckstein, K., Jugert, P., and Noack, P. (in preparation) 'Comparing Barriers of Participation Among Immigrant and Majority Youth in Belgium, Germany, and Turkey.'

Fishbein, M. and Ajzen, I. (1975) *Belief, Attitude, Intention and Behavior: An Introduction to Theory and Research.* Harlow: Longman Higher Education.

Fridkin, K. L. (2006) 'On the margins of democratic life: the impact of race and ethnicity on the political engagement of young people,' *American Politics Research*, 34: 605–26.

Glatzer, W. (2004) 'Integration und Partizipation junger Ausländer vor dem Hintergrund ethnischer und kultureller Identifikation: Ergebnisse des Integrationssurveys des BiB' ['Integration and participation of young foreigners as a function of ethnic and cultural identification: results from the integration survey of the BiB'], *Materialien zur Bevölkerungswissenschaft* [*Materials for Population Science*], 105th edn. Wiesbaden: Bundesinstitut für Bevölkerungsforschung.

Halm, D. and Sauer, M. (2005) *Freiwilliges Engagement von Türkinnen und Türken in Deutschland* [*Volunteering Among Female and Male Turks in Germany*]. Essen: Zentrum für Türkeistudien.

Hart, D. and Atkins, R. (2002) 'Civic competence in urban youth,' *Applied Developmental Science*, 6: 227–36.

Hart, D., Donelly, T. M., Youniss, J., and Atkins, R. (2007) 'High school community service as a predictor of adult voting and volunteering,' *American Education Research Journal*, 44: 197–219.

Haug, S. (2007) 'Soziales Kapital als Ressource im Kontext von Migration und Integration' ['Social capital as a resource in the context of migration and integration'], in J. Lüdicke and M. Diewald (eds), *Soziale Netzwerke und soziale Ungleichheit* [*Social Networks and Social Inequality*]. Wiesbaden: VS Verlag, pp. 67–90.

Jugert, P. and Noack, P. (2013) 'Schlüssel zur Integration oder Weg in die Parallelgesellschaft? Die Wirkung von Partizipation in religiösen Organisationen am Beispiel junger türkischstämmiger Migranten in Deutschland' ['Key to integration or pathway into a parallel society? The effects of participation in religious organizations among young migrants of Turkish origin in Germany'], in Berufsverband Deutscher Psychologen und Psychologinnen (eds), *Inklusion – Integration – Partizipation: Psychologische Beiträge für eine humanere Gesellschaft* [*Inclusion – Integration – Participation: Psychological Contributions to a More Humane Society*]. Berlin: Deutscher Psychologen-Verlag, pp. 32–9.

Jugert, P., Benbow, A., Noack, P., and Eckstein, K. (2011) 'Politische Partizipation und soziales Engagement unter jungen Deutschen, Türken und Spätaussiedlern: Befunde aus einer qualitativen Untersuchung mit Fokusgruppen' ['Political participation and social engagement among young German, Turks, and late resettlers: results from a qualitative study using focus groups'], *Politische Psychologie*, 1: 36–53.

Jugert, P., Eckstein, K., Noack, P., Kuhn, A., and Benbow, A. (2013) 'Offline and online civic engagement among adolescents and young adults from three ethnic groups', *Journal of Youth and Adolescence*, 42: 123–35.

Kriesi, H. (2004) 'Political context and opportunity,' in D. Snow, S. Soule, and H. Kriesi (eds), *The Blackwell Companion to Social Movements*. Malden: Blackwell, pp. 67–90.

Kuhn, H.-P. (2010) 'Adolescent voting for right-wing extremist parties and readiness to use violence in political action: parent and peer contexts,' *Journal of Adolescence*, 27: 561–81.

Leibold, J., Kühnel, S., and Heitmeyer, W. (2006) 'Abschottung von Muslimen durch generalisierte Islamkritik' ['Segregation from Muslims through general criticism of Islam'], *Aus Politik und Zeitgeschichte*, 1–2: 3–10.

Livingston, S., Bober, M., and Helsper, E. J. (2005) 'Active participation or just information? Young people's take-up of opportunities to act and interact on the internet,' *Information, Communication and Society*, 8: 287–314.

Oesterle, S., Johnson, M. K., and Mortimer, J. T. (2004) 'Volunteerism during the transition to adulthood: a life course perspective,' *Social Forces*, 82: 1123–49.

Oswald, H. and Schmid, C. (1998) 'Political participation of young people in East Germany,' *German Politics*, 7: 147–64.

Pattie, C., Seyd, P., and Whiteley, P. (2003) 'Citizenship and civic engagement: attitudes and behavior in Britain,' *Political Studies*, 51: 443–68.

Putnam, R. D. (2000) *Bowling Alone: The Collapse and Revival of American Community*. New York: Simon & Schuster.

Sears, D. O. and Levy, S. (2003) 'Childhood and adult political development,' in D. O. Sears, L. Huddy, and R. Jervis (eds), *Oxford Handbook of Political Psychology*. Oxford: Oxford University Press, pp. 60–109.

Shell (ed.) (2006) *Jugend 2006. 15. Shell Jugendstudie. Einepragmatische Generation* [*Youth 2006. 15th Shell Youth Study. A Pragmatic Generation*]. Frankfurt: Fischer.

Shell (ed.) (2010) *Jugend 2010. 16. Shell Jugendstudie* [*Youth 2010. 16th Shell Youth Study*]. Frankfurt: Fischer.

Sherrod, L. R., Flanagan, C., and Youniss, J. (2002) 'Dimensions of citizenship and opportunities for youth development: the what, why, when, where, and who of citizenship development,' *Applied Developmental Science*, 6 (4): 264–72.

Smith, J. R. and Louis, W. R. (2009) 'Group norms and the attitude-behavior relationship,' *Social and Personality Psychology Compass*, 3 (1): 19–35.

Stallmann, F., Paulsen, F., and Zimmer, A. (2008) 'Das Ehrenamt: erster Schritt in die Lokalpolitik? Zum Nexus von Vereinsengagement und lokalpolitischem Mandat am Beispiel der Stadt Münster' ['The honorary post: first step towards local politics? On the nexus between civic engagement and running for local political office in the town of Munster'], *Zeitschrift für Parlamentsfragen*, 39: 547–60.

Statistisches Bundesamt (2012) *Statistisches Jahrbuch 2012* [*Annual Statistical Report 2012*]. Retrieved from: https://www.destatis.de/DE/Publikationen/StatistischesJahrbuch/StatistischesJahrbuch2012.pdf;jsessionid=F6B0D0A6D0C0134F833F74EFAD576DA2.cae3?__blob=publicationFile.

Stepick, A., Stepick, C. D., and Labissiere, Y. (2008) 'South Florida's immigrant youth and civic engagement: major engagement: minor differences,' *Applied Developmental Science*, 12: 57–65.

Terry, D. J. and Hogg, M. A. (1996) 'Group norms and the attitude-behaviour relationship: a role for group identification,' *Personality and Social Psychology Bulletin*, 22: 776–93.

Torney-Purta, J., Amadeo, J.-A., and Andolina, M. W. (2010) 'A conceptual framework and multi-method approach for research on political socialization and civic engagement,' in L. R. Sherrod, J. Torney-Purta, and C. Flanagan (eds), *Handbook of Research on Civic Engagement in Youth*. New York: Wiley, pp. 497–524.

Torney-Purta, J., Lehmann, R., Oswald, H., and Schulz, W. (2001) *Citizenship and Education in Twenty-Eight Countries: Civic Knowledge and Engagement at Age Fourteen*. Amsterdam: International Association for the Evaluation of Educational Achievement.

Verba, S., Schlozman, K. L., and Brady, H. (1995) *Voice and Equality: Civic Volunteerism in American Politics*. Cambridge, MA: Harvard University Press.

Verkuyten, M. and Masson, K. (1996) 'Culture and gender differences in the perception of friendship by adolescents,' *International Journal of Psychology*, 31: 207–17.

Yeich, S. and Levine, R. (1994) 'Political efficacy: enhancing the construct and its relationship to mobilization of people,' *Journal of Community Psychology*, 22: 259–71.

Zukin, C., Keeter, S., Andolina, M., Jenkins, K., and Delli Carpini, M. X. (2006) *A New Engagement? Political Participation, Civic Life, and the Changing American Citizen*. New York: Oxford University Press.

14

CIVIC ENGAGEMENT AMONG MIGRANT YOUTHS IN SWEDEN

Do parental norms or immigration generation matter?

Yunhwan Kim and Erik Amnå

Introduction

Sweden is becoming a more plural society with a growing number of immigrants, as is the case for many other developed countries in Europe. Indeed, the number of immigrants in Sweden has continued to grow since the 1940s (Statistics Sweden 2013). At the end of 2012, around 1.3 million residents in Sweden were either foreign-born Swedish citizens or Swedish-born citizens having foreign-born parents, consisting of around 14 percent of the whole population (Statistics Sweden 2013). Statistics indicate that the increase in the number of immigrants will continue for the time being, with the number of immigrants having been twice as high as the number of emigrants since 2000 (Statistics Sweden 2013).

Given the scale of the changing population composition, its impact is one of the most urgent social concerns in such societies. For example, a growing number of Latin American immigrants in the United States has been receiving particular attention not only in research but also in society overall (Jensen 2010; Seif 2010). There are various factors which contribute to the change in population composition: increasing longevity, low/high birth rate, and immigration, to mention a few. Among them, at the present time, immigration is a large contributor to the changes in the population composition of Sweden. Immigrant populations present their own characteristics such as socio-economic status, language, and ethnicity, all of which have impacts on the pattern of their lives (Brochman and Hagelund 2012). Accordingly, understanding immigrant populations is becoming important in Sweden, and their civic engagement is one area that requires research attention.

The topic of civic engagement among immigrant youth may be addressed both at a societal level and at an individual level. At the societal level, Sweden has been considered as maintaining a solid democracy (Kekic 2007). However, because

Sweden has been mostly a monocultural (Lutheran/post-Lutheran) society until recently, as it is now changing into a multicultural society how this solid democracy will work in such a context is open to question (Amnå 2011). This has indeed been a major argument behind one of the most extensive state-sponsored integration policies in Europe (Valenta and Bunar 2010). Although changes usually present both a threat and an opportunity, it seems that the current changes are perceived as a potential threat in general. The anxiety shared among those who perceive the change as a threat concerns the clash between different civic cultures as well as the democratic decay caused by the alleged decreasing civic engagement among immigrant populations (Strömblad et al. 2010). In order for the change to constructively lead to a successful transition to a better society, more understanding about the civic engagement of immigrant youth is critical.

Civic engagement among immigrant youth deserves research attention also for the individual adjustment of such youth. Usually, immigrants are more likely to experience discrimination throughout their lives. This is even more likely when immigrants are differentiated from native residents by easily noticeable characteristics such as appearance and ethnicity (Sherrod and Lauckhardt 2009), which is usually the case for immigrants in Sweden. Civic engagement has the potential to assist in overcoming this difficulty, so that immigrant youth can take up their eligible rights as individuals.

In sum, Sweden has been experiencing a change in population composition which has a great impact on society. While understanding immigrants is critical, there is a lack of empirical evidence. Therefore in this chapter, we present our empirical findings on one of the imperative aspects of this issue: the civic engagement of immigrant youth in Sweden.

Immigrant youth and civic engagement

Before proceeding, the key terms to be used in this chapter need to be clarified: immigrant youth and civic engagement. The two terms are variously defined and have their own ongoing arguments revolving around them (Seif 2010). However, for the purposes of this chapter, the term 'immigrant youth' refers either to those who were born outside Sweden having at least one foreign-born parent but who subsequently moved into Sweden (first-generation immigrants), or to those who were born in Sweden but who have at least one foreign-born parent and who identify themselves as immigrants (second-generation immigrants). The youth discussed in this chapter range in age from 16 to 26 years. This age range was chosen because these are likely to be formative years of civic engagement: youth in this age range are mature enough to engage in less institutionalized forms of civic/political engagement such as Internet-based community and political discussions with peers and families as well as more institutionalized forms of civic/political participation such as involvement in youth associations and voting (Ekman and Amnå 2012), but they also have greater plasticity compared to older populations.

'Civic engagement' refers to various core indicators of underlying civic competence. We rely here on Sherrod and Lauckhardt's (2009) suggestion that, across various definitions of civic engagement, common underlying aspects include civic membership, rights, and obligations. While studies in this area conventionally tend to focus on overt political behaviors such as voting and party membership, some scholars argue that including a wider range of underlying, hence often covert, indicators has a potential to better grasp the whole picture of civic engagement (Amnå and Ekman 2014). This perspective seems to be particularly relevant for studies on immigrant youth since their experiences in terms of overt political behaviors are likely to be limited due to their age and civic status (Stepick *et al.* 2008). Therefore, in this chapter, we rely on this recent perspective in order to embrace a wide range of indicators of civic/political engagement. Accordingly, our focus includes both overt and covert indicators which are likely to represent attitudes, beliefs, and behaviors in relation to civic membership, rights, and obligations. Specifically, in this chapter, we focus on youths' perceived parental social norms of civic/political engagement, political interest, actual civic/political participation, effectiveness of civic/political participation, dispositions for civic/political participation, motivation for political participation, collective political efficacy, emotions towards discrimination, and support for minority rights. In the literature, these variables have been considered to play an important role in civic engagement (Sherrod and Lauckhardt 2009).

From passivity to variety

As mentioned earlier, civic engagement among immigrant youth is one of the least studied areas, not only in Sweden but also internationally (Stepick and Stepick 2002), as was well expressed by Sherrod and Lauckhardt (2009): '… addressing the civic engagement of immigrant youth raises more questions than answers …' (p. 400). Although scarce, a view of the civic engagement of immigrants overall (hence including, but not specific to, youth populations) is available from the traditional literature. In this literature, immigrants are usually described as passive in their civic engagement (Martiniello 2005). This picture of passive civic engagement among immigrants is not unrelated to the major cause of immigration at the time, namely the supply of labor. In such a perspective, immigrants were assumed to be interested in their individual concerns such as their domestic economy rather than the current affairs of the settlement society. Furthermore, some realities of the time seemed to contribute to the creation of the image of immigrants being civically passive (Prokic-Breuer *et al.* submitted), with opportunities for immigrants to participate civically often being limited and even prohibited by the host society (as the society of the time tended to restrict immigrants' rights and their impacts on the society).

However, more recent perspectives do not coincide with this older picture of civically passive immigrants. Some have argued that immigrants' seemingly low civic engagement should be interpreted as a sign of acquiescence rather than passivity (Martiniello 2005). In addition, the causes of immigration as well as the civic circumstances of immigrants have changed and improved. Indeed, recent perspectives on civic engagement among immigrants suggest that there is little reason to believe that their civic engagement is less than that of native residents (Seif 2010). Further, some even argue that immigrants may be very active civically, especially when a political situation has been the driving force behind their migration since they are likely to be politically awakened (Martiniello 2005). Hence it seems that research attention is switching its focus from immigrants' alleged passivity to understanding the variety of their activity.

Perceived parental norms of civic engagement among Iraqi and Kurdish youth

One way to understand civic engagement among immigrant youth is through the lens of their country of origin (Jensen 2010). Indeed, the effects of country of origin have been discussed in relation to immigrants' adjustment in general and their civic engagement in particular (Aleksynska 2011; Berry 1997). However, the relationship between the country of origin and the current characteristics of immigrants is not simple to explore, especially among youth. This is because, while it is clear that immigrant youth have a connection with their country of origin, how they connect themselves to that country is relatively obscure, since most of them have only limited first-hand contact with that country (Sherrod and Lauckhardt 2009).

Despite the limited contact, it is still reasonable to assume that one major source from which immigrant youth learn about and experience the cultures and contexts of their country of origin is their parents (McIntosh and Youniss 2010). Parents have been considered to be a major socializing agent in general and in civic engagement specifically (Sherrod and Lauckhardt 2009). Since parents are likely to have spent much of their lives in the contexts of their country of origin, it is also likely that their socializing practices will reflect the social norms of their country of origin in relation to civic/political engagement.

The next question to ask is which countries of origin should be of interest. In our study, we focused specifically on two immigrant youth groups: Iraqi and Kurdish immigrant youth. Two reasons led us to focus on these two particular groups: the size of the groups and the characteristics of their country of origin, especially in relationship to civic engagement.

First, Iraqi and Kurdish immigrants are among the largest immigrant populations in Sweden. Recent statistics in Sweden have revealed the ten largest immigrant populations in Sweden and Iraqis are one of them. Although Kurdish immigrants were not specifically included in the list, this is due to the technical legal status of their country of origin (Taloyan et al. 2008). While the website of one representative Kurdish ethnic group reports their number as being around 50,000 to 60,000, the number is currently believed to be much greater than this.

Second, Iraqi and Kurdish people are assumed to represent characteristically different political orientations of their country of origin. Until quite recently, Iraqi people have lived under a long history of dictatorship. In such a society, civic engagements are highly limited, often discouraged, and in the worst case, incur significant dangers. Parents of Iraqi immigrant youth are likely to have only experienced dictatorship in their country of origin. Thus it is likely that their socializing practices will be civically less active in nature compared to those of parents in societies where circumstances for civic engagement are more favorable. In contrast, Kurdish people are well known for the continuing political movement for their own independent nation state. Hence, parents of Kurdish immigrant youth are likely to provide many civically stimulating and provocative experiences for their offspring. In addition, it is likely that these youths' civic engagement will be well rewarded at least in their communities. Thus the socializing practices of Kurds are likely to be civically more active in nature.

Immigration generation

As immigrants live in the country of settlement, they inevitably go through the process of experiencing the distinctive culture of the host society, and the adaptations which they make to this culture is called the acculturation process (Berry 1997). In acculturation, immigrant youth adapt themselves at least to a certain degree to the culture and orientations of the host society, and questions arise regarding the direction and degree of adaptation. That is, how and how much do they change?

In order to answer these questions, we first need a clear picture of civic engagement in Sweden (Berry 1997). As briefly mentioned earlier, Swedish democracy has a solid foundation and a strong background. Many social systems are suited for democracy, and the levels of various indicators of civic competence among individuals are generally high. However, just as decreasing political participation has been a recent concern for many countries, the weakening legacy of strong democracy has also often been brought to the discussion table in Sweden as well (Amnå 2006). Although conclusions regarding the level of civic engagement among contemporary Swedish youth offer a mixed picture, one recent study by Amnå and Ekman (2014) seems to provide the most well-balanced picture on this issue. These authors argue that civic engagement can be better understood by embracing both overt and covert forms of civic engagement, and they tested this contention using a sample of Swedish youth. They reported that the majority of Swedish youth showed moderate levels of overt forms of civic engagement, which contributes to the creation of a passive connotation regarding the nature of civic engagement among contemporary Swedish youth. However, the authors also highlight that these youth still maintain high levels of civic competence in many areas of covert forms of civic engagement such as political interest, suggesting a new concept, that of the 'standby citizen' (see Amnå and Ekman, Chapter 5 in this volume). Therefore, civically competent youth with moderate levels of behavioral participation seem to provide the most appropriate illustration of current patterns of civic engagement among Swedish youth.

The longer immigrants live in the settlement country, the more likely they are to be immersed into the host society; that is, the degree of adaptation is greater with the duration of stay in the settlement country. Because second-generation immigrants have not spent any time in the country of origin, the effects of the country of origin which may compete with the effects of the country of settlement are expected to be weaker among second-generation immigrants than among their first-generation counterparts. Indeed, it has been found that the civic participation of those who immigrated into the settlement country before their formative years is the same as that of native residents (Li and Jones 2011). In addition, the second generation has some more practical reasons for their easier immersion into the host country, such as their citizenship status and their language proficiency. In sum, second-generation immigrants are expected to manifest more of the characteristics of the settlement country compared to first-generation immigrants.

The current study

The current study compared various civic competence measures among Iraqi and Kurdish immigrant youth groups in Sweden. A group of native Swedish youth was also included for comparison purposes. The study addressed the following issues.

First, we aimed to compare various civic competence measures among three groups of youth: Iraqi immigrants, Kurdish immigrants, and native Swedes. We hypothesized that immigrant youth would not be less active than native residents. In addition, based on the civic engagement culture of the country of origin, which we assumed would be reflected in the youths' perception of parental norms for civic engagement, the Kurdish youth were expected to show higher civic competence than the Iraqi youth.

Second, we aimed to compare first- and second-generation immigrant youth. The expectation was that second-generation youth would be more acculturated than first-generation youth. This hypothesis was tested using two sets of comparisons. First, we compared first- and second-generation immigrant youth within each ethnic group. We expected that second-generation Iraqi youth would be more civically active than their first-generation counterpart. Regarding Kurdish youth, we expected that second-generation youth would be less civically active than their first-generation counterpart. Second, we compared the two ethnic groups by generation. These results were compared with our expectation that the differences between the two groups would be more prevalent among first-generation youth, compared to second-generation youth.

Method

Participants

The participants were 538 youth who were living in two central cities in Sweden at the time of recruitment, the year 2011. Of the participants, 79 (14.7 percent) were Iraqi immigrants, 351 (65.2 percent) were native Swedes, and 108 (20.1 percent) were Kurdish immigrants. The mean age of the participants was 19.8 years ($SD = 4.2$), and

295 of them (54.8 percent) were female. There was no significant difference in terms of gender composition across the three groups. However, the mean age of the Kurdish immigrants (20.8) was significantly higher than those of the remaining two groups (18.7 for Iraqi immigrants and 19.7 for native Swedish).

Among Iraqi immigrant youth, 29.1 percent were second-generation immigrants. For the remaining youth who were first-generation immigrants, the mean age of their arrival in Sweden was 9.7 years ($SD = 5.2$). Among Kurdish immigrant youth, 33.3 percent were second-generation immigrants. For the remaining first-generation immigrants, the mean age of their arrival in Sweden was 7.9 years ($SD = 5.7$). There was no significant difference in the age of arrival between the two groups.

Procedure

The current study was conducted as a part of a larger international project across nine European countries, Processes Influencing Democratic Ownership and Participation (PIDOP). This section only provides information which is relevant to the current study.

Different recruitment methods were used for participants aged between 16 and 18 and for those aged between 20 and 26. For the former group, trained research assistants recruited participants from various places where this age group of youth were likely to congregate such as a football arena, an ethnic student association in the town, and both inside and outside the classrooms of several schools in the town. For the latter group, research assistants approached potentially eligible participants in several public places such as public libraries, cafeterias, and adult education centers where Swedish language courses are offered for immigrants. All participants received a small compensation for their time such as a movie ticket. Participants were asked to complete a questionnaire which contained all of the following measures.

Measures

Parental social norms of civic/political engagement

Perceived parental social norms of civic/political engagement were measured using three items from Ajzen (2002) and Pattie et al. (2003). This measure assessed the youths' perception of their parents' attitude towards their own and their children's civic/political engagement. An example item was 'My parents would approve it if I engaged politically.' The youth reported how much they agreed with the given statements on a five-point Likert scale ranging from 1 (*Not at all*) to 5 (*To a great extent*). The alpha reliability of the measure was 0.62.

Political interest

Political interest was measured using a single item 'I am interested in politics.' The item was obtained from a measure for political interest used in the IEA Civic

Education study (Husfeldt and Torney-Purta 2004). (Two additional items were also used to assess interest, but as these reflected behavioral aspects, only the single item was used in the current study.) The participants provided their rating on a five-point Likert scale ranging from 1 (*Not at all*) to 5 (*To a great extent*).

Motivations for political participation

The measure for motivations for political participation was adopted from Collom (2011). The measure consisted of six items which assessed underlying reasons for political participation such as 'I would participate in a political cause if I felt I could learn new things' and 'I would participate in a political cause because I like helping other people.' The participants provided their ratings in terms of how much they agreed with the given statements on a five-point Likert scale ranging from 1 (*Not at all*) to 5 (*To a great extent*). The alpha reliability of the measure was 0.91.

Actual civic/political participation

The levels of the participants' actual civic/political participation during the past 12 months were measured using 15 items adopted from Lyons (2008). A wide range of behaviors were listed such as 'Attend a public meeting or demonstration dealing with political or social issues,' 'Distribute leaflets with a political content,' and 'Visit a website of a political or civic organization.' The participants provided their ratings on the question 'Have you done the following during the last 12 months?' The response options ranged from 1 (*Never*) to 5 (*Very often*). The alpha reliability of the measure was 0.86.

Effectiveness of civic/political participation

The same set of items as the measure for actual civic/political participation was used to assess the levels of the participants' evaluation of the effectiveness of civic/political participation. The only difference was the content of the stem question and the response options. Specifically, the respondents were asked 'To what extent do you think that these actions are effective for political and social change?' The response options ranged from 1 (*Not at all*) to 5 (*Very effective*). The alpha reliability of the measure was 0.92.

Dispositions for civic/political participation

Again, the same set of items as the measure for actual civic/political participation was used to assess the levels of the participants' likelihood of civic/political participation in the future. The respondents were asked 'How likely are you to take each of these actions in the future?' The response options ranged from 1 (*Not likely at all*) to 5 (*Very likely*). The alpha reliability of the measure was 0.90.

Collective political efficacy

The participants' levels of collective political efficacy as a youth group were measured by two items adopted from Husfeldt and Torney-Purta (2004) and Niemi et al. (1991). The participants provided their level of agreement with the two items 'I think that by working together, young people can change things for the better' and 'By working together, young people are able to influence the decisions which are made by government.' The response options ranged from 1 (*Not at all*) to 5 (*To a great extent*). The correlation between the two items adjusted by the Spearman-Brown formula was 0.86.

Emotions towards discrimination

The measure of emotions towards discrimination was adopted from van Zomeren et al. (2008). The participants provided their ratings of the extent to which they felt the following five emotions about discrimination against minority groups: anger, frustration, hope, worry, and shame. The response options ranged from 1 (*Not at all*) to 5 (*To a great extent*). The alpha reliability of the measure was 0.83.

Support for minority rights

This measure, adopted from Nata and Menezes (2004), assessed the participants' levels of support for minority rights. The measure included 11 items such as 'Ethnic minority/immigrant individuals should be granted the same rights as any other person.' The participants provided their level of agreement with the given statements on a five-point Likert scale ranging from 1 (*Not at all*) to 5 (*To a great extent*). The alpha reliability of the measure was 0.92.

Analysis

Prior to the main analyses, descriptive statistics of all the variables were computed. For the main analyses, ANOVA tests and *t*-tests were used. First, in order to compare the study variables among three groups of youth (Iraqi immigrants, Kurdish immigrants, and native Swedes), a series of ANOVAs was conducted. Second, in order to compare the first and second generations of immigrant youth, a series of independent *t*-tests were conducted, both within individual ethnic groups and across ethnic groups.

Results

Descriptive statistics of all study variables are shown in Tables 14.1 to 14.3. Table 14.1 also presents the results from the ANOVAs that compared the three groups of youth. The results from the *t*-tests that compared first and second generations of immigrant youth are presented in Tables 14.2 and 14.3.

TABLE 14.1 Results from the ANOVAs comparing the three ethnic groups

Variables	Mean (SD)	Mean (SD) by group			F (df)	Effect size
		Iraqi	Swedish	Kurdish		
Parental social norms of civic/political engagement	3.26 (0.94)	2.91ª (1.05)	3.25ᵇ (0.85)	3.56ᶜ (1.05)	11.529*** (2, 532)	0.04
Political interest	2.76 (1.31)	2.54ª (1.27)	2.72 (1.28)	3.04ᵇ (1.40)	3.534* (2, 518)	0.01
Motivations for political participation	3.18 (1.06)	2.96ª (1.11)	3.11ª (1.02)	3.59ᵇ (1.04)	10.622*** (2, 530)	0.04
Actual civic/political participation	1.80 (0.69)	1.77ª (0.69)	1.71ª (0.62)	2.11ᵇ (0.81)	12.670*** (2, 483)	0.05
Dispositions for civic/political participation	2.38 (0.85)	2.25ª (0.85)	2.33ª (0.81)	2.70ᵇ (0.95)	7.377** (2, 449)	0.03
Collective political efficacy	3.41 (1.23)	3.36 (1.36)	3.35 (1.20)	3.66 (1.19)	2.778 (2, 526)	0.01
Effectiveness of civic/political participation	2.43 (0.87)	2.24 (0.84)	2.44 (0.86)	2.52 (0.10)	1.883 (2, 445)	0.01
Emotions towards discrimination	2.96 (1.00)	2.72ª (1.00)	2.92ª (1.01)	3.28ᵇ (0.90)	7.956*** (2, 519)	0.03
Support for minority	3.86 (0.97)	3.81ª (1.05)	3.76ª (1.01)	4.23ᵇ (0.97)	10.027*** (2, 531)	0.04

Note: Different superscript letters indicate significant differences.
*$p < 0.05$; **$p < 0.01$; ***$p < 0.001$

Comparisons between the three groups of youth

As shown in Table 14.1, the ANOVA results were significant in all study variables but two: collective political efficacy and effectiveness of civic/political participation. Post-hoc analyses for the significant variables showed that, in general, Kurdish youth had higher scores than the other two groups of youth. Two exceptions to this trend were found: (1) for parental social norms of civic/political engagement, a significant difference was also found between Swedish youth and Iraqi youth with the former group being higher; (2) for political interest, where the Swedish youth score was in between the scores of the Iraqi and Kurdish youth, but without being significantly different from either of the other two groups.

TABLE 14.2 Results from the *t*-tests comparing the first and second generations within each minority ethnic group

Variables	Iraqi				Kurdish			
	First	Second	t (df)	Effect Size	First	Second	t (df)	Effect Size
Parental social norms of civic/political engagement	2.90 (1.03)	2.91 (1.13)	−0.04 (72)	0.05	3.55 (1.09)	3.59 (0.99)	−0.16 (104)	0.02
Political interest	2.58 (1.33)	2.45 (1.14)	0.38 (72)	0.04	3.06 (1.37)	3.00 (1.48)	0.20 (101)	0.02
Motivations for political participation	3.02 (1.11)	2.79 (1.11)	0.82 (76)	0.09	3.67 (1.05)	3.44 (1.04)	1.09 (102)	0.11
Actual civic/political participation	1.79 (0.72)	1.74 (0.62)	0.25 (65)	0.03	2.14 (0.80)	2.04 (0.84)	0.67 (90)	0.07
Dispositions for civic/political participation	2.29 (0.87)	2.18 (0.82)	0.45 (55)	0.06	2.71 (0.97)	2.70 (0.94)	0.05 (80)	0.01
Collective political efficacy	3.46 (1.36)	3.10 (1.35)	1.06 (74)	0.12	3.83 (1.14)	3.35 (1.25)	2.00* (105)	0.19
Effectiveness of civic/political participation	2.31 (0.87)	2.10 (0.77)	0.90 (59)	0.12	2.60 (0.91)	2.38 (0.95)	1.05 (78)	0.12
Emotions towards discrimination	2.75 (1.00)	2.64 (1.02)	0.46 (74)	0.05	3.24 (0.86)	3.34 (0.97)	−0.52 (102)	0.05
Support for minority rights	3.85 (1.00)	3.71 (1.17)	0.53 (77)	0.06	4.18 (0.69)	4.32 (0.51)	−1.20 (93.8)	0.12

*$p < 0.05$

Comparisons between the first and second generations of immigrant youth

Comparisons within ethnic groups

As shown in Table 14.2, out of a total of 18 comparisons, only one comparison was statistically significant. Specifically, the level of collective political efficacy was different between the first and second generations of Kurdish youth, with first-generation youth having higher efficacy scores.

Comparisons between ethnic groups

As shown in Table 14.3, significant differences between Iraqi and Kurdish immigrant youth were found on six variables. In all of the significant results, Kurdish youth had higher scores than Iraqi youth. On four of these six variables, the differences existed between both first- and second-generation youth. However, for the other two variables (actual participation and dispositions for civic/political

TABLE 14.3 Results from the *t*-tests comparing first and second generations across minority ethnic groups

Variables	First generation				Second generation			
	Iraqi	Kurdish	t (df)	Effect size	Iraqi	Kurdish	t (df)	Effect size
Parental social norms of civic/political engagement	2.90 (1.03)	3.55 (1.09)	−3.40*** (123)	0.29	2.91 (1.13)	3.59 (0.99)	−2.42* (58)	0.30
Political interest	2.58 (1.33)	3.06 (1.37)	−1.93 (118)	0.18	2.45 (1.14)	3.00 (1.48)	−1.56 (52.5)	0.21
Motivations for political participation	3.02 (1.11)	3.67 (1.05)	−3.34*** (122)	0.29	2.79 (1.11)	3.44 (1.04)	−2.23** (56)	0.29
Actual civic/political participation	1.79 (0.72)	2.15 (0.80)	−2.44* (104)	0.23	1.74 (0.62)	2.04 (0.84)	−1.46 (49)	0.20
Dispositions for civic/political participation	2.29 (0.87)	2.71 (0.97)	−2.16* (91)	0.22	2.18 (0.87)	2.70 (0.94)	−1.90 (44)	0.28
Collective political efficacy	3.46 (1.36)	3.83 (1.14)	−1.63 (123)	0.15	3.10 (1.35)	3.35 (1.25)	−0.73 (56)	0.10
Effectiveness of civic/political participation	2.31 (0.87)	2.60 (0.91)	−1.59 (91)	0.16	2.10 (0.77)	2.38 (0.95)	−1.06 (46)	0.15
Emotions towards discrimination	2.75 (1.00)	3.24 (0.86)	−2.91** (120)	0.26	2.64 (1.02)	3.34 (0.97)	−2.64* (56)	0.33
Support for minority rights	3.85 (1.00)	4.18 (0.69)	−2.11* (93.8)	0.21	3.71 (1.17)	4.32 (0.51)	−2.38* (27.3)	0.41

*$p < 0.05$; **$p < 0.01$; ***$p < 0.001$

participation), the significant differences were found only among first-generation youth.

Discussion

The current study was conducted to obtain a deeper understanding of civic engagement among different groups of immigrant youth in Sweden, with native Swedish youth being included as a reference group. The study focused on group differences between immigrant youth whose country of origin differs in terms of civic orientation: Iraqi and Kurdish immigrant youth. In addition, the differences between first- and second-generation immigrant youth were examined. In brief, the comparison with native Swedish youth revealed that immigrant youth are not passive as far as civic engagement is concerned. Also, the study suggests that the civic engagement of immigrant youth reflects the civic culture and orientation of their country of origin. Lastly, some differences between first- and second-generation immigrants were found which require more systematic examination. The implications of these findings will now be discussed.

Comparisons between the three groups of youth

Comparisons between immigrant youth and native Swedish youth

Across all nine indices of civic competence, there was only one measure on which immigrant youth displayed lower scores than native Swedish youth: Iraqi youth reported significantly lower levels of perceived parental social norms of civic/political participation than native Swedish youth. Furthermore, this measure represents perceived parental characteristics in relation to civic engagement rather than those of youth themselves. Thus the study reveals that, as expected, immigrant youth are not passive citizens, which is in line with other recent views that have been expressed on the civic engagement of immigrants (Martiniello 2005; Seif 2010). Indeed, our findings indicate that in most cases, levels of civic competence among Kurdish immigrant youth are significantly higher than those among native Swedish youth.

Thus the traditional view of immigrants as passive citizens does not seem to be valid anymore, which raises the question of why this is the case. Several explanations are possible. For example, as mentioned earlier in this chapter, the driving force of immigration is no longer simply to fulfill labor or employment needs. In cases where there are political or religious reasons for migration, these drivers are connected to fundamental forms of civic engagement (Sherrod and Lauckhardt 2009). Also, opportunities for immigrants to actualize their civic needs seem to have become more favorable than before. Although not yet as ideal as possible in some areas, there has been some improvement in the civic rights of immigrants, as reflected in, for example, their right to vote in local elections and their access to citizenship status. With their increased and increasing civil rights, it seems that their acquiescence is coming to a close.

This finding calls for a reframing of perspectives on the civic engagement of immigrant youth from passive citizens to normative/active citizens. This reframing, in essence, would help to correct the distorted picture of civic engagement among immigrants in the traditional view. This revised picture should spark more fruitful studies and discussions by shifting the focus from passivity to varieties of activity.

Comparisons between Iraqi and Kurdish immigrant youth

Overall, it seems that the characteristics of the country of origin are reflected in civic competence among immigrant youth. As a potential mechanism, we have assumed a socialization effect from parents to children. In order for this contention to be valid, the precondition that has to be met is that different immigrant groups of parents should display distinctive characteristics associated with their country of origin. With regard to this, our data show that Kurdish youth reported significantly higher level of perceived parental social norms of civic/political engagement than Iraqi youth, which is in line with the unique circumstances of civic engagement in the respective countries of origin as outlined earlier in this chapter. Accordingly, this finding indicates that this precondition was met among our sample, although actual parental characteristics are unknown (which will be discussed later).

The civic characteristics of the youth also reflected those of their country of origin. That is, in most of the civic competence measures, the Kurdish youth reported higher levels than the Iraqi youth. Specifically, the Kurdish youth were more interested and motivated to participate in politics than the Iraqi youth. In addition, the Kurdish youth participated in and were planning to participate in civic/political actions more than the Iraqi youth. Also, the Kurdish youth showed stronger emotions toward discrimination and stronger support for immigrant rights. To sum up, these results indicate that Kurdish youth were more behaviorally participatory and showed attitudes and beliefs that were geared towards more active civic engagement. From these findings, and in combination with the results on perceived parental social norms of civic/political engagement, we suggest that parents do indeed serve as a hub through which immigrant youth connect themselves to their country of origin in terms of civic engagement.

Although our comparison between Kurdish and Iraqi youth may convey the impression that Iraqi youth are passive, it should be remembered that these differences were only relative between the two minority groups. Since, as discussed above, the civic competence of Iraqi youth was the same as that of native Swedish youth, it would be overhasty to conclude that civic competence among Iraqi youth is passive in nature. Rather, given that civic competence among Swedish people has been considered to be strong (Kekic 2007), it would be more reasonable to also see Iraqi youth as being civically competent or at least normative.

The exceptions to the above trend are worth noting. There were two variables that were not significantly different between the two groups of youth: collective political efficacy and the evaluated effectiveness of civic/political participation. Considering the characteristics of the two variables in terms of how the sense of efficacy is built and of how effectiveness is evaluated, this finding may provide an insight regarding these immigrant youths' experiences. The sense of efficacy and the evaluation of the effectiveness of actions are strongly influenced by successful experiences in the past (Bandura 1997). Therefore successful experiences regarding civic participation should lead to higher levels of efficacy and effectiveness evaluation. Against this backdrop, given the significantly higher levels of participation reported by the Kurdish youth in this study, it is reasonable to expect higher levels of efficacy and perceived effectiveness of participation among Kurdish youth than Iraqi youth, if their actions do indeed bring about desirable outcomes and successes as expected. However, the findings of this study are not consistent with this expectation. This implies that the civic actions of Kurdish youth may not effectively translate into successes. Alternatively Kurdish youth may have experiences of confronting certain barriers which make them suspect the effectiveness of their efforts.[1] Evaluative beliefs about their own actions, such as political efficacy and the effectiveness of civic/political participation in this study, have been suggested as one of the strong underlying motivational factors for behaviors (Bandura 1997). Therefore, if the high levels of behavioral participation of Kurdish youth are not perceived by them as bringing about substantive impacts, this may contribute to decreasing behavioral participation in the long run, which is the loss of a promising asset for democracy. Therefore this finding calls for further studies to obtain a clearer picture regarding the discrepancy between levels of behavioral participation and evaluative beliefs about participation among Kurdish youth.

Comparisons between the first- and second-generations of immigrant youth

The study revealed only one significant difference between first- and second-generation immigrants from the Kurdish group, with the collective efficacy of first-generation youth being higher than that of second-generation youth. Despite this difference, however, the overall findings indicate that the civic orientation of youth does not differ considerably between first- and second-generation immigrant youth. In addition, there were significant differences between Iraqi and Kurdish youth in actual civic/political participation and disposition for civic/political participation in the future, but only amongst first-generation youth. In other words, these differences were not found among second-generation youth.

As discussed earlier in this chapter, the existence of differences between the first and second generation indicates potential acculturation effects. What makes it more meaningful is the specific pattern of the difference. Our results show that the gaps in behavioral activity levels between the two immigrant youth groups tend to diminish with the generation. This explanation is partly in line with our description of civic engagement among contemporary Swedish youth (Amnå and Ekman 2014). Again, in general, Swedish youth are characterized by high competence in most aspects of civic engagement, but with moderate levels of behavioral aspects. Therefore comparatively high levels of behavioral tendency among Kurdish youth seem to lessen over immigration generations, which may contribute to the decreased gap between the two youth groups among the second generations. Given the decreased gap among the second-generation youth, as hypothesized, this finding seems to indicate the acculturation effect. However, given the discrepancy in results between the within ethnic group and the between ethnic group comparisons, this interpretation needs caution which will be discussed later in this chapter.

Back to the social concern debate

Earlier in this chapter, we addressed the underlying importance of understanding civic engagement among immigration youth in Sweden, at both a societal and an individual level. At the societal level, we raised an issue of general, but unsubstantiated, anxiety that immigrant populations may be a threat to the strong, long-lasting democracy of Sweden. As it is already expressed as 'unsubstantiated,' our results also indicate that there is no evidence to justify the anxiety. Rather, the opposite seems to be more likely. That is, civic competence among immigrant youth seems to be a valuable asset for Swedish society as well. As shown in the results of this study, the levels of civic competence among immigrant youth are, in most cases, equal to or higher than those of native Swedes, which are considered to be desirable attributes for a solid democracy (Sherrod and Lauckhardt 2009).

However, our findings also leave a task to solve. Among the youth whose civic orientation is fairly active, beliefs on the effectiveness of their efforts were not as high as reasonably expected. Therefore it is imperative to understand why this is the case, and to take further action if there is any systematic barrier to discourage active participation among immigrant youth. This may be further justified considering the studies that showed such efforts indeed have potential for higher levels of civic engagement among immigrants (i.e. Aleksynska 2011) and for the political integration of immigrants (i.e. Lödén 2008).

Limitations and future studies

The current study was conducted using a cross-sectional design. Therefore if any of the interpretations above imply causal relationships then they are only theoretical predictions at the present time. Only longitudinal studies permit causal conclusions to be drawn, hence future studies based on longitudinal designs are called for.

In comparing the civic engagement of different groups of immigrant youth we formulated our hypotheses based on the civic characteristics of the country of origin which are assumed to be reflected in the youth's perception of parental social norms. In doing so, the overall discussion has been largely based on the socialization framework. However, it should be noted that the current study: (1) only included youth perceptions, which may not fully represent actual parent characteristics; and (2) did not include a direct measure to substantiate the socialization process. In addition, the reliability of the measure of perceived parental social norms was lower than ideal. Any firm conclusions regarding this specific mechanism can only be drawn when direct measures of actual parental characteristics and socialization processes are included and tested in future studies.

Some methodological and conceptual limitations regarding the comparisons between the first and second generations are also worth noting. Most of all, two types of comparison (within ethnic group and between ethnic group) generated results which did not converge on the same conclusion. Some reasons for this may be found in the methodological simplicity of the current study. For example, the study included only two adjacent generations in the analysis. Depending on the areas of development, the effects of acculturation may appear earlier or later (Portes and Rumbaut 2001). Civic engagement may be an area where acculturation effects appear later, which calls for further studies including multi-generations. In addition, comparison criteria can be further specified in future studies. The comparison between first and second generations may be too crude to show specific acculturation effects, allowing room for potential confounders. For example, studies of post-immigration adjustment have treated the 1.5 generation, who are born outside but are educated in the settlement country, as having distinctive qualities from both the first and the second generation (Jensen 2010). Similarly, there are many indices which are likely to affect the acculturation process such as the specific reasons for immigration, the timing of immigration, and the characteristics of the host society (Berry 1997; Li and Jones 2011). Each deserves to be included for more systematic examination in future studies.

In addition, conceptually, acculturation is essentially a mutual process (Berry 1997). However, the focus of our analyses in this study was given only to the unidirectional path from the characteristics of the settlement society to immigrant youth. Since it is also true that the characteristics that immigration populations bring to the settlement country affect those of the settlement country, future studies should pay attention to the mutual process as well.

Indicators of civic engagement can also be considered further. Although we included a wide range of potential indicators reflecting various types of civic competence, some other important indicators may be further examined. For example, for a certain group, religious affairs explain more of their lives than other groups. Since participating in religious affairs is considered one way to engage with civil society, it should be considered more seriously when examining groups whose lives are greatly attached to religious affairs.[2] In addition, by including a wide range of variables, the present study essentially limited the in-depth analysis of each variable. For example, motivation can be divided into internal vs. external motivation, and participation can be divided into online vs. offline participation.

Strength

Despite the long-lasting debate regarding levels of civic engagement among immigrant populations, empirical evidence is lacking in the literature. The current study has provided empirical evidence regarding this issue among immigrant youth. Further, by conducting the direct comparisons with native Swedish youth, this study provides reliable grounds for drawing conclusions regarding the nature of civic engagement among immigrant youth with higher confidence.

In addition, beyond the traditional notion of passivity, this study provides the unique chance of an initial step to understanding the variety of civic engagement among immigrant youth. Although more systematic studies are called for, this study built and set up the initial evidence and direction for future studies on socialization effects (based on youth perceptions of parental social norms) as well as acculturation effects (by comparing first and second generations) in relation to civic engagement among immigrant youth.

Conclusion

The current study was conducted to understand civic engagement among immigrant youth in Sweden. It has shown that civic engagement among immigrant youth in Sweden is as active as, or more active than, native Swedish youth. The heritage of the country of origin among immigrant youth is a promising factor to help understand the variability among immigrant groups.

At the same time, youth also seem to be affected by the country of settlement. Immigrant youth seem to be a potential for Swedish democracy, rather than a threat. Thus maximizing this potential might be the next task to focus upon in Sweden. Future studies are called for in order to provide more graduated colors in this overall picture.

Notes

1   One example of this scenario is, perhaps, their experience of discrimination, given that perceived discrimination has negative impacts on post-immigration adjustment (Berry 1997; Jensen 2010; Taloyan et al. 2008). Although not included as a main focus of this chapter, our data provides descriptive information on this issue. The perceived experience of discrimination due to ethnicity (assessed by a dichotomous measure of yes/no) was significantly more prevalent among Kurdish youth than the other two groups of youth (χ^2 (2) = 126.41, $p < 0.001$).
2   Among our sample of youth groups, Iraqi immigrant youth may be considered to fall into this category. Therefore, for exploratory purposes, we compared their level of religiousness to those of the other two groups. The result showed that the level of religiousness was significantly higher among Iraqi immigrant youth compared to the remaining two groups ($F_{2, 530}$ = 62.88, $p < 0.001$). Because more specific measures to assess religious activities were not used, it is not possible to analyze this issue any further. Future studies are required.

References

Ajzen, I. (2002) 'Constructing a TpB questionnaire: conceptual and methodological considerations.' Retrieved from: http://people.umass.edu/~aizen/pdf/tpb.measurement.pdf.
Aleksynska, M. (2011) 'Civic participation of immigrants in Europe: assimilation, origin, and destination country effects', *European Journal of Political Economy*, 27: 566–85.
Amnå, E. (2006) 'Playing with fire? Swedish mobilization for participatory democracy,' *Journal of European Public Policy*, 13 (4): 587–606.
Amnå, E. (2011) 'Scandinavian democracies learning diversity,' in K. Sporre and J. Mannberg (eds), *Values, Religions and Education in Changing Societies*. Dordrecht: Springer, pp. 9–22.
Amnå, E. and Ekman, J. (2014) 'Standby citizens: faces of political passivity,' *European Political Science Review*, 6: 261–81.
Bandura, A. (1997) *Self-efficacy: The Exercise of Control*. New York: W. H. Freeman.
Berry, J. W. (1997) 'Immigration, acculturation, and adaptation,' *Applied Psychology: An International Review*, 46 (1): 5–68.

Brochmann, G. and Hagelund, A. (2012) *Immigration Policy and the Scandinavian Welfare State 1945–2010*. Basingstoke: Palgrave Macmillan.

Husfeldt, V. and Torney-Purta, J. (2004) 'Development of the CivED Instruments,' in W. Schulz and H. Sibberns (eds), *IEA Civic Education Study Technical Report*. Amsterdam: Multycopy, pp. 17–26.

Jensen, L. A. (2010) 'Immigrant youth in the United States: coming of age among diverse civic cultures,' in L. R. Sherrod, T. Judith, and C. A. Flanagan (eds), *Handbook of Research on Civic Engagement in Youth*. Hoboken, NJ: John Wiley & Sons, pp. 425–43.

Kekic, L. (2007, May) 'The Economist Intelligence Unit's index of democracy,' *The Economist*. Retrieved from: http://www.economist.com/media/pdf/DEMOCRACY_INDEX_2007_v3.pdf.

Li, R. and Jones, B. (2011) 'Age at Immigration Matters: Explaining Immigrants' Political Participation from a Socialization Perspective.' Unpublished paper presented at American Politics Workshop, Madison, WI, November.

Lödén, H. (2008) 'Swedish: being or becoming? Immigration, national identity and the democratic state,' *International Journal of Human and Social Sciences*, 3 (4): 257–64.

Lyons, E. (2008) *Political Trust and Political Participation Amongst Young People from Ethnic Minorities in the NIS and EU: A Social Psychological Investigation*, Final Report to INTAS. Belfast: Queen's University Belfast.

McIntosh, H. and Youniss, J. (2010) 'Toward a political theory of political socialization of youth,' in L. R. Sherrod, T. Judith, and C. A. Flanagan (eds), *Handbook of Research on Civic Engagement in Youth*. Hoboken, NJ: John Wiley & Sons, pp. 23–41.

Martiniello, M. (2005) *Political Participation, Mobilization and Representation of Immigrants and Their Offspring in Europe*, Willy Brandt Series of Working Papers in International Migration and Ethnic Relations No. 1. Retrieved from http://hdl.handle.net/2043/1495.

Nata, G. and Menezes, I. (2004) *Escala de suporte dos direitos das minorias*. Porto: FPCEUP.

Niemi, R. G., Craig, S. C., and Mattei, F. (1991) 'Measuring internal political efficacy in the 1988 National Election Study,' *American Political Science Review*, 85 (4): 1407–13.

Pattie, C., Seyd, P., and Whiteley, P. (2003) 'Citizenship and civic engagement: attitudes and behavior in Britain,' *Political Studies*, 51: 443–68.

Portes, A. and Rumbaut, R. G. (2001) *Legacies: The Story of the Immigrant Second Generation*. Berkeley, CA: University of California Press.

Prokic-Breuer, T., Vink, M. P., Hutcheson, D., and Jeffers, K. (Submitted) 'Socialization, naturalization, and immigrant political participation in Europe: testing transferability theory.'

Seif, H. (2010) 'The civic life of Latina/o immigrant youth: challenging boundaries and creating safe spaces,' in L. R. Sherrod, T. Judith, and C. A. Flanagan (eds), *Handbook of Research on Civic Engagement in Youth*. Hoboken, NJ: John Wiley & Sons, pp. 445–70.

Sherrod, L. R. and Lauckhardt, J. (2009) 'The development of citizenship,' in R. M. Lerner and L. Steinberg (eds), *Handbook of Adolescent Psychology*, 3rd edn. Hoboken, NJ: John Wiley & Sons, pp. 372–407.

Statistics Sweden (2013) See: http:www.scb.se.

Stepick, A. and Stepick, C. D. (2002) 'Becoming American, constructing ethnicity: immigrant youth and civic engagement,' *Applied Developmental Science*, 6: 246–57.

Stepick, A., Stepick, C. D., and Labissiere, C. Y. (2008) 'South Florida's immigrant youth and civic engagement,' *Applied Developmental Science*, 12 (2): 57–65.

Strömblad, P., Bay, A., and Bengtsson, B. (eds) (2010) *Diversity, Inclusion and Citizenship in Scandinavia*. Newcastle: Cambridge Scholars.

Taloyan, M., Johansson, S., Sundquist, J., Koctürk, T. O., and Johansson, L. M. (2008) 'Psychological distress among Kurdish immigrants in Sweden,' *Scandinavian Journal of Public Health*, 36: 190–6.

Valenta, M. and Bunar, N. (2010) 'State assisted integration: refugee integration policies in Scandinavian welfare states: the Swedish and Norwegian experience,' *Journal of Refugee Studies*, 23 (4): 463–83.

Van Zomeren, M., Postmes, T., and Spears, R. (2008) 'Toward an integrative social identity model of collective action: a quantitative research synthesis of three socio-psychological perspectives,' *Psychological Bulletin*, 134: 504–35.

15

PREDICTORS OF CIVIC AND POLITICAL PARTICIPATION AMONG NATIVE AND MIGRANT YOUTH IN ITALY

The role of organizational membership, sense of community, and perceived social well-being

Cinzia Albanesi, Davide Mazzoni, Elvira Cicognani and Bruna Zani

Introduction

Explaining youths' political (dis)engagement is currently a key research endeavor for different disciplines, including political science, sociology, and social and developmental psychology (Sherrod et al. 2010). In this chapter, we will present data from the Italian sample of the PIDOP project, focusing on the explanatory role of organizational membership, and on how the quality of participation in such organizations affects youth civic and political participation. More importantly, we will test two possible mediating factors of the association between organizational membership and civic and political participation, drawn from theoretical perspectives in community psychology (see Chapter 9 by Cicognani and Zani in the present volume): sense of community and social well-being. We will include data on both native and migrant adolescents and young adults: the latter are an understudied population in Italy still experiencing forms of institutional discrimination as far as citizenship rights are concerned. This will provide an important test for the role of (legal and perceived) institutional and community inclusion in promoting civic and political engagement.

Youth civic and political participation in Italy

Sociological surveys on nationally representative samples of youth conducted in Italy in the last 20 years have documented a constant increase of disgust toward formal politics (Buzzi et al. 2002). The majority of Italian people aged 15–24 perceive themselves as not competent in politics and not interested (De Luca 2007). Initial interpretations of these data pointed to the increasing disaffection toward politics that characterized Italian society as a whole, similar to other countries. More recently, discourses and social narratives among youth have increasingly stressed the role of intergenerational factors, in view of the peculiar demographic trends in South European countries and specifically in Italy, showing a strong imbalance (of power and control) in favor of older groups (as the currently used term *gerontocracy* testifies).

Other perspectives stressed that youths' disaffection toward politics might be balanced by an increasing interest in social issues, which finds expression through different forms of civic engagement. One form of civic engagement is volunteering. According to the Italian National Institute of Statistics (ISTAT 2013), the total number of people donating their time to voluntary organizations for solidarity purposes has increased in the last 20 years from 7 percent (1993) to 10 percent (2012). This percentage, even if it is still low compared to north European countries, is higher among young people aged 14–24 (from 7 to 11.62 percent). Also the percentage of people donating money to support volunteers' organizations had an increasing trend from 1993 to 2010, from 14.1 to 17.6 percent; in 2011 this percentage decreased, probably due to the generalized economic crises. A similar trend was also observed among people aged 14–24: those donating money for volunteers' organizations increased from 8.1 percent in 1993 to 8.5 percent 2010.

Web 2.0 technology has very rapidly taken on a crucial role in enabling youth civic and political participation (e.g. Cammaerts 2007; Juris and Pleyers 2009; Riley *et al.* 2010; Jugert *et al.* 2013) making participatory action easier, faster and more widespread. According to the recent BES report on equitable and sustainable well-being (ISTAT 2013), from 2011 to 2012 the increase in the number of citizens (above 14 years) who participated in online consultations or voting on social or political issues (overall from 4.6 percent to 5.9 percent) is mainly attributable to adolescents and young people up to 24 years of age and appears to be their predominant form of political participation. Web civic and political participation (including talking about politics or looking for information on the web) characterized over 2 million Italian citizens in 2012 (vs. 1 million in 2011), and is mostly concentrated in the 14–24 age range. Such increasing relevance of the web is supported by the study of Cioni and Marinelli (2010) on the attitudes of young people toward the participative opportunities offered by the web (blogs, social networks, etc.). Their findings show that, even if some participants think that social networks can only support already existing personal relationships, for many young people the web is going to overtake TV in terms of relevance for communication on politics. Park *et al.* (2009) found that informational use of social networks was associated with civic engagement and that Facebook facilitated civic action among college students (cf. also Pasek *et al.* 2009).

Considering gender differences, according to ISTAT (2010), the percentage of young people interested in politics ranges from 10 percent of young females to 12 percent of young males, while the percentage of young people who donate their time to volunteers' organizations ranges from 10.66 percent of males to 12.83 percent of females (aged 14–24). Even if there are still gender differences regarding levels of civic and political involvement, the gender gap in the younger generations is lower compared to older generations (cf. Cicognani *et al.* 2012). This could be a consequence of the increased relevance of web civic and political participation among youth: the web supports both males and females practising and learning how to become active citizens, removing some barriers to women's participation (Cassel et al. 2006). Such findings are confirmed by the BES report (ISTAT 2013), according to which no gender differences emerge in civic and political participation among 14- to 19-year-old adolescents. The gender gap increases steadily after 20 years reaching the maximum after 55 years. Civic and political participation, among both males and females, is higher among more educated individuals and those with higher socio-economic background. Only among students do gender differences disappear (67.4 percent of females vs. 69.5 percent of males).

The role of organizational membership in civic and political participation

Involvement in organized group activities is common in young people's experiences. According to the classic study by Hendry et al. (1993), the majority of adolescents participate regularly in organized activities offered by their community, and only a few are not involved in such activities. Similar evidence has been collected in Italy: Albano (2005), analyzing the data collected on a national representative sample of Italian youth, found that 50 percent of young people aged 16–19 belongs to at least one association, while among those aged 20–30 only one out of three belongs. Sport and recreational groups were found to be very popular among young people; religious organizations were less popular, but still involve around 10 percent of young people.

In a study involving 173 leaders of youth associations (Di Gioia et al. 2009), the majority of participants reported that in the previous five years youth participation had increased, and they estimated a further increase in the future. Leone (2011) analyzed participation in a sample of 1,410 young people aged 14–30 (M = 21 years old): she found that only 18 percent had never been involved in any kind of association, while 65 percent had been/were currently involved in one or more associations. Cultural associations were the most popular among young people (27.4 percent), followed by sport and scout groups (ranging from 14 percent to 18 percent). Student organizations and parish groups were less attended. Leone also found a positive correlation between associational experience and participation through the web: members or ex-members of associations participated more in discussions on social issues through the Internet and social networks.

Organizational membership is an important precursor to civic and political participation because of its role in building social capital (Putnam 2000). According to Paxton (1999), social capital increases the likelihood of people being civically and politically engaged because it enhances their capacity for agency.

Involvement in formal and non-formal organizations and groups in the community is central for civic and political socialization (Verba et al. 1995; Sherrod et al. 2010). Such socializing agencies (or *developmental niches*) (Torney-Purta and Amadeo 2011) impact youth's civic and political engagement and participation through different mechanisms (e.g. situated learning; scaffolding by involvement in structured and adult-supervised organizations providing information, training and access to the political system; perspective-taking by involving youth in discussions with people with different perspectives, interests and needs) (McIntosh and Youniss 2010).

There is evidence that adolescent involvement in community organizations offering programmes designed to foster civic and political engagement predicts adult political participation (Larson and Hansen 2005). Youniss et al. (1997) argued that students who participated in high-school activities (such as government and community service projects) were more likely to vote and to join community organizations 15 years later than were young people who did not participate. Similarly, McFarland and Thomas (2006) showed that voluntary participation at a young age stimulates political participation in adulthood. Further, retrospective studies of adults have found that participation in non-formal community youth groups and extracurricular activities is related to engagement in civic associations and political affairs in adulthood (Verba et al. 1995).

Several psychological and psychosocial mediating factors for the impact of organizational membership on civic and political participation have been proposed.

Participating in these organizations enhances youth's feeling that they can influence political decisions and consequently their likelihood to engage in politics (Verba et al. 1995). Membership of voluntary associations creates social trust, which stimulates civic commitment and political participation (Youniss et al. 1997) and increases personal resources and skills (Eggert and Giugni 2010). Voluntary membership gives individuals extra information about social issues as well as politics and policies through communication and personal networks (Parry et al. 1992), and as this information makes people more knowledgeable about politics and social issues, they are more likely to participate (Delli Carpini and Keeter 1996). Membership in voluntary associations encourages the development of skills that are useful in political participation: for example, deliberation, compromise, speaking in public, expressing an opinion, learning to work in groups, and assimilating other people's opinions (Verba et al. 1993; Eden and Roker 2002; Torpe 2003; Checkoway et al. 2005). Satisfaction and integration with volunteers' organizations contribute to an increased willingness to sustain volunteering over time (Marta et al. 2006).

Involvement in community organizations may also enhance the construction of a more complex civic and political identity and sense of ownership and belonging to the community (McMillan and Chavis 1986; Albanesi et al. 2007; Chiessi et al. 2010). In the literature within Community Psychology, there is evidence on the role of a sense of community (SoC) in enhancing participation, both among adults (Wandersman and Florin 2000) and adolescents (cf. Chapter 9 in the present volume). Among young people, it is especially the perception of opportunities for having an influence over the community (one of the SoC dimensions) that plays a stronger role in civic and political participation (Albanesi et al. 2007; Evans 2007).

It is still not clear how organizational characteristics affect participation outcomes (Yang and Pandey 2011). Both the range (e.g. membership of different groups/associations) and intensity of such involvement seem to be important. Quintelier (2008) found that multiple membership is associated with greater civic and political activity among Belgian adolescents, while time spent in associational activities was not. Teney and Hanquinet (2012) found that young people who are more politically active benefit from different forms of social capital (participating in different kinds of voluntary organizations). These results are consistent with the idea that bridging social capital contributes to political participation. Quintelier's findings, however, revealed also that only cultural, deliberative and religious-ethnic organizations increase political participation, whereas youth and expressive organizations do not. She considers that this diversity is related to the different opportunities and skills that young people develop within the organizations, in particular to playing a leadership role and organizing activities. Less relevance was accorded to taking part in the decision-making process. Menezes and colleagues have emphasized the importance of the quality of participatory experiences as an explanatory factor for civic and political participation. The assumption is that the elements of challenge and support, of action and reflection, may be important in getting involved in political parties, social movements, volunteer work in the community, and religious or recreational associations (Ferreira et al. 2012). The combination of opportunities for action and reflection in a supportive environment where pluralism and dissent are valued – i.e. the *quality of participation* – seems not only to characterize many current civic and political experiences, but also to foster relevant participatory attitudes, dispositions and behaviors (Carneiro 2006; Ferreira 2006; Veiga 2008; Azevedo 2009). These findings point to the importance of distinguishing between the quality of participation experiences within community organizations from the range and intensity of such experiences, as they might produce partly different influences on political participation.

Civic and political participation: the case of migrant youth in Italy

In the last decades, the number of immigrants resident in Italy (including adolescents and young people) has steadily increased. According to data from the Italian National Institute of Statistics, there were fewer than 1.5 million in 2002, becoming almost 5 million in 2012. Only 66,000 of them have Italian citizenship. Twenty-one percent of the immigrants living in Italy are under the legal age of 18, and 70 percent of them were born in Italy. The limited number of 'Italians' with different ethnic origins depends on Italy's current laws on citizenship that are among the most restrictive in Western Europe (e.g. children of foreign parents born in Italy are not automatically Italian: they can request Italian citizenship when they are 18 years old only if they remain continually resident in Italy and by going through a complicated bureaucratic process). This situation is experienced as a significant structural barrier to political participation, particularly among the young generation (only

Italian citizens have the right to vote in Italy), as testified in the following quotes extracted from a focus group on democratic ownership and political participation with young Albanians (Albanesi *et al.* 2012).

> I have been living in Italy for 11 years and I cannot vote because I am not allowed to have citizenship yet. We just had elections and I wanted to express my opinion. Italy is very far behind in comparison with other EU countries. Now there is a proposal that foreigners asking for citizenship should take a test on the Italian Constitution, to verify whether they know it. But even many Italians do not know it, so what do they want to do?

> ... the vote is important for citizenship. Italy is very far behind from this point of view, especially for what concerns immigrants' children. They were born here, went to school here, speak Italian perfectly even though they still keep something of their own culture of origin, their traditions, they feel Italian. However, they do not have citizenship, they have to wait to be 18 years old to ask for it and then, at least three years to obtain it.

Institutionalized forms of inequality (e.g. lack of legal citizenship) limit migrants' sense of efficacy and marginalize them, while participation has a central role for their integration: participation can be 'the civic glue that bonds those who would otherwise be divided along racial and ethnic lines' (Putnam 2000: 362). There is an explicit recognition that the active participation of young people, and particularly immigrants, in decisions at both local and national levels is a precondition for the construction of an inclusive society.

Civic and political participation among migrant young people in Italy is an understudied topic. Most research has focused on young people's perspectives on citizenship and their relevance for inclusion (Colombo 2010; Colombo *et al.* 2011): only a few studies have examined the role of migrant and ethnic associations as a context that promotes political participation, but these did not focus specifically on young people's experiences, being more interested in the political role played by associations at the structural (city) level (Caponio 2005). The existence of structural opportunities for immigrant participation (i.e. a hospitable and inclusive community, supportive integration policies) is an important condition in order to build a sense of political agency and identity, as well as confidence in one's own abilities to mobilize and change the circumstances in which one lives. However, in our perspective, personal experiences of participation are also important, besides structural opportunities.

In addition, in Europe, research on civic and political participation among migrant young people is limited (cf. Stepick *et al.* 2008). Some studies suggest a tendency for lower levels of civic and political participation among migrant youths (Norris 2002; Vogel and Triandafyllidou 2005; Burns 2007; Paxton *et al.* 2007), not recognizing the existence of diversity in terms of contexts and forms of engagement (Stepick *et al.* 2008). Other studies that have considered various forms of civic and political participation among several ethnic groups provide a different picture (Quintelier 2009). Among migrant youth, associational membership has the functions of integration and adaptation (Munro 2008; Sonn 2002). Eggert and Giugni (2010) found empirical evidence in a study with migrants of different ethnic origins in Switzerland, and they concluded that political participation represents the behavioral dimension of integration.

Summary of the literature and hypotheses

Summarizing the literature examined so far on majority and migrant youth, we can conclude that both organizational membership and quality of participation experiences within such organizations have a central role in explaining the civic and political participation of both groups; among migrants, the evidence of such association has been found in studies conducted in different countries (with different laws concerning citizenship rights) and with different ethnic groups. Less evidence is available on the psychological and psychosocial mechanisms that may mediate such association, and whether they are similar or different, depending on factors such as legal status (citizens vs. not citizens) or ethnic/cultural background. Considering legal status, from the literature reviewed there are grounds to expect specific mediation pathways for majority (citizens) vs. migrant (non-citizens) youth. In particular, the evidence on migrant youth participation indicates that perceived social integration into the host society (which can be enhanced by organizational membership) is important for explaining the civic and political participation of this population. Such a hypothesis is consistent also with focus group data collected within the PIDOP project (cf. Cicognani *et al.* under review), which showed that, for migrant (Moroccan) adolescents, who mostly were not legally citizens and thus experienced a sort of *institutional discrimination*, the perception of a higher social integration into Italian society is a prerequisite condition for engaging in civic and political action as citizens; the latter is perceived as useless and not meaningful without feeling accepted by the host country.

Italian youth, who do not experience this form of exclusion, should perceive social integration into the larger society as less influential; a more relevant role could be played by the SoC which concerns the perceived quality of the relation with the local community or residential context. In particular, the perception of the existence of opportunities for having an influence over the community is expected to be particularly relevant and to influence current civic and political participation as well as intentions to participate in the future.

The study

The aim of this study was to test the role of organizational membership and quality of participatory experiences in predicting youth's civic and political participation. We focused on traditional forms of civic participation (e.g. volunteering) and modern forms of political participation (e.g. through the web, demonstrating) that are currently most typically adopted by youths in Italy. Specifically, we tested a model of the predictors of participation (Figure 15.1) which includes the role of

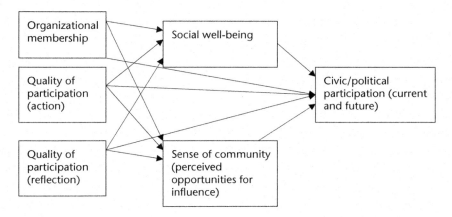

FIGURE 15.1 Theoretical model

organizational membership, of the perceived *quality of participation experience* (action and reflection), and the mediation role of *SoC* (perceived opportunities for influence) and *social well-being* (the latter examined as an indicator of perceived social integration in the host society). The model was tested among both Italian and migrant youth, to assess its predictive role on both current and future civic and political participation.

The model assumes that both organizational membership and quality of participation experiences within organizations are significant predictors of current and future civic/political participation. It also assumes that such influence is mediated by youth's perceptions of having an influence over the local community and perceived social integration into the broader society (social well-being). Specific mediation pathways were expected based on the existing literature and qualitative (focus group) findings from the PIDOP project: specifically, perceptions of opportunities for influence over the local community were expected to significantly mediate the impact of the predictors especially among Italian youth, whereas social well-being was expected to be a more significant mediator among migrant participants.

We also tested the differences in all the variables according to age group, gender and migrant/citizen status. Based on the literature, we expected that, with age, there would be stronger intentions to become civically active and participate in politics. Migrant youth were expected to be less involved in organizations and to score lower on perceived opportunities for influence over the local community and social well-being than majority youth.

Method

The sample comprised a total of 1,145 adolescents and young adults. Their ages ranged from 16 to 26 years old, with 16- and 17-year-olds being classified as adolescents and those aged 18 and over being classified as adults. There were 799 Italians and 346 migrants. The mean age of the Italians was 20.73 years ($SD = 3.09$) and 49.1 percent were males. Among migrants, 173 were Moroccans and 173 Albanians; the mean age was 18.45 years ($SD = 2.88$) and 62.4 percent were males. Results of ANOVA showed a significant interaction between age group and migrant status ($F(1, 1136) = 8.60$, $p < 0.05$, $\eta^2 = 0.007$). Adolescents' mean age was 16.51 ($SD = 0.536$), with no differences between Italians and migrants. Adults' mean age was 21.65 (SD = 2.56), but Italian adults ($M = 21.84$; $SD = 2.48$) were older than migrant adults ($M = 20.99$; $SD = 2.75$). Migrant participants did not have Italian citizenship: 76 percent were first-generation migrants ($N = 291$); second-generation migrants made up only 15.7 percent ($N = 60$): among them there were more adolescents ($N = 38$) than adults ($N = 22$).

Procedure

Participants were recruited from different types of high schools and universities in the region of Emilia Romagna (North Italy). Recruitment of migrant adolescents was conducted in those schools (e.g. vocational schools, technical schools) having higher percentages of migrants. Migrant young adults (20- to 26-year-olds) were approached first at the university. As a second step, several organizations and associations in the community were approached, both youth associations attended by the general youth population (e.g. youth centres, etc.) and migrant associations. To help spread information about the study and ask for collaboration, some media were also used (e.g. the journal *Albania News*, which is very popular among this group), as well as contacts with work contexts (work cooperatives, where many migrants are employed) and thematic social events concerning integration, migration, intercultural dialogue, etc., involving our targets (e.g. meetings of Moroccan and Albanian citizens, a referendum for the election of Moroccan president, etc.). We also used a snowball method, asking those migrant youth willing to complete the questionnaire to provide the names of other members of their networks.

The data on the two migrant groups (Albanian and Moroccan) were collapsed as the crucial variable in this study was migrant/citizenship status.

Measures

Participants completed a paper-and-pencil questionnaire including different sections. For the purposes of this study, the following sections of the questionnaire were used.

Organizational membership

We measured the degree of involvement in eight different kinds of associations and organized groups (trade unions and student associations, political parties and party youth groups, volunteering and charity groups, youth associations or groups, religious associations or groups, associations for the protection of human rights, environmental associations and animal rights groups, leisure and recreational associations or groups). We asked participants whether they took part in the activities of the different groups. Responses were provided on a four-point response scale (1 = 'never', 2 = 'occasionally', 3 = 'less than 6 months', 4 = 'more than 6 months'). The reliability of this scale was acceptable in both the Italian (Cronbach $a = 0.71$) and migrant (Cronbach $a = 0.77$) groups. An average score of involvement was thus computed and adopted in the analysis.

Quality of participation experiences: action and reflection

The Participation Experiences Questionnaire (QOP) (Ferreira et al. 2012) is a self-report measure that operationalizes this theoretical perspective on the quality of participation experiences. Respondents were asked to indicate, with reference to the experience they considered to be the most important (from the list used to measure organizational membership), how frequently they actively engaged in different kinds of *actions* (five items, e.g.: 'to participate in activities such as petitions, protests, parties, meetings, assemblies, debates, public statements; to manage or guide a team having to organize activities, such as petitions, protests, parties, meetings, assemblies, debates, public statements') and how often they felt that certain conditions facilitating *reflection* were present (five items, e.g. 'different perspectives were discussed'; 'conflicting opinions gave rise to new ways of seeing the issues'; 'real and everyday life issues were the focus of the discussions'). Thus the scale was made of two dimensions, the first regarding opportunities for Action (QOP-action) and the second regarding opportunities for Reflection (QOP-reflection). Responses were given on a five-point Likert-type scale ranging from 1 (= 'never') to 5 (= 'very often'). Participants with no organizational membership were assigned the score of 1. Reliability of QOP-action was acceptable in both the Italian ($a = 0.82$) and migrant ($a = 0.84$) groups. Also, the reliability of QOP-reflection was good for both the Italian ($a = 0.91$) and migrant ($a = 0.90$) groups. For the analyses, an average index of QOP-action and a score for QOP-reflection were thus created.

Sense of community (perceived opportunities for influence)

We used the subscale 'perceived opportunities for influence' of the Brief Scale of Sense of Community in Adolescents (Chiessi et al. 2010). The subscale includes four items and responses are provided through a five-point Likert-type scale (ranging from 1 = 'not at all true' to 5 = 'completely true'). Item examples were "Honestly, I feel that if we engage more, we would be able to improve things for young people in this town,' 'I think that people who live here could change things that are not properly working for the community'. The reliability of this scale was good in both the Italian ($a = 0.80$) and migrant ($a = 0.79$) groups. An average score was thus used in the analysis.

Social well-being

We measured social well-being, using Keyes' (2006) brief scale including five items. Item examples were 'The way our society works made sense to you?', 'Our society is becoming a better place?' Answers were provided referring to the last month, on a frequency scale from 1 (= 'never') to 6 (= 'every day'). The reliability of this scale was acceptable in both the Italian ($a = 0.66$) and migrant ($a = 0.74$) groups. An average score was thus used in the analysis.

Current and future civic participation

We measured current and future civic participation through items which included: doing volunteer work, donating money to a cause/organization, taking part in concerts or a fund-raising event. The scale resulted from factor analysis of the participation scale used in the PIDOP study. Answers were provided on a five-point scale. The reliability of the future civic participation scale was acceptable in both the Italian ($a = 0.66$) and migrant ($a = 0.69$) groups; with regard to the actual civic participation scale the reliability was acceptable for the migrant group ($a = 0.60$) but very low for the Italian ($a = 0.49$). However, as we wanted to measure the same phenomenon across groups and over time, we decided to use it. Average scores were thus used in the analysis.

Current and future political participation

We measured current and future political participation through the following items: attending a public meeting or demonstration dealing with political or social issues; boycotting or buying certain products for political, ethical or environmental reasons; linking news or music or videos with a social or political content; discussing societal or political questions on the net; visiting a website of a political or civic organization; participating in online-based protest or boycotting; connecting to a group on Facebook (or similar online social network) dealing with social or political issues. Answers were provided referring to the present and the future on a five-point scale. Factor analysis confirmed the unidimensionality of the scale. The reliability of this scale was acceptable in both the Italian (current: $a = 0.85$; future: $a = 0.87$) and migrant (current: $a = 0.89$; future: $a = 0.89$) groups. Average scores were thus used in the analysis.

Analysis

Firstly, we compared the scores of psychosocial variables according to gender, age, and citizenship status. Bootstrapping, an alternative approach to Baron and Kenny's (1986) causal steps of mediation testing, was then used to test a mediation model with three independent variables and two mediators. The SPSS macro MEDIATE, developed by Preacher and Hayes (2004; Hayes and Preacher 2013), was used.

The variables of organizational membership, QOP-action and QOP-reflection, were inserted as independent variables, and perceived opportunities for influence over the local community and social well-being inserted as mediators. Participation scales (current civic participation, future civic participation, current political participation, future political participation) were inserted as the dependent variable. Gender and age were included in the model as covariates. An estimate of confidence intervals for the indirect effect in each resampled data set was calculated from the sampling distribution. In the current study, 5,000 bootstrap resamples were used to generate 95 percent confidence intervals.

Results

Table 15.1 shows descriptive statistics (mean and standard deviation) of the psychosocial variables under study, separately for citizenship status (native and migrant), gender, and age. Through analysis of variance (ANOVA) the significant main effects of these three variables on each psychosocial variable are pointed out.

Table 15.2 presents correlations between the variables under study. Organizational membership, QOP-action, and QOP-reflection positively correlate with perceived opportunities for influence, social well-being, and civic/political participation (current and future).

The mediation model in Figure 15.1 was thus tested separately in the natives and migrants groups, for each of the four variables of civic and political participation (current and future).

Italians

First we tested the model on *current civic participation*. The bootstrapping procedure yielded an estimate of the indirect effect of organizational membership through perceived opportunities for influence over the local community of 0.0096 ($SE = 0.0070$), with a 95 percent CI ranging from 0.0003 to 0.287. The indirect effect of QOP-reflection through opportunities for influence was 0.0117 ($SE = 0.0056$; CI: 0.0023–0.0247). As these intervals did not contain zero, the indirect effect was significant at $a = 0.05$.

This pattern of results was confirmed on *future civic participation*. The indirect effect of organizational membership (0.0260) was significant through opportunities for influence ($SE = 0.0148$; $CI = 0.0011$–0.0603). The indirect effect of QOP-reflection (0.0320) was significant through opportunities for influence ($SE = 0.0100$; $CI = 0.0158$–0.0555).

These results were confirmed on *current political participation*. The indirect effect of organizational membership (0.0142) was significant through opportunities for influence ($SE = 0.0087$; $CI = 0.0014$–0.0379). The indirect effect of QOP-reflection (0.0174) was significant through opportunities for influence ($SE = 0.0070$; $CI = 0.0058$–0.0338).

TABLE 15.1 Descriptive statistics of psychosocial variables: Italians and migrants, females and males, adolescents and young adults

	Organization membership	QOP-action	QOP-reflection	Opportunities for influence	Social well-being	Current civic participation	Future civic participation	Current political participation	Future political participation
	M (SD)	M (SD)	M (SD)	M (SD)	M (SD)	M (SD)	M (SD)	M (SD)	M (SD)
Citizenship status									
Italians	1.61 (0.52)	2.28 (1.08)	2.92 (1.22)	3.03 (0.86)	2.69 (0.84)	1.80 (0.78)	2.70 (1.00)	2.01 (0.90)	2.40 (1.02)
Migrants	1.60 (0.54)	2.28 (1.05)	2.59 (1.19)	3.00 (0.92)	2.81* (0.97)	1.91** (0.88)	2.57 (1.13)	2.02 (0.98)	2.38 (1.11)
Gender									
Females	1.63 (0.53)	2.30 (1.08)	2.94 (1.25)	3.08 (0.87)	2.72 (0.86)	1.93 (0.79)	2.89 (0.98)	2.05 (0.92)	2.49 (1.04)
Males	1.57 (0.52)	2.26 (1.06)	2.72 (1.19)	2.97 (0.89)	2.73 (0.90)	1.75** (0.82)	2.46** (1.05)	1.98 (0.93)	2.31 (1.05)
Age									
Adolescents (<18)	1.57 (0.52)	2.15 (0.96)	2.58 (1.17)	2.86 (0.89)	2.62 (0.85)	1.75 (0.79)	2.48 (1.09)	1.79 (0.82)	2.16 (1.01)
Young adults (≥18)	1.63 (0.53)	2.34* (1.11)	2.94* (1.23)	3.09** (0.87)	2.77** (0.89)	1.88* (0.82)	2.75* (1.01)	2.12** (0.95)	2.50** (1.05)

Note: *$p < 0.01$; **$p < 0.001$.

TABLE 15.2 Correlations among psychosocial variables among Italians and migrants

	Italians								Migrants							
	2	3	4	5	6	7	8	9	2	3	4	5	6	7	8	9
1. Organizational membership	0.60**	0.51**	0.22**	0.27**	0.48**	0.31**	0.37**	0.29**	0.63**	0.56**	0.25**	0.27**	0.48**	0.29**	0.41**	0.35**
2. QOP-action		0.71**	0.24**	0.32**	0.49**	0.36**	0.51**	0.43**		0.74**	0.33**	0.39**	0.38**	0.30**	0.46**	0.43**
3. QOP-reflection			0.30**	0.34**	0.40**	0.35**	0.43**	0.39**			0.38**	0.34**	0.34**	0.38**	0.39**	0.42**
4. Opportunities for influence				0.30**	0.23**	0.28**	0.24**	0.29**				0.48**	0.19**	0.34**	0.31**	0.35**
5. Social well-being					0.22**	0.17**	0.18**	0.17**					0.35**	0.43**	0.51**	0.51**
6. Current civic participation						0.55**	0.42**	0.33**						0.56**	0.59**	0.43**
7. Future civic participation							0.41**	0.55**							0.48**	0.67**
8. Current political participation								0.85**								0.77**
9. Future political participation								—								—

Note: $^*p < 0.01$; $^{**}p < 0.001$

Finally, this pattern of results was confirmed also on *future political participation*. The indirect effect of organizational membership (0.0283) was significant through opportunities for influence over the local community ($SE = 0.0158$; $CI = 0.0007–0.0642$). The indirect effect of QOP-reflection (0.0348) was significant through opportunities for influence ($SE = 0.0103$; $CI = 0.0174–0.0584$).

For all the four variables (civic and political participation, current and future) the indirect effect of QOP-action through opportunities for influence was not significant. Social well-being did not result as a significant mediator for any independent variables.

Migrants

Among migrants, we firstly tested the model on *current civic participation*. The bootstrapping procedure yielded an estimate of the QOP-action indirect effect through social well-being of 0.0674 ($SE = 0.245$), with a 95 percent CI ranging from 0.0302 to 0.1287. As this interval does not contain zero, the indirect effect is significant at $a = 0.05$. The indirect effects of organizational membership and QOP-reflection through social well-being were not significant. None of the independent variables showed a significant indirect effect through opportunities for influence.

A quite similar pattern of results was confirmed on *future civic participation*. The indirect effect of QOP-action (0.1086) was significant through social well-being ($SE = 0.0361$; $CI = 0.0515–0.1952$). The indirect effect of QOP-reflection (0.0256) was significant through opportunities for influence ($SE = 0.0156$; $CI = 0.0021–0.0642$).

The same model was tested also on *current political participation*. The indirect effect of QOP-action (0.1116) was significant through social well-being ($SE = 0.0340$; $CI = 0.0540–0.1894$). Finally, this pattern of results was confirmed also on *future political participation*. The indirect effect of QOP-action (0.1237) was significant through social well-being ($SE = 0.0385$; $CI = 0.0574–0.2085$).

In brief, among migrants, QOP-action had a significant indirect effect on the four dependent variables through social well-being. In addition, the indirect effect of QOP-reflection was significant through perceived opportunities of influence in only one case (future civic participation).

Tables 15.3 and 15.4 complement these results and present the detailed results of the regressions. Among Italians, organizational membership and QOP-reflection had a positive effect on perceived opportunities of influence which in turn positively affected current/future civic/political participation. Among migrants, QOP-action had a positive effect on social well-being which in turn positively affected current/future civic/political participation.

A significant direct effect was still present for organizational membership on current civic/political participation (Italians and migrants) and on future civic participation (Italians). Moreover, a significant direct effect was present for QOP-action on current/future civic participation (Italians), current political participation (Italians and migrants), and future political participation (Italians). A significant direct effect

TABLE 15.3 Regression results among Italians

Opportunities for influence	B	SE	t
Constant	1.93	0.17	11.11***
Age	0.15	0.07	2.06*
Gender	0.05	0.06	0.85
Organizational membership	0.14	0.07	1.98*
QOP-action	0.01	0.04	0.24
QOP-reflection	0.17	0.03	5.00***
Social well-being			
Constant	1.77	0.17	10.68***
Age	0.10	0.07	1.50
Gender	−0.09	0.06	−1.57
Organizational membership	0.15	0.07	2.27*
QOP-action	0.09	0.04	2.25*
QOP-reflection	0.14	0.03	4.43***
Current civic participation			
Constant	−0.09	0.15	−0.60
Age	0.01	0.06	1.72
Gender	0.18	0.05	3.85***
Organizational membership	0.43	0.06	7.67***
QOP-action	0.19	0.03	5.72***
QOP-reflection	0.02	0.03	0.72
Opportunities for influence	0.07	0.03	2.39*
Social well-being	0.02	0.03	0.79
Future civic participation			
Constant	0.35	0.21	1.70
Age	0.08	0.08	1.01
Gender	0.43	0.06	6.68***
Organizational membership	0.25	0.08	3.25**
QOP-action	0.15	0.04	3.34**
QOP-reflection	0.08	0.04	2.15*
Opportunities for influence	0.19	0.04	4.79***
Social well-being	0.01	0.04	0.24
Current political participation			
Constant	0.17	0.18	0.97
Age	0.32	0.07	4.76**
Gender	−0.06	0.05	−1.08
Organizational membership	0.13	0.07	1.20*
QOP-action	0.30	0.04	7.80***
QOP-reflection	0.08	0.03	2.60**
Opportunities for influence	0.10	0.03	3.03**
Social well-being	−0.03	0.04	−0.93

(Continued)

TABLE 15.3 Regression results among Italians *(Continued)*

Opportunities for influence	B	SE	t
Future political participation			
Constant	0.26	0.21	1.26
Age	0.31	0.08	3.92***
Gender	0.05	0.06	0.84
Organizational membership	0.05	0.08	0.69
QOP-action	0.27	0.04	6.05***
QOP-reflection	0.09	0.04	2.60*
Opportunities for influence	0.20	0.04	5.16***
Social well-being	−0.04	0.04	−0.99

Note: Unstandardized regression coefficients are reported.
*$p < 0.05$; **$p < 0.01$; ***$p < 0.001$.

was also present for QOP-reflection on future civic participation (Italians and migrants), and current/future political participation (Italians). Finally, among Italians a significant direct effect of gender on civic participation (current and future) and a direct effect of age on political participation (current and future) were found.

Discussion

In this chapter, we have examined the role of organizational membership in predicting youth's civic and political participation. One important finding is that organizational membership is strongly related to civic and political participation with different patterns regarding migrants and Italians. Among Italians, despite the mediation effect of SoC, organizational membership still influences directly actual and future civic participation. Among migrants, organizational membership affects directly only current civic participation and has no direct effect on future civic participation. The direct effect of organizational membership on future political participation is absent both among migrants and Italians; it plays a direct significant role only in current political participation. This result is partially in line with the findings of Quintelier (2008). She found that political participation benefits from multiple associational experiences: insofar as we had a global index that kept together the level and variety of associational involvement, we should provisionally assume that a variety of associational experiences promotes 'immediate' civic and political participation, but has a more limited role on future orientation, in particular toward political activity. Further research examining the two measures separately is needed in order to disentangle the specific effects of level and type of associational involvement.

Our results question the assumption regarding the association between organizational membership at a young age and political participation in adulthood: according to our findings, it is not organizational membership per se that stimulates

TABLE 15.4 Regression results among migrants

Opportunities for influence	B	SE	t
Constant	1.77	0.22	8.02***
Age	0.24	0.09	2.56*
Gender	0.07	0.10	0.68
Organizational membership	0.05	0.11	0.42
QOP-action	0.09	0.07	1.26
QOP-reflection	0.20	0.06	3.29**
Social well-being			
Constant	1.41	0.23	6.05***
Age	0.26	0.10	2.63**
Gender	0.11	0.10	1.11
Organizational membership	0.03	0.12	0.27
QOP-action	0.30	0.08	3.94***
QOP-reflection	0.05	0.06	0.78
Current civic participation			
Constant	0.23	0.22	1.05
Age	0.03	0.09	0.30
Gender	0.05	0.09	0.60
Organizational membership	0.61	0.10	6.16***
QOP-action	0.04	0.06	0.55
QOP-reflection	0.012	0.05	0.36
Opportunities for influence	−0.05	0.05	−1.02
Social well-being	0.23	0.05	4.50***
Future civic participation			
Constant	0.33	0.28	1.18
Age	−0.06	0.11	−0.58
Gender	0.18	0.11	1.67
Organizational membership	0.17	0.13	1.29
QOP-action	−0.10	0.08	−1.17
QOP-reflection	0.25	0.07	3.57***
Opportunities for Influence	0.13	0.07	1.87
Social well-being	0.36	0.06	5.51***
Current political participation			
Constant	−0.22	0.23	−0.95
Age	0.09	0.09	1.04
Gender	0.07	0.09	0.80
Organizational membership	0.31	0.10	2.93**
QOP-action	0.19	0.07	2.72**
QOP-reflection	0.00	0.06	0.03
Opportunities for influence	0.02	0.05	0.30
Social well-being	0.37	0.05	6.97***

(Continued)

TABLE 15.4 Regression results among migrants *(Continued)*

Opportunities for influence	B	SE	t
Future political participation			
Constant	−0.08	0.26	−0.31
Age	0.01	0.10	0.06
Gender	0.16	0.10	1.58
Organizational membership	0.14	0.12	1.15
QOP-action	0.14	0.08	1.81
QOP-reflection	0.12	0.07	1.89
Opportunities for influence	0.07	0.06	1.14
Social well-being	0.41	0.06	6.71***

Note: Unstandardized regression coefficients are reported.
*$p < 0.05$; **$p < 0.01$; ***$p < 0.001$.

political participation in adulthood, the last being an effect of the kind of awareness that people can gain within those organizations regarding their position in the community and in their social world.

This leads us to the role of having opportunities for reflection and influence within organizations. Our findings confirm the hypotheses about the mediating role of SoC and, specifically, that perceived opportunities for having an influence over the community (cf. Albanesi et al. 2007; Evans 2007) impact civic and political participation. Moreover, they demonstrate that supporting young people's feelings that they can influence decisions regarding their community is one of the key mechanisms through which organizational membership stimulates political participation. Among Italians, having opportunities for reflection is a key mechanism/experience that makes associations a fertile ground for civic and political participation through opportunities for influence, together with the acquisition of practical skills. Such an effect seems compatible with the possibility that within associations young people have the opportunity to develop a different narrative about themselves and about their place in the society that is reinforced by the experience and the reflection developed within organizations on the opportunities (and the need) for influence. Further empirical evidence should be collected to support our findings using a more reliable measure of current civic participation: the low reliability of this measure in the Italian sample suggests some caution is needed in interpreting these particular results. However, despite the low reliability of this measure, we still think that our findings are robust because our pattern of results regarding the mediational role of SoC is consistent across current and future civic and political participation.

Our results also support the position of those scholars who suggest that acquisition of practical skills is one of the key mechanisms through which associational membership promotes civic and political participation: this seems particularly important for migrant youth who generally have lower SES compared to natives, and who benefit less from recruitment strategies as a means to access the political arena (Myrberg 2011). According to our results, voluntary associations represent for migrants a training ground where they can learn and practice both civic and political skills and behaviors. At the same time, consistent with Eggert and Giugni's (2010) assumptions, such contexts represent a place where the experience of social integration becomes possible and concrete. This explanation fits with the evidence that, among migrant youth, social well-being mediates the relationship between the active role played within the organization and civic and political participation, as hypothesized, further strengthening the findings of qualitative studies (cf. Cicognani et al. under review). It is important to notice also that even if SoC plays a limited role in supporting migrants' participation, it mediates the relationship between having the opportunity to reflect on participatory experience and intention to engage civically in the future, suggesting that experiencing some influence and reflecting about it can have long-term effects, supporting the idea that migrants' will find a valued social position in the local community.

As regards socio-demographic variables, contrary to our expectations, organizational membership did not differ according to gender; one possible explanation is that gender differences characterize only some group memberships, possibly in opposite directions (e.g. males might be more active in political groups and females in volunteer groups). In such cases, the use of an aggregate score (vs. specific group membership) did not allow gender differences in the membership of specific groups to emerge.

With age, stronger intentions to participate in civic issues and politics emerged, as expected. Also, and quite surprisingly, stronger intentions toward future political participation were found among female participants: considering this finding in connection with the general picture of lower actual political participation among females in Italy, a potential explanation is that structural factors (opportunity structures for participation) are responsible for the difficulties of women in translating their intentions to be politically active in the future into concrete actions.

Interestingly, migrant youth reported higher social well-being than majority youth. The lower scores among Italian youth might be explained by the disillusion and powerlessness that they experience toward the future of Italian society (e.g. the subscales of social well-being include the belief that society is moving in a positive direction and is progressing) and the prospects that they envision for their future, which have characterized the overall social climate of Italian society in recent years. Migrant youth, though suffering from perceived discrimination as well as other social and economic difficulties, might have developed a more resilient attitude and thus feel more 'empowered' and optimistic in the possibility that their living conditions might improve, as suggested also by qualitative data (Cicognani et al. 2012).

In conclusion, the findings of this study further support the role of organizational membership in explaining civic and political participation among both majority and migrant youth in Italy. Also, they confirm that the nature and quality of participatory activities and their potential for learning and building competences are crucial factors, especially for migrants. The benefits of organizational involvement for Italian and migrant youth are based on partly different processes: in particular, for the latter, satisfactory participatory experiences within organizations have the potential for building a more positive overview and feelings of social integration. The findings also support the literature on the role of SoC in participation by indicating that perceptions of having opportunities for influence over the community are important in explaining both civic and political participation.

References

Albanesi, C., Cicognani, E., and Zani, B. (2007) 'Sense of community, civic engagement and social well-being in Italian adolescents,' *Journal of Community and Applied Social Psychology*, 17: 387–406.

Albanesi, C., Cicognani, E., and Zani, B. (2012) 'Tra cittadinanza e discriminazione: esperienze e opinioni sulla partecipazione civica e politica di giovani e adolescenti albanesi e marocchini,' in D. Giovannini and L. Vezzali (eds), *Immigrazione, processi interculturali e cittadinanza attiva*. Caserta: Edizioni Melagrana.

Albano, R. (2005) 'I giovani e le nuove forme di partecipazione,' *Il Mulino*, 2: 320–30.

Azevedo, C. N. (2009) 'Experiências de participação dos jovens: Em estudo longitudinal sobre a influência da qualidade de participação no desenvolvimento psicológico.' Unpublished doctoral dissertation, University of Porto, Porto, Portugal.

Baron, R. M. and Kenny, D. A. (1986) 'The moderator-mediator variable distinction in social psychological research: conceptual, strategic, and statistical considerations,' *Journal of Personality and Social Psychology*, 51: 1173–82.

Burns, N. (2007) 'Gender in the aggregate, gender in the individual, gender and political action,' *Politics and Gender*, 3: 104–24.

Buzzi, C., Cavalli, A., and De Lillo, A. (eds) (2002) *Giovani del nuovo secolo: quinto rapporto IARD sulla condizione giovanile in Italia*. Bologna: Il Mulino.

Cammaerts, B. (2007) 'Jamming the political: beyond counter-hegemonic practices,' *Continuum: Journal of Media and Cultural Studies*, 21: 71–90.

Caponio, T. (2005) 'Policy networks and immigrants' associations in Italy: the cases of Milan, Bologna and Naples,' *Journal of Ethnic and Migration Studies*, 31: 931–50.

Carneiro, N. S. (2006) 'Ser, pertencer, participar: Construção da identidade homossexual, redes de apoio e participação comunitária.' Unpublished doctoral dissertation, University of Porto, Porto, Portugal.

Cassell, J., Huffaker, D., Tversky, D., and Ferriman, K. (2006) 'The language of online leadership: gender and youth engagement,' *Developmental Psychology*, 42: 436–49.

Checkoway, B., Allison, T., and Montoya, C. (2005) 'Youth participation in public policy at the municipal level,' *Children and Youth Services Review*, 27: 1149–62.

Chiessi, M., Cicognani, E., and Sonn, C. (2010) 'Assessing sense of community on adolescents: validating the brief scale of sense of community in adolescents (SOCA),' *Journal of Community Psychology*, 38: 276–92.

Cicognani, E., Albanesi, C., Zani, B., and Sonn, C. (under review) 'Identity and belonging: experiences of young Moroccans in Italy.'

Cicognani, E., Zani, B., Fournier, B., Gavray, C., and Born, M. (2012) 'Gender differences in youths' political engagement and participation. The role of parents and of adolescents' social and civic participation,' *Journal of Adolescence*, 35: 561–76.

Cioni, E. and Marinelli, A. (eds) (2010) *Le reti della comunicazione politica: tra televisioni e social network*. Florence: University Press.

Colombo, E. (2010) 'Changing citizenship: everyday representations of membership, belonging and identification among Italian senior secondary school students,' *Italian Journal of Sociology of Education*, 2: 129–53.
Colombo, E., Domaneschi, L., and Marchetti, C. (2011) 'Citizenship and multiple belonging. Representations of inclusion, identification and participation among children of immigrants in Italy,' *Journal of Modern Italian Studies*, 16: 334–47.
De Luca, D. (2007) 'Giovani divisi fuori e dentro la politica,' in C. Buzzi, A. Cavalli, and A. De Lillo (eds), *Rapporto giovani. Sesta indagine dell'Istituto IARD sulla condizione giovanile in Italia*. Bologna: Il Mulino.
Delli Carpini, M. X. and Keeter, S. (1996) *What Americans Know About Politics and Why It Matters*. New Haven, CT: Yale University Press.
Di Gioia, R., Giacomello, L., Inserra, P. P., and Rotondi, S. (2009) *Quando i giovani partecipano. Prima indagine nazionale sulla presenza giovanile nell'associazionismo, nel volontariato e nelle aggregazioni informali*. Roma: Sviluppo Locale Edizioni.
Eden, K. and Roker, D. (2002) '... *Doing something': Young People as Social Actors*. Leicester: National Youth Agency.
Eggert, N. and Giugni, M. (2010) 'Does associational involvement spur political integration? Political interest and participation of three immigrant groups in Zurich,' *Swiss Political Science Review*, 16: 175–210.
Eggert, N., Giugni, M. (2011) 'The impact of religion on the political participation of migrants,' in L. Morales and M. Giugni (eds), *Social Capital, Political Participation and Migration in Europe: Making Multicultural Democracy Work?* Basingstoke: Palgrave.
Evans, S. D. (2007) 'Youth sense of community: voice and power in community contexts,' *Journal of Community Psychology*, 35: 693–709.
Ferreira, P. D. (2006) 'Conceções de direitos ativos e experiências de participação na sociedade civil.' Unpublished doctoral thesis, Universidade do Porto.
Ferreira, P. D., Azevedo, C. N., and Menezes, I. (2012) 'The developmental quality of participation experiences: beyond the rhetoric that "participation is always good!",' *Journal of Adolescence*, 35: 599–610.
Hayes, A. F. and Preacher, K. J. (2013) 'Statistical mediation analysis with a multicategorical independent variable,' *British Journal of Mathematical and Statistical Psychology*. DOI: http://dx.doi.org/10.1111/bmsp.12028.
Hendry, L. B., Shuchsmith, J., Love, J. G., and Glending, A. (1993) *Young People's Leisure and Lifestyles*. London: Routledge.
ISTAT (2010) *La partecipazione politica: differenze di genere e territoriali*. Roma: Istat.
ISTAT (2013) *BES Report on Equitable and Sustainable Well-Being*. Rome: Istat.
Jugert, P., Eckstein, K., Noack, P., Kuhn, A., and Benbow, A. (2013) 'Offline and online civic engagement among adolescents and young adults from three ethnic groups,' *Journal of Youth and Adolescence*, 42: 123–5.
Juris, J. S. and Pleyers, G. H. (2009) 'Alter-activism: emerging cultures of participation among young global justice activists,' *Journal of Youth Studies*, 12: 57–75.
Keyes, C. L. M. (2006) 'The subjective well-being of America's youth. Toward a comprehensive assessment,' *Adolescent and Family Health*, 4: 3–11.
Larson, R. and Hansen, D. (2005) 'The development of strategic thinking: learning to impact human systems in a youth activism program,' *Human Development*, 48: 327–49.
Leone, L. (2011) *FTP forme in trasformazione della partecipazione: Rapporto di ricerca sui processi partecipativi dei giovani e sui loro effetti*. Roma: CEVAS.
McFarland, D. A. and Thomas, R. J. (2006) 'Bowling young: how youth voluntary associations influence adult political participation,' *American Sociological Review*, 71: 401–25.

McIntosh, H. and Youniss, J. (2010) 'Toward a political theory of political socialization of youth: handbook of research on civic engagement in youth,' in L. R. Sherrod, J. Torney-Purta, and C. A. Flanagan (eds), *Handbook of Research on Civic Engagement in Youth*. Hoboken, NJ: John Wiley & Sons.

McMillan, W. D. and Chavis, M. D. (1986) 'Sense of Community: a definition and a theory,' *Journal of Community Psychology*, 14: 6–22.

Marta, E., Guglielmetti, C., and Pozzi, M. (2006) 'Volunteerism during young adulthood: an Italian investigation into motivational patterns,' *Voluntas: International Journal of Voluntary and Nonprofit Organizations*, 17 (3): 221–32.

Munro, D. (2008) 'Integration through participation: non-citizen resident voting rights in an era of globalization,' *International Migration and Integration*, 9: 43–80.

Myrberg, G. (2011) 'Political integration through associational affiliation? Immigrants and native Swedes in Greater Stockholm,' *Journal of Ethnic and Migration Studies*, 37: 99–115.

Norris, P. (2002) *Democratic Phoenix: Reinventing Political Activism*. New York: Cambridge.

Park, N., Kee, K. F., and Valenzuela, S. (2009) 'Being immersed in social networking environment: Facebook groups, uses and gratifications, and social outcomes,' *CyberPsychology and Behavior*, 12 (6): 729–33.

Parry, G., Moyser, G., and Day, N. (1992) *Political Participation and Democracy in Britain*. Cambridge: Cambridge University Press.

Pasek, J., More, E., and Romer, D. (2009) 'Realizing the social Internet? Online social networking meets offline civic engagement,' *Journal of Information Technology and Politics*, 6 (3–4): 197–215.

Paxton, P. (1999) 'Is social capital declining in the United States? A multiple indicator assessment,' *American Journal of Sociology*, 105: 88–127.

Paxton, P., Kunhovich, S., and Hughes, M. (2007) 'Gender in politics,' *Annual Review of Sociology*, 33: 263–84.

Preacher, K. J. and Hayes, A. F. (2004) 'SPSS and SAS procedures for estimating indirect effects in multiple mediator models,' *Behavior Research Methods, Instruments, and Computers*, 37: 717–31.

Putnam, R. D. (2000) *Bowling Alone: The Collapse and Revival of American Community*. New York: Simon & Schuster.

Quintelier, E. (2008) 'Who is politically active: the athlete, the scout member or the environmental activist? Young people, voluntary engagement and political participation,' *Acta Sociologica*, 51: 355–70.

Quintelier, E. (2009) 'The political participation of immigrant youth in Belgium,' *Journal of Ethnic and Migration Studies*, 35: 919–37.

Riley, S., More, Y., and Griffin, C. (2010) 'The "pleasure citizen." Analyzing partying as a form of social and political participation,' *Young: Nordic Journal of Youth Research*, 18: 33–54.

Sherrod, L. R., Torney-Purta, J., and Flanagan, C. A. (2010) *Handbook of Research on Civic Engagement in Youth*. Hoboken, NJ: Wiley.

Simon, B. and Grabow, O. (2010) 'The politicization of migrants: further evidence that politicized collective identity is a dual identity,' *Political Psychology*, 31: 717–38.

Sonn, C. C. (2002) 'Immigration adaptation: understanding the process through sense of community,' in A. T. Fisher, C. C. Sonn, and B. J. Bishop (eds), *Psychological Sense of Community: Research, Applications, and Implications*. New York: Kluwer Academic.

Stepick, A., Stepick, C., and Labissiere, Y. (2008) 'South Florida's immigrant youth and civic engagement: major engagement: minor differences,' *Applied Development Science*, 12: 57–65.

Teney, C. and Hanquinet, L. (2012) 'High political participation, high social capital? A relational analysis of youth social capital and political participation,' *Social Science Research*, 41: 1213–26.

Torney-Purta, J. and Amadeo, J.-A. (2011) 'Participatory niches for emergent citizenship in early adolescence: an international perspective,' *Annals of the American Academy of Political and Social Science*, 633: 180–200.

Torpe, L. (2003) 'Social capital in Denmark: a deviant case?' *Scandinavian Political Studies*, 26: 27–48.

Veiga, S. (2008) 'O Impacto do envolvimento dos estudantes universitários em actividades extra-curriculares no empowerment psicológico e no desenvolvimento cognitivo-vocacional.' Unpublished doctoral dissertation, University of Porto, Portugal.

Verba, S., Schlozman, K. L., and Brady, H. (1995) *Voice and Equality: Civic Voluntarism in American Politics*. Cambridge, MA: Harvard University Press.

Verba, S., Schlozman, K. L., Brady, H., and Nie, N. H. (1993) 'Race, ethnicity and political resources: participation in the United States,' *British Journal of Political Science*, 23: 453–97.

Vogel, D. and Triandafyllidou, A. (2005) *Civic Activation of Immigrants: An Introduction to Conceptual and Theoretical Issues*. Oldenburg: IBKM.

Wandersman, A. and Florin, P. (2000) 'Citizen participation and community organizations,' in J. Rappaport and E. Seidman (eds), *Handbook of Community Psychology*. New York: Kluwer Academic/Plenum.

Yang, K. and Pandey, S. K. (2011) 'Further dissecting the black box of citizen participation: when does citizen involvement lead to good outcomes?' *Public Administration Review*, 71 (6): 880–92.

Youniss, J., McLellan, J. A., and Yates, M. (1997) 'What we know about engendering civic identity,' *American Behavioral Scientist*, 40: 620–31.

16
PARTICIPATION AMONG YOUTH, WOMEN, AND MIGRANTS
Findings from the Wallonia-Brussels Federation of Belgium

Claire Gavray, Michel Born, and Bernard Fournier

Youth participation: the Belgian context

For more than 20 years, the question of participation has represented a strong political challenge for Europe (Giddens 1990). One idea is that youth participation is a strong predictor of involvement in adulthood. Because of the depoliticization of adults and their loss of interest in common goods, there is a necessity to promote political and social participation early in life. A second idea expressed in the White Paper of the European Commission (2001)[1] is that if young people do not behave as active citizens, the political legitimacy of institutions is damaged (Bréchon 1995).

In Belgium, as elsewhere in Europe, we find ambivalent discourses concerning youth and participation (Martelli 2013). According to one account favored by many researchers, youth refuse to engage anymore, being apathetic and apolitical (Putnam 2007). In another account, young people are still significantly involved but in new ways, participation becoming in this case not only a question of the degree but also the type of participation. 'Youth participation does not only mean youth consultation but the acceptance of social change toward new and unknown forms of society, which implies accepting uncertainty' (Muniglia *et al.* 2012: 2). Paakkunainen (2003), for instance, speaks about 'fun, elasticity, play and irony' as a current mode of youth participation. At the same time, participation in demonstrations and protests is one form of contemporary youth participation and must be seen as a denunciation of numerous gaps between rhetorical principles and effective interventions (Shildrick and MacDonald 2006). In previous articles, we have discussed and illustrated this point (Gavray 2012; Gavray *et al.* 2012): non-conventional political participation is significantly correlated with conventional participation. In many countries of the world, young people, reacting against the uneven and inequitable treatment which is reserved for them, do not hesitate to claim a larger stake in fundamental social decision-making. Contrary to the idea that the revolt of young people is an indicator of the ineffectiveness of youth policies (for instance in Spain), Malagón (2011) thinks that the more these programs are effective, the more young people acquire a consciousness as citizens and mobilize themselves, believing that they have a responsibility with regard to the community.

In many countries, researchers notice the contrast between the strong discourse on youth participation (recognized as a fundamental right in the Convention on the Rights of the Child of 1989) and the structural weaknesses of youth policies (Walther *et al.* 2006). In Belgium, the Walloon delegate for children's rights, Bernard De Vos, often deplores the fact that adolescents and youths continue to have few opportunities to participate. A similar observation has been made for Ireland: Leahy and Burgess (2012) note some broadly progressive trends such as the youth work sector and at the same time some 'regressive infantilisation.' Judging from a recent survey, Belgian Francophone youths do not declare a loss of formal participation structures; they judge severely the shortfall from their idealized image of participation. Of course sometimes, at school or in some other structures, they have the right to participate, to give their opinion and to elect their representatives. However, they suspect that adults are hardly interested in their opinion because they do not really listen to them and follow them rarely (OEJAJ 2007: 186).

While disengagement itself may be seen as taking a position (no commitment in a list of activities and responsibilities traditionally considered political or civic participation cannot automatically be interpreted as a sign of apathy), the fact that the criticism of politics does not only concern those who do not participate shows the necessity to renew the mechanisms, authenticity, and efficacy of participation and not only to increase participation rates (Spanning *et al.* 2008).

In fact, a large set of participation types are taken into account and classified today: socially recognized and sanctioned or not, active or passive, bottom-up, top-down, or community, voluntary or not, individual or collective, formal or concrete (Walther *et al.* 2006), inspired by personal interest or identification with a collective interest, framed by 'traditional' techniques of information and communication or by contemporary techniques. Some studies warn us of the danger of thinking that the Internet is a negative tool or a sign of democracy in crisis. Following Stevenson (2001), it is today a tool used by young people to find their own lifestyle, and to assert their generational difference from the parental world. It remains a tool and not a driving force. The real driving force is youth saying that they are disappointed with their life circumstances and that governments are responsible for these circumstances (Bimber *et al.* 2005). Another classification concerns the distinction between political and civic participation. Globally, we consider that political participation refers to the relationship between the person and democratic society, and we define social and civic participation in relation to the public nature of belonging and more concretely the links between the person and the community or the group. Nevertheless, different conceptions may be hidden here. For instance, in some cases political participation only refers to the vote (it is important to note that voting is compulsory for those aged over 18 years in Belgium for municipal, provincial, regional, national, and European elections). In other cases, political participation involves keeping a check on institutions and the political elite, and increasing public debate and direct political action by citizens.

With regard to the specific place given to youth in the public sphere, in some countries it refers more to decision-making (political participation) while in others it refers more to wider active contributions to the community (social/civic participation). Walther *et al.* (2006) classify Belgium as falling into the second group.

Simultaneously, we emphasize the shared identities at the origin of much participation. Quite recently, the idea has emerged that it is impossible to study political/social participation without considering ethnic minorities' participation. Cultural and religious tensions, and the objectives of parity and diversity rather than equality and the fight against discrimination, mean that one cannot study political participation without considering groups classified as minorities. Historically, the classical portrait of the citizen and politician corresponded to a white, middle-aged/ elderly man, native of the territory and occupying a recognized social position. Profiles escaping this category are still thought of and described in terms of minorities and catch-up strategies. This applies particularly to women. In Belgium, although a system of gender quotas was established in 2000 for the constitution of lists for municipal elections, quantitative disparities persist and the hierarchy between men and women re-emerges at other levels. For instance, elected women are often denied mandates involving the highest decision-making powers and are instead assigned matters and responsibilities considered to be 'female.' Furthermore, the dimensions of gender, ethnicity, class, and age are often studied individually, without perceiving the relevance of investigating the articulations between them. However, some scholars think it is particularly important to understand individual, family, and group issues that concern the education and the political participation and commitment of individuals who are defined in terms of the intersections between social categories, for example the education and participation of young immigrant women (Manço and Freyens 2008).

In this chapter, we report some of the findings which were obtained in the Wallonia-Brussels Federation of Belgium as part of the PIDOP project. In particular, we report findings that were obtained in the focus groups and the quantitative survey which were conducted with both ethnic majority and ethnic minority youth.

The choice of minority groups

A debate exists in Belgium concerning the 'integration' and public commitment of second- and even third-generation Muslim youth. For this reason, we chose to study young people of Turkish and Moroccan origin living in Brussels and Wallonia. In 2011, Moroccans were the fourth largest and Turks the eighth largest minority groups living in Belgium. A high proportion of young people of both minorities have Belgian nationality. For instance, in 2011, the total number of people of Turkish origin living in Belgium was around 160,000 but only 40,000 have Turkish nationality; the corresponding numbers of Moroccans are 250,000 and 82,000.[2]

Moroccans and Turks are often amalgamated in the representations of public opinion and of decision-makers because they came to Belgium in the same period and in the same context of economic immigration (to work in the coal mines). Nevertheless, they have developed different integration strategies in response to the negative conditions/perspectives which they have encountered (Manço 1998).

Turks

In 1964, when Belgium needed extra workers a number came from Turkey and were well accepted (Lafleur 2005). Nevertheless, with increasing unemployment and the trend for Turks to organize their own community life, Turks have faced a certain level of prejudice and discrimination, especially in the spheres of housing and employment (Centre pour l'Egalité des Chances et la Lutte contre le Racisme 2009). Young Turks in Brussels today face negative appraisals, with 50 percent of young Turks saying that they suffer from discrimination. This percentage has doubled over the past 20 years. The percentage of young Turks born in Belgium has tripled over the same period (more than 70 percent today). Although initially classified as immigrants, any immigrant can apply for Belgian citizenship after seven years of residency, and the proportion of naturalizations of Turks is high. The Turkish community is concentrated in specific areas, with little assimilation or integration, and the national identity of origin remains very important. In response to unemployment and economic difficulties (more than 40 percent of young Turks are unemployed), family businesses and shops have been set up, which is made possible with the cooperation and financial help of family members in Turkey, often in return for the possibility for a younger family member to immigrate to Belgium through marriage (Feld and Manço 2000). For this reason, the community has not invested much in education. Among the Turkish population, 78 percent have attended secondary school and 12 percent have gained access to higher education levels. Ninety percent of Turks are officially Muslim but only one-third actually practice their religion.

Moroccans

A high proportion of Moroccans are also Muslims, and they have higher levels of religiosity than Turks. In comparison to Turks, a higher proportion of Moroccan young people (including girls) invest in education to achieve social mobility. Employment levels among Moroccans are similar to those among Turks: one-third of Moroccans are unemployed but, unlike Turks, self-employment strategies are not used. Moroccan young people say they would like to have access to the same jobs as Belgians, and they also claim the same rights and opportunities. They react particularly strongly against social injustice and inequalities and spend more time than Turks outside their residential area and community. The attitudes of the 'majority' population toward Moroccans were positive when their families immigrated to work in the 1970s. But, here too, the context has changed and youths today have to face stereotypes (being seen as potential juvenile delinquents) and discrimination in the realms of employment and housing (Banque Nationale de Belgique 2012). Many Moroccan youth were born in Belgium and have applied for Belgian nationality (in 2012, out of 4,838 naturalizations, 709 involved citizens of Moroccan origin).

The field work

For the research, focus groups and a survey were conducted with Belgian, Turkish, and Moroccan participants. Twelve focus groups were conducted, with six to eight participants in each group, and with each group consisting of either 16- to 18-year-olds or 20- to 26-year-olds. In total, 97 persons were recruited through websites, networks, and associations using a snowball technique: among them, more than a third consisted of young people of Moroccan or Turkish origins. In addition, a quantitative survey was conducted with 1,228 people drawn from two age groups (16- to 19-year-olds and 20- to 26-year-olds), both gender groups (557 males and 671 females) and the three national origins (896 Belgians, 156 Turks, and 176 Moroccans); 741 of the participants were aged 16 to 18 years old, and the remainder were aged 20 to 26 years old. Most of the younger groups were recruited from 14 schools in Brussels and Liege. The task of recruiting the older group for the survey was much more difficult. Twenty-one institutions working with native and non-native groups agreed to assist us but gave no guarantee concerning the participation of their members. In addition, a dozen students of Turkish and Moroccan origin were engaged as additional help to reach young people who were no longer students. The questionnaire was filled in by 173 university students. Because of the difficulty in recruiting young adults, the only representative sub-sample was the school students. For this reason, the quantitative results which are presented below are drawn from this younger age group only.

Main findings from the focus groups

A large majority of the participants in the focus groups from all communities thought that voting was an opportunity, a right, and an obligation for them and for the country. Remember that most youths of Turkish or Moroccan origin had Belgian nationality.

They had difficulties in defining what a citizen is: 'someone who feels involved in what happens in the country'; 'someone who participates in everything.' And when asked if they considered themselves citizens, most of the younger participants answered that they were but not totally because they were not adults. They defined themselves as 'pre-citizens,' too young to engage seriously.

None of them felt well informed about the Belgian political system and its priorities. They were a little disappointed about Belgian national political events. The European level was not concrete for them – it was 'too far' from the problems of the population. Perhaps events that had occurred during the period of the focus groups had an influence. Young Turkish people discussed the fact that Turkey was not welcomed in Europe. Some of them thought that joining the European Union was not the best solution for Turkey anyway. No one said that he/she had experience of 'real' political participation, even if he/she had signed petitions, participated in Internet forums, was involved with associations or had experienced democracy at school.

The feeling of discrimination was particularly prevalent among young Turks and Moroccans but at the same time they were not very aware of the institutional mechanisms that generated social inequalities. They were conscious of their luck, knowing that the countries that their families had originated from are not rich and that it is not so easy to live in these countries (e.g. no social security, no Internet, and sometimes no running water). They seemed less concerned about the environment and climate problems than the Belgian participants in the focus groups: 'Anyway it won't make a difference, unless all countries change.' All youths suggested that political and civic participation was more a question of language knowledge and access to useful information than a question of origin or ethnicity. 'Even Belgian people can be uninterested in social questions and civic issues. It's not a question of national or ethnic origin.' Nevertheless, all young participants considered that foreigners had higher risks of social exclusion (Turks, Lebanese, Italians, Spanish, etc.). It is interesting to note that, during the discussions, at no time were women described as a group at 'risk of exclusion or discrimination' or as a group excluded from participatory processes, and at no time were gender stakes or inequality of opportunities between men and women addressed, even in the focus groups including young women. However, group dynamics did involve males talking much more and louder than females, who did not always seem comfortable or authorized to express their opinion. Indeed, it was difficult to find minority young women – especially Turkish ones – who accepted and had permission to participate in the focus groups.

Among the *Turkish youth* the feeling of discrimination was especially high and concerned quality of life and freedom. They did not feel well informed about their rights and obligations as citizens. Most of them felt they were Turks before feeling Belgian, even if 'When you're there [in Turkey], you feel Belgian, but when you're in Belgium, you don't feel Belgian.' They spoke a lot about their country of origin and 'imported' political conflicts or preoccupations. They expressed clear patriotic feelings and ideas, and said that they were ready to become soldiers and to defend their country ... 'and Belgium also, maybe.'

An important theme for them was religion; they described themselves as Muslims and explained that this religion was not evaluated positively by others in Belgium. Some of them said that religious freedom was not a reality in Belgium, that religion and national traditions were not appreciated by the Belgians: 'What I see on the Internet is that Islam is shown as diabolic. But Islam isn't that: some people are doing wrong and live badly and the whole community is stigmatized ... They generalize.' They were proud of their religion and considered religion to be a private matter and solidarity to be an important human value. They were particularly sensitive to the subject of poverty, especially child poverty, and said that they had no choice because of their community, their religion, and their traditions. 'We are obliged to help because it's in our religion; we are obliged to help poor people during Ramadan for example.' At the same time, they appreciated obtaining help and solutions to their problems from within their own community. But they did not feel free enough about their personal choices, with opportunities of expression only being available through the Internet or at school.

Parents were described as their main source of information, power, and influence, followed by religion, brothers, fathers, and finally teachers. They spoke about television and other media but most youths said that they did not trust them: 'I don't know if you've already watched French news and other news, that isn't really objective ... when they are talking about Gaza. They manipulate people, they show what they want and not the truth ...' They did not believe much in the power of demonstrations and did not think that having representatives in Belgian institutions was a strict necessity.

Most *Moroccan youths* felt they were Belgian with a Moroccan origin. They said that they had grown up in Belgium but that they lived their everyday life within Moroccan culture. They said that Belgian people had a negative opinion of Muslims but thought that the messages of Islam were often misunderstood and could be better known. They thought they had more economic and employment difficulties than Belgian people with the same level of education. The eldest pointed out the potential power of demonstrations but said they needed to have real motivation to demonstrate. 'For example, in Belgium, daily life, despite the government's instability, has not changed that much over the past years: there is still food, petrol, etc.... If they see (think) there is no impact, of course people lose interest in politics ... even without government, daily life doesn't change' (when the focus groups were conducted, political parties had been trying to form a federal government for a considerable period of time). One person said that some groups of people could only express their social discomfort using violence through demonstrations or riots. Another person added: 'This is why there is more delinquency in ghettos, because migrants can't express themselves without violence. Nobody listens to them.' Several members of this group stated that they needed to elect representatives from their community (such as educators) who would have more influence on policy-makers than young people. 'It is necessary to encourage representatives coming from our community to engage in politics and to get power: they can listen to young people and help them better.' The Moroccan youths said that they did not feel sufficiently numerous to have real power: they were sensitive to empowerment politics. They felt that policy-makers were 'playing' with youth: "When we talk to the mayor, he says that he will see what he can do but nothing happens. When it is election time, he is coming to the mosque because he needs us ...' Most Moroccan participants said that they had more respect for street educators than for policy-makers who remained too distant. In this group, first school and then religion, television, and the Internet were described as the main sources of political and civic information. The influence of the family, the community, or even religion did not have the same importance as they did for the Turks. The results of the discussions contradict to some extent the hypothesis that religious identity would dominate among Moroccans and national identity among Turks (although this might have been a result of the make-up of the sample). The young Moroccan participants felt insufficiently informed about what is going on in Belgium. They would have liked to have had more debates at school about societal and economic topics. Many participants said that they were ready to invest in concrete projects with youth. They thought that policy-makers and youth (including both Belgian and minority youth) should communicate more. 'A bit like you are doing now with us! The fact to come and ask, to be interested in what the population is thinking.'

Main findings from the quantitative survey

As noted previously, only the data from the secondary school students (aged between 16 and 19 years old) will be reported here because this was the only age group which we consider to be representative. Most of the minority youths held Belgian nationality. However, the majority Belgian group was not homogeneous from the perspective of their parents' countries of origin (see Table 16.1). For this reason, in our main analyses, the four groups shown in Table 16.1 were used (rather than just three). One set of analyses compared all four groups, another set compared those who were of Turkish vs. Moroccan origin, while a third set compared groups 1 and 4. Gender differences were also analysed, but because of the small numbers of minority youth, caution needs to be exercised in interpreting these gender differences. Table A16.1 in the appendix to this chapter summarises the results of some of the main analyses.

With regard to *socio-economic, cultural and family matters*, it was found that groups 1 and 4 had a higher standard of life, while groups 2 and 3 (the Turks and Moroccans) had less well-educated parents and more financial difficulties. As expected, more individuals from groups 1 and 4 lived with only one of their parents, spoke French at home, had more books in the home, had highly educated parents and were students in the 'general' section of secondary school than Turks and Moroccans. In addition, only 42 percent of Turks but 78 percent of Moroccans mainly spoke French at home. Despite the unequal economic and social resources between the

TABLE 16.1 Distribution of young people (16–19 years old) by parents' countries of birth

	Group	N	Proportion of individuals with Belgian nationality
Both parents born in Belgium	1	583 (69%)	100%
At least one parent born in Turkey	2	58 (6%)	62%
At least one parent born in Morocco	3	69 (8%)	69%
At least one parent not born in Belgium, but not in either Turkey or Morocco	4	141 (17%)	81%
Total		851 (100%)	83%

four groups, there were no significant differences in levels of 'feeling happy' or in the subjective evaluation of the financial well-being of their households.

With regard to *discrimination and life perspectives*, most of the young people said that they were optimistic about their own future but had the impression that society was becoming less and less fair. Turks and Moroccans were the most numerous in believing that society is not fair at all, feeling that they were discriminated against due to their national origins and their religion. The Turks felt more discriminated against than the Moroccans concerning their socio-economic conditions. At the same time, most of the youth from all groups said that school was the place where they had already experienced discrimination. Moroccans were the least concerned by this feeling, a potential sign that they rely on the school for their integration and social advancement.

With regard to *political interest, discussions, actions*, groups 1 and 4 discussed social and political issues with their relatives more often than the Turks and Moroccans. They affirmed more often their interest in and understanding of Belgian political events and functioning. Nevertheless, compared to the other three groups, the Moroccans looked for political information the most, especially on the Internet, and were the most likely to say that they had something to say about politics and wanted to express it. The same trend concerned involvement with active groups of discussion about political aims. Turks and Moroccans wrote engaged articles less often than groups 1 and 4, but they had experienced participation in demonstrations more frequently. There was no difference between the four groups in using graffiti to express a point of view. Such behavior was rare in all groups.

With regard to the *effectiveness of different forms of participation*, all youths continued to believe the most in conventional political actions. However, the Turks and Moroccans were less inclined towards boycott actions and online petitions than those in groups 1 and 4. The Moroccans believed the most in political apprenticeship through school and other places/activities of socialization and leisure. This can be interpreted as one more sign of their hope or desire to become part of Belgian society in its functioning. Moroccans also supported positive actions in favor of minorities the most.

With regard to *future investments*, young Turks were slightly more likely than the other groups to say that they would be ready to express their specific problems/needs on the street and through graffiti, while Moroccans were especially mobilized for future issues to do with political discussion and engagement. Moroccans were also the most concerned about problematic situations in other countries (e.g. Palestine), while Turks were more worried about what was happening in their country of origin. Overall, Turks and Moroccans were more proud of their national origins than those in groups 1 and 4. Moroccans identified more with their religion while Turks identified more with their country of origin (a discrepancy with the findings of the focus groups). In addition, only 67 percent of Turks but 81 percent of Moroccans described themselves as Muslim. The same trend was found in relationship to prayer and the reading of religious texts. Most of the youths in groups 1 and 4 distanced themselves from religion and religious authorities.

With regard to *participation in social groups*, one in five of the participants in the survey had never taken part in such groups previously. The youths in groups 1 and 4 were more likely to be members of youth and leisure associations, while the Turks and Moroccans were more likely to be members of religious associations (around 10 percent were active members). In general, youths from groups 1 and 4 were more positive about the value of participating in their main association. In comparison, Moroccans more often than Turks thought that their group activities were aimed at helping with their concrete daily problems and that these activities were a positive experience for them. The Moroccans also thought that their neighborhood gave them good opportunities for meeting other people including people of the opposite gender. This was not the case for the Turks. More Moroccans than Turks who had Belgian nationality felt 'Belgian.' Those young people who had entered politics or taken social action were more likely to have been personally approached by other people who were already members of a political party, social association or youth organization.

With regard to their *feelings about the decisions which they were allowed to make*, the youths in groups 1 and 4 had a greater feeling of freedom of choice: 25 percent of Turkish and Moroccan youth said that they had no freedom concerning contraception or in their choice of friends. Young Turks were the least free on all items and especially concerning school orientation. This confirms the results from the focus groups. Remember that the Turkish community invests in the development of freelance activities and family enterprises, which might explain why the main problem for young Turks is economic while for other groups it is employment. This could also explain why, in the hit parade of motivations, the main one for young Turks to invest in politics is to achieve social power and recognition whereas for the other three groups it is 'to learn' and 'be more effective.' Young Turks were also the most likely to think that a good citizen is someone who has a paid job. There was less self-confidence and poorer knowledge among the Turks and Moroccans than in the other two groups, but at the same time there was more optimism concerning the effectiveness of group mobilization (especially among Moroccans). There were no significant intergroup differences in perceptions of barriers to political engagement.

In the *evaluation of politics, politicians and institutions*, there were no group differences in total levels of institutional trust, but there were differences on some specificities. Moroccans especially invested in European identity, more than Turks (possibly because the latter thought that Turkey was not welcome in the European Union or because of the isolationist nature of their community). Groups 1 and 4 were the most positive toward non-governmental organizations (NGOs) and were also more aware of environmental issues. Unsurprisingly, groups 1 and 4 had more trust 'in others' (social trust), while groups 2 and 3 had more trust in structures and institutions, with exceptions being the police and the courts. In total, all groups thought that the current Belgian political regime was moderately good in spite of its defects.

As far as *rights* were concerned, the Turks and Moroccans placed greater emphasis on the right to preserve their language and traditions than groups 1 and 4.

But simultaneously, Turks and especially Moroccans claimed the individual right to distance themselves from their national traditions and the right to choose their faith and potential religion. Thus Turks and Moroccans had a sense of belonging to a nationality or community, but felt that this community should be open. They were proud of their group, but many did not want to be reduced to it. They were in favor of community initiatives to work together. Moroccans gave the most support to equal rights and positive discrimination in favor of foreign groups, especially concerning educational training. At the same time, the right to choose one's own religion/faith was affirmed most by those in groups 1, 2, and 4. This was less pronounced among Moroccans who had higher levels of religiosity. Gender equality was affirmed to a lesser extent by Turks than by the other three groups.

The data were also analyzed to ascertain *what distinguishes young women from young men*. Although girls' political interest is often found to be lower than that of boys, the Table A16.1 in the appendix to this chapter shows that this is no longer the case in Belgium. Even though they are less politically attentive and have lower levels of internal efficacy, we found that the young women in our sample were simultaneously more positive and confident about politics, politicians, and society. They were significantly more involved in associations and were more engaged in social causes. These young women were also more attentive to common well-being and were more preoccupied by societal problems and discrimination against minorities. In fact, Turkish and Moroccan girls more often said that they were discriminated against and were not treated equally within their family; nearly 100 percent of them wished for an improvement of their status in society and greater autonomy. We also found that a majority of respondents belonging to both minority groups, girls and not only boys, did not want to be prisoners of traditional family decisions nor of stereotyped conceptions.

Table 16.2 shows that, in both minority groups, girls supported more than boys ($p < 0.005$ in each case) the right to keep the group's culture and tradition and to build places of worship as these guarantee the social cohesion of the group. We verify here that girls have internalized their role of guarantor of traditions

TABLE 16.2 Percentage of young people supporting specific rights, by minority group

	Turks		Moroccans	
	Boys	Girls	Boys	Girls
The right to keep their group's culture and tradition	46%	69%	53%	67%
The right to build places of worship as they guarantee the social cohesion of the group	44%	67%	59%	78%
The right to be distanced from strict traditions	38%	71%	50%	59%
The right to be distanced from religion when it is not a private choice of faith	34%	67%	62%	66%

and values. At the same time, girls were also more likely to support the right to be distanced from strict traditions and from religion when it is not a private choice of faith. Girls (especially Moroccan girls) seemed conscious of the evolution of potential opportunities for them in society: 45 percent of boys and 65 percent of girls of Moroccan origin think that gender equality is desirable, while corresponding figures in the Turkish group were 20 percent and 58 percent. At the same time, the girls accepted more than the boys the control and constraints of their family and not always having a free choice. These gendered social pressures were more pronounced in the minorities than in the majority group. Boys from the minority groups believed more in the collective efficacy of their gender group than the other sub-groups in the sample. Those results confirm the apparently contradictory movement/dynamic described by Kaufmann (2001) concerning contemporary girls: on one hand, they accept their role as the guardians of morality and culture; on the other hand, they help conventions to change and they behave as full social actors.

The girls in our sample were found to be more involved with organized social activities while the boys participated more in sport and leisure activities (a prolongation of the gendered specialization of spheres of activity). Some girls – mainly Turkish and Moroccan – still had no right to participate in any activity outside the home. However, they were not passive and disengaged. Because they were more confined to the domestic sphere, they used the Internet and other news communication tools more often to be in contact with others and to stay informed about what is going on in the world. They reported wearing protest bracelets and boycotted more often than boys in all groups. Even if their self-confidence was confirmed as being lower on average in comparison to boys, the girls were much more optimistic and positive concerning NGOs and politics than boys in each group. They believed in collective action and they were more proud than boys of their national identity. The minority girls were invested in positive perspectives about the future and in school to gain independence and freedom and to build a better society. They assigned high importance to voting, even the compulsory vote. The girls were mobilized for present and future actions more than for discourse. They had internalized a society which should give equal rights and obligations, and said that they wanted to participate to improve society more than for their own promotion, although this was possibly less true in the two minority groups where the girls had to fight more over their day-to-day lives which they described as unfair for girls and women. Even though the young women said that there are more obstacles and barriers to their involvement and engagement in politics, at the same time they thought more than boys that they would be encouraged by friends and parents if they did engage in such activities and causes. This is perhaps an effect of the feminization of the political sphere and authorities (through a better ratio of women), or perhaps an expression of the valorization of new political goals (with a greater place for emotion). It could also illustrate the fact that today, among minority groups, young women represent the best investment for the social mobility of the family group because they believe in school and education.

Conclusions

A major conclusion from our quantitative data is that the way youths conceive and apply political and civic engagement is not independent of the economic, social, and historical opportunities and strategies of the different groups to which they belong. But if gendered socialization continues to influence the distribution of roles and motivations (defense of prosocial or pro-traditional values for girls), young women are also determined to distance themselves with regard to gender-stereotyped choices.

We have also confirmed the cultural and sociological differences between, and separate strategies and reactions of, young Turks and Moroccans that have been described earlier by Manço (2009). Our study shows the relevance of studying Moroccans and Turks separately. Turks relate more to their own community and traditions and they develop collective strategies, while Moroccans are more open to diversity and want to find their place in and to take advantage of the opportunities given by Belgian society. They rely on conventional institutions like the school and the labor market. This is also true for girls. Even among Turks and Moroccans, girls say they want to distance themselves from tradition and religion. They are also more likely than the two other groups (Belgian and other origin) to think that gender equality has not been realized but is very important. Their responses show that they want to benefit from the historical opportunities which are offered by Belgian society. And they invest in the web to talk and get information (the private sphere being more legitimized for them).

Other results also concern the gender dimension and gender stakes. The research confirms that boys put less trust in democratic governance, irrespective of their national origins. They are also more skeptical than girls about the importance of gender equality and social justice, and they undertake more non-conventional political actions. They also believe, more readily than girls, that they are not free to choose friends or partners and that they suffer from social, religious, or statutory discrimination. With regards to political interest and investment, we see that girls play an active and positive role in both political and social spheres and projects.

Recommendations

The data which we collected in Belgium in the PIDOP project are consistent with the theory of societal vulnerability of Vettenburg (1988). Both groups and individuals in society are defined as 'societally vulnerable' when they derive little benefit from their contacts with societal institutions and additionally are mainly and recurrently confronted with the negative effects of these institutions. Political/civic interests, opinions, and (current or future) commitments are mostly linked to everyday needs and experiences in their objective and subjective dimensions. Youths express a significant desire for community and personal recognition in the private and public spheres, and this impacts on their political and civic attitudes. This has been put forward in Honneth's theory of recognition (1992). We would recommend not to neglect or misinterpret the message given in non-conventional ways. European young people still feel responsible within and for society. They want a future but some are very disenchanted and discouraged. European national authorities must listen to youths and place them more concretely in the centre of their preoccupations. This does not mean attempting to convince them through theoretical or rational arguments and moralizing, but giving them real opportunities and responsibilities. It seems important to inform youths about the injustices in the world (malnutrition, exploitation, violence) and to explain to them the role that may be played by peaceful civic disobedience (e.g. Luther King, Gandhi, etc.). The aim should be to fight against fatalism and the temptation to close one's eyes to injustices.

Our research leads us to emphasize the idea and the reality of the 'native majority' population. However, it is extremely difficult to decide who is a member of this group in Belgium because of the large number of young people from various foreign origins who have been born in Belgium and are often naturalized. Our data show that young people with parents who have been born elsewhere but not in either Morocco or Turkey could be classified as part of the majority Belgian group because they have similar characteristics while being distinctive from youths of these two minority groups. At the same time, our results confirm that Turks and Moroccans do not comprise a single group, even if they have a similar immigration history and the same religion. Even though they might live in quite similar economic and social situations, their groups have developed different strategies to cope with problems of unemployment or social inclusion.

Young Turks are protected but also controlled by their community. If they are interested in politics, this interest still mainly concerns Turkey. Until now, they have not invested much in school qualifications and they do not frequently meet young people of other national origins. But things are changing. If they are proud of the solidarity and other values of their national group, at the same time they express disappointment in suffering today from a lack of personal freedom. In comparison, young Moroccans invest more in Belgian society and its institutions. They invest more in the school and want to reach the same jobs and positions as Belgian people. They feel both Belgian and Moroccan and most of them like to repeat that they have Belgian nationality. This is why they feel more injustice and discrimination when they cannot valorize their diplomas and remain unemployed. They invest in the political field more than Turks and not mainly in order to defend their own community. They believe that it is important to reinforce the links between the Moroccan and Belgian communities. They think that educators and social associations have a bigger place to take in this dialogue. Moroccan girls are allowed to take part in the public sphere and in politics more than Turkish girls. We recommend keeping these differences in mind when conceiving new ways to deal with young people from minority groups. It is important to understand their current specific needs and uneasy feelings. At the same time, all groups must be considered as being in a process of transformation, and stereotypes should be challenged while giving young people the tools to understand the social and gender issues which affect them.

Although differences clearly do exist between the two minority groups that we have studied, it is important to not overlook interpersonal and intragroup diversity while focusing on intergroup diversity. This issue is particularly important for the females within each ethnic group. Our results confirm that girls are not in fact less interested in politics. Most young women are not passive, even when they are not allowed to invest in any public space at any time. Most of them use the Internet to get useful information and to share their opinions. In fact, we see that traditional indicators created and used to measure interest or involvement are still gender-colored. They allow the assessment of boys' values, conceptions, and actions more easily than those of girls. In the results of the survey, we also found clear tracks of gendered social relations and of separate socialization injunctions addressed to each gender group in terms of implications in the public sphere.

We also found that a large majority of young pupils who went into politics or took on responsibilities in a social association had been approached by other persons who were already involved in a political party or social organization. Without personal experiences and networks and without such stimulation, these young people would not have gone into politics. It seems important to give information and to promote social relations between younger and older people who are already involved in public life. Role models are essential. Young Moroccans insist on this fact, on the impact of school, teachers, and other professionals. In the survey, many respondents told us that if they had not been involved, it was because nobody had asked them.

We recommend continuing to invest in democratic school functioning and in inclusive pedagogic initiatives because school is described by young people as a 'laboratory of democracy' which impacts on their future political interest and investment. It is even more important because school is described as the main place where young people experience discrimination today. The school system must take care of the well-being of youths – especially the most socially and culturally deprived youths – not only their instruction and employability. One of the experts we interviewed said to us: 'We must admit there is no real place reserved for students' reflection and experimentation about environmental or societal issues, about values ... Every teacher, every school, has the choice to tackle those questions or not, to practise dialogue and democracy or not.'

We conclude that youths' dreams, demands, and opinions about 'what works or not' are not so different from those of adults. Even if young people use new technologies and the Internet to inform themselves and to discuss issues, they still think that the most traditional ways of social and political involvement – which require human and social contact – are the most effective. Both tracks must be encouraged. It is recommended not to rely on e-action alone but, at the same time, to view the Internet as a real opportunity to reach girls belonging to specific groups who may not be allowed to invest in the public sphere physically. Girls do not want to be the losers of the European adventure and do not consider themselves to be a minority.

Appendix

Table A16.1 presents general comparisons between ethnic groups and gender groups.

TABLE A16.1 General comparisons between ethnic groups (columns 1 and 2) and between gender groups (column 3)

Items/Scales	Significant differences between Belgian (A) and minority (Turkish and Moroccan) youth (B)		Significant differences between Turkish (T) and Moroccan (M) youth		Significant differences between gender groups (M+ = higher male scores, F+ = higher female scores)	
Political interest	0.006	A > B	NS		NS	
Political attentiveness	0.02	B > A	0.01		0.0008	M+
Political participation (excluding 'voting')	< 0.0001	B > A	NS		NS	
Level of involvement in civic/social organizations	0.02	A > B	NS		NS	
Feelings about previous participation	0.03	A > B	0.04	M > T	NS	
Feelings of freedom in own choices	< 0.0001	A > B	0.02	M > T	< 0.0001	F+
Prosocial motivations	NS		NS		< 0.0001	F+
Willing to participate in social change	NS		NS		< 0.0001	F+
Barriers to involvement	NS		NS		0.0001	F+
Internal political efficacy	NS		0.04	M > T	< 0.0001	M+
External political efficacy	0.03	A > B	NS		0.04	M+
Collective efficacy of the ethnic group	0.003	B > A	0.003	M > T	NS	
Collective efficacy of the gender group	0.0007	B > A	NS		NS	
Trust in form of governance	NS		NS		0.0012	
Emotions about environmental problems	0.02	A > B	NS		NS	
Emotions about discrimination	NS		S		0.0026	F+
Collective community power of change	NS		0.001	M > T	0.03	F+
Proud of national identity	0.01	B > A	NS		0.01	F+
Strength of EU identity	NS		0.02	M > T	NS	
Religiosity	< 0.0001	B > A	0.002	M > T	NS	
Fight against discriminations toward minorities	NS		0.01	M > T	<0.0001	F+
Defense of cultural rights for minorities	< 0.0001	B > A	NS		NS	
Demand for positive actions for the benefit of minorities	< 0.0001	B > A	0.04	M > T	NS	

Note: Numbers are significance levels; NS = not significant.

Notes

1 http://www.linguee.fr/francaisanglais/search?source=auto&query=commission%27s+white+paper+youth+participation
2 http://www.belgium.be/fr/la_belgique/connaitre_le_pays/Population/

References

Banque Nationale de Belgique (2012) *Rapport annuel*. December.
Bimber, B., Flanagin, A. J., and Stohl, C. (2005) 'Reconceptualizing collective action in the contemporary media environment,' *Communication Theory*, 15: 365–88.
Bréchon, P. (1995) 'Politisation et vote des jeunes' ['Politicization and vote of the youth'], *Agora débats/jeunesses*, 2 (2): 9–21.
Centre pour l'Egalité des Chances et la Lutte Contre le Racisme (2009) *Rapport annuel Migration 2008*. Brussels. Retrieved from: http://www.diversite.be.
Coenen, M.-T. (2002) *De l'égalité à la parité: le difficile accès des femmes à la citoyenneté* [*From Equality to Parity: the Difficult Access of Women to Citizenship*]. Brussels: Labor.
Coenen, M.-T. (2005) *La parité* [*The parity*], Publications et Analyses, No. 29. Brussels: Université des femmes. Retrieved from: http://www.universitedesfemmes.be/041_publications-feministes.php?idpub=28anddebut.
Coffé, H. and Bolzendahl, C. (2010) 'Same game, different rules? Gender differences in political participation,' *Sex Roles*, 62 (5/6), 318–33.
Ekman, J. and Amnå, E. (2012) 'Political participation and civic engagement: towards a new typology,' *Human Affairs*, 22 (3): 283–300.
Feld, S. and Manço, A. (2000) *L'intégration des jeunes d'origine étrangère dans une société en mutation* [*The Integration of Non-native Youths in a Changing Society*]. Paris: L'Harmattan.
Gavray, C. (2012) 'Mieux comprendre les modes non conventionnels d'expression politique et civique des adolescents et adolescentes. Apport de la théorie de la vulnérabilité sociétale et de la théorie de la reconnaissance' ['The unconventional modes of political and civic expression of male and female teenagers. Contribution of the theory of the societal vulnerability and of the theory of recognition'], in M. de Bie, R. Roose, and M. Vandenbroeck (eds), *Maatschappelijk engagement: een besef van kwetsbaarheid: liber amicorum voor Nicole Vettenburg*. Ghent, Belgium: Academia Press, pp. 13–34.
Gavray, C., Born, M., and Waxweiler, C. (2012) 'La dimension de genre dans l'étude de la participation sociale, civique et politique' ['The gender dimension in the study of social, civic, and political participation'], in B. Fournier and R. Hudon (eds), *Engagements citoyens et politiques des jeunes: bilans et expériences au Canada et en Europe* [*Civic and Political Involvements of Young People*]. Quebec City: Les Presses de l'Université Laval, pp. 65–79.
Gavray, C., Fournier, B., and Born, M. (2012) 'Non-conventional/illegal political participation of male and female youths,' *Human Affairs*, 22 (3): 405–18.
Giddens, A. (1990) *The Consequences of Modernity*. Cambridge: Polity Press.
Honneth, A. (1992) 'Integrity and disrespect: principles of a conception of morality based on the theory of recognition,' *Political Theory*, 20 (2): 187–201.
Hudon, R. (2012) 'Introduction,' in B. Fournier and R. Hudon, *Engagements citoyens et politiques des jeunes: bilans et expériences au Canada et en Europe* [*Civic and Political Involvements of Young People in Canada and in Europe*]. Quebec City: Les Presses de l'Université Laval, pp. 1–9.
Jacobs, D., Rea, A., and Martiniello, M. (2000) 'Changing patterns of political participation of citizens of immigrant origin in the Brussels capital region: the October 2000 elections,' *Journal of International Migration and Integration*, 3 (2): 201–21.

Kaufmann, J. C. (2001) *Ego. Pour une sociologie de l'individu. Une autre vision de l'homme et de la construction du sujet* [*Ego. For a Sociology of the Individual*]. Paris: Nathan.

Lafleur, J. M. (2005) *Le transnationalisme politique. Pouvoir des communautés immigrées dans leurs pays d'accueil et pays d'origine* [*Political Transnationalism. The Power of Migrant Communities in Their Home and Host Societies*]. Louvain-La-Neuve: Academia Bruylant, Cahiers Migration.

Leahy, P. and Burgess, P. (2012) 'Barriers to participation within a recessionary state: impediments confronting Irish youth,' in P. Loncle, M. Cuconato, V. Muniglia, and A. Walther (eds), *Youth Participation in Europe: Beyond Discourses, Practices and Realities*. Cambridge: Policy Press, pp. 109–24.

Lister, R. (1990) 'Women, economic dependency and citizenship,' *Journal of Social Policy*, 4: 445–67.

Malagón, J. (2011) 'Guide for the design and implementation of participation projects and civic training of children and young people' [*Guía para el diseño y ejecucío de proyectos de participación y capacitación cívica de la infancia y la adolescencia*]. Madrid: Ayuntamiento de Rivas Vaciamadrid. Retrieved from: http://www.rivasciudad.es/portal/RecursosWeb/DOCUMENTOS/1/0_2307_1.pdf.

Manço, A. (1998) *Valeurs et projets des jeunes issus de l'immigration* [*Values and Projects of Young People from Migrant Descent*]. Brussels: L'Harmattan, Collection Logiques sociales.

Manço, A. and Freyens, F. (2008) 'Connaître, reconnaître et développer les ressources identitaires des jeunes filles issues de l'immigration musulmane: de la recherche à l'action scolaire preventive' ['Knowing, recognizing, and developing the identity resources of the girls from Muslim migrant descent: from the research to the preventive school action'], *Revue des Sciences de l'Education*, 34 (2): 399–417. Retrieved from: http://www.erudit.org/revue/rse/2008/v34/n2/019687ar.html.

Martelli, A. (2013) 'The debate on young people and participatory citizenship: questions and research prospects,' *International Review of Sociology*, 12 July [online].

Martiniello, M. (2005) *Political Participation, Mobilisation and Representation of Immigrants and Their Offspring in Europe*, Willy Brandt Series of Working Papers in International Migration and Ethnic Relations, No. 1/05. Malmö: Malmö University.

Martiniello, M. and Statham, P. (1999) 'Introduction,' *Journal of Ethnic and Migration Studies*, 25 (4): 565–73.

Menezes, I. (2003) 'Participation experiences and civic concepts, attitudes and engagement: implications for citizenship education projects,' *European Educational Research Journal*, 2 (3): 430–45.

Muniglia, V., Cuconato, M., Loncle, P., and Walther, A. (2012) 'The analysis of youth participation in contemporary literature: a European perspective,' in P. Loncle, M. Cuconato, V. Muniglia, and A. Walther (eds), *Youth Participation in Europe. Beyond Discourses, Practices and Realities*. Bristol: Policy Press, pp. 1–17.

OEJAJ (Observatoire de l'enfance, de la jeunesse et de l'aide à la jeunesse de la Communauté Française) (2007) *Conclusion of the Final Report of the Survey About Children and Youth (10–18) Participation*, April. Retrieved from: http://www.oejaj.cfwb.be/index.php?eID=tx_nawsecuredlandu=0andfile=fileadmin/sites/oejaj/upload/oejaj_super_editor/oejaj_editor/pdf/rapport_final_participation_10_18_ultra_light.pdfandhash=9ac69931abe22c03425608443e5a05867d0194fc.

Paakkunainen, K. (2003) *Yes to Politics, But ...* [in Finnish]. Finnish Youth Research Network.

Paxton, P., Kunhovich, S., and Hughes, M. (2007) 'Gender in politics,' *Annual Review of Sociology*, 33: 263–84.

Putnam, R. (2007) 'E pluribus unum: diversity and community in the twenty-first century. The 2006 Johan Skytte Prize Lecture,' *Scandinavian Political Studies*, 30 (2): 137–74.

Schildrick, T. and MacDonald, R. (2006) 'In defence of subculture: young people, leisure and social division,' *Journal of Youth Studies*, 9 (2): 125–40.

Spanning, R., Ogris, G., and Gaiser, W. (eds) (2008) *Youth and Political Participation in Europe. Results of the Comparative Study* (EUYOUPART). Opladen: Barbara Budrich.

Stevenson, N. (2001) *Culture and Citizenship*. London: Sage.

Van Berkel, R. and Hornemann-Möller, I. (eds) (2002) *Active and Social Policies in the EU: Inclusion Through Participation?* Bristol: Policy Press.

Vettenburg, N. (1988) *Schoolervaringen, delinquentie en maatschappelijke kwetsbaarheid* [*School Delinquency and Societal Vulnerability*]. Leuven: Onderzoeksgroep Jeugdcriminologie.

Walther, A., Du Bois-Reymond, M., and Biggardt, A. (eds) (2006) *Participation in Transition: Motivation of Young People in Europe for Learning and Working*. Frankfurt am Main: Lang.

17
PARTICIPATION AMONG YOUTH, WOMEN AND MIGRANTS

Findings from Portugal

Maria Fernandes-Jesus, Carla Malafaia, Norberto Ribeiro and Isabel Menezes

Introduction

In the past few decades, there has been an increasing interest in understanding and promoting youth civic and political participation, due to a series of studies that have defined young people as being at risk of becoming apathetic and apolitical (e.g. Forbrig 2005; Galston 2001; Perliger *et al.* 2006; Putnam 2000). Thus there is a call to revitalise young people's participation as a condition for the legitimacy and quality of democratic systems (Sullivan and Transue 1999). Taking into account that civic and political participation during youth is a predictor of involvement in adulthood, and youth is a formative phase for civic attitudes and behaviours (Jennings and Stoker 2004; Youniss *et al.* 1997), the number of efforts to understand young people's participation is not surprising.

In this context, several studies claim that the participatory 'crisis' that has been denounced for many decades is clearly exaggerated, as recent research has shown an increase in non-conventional types of participation that are more creative and less institutional (Forbrig 2005; Haste and Hogan 2006; Stolle *et al.* 2005; Zukin *et al.* 2006). These studies reveal that conclusions about young people participation were based on research that used conventional measures of participation such as voter turnout or party membership (Beaton and Deveau 2005; Harris *et al.* 2010; Van Deth and Elff 2004), which tends to exclude several types of participation in which young people are currently engaged (see Bang 2005; Ferreira *et al.* 2012; Harris *et al.* 2010; Juris and Pleyers 2009; Vromen and Collin 2010; Zukin *et al.* 2006). In this vein, O'Toole *et al.* (2003) argue that most of the research on civic and political participation tends to overlook generational effects, assuming frequently that if young people do not engage in activities that researchers consider representative of political participation, then they are politically apathetic. This trend has created several obstacles to the process of understanding political behaviour (Haste and Hogan 2006).

Farthing (2010) claims that discourse about youth participation needs to move on, accepting that both 'engagement and disengagement are simultaneously occurring as young people navigate an entirely new world' (p. 182). Therefore research on youth participation needs to consider young people as a specific group with their own particular circumstances, concerns and characteristics.

But young people are not the only group that are often studied as homogeneous, underestimating their specificities, singularities and internal diversity. Research on immigrant groups also tends to be inadequate in this respect. In fact, the discussion about civic and political participation must be related to the debate on cultural diversity – which is growing in Europe, especially due to the increased number of immigrants, and therefore the debate on the political integration of immigrants can no longer exclude political integration (Martiniello 2005), as the role of civic and political participation on immigrants' integration seems to be crucial (Munro 2008).

Similar to perspectives on youth participation, research on immigrants' civic and political participation has been dominated by two perspectives. Firstly, for many decades, people of immigrant background were considered apolitical and apathetic in relation to politics (Martiniello 2005). Such beliefs were supported by several studies reporting immigrants as having lower levels of civic and political participation when compared with non-immigrants (Vogel and Triandafyllidou 2005; Putnam 2000; Couton and Gaudet 2008). In opposition to this perspective, Simon (2011) argues that migrants are increasingly making political claims and are mobilising for collective action in support of their claims; however, not all ethnic/migrant groups are the same. For instance, Stoll and Wong (2007) found that Whites, Blacks, Latinos and Asians are characterised by differential rates of participation. Fennema and Tillie (1999) also found differences among immigrant groups, suggesting the need to consider the diversity in ethnic minority political participation. Regarding immigrant youths' participation, Marcelo et al. (2007) found that African-American youth are the most politically engaged, and Asian-American youth are among the most engaged in civic activities such as volunteering. In addition, Latinos seems to be more involved in protesting (Dávila and Mora 2007). A number of studies tend to argue that the participation of immigrants varies, and that we need to look at differences between migrant groups.

Although there is a growing recognition of the importance of civic and political participation of immigrants as a promoter of social integration, socialisation and strengthening of community ties (Eggert and Giugni 2010; Kelly 2009; Munro 2008; Vogel and Triandafyllidou 2005), several gaps still persist in the literature regarding the civic and political participation of immigrants (Martiniello 2005). First of all, few studies have examined the issue of immigrants' participation (Simon and Grabow 2010) and even fewer consider the specific case of young immigrants (Stepick et al. 2008). Secondly, most of the research focused on European migrants highlights factors such as the labour market and the demographic effects of migration and we rarely find gender sufficiently explored (Martiniello 2005). These gaps in the literature about young people's participation have promoted theories of participation that are generalised to all groups, but are tested and developed almost exclusively from majority populations (Myrberg 2011).

Similarly, in Portugal, studies about the immigrant population are merely demographic (Teixeira and Albuquerque 2005); none focuses on youth, very few consider the gender dimension (Miranda 2009) and there are no studies comparing nationals and non-nationals in terms of civic and political participation (Teixeira and Albuquerque 2005). For all these reasons, a study on young people's participation seems to be urgently required and, in this regard, PIDOP has contributed to filling this gap. The purpose of this chapter is to report the findings from Portugal regarding participation among youth, women and migrants. We present some of the findings from the focus groups and from the survey. Regarding the focus groups, perceptions about disadvantages in civic and political participation are discussed. Then, using data from the survey, patterns of civic and political participation among young people are reported, considering age, gender, books at home and immigrant background.

Youth participation in Portugal

In spite of the recent recognition of diversity in participatory experiences, the major tendency of research, mostly in western democracies, is to point out the low levels of interest and participation of young people in political and civic matters. Such results have been stressed by several scholars and also by the European Commission, which warns that young people do not invest in the traditional structures of political action (Galston 2001; Putnam 2000; European Commission 2001). Portugal is not an exception in this respect – on the contrary. Due to its recent democratic system – implemented after the Revolution in 1974 – research has emphasised the low political development and the fragile political culture (Braga da Cruz 1985). This justifies concerns about the democratic knowledge and political attitudes of younger generations, and also about the reasons behind the withdrawal of political mechanisms, and if such a tendency really means their 'depoliticisation' (Augusto 2008). In addition, the lack of commitment in the civic and political realms often creates a vicious cycle, in which the disbelief of society regarding young people (Pais 1990), commonly called the 'lost generation', finds a correspondence in the young people themselves, who often internalise such guilt (Silva 2012).

Research in this area clearly shows the low levels of democratic satisfaction and political involvement of young people (Magalhães and Moral 2008). In this respect, it also highlights youth scepticism about the efficacy of conventional political participation – with the exception of voting – (Augusto 2008; Magalhães and Moral 2008), even if levels of social participation, for example in voluntary associations, are relatively high (Magalhães and Moral 2008), as is involvement in the school context, particularly students' councils and environmental organisations (Menezes 2003; Dias and Menezes 2013).

In fact, there is a clear deinstitutionalisation of youth political practices and a preference among youth for horizontal decision-making mechanisms, far from political parties and closer to membership association, namely sport, cultural or recreational types (Augusto 2008; Menezes 2003). Paradoxically, it is also important to consider the decrease in the perceived efficacy of non-conventional participation in older groups of young people (Magalhães and Moral 2008), which suggest that some mediating factors, such as social structures, play important roles in this relationship between young people and participation (Augusto 2008). The structural conditions, the political socialisation and the increasing institutionalisation of the relationship models with the political system are also important elements that must be taken into consideration when studying opportunities to participate (Teixeira and Albuquerque 2005). Moreover, the recent events of the current and previous year (2012 and 2013) are quite interesting concerning the participation of Portuguese young people who often have been occupying the forefront of several protests and demonstrations (e.g. the 'Indignados' protests and the 'Que se lixe a troika' movements).

Gender and participation

Similar to youth, women have been identified as having low levels of participation in civic and political domains compared to men. For instance, Paxton et al. (2007) conducted a comparative study in several countries, concluding that women continue to be unrepresented in the political systems. Similarly, Atkeson and Rapoport (2003) argue that, despite the increase in political resources, women continue to have lower levels of political knowledge. Other studies report that women contact political candidates less (Verba et al. 1995; Rosenstone and Hansen 1993), discuss political issues less frequently and know less about politics (Huckfeldt and Sprague 1995). All these studies seem to indicate a persistent gender gap on participation, especially regarding the formal and public domains (see also Chapter 3 by Galligan in this volume).

From another point of view, some authors point out that the gender gap in participation is a matter of contexts of participation instead of levels (Paxton et al. 2007), suggesting the need to look for diversity in women's participation. In Portugal, as far as we know, studies about women's participation are quite rare; however, one study reports that inequalities in terms of gender are only significant in non-conventional participation, while in electoral and extra-electoral forms there are no significant differences between men and women (Espírito-Santo and Baum 2004).

Concerning women with immigrant background, the research gap is even wider, as there is very little attention to the role of gender in migration (Miranda 2009). In this sense, the recognition of a growing increase of migrant women (Yamanaka and Piper 2006; Kofman et al. 2000) and insufficient exploration of the gender dimension of immigrants' civic and political participation (Martiniello 2005) justifies the inclusion of gender on our analysis.

Migration background and civic and political participation in Portugal

Historically a country of emigration, after the collapse of the dictatorial regime and the independence of the Portuguese colonies in Africa (1974), Portugal has exponentially increased the number of immigrants, especially those coming from former African colonies. In the 1990s, Portugal also became attractive for Brazilian immigrants, and more recently the migration influxes from Eastern Europe have quickly increased (Foreigners and Border Services (SEF) 2012). By the end of 2011 (SEF 2012), the foreign population resident in Portugal totalled 436,822 people. About half (47.9 per cent) are native from Portuguese-speaking countries such as Brazil (25.5 per cent), Cape Verde (10.1 per cent), Angola (4.9 per cent) and Guinea-Bissau (4.2 per cent). The other relevant nationalities are Ukraine (11 per cent) and Romania (9 per cent). The integration of immigrants from former colonies has been favoured in some countries (Vogel and Leiprecht 2008), including Portugal. For example, several bilateral agreements between Portugal and Brazil have contributed to the stabilisation and strengthening of the migration systems between Portugal and Brazil (Baganha 2009).

The promotion of the civic and political participation of immigrants is a recent topic in the Portuguese context; however, it seems that Portuguese policies have already been creating favourable contexts and opportunities for participation (Ramalho and Trovão 2010). Yet it is not clear how immigrants in Portugal are using the opportunities to be involved. It seems that in the civil society sphere, the main actors encouraging immigrants' civic participation are immigrants' associations (Teixeira and Alburquerque 2005), but there is not enough research on how immigrants engage in these associations. In addition, as far as we know, before PIDOP there was no research on civic and political participation of Brazilians and Angolans in Portugal, two representative communities of immigrants that are relevant to understanding the way these communities are living in Portugal. The strong migration systems between Portugal and Brazil (Baganha 2009) and the large presence of Brazilians in Portugal clearly justify the choice to include the Brazilian group in our analysis. In addition, the option to study youth of Angolan origin was determined by the relatively recent history of decolonisation (Grillo and Mazzucato 2008), and the fact that many young Angolans are, in fact, second- and third-generation immigrants who have Portuguese citizenship.

Here we consider the qualitative and quantitative data collected from young people of immigrant (Brazilian origin and Angolan origin) and non-migrant background living in Portugal, exploring the interplay between immigrant status, gender, books at home (as an indicator of cultural capital) and age, and differences in civic and political participation, political interest and attentiveness.

Methodology

Participants

Data were collected under the PIDOP Project and the results reported here are drawn from two phases of the project. In phase one, we conducted focus group discussions with young people of Portuguese origin, Angolan origin (mostly second- and third-generation migrants) and Brazilian origin (from a more recent wave of immigration, the majority of whom were not born in Portugal), all aged from 16 to 26 years old. Altogether, 14 focus groups involving 94 young participants (44 male, 50 female) were carried out: five groups of Angolan immigrants, five groups of Brazilian immigrants and four groups of Portuguese nationals.

In phase two, 1,010 young people participated in a survey study. Participants were from the three backgrounds (Portuguese origin = 388; Angolan origin = 255; Brazilian origin = 367) from both genders (Portuguese origin: female = 222; male = 166; Angolan origin: female = 134, male = 121; Brazilian origin: female = 209, male = 158) and from two age ranges: young people aged 15 to 18 years old (young adolescents = 375) and young people aged 19 to 29 years old (young adults = 635). Both age groups were also represented in all the sample groups (Portuguese origin: adolescents = 158, young adults = 230; Angolan origin: adolescents = 125, young adults = 130; Brazilian origin: adolescents = 92, young adults = 275). Regarding citizenship status, 29.4 per cent of young people of Angolan origin had Portuguese nationality, 14 per cent dual citizenship (Portuguese and Angolan) and 55.3 per cent had Angolan citizenship. In turn, 85.6 per cent of young Brazilians were citizens of Brazil and 13.6 per cent had dual citizenship (Portuguese and Brazilian).

Procedures and instruments

In both phases, data were collected mainly in the two main metropolitan areas, Lisbon and Porto, in a variety of contexts: religious associations, immigrant associations, youth organisations, regular and vocational schools and higher education institutions. For the questionnaire we also collected data at the National Centres of Immigrant Support (CNAI), where immigrants usually go to deal with bureaucratic issues, recruiting individual immigrants while they were in the waiting room.

In the first phase of this study, in order to facilitate the discussion and to focus the participants' attention and discussion on certain topics, we used a script in all focus groups (Tonkiss 2006). This script was divided into different blocks: the relevance of civic and political participation for young people; sources of information and knowledge; personal and group experiences; and proposals for inclusion. All the focus groups were taped, transcribed and analysed with the software NVivo9. Based on the qualitative study, we elaborated the survey to explore forms of participation and political attitudes among young people. During data collection, we started by presenting the aims of the study to participants and obtained their consent. We also had an online version of the questionnaire that was disseminated through online social networks.

Groups' background, age, books at home and gender were added as factors that might influence the levels of civic and political participation (as participants reported during the focus group discussions). Gender (1 = male; 2 = female) and group membership (1 = Portuguese origin, 2 = Angolan origin and 3 = Brazilian origin) were nominal variables so they were added as such. In addition, we transformed the 'age' variable into a nominal variable (1 = adolescents 15–18 years old; 2 = young adults 19–29 years old). The inclusion of age (adolescence and young adults) as a factor that might differentiate patterns of participation was based on studies that show that participation is lower during young adulthood compared with adolescence and later adulthood (Jennings and Stoker 2004; Planty et al. 2006; Snell 2010). Indeed, adolescence is an important phase of life in terms of the development of cultural orientations (Vollebergh et al. 2001) such as those related to political issues. Furthermore, our goal was to compare patterns of participation across young people who were old enough to legally engage in all types of participation and young people who were less than 18 years old.

Finally, we also included books at home as a factor. The number of books at home has been suggested as a strong indicator of parental resources and cultural capital and has been used in international studies (Torney-Purta et al. 2001).

Multivariate analyses of variance (MANOVA) were run for current civic and political participation and also for political interest and attentiveness. We should add that indicators were computed using the weighted means of the values for scale items.

Current civic and political participation

$\chi^2(60) = 225.27$, $p < 0.001$; $\chi^2/df = 3.75$; CFI = 0.94; GFI = 0.93; RMSEA = 0.074; p(RMSEA ≤ 0.05) < 0.001

Four forms of participation emerged in our analysis: online (Portuguese: $\alpha = 0.76$; Angolan, $\alpha = 0.91$, Brazilian: $\alpha = 0.84$), social (Portuguese $\alpha = 0.76$; Angolans $\alpha = 0.78$; Brazilian $\alpha = 0.60$), activism (Portuguese $\alpha = 0.77$; Angolans $\alpha = 0.85$; Brazilian $\alpha = 0.67$), and the single-item 'vote in elections'. Online participation included four items: discuss social or political issues on the Internet; visit a website of a political or civic organisation; participate in online based petition, protest or boycotting; connect to a group on Facebook (or similar online social network) dealing with social or political issues. Social participation was composed of three items: volunteer work; boycott or buy certain products for political, ethical or environmental reasons; and donate money to a social or political cause/organisation. The activism scale comprised five items and covered a range of activities such as: attend a public meeting or demonstration dealing with political or social issues; distribute leaflets with a political content; take part in concerts or a fund-raising event with a social or political cause; write political messages or graffiti on walls; and participate in political actions that might be considered illegal.

Political interest and attentiveness

$\chi^2(4) = 17.93$, $p = 0.001$; $\chi^2/df = 4.48$; CFI = 0.991; GFI = 0.99; RMSEA = 0.08; p(RMSEA ≤ 0.05) = 0.066

Political interest comprised the following two items (Portuguese $r = 0.75$, $p \leq 0.0001$; Angolan $r = 0.76$, $p \leq 0.0001$; Brazilian $r = 0.74$, $p \leq 0.0001$): I discuss social and political issues with friends and acquaintances; I bring political and social issues into discussions with others. In turn, political attentiveness was constituted by three items (Portuguese α = 0.78; Angolans α = 0.87; Brazilian α = 0.83): I follow what is going on in politics by reading articles in newspapers or magazines; I watch television programmes or listen to radio broadcasts that deal with political issues; I pay attention to information on the Internet that is about politics.

Findings from the focus group discussions

We focus here on the perceptions of the main disadvantages regarding civic and political participation reported by the participants. During the focus group discussions, gender, age, immigrant background and family resources emerged as factors of discrimination and disadvantage that could influence civic and political participation. Below, we present some of the discourses of young people expressing these perceptions of disadvantage.

Age

The feeling that societies do not take young people seriously into account and that age is one factor of discrimination was shared by all groups of adolescents and young people. Discrimination was apparent in several contexts and dimensions such criminality, employment and also participation. One of the adolescents of Portuguese origin said that

> with the increase of criminality in Portugal, people associate it with youth … I am walking in the street and people look at me in a strange way … and only because I am young. (Male, 18 years old)

Additionally, some of the youth did not feel they were citizens with full rights and claimed that youth

> are not fully represented; I think that people and the state (…) look at us as mere adolescents that are protesting just as an excuse to miss classes (Male, 18 years old)

and that

> we have a low status, we don't have much influence, we don't have a direct impact on the state, that is the reality. (Female, 18 years old)

An adolescent of Angolan origin added that

> concerning youth, people listen and realise they are right, however they pretend not to hear, and it is necessary to repeat several times for people to hear you. (Male, 19 years old)

One young adult of Brazilian origin agreed that age creates disadvantages and obstacles to participation:

> The question is to speak for whom; because if you need more information you have to access it, youth don't have access to how to do things. There has to be a way to get such information, because young people themselves will hardly be able to reach it. (Male, 23 years old)

On the one hand, Brazilian adolescents seemed to agree that there are few opportunities for young people to participate, but on the other hand there was also a lack of interest in political issues:

> not all of them, but I think that many youth are not interested. (Female, 16 years old)

Simultaneously, young people of Portuguese origin criticised youth especially because sometimes

> young people don't have enough knowledge about politics (Female, 18 years old)

which in part is due to low contact with politics:

> We don't have enough direct contact with politics. (Female, 18 years old)

For some of the participants this fact led to political actions developed by young people being

> poorly organised and cohesive. (Female, 18 years old)

An adolescent of Portuguese origin emphasised the fact that there are few opportunities in school to discuss these kinds of topics:

> The debate that we are having here might be the first in the school (...). On the other hand, I think that few people join this (...) and the reason is laziness ... but simultaneously there are not so many opportunities ... (Male, 18 years old)

Young adults of Angolan origin adults seemed to agree, saying that:

> We have both: youth that invest in participation, but we also have youth that easily accept things and don't want more, do not fight. (Female, 25 years old)

Immigrant background

Racism, prejudice and discrimination were topics that arose very frequently in the focus group discussions, especially those with the young people of immigrant background. Although the immigrants of Angolan origin emphasised a double disadvantage due to immigrant status and black skin, it seemed consensual that immigrant status by itself was a motive for discrimination. For instance, a young adult of Angolan origin said

> Ukrainian people suffer much more than the Africans especially because of the language. (Male, 23 years old)

However, the main bias recognised by all the Angolan origin youth was the association between Angolan people and theft:

> If someone is black/African he/she is a robber (Female, 25 years old)

while in the case of Brazilians, the young people acknowledged the tendency to consider Brazilian women as prostitutes:

> Society has these prejudices and bias. (Female, 25 years old)

In turn, adolescents of Brazilian origin believed that all the immigrants from China, Africa and Japan suffered racism which was not only because of 'black colour':

> The ones who suffer more are the ones that you look at and you can see that they are immigrants; for example, the Japanese have that eyes' shape. (Female, 17 years old)

In terms of participation, young people of Brazilian origin believed that young immigrants have the same opportunities for participation as other groups in society. One of the participants said that:

> Prejudice exists in any place, but I don't believe that if you wanted to get involved politically you cannot because of that [being immigrant], I believe you have the same rights and opportunities. (Male, 24 years old)

Some young people of Angolan origin also believed that there are opportunities to participate in political and civic organisations, but others reported some obstacles, for example regarding participation in sport groups. A youngster of Angolan origin said:

> The opportunities are not the same, there are always differences. (Female, 17 years old)

Regarding the right to vote, adolescents of Angolan origin advocated that everybody should have the right to vote

> because, I know that foreign people could not vote in Portugal, (...) while you are in an irregular situation. (Male, 19 years old)

Family resources

For young people of Portuguese origin, not all youth are equal. For some, young people are only taken into consideration if they are from a high status:

> If I am the son of the prime minister and if you are the son of a poor person, who is heard? The son of the prime minister, for sure! He has the power, even if he doesn't have any ideas. (Male, 20 years old)

Young adults of Brazilian origin reported that even between the immigrant groups 'there is segregation' due to education:

> Africans are the ones who might suffer from more discrimination in any place of the world (...) culturally Africans are less educated, and have less access to education and culture. (Male, 26 years old)

Some of them related these factors to the 'colour of the skin' (male, 21 years old), and others to the fact that 'they are coming from a poor country' (female, 25 years old). Adolescents of Angolan origin said that:

> Even Portuguese young people suffer a lot; especially those who haven't studied. (Male, 21 years old)

But even so:

> They prefer to give a job to a white person without studies than to a black person educated. (Female, 18 years old)

Gender

Gender differences were recognised in all groups. In general, women were seen as having less power and influence in several fields, such as employment, salary, leadership positions and domestic tasks. The adolescents of Portuguese origin recognised the history and evolution of women rights; however, all of them agreed that women suffer more discrimination than men:

> Our rights are segregated comparing with men's rights, in politics there is a higher number of male deputies in the Parliament. (Female, 18 years old)

The young adults of Portuguese origin tended to naturalise the discrimination against women:

> It's like racism, such things could be attenuated, but there will always be some, because it is a cultural issue. (Male, 24 years old)

They emphasised that even if women have the same political opportunities as men and if

> they can run for a political position like a man, [they are] not taken seriously. (Male, 20 years old)

Young adults of Brazilian origin also reported discrimination against women, especially because they were associated with sexual work:

> I think that in practical terms there is more prejudice against women. (Male, 24 years old)

Findings from the survey

In order to explore the group differences in civic and political participation and political interest and attentiveness, we ran several analyses of variance, using books at home, immigrant background, age and gender as differentiating factors – that is, the factors that young people had mentioned in the focus groups as motives for discrimination and disadvantage.

Civic and political participation

Multivariate tests revealed a significant effect from the number of books at home (Pillai's trace = 0.069; $F(8,1850)$ = 8.207; $p \leq 0.0001$), age (Pillai's trace = 0.073; $F(4,924)$ = 18.100; $p \leq 0.0001$), group background (Pillai's trace = 0.067; $F(8,1850)$ = 8.051; $p \leq 0.0001$) and gender (Pillai's trace = 0.012; $F(4,924)$ = 2.775; p = 0.026). There were also significant interactions between books at home * age (Pillai's trace = 0.022; $F(8,1850)$ = 2.532; p = 0.010) and gender * group background (Pillai's trace = 0.018; $F(8,1850)$ = 2.105; p = 0.032). Tests of between-subjects effects showed this effect was significant for all the forms of participation in the analysis for the following factors: age, books, group and books at home*age (see Table 17.1). Concerning the effect of gender, there was a significant effect only for social participation. The interaction between gender and group was significant for vote and activism.

The effect of books at home seemed to be linear, as levels of participation in all its forms increased when the number of books at home increased (see Figure 17.1). However, pairwise comparisons revealed that differences in terms of means were not significant between all the groups for the following variables: activism and vote

Participation of youth, women and migrants in Portugal 323

TABLE 17.1 Test of between-subjects effects – civic and political participation

Source	Dependent variable	df	F	Sig.
Gender	Social	1	80,398	**0.004***
	Activism	1	20,844	0.092
	Internet	1	10,480	0.224
	Vote in elections	1	610	0.435
Group	Social	2	250,381	**0.000***
	Activism	2	120,181	**0.000***
	Internet	2	130,171	**0.000***
	Vote in elections	2	30,728	**0.024***
Age	Social	1	490,022	**0.000***
	Activism	1	130,166	**0.000***
	Internet	1	160,920	**0.000***
	Vote in elections	1	420,157	**0.000***
Books at home	Social	2	280,474	**0.000***
	Activism	2	50,140	**0.006***
	Internet	2	90,531	**0.000***
	Vote in elections	2	80,004	**0.000***
Gender * group	Social	2	431	0.650
	Activism	2	30,328	**0.036***
	Internet	2	10,610	0.200
	Vote in elections	2	40,594	**0.010***
Age * books	Social	2	60,130	**0.002***
	Activism	2	30,970	**0.019***
	Internet	2	40,369	**0.013***
	Vote in elections	2	30,114	**0.045***

*p ≤ 0.050

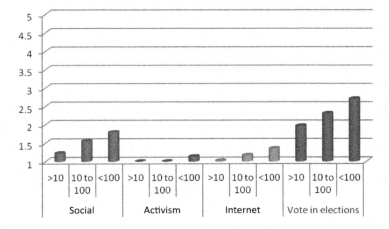

FIGURE 17.1 Effect of books at home on participation

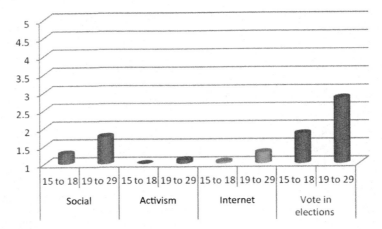

FIGURE 17.2 Effect of age on participation

in elections. Regarding activism, differences were not significant between the groups with few books at home (p = 0.121). In turn, concerning vote in elections, there was no significant difference between the groups with 10 to 100 books and the group with more than 100 books (p = 0.063).

Concerning the impact of age, the analysis of variance revealed that young adults participate more than young adolescents in all forms of participation (see Figure 17.2).

Likewise, on the interaction between books at home and age, results revealed that the older groups with more books at home reported higher levels of participation (see Figure 17.3).

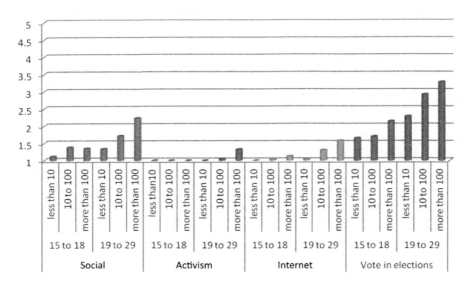

FIGURE 17.3 Effect of age * books at home on participation

Participation of youth, women and migrants in Portugal **325**

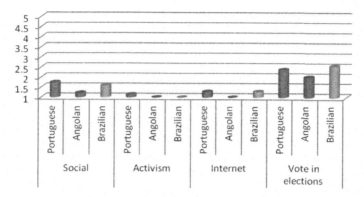

FIGURE 17.4 Effect of immigrant background on participation

Group differences concerning immigrant background showed that young people of Portuguese origin had significantly higher levels of social participation and activism. On vote in elections (p = 0.316) and participation through the Internet (p = 0.999) there were no significant differences between the young people of Brazilian origin when compared to the young people of Portuguese origin. In all forms of participation, young people of Angolan origin had significantly lower levels of participation (see Figure 17.4).

Concerning the impact of gender, the effect was significant only on social participation, with women having higher levels of involvement. In turn, the significant interaction between gender and immigrant background showed that women of immigrant origin exhibited higher activism compared to men. On the contrary, males of Portuguese origin showed higher levels of activism than females. Regarding levels of voting, females of Angolan origin vote more frequently than males, and women of Brazilian origin vote less frequently than men (see Figure 17.5).

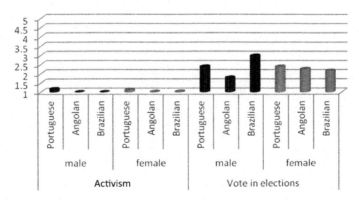

FIGURE 17.5 Effect of gender * immigrant background on participation

Political interest and attentiveness

The multivariate tests showed a significant effect for number of books at home (Pillai's trace = 0.040; F(4,1928) = 9.933; p ≤ 0.0001), age (Pillai's trace = 0.031; F(2,963) = 15.306; p ≤ 0.0001) and group background (Pillai's trace = 0.147; F(4,1928) = 38.256; p ≤ 0.0001) on political interest and attentiveness (see Table 17.2). The effect of gender was not significant (Pillai's trace = 0.003; F(2,963) = 1.389; p = 0.250), as was the interaction between the factors.

Young people of Portuguese origin revealed significantly higher levels of political interest compared to both immigrant groups. As regards political attentiveness, pairwise comparisons showed a significant difference between the group of Portuguese origin and the group of Angolan origin (see Figure 17.6).

TABLE 17.2 Test of between subjects effects – political interest and attentiveness

Source	Dependent variable	df	F	Sig.
Group	Political interest	2	690,080	**0.000***
	Political attentiveness	2	590,515	**0.000***
Age	Political interest	1	290,614	**0.000***
	Poltical attentiveness	1	160,943	**0.000***
Books at home	Political interest	2	130,707	**0.000***
	Political attentiveness	2	140,059	**0.000***

*p ≤ 0.050

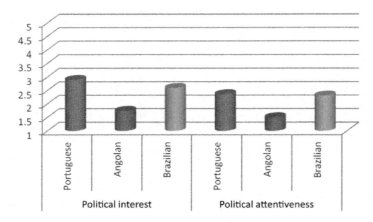

FIGURE 17.6 Effect of immigrant background on political interest and attentiveness

Participation of youth, women and migrants in Portugal **327**

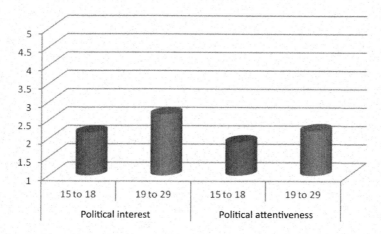

FIGURE 17.7 Effect of age on political interest and attentiveness

Concerning the age of participants, we found that young adults had higher levels of political interest and also political attentiveness compared to young adolescents (see Figure 17.7).

Concerning the relation between the number of books at home and levels of political interest and attentiveness, again when the number of books at home increased, so did levels of interest and attentiveness. Concerning political interest, pairwise comparisons revealed that differences between the participants with 10 to 100 books at home with those with more than 100 books was not significant (p = 0.204) (see Figure 17.8).

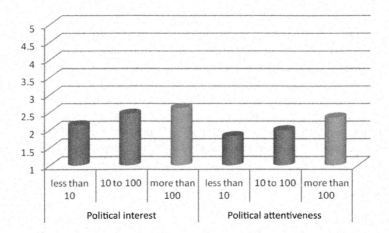

FIGURE 17.8 Effect of books at home on political interest and attentiveness

Discussion

Based on the findings from both the qualitative and quantitative studies, we tried to understand the patterns of civic and political participation among young people of Portuguese, Angolan and Brazilian origin living in Portugal. It was found that discrimination based on age was mentioned by all three groups (young people of Portuguese, Angolan and Brazilian origin). All of them stressed that young people are usually perceived as having no credibility in the public sphere, which leads to a feeling of having no opportunities to participate. This is in line with a notion of citizenship based on an adulthood standard (Castro 2001), which views youth as an age group that is still under construction. In fact, the young people stressed the need to promote access to more information and to stimulate the contact of youth with the political sphere, favouring access to more institutionalised forms of relationship with politics (Augusto 2008). However, youth discourses showed ambivalence on this issue, as the three groups also said that young people are unstable, are always changing their minds and show a lack of interest in civic and political matters. Therefore it is important to understand this ambivalence that might reflect (or cause) the internalisation of a concept of youth conveyed by society that is related to a lack of 'political competence' (Silva 2012) and the difficulty in articulating rights and responsibilities (Lister et al. 2003).

Moreover, as youth has been defined as an important stage for the development of political attitudes and behaviours (Braungart and Braungart 1986), age-related patterns of political behaviour were studied. In this regard, our quantitative findings suggest that young adults participate more than adolescents in all forms of participation, and they also exhibit the highest levels of political interest and attentiveness. Contrary to some studies that show that participation is lower during young adulthood compared with adolescence and later adulthood (Jennings and Stoker 2004; Planty et al. 2006; Snell 2010), our data reveal that young people are delaying the experiences of civic and political participation. Indeed, considering that young people struggle daily with uncertainty in all contexts and aspects of their lives – Arnett has been arguing that we should considered this period of life as 'emerging adulthood' (2004) – this might lead to a postponement of the first experiences of civic and political participation. Moreover, young adulthood is the time when people are old enough to legally engage in all types of participation and, as some studies have hypothesised, those who participate in formal and conventional settings are much more likely to invest in other forms of civic and political activism (Bakker and Vreese 2011; Smith et al. 2009; Van den Bos and Nell 2006). Thus we suggest that different forms of participation might be related, emerging and rising simultaneously.

At the same time, the effect of age seems to be influenced by other factors, such as the resources that each individual and her/his family have. In other words, the three groups of this study considered that economic and educational resources had a significant impact on their self-conception as political actors – however, this was clearly stronger in the discourse of young people of Portuguese origin. Thus opportunities to participate are perceived as influenced by socio-economic status, as already suggested by other studies (Gibson, Lusoli, and Ward 2005). This correlation between the cultural capital resources of youngsters' families and their political and civic participation is clearly demonstrated by the quantitative study: the more books at home, the more they participated (in all its forms) and the more interested and attentive they were to civic and political issues. However, despite the groups of Angolan and Brazilian origin acknowledging this influence, both groups agreed that any drawback caused by low levels of social, cultural and economic resources was definitely supplanted by the disadvantages related to the discrimination they suffered for being of immigrant origin. An adolescent of Angolan origin illustrated this point, giving the example of applying for a job, where the black person will always be disadvantaged when compared with white people, regardless of their level of education. As some of the young people argued, discrimination might also lead to obstacles in terms of civic and political participation.

Results from the survey were consistent with previous work that has demonstrated ethnic heterogeneity in developmental patterns of civic engagement across young adulthood (Finlay et al. 2011). In fact, our findings show different levels of civic and political participation – and also political interest and attentiveness – among non-migrants and migrants in Portugal. These disparities do not represent a clear disadvantage for migrants, but instead reveal that patterns of involvement change across groups. Youth of Portuguese origin exhibit the highest levels of activism, social participation and political interest. However, young people of Brazilian origin are the ones who vote more – which may be primarily due to the fact that voting in Brazil is compulsory – and also participate more on the Internet. This draws attention to the important role that alternative political spheres might have for groups that feel strongly discriminated against in traditional public spaces, as the young people of Angolan and Brazilian origin emphasised concerning their immigrant background. Nevertheless, young people of Angolan origin clearly appeared to be less engaged in all forms of participation and also displayed less interest in political and civic issues, which might be related to discrimination and racism. In fact, some research has found that participation might be influenced by the levels of discrimination and racism (Cesari 2006). In Portugal the immigration influxes from the former colonies have strengthened the colonial hierarchies, with Brazil occupying an intermediate place between Africans and Portuguese (Machado 2006). In addition, some studies suggest that acceptance of African immigrants is lower than that of white and poor immigrants, such as those who recently came from Eastern Europe (Lages and Policarpo 2003). Still, these theories are not enough to fully explain these results and more research is necessary to achieve a full understanding of the factors which explain the civic and political participation of migrant youth in Portugal.

Furthermore, we found the same patterns of political interest and political attentiveness as levels of civic and political participation, suggesting a link between these dimensions and levels of civic and political participation, as reported in previous research (Chaffee et al. 1970; Torney-Purta et al. 2001; Zukin et al. 2006). But, despite the lower levels of participation, the substantially higher levels of political interest and attentiveness should be emphasised, suggesting that young people care about civic and politic issues, even if they do not participate (as yet).

Interestingly – and although some studies stress the double disadvantage of women of immigrant background (Kofman et al. 2000) – our outcomes show a decrease – and even a reverse – of gender gaps. In fact, women of all groups showed higher levels of social participation and similar levels of political interest and attentiveness. In addition, women of immigrant background reported higher levels of activism than men of immigrant origin, and women of Angolan origin tended to vote more frequently than men. Marien et al. (2010) suggested that non-institutionalised forms of participation reduce or even reverse gender inequalities – which, we believe, might happen in this context.

In conclusion, our findings reveal that perceptions of discrimination and disadvantage identified by youth during the focus groups discussions were also linked to levels of civic and political participation across migrants and non-migrants. Considering that participation is 'the civic glue that bonds those who would otherwise be divided along racial and ethnic lines' (Putnam 2000: 362), further investigation should continue to strive for a deeper understanding of the multiple factors than seem to interact to explain the patterns of civic and political participation among young people from diverse backgrounds in our society.

References

Arnett, J. J. (2004) *Emerging Adulthood: The Winding Road from the Late Teens through the Twenties*. New York: Oxford University Press.

Atkeson, L. and Rapoport, R. (2003) 'The more things change the more they stay the same: examining gender differences in political communication by men and women, 1952 through 2000', *Public Opinion Quarterly*, 67: 495–521.

Augusto, N. M. (2008) 'A juventude e a(s) política(s): Desinstitucionalização e individualização', *Revista Crítica de Ciências Sociais*, 81: 155–77.

Baganha, M. I. (2009) 'The Lusophone migratory system: patterns and trends', *International Migration*, 47(3): 5–20.

Bakker, T. P. and Vreese, C. H. (2011) 'Good news for the future? Young people, Internet use, and political participation', *Communication Research*, 38 (4): 451–70.

Bang, H. (2005) 'Among everyday makers and expert citizens', in J. Newman (ed.), *Remaking Governance: Peoples, Politics and the Public Sphere*. Bristol: Policy Press, pp. 159–79.

Beaton, A. M. and Deveau, M. (2005) 'Helping the less fortunate: a predictive model of collective action', *Journal of Applied Social Psychology*, 35 (8): 1609–29.

Braga da Cruz, M. (1985) 'A participação política da juventude em Portugal', *Análise Social*, XXI (87-88-89), 3/4/5: 1067–88.

Braungart, R. and Braungart, M. (1986) 'Life-course and generational politics', *Annual Review of Sociology*, 12: 205–31.

Castro, L. R. (2001) *Subjectividade e Cidadania*. Rio de Janeiro: Lidador.

Cesari, J. (2006) *Securitization and Religious Divide in Europe: Muslims in Western Europe after 9/11: Why the Term Islamophobia Is More a Predicament than an Explanation*. Submission to the Changing Landscape of Citizenship and Security 6th PCRD of European Commission. Retrieved from: http://www.libertysecurity.org/rubrique20.html.

Chaffee, S., Ward, S. and Tipton, L. (1970) 'Mass communication and political socialization', *Journalism Quarterly*, 47: 647–59.

Couton, P. and Gaudet, S. (2008) 'Rethinking social participation: the case of immigrants in Canada', *Journal of International Migration and Integration*, 9 (1): 21–44.

Dávila, A. and Mora, M.T. (2007) *Do Gender and Ethnicity Affect Civic Engagement and Academic Progress?* Working Paper 52. Retrieved from Tufts University, Center for Information and Research on Civic Learning and Engagement, at: http://www.eric.ed.gov/PDFS/ED495764.pdf.

Dias, T. S. and Menezes, I. (2013) 'The role of classroom experiences and school ethos in the development of children as political actors: confronting the vision of pupils and teachers', *Educational and Child Psychology*, 30 (1): 26–37.

Eggert, N. and Giugni, M. (2010) 'Does associational involvement spur political integration? Political interest and participation of three immigrant groups in Zurich', *Swiss Political Science Review*, 16 (2): 175–210.

Espírito-Santo, A. and Baum, M. (2004) *A participação feminina em Portugal numa perspectiva longitudinal.* Actas do V Congresso Português de Sociologia – Sociedades Contemporâneas – Reflexividade e Acção. Braga: Universidade do Minho.

European Commission (2001) *Livre Blanc de la Commission Européenne: un nouvel élan pour la jeunesse européenne.* Brussels: European Commission.

Farthing, R. (2010) 'The politics of youthful antipolitics: representing the issue of youth participation in politics', *Journal of Youth Studies*, 13 (2): 181–95.

Fennema, M. and Tillie, J. (1999) 'Political participation and political trust in Amsterdam: civic communities and ethnic networks', *Journal of Ethnic and Migration Studies*, 25 (4): 703–26.

Ferreira, P. D., Azevedo, C., and Menezes, I. (2012) 'The developmental quality of participation experiences: beyond the rhetoric that "participation is always good!"', *Journal of Adolescence*, 35 (3): 599–610.

Finlay, A., Flanagan, C. and Wray-Lake, L. (2011) 'Civic engagement patterns and transitions over 8 years: the AmeriCorps National Study', *Developmental Psychology*, 47 (6): 1728–43.

Forbrig, J. (ed.) (2005) *Revisiting Youth Political Participation.* Strasbourg: Council of Europe.

Galston, W. A. (2001) 'Political knowledge, political engagement, and civic education', *Annual Review of Political Science*, 4: 217–34.

Gibson, R. K., Lusoli, W. and Ward, S. (2005) 'Online participation in the UK: testing a "contextualised" model of Internet effects', *British Journal of Politics and International Relations*, 7 (4): 561–83.

Grillo, R. and Mazzucato, V. (2008) 'Africa <> Europe: a double engagement', *Journal of Ethnic and Migration Studies*, 34 (2): 175–98.

Harris, A., Wyn, J. and Younes, S. (2010) 'Beyond apathetic or activist youth: "ordinary" young people and contemporary forms of participation', *Young: Nordic Journal of Youth Research*, 18 (1): 9–32.

Haste, H. and Hogan, A. (2006) 'Beyond conventional civic participation, beyond the moral political divide: young people and contemporary debates about citizenship', *Journal of Moral Education*, 35 (4): 473–93.

Huckfeldt, R. and Sprague, J. (1995) *Citizens, Politics, and Social Communications: Information and Influence in an Election Campaign.* Cambridge: Cambridge University Press.

Jennings, M. K. and Stoker, L. (2004) 'Social trust and civic engagement across time and generations', *Acta Politica*, 39: 342–79.

Juris, J. S. and Pleyers, G. (2009) 'Alter-activism: emerging cultures of participation among young global justice activists', *Journal of Youth Studies*, 12 (1): 57–75.

Kelly, C. (2009) 'In preparation for adulthood: exploring civic participation and social trust among youth minorities', *Youth and Society*, 40 (4): 526–40.

Kofman, E., Phizacklea, A., Raghuram, P. and Sales, R. (2000) *Gender and International Migration in Europe: Employment, Welfare and Politics*. London: Routledge.

Lages, M. and Policarpo, V. (2003) *Atitudes e Valores Perante a Imigração*. Lisbon: Alto Comissariado para a Imigração e Minorias Étnicas.

Lister, R., Smith, N., Middleton, S. and Cox, L. (2003) 'Young people talk about citizenship: empirical perspectives on theoretical and political debates', *Citizenship Studies*, 7 (2): 235–53.

Machado, I. J. (2006) 'Imigração em Portugal', *Estudos Avançados*, 20 (57): 119–35.

Magalhães, P. and Moral, J. S. (2008) *Os Jovens e a Política*. Lisbon: CESOP.

Marcelo, K. B, Lopez, M. H. and Kirby, E. H. (2007) 'Civic engagement among young men and women'. Retrieved from Tufts University, Center for Information and Research on Civic Learning and Engagement, at: http://www.civicyouth.org/PopUps/FactSheets/FS07_Gender_CE.pdf.

Marien, S., Hooghe, M. and Quintelier, E. (2010) 'Inequalities in non-institutionalised forms of political participation: a multi-level analysis of 25 countries', *Political Studies*, 58 (1): 187–213.

Martiniello, M. (2005) *Political Participation, Mobilisation and Representation of Immigrants and Their Offspring in Europe*, Willy Brandt Series of Working Papers in International Migration and Ethnic Relations (1/05) Malmö: Malmö University.

Menezes, I. (2003) 'Participation experiences and civic concepts, attitudes and engagement: implications for citizenship education projects', *European Educational Research Journal*, 2 (3): 430–45.

Miranda, J. (2009) *Mulheres imigrantes em Portugal. Memórias, dificuldades de Integração e projectos de vida*. Lisbon: Observatório da Imigração.

Munro, D. (2008) 'Integration through participation: non-citizen resident voting rights in an era of globalization', *International Migration and Integration*, 9: 43–80.

Myrberg, G. (2011) 'Political integration through associational affiliation? Immigrants and native Swedes in Greater Stockholm', *Journal of Ethnic and Migration Studies*, 37 (1): 99–115.

O'Toole, T., Lister, M., Marsh, D., Jones, S. and Mcdonagh, A. (2003) 'Tuning out or left out? Participation and non-participation among young people', *Contemporary Politics*, 9 (1): 45–61.

Pais, J. M. (1990) 'A construção sociológica da juventude – alguns contributos', *Análise Social*, XXV: 139–65.

Paxton, P., Kunovich, S. and Hughes, M. (2007) 'Gender in politics', *Annual Review of Sociology*, 33: 263–84.

Perliger, A., Canetti-Nisim, D. and Pedahzur, A. (2006) 'Democratic attitudes among high-school pupils: the role of played by perceptions of class climate', *School Effectiveness and School Improvement*, 17 (1): 119–40.

Planty, M., Bozick, R. and Regnier, M. (2006) 'Helping because you have to or helping because you want to? Sustaining participation in service work from adolescence through young adulthood', *Youth and Society*, 38: 177–202.

Putnam, R. D. (2000) *Bowling Alone: The Collapse and Revival of American Community*. New York: Simon & Schuster.

Ramalho, S. and Trovão, S. (2010) *Repertórios Femininos em Construção num Contexto Migratório Pós-Colonia. Modalidades de Participação Cívica*. Lisbon: Observatório da Imigração.

Rosenstone, S. and Hansen, J. (1993) *Mobilization, Participation, and Democracy in America*. New York: Macmillan.

SEF (Foreigners and Border Services) (2012) *Relatório de Imigração Fronteiras e Asilo 2011*. Oeiras: SEF. Retrieved from: http://sefstat.sef.pt/Docs/Rifa_2011.pdf.

Silva, S. M. (2012) 'Contributos do PIDOP para uma reflexão sobre as juventudes em tempos de descrença', in I. Menezes, N. Ribeiro, M. Fernandes-Jesus, C. Malafaia and P. D. Ferreira (eds), *Agência e participação cívica e política: Jovens e imigrantes na construção da democracia*. Porto: Livpsic, pp. 155–7.

Simon, B. (2011) 'Collective identity and political engagement', in A. E. Azzi, X. Chryssochoou, B. Klandermans and B. Simon (eds), *Identity and Participation in Culturally Diverse Societies: A Multidisciplinary Perspective*. Oxford: Wiley-Blackwell, pp. 89–93.

Simon, B. and Grabow, O. (2010) 'The politicization of migrants: further evidence that politicized collective identity is a dual identity', *Political Psychology*, 31 (5): 717–38.

Smith, A., Schlozman, K. L., Verba, S. and Brady, H. (2009) *The Internet and Civic Engagement*. Washington, DC: Pew Internet and American Life Project.

Snell, P. (2010) 'Emerging adult civic and political disengagement: a longitudinal analysis of lack of involvement with politics', *Journal of Adolescent Research*, 25 (2): 258–87.

Stepick, A., Stepick, C. and Labissiere, Y. (2008) 'South Florida's immigrant youth and civic engagement: major engagement: minor differences', *Applied Development Science*, 12 (2): 57–65.

Stoll, M. and Wong, J. (2007) 'Immigration and civic participation in a multiracial and multi-ethnic context', *International Migration Review*, 4 (4): 880–908.

Stolle, D., Hooghe, M. and Micheletti, M. (2005) 'Politics in the supermarket: political consumerism as a form of political participation', *International Political Science Review*, 26: 245–69.

Sullivan, J. and Transue, J. (1999) 'The psychological underpinnings of democracy: a selective review of research on political tolerance, interpersonal trust, and social capital', *Annual Review of Psychology*, 50: 625–50.

Teixeira, A. and Albuquerque, T. (2005) *Active Civic Participation of Immigrants in Portugal*. Country Report, Politis Project, University of Oldenburg.

Tonkiss, F. (2006) 'Using focus groups', in C. Seale (ed.), *Researching Society and Culture*. London: Sage, pp. 193–206.

Torney-Purta, J., Lehman, R., Oswald, H. and Schulz, W. (2001) *Citizenship and Education in Twenty-Eight Countries: Civic Knowledge and Engagement at Age Fourteen*. Amsterdam: IEA.

Van den Bos, M. and Nell, L. (2006) 'Territorial bounds to virtual space. Transnational online and offline networks of Iranian and Turkish-Kurdish immigrants in the Netherlands', *Global Networks*, 6 (2): 201–20.

Van Deth, J. W. and Elff, M. (2004) 'Politicisation, economic development and political interest in Europe', *European Journal of Political Research*, 43 (3): 477–508.

Verba, S., Schlozman, K. L. and Brady, H. (1995) *Voice and Equality: Civic Voluntarism in American Politics*. Cambridge, MA: Harvard University Press.

Vogel, D. and Leiprecht, R. (2008) *Part II: Europe as the Positive Other for Immigrants?* Final Activity Report, Politis Project, University of Oldenburg, pp. 25–32.

Vogel, D. and Triandafyllidou, A. (2005) *Civic Activation of Immigrants – An Introduction to Conceptual and Theoretical Issues*, Working Paper 1. University of Oldenburg: POLITIS.

Vollebergh, W. A., Iedema, J. and Raaijmakers, Q. A. (2001) 'Intergenerational transmission and the formation of cultural orientations in adolescence and young adulthood', *Journal of Marriage and Family*, 63 (4): 1185–98.

Vromen, A. and Collin, P. (2010) 'Everyday youth participation? Contrasting views from Australian policymakers and young people', *Young*, 18 (1): 97–112.

Yamanaka, K. and Piper, N. (2006) *Feminised Migration in East and Southeast Asia: Policies, Actions and Empowerment*, UNRISD Occasional Paper No. 11. Geneva: UNRISD.

Youniss, J., McLellan, J. and Yates, M. (1997) 'What we know about engendering civic identity', *American Behavioral Scientist*, 40 (5): 620–31.

Zukin, C., Keeter, S., Andolina, M., Jenkins, K. and Delli Carpini, M. X. (2006) *A New Engagement? Political Participation, Civic Life, and the Changing American Citizen*. New York: Oxford University Press.

18

PARTICIPATION AMONG TURKISH, ROMA, AND BULGARIAN RESETTLER YOUTH LIVING IN TURKEY

Tülin Şener[1]

Research has revealed that many people today are participating less in various kinds of shared endeavors than in the past, from unions and political parties to other sorts of voluntary membership organizations, and that voting rates are also dropping (International IDEA 2004; Putnam 2000). However, levels of social and political participation also show variation according to nation and life context (Skocpol and Fiorina 1999), with young people and ethnic minorities having been identified as particular groups that are at risk of social and political disengagement (Ahmad and Pinnock 2007; Martiniello 2005; Putnam 2000). While there has been a great deal of research on youth and minority participation in North America and some European countries (e.g. Forbrig 2005; Jensen and Flanagan 2008; Sherrod et al. 2010), relatively little research on participation by young people and ethnic minorities has been conducted in Turkey. This chapter reports research which was conducted in Turkey as part of the PIDOP project, and focuses particularly on participation by Turkish, Roma, and Bulgarian resettler youth who are living in Turkey.

Turkey exhibits considerable linguistic, religious, and ethnic diversity. It is home to millions of people with different ethnic identities, including Alevis, Ezidis, Assyrians, Laz, Caferis, Roma, Rum (Greek Orthodox), Caucasians, and Jews, as well as Turks, Kurds, and Armenians (Minority Rights Group International 2007). Turkey prioritizes territorial integrity and unity above group rights, minority rights, or identities, whether these are ethnic, religious, linguistic, or cultural in nature. By the same token, Turkish citizenship is defined as universal (Kolukirik and Toktas 2007). It is claimed that Turkish nation-building involved democratic norms and that unification was achieved by the equality principle of citizenship, which resolved the minority question in the country by placing all the inhabitants of Turkey on the same and equal footing (Toktas and Aras 2009). On the other hand, this approach may be viewed as providing room for the suppression of differences which are seen to be threatening to the political stability of the country. As a result, the concept of citizenship does not include any reference to individuals' ethnic and/ or religious identities. That is to say, the concepts of 'majority' and 'minority' do not form a part of Turkish legal citizenship, rights, or obligations. In parallel with this, the minorities excluded from the rights established by the Treaty of Lausanne have been banned from using their own language in schools and in the media (Minority Rights Group International 2007). The United Nations and the European Union consider minority rights, alongside human rights, as part of truly democratic and politically stable societies (Tasch 2010). This situation raises questions about the definitions of minorities in Turkey, and highlights the underestimated difficulties that minorities in Turkey face. Due to the lack of official recognition of minority groups, it is also difficult to find reliable data about such groups. The two minority groups in Turkey that were studied in the PIDOP project were Turks who previously lived in Bulgaria but have now migrated back to Turkey, and Roma. In addition, members of the national majority group of Turks were studied. The basic characteristics of these three groups are as follows.

Turkish resettlers from Bulgaria

The first migrations of Turks from Bulgaria to Turkey started just after the Ottoman-Russian war in 1877 to 1878 and have continued until the present day (Çetin 2009). Even though a series of agreements was set to protect the rights of Turks living in Bulgaria, Turks have continually been forced to migrate as part of Bulgarian government policy. The years 1912–20, 1950–1, 1968–78, and 1989 were the times when the biggest migrations took place from Bulgaria to Turkey (Çetin 2009). Within Bulgaria, the fast growth of the Turkish population had led to it becoming almost half of the overall population, and there were ethnic tensions between the Bulgarian majority and Turks in Bulgaria which took the form of conflicts between Muslims and Christians (Vasileva 1992). In 1989, a very large number of Turks migrated from Bulgaria to Turkey for three main reasons: to escape from persecution; to rejoin families and relatives back in Turkey; and to live more freely, particularly in terms of language use (Çetin 2009). Workers and secondary school graduates constituted the main groups of emigrants from Bulgaria to Turkey in 1989, but they experienced difficulties in finding accommodation and jobs after their migration (Çetin 2009) and within a year 42 percent of the Bulgarian immigrants returned to Bulgaria (Vasileva 1992). For a long period of time, the Bulgarian resettlers who remained in Turkey were regarded as foreigners by the local population. However, those who had good connections with relatives or had occupational skills managed to integrate better into mainstream society, but others experienced the disadvantages of immigration.

Between 1878 and 1989, the total number of registered immigrants from Bulgaria to Turkey was around 1.5 million (Vasileva 1992). The migration also continued after 1989. Unlike the large wave of Bulgarian immigrants in 1989, the subsequent waves of Bulgarian immigrants have had little political motivation behind their decision to move, with their migration being economically driven instead. While the immigrants from 1989 and earlier view Turkey as their homeland, post-1990 migrants do not share their feelings of homecoming despite their ethnic affiliations with Turkey and their self-ascription of Turkishness (Suter 2008).

In today's Turkey, there are around one million Bulgarian resettlers. Although official figures do not exist, a high proportion of these resettlers attend secondary and higher education in Turkey, and members of this group are generally better educated than the Roma – and indeed better than the majority. They also tend to occupy a relatively high socio-economic status. Majority group Turks tend to perceive the Turkish resettlers from Bulgaria favorably when comparing them to other minority groups, as they regard them as members of their own ethnic group. However, the resettlers are also marginalized to a certain extent by the local population since they are also seen as 'Bulgarian' (Parla 2007). They are officially classed as immigrants, but citizenship used to be granted on arrival (Doganay 1996). At present, many of the Turkish resettlers from Bulgaria who have attained Turkish citizenship tend to hold both Turkish and Bulgarian citizenship (Suter 2008).

Roma people

Turkish Roma, due to their Islamic identity, which in the Ottoman Empire brought them within the Muslim community, were not granted minority status (Kolukirik and Toktas 2007). Therefore no specific rights were granted to Turkish Roma. The perception of the Roma population is strikingly different in Turkey and in the rest of Europe. In Turkey, the idea of regarding Roma as a separate ethnic minority is largely rejected, even by Roma themselves, as it is seen as divisive and therefore discriminatory (Marsh and Strand 2005). Neither passive nor particularly assertive (in comparative terms) about their identity, their preferred and primary identification is Turkish (Marsh and Strand 2005). The Roma of Turkey have increasingly started to become organized after 1990 through the founding of communal associations (Kolukirik and Toktas 2007). The number of Roma people living in the country is unclear as the Roma, just like the Bulgarian resettlers, are not officially recognized as a minority group. Statistics about the Roma in Turkey are limited, but numbers are estimated unofficially to stand at about two million (Minority Rights Group International 2007).

Most Roma in Turkey are sedentary and are found in settlements in larger cities and towns, but some are still nomadic and follow pre-established itineraries across the country. Similarly to the Bulgarian resettlers, Roma people generally tend to subscribe to Islam but there is also a small number of Christian Roma (International Helsinki Federation for Human Rights 2006). Education levels tend to be low. Illiteracy, for instance, is a prevalent feature and participation levels in secondary school and higher education are lower than for other groups in Turkey (Minority Rights Group International 2007). Members of this group tend to suffer from financial destitution and generally take up employment that is low paid and low skilled (Kolukirik and Toktas 2007). The majority of the population usually perceive Roma unfavorably and see them as highly involved in the perpetration of criminal acts (Kolukirik and Toktas 2007). According to the European Roma Rights Center (ERRC), they sometimes experience acute social exclusion, amounting to a variety of violations of economic, social and cultural rights, including having difficulty accessing personal documents which subsequently affects their ability to access social welfare, medical care and legal marriage. Simply put, Roma people in Turkey today are more consistently under-educated, under-employed, suffer much higher levels of ill-health, have poorer housing, and experience higher levels of discrimination on the basis of their ethnicity than any other group in Turkey (Marsh and Strand 2005).

Majority Turks

The Turkish majority group comprises perhaps 70–75 percent of the population in Turkey (once again, precise figures are difficult to establish due to the lack of official information about minority groups within the country). Turks are primarily made up of Sunni Muslims, but they have varying degrees of devoutness and many live entirely secular lifestyles. Officially, Turkey has been a secular state since 1928, although the current governing party, the Justice and Development Party, is often charged with pursuing an Islamist agenda and Turkey's secular status is frequently a source of tension. A high percentage of Turkish youth has at least the mandatory level of school education. Young Turks typically have a better educational, occupational, and income level, and better parental education and income, than young Roma people.

The background to the present study

In Turkey, political and civic engagement and participation as a way of expressing ethnic, cultural, or social identities are important not only for minorities but also for other segments of society such as young men and women. However, only limited evidence on political and civic participation is available within the country. Previous research includes several surveys which have been carried out to gather information on youth attitudes towards participation, especially in order to identify the motivations of the young population, and the barriers which they encounter, for participating in politics and the policy-making processes (e.g. Cankurtaran-Ontaş et al. 2013; Artan et al. 2005; Kılıç 2009; Şener, 2011, 2012, 2014; Yentürk 2008). This research has mostly shown that the representation of women, youth, and ethnic and religious groups as citizens with distinct political identities is virtually non-existent. The political history of Turkey reveals the effects of the 1980 Military Coup, which resulted in the depoliticization and alienation of not only young people but also elderly people, and young people have been deterred from political activity, including reading political books and newspapers, through the fear of getting arrested.

The Turkish PIDOP team began its work by exploring majority and minority youth participation in Turkey through a qualitative study in which focus groups were used to explore young people's levels of civic and political participation, the nature of their participation experiences, and their perceptions of the various factors which have influenced their patterns of participation and non-participation. Twelve focus groups were conducted in total, four with young Turks, four with young Roma, and four with young Bulgarian resettlers; for each ethnic group, two focus groups were conducted with 16- to 18-year-olds and two with 20- to 26-year-olds. In total, 80 individuals participated in these focus groups.

It was found that civic and political participation levels were low. Unemployment and poverty formed the major impediment for male Roma engagement, involvement, and participation. For female Roma, early marriage and poverty constituted the main impediments. Similar issues did not emerge among the Turkish and Bulgarian resettler groups. Among these two groups, the younger participants instead listed time spent studying for university entrance exams, lack of economic independence, parents' prohibitive attitudes, and the existence of hostile police interventions against those who engage in demonstrations as the major disincentives which discourage their participation. The older Turkish and Bulgarian resettler participants described similar discouraging factors (with the exception of university entrance exams), but also emphasized their own sense of a lack of personal efficacy.

For most participants, regardless of ethnicity, the most important sources of influence appeared to be family members (especially fathers) and friends. Family elders were also frequently mentioned. The media (particularly TV rather than printed) and the Internet were cited as the most influential sources of information. However, Roma participants in general and 20- to 26-year-old female Bulgarian resettlers were exceptions in this regard: they generally spent high amounts of time in front of the TV, but they reported that they did not for the most part follow news or TV programs on civic and political issues; they also had no or limited access to the Internet.

Participants aged between 20 and 26 years were more cautious with respect to civic and political participation, in that they tended to condemn different forms of action and protest such as marches, demonstrations, and graffiti in strong terms. They tended to regard these as deviant behaviors and they also emphasized their ineffectiveness and inconvenience. Although the participants generally thought that civic and political participation is important for being a member of society, they personally had very little experience of participation. The 16- to 18-year-old male Turkish and Bulgarian resettler participants appeared to be the most engaged.

For a more detailed report of the findings which emerged specifically from the Turkish and Roma focus groups, see Ataman et al. (2012).

The quantitative study conducted in Turkey

Against the background of these findings from the focus groups, a quantitative questionnaire designed by the PIDOP project (see Appendix C at the end of this book) was subsequently administered to much larger samples of Turkish, Roma, and

Bulgarian resettler youth in Turkey. The questionnaire collected data on the respondents' patterns of civic and political participation, the quality of their participation experiences, political interest, political attentiveness, political knowledge, internal and external efficacy, trust in institutions and in government, motivations and emotions regarding participation, perceived barriers to participation, perceived social norms, social well-being and interpersonal trust, sense of community, strength of national, ethnic, and religious identifications, level of religiosity, and support for minority rights. In addition, detailed demographic information was collected from each participant.

Participants

In total, 732 young people aged between 16 and 26 years participated in the study, 34.6 percent of whom were Turkish, 32.4 percent Roma, and 33.1 percent Bulgarian resettlers (see Table 18.1). To help recruit the Bulgarian resettlers and the Roma participants, non-governmental institutional actors working on minority issues in different cities in the country were asked to collaborate in the data collection process. The majority group was reached by snowball sampling from secondary schools, universities, and private establishments called 'dershane' which prepare students for special examinations such as those for university entrance. In the process of composing the groups, the research team attempted to recruit participants having different characteristics in terms of their socio-economic and educational status as well as their levels of civic and political participation. The distribution of the participants according to age and gender in the three ethnic groups is presented in Table 18.1.

While an attempt was made to keep the socio-demographic characteristics of each group as similar as possible, the responses to the demographic questions revealed several differences between the three groups. Not surprisingly, the Bulgarian resettlers had the highest rate of being born outside Turkey (41 percent), of holding citizenship of another country (8.47 percent), and of double citizenship (9.29 percent). However, only 4.3 percent of the Bulgarian resettlers spoke a language at home other than Turkish, while the corresponding figure for the Roma was 13.9 percent. The Roma exhibited the lowest levels of education. Thus 61 percent of them had

TABLE 18.1 The distribution of participants according to gender and age for each of the three ethnic groups

		Turkish	*Bulgarian*	*Roma*	*Total*
Gender	*Female*	153	87	120	360
	Male	100	150	122	372
Total		253	237	242	**732**
Age	*16–19*	124	133	66	323
	20–26	129	104	176	409
Total		253	237	242	**732**

only primary education, while more than half of the Bulgarian resettlers (51 percent) had completed secondary (mandatory) education.[2] More than 80 percent of the Turks had completed secondary education. Finally, and unexpectedly, the Bulgarian resettler group reported having had the highest incidence of family financial difficulties before the age of 14.

Procedure

Translation and back-translation of the original PIDOP questionnaire (which had been prepared in English) was completed carefully (see Appendix C for a copy of the questionnaire in English). The Turkish version of the questionnaire was given to each participant individually with a brief introduction and explanation. Some questionnaires were distributed with the help of the representatives of the contact organizations in different parts of the country, especially in Antalya, Bartın, Bursa, and Eskişehir. Illiterate participants, who were mostly from the Roma group, were interviewed individually using exactly the same questions; they were asked each question and provided with the possible response options orally, and were also provided with all necessary explanations orally.

All scaled questions were answered using scales which ran from 1 to 5. In all cases except one, high scores represented high levels of the variable being measured. The single exception involved the two questions measuring external efficacy, where high scores represented low levels of efficacy. For this reason, the external efficacy items were reverse scored prior to running the analyses.

Scales which were used in the present analyses

For the purposes of this chapter, only a subset of the data from the questionnaires was used in the analyses. Because the overall aim was to identify possible differences between the three ethnic groups, only data derived from scales which exhibited high internal reliability in each of the three ethnic groups individually were used. In addition, it was decided to focus primarily on psychological (rather than social or demographic) variables. The scales that were used for the present analyses, and their internal reliabilities, are listed in Table 18.2.

Results

Mean scores (and standard deviations) for all 18 variables for each of the three ethnic groups are shown in Table 18.3. One-way ANOVAs were run to see whether there were any significant differences between the three ethnic groups, and Scheffe tests were used to locate where any significant differences fell. These results are also shown in Table 18.3.

Table 18.3 reveals that the significant differences between the three ethnic groups differed from one variable to another. For example, Turks showed the lowest levels of participation over the previous 12 months, Bulgarian resettlers showed the

Youth participation in Turkey 341

TABLE 18.2 Scales used in the analyses, together with their internal reliabilities (Cronbach alphas) for the sample as a whole and for each of the three ethnic groups individually

Scale	Number of items on scale	Total sample alpha	Turks alpha	Roma alpha	Bulgarian resettlers alpha
Participation in last 12 months	15	0.89	0.84	0.90	0.90
Perceived quality of participation (action)	4	0.86	0.79	0.91	0.85
Perceived quality of participation (reflection)	4	0.90	0.86	0.91	0.91
Political interest	3	0.84	0.83	0.84	0.86
Political attentiveness	3	0.85	0.83	0.86	0.88
Motivations to participate	6	0.92	0.90	0.93	0.94
Perceived barriers to participation	4	0.81	0.75	0.86	0.84
Internal efficacy	2	0.83	0.81	0.84	0.85
External efficacy	2	0.73	0.68	0.72	0.81
Collective efficacy of young people	2	0.80	0.71	0.85	0.86
Collective efficacy of ethnic group	2	0.81	0.83	0.76	0.85
Perceived social norm support for participation	8	0.74	0.85	0.87	0.88
Institutional trust	14	0.91	0.85	0.91	0.92
Trust in government	6	0.86	0.82	0.88	0.85
Social trust	1	–	–	–	–
Negative emotions about social problems	8	0.89	0.84	0.89	0.91
Sense of community (positive feelings about community)	4	0.86	0.87	0.81	0.89
Sense of community (provides opportunities to achieve change)	4	0.84	0.70	0.86	0.88

highest levels, with Roma being in between. However, Turks showed significantly higher levels of political interest than Roma, and had a greater belief in the collective efficacy of young people than Bulgarian resettlers. Conversely, Bulgarian resettlers had lower levels of motivation to participate than the Roma, and lower levels of negative emotions about social issues (such as anger and worry, which might be expected to motivate action) than either the Roma or the Turks. Meanwhile, the Roma youth had the highest levels of trust in government as well as the highest levels of social and institutional trust, while the Turks had the highest levels of sense of community (both positive feelings about their community as well as perceiving opportunities to achieve change in their community). However,

TABLE 18.3 Ethnic group means (M) and standard deviations (SD) on the various scales, and the results of the one-way ANOVAs and Scheffe tests (ns = not significant)

		Turks (a)	Roma (b)	Bulgarian resettlers (c)	One-way ANOVA results	Significantly different (Scheffe)
Participation in last	M	20.05	20.37	20.57	$F(2, 690) = 220.63$	a – b
12 months	SD	0.71	10.11	0.78	$p < 0.001$	a – c
						b – c
Perceived quality of	M	20.14	20.27	20.68	$F(2, 495) = 90.45$	a – c
participation (action)	SD	10.02	10.42	10.00	$p < 0.001$	b – c
Perceived quality of	M	30.31	30.02	30.11	$F(2, 487) = 20.01$	–
participation (reflection)	SD	10.10	10.44	10.06	ns	
Political interest	M	30.07	20.75	20.95	$F(2, 687) = 40.69$	a – b
	SD	10.04	10.34	10.05	$p = 0.009$	
Political attentiveness	M	20.94	20.80	30.02	$F(2, 678) = 10.82$	–
	SD	10.09	10.40	10.10	ns	
Motivations to	M	30.04	30.23	20.88	$F(2, 699) = 50.26$	b – c
participate	SD	10.09	10.34	10.06	$p = 0.005$	
Perceived barriers to	M	20.43	20.67	20.47	$F(2, 699) = 20.67$	–
participation	SD	10.16	10.40	0.98	ns	
Internal efficacy	M	20.75	20.60	20.90	$F(2, 705) = 30.69$	b – c
	SD	10.11	10.31	10.01	$p = 0.026$	
External efficacy	M	20.73	20.98	30.03	$F(2, 703) = 40.36$	a – c
	SD	10.17	10.31	10.07	$p = 0.013$	
Collective efficacy of	M	30.66	30.53	30.32	$F(2, 706) = 50.08$	a – c
young people	SD	10.07	10.34	10.16	$p = 0.006$	
Collective efficacy of	M	20.96	30.42	30.09	$F(2, 691) = 80.56$	a – b
ethnic group	SD	10.19	10.31	10.56	$p < 0.001$	b – c
Perceived social norm	M	20.44	20.68	20.73	$F(2, 717) = 60.54$	a – b
support for participation	SD	0.89	10.12	0.88	$p = 0.002$	a – c
Institutional trust	M	20.60	30.37	20.75	$F(2, 724) = 570.71$	a – b
	SD	0.71	0.97	0.81	$p < 0.001$	b – c
Trust in government	M	20.63	30.17	20.45	$F(2, 707) = 330.04$	a – b
	SD	0.92	10.16	0.86	$p < 0.001$	b – c
Social trust	M	20.54	20.98	20.60	$F(2, 713) = 100.16$	a – b
	SD	0.99	10.41	10.02	$p < 0.001$	b – c
Negative emotions about	M	30.45	30.37	20.83	$F(2, 707) = 240.25$	a – c
social problems	SD	0.90	10.18	10.11	$p < 0.001$	b – c
Sense of community	M	30.21	20.69	20.67	$F(2, 709) = 190.37$	a – b
(positive feelings about	SD	10.03	10.21	10.02	$p < 0.001$	a – c
community)						
Sense of community	M	30.41	30.13	20.93	$F(2, 701) = 130.34$	a – b
(provides opportunities	SD	0.80	10.25	0.99	$p < 0.001$	a – c
to achieve change)						

perceived social norm support for participation was lowest among the Turkish youth. Bulgarian resettlers showed higher levels of internal efficacy than the Roma, and higher external efficacy than the Turkish majority.

In order to obtain more insight into the relationships between variables, Pearson correlation coefficients between all 18 variables were calculated for each ethnic group individually. The results are presented in Tables 18.4, 18.5, and 18.6.

Tables 18.4, 18.5, and 18.6 reveal that there were different patterns of relationships between the variables for the majority Turkish ethnic group vs. the two minority groups. For example, among the Roma, levels of participation in the previous 12 months were systematically related to every other variable; for the Bulgarian resettlers, a similar pattern occurred with the sole exception of negative emotions which were unrelated to participation. By contrast, among the Turks, there were five variables which were not related to participation. Interestingly, perceived barriers to participation, social trust, and sense of community (positive feelings about community) were all related to relatively few other variables in the case of the Turks; however, all three of these variables were consistently related to many other variables in the cases of both the Roma and the Bulgarian resettlers. Also, external efficacy was (unexpectedly) *negatively* related to many other variables in all three groups, but was positively related to both institutional trust and trust in the government in the Turkish majority group (but not in the two minority groups).

Among the Turks, the highest correlation was between political interest and attentiveness, and these two variables were both strongly and positively correlated with internal efficacy; the relationship between political interest, attentiveness, and internal efficacy was also high in both the Roma and Bulgarian resettler youth. Similarly, the perceived quality of previous participation experiences (both the quality of action and the quality of reflection) was positively correlated with the level of participation in the previous 12 months in all three groups.

In order to clarify further the relationship between the incidence of participation in the previous 12 months and all the other variables, three stepwise regression analyses were performed, one for each ethnic group individually, with participation in the previous 12 months as the dependent variable. The regression for the Turkish majority youth revealed that the main predictors of participation were the quality of the action in previous participation experiences ($\beta = 0.56$, $p < 0.001$), political interest ($\beta = 0.25$, $p = 0.001$) and (negatively) external efficacy ($\beta = -0.14$, $p < 0.05$) ($R^2 = 0.51$, $F(3, 109) = 40.36$, $p < 0.001$). The regression for the Roma youth revealed that the main predictors of participation were the quality of the action in previous participation experiences ($\beta = 0.46$, $p < 0.001$), the quality of the reflection in previous participation experiences ($\beta = 0.22$, $p = 0.005$), and the strength of the negative emotions which were felt about issues ($\beta = 0.18$, $p = 0.005$) ($R^2 = 0.46$, $F(3, 156) = 45.20$, $p < 0.001$). The regression for the Bulgarian resettler youth revealed that the main predictors of participation were the quality of the action in previous participation experiences ($\beta = 0.55$, $p < 0.001$) and institutional trust ($\beta = 0.27$, $p < 0.001$) ($R^2 = 0.37$, $F(2, 179) = 54.66$, $p < 0.001$). In other words, in all three ethnic groups, the quality of the action which had been taken in previous

TABLE 18.4 Correlations between the variables for the Turks

	1.	2.	3.	4.	5.	6.	7.	8.	9.	10.	11.	12.	13.	14.	15.	16.	17.
1. Participation in last 12 months																	
2. Perceived quality of participation (action)	0.66**																
3. Perceived quality of participation (reflection)	0.49**	0.55**															
4. Political interest	0.49**	0.36**	0.29**														
5. Political attentiveness	0.48**	0.44**	0.30**	0.69**													
6. Motivations to participate	0.47**	0.47**	0.21**	0.55**	0.53**												
7. Perceived barriers to participation	−0.01	−0.09	0.04	−0.08	−0.01	0.01											
8. Internal efficacy	0.45**	0.47**	0.32**	0.65**	0.64**	0.52**	−0.01										
9. External efficacy	−0.27**	−0.11	−0.14	−0.27**	−0.29**	−0.32**	−0.07	−0.38**									
10. Collective efficacy of young people	0.22**	0.24**	0.14	0.23**	0.26**	0.41**	−0.04	0.29**	−0.35**								
11. Collective efficacy of ethnic group	0.16*	0.25**	0.01	0.10	0.16*	0.35**	−0.04	0.17**	−0.15	0.47**							
12. Perceived social norm support for participation	0.54**	0.58**	0.40**	0.45**	0.46**	0.51**	0.14*	0.52**	−0.32**	0.28**	0.29**						
13. Institutional trust	−0.12	−0.17	−0.15	−0.14*	−0.15*	−0.14*	0.10	−0.21**	0.30**	−0.10	−0.08	−0.16*					
14. Trust in government	−0.08	−0.15	−0.20**	−0.02	−0.02	−0.05	0.04	−0.08	0.28**	−0.13*	0.01	−0.12	0.57**				
15. Social trust	0.09	0.03	0.17	0.02	0.05	0.06	−0.06	0.05	−0.01	−0.02	0.00	0.10	0.11	0.15*			
16. Negative emotions about social problems	0.15*	0.20*	0.10	0.14*	0.17**	0.17**	0.03	0.07	−0.20**	0.21**	0.13	0.20**	−0.07	−0.10	0.02		
17. Sense of community (positive feelings about community)	0.11	0.12	0.00	−0.01	0.01	−0.02	0.02	−0.04	−0.09	0.03	0.10	0.16*	0.13*	0.19**	0.22**	−0.01	
18. Sense of community (provides opportunities to achieve change)	0.33**	0.43**	0.18	0.22**	0.28**	0.43**	−0.02	0.32**	−0.12	0.37**	0.33**	0.41**	0.06	0.01	0.12	0.16*	0.32**

TABLE 18.5 Correlations between the variables for the Roma

	1.	2.	3.	4.	5.	6.	7.	8.	9.	10.	11.	12.	13.	14.	15.	16.	17.
1. Participation in last 12 months																	
2. Perceived quality of participation (action)	0.63**																
3. Perceived quality of participation (reflection)	0.55**	0.62**															
4. Political interest	0.35**	0.42**	0.44**														
5. Political attentiveness	0.45**	0.50**	0.46**	0.77**													
6. Motivations to participate	0.42**	0.40**	0.60**	0.49**	0.48**												
7. Perceived barriers to participation	0.27**	0.36**	0.40**	0.34**	0.36**	0.48**											
8. Internal efficacy	0.37**	0.44**	0.39**	0.60**	0.59**	0.46**	0.32**										
9. External efficacy	−0.24**	−0.27**	−0.25**	−0.30**	−0.37**	−0.27**	−0.29**	−0.43**									
10. Collective efficacy of young people	0.34**	0.28**	0.35**	0.33**	0.39**	0.49**	0.27**	0.33**	−0.44**								
11. Collective efficacy of ethnic group	0.32**	0.25**	0.30**	0.31**	0.43**	0.41**	0.25**	0.35**	−0.50**	0.68**							
12. Perceived social norm support for participation	0.47**	0.55**	0.50**	0.55**	0.63**	0.56**	0.48**	0.57**	−0.43**	0.44**	0.54**						
13. Institutional trust	0.25**	0.16*	0.18*	0.33**	0.33**	0.32**	0.39**	0.28**	−0.23**	0.48**	0.38**	0.43**					
14. Trust in government	0.18*	0.13	0.23**	0.19**	0.25**	0.33**	0.21**	0.08	−0.21**	0.34**	0.34**	0.31**	0.56**				
15. Social trust	0.18*	0.11	0.17*	0.17*	0.17*	0.14*	0.12	0.24**	−0.11	0.19**	0.12	0.28**	0.40**	0.23**			
16. Negative emotions about social problems	0.32**	0.18*	0.30**	0.25**	0.32**	0.46**	0.24**	0.26**	−0.28**	0.57**	0.55**	0.43**	0.34**	0.32**	0.18**		
17. Sense of community (positive feelings about community)	0.31**	0.27**	0.26**	0.29**	0.33**	0.18**	0.21**	0.26**	−0.16*	0.28**	0.23**	0.28**	0.33**	0.39**	0.25**	0.25**	
18. Sense of community (provides opportunities to achieve change)	0.24**	0.29**	0.42**	0.33**	0.41**	0.45**	0.24**	0.27**	−0.29**	0.43**	0.48**	0.38**	0.26**	0.36**	0.19**	0.40**	0.51**

*p < 0.05; **p < 0.01

TABLE 18.6 Correlations between the variables for the Bulgarian resettlers

	1.	2.	3.	4.	5.	6.	7.	8.	9.	10.	11.	12.	13.	14.	15.	16.	17.
1. Participation in last 12 months																	
2. Perceived quality of participation (action)	0.55**																
3. Perceived quality of participation (reflection)	0.35**	0.51**															
4. Political interest	0.27**	0.32**	0.36**														
5. Political attentiveness	0.28**	0.25**	0.28**	0.72**													
6. Motivations to participate	0.28**	0.30**	0.46**	0.53**	0.46**												
7. Perceived barriers to participation	0.24**	0.29**	0.25**	0.25**	0.18**	0.43**											
8. Internal efficacy	0.28**	0.30**	0.50**	0.58**	0.42**	0.60**	0.25**										
9. External efficacy	−0.16*	−0.15*	−0.40**	−0.36**	−0.24**	−0.44**	−0.20**	−0.54**									
10. Collective efficacy of young people	0.16*	0.14	0.40**	0.42**	0.33**	0.60**	0.19**	0.53**	−0.56**								
11. Collective efficacy of ethnic group	0.27**	0.15*	0.30**	0.42**	0.34**	0.60**	0.33**	0.47**	−0.44**	0.75**							
12. Perceived social norm support for participation	0.41**	0.43**	0.49**	0.51**	0.39**	0.65**	0.39**	0.53**	−0.42**	0.53**	0.53**						
13. Institutional trust	0.28**	0.02	0.13	0.15*	0.21**	0.27**	0.24**	0.21**	−0.23**	0.31**	0.31**	0.32**					
14. Trust in government	0.20**	0.09	0.24**	0.29**	0.35**	0.39**	0.28**	0.27**	−0.22**	0.32**	0.34**	0.42**	0.57**				
15. Social trust	0.30**	0.18*	0.23**	0.28**	0.18**	0.33**	0.25**	0.36**	−0.25**	0.23**	0.35**	0.39**	0.41**				
16. Negative emotions about social problems	0.04	−0.20**	0.13	0.19**	0.24**	0.39**	0.10	0.27**	−0.34**	0.37**	0.28**	0.21**	0.29**	0.34**	0.20**		
17. Sense of community (positive feelings about community)	0.22**	0.15	0.34**	0.43**	0.38**	0.43**	0.25**	0.34**	−0.27**	0.33**	0.33**	0.41**	0.32**	0.43**	0.43**	0.20**	
18. Sense of community (provides opportunities to achieve change)	0.17*	0.12	0.40**	0.48**	0.41**	0.59**	0.25**	0.41**	−0.41**	0.50**	0.47**	0.53**	0.32**	0.49**	0.39**	0.37**	0.78**

*p < 0.05; **p < 0.01

participation experiences was a strong and consistent predictor of levels of participation; however, the other significant predictors differed across the three ethnic groups. Furthermore, and notably, in the Turkish majority youth only, the *less* responsive that government was perceived as being towards the views of citizens, the *higher* the levels of participation by the individual in the previous 12 months.

Discussion

This study has shown that there are significant differences both in participation and in the predictors of participation between the three ethnic groups that were studied. It is especially noteworthy that the Turkish group showed lower participation levels than the two minority groups over the previous 12 months. Previous research has suggested that minority ethnic groups can have higher rates of participation than the majority group in some cultural settings (Torgerson *et al.* 2008; Muller and Vothknecht 2011), and it is possible that perceptions of inequalities enhance their levels of participation (Uslaner and Brown 2003), coupled with the fact that they perceive that their views will not be presented or considered if they do not take action themselves.

Many researchers (e.g. Niemi *et al.* 1991; Schulz 2005; Kenski and Stroud 2006) have argued that both internal and external efficacy are important predictors of participation. However, internal efficacy did not emerge as a significant predictor for any of the three groups in the regression analyses (and it is notable that internal efficacy did not emerge as a significant predictor of participation for any of the three groups in a second set of regressions in which the enter method was used instead of the stepwise method). By contrast, external efficacy did emerge as a significant *negative* predictor of participation in the Turkish majority group (but this variable did not predict participation in either of the two minority groups). This finding is extremely interesting and possibly explains why Turkish youth engaged in significant protests and demonstrations in Gezi Park in Istanbul in June 2013, when thousands of young people protested against the government: these protests erupted precisely when the government appeared totally intransigent and unresponsive to citizens' views over its plans to demolish Gezi Park in order to redevelop it into a replica of an Ottoman army barracks with a shopping mall on the ground floor. In other words, the present study suggests that it was precisely the lack of responsiveness of the government to citizens' views which precipitated Turkish youth into collective action over this issue. Note that the data for the present study were collected in 2011, two years prior to the Gezi Park protests.

As far as the Roma youth were concerned, it is interesting to see that trust in all its forms (institutional, governmental and social) was relatively high among these individuals. Previous research has shown that being a member of a minority group often impacts negatively on the levels of trust in the government (Fennema and Tillie 1999, 2001). However, in the case of Turkey, Roma youth, who usually have a relatively right-wing and conservative political orientation (Kolukirik and Toktas 2007), distrust the system, questioning the discrimination they face every day, while simultaneously wanting to 'stay loyal to the country' (Ataman et al. 2012: 426), strongly emphasizing that they do not want to be perceived as 'others.' They wish to be part of the national community and also want to believe in the leaders who run the government and that they will have equal access to rights as other citizens. It is therefore not surprising to see that Roma youth have relatively high levels of both governmental and institutional trust. It is important to note that the Roma participants also had higher levels of collective efficacy in relationship to their own *ethnic* group when compared to the other two groups. As Roma people live in collectivist groups comprising 'neighborhoods for gypsies' all over Turkey, and especially in Istanbul, they tend to connect with each other in many different cultural, religious, and social ways. Thus it is possible that this mode of living leads these individuals to believe that, by working together as a group, they can achieve civic and political change. This pattern is consistent with the argument of Emler (Chapter 9 this volume) that individuals engage with political life largely when they come together to influence one another and encourage and support each other to act in a collective way.

As far as the Bulgarian resettlers were concerned, their participation over the previous 12 months, as well as the perceived quality of participation in terms of action, was the highest among these individuals. As most of the Bulgarian resettlers held double citizenship, they might well have identified as being Turkish (Suter 2008), possibly did not experience feelings of discrimination, and probably felt more positively regarded than Roma youth. However, it is interesting to see that their sense of community was significantly lower than that of the majority Turkish group. Although the Bulgarian resettlers, on average, did not have such high levels of institutional trust as the Roma, institutional trust emerged as a significant predictor of participation for these youth: the higher their levels of trust, the higher their levels of participation.

One of the most striking findings of this study was the positive relationship, in all three groups, between the perceived quality of previous participation experiences and participation within the last 12 months. This finding is consistent with previous research. Fernandes-Jesus et al. (2012) argue that the quality of participation experiences directly affects political attitudes and suggest that the relationship between participation and empowerment is complex and probably bi-directional. At this point, it is important to stress not only the positive aspects of participation (e.g. empowerment) but also its possible negative effects such as opening oneself to stereotyping, conformity, skepticism, and distrust. During the protests in Gezi Park in Istanbul in 2013, thousands of young people protested against the government. Throughout these protests, Prime Minister Erdogan labelled the protesting youth as 'a few çapulcu' which can be translated as 'looters.' Although the Prime Minister had put a strongly negative impact on 'çapulcus,' the word was quickly appropriated by the protestors and became a word denoting fighting for your rights. Soon afterwards, 'chapulling' was used widely, and many took the concept still further by redefining it to mean: 'to act towards taking the democracy of a nation to the next step by reminding governments of their reason for existence in a peaceful and humorous manner'[3]. This illustrates the shift from distrust, through positive experience of participation, to empowerment. When young people are treated as active citizens (rather than as 'a few looters') who have the power to act in a considerable manner and also to take responsibility for the protection of a city park in a manner which involves searching for relevant information, organizing activities, and participating in group decision-making (three of the PIDOP items which were used to measure the quality of participation), then their political empowerment is enhanced as well as their feelings of positive psychological consequences (Flanagan and Sherrod 1998; Menezes 2003).

Finally, the present results show discrepancies in the levels and the types of participation according to ethnic status, although all groups demonstrated relatively low levels of participation and civic engagement activities. It is important to note that, despite these differences, the recognition of the groups does not differ in terms of Turkish legal arrangements. Most of the participants in the sample held Turkish citizenship. There are no minority laws in Turkey and pseudo-egalitarianism brings all citizens equal rights and responsibilities. However, although legal opportunities seem to be equal, macro factors such as institutional and cultural, historic and economic factors nevertheless impact differentially on levels of political and civic participation by the members of different ethnic groups (as discussed in Barrett's Chapter 10 in the present book). The unification process through nation-building (Toktas and Aras 2009) equalizes the formal rights of different ethnic groups but at the same time it masks the mosaic of cultural and ethnic differences (including differential incomes, educational levels and political orientations) which impact significantly on the demographic and psychosocial situations of ethnic groups, and hence on their patterns of civic and political participation.

Notes

1 The work reported in this chapter was conducted through teamwork. I would like to thank my team members, Professor Figen Çok, Sümercan Bozkurt and Ayşenur Ataman, for their great contributions to the project.
2 In Turkey, mandatory education used to consist of eight years, with the first five grades belonging to primary education and the sixth to eighth grades belonging to secondary education. However, the system changed in 2012 with the new Education Law which implemented a '4+4+4' system, consisting of four years primary education, four years secondary education and four years of high school.
3 See http://en.wikipedia.org/wiki/Chapulling and http://www.ibtimes.com/what-capuling-everyday-im-capuling-turkish-protest-video-goes-viral-1291541 (date both sites accessed 4 January 2014).

References

Ahmad, N. and Pinnock, K. (2007) *Civic Participation: Potential Differences between Ethnic Groups*. London: Commission for Racial Equality.
Artan, İ. E., Börü, D., İslamoğlu, G., Yurtkoru, S., Sipahi, B., Çalışkan, K., and Ergun, S. (2005) *Üniversite Gençliği Değerleri: Korkular ve Umutlar*. Istanbul: TESEV Yayınları.

Ataman, A., Çok, F. and Şener, T. (2012) 'Understanding civic engagement among young Roma and young Turkish people in Turkey,' *Human Affairs*, 22 (3): 419–33.
Cankurtaran-Ontas, A., Buz, S., and Hatiboğlu, B. (2013) 'Youth and political participation: case in Turkey,' *European Journal of Social Work*, 16 (2), 249–62.
Çetin, T. (2009) 'The socio-economic characteristics of the Turkish people who immigrated from Bulgaria,' *Ekev Akademi Dergisi*, 13: 395–412.
Doganay, F. (1996) *Türkiye'ye göçmen olarak gelenlerin yerleşimi*. Ankara: State Planning Organization.
Fennema, M. and Tillie, J. (2001) 'Civic community, political participation and political trust of ethnic groups,' *Connections*, 24 (1): 26–41.
Fennema, M. and Tillie, J. (1999) 'Political participation and political trust in Amsterdam: civic communities and ethnic networks,' *Journal of Ethnic and Migration Studies*, 25 (4): 703–26.
Fernandes-Jesus, M., Malafaia, C., Ferreira, P., Cicognani, E., and Menezes, I. (2012) 'The many faces of Hermes: the quality of participation experiences and its effects on migrant and non-migrant youth,' *Human Affairs*, 22 (3): 434–47.
Flanagan, C. and Sherrod, L. R. (1998) 'Youth political development: an introduction,' *Journal of Social Issues*, 54: 447–56.
Forbrig, J. (ed.) (2005) *Revisiting Youth Political Participation*. Strasbourg: Council of Europe Publishing.
International Helsinki Federation for Human Rights (2006) *International Helsinki Federation Annual Report on Human Rights Violations: Turkey*. Helsinki: International Helsinki Federation for Human Rights (IHF).
International IDEA (Institute for Democracy and Electoral Assistance) (2004) *Voter Turnout in Western Europe since 1945: A Regional Report*. Stockholm: International IDEA.
Jensen, L. A. and Flanagan, C. A. (eds) (2008) *Immigrant Civic Engagement: New Translations*. Special Issue, *Applied Developmental Science*, 12.
Kenski, K. and Stroud, N. J. (2006) 'Connections between internet use and political efficacy, knowledge, and participation,' *Journal of Broadcasting and Electronic Media*, 50 (2): 173–92.
Kılıç, K. (2009) 'Kentsel Gençlik Araştırması Anketi Bağlamında Gençlerin Siyasal Eğilimlerini Etkileyen Faktörler,' in C. Boyraz (ed.), *Gençler Tartışıyor: Siyasete Katılım, Sorunlar ve Çözüm Önerileri*. Istanbul: TUSES.
Kolukirik, S. and Toktas, S. (2007) 'Turkey's Roma: political participation and organization,' *Middle Eastern Studies*, 43 (5): 761–77.
Marsh, A. R. and Strand, E. (2005) *Reaching the 'Romanlar': A Report on the Feasibility Studies 'Mapping' a Number of Roman (Gypsy) Communities in İstanbul*. Istanbul: International Romani Studies Network.
Martiniello, M. (2005) *Political Participation, Mobilisation and Representation of Immigrants and Their Offspring in Europe*, Willy Brandt Series of Working Papers in International Migration and Ethnic Relations, 1/05. Malmö: Malmö University.
Menezes, I. (2003) 'Participation experiences and civic concepts, attitudes and engagement: implications for citizenship education projects,' *European Educational Research Journal*, 2: 430–45.
Minority Rights Group International (2007) *A Quest for Equality: Minorities in Turkey*. MRG.
Muller, C. and Vothknecht, M. (2011) *Group Violence, Ethnic Diversity, and Citizen Participation: Evidence from Indonesia*, MICROCON Research Working Paper 48. Brighton: MICROCON.
Niemi, R. G., Craig, S. C., and Mattei, F. (1991) 'Measuring internal political efficacy in the 1988 National Election Study,' *American Political Science Review*, 85: 1407–13.
Parla, A. (2007) *Longing, Belonging and Locations of Homeland among Turkish Immigrants from Bulgaria*, CAS Sofia Working Paper Series, No. 1, pp. 1–18.

Putnam, R. D. (2000) *Bowling Alone: The Collapse and Revival of American Community*. New York: Simon & Schuster.
Schulz, W. (2005) *Political Efficacy and Expected Participation Among Lower and Upper Secondary Students. A Comparative Analysis with data from the IEA Civic Education Study*. Paper presented at the ECPR General Conference, Budapest, 8–10 September 2005.
Şener, T. (2011) 'The effects of experiences of participation among Turkish youth,' in *XV European Conference on Developmental Psychology ECDP*. Bologna: Medimond, pp. 435–40.
Şener, T. (2012) 'Civic engagement of future teachers,' *Procedia Technology*, 1: 4–9.
Şener, T. (2014) 'Civic and political participation of women and youth in Turkey: an examination of perspectives of public authorities and NGOs,' *Journal of Civil Society*, 10: 69–81.
Sherrod, L. R., Torney-Purta, J., and Flanagan, C. A. (eds) (2010) *Handbook of Research on Civic Engagement in Youth*. Hoboken, NJ: John Wiley & Sons.
Skocpol, T. and Fiorina, M. P. (1999) *Civic Engagement in American Society*. Washington D.C. Brookings Institution Press.
Suter, B. (2008) 'The Different Perception of Migration from Eastern Europe to Turkey: The Case of Moldovan and Bulgarian Domestic Workers,' *migrationonline.cz*, May 2008.
Tasch, L. (2010) 'The EU enlargement policy and national majority-minority dynamics in potential European Union members: the example of Turkey,' *Mediterranean Quarterly*, 21 (2): 18–46.
Toktas, S. and Aras, B. (2009) 'The EU and minority rights in Turkey,' *Political Science Quarterly*, 124: 697–720.
Torgerson, C. J., Gorard, S., Low, G., Ainsworth, H., See, B. H., and Wright, K. (2008) 'What are the factors that promote high post-16 participation of many minority ethnic groups? A focused review of the UK-based aspirations literature,' in *Research Evidence in Education Library*. London: EPPI-Centre, Social Science Research Unit, Institute of Education, University of London.
Uslaner, E. M. and Brown, M. (2003) 'Inequality, trust, and civic engagement,' *American Politics Research*, 33: 868–94.
Vasileva, D. (1992) 'Bulgarian Turkish emigration and return,' *International Migration Review*, 26 (2): 342–52.
Yentürk, N. (2008) 'Youth policy proposals in area surrounding the lives of young people,' in N. Yentürk, Y. Kurtaran, and G. Nemutlu (eds), *Youth Work and Policy in Turkey*, Youth Study Unit Research Paper No. 3. Istanbul: Istanbul Bilgi University, pp. 41–69.

19
THE EXPECTATIONS AND UNDERSTANDINGS OF INFLUENTIAL OTHERS WHO CAN MOBILISE YOUTH PARTICIPATION

Findings from England

Dimitra Pachi and Martyn Barrett

This chapter reports the findings of a study that explored the expectations and understandings held by significant others who are in a position to influence young people's political and civic participation. In particular, the study explored the expectations and understandings held by parents, teachers, youth workers, church youth leaders and international hip hop/rap musicians (through their lyrics). All of these individuals are able to affect political and civic participation by young people, as has been revealed by previous research. In this chapter, a conceptual distinction is drawn between political and civic participation. We use the term 'political participation' to refer to behaviours which have the intent or the effect of influencing governance, whether this be through conventional means involving electoral processes (e.g. voting, standing for office, etc.) or through non-conventional means which occur outside electoral processes (e.g. demonstrating, signing petitions, etc.). We use the term 'civic participation' to refer to voluntary activity focused on helping others, achieving a public good or solving community problems (e.g. raising money for charity, helping neighbours, community volunteering, etc.).

As far as parents are concerned, there is an extensive research literature which has shown that parents and family life can have a significant influence on young people's patterns of participation. This influence has been examined in four main ways:

1. In terms of the impact of parents' political attitudes, interest and/or political party preferences, which have been found to be linked to the attitudes, interest and preferences of their offspring (Gniewosz *et al.* 2009; Jennings 1996; Jennings and Niemi 1968; Niemi and Jennings 1991).
2. In terms of parents' practices, such as their engagement in political discussions, voting, charity work, etc. Research has revealed that parents who engage in these activities bring up children who engage in similar activities (Jennings 2002; Verba *et al.* 1995; Zukin *et al.* 2006).

3. In terms of the values related to pro-social activity and political/civic participation, such as empathy, social responsibility and social trust. Studies have shown that individuals with high levels of political and civic engagement are often brought up in families where these values have had a central role (Flanagan et al. 1998; Franz and McClelland 1994; Oliner and Oliner 1998).
4. In terms of family climate. Family cohesion/expressivity, cultural/intellectual orientation and organisation/control have been found to predict young people's political literacy, civic knowledge, trust in institutions and political efficacy (Azevedo and Menezes 2007).

The influence of parents on political and civic participation has been found to occur not only in ethnic majority youth but also in ethnic minority and immigrant youth (Bloemraad and Trost 2008; Pachi and Barrett 2011; Pachi et al. in press). The family plays an additional role for ethnic minority or immigrant youth in cases where the family culture differs from the culture of the country of residence, especially when the two cultures are very different both in terms of their core moral values and their perceptions of political and civic participation (Pachi and Barrett 2011; Stepick and Stepick 2002). The differences between the two cultures may act either as a barrier to young people's participation or as a motivator, sometimes even leading to a reverse direction of influence from children to parents, depending on the specific issue concerned and the means of participation (Bloemraad and Trost 2008; Pachi and Barrett 2014).

Teachers and the school are also known to be further important influences on youth participation. Research has shown that the curriculum of the school, the rules of the functioning of the school, classroom climate, as well as the teaching strategies and characters of teachers, all affect young people's political socialisation (Flanagan et al. 2007; Flanagan et al. 2010; Niemi and Junn 1998; Torney-Purta et al. 2001; Zukin et al. 2006). Much research has been conducted on the role of classroom climate on young people's political/civic participation. The opportunity to take part in open discussions on social issues and to be listened to with respect has been found repeatedly to be related to young people's political interest, civic knowledge, political trust, political efficacy and the likelihood of voting in the future (Azevedo and Menezes 2007; Hahn 1998; Torney-Purta et al. 2001), while perceptions of teachers' practices, in terms of the level of democratic ethos within the classroom, predict social justice beliefs and levels of civic commitment (Flanagan et al. 2007).

Apart from the family and the school, membership of civic, community and religious organisations is also important for engagement and participation by adults and young people alike (Fennema and Tillie 2001; Hart and Atkins 2002; Mercer and Page 2010; Putnam 2000; Smith 1999; Verba et al. 1995; Youniss et al. 1997). Among youth, participation in extracurricular activities plays a particularly important role in fostering both civic and political participation (Glanville 1999; Hart et al. 2007; Zaff et al. 2003). The link between civic activity during adolescence and adult political and civic activity has been repeatedly confirmed in the literature (e.g. Hart et al. 2007; Smith 1999), while religious participation has also been linked with later civic and political participation (Smith 1999). Youth workers' activities in youth centres can also play an important role in youth participation. Youth workers' efforts to develop a trustful and meaningful relationship with young people (Young 1999) are appreciated by young people, whose motivation towards civic participation can change in response to this relationship (Pearce and Larson 2006).

Finally, music also plays an important part in youth culture. Research with American youth has found that hip hop/rap music in particular is connected to political and civic action and expression (Flores-Gonzalez et al. 2006; Stapleton 1998; Tyson 2004). This genre of music, which began among the African-American population, is now an international multi-billion dollar industry with fans across all ethnic groups, not only in the US but also around the world (Tyson 2004). The social media that young people use for both entertainment and information have contributed to this expansion, transferring the messages of popular singers/artists to young people across the globe. The analysis of rap/hip hop lyrics shows that they sometimes act as a form of political protest aimed at raising political awareness for the socio-economic plight of African-Americans in the US; issues of poverty, discrimination, injustice and institutional brutality are all addressed by these lyrics (Ginwright and Cammarota 2002; Stapleton 1998). Such lyrics therefore provide a further potential influence on young people's engagement with these issues.

The present study explored the expectations, understandings and perceptions held by parents, teachers, youth workers, church youth leaders and international hip hop/rap artists about youth political and civic participation. These specific sources of influence were chosen for examination because in our previous work (Pachi and Barrett 2011, 2012), which involved focus groups that were conducted with English, Congolese and Bangladeshi youth living in London, the youth themselves explicitly identified all of these as the principal sources of influence on their own participatory behaviours.[1]

Consequently, in the present study, interviews were conducted with these individuals who had been identified in the focus groups as influences on the youths' levels and patterns of participation; in the case of the hip hop/rap artists, the lyrics of songs by artists who had been cited as being influential were analysed. In-depth qualitative interviews were conducted with parents, teachers, youth workers and religious leaders, the aim being to examine how these influential others themselves viewed young people's political and civic participation, the levels and kinds of political and civic participation which these individuals expected from youth, the strategies which they employed in order to encourage youth to participate, and the barriers which they perceived to youth participation. In the case of the song lyrics, these were examined for evidence of the orientation of the artist on these various issues.

Method

The selection of participants and lyrics

The focus groups conducted with the Bangladeshi youth revealed the importance of youth workers and international hip hop/rap songs in particular as influences on the participants' patterns of participation. Consequently, for the present study, two youth workers were interviewed who worked in a youth centre attended by young people from all three ethnic groups: Bangladeshi, Congolese and English. Both youth workers were male in their late 30s. One of them was British Bangladeshi and the other was British Cypriot. In addition, the lyrics of eight songs by the American hip hop artist and music producer Jay-Z (Shawn Corey Carter, born in 1969) and the lyrics of six songs by the American hip hop artist Tupac (Tupac Amaru Shakur, 1971–96) were analysed using thematic analysis. These two artists were chosen because both were explicitly mentioned as important influences by the focus group participants. The choice of songs was based on the chart position and the certification of the artists' singles in the American and British charts in the period 1995–2013 for Jay-Z and 1991–2006 for Tupac. The songs of Jay-Z which were analysed were: *Ain't No Nigga, Can't Knock the Hustle, Dead Presidents (Part 1), It's the Hard Knock Life, Bonnie and Clyde, Empire State of Mind, Run This Town* and *99 Problems*. The songs of Tupac which were analysed were: *If My Homie Calls, Brenda's Got a Baby, Keep Ya Head Up, Dear Mama, Ghetto Gospel* and *Until the End of Time*.

The results of the focus groups with the Congolese youth revealed the importance of parents and church leaders in particular. Consequently, two parents, a father and a mother of two of the focus group participants, were interviewed; they were both in their late 40s. Both parents had migrated to the UK in the early 1990s. In addition, two church youth leaders from a Kimbanguist church were interviewed. The first church youth leader was male and 36 years old. He arrived in Europe in 1979 in France and then migrated to the UK at the end of the 1990s. The second church youth leader was female and 20 years old and studied law. She arrived in the UK at the age of six months in the early 1990s.

Finally, the results of the focus groups with the English youth revealed the importance of parents and teachers in particular. Consequently, two parents of participants in the English focus groups were interviewed. The first English parent was female and was in her early 40s, while the second English parent was male and was in his early 50s. In addition, two college teachers who had been mentioned by the focus group participants were interviewed. Both of these colleges were attended by Bangladeshi, Congolese and English young people. The first teacher was female and taught anthropology, while the second teacher was male and taught mathematics although he had a degree in Engineering from the Democratic Republic of the Congo. Both teachers were teaching at sixth-form college level (typically attended by 16- to 18-year-olds). The mathematics teacher was Congolese, and he had arrived in the UK in the late 1990s, while the anthropology teacher was English.

Procedure

The participants were contacted and asked to participate in an individual interview which would last approximately one hour and which could be conducted in a location that was convenient to them. The semi-structured interview schedule (see Appendix B at the end of this book for the complete interview schedule) included a range of open-ended questions on:

1. The participants' expectations of youth participation in general and more specifically their expectations of youth participation in relationship to their immediate environment.
2. The strategies which were used by the participant and by the organisation to which the participant belonged to support and encourage youth participation.
3. The barriers to youth participation which they perceived.

Both the interview data and the song lyrics were analysed qualitatively, using the principles of thematic analysis as described by Braun and Clarke (2006) and Joffe and Yardley (2004). Both semantic and latent themes were identified in the data.

Findings

Expectations of youth participation

Looking initially at the expectations of significant others in relation to civic and political participation, the English parents we interviewed expected their children to participate politically by voting, and also civically by engaging with environmental and charity activities:

> 'Yeah, what, to vote? Yeah, as long as he has, he can, what happens in this situation you have the power to vote to change it, so I think that's important that he exercises that right.' (English parent)

> 'We are quite active in our local Church and there is often various, you know, charitable things where you are supporting an initiative or a petition, or … raising money through whatever it is, you know, some jumble sale or something, and you try to get involved and get the children involved as well … (…) Yes we do recycle a lot and we try to purchase fair-trade in the majority of instances, ermm, strange enough they are quite … they are not … as enthusiastic as I hoped they would be to be honest …' (English parent)

On the other hand, the Congolese parents we interviewed appeared to have expectations only in regard to civic participation, and this was mainly in relation to the country of origin. The return to the Congo, which has gradually become a 'dream' for many parents (Stefansson 2004; Wessendorf 2007), was being projected onto their children. The expectation of their children's return to the Congo in order to help the country was considered possible despite the children's lack of a relationship with the country of origin:

> *Interviewer*:
> 'But, can they organise a charity from here?'
> *Congolese parent*:
> 'Yes they do … they spoke on TV asking if you have anything to send to Africa … a woman and a man here they organised a container, collected

clothes, shoes, for orphans in Kinshasa … they sent this (…) One day our children will go there to help, our children … it will come …'

On the other hand, the youth workers, the teachers and the church youth leaders we interviewed did not express strong expectations of either political participation or charity work. This could be related to the lack of projects on these issues in the youth organisations and the schools. The youth workers and the teachers talked about their expectations of how young people should behave in an environmentally friendly way and should also know about values such as equality and freedom of speech:

> 'Right, err … I mean we always try to promote to them that they are equal citizens, they are equal to everyone in this country (…) we try to encourage young people kind of really participate and value equality, and see that everyone is equal in life, you know, no one is you know, no one is better than the other person, everyone on an equal footing.' (Youth worker)

They wanted young people to be responsible for their actions and their views and to take informed decisions. In this regard, they respected young people who did not want to engage with a certain issue or had other plans or interests, as long as there was some initial level of cognitive engagement:

> 'I encourage them to participate (…) it depends, even if they, if that was an activity I know they don't like, even if they spent 3 minutes sat down listen … you know and try and they still say no, I don't like it, it's not for me, then fine, at least they tried, as long as they try to participate that's good.' (Youth worker)

While there was no expectation of active participation among the youth workers, teachers and church youth leaders, there was also no discouragement of participation either. Participation was seen positively in the current climate of perceived youth disengagement:

> 'No … I wouldn't see it as a bad thing. If some of them decide to march … cause one of the bad things you have in youth, I mean, many of them don't give a damn about anything. You tell them 'OK there's war in Iraq', they don't care. 'OK there's people dying in Africa – oh …' as long as it doesn't touch them, they are so passive, many of them.' (Church youth leader)

Another type of expectation that was expressed by the church youth leaders and the parents concerned the moral and psychological well-being of young people. The English parents we interviewed wanted their children to be happy in their lives whatever their choices, while the Congolese and English parents and the church youth leaders expressed the expectation that their children and young people in general should live and behave morally. The Congolese parents and the church youth leaders perceived morality differently from the English/British participants (Verhoef and Michel 1997), perceiving it primarily in religious terms (Amadiume 1997) and through the ability to distinguish 'good' from 'bad' and to follow God's will, which also included being committed to social/political order:

> 'Of course ... as you said in your question, it's based on the morals ... we often stress the [10] commandments and we also stress the fact that following the commandments not only puts you in peace with God but also in peace with society... we also have that big commandment from our spiritual leader: 'be in good terms with the state where you live'. So it all goes together really. Not only be in peace spiritually but also be in peace as a person in society ...' (Church youth leader)

On the other hand, the two English parents perceived morality independently from religion, seeing it in legal terms (i.e. not breaking the law). It is notable that all of the parents, youth workers, teachers and church youth leaders we interviewed, irrespective of their cultural background, expected young people not to participate in illegal activity, based on grounds of both morality and personal well-being:

> 'Yes, I would discourage them from breaking the law, so something like graffiti, it's breaking the law, so ... (...) Yeah, yeah, I am ... trying not to duck it, but I would have said both, it is, you know some things are right and some things are wrong... it's like erm, you know, you can support non-violent protest but you wouldn't advocate violent protest, erm, you know, because some things are right and some things are wrong, it's not everything going to be relative ... and ... but also, just think that they would be ... I wouldn't encourage them into things which would draw down you know a lot of problems on top of them, I don't think that would be a very responsible thing to do ...' (English parent)

> 'No ... I would advise them not to get personally in trouble ... but I wouldn't see it as a bad thing [to participate in a political rally]' (Church youth leader)

In contrast, there were neither implicit nor explicit expressions of expectations of political or civic action in the hip hop lyrics, with both artists referring to religion as a way of enduring the cruelty of society (discrimination, social injustice, poverty, etc.):

> 'If I upset you, don't stress, never forget, that God hasn't finished with me yet, I feel his hand on my brain, when I write rhymes I go blind, and let the Lord do his thing, but am I less holy, cause I choose to puff a blunt and drink a beer

with my homies, before we find world peace, we gotta find peace and end the
war on the streets, my ghetto gospel
...
Lord can you hear me speak!
To pay the price of being hell bound'

(Tupac, featuring Elton John, Ghetto Gospel*)*

The most prevalent expectation in both artists' work in response to a disappointing social and political system was individual empowerment through affluence, which in the case of Jay-Z appeared to be the way out of everyday hardships:

'I see you vision mama, I put my money on the longshots,
All my ballers thar's born to clock,
Now I might be on top whether I perform or not
I went from lukewarm to hot, sleeping on futons and cots
To King size, dream machines, the green fives'

(Jay-Z, It's the Hard Knock Life*)*

Tupac referred to the struggles of Malcolm X and Bobby Hutton, but did not encourage young people to engage in any form of collective action to fight for the rights of young black people or to escape from the conditions in which they live. This was perceived to be exclusively an individual struggle, with family as the only ally:

'I moved out and started really hangin
I needed money of my own so I started slangin
I ain't guilty cause, even though I sell rocks
It feels good putting money in your mailbox
I love payin rent when the rent's due
I hope ya got the diamond necklace I sent to you
Cause when I was low you was there for me
And never left me alone cause you cared for me
And I could see you coming home after work late ...'

(Tupac, Dear Mama*)*

The strategies used for encouraging participation

Concerning the strategies which were used to encourage participation, all three classic strategies of teaching young people to be helpful were identified in the significant others' discourses: giving direct instructions (Grusec *et al.* 1978), using reinforcement (Grusec 1991) and exposing them to role models (Bandura 1973). Among the three strategies, the most common was giving direct instructions. Some of our interviewees did this in an authoritarian way, others in an encouraging way and others with an explanation of why they should follow these instructions:

> *English parent*:
> 'Oh yes, not that he does, but yes, "turn your lights off, you don't need all of them" or "take that down to the recycling bin"
> (laughing)'
> *Interviewer*:
> 'So this is a continuous discussion in the house?'
> *English parent*:
> 'Continuous yes, all the time'

'It was our encouragement to go and vote' (English parent)

'Yeah, I do encourage them actually … obviously, we need to encourage them, in a good way … I don't know … nowadays … To encourage someone to do something, you need to know why you're encouraging them. To tell "not to do this", you need to know why you are telling them not to do that. Because when we were young, when our parents used to say "don't do that" we wouldn't ask questions. We would be like "alright then". But nowadays, they challenge. We tell the youngster "don't do that" they wanna know why … so I am telling someone "don't do that" and then I don't know why I am telling them not to do that. It doesn't make sense. So when I am telling someone "don't do that, don't do that" I have a reason behind it. So I do tell them about the reason why "you can't do that" … because of this … "this would happen if you do this". So they understand more…they know when they growing up, they are getting wise …' (Church youth leader)

Another strategy which was used by the parents and the youth workers we interviewed was role modelling. The youth workers, through the way they ran the youth centre, showed young people how they should behave in society, while the parents reported that their children were following in their steps and were engaged with the type of activities with which their parents were also engaged:

'I think to a degree it's an example type of thing, they, we are quite active in our local Church and there is often various … you know, charitable things where you are supporting an initiative or a petition, or … raising money through whatever it is, you know, some jumble sale or something, and you try to get involved and get the children involved as well, my youngest, you know if something catches their imagination, the youngest one, the 13 year old raised quite a lot of money for cancer research, because a teacher at her school died of cancer, who she was very fond of, so it was something that you know, it was a situation which, you know the right thing at the right time, she was able to do some sponsored events and she did it off her own ... she wasn't actively encouraged by us to do that, she did that on her own initiative.' (English parent)

Role modelling (either on themselves or on other important figures in American history) was also used by the two hip hop artists. In their lyrics, they described both their own earlier experiences of socio-economic difficulties and their latest experiences of economic affluence, which they displayed as an example for people to follow. Jay-Z also called on young people to follow him in his new discovery, which was Masonry; Masonry was portrayed as a form of religion with the God of Peace as a central figure:

'We are, Yeah I said it, We are, You can call me Caesar, in a dark Czar, Please follow the leader, So Eric B. we are Microphone fiend, it's the return of the God, Peace God ... And ain't nobody fresher, I am in Mason'
(Jay-Z, featuring Rihanna, Run This Town)

One important factor mentioned only by the parents was that all of these strategies of encouragement are only effective gradually, not immediately, and not to their full potential but only on average. Furthermore, the parents also reported that the effectiveness of particular strategies depended heavily on the personality of the young person and the issue of participation.

Additionally, in some cases, parents reported that offering rewards (as reinforcements) could also be a successful strategy to persuade young people to participate (Grusec 1991):

'Yeah, they do it a little bit, it's, that's the way with children, isn't it? You sort of encourage them and slowly they pick it up and they get ... I think they get habituated to ... and make it a habit, and educate their thinking I suppose.' (English parent)

'Some people could be bribed to go and do something, will you go and do and I will buy you a take away, on whatever level, some people can be bribed to do things.' (English parent)

The teachers and the youth workers also used additional strategies. For example, they reported giving advice to young people rather than instructions, they would be less directional, and they would also encourage young people to question social phenomena (Batten and Batten 1967):

'All I can do, is try to open their minds, try to make them ask questions, about everything they see, not just drugs and laws, everything.' (Youth worker)

They would also hold discussions with young people when young people requested this. The teachers we interviewed also reported holding discussions with young people about environmental and political issues in their classes but only in the context of the subject they were teaching; due to the pressure to follow the school curriculum, there was no room or time for extra discussions or encouragement for participation. Encouragement for participation was only done personally, when a discussion was initiated by the students:

> *Teacher:*
> 'People, I think they do, I think erm some people have those discussions, because I teach anthropology we have discussions about universal human rights, for example. And ... yeah so that happens, that must happen in the law as well, in the law, in the law classes about environmental issues, and the global issue of environmentalism, you know so important in terms of Bangladesh ... And the rising sea level, the rising sea level. The unpredictability of the climate, plastic bags, you know all of this.'
> *Interviewer:*
> 'Is it something that you have found yourself, talking about it or promoting recycling or ... you know giving this sort of advice?'
> *Teacher:*
> 'Er, I do personally, I don't do it at work.'

An important characteristic of all the above strategies is that they were used to encourage individual action rather than collective action. The parents, the youth workers, the teachers, the church youth leaders and also the hip hop artists were all found to talk about individual agency, not collective agency (Zukin *et al.* 2006):

> '... and all I had to give her was my pipe dream
> of how I'd rock the mic, and make it to that bright screen
> I'm trying to make a dollar out of fifteen cents
> It's hard to be legit and still pay the rent
> ...
> it's gonna take the man in me to conquer this insanity
> it seems that rain 'll never let up
> I try to keep my head up, and still keep from getting wet up
> You know it's funny when it rains it pours,
> They got money for wars, but can't feed the poor'
> *(Tupac,* Keep Ya Head Up*)*

The perceived barriers to participation

Finally, the third major theme examined was the perceived barriers to youth participation. Interestingly, while the youth workers and the parents among our participants believed that the school had the primary responsibility for providing civic education and for encouraging civic and political participation, the teachers themselves believed that their primary role was teaching the curriculum, with the pressure of covering the curriculum preventing them from discussing civic or political participation at school:

> 'it [political participation] usually comes through school and they associate it with school and schoolwork and things like that ...' (English parent)

> 'I think anyone is informed about their rights yeah ... I think so yes, school comes in for this stuff ... Yeah, they do erm, they have certain lessons that they have, that they cover that kind of thing.' (Youth worker)

> 'Yeah, yeah, yeah. Erm I guess that I don't now [encourage participation with activities] because my job is teaching and erm there is people I work with, they've got 9 months and they've got to get through their course and get to university.' (Teacher)

There was also considerable variability across the interviewees in the opportunities which they perceived to be available for youth participation. The parents, the youth workers, the teachers and the church youth leaders held differing views on whether opportunities and information on youth participation were made available to young people. Some of them thought that there were sufficient opportunities, while others thought either that there were not enough opportunities or that the existing opportunities are not communicated effectively to young people:

> 'I think, there is a lot of information out there but I don't think it's getting through to young people, I don't think the ... we are using as adults the right kind of media channels to get the message across to young people ...' (Youth worker)

> 'they [young people] know their rights anyway, from school, from what they learn at school in PSHE,[2] and they know that from the age of 18 they have the right to live their life the way they want to ... on legal level ... They are aware of that ...' (Church youth leader)

A divide was observed between most of the Congolese participants and the remainder of the interviewees. The Congolese parents and teacher strongly believed that the British society/political system offers sufficient opportunities for young people to participate, in contrast to the Congolese system which has less infrastructure and high levels of political corruption. The culture of origin and the experience of immigration appeared to play an important role in this respect:

> 'In Africa, young people have the love of work, because there are not many opportunities, people suffer ... If there were many opportunities like in

England, they give to the children, then it would be different, we would have many intellectuals, people working, and not criminals on the street.' (Congolese parent)

However, affluence alone was not perceived as leading to youth participation. The Congolese parents and teacher believed that affluence together with a legal system which is not strict with young people leads to amorality, which in turn leads to a lack of youth participation. British laws and practices were considered too permissive by the two Congolese parents, who said that they were used to a more authoritarian parenting style. This difference was perceived to stem from 'cultural differences' between the two societies, and both parents were keen to draw a boundary between the two antithetical models of education, authority and values. In contrast to Europe, the education of young people in the Congo was described as linked to the importance of the extended family and a (mainly Christian) religious ethos which promotes family values, authority and a respect for elders. Young people were then expected to be more respectful, more compliant and less argumentative towards their parents and elder members of the community (Verhoef and Michel 1997):

'Obviously they have more a European mentality than an African one … so the view of the adults is different … I know that for instance that teachers are considered in Africa… adults are considered is different than here … We are scared of teachers in Africa, we are mortified when a teacher comes in because he's an adult, because he is in power … but here … you are not that scared when you see an adult… and now you see adults the way they act, so we can make fun of them, maybe you wouldn't dare doing that in Africa …' (Church youth leader)

This difference between the two cultures was also reported by both youth workers who were younger than the parents and were in contact with a lot of young people. However, their approach to this cultural difference was more positive; they believed in the reconciliation of the two cultures by selecting and retaining the best features of each.

Another important factor that was reported as limiting the impact of significant others' efforts was the stereotypical view of young people: young people's tendency to contest adult instructions, their apathy towards their parents' or teachers' role modelling, their adherence to a youth culture which expects young people to be disengaged towards political issues, and young people's different interests and use of different means of information and communication from those of adults (Farthing 2010; Zukin et al. 2006):

'But in general, with the politics and all of that, young people won't really watch the news, so we don't really know what's going on, and actually, get a newspaper and read it, some youngsters find it is a waste of time, so we would prefer if we were more involved.' (Church youth leader)

'Erm ... that's a good question ... well ... I would guess that they are apathetic because it's not very cool, it's not very fashionable, they do not appear to be, the... excitement of say radical politics ...' (English parent)

One further theme that emerged from the analysis of the song lyrics was people's inner 'obstacles'; despite their fame and wealth, the two hip hop artists presented an image of themselves as having been stigmatised by their childhood and of having survived their violent and deprived environments, which acted as an inner impediment to societal engagement. When role models claim not to be able to change themselves or the society in which they live, it is unlikely that the young people who look up to these role models will believe that their participation can bring about any change:

'I've been sinnin since you been playin with Barbie and Ken in
you can't change a player's game in the 9th inning?'
(Jay-Z, featuring Roxy Brown, Ain't No Nigga)

'I don't know how to sleep, I gotta eat, stay on my toes,
gotta a lot of beef, so logically, I prey on my foes,
hustling's still inside of me'
(Jay-Z, It's the Hard Knock Life)

'... until we even, thieving, as long as I'm breathing, can't knock the way a nigga eating ...'

(Jay-Z, Can't Knock the Hustle)

'it never stop, when my mama ask me will I change
I tell her yeah, but it's clear I'll always be the same
Until the end of time'
(Tupac, Until the End of Time)

Inability to effect any changes, together with these artists' grim portrayal of a society characterised by social deprivation, poverty, unemployment, criminality, prostitution, an unfair and discriminatory justice system as well as an unresponsive social and political system, convey a fatalistic and negative message. It is notable that the English and Bangladeshi male participants in the focus groups which were conducted prior to the present study also referred to social deprivation, unemployment and their unfair treatment by the police (especially being stopped and searched repeatedly on the streets) as reasons for not being engaged. Negative representations in the hip hop artists' lyrics included:

'I hear Brenda's got a baby
But Brenda's barely got a brain

A damn shame
The girl can hardly spell her name
That's not our problem, that's up to Brenda's family
Well let me show ya how it affects the whole community …'

(Tupac, Brenda's Got a Baby*)*

'So I pull over to the side of the road
I heard "Son do you know why I'm stoppin' you for?"
Cause I'm young and I'm black and my hat's real low?
Do I look like a mind reader sir, I don't know …'

(Jay-Z, 99 Problems*)*

This overridingly negative message about society is also conveyed through references to religion in the lyrics. For Tupac, religion was not a motivator to escape from an illegal life; it was an internal 'refuge' from the violence experienced in everyday life, a 'refuge' which is based on a system of punishment/reward by God. In front of this 'higher' and powerful system of judgement, a feeling of fatality and inability to act against one's fate and one's past emerges for the individual, which could be related to the inability reported by both artists to change their lives completely:

'Please Lord forgive me for my life of sin, My hard stare seem to scare all my sisters' kids, So you know I don't hang around the house much … Now, who's to say if I was right or wrong? To live my life as an outlaw all along, remain strong in this planet full of player haters …' (*Tupac,* Until the End of Time)

Discussion

The overall picture which emerged from the analysis was one in which these significant others did not hold particularly high expectations of either political or civic participation by young people. It was mainly the English parents, among our participants, who expected their children to participate politically through voting and civically through engaging with environmental and charitable causes, while the Congolese parents expected their children to be primarily engaged with civic issues concerning their country of origin. Otherwise, the youth workers, the teachers, the church youth leaders and the hip hop artists did not hold particularly high expectations of youth in regard to either political or civic participation. These low expectations may have been due, in part, to the fact that many of the interviewees held a stereotypical view of youth as being disengaged and apathetic towards civic and political matters. However, although the interviewees held rather low expectations of participation by young people, they did not discourage participation by youth (other than participation in illegal acts) and tended to view participation in a positive light.

Although these significant others did not hold particularly high expectations for participation, they did hold a range of other expectations of young people, from becoming professionally successful to gaining a lot of money and staying faithful to one's culture's morals. This shows that: (1) young people may have a great deal to live up to, which can be problematic especially in cases where these expectations are perceived as antithetical or incompatible (i.e. being both successful and moral); and (2) ethnic minority youth sometimes have to deal with a conflict between their parents' expectations in relation to their culture of origin and the expectations of the country of residence, which can be time-consuming, destabilising and a further barrier to active participation (Pachi and Barrett 2014).

Rather worryingly, in our sample, the parents and the youth workers tended to assume that it was not their responsibility but that of the school to provide civic education and to encourage participation, while the teachers themselves reported that they did not have sufficient time in a highly pressured curriculum for encouraging either civic or political participation. It should be noted that England only introduced citizenship education into state schools in 2002 for pupils aged 11–16 years, with schools being allowed considerable discretion in how it is delivered. As a result, the delivery of citizenship education varies considerably across schools and is sometimes very weak due to the low status of the subject, the lack of curriculum time, and poor coordination and implementation (Keating *et al.* 2009). Furthermore, given that this statutory requirement on schools to deliver citizenship education ends at age 16, it is perhaps not surprising that the teachers in this study, who mainly taught 16- to 18-year-olds, gave little attention to issues concerning political and civic participation in their own classrooms.

That said, the parents, the youth workers, the teachers and the church youth leaders in our study all reported that they did use a variety of strategies to encourage participation, including giving direct instructions, role modelling and discussing issues with youth. Instruction for individual economic success and role modelling were also implied by the hip hop lyrics. It is noteworthy that both teachers reported that they tended to engage in discussions on a one-to-one basis rather than in the classroom unless the issues concerned were directly relevant to the material that was being taught. It is also of note that all of the strategies that were used were aimed at encouraging individual rather than collective action. The youth workers, teachers and church leaders appeared to be more flexible in their methods of encouragement; instead of prescribing to young people how to behave, the majority aimed to put young people in a position where they could decide for themselves (Kidd *et al.* 2007; Yohalem 2003). By contrast, the parents were more instructive and directional, having more precise expectations and a clear idea about how their children should behave.

The overall picture which emerges from this study into the various influences on young people is rather negative, with many significant others having low expectations of youth and the assignment of considerable responsibility to teachers who, however, are unable to fulfil this responsibility. This negative picture is further compounded by the representations that are promulgated by the lyrics of the two hip hop artists. These lyrics convey a bleak and negative image of a society in which it is difficult to effect any change through action. Furthermore, the evidence from the preceding focus groups suggested that these messages from the hip hop artists about social deprivation, unemployment and unfair treatment by the police are indeed taken up by English and Bangladeshi youth as a justification for their own disengagement and non-participation. Thus these artists, instead of mobilising young people, appear to be reinforcing a passive stance towards society, the state and its institutions.

That said, it is important to bear in mind that young people during adolescence and emerging/early adulthood are not passive recipients of environmental influences. Instead, young people attend selectively to the messages, instructions, suggestions and information which they receive from significant others in their environment, make their own inferences based on this information, and take decisions that are motivated by their own current interests, concerns and motivational needs (Arnett 2004; Schaffer 1996). This applies across all social domains, including political and civic engagement and participation (Barrett 2007; McDevitt and Chaffee 2002; Niemi and Hepburn 1995; Yates and Youniss 1998; see also Chapter 10 by Barrett in the present volume).

There are, of course, some significant limitations to the present study, not least the very small sample size that was used and the fact that the design of the study was driven by previous findings on the participation of youth from just three ethnic groups, namely English, Congolese and Bangladeshi, all of whom were living in just one particular location (London). Furthermore, the very clear differences in orientation between the Congolese vs. the other interviewees, with the former regarding the British political and societal systems in a positive light when compared to systems in the Congo, suggest that understandings and interpretations of youth participation can be dependent on the specific cultural positioning of the individuals involved. These differences underline the fact that the present findings cannot be directly extrapolated to other ethnic groups and to other national contexts.

In conclusion, this study helps to provide an explanation of why many of the youth who participated in the preceding focus groups sometimes held rather negative attitudes towards both political and civic participation (Pachi and Barrett 2011, 2012). In those focus groups, low external efficacy emerged as a major factor which was driving perceptions of the ineffectiveness of many forms of participation, which in turn was used to justify youths' own disengagement and non-participation. The results of the present analysis suggest a broader picture in which these young people are embedded in a network of social influences which do little to disconfirm (and which, in the case of the hip hop lyrics, explicitly reinforce) the view that political and civic participation is unlikely to effect any real change in the world.

Notes

1 This previous study involved 14 focus groups which were conducted with 16- to 26-year-old English, Congolese and Bangladeshi young people living in London (Pachi and Barrett 2011, 2012). These ethnic-specific focus groups discussed issues related to

the participants' perceptions of citizenship, the participants' levels and quality of civic and political participation, and the role of significant others in relationship to their civic and political participation (Pachi and Barrett 2011).
2 *Personal, Social and Health Education*, a module of the National Curriculum in secondary education in the UK.

References

Amadiume, I. (1997) *Re-inventing Africa: Matriarchy, Religion and Culture*. London: Zed Books.
Arnett, J. J. (2004) *Emerging Adulthood: The Winding Road from the Late Teens Through the Twenties*. Oxford: Oxford University Press.
Azevedo, C. N. and Menezes, I. (2007) 'Learning politics beyond cognition: the role of experience and participation in political development', in N. Kryger and B. Ravn (eds), *Learning Beyond Cognition*. Copenhagen: Danish University of Education, pp. 95–114.
Bandura, A. (1973) *Aggression: A Social Learning Analysis*. Englewood Cliffs, NJ: Prentice-Hall.
Barrett, M. (2007) *Children's Knowledge, Beliefs and Feelings About Nations and National Groups*. Hove: Psychology Press.
Batten, T. R. and Batten, M. (1967) *The Non-directive Approach in Group and Community Work*. New York: Oxford University Press.
Bloemraad, I. and Trost, C. (2008) 'It's a family affair: inter-generational mobilization in the spring 2006 protests', *American Behavioral Scientist*, 52 (4): 507–32.
Braun, V. and Clarke, V. (2006) 'Using thematic analysis in psychology', *Qualitative Research in Psychology*, 3 (2): 77–101.
Farthing, R. (2010) 'The politics of youthful antipolitics: representing the "issue" of youth participation in politics', *Journal of Youth Studies*, 13 (2): 181–95.
Fennema, M. and Tillie, J. (2001) 'Civic community, political participation and political trust of ethnic groups', *Connections*, 24: 26–41.
Flanagan, C. A., Bowes, J. M., Jonsson, B., Csapo, B. and Sheblanova, E. (1998) 'Ties that bind: correlates of adolescents' civic commitments in seven countries', *Journal of Social Issues*, 54: 457–75.
Flanagan, C., Cumsille, P., Gill, S. and Gallay, L. (2007) 'School and community climates and civic commitments: patterns for ethnic minority and majority students', *Journal of Educational Psychology*, 99: 421–31.
Flanagan, C., Stoppa, T., Syvertsen, A. K. and Stout, M. (2010) 'Schools and social trust', in L. R. Sherrod, J. Torney-Purta and C. A. Flanagan (eds), *Handbook of Research on Civic Engagement in Youth*. Hoboken, NJ: John Wiley & Sons, pp. 307–29.
Flores-Gonzalez, N., Rodriguez, M. and Rodriguez-Muniz, M. (2006) 'From hip-hop to humanization: Batey Urbano as a space for Latino youth culture and community action', in P. Noguera, J. Cammarota and S. Ginwright (eds), *Beyond Resistance*. New York: Routledge, pp. 175–96.
Franz, C. E. and McClelland, D. C. (1994) 'Lives of women and men active in the social protests of the 1960s: a longitudinal study', *Journal of Personality and Social Psychology*, 66 (1): 196–205.
Ginwright, S. and Cammarota, J. (2002) 'New terrain in youth development: the promise of a social justice approach', *Social Justice*, 29: 82–95.
Glanville, J. L. (1999) 'Political socialization or selection? Adolescent extracurricular participation and political activity in early adulthood', *Social Science Quarterly*, 80: 279–90.
Gniewosz, B., Noack, P. and Buhl, M. (2009) 'Political alienation in adolescence: associations with parental role models, parenting styles and classroom climate', *International Journal of Behavioral Development*, 3: 337–46.

Grusec, J. (1991) 'The socialisation of altruism', in M. S. Clark (ed.), *Prosocial Behaviour*. New York: Sage, pp. 9–33.
Grusec, J., Kuczynski, L., Rushton, J. and Simutis, Z. M. (1978) 'Modelling, direct instruction, and attributions: effects on altruism', *Developmental Psychology*, 14: 51–7.
Hahn, C. (1998) *Becoming Political: Comparative Perspectives on Citizenship Education*. Albany, NY: State University of New York Press.
Hart, D. and Atkins, R. (2002) 'Civic competence in urban youth', *Applied Developmental Science*, 6 (4): 227–36.
Hart, D., Donnelly, T. M., Youniss, J. and Atkins, R. (2007) 'High school community service as a predictor of adult voting and volunteering', *American Educational Research Journal*, 44 (1): 197–219.
Jennings, M. K. (1996) 'Political knowledge over time and across generations', *Political Opinion Quarterly*, 60: 228–52.
Jennings, M. K. (2002) 'Generation units and the student protest movement in the United States: an intra- and intergenerational analysis', *Political Psychology*, 23: 303–24.
Jennings, M. K. and Niemi, R. G. (1968) 'The transmission of political values from parent to child', *American Political Science Review*, 62: 169–84.
Joffe, H. and Yardley, L. (2004) 'Content and thematic analysis', in D. F. Marks and L. Yardley (eds), *Research Methods for Clinical and Health Psychology*. London: Sage, pp. 56–68.
Keating, A., Kerr, D., Lopes, J., Featherstone, G. and Benton, T. (2009) *Embedding Citizenship Education in Secondary Schools in England (2002–08): Citizenship Education Longitudinal Study, Seventh Annual Report*, DCSF Research Report 172. London: DCSF.
Kidd, S. A., Miner, S., Walker, D. and Davidson, L. (2007) 'Stories of working with homeless youth: on being "mind-boggling"', *Children and Youth Services Review*, 29 (1): 16–34.
McDevitt, M. and Chaffee, S. (2002) 'From top-down to trickle-up influence: revisiting assumptions about the family in political socialization', *Political Communication*, 19 (3): 281–301.
Mercer, C. and Page, B. (2010) 'African home associations in Britain: between political belonging and moral conviviality', *African Diaspora*, 3 (1): 110–30.
Niemi, R.G. and Hepburn, M.A. (1995) 'The rebirth of political socialization', *Perspectives on Political Science*, 24: 7–16.
Niemi, R. G. and Jennings, M. K. (1991) 'Issues and inheritance in the formation of party identification', *American Journal of Political Science*, 35: 970–88.
Niemi, R. G. and Junn, J. (1998) *Civic Education: What Makes Students Learn?* New Haven, CT: Yale University Press.
Oliner, S. and Oliner, P. (1998) *The Altruistic Personality*. New York: Free Press.
Pachi, D. and Barrett, M. (2011) 'Focus Groups with Young British Bangladeshi, Congolese and English People Living in London'. Unpublished paper, Work Package 6, PIDOP Project.
Pachi, D. and Barrett, M. (2012) 'Perceived effectiveness of conventional, non-conventional and civic forms of participation among minority and majority youth', *Human Affairs*, 22: 345–59.
Pachi, D. and Barrett, M. (2014) 'Civic and political engagement amongst ethnic minority and migrant youth', in R. Dimitrova, M. Bender and F. van de Vijver (eds), *Global Perspectives on Well-being in Immigrant Families*. New York: Springer, pp. 189–211.
Pachi, D., Chrysanthaki, T. and Barrett, M. (in press) 'Political and civic participation among ethnic majority and minority youth', in T. Capelos, H. Dekker, C. Kinnvall and P. Nesbitt-Larking (eds), *Palgrave Handbook of Global Political Psychology*. Basingstoke: Palgrave.
Pearce, N. and Larson, R. W. (2006) 'How youth become engaged in youth programs: the process of motivational change', *Applied Developmental Science*, 10: 121–31.

Putnam, R. D. (2000) *Bowling Alone: The Collapse and Revival of American Community*. New York: Simon & Schuster.
Schaffer, H. R. (1996) *Social Development*. Oxford: Blackwell.
Smith, E. S. (1999) 'The effects of investments in the social capital of youth on political and civic behavior in young adulthood: a longitudinal analysis', *Political Psychology*, 20 (3): 553–80.
Stapleton, K. R. (1998) 'From the margins to mainstream: the political power of hip-hop', *Media, Culture and Society*, 20 (2): 219–34.
Stefansson, A. H. (2004) 'Homecomings to the future: from diasporic mythographies to social projects of return', in F. Markowitz and A. H. Stefansson (eds), *Homecomings: Unsettling Paths of Return*. Lanham, MD and Boulder, CO: Lexington Books, pp. 2–20.
Stepick, A. and Stepick, C. D. (2002) 'Becoming American, constructing ethnicity: immigrant youth and civic engagement', *Applied Developmental Science*, 6: 246–57.
Torney-Purta, J., Lehmann, R., Oswald, H. and Schulz, W. (2001) *Citizenship and Education in Twenty-Eight Countries: Civic Knowledge and Engagement at Age Fourteen*. Amsterdam: IEA.
Tyson, E. H. (2004) 'Rap music in social work practice with African-American and Latino youth', *Journal of Human Behavior in the Social Environment*, 8 (4): 1–21.
Verba, S., Schlozman, K. L. and Brady, H. E. (1995) *Voice and Equality: Civic Voluntarism in American Politics*. Cambridge, MA: Harvard University Press.
Verhoef, H. and Michel, C. (1997) 'Studying morality within the African context: a model of moral analysis and construction', *Journal of Moral Education*, 26 (4): 389–407.
Wessendorf, S. (2007) '"Roots migrants": Transnationalism and "return" among second generation Italians in Switzerland', *Journal of Ethnic and Migration Studies*, 33 (7): 1083–102.
Yates, M. and Youniss, J. (1998) 'Community service and political identity development in adolescence', *Journal of Social Issues*, 54: 495–512.
Yohalem, N. (2003) 'Adults who make a difference: identifying the skills and characteristics of successful youth workers', in F. A. Villarruel, D. F. Perkins, L. Borden and J. G. Keith (eds), *Community Youth Development: Programs, Policies, and Practices*. Thousand Oaks, CA: Sage, pp. 358–72.
Young, K. (1999) *The Art of Youth Work*. Lyme Regis: Russell House.
Youniss, J., McLellan, J. A. and Yates, M. (1997) 'What we know about engendering civic identity', *American Behavioral Scientist*, 40: 620–31.
Zaff, J. F., Moore, K. A., Papillo, A. R. and Williams, S. (2003) 'Implications of extracurricular activity participation during adolescence on positive outcomes', *Journal of Adolescent Research*, 18: 599–630.
Zukin, C., Keeter, S., Andolina, M., Jenkins, K., and Delli Carpini, M. X. (2006) *A New Engagement, Political Participation, Civic Life, and the Changing American Citizen*. New York: Oxford University Press.

PART IV
Policies

This part is devoted to policies on citizens' political and civic engagement. These policies have been developed at many levels of governance and also by numerous non-governmental organisations (NGOs). In the following four chapters, policies at the national and European governance levels are examined. These policies form an important part of the institutional macro context within which citizen engagement occurs, and they help to frame the debates which take place within individual countries about citizen engagement. As these chapters show, different approaches are taken to engagement and participation in different countries. Government policies provide an important indication of the perspectives of official authorities on citizen engagement and participation, and help to shape government spending priorities and the allocation of resources. That said, there is often a gap between official rhetorical statements in policy documents and the actual measures which are implemented in practice to translate policy goals into outcomes. There can also be a further gap between, on the one hand, the actions that are formally implemented and, on the other hand, citizens' perceptions of these actions and of government intentions. While the chapters in this part scrutinise the contents of policy documents at the European and national levels, the final chapter also examines the perceptions of national and European policies by civic activists in Italy and the UK.

In Chapter 20, **Cristiano Bee and Roberta Guerrina** provide an analysis of the *European Commission's policies* on political participation and active citizenship. Policy documents published by the European Commission between 2004 and 2010 were examined in this analysis. This period was characterised by increased scepticism in many European countries towards the European project (i.e. the vision of the development of a broad European civil society based on citizens' full engagement through a system of deliberative democracy). This period was also pivotal in the history of EU governance reforms. Bee and Guerrina's analysis focuses in particular on policies targeting the traditionally marginalised groups of *youth, women,* *ethnic minorities and migrants*. Their findings suggest that the European Commission has an ambivalent approach to the issue of active citizenship. While young people are viewed in these policy documents as having a central role to play in the public sphere and as being key for the enhancement of European democracy, the engagement and participation of women, minorities and migrants is treated in policy documents in a much more fragmentary way, with these groups effectively being treated as more peripheral to the public sphere and to EU policies.

The subsequent three chapters discuss policies on citizen engagement and participation in four of the countries which participated in the PIDOP project: Portugal, Turkey, Italy and the UK. In Chapter 21, **Norberto Ribeiro, Pedro Ferreira, Carla Malafaia and Isabel Menezes** analyse *gender policies* in Portugal. It is important to recall that Portugal was governed by a dictatorship from 1928 to 1974. Under this regime, women were assigned traditional roles as caregivers and mothers and were denied many political, civil and social rights. Ribeiro and colleagues begin by examining recent changes in Portuguese society regarding gender equality. Their findings suggest that profound transformations have occurred to women's rights since 1974, although politics itself is still predominantly a male arena. Analysing public policy documents produced by the government and by NGOs as well as an interview with a representative of an NGO, they explore the discourses that currently underlie policies on active citizenship and democratic participation by women. Their findings suggest that Portuguese national policies tend to be aligned with EU policies. Gender inequality and violence against women are the two primary areas that are identified in the policy documents as still requiring further action.

In Chapter 22, **Sümercan Bozkurt, Figen Çok and Tülin Şener** provide an analysis of government reports, plans and policy documents on the civic and political participation of *women* and *youth* in Turkey. These documents have been produced against a backdrop of generally low rates of participation by both women and youth in Turkey, which is a legacy of the 1980 military *coup d'état* which brought in restrictive measures to limit and in some cases prohibit various forms of political participation. The analysis by Bozkurt and colleagues reveals that women's participation tends to be construed in government documents solely in terms of electoral/conventional forms of political participation. By contrast, youth are construed as a group that needs to be controlled and protected rather than encouraged to participate in political and civic life. Commenting on the widespread youth demonstrations and protests which suddenly erupted in Turkey in the summer of 2013, Bozkurt *et al*. note that these events reveal that, despite their traditionally low levels of participation in conventional politics, youth in Turkey are neither apolitical nor disengaged – on the contrary, they have strong concerns about state restrictions on their freedoms and many are prepared to engage in collective acts of defiance in order to make their voices heard.

In the final chapter in this part, **Cristiano Bee and Paola Villano** compare the *views of civic activists* in Italy and the UK, in particular their attitudes towards national and European policies on political participation and active citizenship.

Bee and Villano begin by providing an account of the very different political contexts and perspectives which have shaped the policy approaches which are taken to active citizenship and participation in Italy and the UK. They then report the findings which emerged from interviews which they conducted with NGO activists in both countries. A number of convergences as well as divergences were found. For example, while activists in both countries discussed the need for much greater citizen engagement with political decision-making, those in Italy emphasised the framing of active citizenship through both institutionalised top-down and non-institutionalised bottom-up practices, while those in the UK focused much more on just top-down mechanisms from government for the construction of active citizenship. Interestingly, European policies on citizen engagement were viewed very differently in the two countries. While the British activists generally recognised and appreciated the role which was played by the EU in fostering and encouraging active citizenship, the Italian activists were much more critical, viewing EU policy as top-down only and exhibiting an exclusionary orientation towards weaker groups in society.

These four chapters, taken together, provide a fascinating window on the different constructions of political and civic engagement which can be present in the policies formulated in different national contexts. They also serve to illustrate the complex and multi-layered nature of policy discourses about citizen engagement and participation within Europe.

20
EUROPEANISATION OF POLICY DISCOURSES ON PARTICIPATION AND ACTIVE CITIZENSHIP

Cristiano Bee and Roberta Guerrina

Introduction

The main aim of this chapter is to map dominant discourses on political participation and active citizenship emerging at the European level by looking at policies targeting traditionally marginalised groups (such as women, young people, minorities and migrants). In particular, we will establish whether new rules, procedures and norms aimed at engaging civil society in the policy-making process are under construction, by framing the actual position of the European institutions in developing the policy agenda. For these reasons the chapter is focused on the emerging discourses representing specific policy frames in the three subgroups. The analysis presented here is based on a policy analysis of public documents published by the European Commission in the period of time 2004–10. This time frame has been chosen because of its relevance for the enhancement and shaping of specific policies of active citizenship by the European Union. This broader discourse, as we argue in the chapter, has emerged for two reasons. First of all, it represents an attempt to overcome the limitations that can be found in the status of European citizenship formalised by the Maastricht Treaty in 1993. Second, it has been shaped by the need to ensure the full implementation of the governance reform started by the European Commission in 2001. This established a European project based on citizens' full engagement and participation in a system of deliberative democracy and entailed the fostering of a broad European civil society.

The political context that drives our analysis is particularly important because it has been characterised by the democratic crisis of Europe, with the consequent rise of euro-sceptical forces that have questioned the viability of the European project as a whole. This crisis has, on the one hand, enhanced the EU's democratic and social deficits and, on the other hand, worsened the impact of the financial crisis in the euro-zone. Between 2004 and 2010, the European Commission, also known as the Barroso I, initiated an impressive series of measures targeting NGOs at the EU level and in the member states. Codes of conduct, guidelines and workshops for civil society actors were organised in order to enhance dialogic interactions and to shape a policy process based on participatory practices. All of these measures have been subject to public scrutiny and criticism, as we outline in this chapter.

This chapter therefore looks at this context and focuses on the emerging discourses surrounding active citizenship put forward by the European Commission. Our analysis provides emphasis on the main Discursive Nodal Points that provide meaning and establish precise policy priorities at the EU level. In the first section of the chapter, we frame the debate in the light of the European discourse on citizenship. In particular, we focus on the main scholarly discussion that has analysed the impact of the status of European citizenship established by the Maastricht Treaty. In the second section of the chapter, we look at the recent characteristics surrounding the policy development of the European citizenship at the EU level, by focusing more precisely on the recent attempts to shape a European model of governance based on participatory democracy. In this section, we will focus on criticism emerging from the literature on civil society in order to outline some ambiguities that underlie this model. In section three of our chapter, we outline the methodological approach that we used in the PIDOP project and describe the analytical model that we developed in order to compare Discursive Nodal Points. In the final section of the chapter, we discuss the findings of our analysis and unpack some of the ambiguities surrounding this notion. As we argue in the chapter, our evidence shows the persistence of an ambiguous and ambivalent approach to active citizenship in respect to different social groups. While youth are involved in deliberative processes, the engagement of women, migrants and minorities still appears to be fragmented and not yet fully inclusive.

European citizenship: a limited concept?

The development of European citizenship has been on the top of the European agenda since at least the early 1980s, when a number of measures were initiated in order to shape a better relationship with the European citizenry. The perceived social and political needs at the time were to transform the widespread perception of the EU as being a merely economic enterprise into a cultural and political entity. Of significance in this time-context was the constitution, at the Fontainebleau European Council Meeting, of the 'Adonnino Committee' that had the task of exploring measures regarding a new area of policies called 'citizens of Europe', with the overall aim of enforcing European identity and the sense of belonging to a wider European territorial space. The outcomes of the work of the Adonnino Committee can be found in the report published by the European Commission (CEC 1985) that provides recommendations in a number of areas (culture, communication, education, mobility, etc.) and a first formulation of the special rights aimed at guaranteeing the full inclusion and participation of citizens in European political processes. Following the evaluations of a number of scholars, it can be argued that the report provides a wide variety of instruments aimed at the fostering of an imagined Europe and the development of a perception of a homogenous European public space (Shore 1994, 2000; Sassatelli 2002). In addition, as O'Keeffe underlines, 'the Adonnino report on "a People's Europe" concretely dealt with the special rights of Community citizens, from the stance of education, culture, exchanges and identity of the Community. Proposals for conferring special rights on Community nationals considered free movement as one of the keystones of the rights of Community citizens' (O'Keeffe 1994: 88). The report thus includes the first concrete reflections regarding the status of European Citizenship that was subsequently shaped within the Maastricht Treaty in 1992.

The literature emerging in the 1990s discussing the actual value of European citizenship is clearly divided when it comes to its evaluation, as explained for example by Weiler: 'For many the concept is considered one of the least successful aspects of Maastricht, trivial and empty, and hence irrelevant [...] For others, European citizenship is an important symbol with far-reaching potential and dangers' (Weiler 1999: 495). It can therefore be argued that, on the one hand, a broad set of scholars pointed to the limitations of European citizenship, because of the scarce implications entailed by this set of rights for the everyday lives of citizens, for its neo-liberal shape and for the highly exclusionary value inherent to its selective attribution to current member states' nationals (see, for example, Closa 1992; Roche 1997; Lehning 1997). On the other hand, a number of scholars, commenting later in the 1990s, interpreted the status of European citizenship in respect to wider considerations regarding practices and implications in regard to the actual possibilities to engage and participate in European politics (Wiener 1998; Kostakopulou 2001, 2008)

For the first strand of literature, the status of European citizenship was considered market-based and largely influenced by the need to strengthen one of the core liberties formalised in the 1950s with the Treaty of Rome, which is the freedom of movement for workers within the EU. The political dimension of European citizenship, consisting of the right to stand and vote at local elections in any country of residence, was certainly not considered to be guaranteeing full civic inclusion and motivation for the engagement of citizens in public affairs. Moreover, the lack of account of the social dimension was considered to be one of the most relevant limitations of this status (O'Leary 1995; Meehan 1997; Sykes 1997), accentuating even more prominently its neo-liberal connotation.

Closa, in one of the many articles published at the time, in commenting upon the highly exclusionary character of European citizenship, raised the concern that 'citizenship of the Union may not be individually acquired and, therefore, individuals who are not nationals of a Member State may thus not be considered citizens of the Union and, as a consequence, experience their possible exclusion from the catalogue of rights of citizenship' (Closa 1995: 509). Follesdal (2001) instead points at the contradictions inherent in European citizenship, by arguing that its establishment solidified the democratic deficit, because it raised issues regarding the lack of legitimacy of the European project as a whole. This question looks directly at the development, or lack, of a demos and opens up questions regarding the political identification with a wider community (see, for example, Faist 2001; Lehning 1997). This first strand of comments and evaluations about European citizenship is thus based on the argument that both democratic and social deficits were enhanced, rather than challenged, as a consequence of the establishment of this status. Roche, in commenting upon the highly egalitarian character of the European integration process and by consequence of the status of citizenship, argued that 'we are all, to a greater or lesser extent "denizens" rather than citizens in Europe [...] we are all significantly excluded from full civil-political citizenship and also from social citizenship' (Roche 1997: 8).

The literature emerging at the end of the 1990s, acknowledging some of the criticism directed at the value and implications of European citizenship, argued that the missing link in these evaluations was the lack of account of 'the transformative resources entailed by European citizenship' (Kostakopolou 2008). This literature evaluated this status in the light of a broader set of practices and policies that are involved and are relevant for social and political identification with the European polity. Social constructivist scholars (Checkel 2001, 2009; Christiansen et al. 1999; Laffan 2004) in particular have shaped a research agenda that has been looking at the effects of European integration in changing the sense of belonging and the patterns of identification with a wider public and social space. The dynamic role of citizenship (Wiener 2007) is better understood if we take into account the sociopolitical notion of citizenship as a social construct that is shaped through social interaction and practices of political socialisation within the European polity. In this light, a prominent interpretation of European citizenship looks at civic republican elements (Bellamy 2000) and associates it with the various conditions for the actual development of a European demos, such as a public sphere, a civil society and a shared political culture (Habermas 1994, 2001). According to the civic republican reading (Miller 2000; Bellamy 2000), citizenship is a civic virtue that entails the individual's active participation in political and social life and his/her full integration into the community. Mouffe, for example, describes active citizens in the following terms: '... a radical democratic citizen is somebody who acts as a citizen, who conceives of herself as a participant in a collective undertaking ...' (Mouffe 1992: 234). The key research question was subsequently oriented at understanding the conditions that were enabling, or not, the development of a post-national model of citizenship based on an active sense of participation in democratic processes of governance with the individual assuming a set of responsibilities in balance with a prescribed set of rights.

According to this perspective, it can be argued that European citizenship and its value can be better understood if linked to the actual practices that it entails and the consequences in terms of political, cultural and social transformation. As argued by Wiener (1998, 2007) citizenship practice

> sets the terms for the institutionalized relation between the citizens and the political community. The institutions which regulate the practice of citizenship

include principles of justice, the adherence to formal political and legal procedures, as well as a set of norms and values. All contribute to establish the procedures of political participation and day-to-day practices of citizen participation within a particular politically defined community. (Wiener 2007: 11)

The social constructivist agenda has therefore influenced a whole set of research that has been taking place in the last decade and that has been looking, besides other aspects, at the drivers of engagement and participation in the European public sphere (Eriksen 2004; Schlesinger 2003; Trenz 2010), at the transformative aspects entailed by an increased spatial mobility within the European territorial space (Favell and Recchi 2011), at the role of European cultural and educational programmes in fostering a sense of European-ness (Sassatelli 2009), and at the development of the social dimension of European citizenship with a particular focus on gender equality (Guerrina 2005, 2006; Kantola 2010). Overall, it is worth emphasising that some common research questions that characterise this set of academic work look at the actual implications of European integration in developing, or not, patterns of European political, social and cultural identification (Checkel 2009; Risse 2010) and give relevance to the processes of political socialisation and at the determinants of active participation of citizens at the EU level (Warleigh 2001; Sánchez-Salgado 2007), in the form of either coalitions of organised interests, pressure groups or social movements (Greenwood 2007; Ruzza 2004). The discussion on active citizenship has thus become prominent in the last few years (Bee and Guerrina 2014; Boje 2010; Hoskins and Kerr 2010), with a focus on the factors that motivate the engagement and participation of citizens in organised civil society.

Our investigation fits with this research agenda but provides an emphasis on a rather neglected area of study, which is the positioning of traditionally marginalised social groups in the public sphere. The analysis presented in this chapter looks in particular at the development of a European discourse about the need to engage and include these groups in public policy-making. As we will see below, European institutions, and the European Commission in particular, have played a key role in shaping the policy agenda on target groups such as young people, women, minorities and migrants.

European citizenship, civil society and political participation: current policies and development

The scholarly debate on the development and value of European citizenship has been accompanied by an institutional self-reflectivity on the functionality of this status for improving the legitimacy of the EU. A key player in pushing the institutional agenda on the definition of European citizenship has undoubtedly been the European Commission which, especially since 2000, has produced a wide official discourse on the best way to face the aforementioned deficits afflicting European integration. This positioning of the European Commission has been particularly evident since the governance reform of 2001, when it was recognised that:

> We have European Union but citizenship of the Union is much more a legal than political reality. Despite well-established supranational political institutions, citizens have little in the way of a European political consciousness and are not given much encouragement nor facility to engage in a consistent political dialogue with these institutions. The Union's institutions do not have a relationship with the general public that remotely compares with that of national institutions. This is part of the 'democratic deficit'. (CEC 2001a: 7)

As we will remark again later, the governance reform played a central role in fostering a new approach to policy-making based on open and transparent participation by civil society. In this context, information and communication have become priorities for the European Commission, which has focused on improving structures, increasing resources and developing routines for better and fuller communication with the citizens of Europe (see also CEC 2001b, 2001c). In some ways, the 'governance reform' of 2001 (CEC 2001a) and the subsequent 'period of reflection' that began in 2005 led the European Commission into promoting the use of dialogic and interactive instruments in its approach to citizenship, by fostering a communication policy (Bee 2010).

More recently, the publication of the Plan D for Democracy, Dialogue and Debate (CEC 2005a) and the White Paper on a European Communication Policy (CEC 2006a) show a renewed attempt to develop a two-way model of institutional communication in the EU, based on active citizenship. The engagement with civil society actors has become extremely relevant in order to improve standards in terms of input legitimacy to public policies and by consequence to promote outputs based on participatory approaches. The legitimacy function performed by this increasing role given to civil society organisations is rather evident as, for example, Kohler-Koch, in commenting upon the different traditions of studies on civil society, describes:

> Civil society brings added value to EU decision-making since it presents the plurality of interests, values and tastes of the Europeans. EU institutions are not just looking for transmission belts which convey demands and concerns from the grass roots to the upper levels of decision-making but for transnational structures able to distil and aggregate interests across borders. By giving citizens a voice and by bringing additional knowledge to the decision-making process, organised civil society is expected to contribute both to the input and output legitimacy of the EU system. (Kohler-Koch 2009: 50)

As research shows, it can thus be argued that policy actions aimed at developing a system of participatory democracy pushed forward by the European Commission (CEC 2005a; CEC 2006a; CEC 2008a) are characterised by the attempt to improve engagement with organised civil society (Kohler-Koch and Rittberger 2007; Greenwood and Halpin 2007) in order to provide a better basis of legitimisation for policy processes. The goal declared by the European Commission is to develop a basis for a civic republican model of civic engagement based on a citizen-centred approach (CEC 2006a: 4) and on the development of a European-wide public sphere. The aim is to establish the means to engage more and better citizens with European affairs.

The launch of the Citizenship Programme 2007–13 fits in this context and enhances the principles established by the previous framework for shaping European Active Citizenship coordinated by the DG Education and Culture from 2004 to 2006. The new strategic supervision of the programme under the DG Communication is worth noticing and is coherent with the overall strategy undertaken by the European Commission with the Plan D and White Paper on Communication. Overall, the DG Communication, under the direction of Ms Margot Wallström, vice-president of the European Commission in the period 2004–10, has played an active role in the attempt to equate the democratic deficit with a communication deficit to be challenged by improving political participation and engagement in public policy processes.

As remarked in the programme, the new actions regarding active citizenship are meant to shape the institutional relationship with the citizenry of the European Union and 'materialises the legal framework to support a wide range of activities and organisations promoting "active European citizenship", i.e. the involvement of citizens and civil society organisations in the process of European integration' (CEC 2007a: 3). The strengthening of the dialogic and communicative relationship between citizens and institutions is widely reaffirmed in this programme. Between the four core aims of the Citizenship Programme 2007–13, it is relevant to point out the recognition of the necessity to give citizens the 'opportunity to interact and participate in constructing an ever closer Europe, which is democratic and world-oriented, united in and enriched through its cultural diversity, thus developing citizenship of the European Union' (CEC 2007a: 4)

This dialogic relationship between institutions on the one hand and civil society on the other has recently been formalised by Article 11 of the Lisbon Treaty. This established that 'The institutions shall maintain an open, transparent and regular dialogue with representative associations and civil society' (Article 11.2) and that 'The European Commission shall carry out broad consultations with parties concerned in order to ensure that the Union's actions are coherent and transparent' (Article 11.3). It is worth mentioning, however, that engagement in public consultations has been a common practice by the European Commission at least since the governance reform of 2001. In this regard, Article 11 therefore simply formalises an already existing practice of engagement between institutions and civil society.

In evaluating this approach to civic engagement and active citizenship, it is worth underlining that, even if welcomed, the strategy undertaken by the European institutions and the European Commission in particular has been subject to criticism in the literature on governance studies (Magnette 2003; Kohler-Koch 2009; Smismans 2007, 2009). Overall, it is argued that the approach to governance followed by the European Commission suffers from being an account of political and civic participation that could be considered as being selectivist rather than inclusive of the whole of civil society. The emphasis on the term *organised civil society* is representative of this approach. This is a danger that Magnette noted when commenting on the principles of governance and the measures put in place to enhance civic and political participation in the time-context following the governance reform. The scholar argued that these instruments 'are only designed to stimulate the involvement of active citizens and groups in some precise procedures, and not to enhance the general level of civic consciousness and participation' (Magnette 2003: 5).

Moreover, as a consequence of the preceding consideration, another element for discussion emerging in the literature has to be noted. As Heidbreder argues, for example, the 'increased participation of civil society was not primarily the result of a bottom-up process in which civil society pressured for access into EU decision-making' (Heidbreder 2012: 16). This top-down development of organised civil society is thus stimulated by the European Commission's necessity to formalise procedures, norms and practices that enhance the possibilities to actually participate in the governance of the EU rather than stimulate an open and transparent system of participatory democracy. The limitations and the ambiguities of this approach to active citizenship are thus widely remarked. Kohler-Koch, on this account, expresses quite clearly this evaluation by arguing that: 'though European citizenship is a cherished concept in the EU, it is not linked to the idea of a politically active European civil society' (2009: 55). The analysis that we conducted was aimed at understanding whether these considerations are true and whether the European approach to active citizenship is based on a simple formalisation of procedures and principles of mutual engagement, or whether, instead, there is a practice of active citizenship under development.

Integrating structuralism and critical discourse analysis: the construction of discursive nodal points

The methodological approach that we adopted is qualitative and focuses on the application of discourse analysis (DA) to EU policy documents. The main aim of DA is to understand the role of language and communications in shaping the social world and influencing social action and policies (Dryzek 2008; Hajer 2002; Howart and Torfing 2005). In this chapter, we focus on public discourses emerging at the European level in order to understand the positioning of institutional actors in regard to policies of active citizenship. In order to carry out the analysis, we constructed a methodology based on insights derived from different traditions of discourse analysis that, in our point of view, are complementary.

Philips and Hardy (2002) identify at least four mainstream traditions of discourse analysis that emerge from the literature (see Figure 20.1). As represented in Figure 20.1, the horizontal continuum divides approaches to discourse analysis on the basis of their analytical focus on either the role that language and structures play in the social construction of the reality (on the left side) or on the power relations between a variety of policy actors that shape dominant meanings of specific political concepts (on the right side). On the vertical continuum, we can instead divide

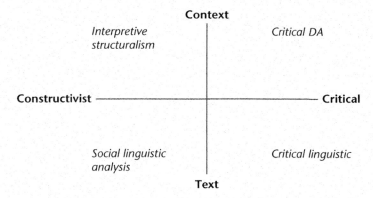

FIGURE 20.1 Traditions of discourse analysis
Source: Philips and Hardy (2002: 20).

discourse analysis traditions by looking at the importance given either to the text that describes the significance of a specific idea or the context in which meaning is produced and shaped.

In the model of policy analysis that we present in this chapter (see also Bee and Guerrina 2014) we looked at the development of various stages of the policy cycle, with a focus on the construction of the agenda setting by different institutional policy actors. We developed our model of discourse analysis by integrating insights from structuralism and critical discourse analysis. In regard to the former, we looked at the importance played by the power relations existing between various policy actors and at their struggle to shape meaning on specific policy concepts that become 'discursive nodal points' (DNPs). In regard to the latter, we looked at the importance that the political context plays in shaping DNPs and in orientating the political strategies of public institutions.

On the one hand, the context of the production of meaning around key political concepts is particularly important in critical discourse analysis (CDA) (Wodak and Fairclough 1997). Following the suggestions of CDA scholars, our analytical framework looked at the specific events that shaped the priority to develop policies of active engagement by the European institutions and by the European Commission in particular (see Table 20.1).

On the other hand, structuralist scholars attempt to understand who imposes specific meanings on social realities and, in short, who participates (or not) in the framing of public discourses and in the social construction of reality. The concept of hegemonic discourse, elaborated by Laclau and Mouffe, is central in this account (Laclau and Mouffe 1985). Different discourses in fact take place at the same time, competing with each other, challenging each other and often overlapping each other. In analytical terms, our scope is to understand why particular meanings become dominant and authoritative, while others are discredited in a precise time context. Diez (2001) refers to Europe as a 'discursive battleground' to represent the

TABLE 20.1 Micro-events in the period 2004–10

Date	Key event	Impact on constitutional debate
May 2004	Enlargement	Accession of 12 new member states
June 2005	Failure of referenda in France and the Netherlands	Start of the 'crisis of Europe'
October 2005	Negotiations with Turkey	Discussion about European boundaries
November 2005	Elections in Germany	Emergence of Merkel as a central political figure for bringing Europe out of crisis
December 2005	European Council under British presidency	Discussion on the divisions between different visions of Europe
February 2006	Approval of the Bokenstein Directive	Discussion on the 'costs of the enlargement' and their part in the European crisis
September 2006	Sarkozy advocates for a Mini Treaty	Start of the discussion on the future of Europe
January 2007	Enlargement	Accession of two member states (Bulgaria and Romania)
March 2007	Celebrations of the Rome Treaty	Discussion on the values of Europe and draft of the Berlin declaration
June 2007	Brussels meeting	Discussion on the results of the European Council
June 2008	Irish rejection of Lisbon Treaty	Discussion on the future of European integration
June 2009	European elections	Discussion on the EU's political identity
October 2009	Change of Commission Presidency	End of Barroso Commission
October 2009	New referendum in Ireland on the Lisbon Treaty	Approval of the Lisbon Treaty/ re-launch of the European Project
March 2010	Europe 2020	Proposal on Europe 2020 by the European Commission

idea of the different ongoing struggles over the shaping of meaning in public discourses related to key policy concepts, which can be considered to form DNPs (Diez 2001: 16). Diez refers to the idea of 'articulation' elaborated by Laclau and Mouffe (1985) in order to describe the set of discursive practices and metanarratives that fix the precise meaning of a DNP.

In our approach, DNPs are defined by a combination of variables such as context, policy priorities and metanarratives (see Figure 20.2). We argue that active

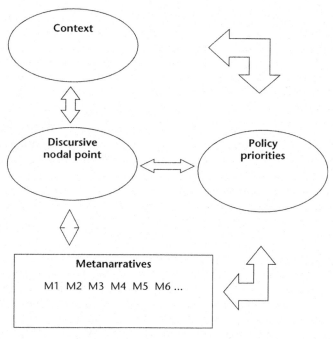

FIGURE 20.2 The structure of discursive nodal points (DNPs)

citizenship as a European Commission-sponsored policy is introduced into the policy agenda because of the combination of four DNPs:

- democratisation and public sphere;
- Europeanisation and transnationalisation;
- political participation and civil dialogue;
- European social dimension.

The discursive bargaining takes place between a number of institutional and non-institutional actors in order to shape meaning – thus the DNPs provide useful insights on convergence as well as fragmentation in the agenda-setting process at the EU level. These nodes appear across a range of documents of the European Commission during Barroso 1. They can therefore be identified as key policy priorities and preoccupations for the organisation. In the following section, we provide an account of the discourse elaborated by the European Commission in order to associate meaning with these four DNPs.

Policy areas: youth, women, migrants and minorities

This section seeks to provide an overview of the main European policy priorities in the project's time frame. It sets out the aims of key policies and provides a brief analysis of the dominant discourses emerging at the European level targeting the four main social groups that were of interest in the broader PIDOP project (i.e. youth, women, migrants and minorities).

European discourses on youth

In the last few years, youth policy has received growing attention from the European institutions, particularly the European Commission. The DG Education and Culture (DG EAC) has the main responsibility for implementing the policy. This comprises two youth units: Unit D1 is responsible for the policy aspects while Unit D2 is in charge of the management of the Youth in Action programme. In terms of historical background, the shaping of the policy itself has been going on since 2001, when the European Commission published a White Paper on Youth (CEC 2001d). This document is particularly relevant for the discussion presented here as it is an example of a *participatory* approach to policy-making. A number of European organisations were included in the drafting process and were invited to Brussels to contribute to the framing of the entire policy. A fundamental concept which drives the implementation of the Youth Policy is the enhancement of active citizenship as a key principle that should encompass all actions in this area.

The Youth in Action programme (2007–13) is the specific financial instrument in the youth field that has supported the political processes launched at the European level in recent years. This programme is oriented at financing actions in various fields and, from an analytical point of view, is central because it activates processes of transnationalisation between different organisations in Europe. Youth in Action is oriented at financing actions in the following areas: Action 1 – Youth for Europe; Action 2 – European Voluntary Service; Action 3 – Youth in the World; Action 4 – Youth Support Systems; Action 5 – Support for European Cooperation in the Youth Field. A number of policy fields are currently covered in the programme and relate to actions to be taken to improve the European social dimension (for example in domains such as education, employment, health and social inclusion). Youth policies are also currently part of the newly launched Europe 2020 programme, Youth on the Move being one of its key flagship initiatives.

The emphasis on practices of civic engagement, active citizenship and civil dialogue is recurrent in our analysis. The sample that we included consisted of official documents that have been produced by the European Commission in the time period 2004–10. The documents provide an emphasis on metanarratives oriented at shaping meaning around the four PIDOP DNPs described above. Table 20.2 shows a summary of the dominant narratives that surround these four DNPs.

The DNP *democratisation and public sphere* is established as an umbrella dominant discourse that surrounds the overall sample of policy documents that we analysed. The centrality of this policy discourse is thus often remarked upon. Young people are seen as key actors in the process of shaping the EU's democratisation:

TABLE 20.2 Emerging discourses and policy development in youth policy

Processes (DNPs)	Dominant narratives
Democratisation and public sphere	Recognition of young people's centrality in the development of the public sphere
Europeanisation and transnationalisation	Enhancement of transnational cooperation between organisations representing young people
Political participation	Mechanisms to foster active engagement
European social dimension	Priority areas: education and training, employment and social inclusion, health and anti-discrimination

Youth participation in democratic institutions and in a continuous dialogue with policy makers is essential to the sound functioning of our democracies and the sustainability of policies which impact on young people's lives. The Commission recently called on Member States to continue their efforts to increase youth participation and formulate coherent information strategies for young people. The Commission also launched a genuine dialogue with young people, structured from the local through to the European level, which needs to be fully implemented. The European Youth Summit 'Your Europe' held in Rome in March 2007, the European Youth Week and regular Presidency Youth events are positive steps towards such a structured dialogue with young people. Involvement in cultural activities can also enable young people to express their creative energy and contribute to fostering active citizenship. (CEC 2007b: 9)

The DNP is enforced by the link with the processes of *Europeanisation and transnationalisation*, the second discourse that emerges as dominant in our analysis and is transversal across our sample. The shaping of collaborations and interchange between youth organisations in Europe, the promotion of European cooperation in the youth field as well as the enhancement of the European voluntary service are seen as cornerstones of the youth programmes. This clearly has the function – coherently with a number of European mobility programmes – to favour an exchange of practices, knowledge and ideas that is pivotal for favouring social interaction and socialisation processes in the wider European territory. It can therefore be argued that these two DNPs are closely interlinked. It is not by chance that it is often stated by the European Commission that youth policy should be based on a dual strategy that includes actions in two areas: *Investing in Youth* and *Empowering Youth* (CEC 2009a: 4).

In the overall discourse, the presence of a high number of metanarratives aimed at improving *political participation* in the EU – our third DNP – and at shaping the *European social dimension* – our fourth DNP – is extremely relevant. Youth policy is considered to be the flagship initiative (as noted further by the European Commission in programmes such as the new Europe 2020) in order to develop further a specific meaning regarding active citizenship.

A direct link between the fostering of European active citizenship and the fight against discrimination is addressed in the *Decision Establishing the Youth in Action Programme for the period 2007 to 2013*. The stated policy priority is to intertwine these two dimensions:

> There is a need to promote active citizenship and, when implementing the action lines, step up the fight against exclusion and discrimination in all their forms, including those based on sex, racial or ethnic origin, religion or belief, disability, age or sexual orientation, in accordance with Article 13(1) of the Treaty. (CEC 2006b: 2)

In terms of overall purposes, we find this strategy to be coherent with the European Commission's design of European citizenship. As we remarked in the second section of this chapter, this is oriented at shaping a consciousness of belonging to a transnational public space that should be complementary to the identification with the national space. In this framework, social responsibility, a key component of civic-republican interpretations of citizenship, is a key factor that needs to be stimulated because it motivates social inclusion and mutual solidarity between young people in Europe. The link with the overall discourse regarding the European Social Dimension is therefore extremely relevant. Recurrent narratives in the documents analysed outline the need to favour social inclusion and to promote an inclusive approach to youth policy that is meant to target especially young people in disadvantaged positions as well as the key target group of women. Intersectionality is thus an issue that is taken into account but, in our point of view, is not fully developed in European discourse, as we will argue later. Youth engagement, at this stage of development, seems to be regarding youth organisations in general, with a less prominent role given to more specific groups. Evidence from our documents show that the metanarratives shaping this DNP slightly change in the documentation produced in 2010 that opened more convincingly the way for a concern towards the issue of intersectionality.

European discourses on women

Gender equality has a long history within the EU, having been included within the founding treaties. Since then it has received a substantial amount of policy attention, making it one of the most widely developed areas in the field of European social policy. Within the European Commission, the body responsible for leading policy developments in this field is DG Employment, Social Affairs and Equal Opportunities. The stated aims of this body are to work towards the *creation of more and better jobs, an inclusive society and equal opportunities for all*. Examples of the areas in which this DG is active include support for improving the quality and quantity of employment opportunities for women through the European Employment Strategy; the free movement of workers and coordination of social security schemes; the improvement of working conditions; the development of social dialogue at European level; the modernisation of labour relations and providing assistance to EU workers who want to be mobile; social inclusion and non-discrimination; and the support and promotion of equality between men and women. This set of actions highlights the wide-reaching policy agenda bestowed upon this DG. In the field of gender equality, it has sought to consolidate the overall objectives entrenched within the Treaties through action programmes, directives and regulations as well as a number of other soft policy measures that seek to expand the reach of European policies in this field.

Particularly important in the context of the analysis presented here is *The Roadmap for Gender Equality (2006–2010)*. The Roadmap seeks to promote a broad-based approach to equality that moves beyond formal rights. It identifies six priority areas:

1. Economic Independence
2. Reconciliation between Work and Family Life
3. Representation in Decision-Making
4. Gender-Based Violence
5. Gender Stereotypes
6. Promoting Gender Norms in External Relations.

The sample of articles included in our analysis comprises official documents that have been produced by the European institutions in the time period 2004–10. Table 20.3 shows a summary of the dominant narratives that surround these four DNPs.

The core documents produced in the time period 2004–10 are coherent with the principles established in the Roadmap. It is also worth noticing that much of the rhetoric that underpins the Roadmap has appeared before in various European-level policy documents, and thus it represents as much a reaffirmation of well-rehearsed European objectives in the field of equality between men and women, as a departure from the equality agenda established over the last 30 years. Enhancing

TABLE 20.3 Emerging discourses and policy development in gender policy

Processes (DNPs)	*Dominant narratives*
Democratisation and public sphere	Enhancement of women's participation in policy-making processes
Europeanisation and transnationalisation	Recognition of the need to start partnerships with the civil society
Political participation	Active engagement seen as functional to policy-making processes
European social dimension	Priority areas: gender mainstreaming, gender equality, social inclusion, gender violence, employment

women's voice in decision-making is part of the wider drive by the EU to improve democratic governance and thus needs to be seen in the context of current debates about improving the links between the EU and its citizens. This has recently been reaffirmed in the new *Strategy for equality between women and men 2010–2015*, where it is stated that:

> In most Member States, women continue to be under-represented in decision-making processes and positions, in particular at the highest levels, despite the fact that they make up nearly half the workforce and more than half of new university graduates in the EU. (CEC 2010a: 7)

This socio-political need, ensuring participation in the policy-making, is constituted by a set of similar metanarratives that shape meaning regarding the DNP on *democratisation and public sphere*. Ensuring the right to participate is considered to be a fundamental right that frames the European discourse on gender policy and it is key in terms of democratic performance. However, it is worth noticing that there are no narratives that identify women as a group as an active actor in the public sphere; instead, much of the discussion is concentrated on the modalities to ensure participation in decision-making. This distinction, we believe, is important, because it emerges from the necessity to ensure public participation as a key factor. However this is not established as a democratic principle in the full sense, since there is no mention of the potential role that the subgroup could play in the wider public sphere.

These considerations are key for introducing the discussion regarding our second DNP, which is *Europeanisation and transnationalisation*. While in the case of youth it was quite evident that there was a need to stimulate a set of organised interests at the transnational level around the policy, in this case we can identify a lack of concern regarding the mobilisation of groups of civil society around gender issues. This is important as well in regard to the political participation of women. Principles of social justice and gender equality are seen as fundamental rights to be achievable through the active participation of women in policy-making processes. It appears quite evident, however, that there is no consciousness by the European Commission of what active participation for women should entail and that this endeavour is still an object of reflection at the European level. The framing of the DNP *political participation* is thus characterised by a set of metanarratives that provides emphasis on the functionality of increasing women's participation in the policy process, without providing a better orientation for the actual engagement with civil society organisations. The vagueness of this approach is well expressed in the following extract taken from the Roadmap, where the Commission recognises that:

> Major progress still has to be achieved in the key areas identified in this Roadmap and this requires better governance at all levels: EU institutions, Member States, parliaments, social partners and civil society. (CEC 2006c: 11)

The urgency of starting a better and more inclusive dialogue with civil society, and more precisely with specific stakeholders, is commented on in the Mid Term Progress Report of 2008, which states that:

> Policies always have an impact on women and men where they involve the citizen, the economy and society. Nevertheless, insufficient account is often taken of such impacts in some fields covered by Community policies. It is in those fields where less attention has traditionally been paid to equality issues that particular vigilance is required and the awareness of stakeholders must be raised. (CEC 2008b: 9)

The need to reinforce cooperation with civil society is thus remarked quite extensively in our sample, showing, however, evidence of delay in enhancing a structured dialogue between institutions and NGOs. This raises issues regarding the governance of gender policy at the EU level, which, from our point of view, is still not fully inclusive and based on participatory means.

The final issue that we want to unpack regarding the fourth DNP, *European social dimension*, consists of recurrent metanarratives in the documents analysed. The eradication of gender-based violence, the improvement of working conditions, the elimination of gender stereotypes and gender mainstreaming are perhaps the most ambitious policy goals outlined in the EU's discourse. Gender equality is considered a core value that should orient the future elaboration of public policies at the EU level. This is remarked, for example, in the 2010 Women's Charter:

> Discrimination, educational stereotypes, labour market segregation, precarious employment conditions, involuntary part-time work and the unbalanced sharing of care responsibilities with men affect the life choices and the economic independence of many women. We reaffirm our commitment to ensure the full realisation of women's potential and the full use of their skills, to facilitate a better gender distribution on the labour market and more quality jobs for women. We will resolutely promote gender equality in the Europe 2020 strategy, consider quantified targets where appropriate, and promote genuine opportunities for both women and men to enjoy a work-life balance. (CEC 2010b: 3)

The need to ensure social protection for women is clearly elaborated in respect to the current context of the socio-economic crisis. In this regard, the wide concern about the possible consequences of the crisis for women is remarked by Barroso who, in presenting the Charter in a press conference, commented that: 'Especially in times of crisis, we need to incorporate the gender dimension in all of our policies, for the benefit of both women and men' (CEC 2010c: 1). The stress on the importance of gender mainstreaming is certainly remarkable. In our view, however, the ambiguous approach regarding women's active citizenship undermines the actual practice of this principle.

European discourses on migrants and minorities

The core institutional actor that deals with this social group within the European Commission is the DG Employment, Social Affairs and Equal Opportunities. From a historical point of view, it is worth underlining that drawing on the wide range of policies, EU legislation takes a broad approach to the issue of migrants and minorities and much of the policy discourse is to be found in the anti-discrimination set of policies. In particular, Article 13 of the Amsterdam Treaty 'gives the Community specific powers to take action to combat discrimination based on sex, racial or ethnic origin, religion or belief, disability, age or sexual orientation'. In general terms the following objectives have been established: to improve knowledge of discrimination, and to raise awareness of citizens' rights and the benefits of diversity (as well as the cost of non-equality). Some recent actions and directives that frame anti-discrimination policies are:

1. The Framework Decision on Combating Racism and Xenophobia of 2008
2. The Campaign 'For Diversity. Against Discrimination' launched in 2003 and shaped more prominently after 2005
3. The Hague Programme (2005–10).

These policies have similar priorities and seek to support and strengthen the principles established within the treaties. The Framework Decision on Combating Racism and Xenophobia ensures that racism and xenophobia are punishable by effective, proportionate and dissuasive criminal penalties in the European Union. Furthermore, it aims to improve and encourage judicial cooperation in this field. The purpose of the Campaign 'For Diversity. Against Discrimination' is to raise awareness of discrimination and increase understanding of the EU laws. It also strives to generate debate on the theme of diversity. Finally, the Hague Programme 2005–10 fixes the priorities for an area of freedom, security and justice. It is worth mentioning the great emphasis that is given to ensuring the full development of policies enhancing citizenship, monitoring and promoting respect for fundamental rights, improvements and shaping of integration policies.

In our sample we looked at a number of documents that deal with anti-discrimination policy and that target specifically migrants and minorities as a core social group. Table 20.4 summarises the dominant narratives that frame the four relevant DNPs for our analysis.

Discrimination is seen as the principal factor that undermines the full engagement of minority groups and migrants in the EU's public policy process. On this account, it can be argued that the narratives framing our first DNP are directed towards the fight against any discriminatory practice that hinders minority groups from being fully included in policy-making. Migrants and minorities are mirrored as a weak social group that do not play a key role in the EU's policy-making because of the scarce possibilities to engage, interact, exchange practices and have an impact. With regard to the second DNP, the sample provides evidence of a

TABLE 20.4 Emerging discourses and policy development in anti-discrimination policy

Processes (DNPs)	Dominant narratives
Democratisation and public sphere	Anti-discrimination as a fundamental right for the democratisation process
Europeanisation and transnationalisation	Promotion of European norms in the member states to raise awareness of anti-discrimination
Political participation	Engagement with NGOs to ensure a better governance of the policy
European social dimension	Promotion of social inclusion and anti-discrimination in a number of policy fields

wide discussion regarding the *Europeanisation* of public communication in the anti-discrimination field and on the need to bridge between different policy networks currently acting in Europe in order to raise awareness of the harm produced by discrimination. In this regard, we found evidence of a set of narratives promoting a process of top-down Europeanisation. This is characterised by the European Commission attempting to dictate standards though soft law mechanisms both to national governments and civil society actors. An example that is highly representative of this scenario can be taken from this extract, emerging from the analysis of the document *Communicating equality and non-discrimination in the European Union*:

> Getting the message across that Europe values diversity and is taking discrimination seriously is crucial for the successful implementation of the legislative and policy framework put in place at EU and national levels. Firstly, rights and obligations have to be known and understood to be effective. Information about the law is vital for potential victims to make real use of legislation and for employers, service providers or administrations to know their duties in this field. Secondly, beyond the application of rights, prejudice can destroy people's lives. Fighting stereotypes and deeply rooted patterns of thinking based on fear and lack of knowledge is difficult but crucial. The EU has set aside funding to raise awareness of the legislative framework amongst the general public as well as people working in the anti-discrimination field. (CEC 2008c: 3)

Seeking support from NGOs and more broadly from civil society is seen as key for the European Commission in the attempt to fight discrimination across Europe. For this reason, the metanarratives framing the DNP on *political participation* are quite directly oriented at stimulating a dialogic approach with the scope of fighting discrimination. The focus on social partners and civil society is seen as particularly important as they are the main actors in implementing the core policy objectives entrenched within the anti-discriminatory framework to support the development of equality policies at the national level and encourage exchange of good practices between member states:

> The European Commission values the importance of working with and bringing together a broad range of organisations representing minority groups in Europe. These organisations form the vital link in informing not only the groups they represent but also of raising awareness amongst the general public at large. (CEC 2008c: 6)

> Equality and non-discrimination non-governmental organisations (NGOs) play a dual role in combating discrimination. First, they often provide direct support and advice to victims of discrimination and those most at risk of unfair treatment. They also use their on-the-ground experience to provide invaluable input to anti-discrimination policy at all levels. European level cooperation with NGOs and NGO networks is mutually beneficial in both of these areas. (CEC 2009b: 13)

In line with the considerations that we outlined in the second section of this chapter, civil society is seen as functional in order to provide a better and more appropriate engagement in the drafting of public policies rather than as an active actor to be included in broader participatory processes. In other words, as it emerges from the reading of the second extract, civil society is key in providing inputs. Yet, as in the case study outlined above, the instruments to ensure full participation in the public sphere are not addressed.

Anti-discrimination policy is driven by the need to enhance the *European social dimension* and in this regard we find a large number of metanarratives that are key in order to shape meaning on the fourth DNP. The overall aims to enhance social inclusion and by consequence to combat any form of social exclusion underpin all debates and developments seeking to address access to employment and political participation for migrants and minorities.

The European Commission has clearly remarked that social exclusion in a number of key areas (such as employment, health, housing, education) is still undermining the possibilities for minorities to be fully integrated. In the *New framework for the open coordination of social protection and inclusion policies in the European Union* the European Commission outlines a number of key policy areas, trying to bring them to the attention of the member states:

> Particularly for social inclusion, the more general presentation of objectives should allow Member States to focus on the policy priorities most important in each national context, for example, homelessness, child poverty and the alienation of youth, immigrants and ethnic minorities, disability, e-inclusion or inequalities in education and training. (CEC 2005b: 5)

The *New framework* is important for shaping the DNP because it establishes the overall policy objective of ensuring *active social inclusion*. Besides, it addresses the issue of intersectionality, prioritising the necessity to provide the basis for activating a full concern regarding gender mainstreaming. It is in fact remarked that the European Commission action should:

> Ensure that social inclusion policies are well-coordinated and involve all levels of government and relevant actors, including people experiencing poverty, that they are efficient and effective and mainstreamed into all relevant public policies, including economic, budgetary, education and training policies and structural fund (notably ESF) programmes and that they are gender mainstreamed. (CEC 2005b: 6)

This is a very important point in the light of the above discussion, since it establishes cross-sectional measures between policy programmes in order to guarantee full participation and inclusion in policy-making. It is, however, worth noticing that, in our view, according to the data we analysed, this is not a fully developed issue in the policy documentation published in the time-context of our concern. This means that gender mainstreaming is affirmed as a principle but, given the lack of indication of the actual instruments to be adopted, it can hardly be conceived as a working practice.

Conclusion

The analysis that we have presented in this chapter shows evidence of an ambiguous and rather ambivalent approach by the European Commission towards the issue of active citizenship. The reflection upon participatory democracy is a key discourse in the background of the framing of youth policy. Young people are seen as active agents in the public sphere, central for enhancing the democratisation process and functional in the prospect of fostering the European social dimension. However, our analysis provides evidence of the fact that when it comes to discussing the role of women, migrants and minorities, the approach undertaken by the European Commission is still at an initial stage and based mostly on a wider reflection on the best ways to collaborate with civil society for improving European governance, rather than ensuring their full participation in European politics and, more generally, in the public sphere. In the field of anti-discrimination policy, however, the role of civil society is seen as being fundamental in order to provide a more inclusive style of policy-making, whereas in the field of gender policy this approach is still at an initial stage and is not fully developed. The scenario emerging from our assessment clearly emphasises a passive rather than an active role played by civil society in policy-making processes. This is in line with the findings of studies on European civil society that we addressed in the second section of this chapter.

However, we discuss elsewhere the actual engagement of organised civil society at the EU level (based on further empirical work that was conducted as part of the

PIDOP project), and there we provide an account of the counter-discourses that challenge dominant institutional frames (Bee and Guerrina 2014). Our research provides evidence of a 'proactivity' played by the organisations in Brussels in shaping the policy agenda in the time-context in which our analysis was conducted. In short, we looked at the whole set of the pressures emerging from umbrella organisations in Brussels to challenge this dominant top-down vision of a civil society at the service of the European institutions. Social NGOs (such as the European Women's Lobby, the Social Platform, the European Youth Forum and the European Network Against Racism) have been widely reflecting on their role in the broader European constituency and confronting each other on the bottom-up processes that could drive the change from a system based on participation in EU governance to a system of European participatory democracy. As we argue, however, the possibilities to actually produce counter discourse regarding democratic participation are still limited and not fully taken into account by the European Commission. Overall, it is worth underlining, as we argue in the fourth section of this chapter, that the emphasis on active citizenship proposed by the European Commission is still highly exclusionary and does not take the role of marginalised groups into account. Using the formulation of Roche (1997) that we referred to in the first section of this chapter, we can argue that a wide number of 'denizens' are still excluded from policy processes at the EU level, but more importantly they still remain at the periphery, considered as marginal and weak groups, not fully integrated in the public sphere and not entitled to act as active citizens. Here, from our point of view, stand all the limitations to the European approach to civic engagement and active citizenship.

List of official documents

CEC (1985) *A People's Europe. Reports from the ad hoc Committee*. Bulletin of the European Communities, Supplement 7/85.
CEC (2001a) *European Governance: A White Paper*. COM (2001) 428 final.
CEC (2001b) *White Paper on European Governance: Work Area n. 1: Report of Working Group on broadening and enriching the public debate on European matters* (Group 1a) June 2001.
CEC (2001c) *White Paper on European Governance: Work Area n. 4: Report of Working Group on networking people for a good governance in Europe* (Group 4b) May 2001.
CEC (2001d) *White Paper: A new impetus for European youth*. COM (2001) 681 final.
CEC (2005a) *The Commission's contribution to the period of reflection and beyond: Plan-D for Democracy, Dialogue and Debate*. COM (2005) 494 final.
CEC (2005b) *Working together, working better: A new framework for the open coordination of social protection and inclusion policies in the European Union*. COM (2005) 706 final.
CEC (2006a) *White Paper on a European Communication Policy*. COM (2006) 35 final.
CEC (2006b) Decision No. 1719/2006/EC of the European Parliament and of the Council of 15 November 2006 establishing the Youth in Action programme for the period 2007 to 2013. *Official Journal of the European Union*, 24.11.2006.
CEC (2006c) *A Roadmap for equality between women and men 2006–2010*. COM/2006/0092 final.
CEC (2007a) *Europe for Citizens Programme 2007–2013*. Europe for Citizens – Programme Guide – version – December 2007.

CEC (2007b) *Promoting young people's full participation in education, employment and society.* COM (2007) 498 final.
CEC (2008a) *Debate Europe — building on the experience of Plan D for Democracy, Dialogue and Debate.* COM (2008) 158.
CEC (2008b) *Mid-term progress report on the roadmap for equality between women and men (2006–2010).*
CEC (2008c) *Communicating Equality and Non-discrimination in the European Union.* Directorate-General for Employment, Social Affairs and Equal Opportunities Unit G.4.
CEC (2009a) *An EU Strategy for Youth – Investing and Empowering: A renewed open method of coordination to address youth challenges and opportunities.* COM (2009) 200 final.
CEC (2009b) *EU action against discrimination: Activity report 2007–08.* Directorate-General for Employment, Social Affairs and Equal Opportunities Unit G4.
CEC (2010a) *Strategy for equality between women and men 2010–2015.* COM (2010) 491 final.
CEC (2010b) *A strengthened commitment to equality between women and men: A women's charter.* COM (2010) 78 final.
CEC (2010c) *European Commission strengthens its commitment to equality between women and men.* IP/10/237, Brussels, 5 March 2010.

References

Bee, C. (2010) 'Understanding the EU's institutional communication. Principles and structure of a contested policy', in C. Bee and E. Bozzini (eds), *Mapping the European Public Sphere: Institutions, Media and Civil Society.* London: Ashgate.
Bee, C. and Guerrina, R. (2014) 'Participation, dialogue, and civic engagement: understanding the role of organized civil society in promoting active citizenship in the European Union', *Journal of Civil Society*, 10 (1): 29–50.
Bellamy, R. (2000) *Rethinking Liberalism.* London: Pinter.
Boje, T. (2010) 'Commentary: participatory democracy, active citizenship, and civic organizations – conditions for volunteering and activism', *Journal of Civil Society*, 6 (2): 189–92.
Checkel, J. (2001) 'The Europeanization of citizenship?', in J. Caporaso, M. Cowles and T. Risse (eds), *Transforming Europe: Europeanization and Domestic Change.* Ithaca, NY: Cornell University Press.
Checkel, J. (2009) *European Identity.* Cambridge: Cambridge University Press.
Christiansen, T., Jorgensen, K. E. and Wiener, A. (1999) 'The social construction of Europe', *Journal of European Public Policy*, 6 (4), Special Issue.
Closa, C. (1992) 'The concept of citizenship in the Treaty on EU', *Common Market Law Review*, 29.
Closa, C. (1995) 'Citizenship of the Union and nationality of the Member States'. In: *Common Market Law Review* 32.
Diez, T. (2001) 'Europe as a discursive battleground discourse analysis and European integration studies', *Cooperation and Conflict*, 36 (1): 5–38.
Dryzek, J. S. (2008) 'Policy analysis as critique', in M. Moran et al. (eds), *The Oxford Handbook of Public Policy.* Oxford: Oxford University Press.
Eriksen, E. (2004) *Conceptualizing European Public Spheres: General, Segmented and Strong Publics*, ARENA Working Paper 3/04. Available from: http//:www.arena.uio.no/publications/wp_04_03.pdf (last accessed 30 March 2010).
Faist, T. (2001) 'Social citizenship in the European Union: nested membership', *Journal of Common Market Studies*, 39 (1): 39–60.

Favell, A. and Recchi, E. (2011) 'Social mobility and spatial mobility', in A. Favell and V. Guiradon (eds) *Sociology of the European Union*. Basingstoke: Palgrave, pp. 50–76.

Follesdal, A. (2001) *Union Citizenship. Unpacking the Beast of Burden*, Arena Working Papers WP 01/9.

Greenwood, J. (2007) *Interest Representation in the European Union*. Basingstoke: Palgrave Macmillan.

Greenwood, J. and Halpin, D. (2007) 'The European Commission and the Public Governance of Interest Groups in the European Union: seeking a niche between accreditation and laissez-faire', *Perspectives on European Politics and Society*, 8 (2): 190–211.

Guerrina, R. (2005) *Mothering the Union: Gender Politics in the EU*. Manchester: Manchester University Press.

Guerrina, R. (2006) 'Constitutional politics in Europe: continuing trends in the politics of gender', *Identities: Journal for Politics Gender and Culture*, 4 (8/9): 9–35.

Habermas, J. (1994) 'Citizenship and national identity', in B. Van Steenbergen (ed.), *The Condition of Citizenship*. London: Sage, pp. 20–35.

Habermas, J. (2001) *The Postnational Constellation: Political Essays*. Cambridge: Polity Press.

Hajer, M. A. (2002) 'Discourse analysis and the study of policy making', *European Political Science*, 2 (1). Available online from: http://www.essex.ac.uk/ECPR/publications/eps/onlineissues/autumn2002/research/hajer.htm (last accessed 30 March 2010).

Heidbreder, E. G. (2012) 'Civil society participation in EU governance,' *Living Reviews in European Governance*, 7 (2).

Hoskins, B. and Kerr, D. (2012) *Final Study Summary and Policy Recommendations: Participatory Citizenship in the European Union*. Southampton: University of Southampton Education School. Available online at: http://eprints.soton.ac.uk/351210/1/__soton.ac.uk_ude_PersonalFiles_Users_aw2w07_mydocuments_Hoskins_Report%204%20Final%20study%20summary%20and%20policy%20recommendations%20.pdf (last accessed 20 September 2013).

Howart, D. and Torfing, J. (2005) *Discourse Theory in European Politics*. Basingstoke: Palgrave Macmillan.

Kantola, J. (2010) *Gender and the European Union*. Basingstoke: Palgrave Macmillan.

Kohler-Koch, B. (2009) 'The three worlds of European civil society – what role for civil society for what kind of Europe?', *Policy and Society*, 28: 47–57.

Kohler-Koch, B. and Rittberger, B. (eds) (2007) *Debating the Democratic Legitimacy of the European Union*. Lanham, MD: Rowman & Littlefield.

Kostakopolou, D. (2001) *Citizenship, Identity, and Immigration in the European Union: Between Past and Future*. Manchester and New York: Manchester University Press.

Kostakopoulou, D. (2008) 'The evolution of European Union citizenship', *European Political Science*, 7: 285–95.

Laclau, E. and Mouffe, C. (1985) *Hegemony and Socialist Strategy: Toward a Radical Democratic Politics*, 2nd edn. London: Verso.

Laffan, B. (2004) 'The European Union and its institutions as identity builders', in R. K. Herrmann, T. Risse and M. B. Brewer (eds), *Transnational Identities. Becoming European in the EU*. New York: Rowman & Littlefield.

Lehning, P. B. (1997) 'European citizenship: a mirage?', in P. B. Lehning and A. Weale (eds), *Citizenship, Democracy and Justice in the New Europe*. London: Routledge.

Magnette, P. (2003) 'European governance and civic participation: beyond elitist citizenship?', *Political Studies*, 51: 1–17.

Meehan, E. (1997) 'Citizenship and social inclusion in the European Union', in M. Roche and R. Van Berkel (eds), *European Citizenship and Social Exclusion*. Aldershot: Ashgate, pp. 23–34.

Miller, D. (2000) *Citizenship and National Identity*. Cambridge: Polity Press.
Mouffe, C. (1992) 'Democratic citizenship and the political community', in C. Mouffe (ed.), *Dimensions of Radical Democracy: Pluralism, Citizenship, Community*. London: Verso, pp. 225–39.
O'Keeffe, D. (1994) 'Union citizenship', in D. O'Keeffe and P. Twomey (eds), *Legal issues of the Maastricht Treaty*. West Sussex: Chancery Law Publishing.
O'Leary, S. (1995) 'The social dimension of community citizenship', in A. Rosas and A. Esko (eds), *A Citizens' Europe. In Search of a New Order*. London: Sage.
Philips, N. and Hardy, C. (2002) *Discourse Analysis: Investigating Processes of Social Construction*. London: Sage.
Risse, T. (2010) *A Community of Europeans? Transnational Identities and Public Spheres*. Ithaca, NY: Cornell University Press.
Roche, M. (1997) 'Citizenship and exclusion: reconstructing the European Union', in M. Roche and R. Van Berkel R. (eds), *European Citizenship and Social Exclusion*. Aldershot: Ashgate, pp. 3–22.
Roche, M. and Van Berkel, R. (eds) (1997) *European Citizenship and Social Exclusion*. Aldershot: Ashgate.
Ruzza, C. (2004) *Europe and Civil Society: Movements Coalitions and European Governance*. Manchester: Manchester University Press.
Sánchez-Salgado, R. (2007) 'Giving a European dimension to civil society organisations', *Journal of Civil Society*, 3 (3): 253–69.
Sassatelli, M. (2002) 'Imagined Europe: the shaping of a European cultural identity through EU cultural policy', *European Journal of Social Theory*, 5: 435–51.
Sassatelli, M. (2009) *Becoming Europeans: Cultural Identity and Cultural Policies*. Basingstoke: Palgrave Macmillan.
Schlesinger, P. (2003) *The Babel of Europe. An Essay on Networks and Communicative Spaces*, Arena Working Paper No. 22.
Shore, C. (1994) 'Citizens' Europe and the construction of European identity', in V. A. Goddard, J. R. Llobera and C. Shore (eds), *The Anthropology of Europe. Identities and Boundaries in Conflict*. Oxford: Berg.
Shore, C. (2000) *Building Europe. The Cultural Politics of European Integration*. London: Routledge.
Smismans, S. (2007) 'New governance – the solution for active European citizenship, or the end of citizenship?', *Columbia Journal of European Law*, 13 (3): 595–622.
Smismans, S. (2008) 'New modes of governance and the participatory myth', *West European Politics*, 32 (5): 87495.
Smismans, S. (2009) 'European civil society and citizenship: complementary or exclusionary concepts?', *Policy and Society*, 27 (4): 59–70.
Sykes, R. (1997) 'Social policy, social exclusion and citizenship in the European Union. The right to be unequal?', in M. Roche and R. Van Berkel (eds), *European Citizenship and Social Exclusion*. Aldershot: Ashgate, pp. 138–50.
Trenz, H.-J. (2010) 'The Europeanisation of political communication: conceptual clarifications and empirical measurements', in C. Bee and E. Bozzini (eds), *Mapping the European Public Sphere: Institutions, Media and Civil Society*. London: Ashgate, pp. 15–29.
Warleigh, A. (2001) 'Europeanizing civil society: NGOs as agents of political socialization in the European Union', *Journal of Common Market Studies*, 39 (4): 619–39.
Weiler, J. H. H. (1999) *The Constitution of Europe*. Cambridge: Cambridge University Press.
Wiener, A. (1998) *European Citizenship Practice. Building Institutions of a Non State*. Oxford: Westview Press.

Wiener, A. (2007) *European Citizenship Practice*. Paper prepared for presentation at the European Union Studies Association (EUSA) Tenth Biennial International Conference in Montreal, Quebec, Canada, 17–19 May.

Wodak, R. and Fairclough, N. (1997) 'Critical discourse analysis', in T. A. van Dijk (ed.), *Discourse as Social Interaction*. London: Sage, pp. 258–84.

21

THE 'EUROPEANISATION' OF GENDER POLICIES IN PORTUGAL

Transformations in women's access to civil, political, and social rights

Norberto Ribeiro, Pedro D. Ferreira, Carla Malafaia, and Isabel Menezes

After some decades of intermittent relevance, the concept of citizenship re-emerged in academic discourses during the 1990s, and there were many who stated and promoted its revival. As Beiner (1995) pointed out, the topic seems to be growing every day and is now considered to be one of the key concepts in contemporary political theorizing and analysis (Heater 1990; Ignatieff 1995; Janoski 1998; Kymlicka and Norman 1995; Mouffe 1996b; Steenbergen 1994; Turner 1993). More than just revived, citizenship vocabulary has become so attractive that political parties, policy-makers and applied disciplines often use it: 'People sense that there is something in citizenship that defines the needs of the future – in this they are right – but proceed to bend the term to their own predilections' and between the 'ideological abuses' and the 'vacuous label' one 'begins to wonder if it can be rescued' (Dahrendorf 1994: 12–13). When regarding the concept of citizenship, we must not, therefore, ignore the tensions it entails, just as we must not consider its true meaning as being fixed or attainable – as Foucault (1980) points out, definitions do not reflect any natural or objective order in reality, they are produced, not discovered. Discourse operates 'as a strategic field, as a field of battle and not simply as a reflection of something already constituted and pre-existent' (Davidson 1997: 4). Creating new uses for key terms and using them in new language games makes new ways of life possible (Clarke 2000; Mouffe 1996a) and excludes others.

Nonetheless, citizenship 'from its inception (...) was an exclusionary category (...), justifying the coercive rule of the included over the excluded' (Ignatieff 1995: 56) – that is 'the other', as defined by gender, age, race ..., 'categories' that were frequently naturalized and essentialized for the justification and maintenance of oppression (Benhabib 1999; Dietz 2003; Phillips 2004). This explains criticisms of citizenship as a (hopelessly?) masculine, white and heterosexual concept (Lister 2002; Dietz 2003) that denies diversity and hides a pressure for homogeneity behind the mask of universality (Young 1995). For Ruth Lister, the exclusion of women from citizenship results from both the abstract, disembodied individual on whose shoulders the cloak of citizenship sits, and the public-private divide which has facilitated the relegation to the private sphere of all the functions and qualities deemed incompatible with the exercise of citizenship in the 'public.' (1997: 69)

This has been an instrument, as Carole Pateman states, of 'women's subordination' (1992: 28) that restricts access to the public sphere and women's chances of political equality (Phillips 2004; Kofman et al. 2000), leading Voet to speak of a condemnation to 'partial citizenship' (1998: 11). Not surprisingly, research reveals the tendency for a clear gender gap in conventional forms of participation (Burns 2007; Dalton 2008; Norris 2002), suggesting a greater distance from politics, especially in Europe (Vala and Torres 2007), with women being more intensively engaged in informal politics at local or community levels (Burns 2007; Harrison and Munn 2007; Paxton et al. 2007). Given this situation, it is understandable why public policies have started to strongly emphasize gender equality, recognizing the importance of eliminating both the cultural and structural barriers that impede a real equity between men and women (Dahlerup and Freidenvall 2005; Paxton et al. 2007).

It is beyond the scope of this chapter to consider in detail European Union policies regarding gender equality – but, as Verloo and Lombardo (2007) recognize, 'gender equality is [also] a contested notion (…) [that relates to] at least three main different visions of gender equality, which then can translate into different political strategies' (pp. 22–3): equality, difference or transformation. However, they also underline that the way these policy strategies are translated into actual policies at the national level is extremely diverse across countries, as becomes obvious regarding topics such as gender violence or prostitution. Moreover, there is a clear recognition of the gap between policy and practice:

> While EU gender policy has been admired as the most innovative aspect of its social policy, gender equality is far from achieved: women's incomes across Europe are well below men's; policies for supporting unpaid care work have developed modestly compared with labour market activation policies. (Pascall and Lewis 2004: 373)

The case of Portugal is of particular interest to this discussion given the very rapid evolution of the country in the last four decades, from dictatorship to democracy and from isolation to a full integration in the European Union – an evolution that also implied major transformations in women's access to civil, political and social rights (Rêgo 2012). Therefore we will begin by considering the changes in Portuguese society regarding gender equality, based on previous literature and demographic data provided by statistical sources such as PORDATA[1] and the National Institute of Statistics (INE). We will then proceed by exploring current institutional and civil society discourses about European and national policies concerning active citizenship and the democratic participation of women.

Women's access to civil, political and social rights in Portugal: equality, difference, or transformation?

Portugal lived under a dictatorial regime of fascist inspiration from 1928 to 1974, characterized by a strong emphasis on traditional values, with a vision of women's role as caregivers and mothers in the family which the law recognized, as late as 1967, to be ruled by the man, as the 'head of family'; until 1969 women could not vote (unless they had a higher education degree), nor leave the country without the formal permission of their fathers/husbands. Divorce was forbidden and attitudes towards gender violence were of silence and resignation. The revolution that instituted democracy in 1974 generated new legislation and a recognition of women's civil, political, and social rights, even though it resulted from a 'top to bottom' movement, meaning that this was a problem more acknowledged by political elites than by the people (Ferreira 2000). In the participatory period that followed the revolution, women were actively involved, but access to positions of power was not easy and women's issues were ultimately belittled in political agendas (Tavares 2000). But nevertheless, profound transformations occurred.

After the revolution, the country evolved quite rapidly from a traditional male breadwinner to a dual-earner model (see Figure 21.1), even if women tend to earn less (Figure 21.2) – a discrepancy that, curiously, increases with the level of qualification – and, until recently, were more frequently unemployed (Figure 21.3).

Access to education in general, and higher education in particular, is impressive, with the majority of graduates being women (Figure 21.4), including PhDs (Figure 21.5), even if the higher positions within universities are still mostly occupied by men (Araújo 2009; Bettencourt et al. 2000).

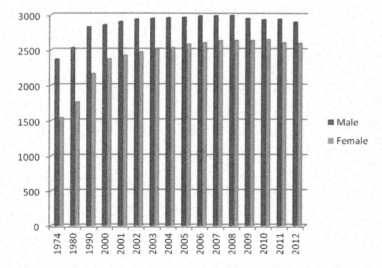

FIGURE 21.1 Working population: by gender – in thousands
Source: PORDATA

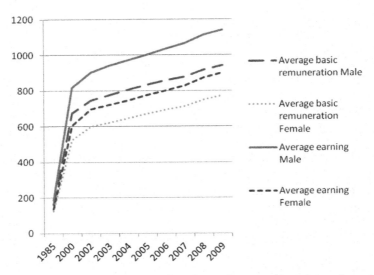

FIGURE 21.2 Average monthly salary of employee: basic remuneration and earnings (€) by gender
Source: PORDATA

However, politics is still typically a masculine space, leading Santos and Amâncio (2012) to speak of a *genderization of politics* – women show higher levels of political demobilization and distance-to-power (Villaverde Cabral 1997), experience more barriers, and hold less significant resources, such as time, due to their dual role as earners

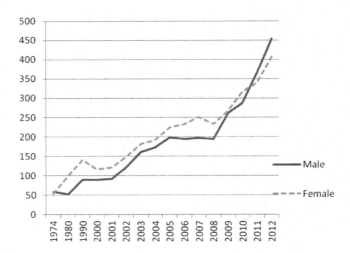

FIGURE 21.3 Unemployment population: by gender – in thousands
Source: PORDATA

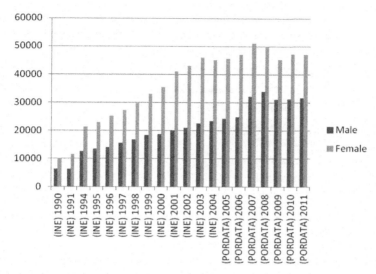

FIGURE 21.4 Graduates in higher education by gender
Sources: INE/PORDATA

and caretakers (Jordão 2000), and there are, in fact, fewer female representatives in political positions, such as the Parliament (Figure 21.6), in government (Figure 21.7), or even in municipalities (Figure 21.8). Nevertheless, there seems to be a tendency for a dilution of gender differences in both conventional and non-conventional political

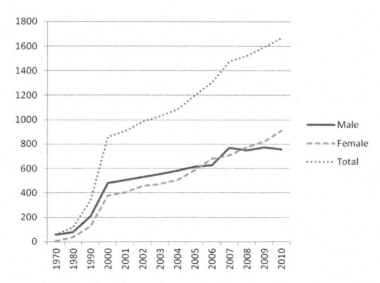

FIGURE 21.5 PhDs: total and by gender
Source: PORDATA

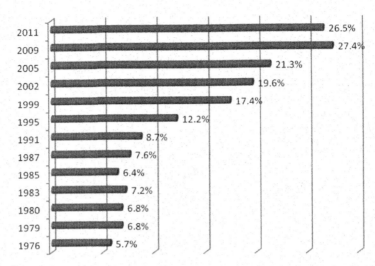

FIGURE 21.6 Mandates in the elections to the national Parliament: % of total of female members by years
Source: PORDATA

participation (Espírito-Santo and Baum 2004) and legislation now demands a quota of 30 percent women candidates.

Therefore, it is not surprising that women still have a higher risk of poverty than men (Figure 21.9).

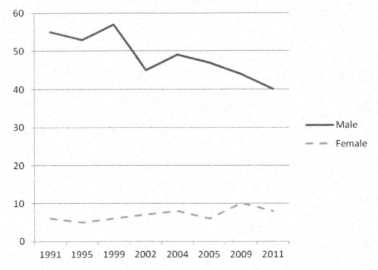

FIGURE 21.7 Members of central government (no.) by gender
Source: INE

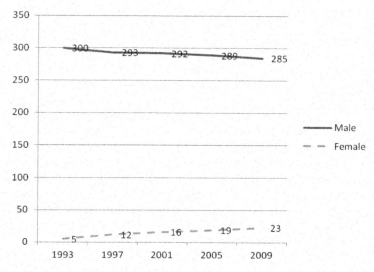

FIGURE 21.8 Presidents of municipalities (no.) by gender
Source: INE

The fact that democracy in Portugal displays an undeniable evolution in women's access to civil, political, and social rights – even more so because the level of access to these rights during the dictatorship was non-existent – clearly does not mean that Portuguese women's equality in the eyes of the law has resulted in inclusion, recognition, or voice in daily life. But undoubtedly Portugal becoming a

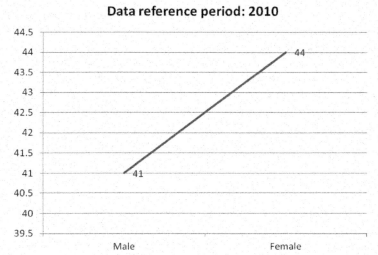

FIGURE 21.9 At-risk-of-poverty rate (before social transfers – %) by gender
Source: INE

member of the European Union has played an important role in this process of transformation – and therefore it is important to understand how institutional and civil society discourses consider European and national policies regarding gender equality.

Institutional and civil society discourses about gender equality

This section contrasts two different levels of analysis, the institutional and that of civil society. On the one hand, we consider the legal framework related to women's rights, i.e. the written texts of Portuguese policy documents concerning women. On the other hand, we consider the official documents of public institutions and NGOs, and an interview with a representative of an NGO. The document analysis was intended to explore how national policies have been influenced by the process of Europeanisation in the promotion of civic and political participation, especially of women. The analysis focused specifically on the following political issues: (1) the visibility of European issues; (2) the alignment of national policies with European standards; (3) criticism of European and national policies; and (4) the development of the 'European dimension.' In practice, the alignment of national policies with European policies, and criticism of both European and national policies, were emphasised most in the analysis. The interview analysis, in turn, had the objective of examining different levels of discourse in order to identify potential discrepancies. The interview was intended to: (1) map the convergence of European priorities and national priorities; (2) define patterns of Europeanisation in the context of national policies; (3) identify the visibility of European policies at the national level; and (4) evaluate the impact of European legislation and policy-making at the national level. In the discussion of these political issues, the interviewee adopted a discourse that relied, fundamentally, on criticism of national and European policies.

To analyse the documents and the interview, we adopted a qualitative approach based on discourse analysis (DA). This theoretical-methodological approach enabled the exploration of discourses concerning the role of language in shaping the social world and influencing social action and policies (cf. Hajer 2002, 2005; Howarth and Torfing 2005). In particular, DA was used to analyse both the documents and the interview in order to allow a better understanding of the impact of supranational dominant discourses over the national policy outcomes and social practices. As Hajer (2002) argues, 'discourse is defined here as an ensemble of ideas, concepts, and categories through which meaning is given to social and physical phenomena, and which is produced and reproduced through an identifiable set of practices' (p. 300). One interview was conducted with a representative of the NGO Union of Women Alternative and Response (UMAR).[2] Eleven documents were analysed, five from public institutions and six from NGOs. The following documents were from public institutions:

- National Action Plan for Inclusion 2006–2008 (PNAI)[3]
- III National Plan Against Domestic Violence (2007–2010)[4]
- I National Action Plan against Human Trafficking (2007–2010)[5]

- III National Plan for Equality – Citizenship and Gender (2007–2010)[6]
- Speech of the Minister of the Presidency (Pedro Silva Pereira) to the Commission on Women's Rights and Gender Equality and to the European Parliament (2007).[7]

From NGOs, the following documents were analysed:

- Association Solidarity International: SIMM Project – Awareness and Integration of Migrant and Marginalised Women: On the Road to Equality[8]
- Amnesty International: report of the campaign Stop Violence Against Women: (In)Visible Women[9]
- Doctors of the World (MdM): News Bulletin, No. 8: Violence Against Women: A reality that it is necessary to stop![10]
- Action for Justice and Peace (AJP): the future is not the present's improvement: it is something else – Annual Activities Plan 2008[11]
- Portuguese Platform for Women's Rights: Activities Report (2008)[12]
- Portuguese Network of Young People for Equality of Opportunities between Women and Men: speech for gender equality – to understand and to know what we are talking about.[13]

The institutional level

The support of gender equality and real equal opportunities for men and women dominates the discourses in the documents from both the public institutions and the NGOs. Public authorities highlight a set of core issues in this field that have been pointed out at national and European levels. The National Action Plan for Inclusion 2006–2008 (PNAI) stresses, for instance, social protection and social inclusion and cohesion in areas such as employment, education, health, etc., '*taking into account the perspective of equality between men and women*' (2006: 49). The document points out that the highest incidence of low income among women leads in Portugal, like in most countries, to the feminization of poverty (p. 13). It is fundamental for achieving a democratic society to ensure that the rights of discriminated persons are made effective, and that strategic agents of social intervention, and the general population, develop skills for the fuller exercise of citizenship (p. 68). Additionally, the documents of public institutions are focused on the importance of fighting domestic violence, promoting the empowerment of victims (III National Plan Against Domestic Violence, 2007–2010), and combating human trafficking. Regarding the latter issue, the I National Action Plan against Human Trafficking (2007–2010) states 'it is critical to adopt a set of areas, which share as their common denominator, the concerns and interests of victims' (p. 7). As indispensable elements for the promotion of an effective human rights policy, the document points out:

> the granting of residential permits; access to official programs dedicated to the inclusion of trafficking victims in social life; psychological and judicial

support and the voluntary and safe return of trafficked victims to their country of origin. Ensuring the most adequate witness protection mechanisms in criminal investigations/judicial processes is another aspect to consider when promoting a just and effective fight against human trafficking. (pp. 7–8)

In line with the documents, the speech of the Minister of the Presidency (Pedro Silva Pereira) to the Commission on Women's Rights and Gender Equality and to the European Parliament (2007) highlights the importance of developing 'gender mainstreaming' through: the valorisation of gender issues in different policy areas, the promotion of gender employability and entrepreneurship for effective equal opportunities, and the development of further conditions for the reconciliation of professional and personal life and family (p. 2).

Gender equality and equal opportunities are also the dominant discourses in the NGOs' documents. Drawing particular attention to immigrant women, the SIMM Project (2007) considers that there is still a more or less visible gender gap depending on the country of origin and the cultural identity of each individual, mentioning that gender inequalities tend to increase in the case of immigrants. The document indicates some priorities to address this situation, such as: the recognition of the educational qualifications of immigrants; psychological counseling for migrant women; conciliation between work and family life; the development of employability skills among migrant women and initiatives to promote professional careers for women; the dissemination of good practices in health; and the end of domestic violence (SIMM Project, 2007). In the same vein, the document of Amnesty International (2004) also points out the importance of providing information about violence against women in order to foster awareness about this issue among civil society, governments, and NGOs. With a view to better explaining how violence against women and gender discrimination has developed, Amnesty International (2004) hopes to encourage tolerance and equality, and to promote human rights in Portugal and worldwide.

With regard to the European dimension, the documents showed, in general, a clear alignment with European policies that emphasise equality of opportunity for all, particularly for women. References relating to the field of gender equality are framed by events and facts, such as: (1) the Lisbon Strategy, (2) the European Year of Equal Opportunities for All, (3) the Council of Europe Convention concerning the fight against trafficking in human beings, (4) the Roadmap for Equality between Men and Women, (5) the National Plan Against Domestic Violence, (6) the Pan-European Strategy on domestic violence against women, etc. This alignment with EU political priorities is expressed by the III National Plan for Equality (2007), when it states that:

[s]everal international declarations and recommendations, particularly those of the European Council and European Union, have considered

gender-based violence as an assault against human rights, appealing to the need for governments to develop efficient strategies in favour of its elimination (p. 42)

and also by the III National Plan Against Domestic Violence (2007):

> Within the scope of the European Union, the eradication of all forms of gender violence constitutes one of the six priority areas of intervention included in the Guide for Equality between Men and Women for the period 2006–2010. We urge the Member States to eliminate all forms of violence against women, since this constitutes a violation of fundamental rights. (p. 4)

This alignment is also reinforced by the speech of the Minister of the Presidency (Pedro Silva Pereira) to the Commission on Women's Rights and Gender Equality and to the European Parliament (2007), which argues that:

> the social dimension of the Lisbon strategy serving a more competitive and inclusive society contains a clear requirement to promote gender equality and effective equality of opportunities [...] The Portuguese presidency aims to tackle this serious problem requiring urgent responses in line with what is advocated in the Convention of the Council of Europe on Human Trafficking, by the EU Roadmap on equality between men and women and by the recent Action Plan on best practices on confronting and preventing human trafficking. (pp. 1–4)

The vision of civil society

Alignment with EU policies is indicated by the absence of criticism of such policies and by the policy recommendations of public institutions. Only the NGOs express some criticisms, mainly regarding investment in more effective policies to prevent violence and to help the victims of violence. Amnesty International (2004) believes that policy-makers must become more aware and ready to protect women from domestic violence, since that is a crime which is not always visible and punishable. This NGO urges governments to work closely with victims in order to understand and help them more effectively. In addition, Amnesty International (2004) considers that the EU's internal and judicial policies need to be more effective, punishing aggressors and controlling crime. In summary, the criticisms from NGOs highlight mainly the fact that many women still suffer in silence and that official policies do not provide sufficient protection and safety, as stated in the document of Doctors of the World (MdM) (2004):

> The biggest accomplice of gender violence is the silence of those who suffer [...] despite the policies adopted, the numbers remain worrisome. According

to official Portuguese data, about five women die every month on average as direct or indirect consequence of domestic violence. If we all know it exists, if governments adopt measures aimed at its elimination, what makes violence against women continue to exist? (p. 3)

In the interview, the representative of the NGO UMAR, a Portuguese feminist organization, presented a clear critical vision about EU policies. Despite the NGO's assessment of EU policies on gender and women issues as being positive in general, the interviewee considered that 'the EU remains tied symbolically, on all sides, to a development model that is a model of capitalist development'. The interviewee criticized the fact that the EU political model gives priority to economic and financial concerns, as well as to the security dimension, over social interests that can effectively promote greater equality and social justice for strengthening European democracy. These priorities should be unemployment, poverty, and inequality in general. In addition, the interviewee argued that equality in terms of political participation needs to be complemented by policies for economic equality and, therefore, for the genuine economic empowerment of women. In fact, this idea of equality was grounded on an understanding of citizenship that 'goes beyond the borders of a State or a government, and has more to do with an ontological perspective of being a person. Citizenship, being a citizen, being an inhabitant of a city that has access to all rights and all duties in whatever its condition, diversity, plurality of human beings' – this is a view which is in line with what several authors have been referring to as post-national citizenship (cf. Benhabib 1999; Janoski 2000; Carvalhais 2004) and transnational citizenship (Keck and Sikkin 1998).

In particular, the representative of UMAR considered that national policies are aligned with the EU policy priorities, although without significant impact on the daily life of citizens. In other words, the interviewee considered that there is a gap between rhetoric and reality. In this context, she criticized Portuguese governments for being uncritical, 'good students,' not taking into account the Portuguese reality:

> Plans, great policies, great measures, extensive legislation but little practice. A lot of showing-off, many openings and campaigns, but in practice the development of quality of life and of the improving of the real quality of life of Portuguese is little. It is little ... because this rhetoric that does not apply in practice, is the idea to be considered by the EU as obedient and compliant, as good students [...] Our governments like to give the idea that they are good students and accountable. And often they do not have an understanding of the impact of some laws that are made from the indications of the EU without regard to the Portuguese reality (UMAR).

To overcome the gap, the interviewee mentioned that resources are required. Without allocation of resources, there is no real monitoring whether the laws are indeed producing real effects. The interviewee emphasised that it is just rhetoric without supervision because there is no allocation of resources:

it is necessary that these policies have one thing that is important for implementation – that is the resources. Without resources, things are not done. Are not done! [...] It's the first question, the resources! The second issue is the monitoring, because you have to do surveillance, for example. No need to monitor because there is no allocation of resources, we are only in rhetoric. (UMAR)

Continuing with the same critical content, the representative of UMAR mentioned that the Lisbon Treaty was a fragile consensus which was fragmented because the relationship between political forces in the EU had weakened with right-wing and conservative governments coming to power, and also because the Lisbon Treaty itself had not mobilized some of the aspirations of some sectors. Furthermore, the interviewee criticized the EU for being far from democratic. It was, at best, a representative democracy, but not in all areas, since some EU bodies are not the result of direct elections and are therefore not subject to the scrutiny of European citizens:

Now, we continue on the basis of electoral democracy, there is some democracy, but it is far from being a democracy that would lead to participation and citizenship with greater rights for all people [...] It is a liberal representative democracy and, even so, not in all its scope, because some of the organs of the EU are not from direct election. Therefore, not being from direct election they escape from our control, they escape the scrutiny of the European citizens. To that extent, there is much to do because they want to ensure that the reproduction of the powers remains in some central countries like France and [Germany]. (UMAR)

Conclusion

Europe has witnessed, across the twentieth century, women's growing access to civil, political, and social rights. However, this path has been delayed in countries with regimes of fascist inspiration, such as Portugal, where the principle of gender equality was included in the constitution only after the 1974 revolution. The data presented here show the immense transformation that has taken place in Portuguese society over the recent decades. It is most clear when we look at how women have entered the labor market and achieved higher education degrees. Still, access to rights, work, and education has not been sufficient to guarantee, as we said before, de facto inclusion, recognition, or voice, as illustrated by women's lower access to elected positions, lower access to income, and higher risk of poverty and of gender-based violence. This makes Portugal a particularly interesting case for an analysis of the flow of influence between European and national policies.

As a whole, both the document analysis and the interview suggest that national policies tend to be aligned with EU policies. The impact of supranational discourses seems to be highest at the national policy level. Present in policy documents, as in the speeches of officials, the issues of gender inequality and victimization now have their official place in what needs to be changed. The discourses presented in the NGOs' documents and in the interview bring, however, a critical perspective on existing policies, and how they translate into social practice. On the one hand, these discourses argue that policies need to take into account the Portuguese reality; on the other hand, they state that it is necessary to invest in more effective policies. The lack of European and national policies on the everyday reproduction of inequality is stressed, as is the lack of action in the face of apparent failure, as noted by Doctors of the World regarding the failure to challenge the prevalence and the effects of domestic violence. Both the NGOs and the interviewee criticised the gap between rhetoric and reality, arguing that it is necessary for policies to have a real impact on the daily life of citizens, especially women. This impact, as our interviewee pointed out, should be monitored and assessed, otherwise policy changes can easily be no more than rhetorical declarations of little consequence. Such monitoring would need the allocation of economic resources, and that means that other values would have to be attached to the issue of gender equality. To promote the efficacy of the policies and to challenge economic and political inequality between women and men, issues of power and distribution would have to be brought to the table, perhaps in a manner that is more inclusive, more informed by everyday life, and more focused on bringing to the hands of ordinary women the economic and political power which is necessary for them to change their lives and our societies in ways that do not make things different so that some things can stay the same.

Notes

1 PORDATA (database of contemporary Portugal) is a public service of statistical information created by the Francisco Manuel dos Santos Foundation. For more details see: http://www.pordata.pt/.
2 UMAR – the Union of Women Alternative and Response – is an association of women formed on 12 September 1976. It was born from women's active participation in the Portuguese revolution on 25 April 1974, and the need to create an association to fight for their rights in that new political context. For more details see: http://umar.no.sapo.pt/umar/historial/historial.htm.
3 Given the common goals of social inclusion defined by the European Union, the 'PNAI 2006–2008 is a reference document guiding the diversity of interventions required in the national social inclusion process for politicians, and citizens in general. The document is intended as an instrument capable of contributing to reversing, with greater efficiency, poverty and social exclusion (phenomena of the past and even the present) in the future, in the direction of a Portuguese society more just, more socially cohesive and with more sustainable development' (p. 9). Available at the website: http://www.pnai.pt/docs/PNAI%202006-2008%20-%20portugu%C3%AAs.pdf.
4 Available at the website: http://195.23.38.178/cig/portalcig/bo/documentos/III%20National%20Plan%20Against%20Domestic%20Violence.pdf.
5 Available at the website: http://www.ungift.org/doc/knowledgehub/resource-centre/Governments/Portugal_National_Action_Plan_Against_Trafficking_en_2007_2010.pdf.
6 Available at the website: http://195.23.38.178/cig/portalcig/bo/documentos/III%20National%20Plan%20For%20Equality%20Citizenship%20and%20Gender.pdf.

7 Available at the website: http://www.eu2007.pt/NR/rdonlyres/4728DF02-3635-4438-828F-84CC47A0C1E6/0/PEIgualdade_MP.pdf.
8 SIMM (*Sensibilização e Integração de Mulheres Migrantes e Marginalizadas: No Caminho para a Igualdade* – Awareness and Integration of Migrant and Marginalised Women: On the Road to Equality) was a project held by the Association Solidarity International. This project developed a personalized service to deal with topics related to the social and labor integration of the immigrant population, particularly women. The main aim of this project was to reduce inequalities between men and women, particularly in the case of migrants and ethnic minorities. Available at the website: http://www.asi.pt/images/pdf/estruturapsicossocial.pdf.
9 Available at the website: http://www.amnistia-internacional.pt/dmdocuments/Relatorio_das_Mulheres.pdf.
10 Doctors of the World (MdM) (2004) 'Violence Against Women: A Reality that It Is Necessary to Stop!' *News Bulletin*, No. 8, February. For information on the NGO, see the website: http://www.medicosdomundo.pt/pt.
11 The document was accessed in December 2009 at the website: http://www.ajpaz.org.pt/.
12 Available at the website: http://afem.itane.com/DOCUMENTS/Portugais/Les%20Nouvelles%20de%20AFEM/Relatorio-Actividades-2008-PPDM.pdf.
13 Available at the website: http://www.redejovensigualdade.org.pt/dmpm1/docs/argumentario.pdf.

References

Araújo, H. C. (2009) 'Participação das mulheres e democracia na Universidade,' in T. S. Brabo (ed.), *Gênero, educação e política: múltiplos olhar*. São Paulo (BR): Icone, pp. 59–72.
Beiner, R. (1995) 'Introduction,' in R. Beiner (ed.), *Theorizing Citizenship*. New York: State University of New York Press, pp. 1–28.
Benhabib, S. (1999) 'Citizens, residents and aliens in a changing world: political membership in a global era,' *Social Research*, 66 (3): 709–44.
Bettencourt, A., Campos, J., and Fragateiro, L. (2000) *Educação para a cidadania*. Lisboa: Comissão para a Igualdade e para os Direitos das Mulheres.
Burns, N. (2007) 'Gender in the aggregate, gender in the individual, gender and political action,' *Politics and Gender*, 3 (1): 104–24.
Carvalhais, I. E. (2004) *Os desafios da cidadania pós-nacional*. Porto: Afrontamento.
Clarke, P. B. (2000) 'A política e o político: Consciência e mito, mística e praxis,' trans. V. Gil, in R. del Águila, P. B. Clarke, A. S. Silva, and N. Tenzer (eds), *A política: ensaios de uma definição*. Madrid: Sequitur, pp. 19–58.
Dahlerup, D. and Freidenvall, L. (2005) 'Quotas as a fast track to equal representation for women,' *International Feminist Journal of Politics*, 7 (1): 26–48.
Dahrendorf, R. (1994) 'The changing quality of citizenship,' in B. van Steenbergen (ed.), *The Condition of Citizenship*. Newbury Park, CA: Sage.
Dalton, R. J. (2008) 'Citizenship norms and the expansion of political participation,' *Political Studies*, 56: 76–98.
Davidson, A. (1997) 'Structures and strategies of discourse: remarks toward a history of Foucault's philosophy of language,' in A. Davidson (ed.), *Foucault and His Interlocutors*. Chicago: University of Chicago Press.
Dietz, M. G. (2003) 'Current controversies in feminist theory', *Annual Review of Political Science*, 6: 399–431.
Espírito-Santo, A. and Baum, M. (2004) 'A participação feminina em Portugal numa perspectiva longitudinal,' *Actas do V Congresso Português de Sociologia – Sociedades Contemporâneas – Reflexividade e Acção*. Braga: Universidade do Minho.

Ferreira, V. (2000) 'Sexualizando Portugal: mudança social, políticas estatais e mobilização das mulheres,' in A. Costa Pinto (ed.), *Portugal Contemporâneo*. Madrid: Ed. Sequitur, pp. 180–212.

Foucault, M. (1980) *Power/Knowledge: Selected Interviews and Other Writings 1972–1977*. London: Harvester Press.

Hajer, M. A. (2002) 'Discourse analysis and the study of policy making,' *European Political Science*, 2 (1): 61–5.

Hajer, M. A. (2005) 'Coalitions, practices, and meaning in environmental politics: from acid rain to BSE,' in D. Howarth and J. Torfing (eds), *Discourse Theory in European Politics. Identity, Policy and Governance*. Basingstoke: Palgrave, pp. 297–315.

Harrison, L. and Munn, J. (2007) 'Gendered (non) participants? What constructions of citizenship tell us about democratic governance in the twenty-first century,' *Parliamentary Affairs*, 60 (3): 426–36.

Heater, D. (1990) *Citizenship: The Civic Ideal in the World. History, Politics and Education*. New York: Longman.

Howarth, D. and Torfing, J. (eds) (2005) *Discourse Theory in European Politics. Identity, Policy and Governance*. Basingstoke: Palgrave.

Ignatieff, M. (1995) 'The myth of citizenship,' in R. Beiner (ed.), *Theorizing Citizenship*. New York: State University of New York Press, pp. 53–77.

Janoski, T. (1998) *Citizenship and Civil Society*. Cambridge: Cambridge University Press.

Janoski, T. (2000) *Citizenship and Civil Society: A Framework of Rights and Obligations in Liberal, Traditional and Social Democratic Regimes*. Cambridge: Cambridge University Press.

Jordão, A. (2000) 'Protagonistas do poder local: obstáculos e oportunidades,' *ex-aequo*, 2/3: 117–23.

Keck, M. and Sikkin, K. (1998) *Activists Beyond Borders: Advocacy Networks in International Politics*. Ithaca, NY: Cornell University Press.

Kofman, E., Phizacklea, A., Raghuram, P., and Sales, R. (2000) *Gender and International Migration in Europe: Employment, Welfare and Politics*. London: Routledge.

Kymlicka, W. and Norman, W. (1995) 'Return of the citizen: a survey of recent work on citizenship theory,' in R. Beiner (ed.), *Theorizing Citizenship*. New York: State University of New York Press, pp. 283–322.

Lister, R. (1997) *Citizenship – Feminist Perspectives*. London: Routledge.

Lister, R. (2002) 'Cidadania: Um desafio e uma oportunidade para as feministas,' *ex-aequo*, 7: 165–78.

Mouffe, C. (1996a) *O regresso do político*, trans. A. C. Simões. Lisbon: Gradiva.

Mouffe, C. (1996b) 'Radical democracy or liberal democracy,' in D. Trend (ed.), *Radical Democracy: Identity, Citizenship and the State*. New York: Routledge, pp. 19–26.

Norris, P. (2002) *Democratic Phoenix: Reinventing Political Activism*. Cambridge: Cambridge University Press.

Pascall, G. and Lewis, J. (2004) 'Emerging gender regimes and policies for gender equality in a wider Europe,' *Journal of Social Policy*, 33 (3): 373–94.

Pateman, C. (1992) 'Equality, difference, subordination: the politics of motherhood and women's citizenship,' in G. Bock and S. James (eds), *Beyond Equality and Difference: Citizenship, Feminist Politics and Female Subjectivity*. London: Routledge, pp. 14–27.

Paxton, P., Kunovich, S., and Hughes, M. M. (2007) 'Gender in politics,' *Annual Review of Sociology*, 33: 263–84.

Phillips, A. (2004) 'Defending equality of outcome,' *Journal of Political Philosophy*, 12 (1): 1–19.

Rêgo, M. C. C. (2012) 'Políticas de igualdade de género na União Europeia e em Portugal: Influências e incoerências,' *ex aequo*, 25: 29–44.

Santos, M. H. and Amâncio, L. (2012) 'Género e política: análise sobre as resistências nos discursos e nas práticas sociais face à Lei da Paridade,' *Sociologia, Problemas e Práticas*, 68: 79–101.

Steenbergen, B. v. (1994) *The Condition of Citizenship*. Newbury Park, CA: Sage.

Tavares, M. (2000) *Movimentos de Mulheres em Portugal, nas décadas de 70 e 80*. Lisboa: Livros Horizonte.

Turner, B. (1993) 'Contemporary problems in the theory of citizenship,' in B. Turner (ed.), *Citizenship and Social Theory*. Newbury Park, CA: Sage.

Vala, J. and Torres, A. (2007) *Contextos e atitudes sociais na Europa. Atitudes sociais dos Portugueses 6*. Lisbon: Imprensa de Ciências Sociais.

Verloo, M. and Lombardo, E. (2007) 'Contested gender equality and policy variety in Europe: introducing a critical frame analysis approach,' in M. Verloo (ed.), *Multiple Meanings of Gender Equality*. Budapest: Central European University, pp. 21–46.

Villaverde Cabral, M. (1997) *Cidadania política e equidade social em Portugal*. Oeiras: Celta.

Voet, R. (1998) *Feminism and Citizenship*. London: Sage.

Young, I. M. (1995) 'Polity and group difference: a critique of the ideal of universal citizenship,' in R. Beiner (ed.), *Theorizing Citizenship*. New York: State University of New York Press, pp. 175–207.

22
GOVERNMENT PERSPECTIVES ON CIVIC AND POLITICAL PARTICIPATION OF YOUTH AND WOMEN IN TURKEY

Deriving insights from policy documents

Sümercan Bozkurt, Figen Çok, and Tülin Şener

Introduction

The concept of political participation has witnessed a variety of reconceptualizations over recent decades in order to transcend narrower definitions of the concept and encompass wider forms of participation aimed at influencing political outcomes and/or the political agenda (see, for example, Brady 1999; Ekman and Amna 2012; Parry *et al.* 1992; Teorell *et al.* 2007). These broader definitions, given the potential operational drawbacks, are attempts to classify participation into different categories such as conventional/non-conventional, parliamentary/extra-parliamentary, electoral/non-electoral and formal/informal. Although these dichotomies do not always overlap exactly, there has nevertheless been an increasing argument that conventional/parliamentary/electoral/formal means of participation have been in decline in many contemporary democracies (Ekman and Amnå 2012: 297; Kriesi 2008: 147; Vráblíková 2014: 3). While many studies have been conducted using such classifications in relation to different societies and groups, there have been fewer studies into government perspectives and those of public bodies on civic and political participation. However, together with the socio-economic, historical and cultural landscape, the political and institutional framework constitutes an important factor that sets the ground for different forms of participation (cf. Zani and Barrett 2012: 280). Although there are important studies on the incentives and disincentives provided by, and the degree of openness of, the 'political opportunity structure' (see, for example, Diani and McAdam 2003; Gamson and Meyer 1996; Kitschelt 1986; Koopmans 1999; Kriesi *et al.* 1992; Tarrow 1996), perspectives on political participation that are taken by public authorities have not been taken into account and examined with sufficient frequency.

This chapter attempts to provide insights into the political/institutional framework in relationship to the civic and political participation of youth and women in Turkey, by examining one important aspect of this framework, namely the perspectives of government and related public bodies as expressed in their policy documents. The examination is based upon the reports, plans, and other policy documents released by public authorities in Turkey between 2004 and 2013. While initially the study was intended to examine documents on the civic and political participation of minority and immigrant groups as well, these groups have been excluded from this chapter, mainly because it was found that civic and political participation by minorities and immigrants are almost entirely neglected in these documents. Although the civic and political participation of youth and women has been given more space on the agendas of public bodies, it can be argued that this space still remains very limited. Yet, as will be seen in this chapter, it is nevertheless possible to identify general orientations and broad perspectives in relationship to participation by youth and women.

Undoubtedly, the main limitation of an examination of policy documents is the possible implementation gap between statements and promises on the one hand and actual practices on the other hand. Despite this limitation, we believe that an examination of documents produced by public authorities can nevertheless provide important information about the perspectives of these institutions on civic and political participation. Throughout this chapter, while the term 'political participation' will be used to refer to both conventional/electoral (voting, political party membership, running for office, deliberately abstaining from voting, blank voting, etc.) and non-conventional/non-electoral (demonstrations, protests, boycotts, strikes, signing petitions, etc.) forms of participation that are aimed at influencing the political agenda and/or outcomes, the term 'civic participation' will be used to denote associational involvement and voluntary work (cf. Ekman and Amnå, 2012). It will be argued that, throughout the period examined, women's participation in Turkey has mainly been framed and conceived by the public authorities with reference to electoral forms of political participation, in particular with reference to their 'political representation' in conventional political processes and institutions. Youth participation, on the other hand, has not been regarded as an issue of primary concern. Furthermore, the perspectives that are expressed by public authorities in Turkey reveal tensions between the conservative ideals which are attributed to women and youth and their civic and political participation.

This chapter is organized into four sections, including this introduction and the concluding remarks. The following section is devoted to describing the general situation of youth and women in Turkey in order to reveal the broader context in which their civic and political participation, and government perspectives on these, have been shaped. The third section of the chapter examines documents published by public institutions, with the aim of mapping the different perspectives on the issue. Finally, the concluding section will gather together the main conclusions that may be drawn from the analysis.

Youth and women's participation in Turkish society and politics

The present status of youth

Turkey has a large young population consisting of about 12.5 million people aged between 15 and 24. This constitutes 16.6 percent of the total population, according to the 2012 data of the Turkish Statistical Institute.[1] The socio-economic context and the youth-related policies shaped by historical legacies have played important roles with regard to youth civic and political participation in Turkey. The education system, employment dynamics, living conditions and family structures have all had crucial impacts on political participation, as has the 1980 *coup d'état*. As Kurtaran et al. (2008: 9) have shown, the 1980 coup led young people to stay away from political structures such as political parties, associations, trade unions, and collective action. Among the most prominent legal regulations realized after the *coup d'état* that restricted youth political participation there were the closure and banning of the youth branches of political parties and the prohibition of 'being involved in political activities, distributing leaflets, possessing, duplicating or distributing posters and banners, making verbal or written ideological propaganda inside the higher education institutions' by the Student Disciplinary Statute of the Council of Higher Education (Yentürk 2008: 63). In the 1960s and especially the 1970s, young people's political socialization reached its peak, especially among university students in Turkey, among whom political activism was very common. However, with the 1980 military coup, the political participation of young people was severely repressed and remained confined mostly to voting in the 1980s and 1990s (cf. Göksel 2009: 18). The legal regulations discouraging participation were also accompanied by familial attitudes shaped by the rationale of 'keeping children away from politics' (Yentürk, cited in Göksel 2009: 18). In the 1980s and 1990s, young people's political attitudes were framed through the influence of this prominent parental stance (Celen and Çok 2007). Although not the majority of youth, by the 2000s, many young people in Turkey were involved in NGO work and more organized activities (cf. Göksel 2009: 18). The impact of international organizations was notable in this respect. Thus one important aspect of youth policy in Turkey has been the involvement of international organizations in cooperation with NGOs. While some of those cooperation schemes have brought issues of youth policy onto the agenda, some other international programs became more effective in the development of national, regional, and international youth work. To the extent that such cooperation requires partnerships between public authorities and civil society, youth organizations have become more popular. As Kuzmanovic (2010: 429) argues, in relation to civic activism in Turkey in general, the involvement of international and supranational organizations has been accompanied by the increased significance of the project culture for civic activism and thereby its professionalization.

Recent studies of youth civic and political participation show that conventional forms of participation among young people in Turkey have remained very limited. In a 2007 survey encompassing 1,203 young people aged 16–29, only 9 percent of the respondents stated that they were closely interested in politics (Kılıç 2009: 58).

According to the results of the survey, the proportion of those who were members of a political party was 4.3 percent (Kılıç 2009: 59). Furthermore, data gathered by the Turkish Statistical Institute (TSI 2011: 137) show that the rate of participation in voluntary work and meetings among youth was 1.5 percent in 2006. It can be argued that discouraging factors behind this low participation rate include various disadvantages surrounding young people's lives, alongside the legacies of the 1980 military coup and the ensuing political environment that has severely restricted youth political participation. Education constitutes one of these factors. Although the average schooling rate in Turkey was 98.4 percent at the primary educational level in 2011, the ratios were 67.3 percent and 33 percent at the secondary and higher educational levels in the same year, respectively.[2] Furthermore, the contents of, and the methods applied in, the curricula at different levels of education have hardly been sensitive to participation. Accordingly, while important reorganizations have been made to the national education system over the past decade – including the consideration of a constructivist learning approach, multiple intelligences, learner-centered learning, learner participation, and individual differences (Kaymakcan 2007) – the hierarchical structure of education and respect-based understanding seem to have had a negative impact on active participation in schools. It has also been found that students of teacher education programs have little knowledge about the civic institutions, activities and implementation of youth work and youth participation in Turkey (Şener 2012).

High rates of unemployment, insecurity and flexible working conditions in Turkey are other important phenomena surrounding young people's lives that also impact upon their civic and political participation.[3] Family structure and dependency on parents also constitute important factors in this respect. As stressed by Göksel (2009: 15), most young people live and spend most of their time with their families, and this increases parental control and influence and youths' dependency on their parents. In research conducted by the Turkish Economic and Social Studies Foundation (TESEV) with 2,200 university students from 27 universities in Turkey (Artan *et al.* 2005), it was found that the values of young people are related more to their families and living conditions than to their education. It was also found in a survey that the participation of young people in family decision-making processes is low, even in decisions about everyday matters such as the determination of which TV channel should be watched (55 percent) and the form of leisure activities that should be undertaken together (52 percent) (UNDP 2008: 78).

All of these factors which directly or indirectly impact upon young people's civic and political participation imply important differences between different categories of youth, with gender, class, and ethnicity all playing roles in young people's access to education and employment and their positioning within the family. This broad picture of the socio-economic context surrounding youth in Turkey implies that there have been important disadvantages in different fields of life for different categories of youth. While it is possible to argue that these disadvantages play different roles in young people's political participation, existing studies have provided few insights into the relationship between participation and the disadvantages of, vulnerabilities of, and exclusionary attitudes towards different categories of youth in Turkey (Enneli 2010).

While the above-mentioned factors may have played different roles in young people's limited participation in conventional civic and political life, the uprisings of June 2013, which started as a protest against the government's agenda to build a replica of an Ottoman army barracks in Taksim that would involve the demolition of Gezi Park but then transformed into much wider anti-government protests in different cities across the country, suggest the need to take into account other factors, needs, and non-conventional forms of action in relation to young people's political participation. According to the results of a survey conducted during the first days of the protests with 4,411 protesters in Gezi Park, almost 80 percent stated that they were not members of any political party or civil society organizations such as associations, foundations, and platforms (KONDA 2013).[4] While the average age of the respondents was 27, the ratio of women was 50.8 percent (KONDA 2013). More than half of the protesters (58 percent) taking part in the survey also indicated that the reason for their participation in the protests was the restriction of their freedoms (KONDA 2013). Another remarkable characteristic of the protests was the extensive use of social media, both for organizational purposes and to share information.[5] It should also be noted that humor, which was reflected in a variety of sight gags, banners, and graffiti, became an important tool for the young people's protests. Furthermore, the protestors became active participants of popular assemblies that were organized as park forums accompanying the protests. Park forums constituted important channels of political participation through which participants engaged in dialogue with their fellows on a variety of political issues.[6] Active involvement of youth in the uprisings and the formation of popular assemblies in Turkey have clearly shown that it is incorrect to regard them as apolitical and disengaged merely on the basis of their levels of political party or NGO membership.

As will be pointed out below in the third section of this chapter, government and public policies on youth participation are not compatible with this picture. However, before engaging in this discussion, we need to describe the context and status of women's participation in social and political life in Turkey.

The present status of women

The participation of women in local and national electoral processes was recognized and enabled in the 1930s, first by the enactment of their right to vote and to be elected in local elections in 1930, and then in the Turkish Grand National Assembly in 1934. Although in the early Republican period many other reforms in the fields of education and fundamental rights were realized in line with the equality of women and men on legal grounds, there have been extensive problems in relation to the attainment of gender equality in Turkey. Important factors include the traditional roles assigned to women in the household, social and political barriers hindering women's access to qualified education and decent jobs, and the widespread violence against women, all of which have played restricting roles against women's civic and political participation. These factors have been even more pronounced with respect to young women. To give an example, a study on 'house girls' in Turkey, who are single and between the ages of 18 and 24 and who participate neither in the educational system nor in the labor market, shows that the lives of these young women are restricted to the private sphere and their full participation in the social and political life is rather limited (Çelik and Lüküslü 2012: 29). Another vital problem that has recently started to register on the political agenda and in the media is violence against women, due to the politicization of its different forms, including 'honor killings,' by elements of the women's movement. Furthermore, similar to youth political participation discussed above, the 1980 *coup d'état* brought restrictive measures also in relation to women's participation in politics. Alongside the general regulations discouraging political participation and involvement, the coup was also followed by the banning of women's branches of political parties until 1995 (Marshall 2010: 575).

Many legal amendments have been introduced during the 2000s in line with gender equality in Turkey, including the amendment in 2004 of Article 10 of the Constitution on equality before the law as 'Men and women have equal rights and the state is responsible for the measures to implement those rights,' and the amendment of Article 90 in the same year ensuring that in case of conflict with the national law CEDAW[7] has precedency (Muftuler-Bac 2012: 5). Alongside the establishment of the Equality of Opportunity of Men and Women Commission in parliament in 2009, which evaluates legal proposals and amendments on the grounds of gender equality and considers complaints about gender-related discrimination, amendments have also been realized in the civil and penal codes for the strengthening of gender equality (CEDAW 2008; Muftuler-Bac 2012: 5–6). These developments have had positive but limited impact on the enhancement of gender equality due to the existence of implementation problems.

Furthermore, although there are no provisions that lead to gender discrimination in terms of political rights in Turkey, there is great inequality between men and women in terms of their presence in the political decision-making processes in practice (CEDAW 2008: 25). The ratio of women members of parliament has only increased from 9.1 percent to 14.3 percent following the 2011 general elections in Turkey. Despite campaigns by different women's organizations for increasing the number of women parliamentarians, the ratios have remained quite restricted. Furthermore, the presence of women at different levels of party management has been limited due to the internal rules and operations of political parties that do not foster women's active involvement (European Parliament 2012: 16). Local politics also do not enable women to become active participants in decision-making processes. Thus, after the 2009 local elections, only 0.42 percent of the seats in municipal councils were held by women, and women constitute only 0.9 percent of the mayors in Turkey (Muftuler-Bac 2012: 12).

Gender quotas have been proposed and brought to the public agenda by the feminist movement since the 1990s as a tool for increasing women's political participation. However, the attempt to incorporate a clause in the Constitution that establishes gender quotas was rejected in 2004, as the deputies from the governing party voted overwhelmingly against it (Marshall 2010: 573). In an interview, the Head of the Parliamentary Commission for Equal Opportunity for Women and Men also expressed the view that gender quotas can be regarded as being against Article 10 of the Constitution according to which 'Men and women have equal rights. The State shall have the obligation to ensure that this equality exists in practice.'[8]

This picture shows that there have been important de facto restrictions against conventional/electoral forms of political participation by women in Turkey. Furthermore, although there are no comprehensive studies on women's civic and non-conventional political participation, it can be argued that, despite the existence of a women's movement that has become more powerful over the past decades with its different components, there have also been important social and political barriers against women's civic and non-conventional political participation. 'Domestic responsibilities' ascribed to women, patriarchal gender roles in different fields of public life, and widespread domestic violence, have all been detrimental in this respect. Having said this, it is important to note that women have increasingly attempted to overcome these barriers and expand the scope of their civic and political participation. One recent example was their active involvement in the Gezi Park protests and the public forums. Together with youth, women have widely been regarded as active participants in the process.

Inferences from documents released by the public authorities

In this section, we examine the discourses and perspectives of public authorities on women's and youths' civic and political participation, drawing on documents published by institutions at the level of government as well as by related public bodies such as ministries and general directorates.

Five-year development plans have been published since the 1960s in Turkey and can be regarded as documents reflecting the main policy framework and strategic priorities of the governments by which they were developed and published. The Ninth Development Plan (2007–13), which was prepared by the State Planning Organization (SPO) and approved in the parliament in 2006, consists of a framework portraying the perspectives of the JDP governments on youths' and women's civic and political participation. Examination of the Plan reveals that particular aspects of youths' and women's participation are given prominence. These aspects are mostly secondary and at best indirectly related to civic and political participation. In this regard, participation of women and youth in the labor force and employment is emphasized as a mechanism that will lead to their participation in social life (SPO 2006: 98, 103). While the political participation of women is associated with the 'rate of women's representation in the parliament' and is regarded as inadequate in Turkey (SPO 2006: 53), political participation by youth is not even mentioned. Rather, alongside the emphasis on the importance of their participation in the labor market, evaluations of and strategies for youth are framed with reference to their roles in the family and society. Thus the Plan states that:

Diversification in mass communication, inability to leave traditional methods in communication within the family, and insurmountable problems of the education system have increased the problems young people face such as breaking away from their families, becoming insensitive to social problems, hopelessness and lack of self-confidence and, consequently, increased the crime proneness among young people. On the other hand, increase in communication opportunities and development of non-governmental organizations enable the young people to clearly express their personal demands. (SPO 2006: 55)

Furthermore, in line with the former five-year development plans, the plan does not propose any concrete measures or action plans for tackling the existing problems of youth in Turkey, although it does mention the importance of youth for the development of the country (cf. Acar 2008: 6).

The National Program for the Adoption of the EU Acquis released in 2008 by the General Secretariat for European Union (GSEU) again hardly includes any explicit perspective on civic and political participation. Women's participation in education, the labor force, and social and political life is claimed to be strengthened mainly by furthering the support provided to women's organizations (GSEU 2008: 10). Apart from this, although it is indicated that further measures will be taken to hinder violence against women and honor killings and to increase women's participation in the labor force (GSEU 2008: 10, 19), the relation between these and the civic and political participation of women is not covered. Youth is again mentioned mainly in relation to high rates of youth unemployment (GSEU 2008: 19) and no perspective on youth participation is offered.

The Human Rights Report of Turkey, released by the Prime Ministry Human Rights Presidency (PMHRP) in 2008 as the first report published at the level of the Prime Ministry on human rights in Turkey, does not mention the rights of young people. Although highly limited, a perspective on women rights is nevertheless offered. The low ratios of women applicants claiming human rights violations and the limited number of 'complaints about women's rights' are highlighted (PMHPR 2008: 26). The reasons given for this are that women are given less opportunity to receive education leading to qualifications and financial independence, or to seek their rights (PMHPR 2008: 26). It is also stated with reference to women that 'the people whose rights are most violated are those that have the least opportunity or means to search for their rights' (PMHPR 2008: 26).

Apart from the above-mentioned documents that concern the generic social, political, and economic situation of the country and the strategic priorities of the consecutive Justice and Development Party (JDP) governments, there are also reports and action plans produced by women- and youth-related public bodies.

The Directorate General on the Status of Women (DGSW) is the public institution that is directly concerned with women's policies in Turkey. The Directorate General was organised under the Prime Ministry of Turkey before its attachment to the Ministry of Family and Social Policies that was established in 2011. This institution has produced national action plans and reports on women's issues such as gender equality and violence against women. The Gender Equality National Action Plan 2008–13 released in 2008 includes references to the political participation of women and their involvement in the power and decision-making processes alongside issues such as women's access to education, health services and employment and violence against women. It is stated in relation to women's participation that:

> […] women's representation in politics is far below of what it should actually be. Representation of women at the local level, constituting the first step of participation in political life, is even lower than at the national level. Women's participation in politics at the local level should be encouraged and increased. Women are also clearly underrepresented at decision-making positions outside the scope of political participation. (DGSW 2008: 14)

It is also stressed that the active participation of women at all levels of political decision-making is important to provide effective solutions to the problems of women (DGSW 2008: 47). Having said this, the 'political domain' is almost entirely identified with the conventional political bodies such as the National Assembly and local authorities, and women's participation is handled with reference to their low representation in these bodies and their limited existence in leadership positions in public institutions and in the private sector (DGSW 2008: 47–51). The Action Plan also contains concrete strategies to enhance women's political participation such as awareness-raising activities among women and the general public about women's political participation, the promotion of female role models in decision-making processes, and increasing the number of women's councils, etc. (DGSW 2008: 53–4). It also identifies institutions/organizations that are responsible for the implementation of these policies. A report prepared within the scope of the evaluation and monitoring of the National Action Plan (DGSW 2011a) shows that activities and projects have been realized to achieve these aims. Furthermore, although the Action Plan mentions quotas as a strategy for increasing women's political participation, it does not state a perspective on any form of quotas (DGSW 2008: 52). Similarly, the Activity Report prepared by the Grand National Assembly Commission on Equality of Opportunity of Men and Women[9] that encompasses the period between October 2010 and June 2011 indicates, but without expressing any perspective or position on the issue, that different forms of quota should be discussed and evaluated by the Commission (CEOMW 2011: 8). The then head of the Commission stated in an interview conducted by the authors that:[10]

> For now, there is about 8–9% of women parliamentarians at the Grand National Assembly which is too low. Our primary goal should be to increase this ratio. Other countries put quotas, which is not a consistent way of increasing women's participation in politics. It can be a temporary solution. Men love politics and they are dominant in politics and do not want to leave. Even in my party women's participation is low.

The only document where a more specific emphasis on the importance of the political participation of women can be found is the *State of Women in Turkey* Report prepared by the DGSW (2011b). In the report, political participation is defined in a more extensive manner encompassing activities such as following political developments, being informed about political issues, and engaging in political actions, alongside more conventional methods of participation such as voting and running for office (DGSW 2011b: 31). It is also stressed that the equal participation of women in decision-making processes should not only be regarded as a claim for justice and democracy but should also be regarded as a necessary condition for the enhancement of the status of women (DGSW 2011b: 31).

With the exception of this report, it can be argued that the weight of civic and political participation within the documents published by public authorities in relation to women in Turkey remains rather restricted and confined to their 'political representation' in conventional political institutions. Even in that respect, no explicit strategies have been articulated. This should be considered in conjunction with the emphasis on the 'family', which is often prioritized more markedly than 'women.' An important manifestation of this is the organization of the Directorate General on the Status of Women under the Ministry of Family and Social Policies. Furthermore, the ministry as well as the government in general have been persistent in their conservative approach to womanhood that prioritizes the familial sphere, although they have had some dialogue with different elements of the women's movement (Coşar and Yeğenoğlu 2011: 557). One of the reflections of this approach was the government's attempt in 2013 to propose a legal amendment that would restrict women's access to abortion which was withdrawn following the opposition of, and protests organized by, women's organizations.[11]

The political engagement of youth has traditionally been regarded as 'dangerous' in Turkey. The General Directorate of Youth and Sports (GDYS) was the principal institution charged with the implementation of youth policies, before the establishment of the Ministry of Youth and Sports (MYS) in 2011 by governmental decree. Documents released and activities realized by this institution indicate that 'control' and 'protection' rather than 'promotion' have formed the main perspective on civic and political participation by young people in Turkey. In the strategic plan of the GDYS (2010: 11–12), the institution is primarily identified with functions such as the promotion and organization of sports activities, conducting services relating to youths' leisure time, strengthening youths' commitment to Atatürk's principles, patriotism among them, and taking necessary precautions for the protection of youth from 'bad habits.' As reflected by this statement, the promotion of youth civic and political participation has not been adopted as a strategic priority by this institution.

Another youth-related institutional setting is the Grand National Assembly Commission on National Education, Culture, Youth, and Sports, which has mainly been responsible for discussing and negotiating parliamentary bills in these areas. The impact of opposition parties in the development of the Commission's agenda is limited as the majority of its members are deputies from the governing party (the

Justice and Development Party (JDP)). It has been indicated by a member of the Commission from the main opposition party (the Republican People's Party (RPP)) that it does not have a vision of, or take any actions for, increasing youth civic and political participation, and it also serves as a consenting/validating body for the policies produced by the government.[12]

Until very recently, there was no document that comprehensively reflected youth policy in Turkey. The National Youth and Sports Policy Document published by the Ministry of Youth and Sports (MYS 2013a) in 2013 is the first document that has encompassed perspectives and strategies in relation to youth. The Ministry of Youth and Sports, established in 2011 by government decree, adopts a more extensive perspective in relation to youth. The 2013–17 Strategic Plan of the Ministry implies a reorganization of youth services in general and the adoption of a more comprehensive approach to youth policies that transcends the above-mentioned emphasis on 'control' and protection' to a certain extent (MYS 2013b). Furthermore, the National Youth and Sports Policy Document produced by the Ministry takes into consideration a variety of aspects, including access to education and employment, sports, the place of youth within the family, the problems faced by disadvantaged young people, and youth health. The report also includes a section on 'democratic participation and civic consciousness' where youth participation is identified as indispensable for an advanced democracy (MYS 2013a: 29). It is stated that 'in order to have a participatory youth with high civic consciousness, it is necessary to firstly make sure that young people have a say in the social processes by identifying obstacles in the way of their participation' (MYS 2013a: 29). The incorporation of tools into educational and training policies that would strengthen democratic consciousness among young people, the enhancement of youth participation in national and local assemblies, the removal of the communication gap between young people and local authorities, and the encouragement of youth to get involved in non-governmental organizations, are identified as policies to be pursued (MYS 2013a: 29–31). Yet despite the existence of a discourse promoting youth participation, it is too soon at the time of writing to argue that implementation is compatible with these statements. Furthermore, there are also important signs indicating the continuation of the government perspective that considers youth as a category to be shaped, controlled, and protected rather than as active participants in all decision-making processes concerning themselves and society in general. Traces of this perspective can be found in the National Youth and Sports Policy Document's sections on issues such as the protection of youth from bad habits, and the prevention of the alienation of young people from national and moral values (MYS 2013a: 11–12, 24). In line with this, it is stated that 'young people should be seen as a unique group requiring attention because of their vulnerability and openness to abuse during the most important period of their lives' (MYS 2013a: 5). It is also stressed that 'parents do not convey the values and culture of the society they live in to their children [which] increases the possibility of the alienation of young people from the society and this results in young people becoming prone to crime' (MYS 2013a: 12).

Government perspectives are also reflected in documents produced by the Justice and Development Party given that it has been the ruling party since the 2002 General Elections. In a document entitled *Political Vision of Ak Parti* (JDP 2012: 35), it is stated: 'Our youth are the spirit of our present and the assurance of our future. The youth is a nation's most precious treasure. Our country has more of this treasure than other countries.' The main mission ascribed to the youth is being 'virtuous' and 'exemplary' (JDP 2012: 36). It is also claimed that the party will launch initiatives to increase and enhance youth participation in decision-making mechanisms (JDP 2012: 36). It is remarkable that this document, which is claimed to portray the 2023 vision of the party, does not include any statement regarding the civic and political participation of women. The latest party program[13] of the JDP includes sections devoted to promises in relation to youth and women. The statement 'Not because women make up half of our population, they should be considered as individuals before everything else primarily effective for the raising of healthy generations' in the party program can be read as an indication of the party's vision about women as 'mothers.' This perspective can be regarded as being in tension with other statements that are in line with the promotion of women's participation in social and political life such as: 'All necessary measures shall be taken to encourage women to participate in public life,' 'Women shall be encouraged to enrol as members of our Party and to play an active role in politics' and 'Support shall be provided to associations, foundations and non-governmental organizations related to women.' In the party program it is claimed that while young people in Turkey were not given the right to speak, were not trusted and were seen as threats before, their participation in national political decision-making processes has been ensured under JDP rule. Yet despite this claim, the 2013 June uprisings in Turkey have revealed that public institutions and decision-making processes have not been open to young people's political participation, especially to more non-conventional forms of participation. As an indication of this, young people participating in the protests have been differentiated from the conservative, 'silent', majority youth, with the former being regarded as marginal by government authorities.

Concluding remarks and prospects for further research

This chapter has attempted to describe the perspectives on civic and political participation of women and youth which are reflected in the policy documents published by public authorities in Turkey between 2004 and 2013. Despite their restricted reference to the issue, the documents examined nevertheless give insights into the general orientation. In this respect, it is possible to argue that women's participation has mainly been understood and framed within the scope of conventional/electoral forms of political participation. Although the importance of their higher 'representation' in electoral bodies and public offices has been acknowledged, no explicit strategy for the achievement of this has been adopted. Youth, on the other hand, have mainly been perceived as a group of people to be controlled and protected, the civic and political participation of whom has not been regarded as an issue to be specifically concerned with. Furthermore, it may be inferred from government perspectives on the civic and political participation of youth and women that there is a tension between the emphasis on conservative values and the participation of these two groups in civic and political life. With regard to women's participation, this shows itself as a tension underlined by the family-centered outlook that identifies womanhood with reference to 'domestic responsibilities'; in terms of youth participation, the prevailing understanding of youth as a category to be shaped, controlled and protected constitutes an important source of tension. It can be argued that these tensions that also mark the policy documents examined within the scope of this study have had important impacts upon youth's and women's involvement in the Gezi Park protests.

As indicated at the very beginning of this chapter, the main limitation of an examination of policy documents such as the one presented here is the existence of a gap between statements and promises on the one hand and practices on the other. Further research on this gap, as well as on how the perspectives of public authorities impact upon women's and youths' civic and political participation, is required to enhance our knowledge of this issue.

Notes

1 Turkish Statistical Institute, Address Based Population Registration System Database. Online at: http://www.tuik.gov.tr/PreTablo.do?alt_id=39.
2 Turkish Statistical Institute, Address Based Population Registration System Database. See http://www.tuik.gov.tr/Gosterge.do?id=3642&metod=IlgiliGosterge for primary and secondary education and see http://www.tuik.gov.tr/Gosterge.do?id=3644&metod=IlgiliGosterge for higher education (retrieved on 10 June 2013).
3 The youth unemployment rate was 20.7 percent in January 2013 and the related ratio is remarkably higher in terms of young women compared to men. (Turkish Statistical Institute, http://www.tuik.gov.tr/Gosterge.do?id=3538&metod=IlgiliGosterge, retrieved on 15 June 2013).
4 Similarly, only 15.3 percent of the respondents of an online questionnaire that was completed by 3,008 individuals stated that they felt themselves close to a political party (Bilgiç and Kafkaslı 2013: 7).
5 In the first 14 days of the protests, the total number of Twitter messages related to the protests was about 13.5 million. See http://www.cnbce.com/yasam-ve-teknoloji/sosyal-medya/gezi--icin-135-milyon-tweet for details.
6 See http://www.whatishappeninginistanbul.com/?p=640 for a detailed narrative.
7 Turkey became a part of the United Nations Convention on the Elimination of All Forms of Discrimination Against Women (CEDAW) in 1985.
8 Interview conducted by the authors on 7 April 2010.
9 The Commission was established in 2009.
10 Interview conducted by the authors with the President of the Grand National Assembly Commission on Equality of Opportunity of Men and Women on 7 April 2010.
11 See Unal and Cindoglu (2013) for a detailed examination of the abortion debate that started in May 2012 when the Prime Minister declared that 'Every abortion is a murder.'
12 Interview conducted by the authors on 7 April 2010.
13 The party program is only available in electronic form. See http://www.akparti.org.tr/english/akparti/parti-programme#bolum_.

References

Acar, H. (2008) 'Türkiye'nin Ulusal Gençlik Politikası Nasıl Yapılandırılmalıdır?' *Uluslararası İnsan Bilimleri Dergisi*, 5 (1): 1–20.
Artan, İ. E. *et al.* (2005) *Üniversite Gençliği Değerleri: Korkular ve Umutlar*. Istanbul: TESEV Yayınları.
Bilgiç, E. E. and Kafkaslı, Z. (2013) *Gencim, Özgürlükçüyüm, Ne İstiyorum? Direngeziparkı Anket Sonuç Raporu*. İstanbul: Istanbul Bilgi University Press.
Brady, H. (1999) 'Political participation,' in J. P. Robinson, P. R. Shaver, and L. S. Wrightsman (eds), *Measures of Political Attitudes*. San Diego, CA: Academic Press, pp. 737–801.
CEDAW (Convention on the Elimination of All Forms of Discrimination Against Women) (2008) *Six Periodic Reports of State Parties: Turkey*. United Nations, November.
Çelen, N. and Çok, F. (2007) Chapter on Turke, in J. J. Arnett (ed.), *International Encyclopedia of Adolescence*. New York: Routledge, pp. 1010–24.
Çelik, K. and Lüküslü., (2012) 'Spotlighting a silent category of young females: the life experiences of "house girls" in Turkey,' *Youth and Society*, 44 (1): 28–48.
CEOMW (Grand National Assembly Commission on Equality of Opportunity of Men and Women) (2011) Faaliyet Raporu 23. Donem 5. Yasama Yili. Ekim 2010– Haziran 2011, Ankara.
Coşar, S. and Yeğenoğlu, M. (2011) 'New grounds for patriarchy in Turkey? Gender policy in the age of AKP', *South European Society and Politics*, 16 (4): 555–73.
DGSW (Directorate General on the Status of Women) (2008) *National Action Plan: Gender Equality in Turkey*. The Republic of Turkey, Prime Ministry, Ankara, September.
DGSW (Directorate General on the Status of Women) (2011a) *Toplumsal Cinsiyet Esitligi Ulusal Eylem Plani (2008–2013) 2010 Yili Birlesik Raporu*. Kadinin Statusu Genel Mudurlugu, Haziran, Ankara.
DGSW (Directorate General on the Status of Women) (2011b) *Turkiye'de Kadinin Durumu*. Kadinin Statusu Genel Mudurlugu, Temmuz, Ankara.
Diani, M. and McAdam, D. (2003) *Social Movements and Networks: Relational Approaches to Collective Action*. New York: Oxford University Press.
Ekman, J. and Amnå, E. (2012) 'Political participation and civic engagement: towards a new typology,' *Human Affairs*, 22: 283–300.
Enneli, P. (2010) 'Türkiye'de Toplumsal Bir Kategori Olarak Yoksul Gençlik,' *Antropoloji*, 23: 41–67.
European Parliament (2012) Report (2009–2014) on a 2020 Perspective for Women in Turkey. Prepared by the Committee on Women's Rights and Gender Equality, Rapporteur: Emine Bozkurt, 12 April.
Gamson, W. A. and Meyer, D. S. (1996) 'Framing political opportunity,' in D. McAdam, J. D. McCarthy, and M. N. Zald (eds), *Comparative Perspectives on Social Movements: Political Opportunities, Mobilizing Structures, and Cultural Framings*. Cambridge: Cambridge University Press, pp. 275–90.
GDYS (General Directorate of Youth and Sports) (2010) *Genclik ve Spor Genel Mudurlugu 2010–2014 Stratejik Plani*. Genclik ve Spor Genel Mudurlugu, Ankara.
Göksel, A. (2009) *Studies on Youth Policies in the Mediterranean Partner Countries: Turkey*. Report prepared for the EuroMed Youth III Programme.
GSEU (General Secretariat for European Union) (2008) *National Programme of Turkey for the Adoption of Acquis*. December, Ankara.
JDP (Justice and Development Party) (2012) *Political Vision of Ak Parti 2023: Politics, Society and the World*. 30 September.
Kaymakcan, R. (2007) 'Turkish religious education: evaluation of recent learning curriculum of religious culture and ethical knowledge,' *Educational Sciences: Theory and Practice*, 7 (1): 202–10.

Kılıç, K. (2009) 'Kentsel Genclik Arastirmasi Anketi Baglamında Genclerin Siyasal Egilimlerini Etkileyen Faktorler,' in C. Boyraz (ed.), *Gencler Tartisiyor: Siyasete Katilim, Sorunlar ve Cozum Onerileri*. Istanbul: TUSES.

Kitschelt, H. P. (1986) 'Political opportunity structures and political protest: anti-nuclear movements in four democracies,' *British Journal of Political Science*, 16: 57–86.

KONDA (2013) Gezi Parki Arastirmasi. See http://www.konda.com.tr/ (retrieved 14 June 2013).

Koopmans, R. (1999) 'Political opportunity structure: some splitting to balance the lumping,' *Sociological Forum*, 14: 93–105.

Kriesi, H. (2008) 'Political mobilization, political participation and the power of the vote,' *West European Politics*, 31 (1–2): 147–68.

Kriesi, H., Koopmans, Duyvendak, J. W., and Giugni, M. (1992) 'New social movements and political opportunities in Western Europe,' *European Journal of Political Research*, 22: 219–44.

Kurtaran, Y., Nemutlu, G., and Yentürk, N. (2008) 'About, for and together with youth: a summary of *Youth Work and Policy in Turkey*,' in N. Yentürk, Y. Kurtaran, and G. Nemutlu (eds), *Youth Work and Policy in Turkey*, Youth Study Unit Research Paper No. 3. Istanbul: Istanbul Bilgi University, pp. 6–20.

Kuzmanovic, D. (2010) 'Project culture and Turkish civil society,' *Turkish Studies*, 11 (3): 429–44.

Marshall, G. A. (2010) 'Gender quotas and the press in Turkey: public debate in the age of AKP government,' *South European Society and Politics*, 15 (4): 573–91.

Muftuler-Bac, M. (2012) *Gender Equality in Turkey*. Note prepared for the Directorate General for Internal Policies, Policy Department C: Cizitens' Rights and Constitutional Affairs, January, Brussels.

MYS (Ministry of Youth and Sports) (2013a) *The National Youth and Sports Policy Document*. Ankara: Ministry of Youth and Sports.

MYS (Ministry of Youth and Sports) (2013b) *Genclik ve Spor Bakanligi Stratejik Plani: 2013–2017*. Ankara: Genclik ve Spor Bakanligi.

Parry, G., Moyser, G., and Day, N. (1992) *Political Participation and Democracy in Britain*. Cambridge: Cambridge University Press.

PMHPR (Prime Ministry Human Rights Presidency) (2008) *Human Rights Report of Turkey*. 2 July, Ankara.

Şener, T. (2012) 'Civic engagement of future teachers,' *Procedia Technology*, 1: 4–9.

SPO (State Planning Organization) (2006) *Ninth Development Plan: 2007–2013*. T. R. Prime Ministry State Planning Organization, Ankara.

Tarrow, S. (1996) 'States and opportunities: the political structuring of social movements,' in D. McAdam, J. D. McCarthy, and N. M. Zald (eds), *Comparative Perspectives on Social Movements: Political Opportunities, Mobilizing Structures, and Cultural Framings*. Cambridge: Cambridge University Press, pp. 41–61.

Teorell, J. et al. (2007) 'Political participation: mapping the terrain,' in J. W. Van Deth, J. R. Montero, and A. Westholm (eds), *Citizenship and Involvement in European Democracies: A Comparative Analysis*. London and New York: Routledge, pp. 334–57.

TSI (Turkish Statistical Institute) (2011) *Youth in Statistics, 2011*. Ankara: Turkish Statistical Institute.

Unal, D. and Cindoglu, D. (2013) 'Reproductive citizenship in Turkey: abortion chronicles,' *Women's Studies International Forum*, 38: 21–31.

UNDP (2008) *Human Development Report – Turkey 2008: Youth in Turkey*. Ankara.

Vráblíková, K. (2014) 'How context matters? Mobilization, political opportunity structures, and nonelectoral political participation in old and new democracies,' *Comparative Political Studies*, 20 (10): 1–27.

Yentürk, N. (2008) 'Youth policy proposals in area surrounding the lives of young people,' in N. Yentürk, Y. Kurtaran, and G. Nemutlu (eds), *Youth Work and Policy in Turkey*, Youth Study Unit Research Paper No. 3. Istanbul: Istanbul Bilgi University, pp. 41–69.

Zani, B. and Barrett, M. (2012) 'Engaged citizens? Political participation and social engagement among youth, women, minorities, and migrants,' *Human Affairs*, 22: 273–82.

23
ACTIVE CITIZENSHIP IN ITALY AND THE UK

Comparing political discourse and practices of political participation, civic activism and engagement in policy processes

Cristiano Bee and Paola Villano

Introduction

This chapter compares policy discussions regarding active citizenship in the UK and Italy, and provides an assessment of the ongoing process of Europeanisation by looking at the frames, ideas, opinions and evaluations of a number of activists interviewed in the two countries in 2011. The choice to focus on these two apparently disjointed dimensions – the national development of active citizenship on the one hand, and the value attributed to European citizenship on the other – for this comparison is justified for at least two reasons. In particular we first want to map out the characteristics of two approaches to active citizenship that have emerged in reaction to specific social and political needs in the Italian and British contexts. We believe that the two models represent exceptional cases for reflection on active citizenship and political participation because of the many commonalities they share, as well as their dissimilarities. The Italian model is marked by a process that intertwines an attempt to restructure the public administration throughout via a top-down process of institutionalisation of practices of active citizenship with bottom-up processes where civic activism is an essential component of the country's socio-economic context. The British case is characterised by a process in which different key politicians belonging to opposite ideologies have been debating the meaning of active citizenship at least since the end of the 1980s, and is marked by an ongoing institutional and political attempt to stimulate active citizenship and civic participation at the communitarian level. In both cases, as we will explain in this chapter, this has happened in response to precise public and social problems that have been afflicting these countries. In the Italian case, it can be argued that the deficit in the public administration, the lack of transparency that affects public institutions, as well as the need to ensure social interventions wherever public actions are lacking, are drivers and components of this wide reflection on active citizenship. In the British case, it can be argued instead that the 'pattern of citizenship' has been pursued in order to answer specific social problems that have emerged throughout the UK over time. The lack of integration between social groups has fostered in the policy agenda the need to shape integration starting from civic engagement and active citizenship, thereby stimulating bottom-up processes. We believe that both approaches have commonalities with the EU approach to active citizenship (see Chapter 20 by Bee and Guerrina in the present volume) as well as differences. This is the reason why we need to take into account the forces of the Europeanisation process by focusing on the impact this might have on domestic political discourses, by looking at the challenge to dominant frames regarding citizenship. We therefore argue that the discussions regarding active citizenship in the two countries needs to be mirrored and confronted with European discourse, because of the impact that European citizenship has had in changing patterns of identification and belonging to the national arenas. We will show, in our analysis, that this construct, European citizenship, is perceived both as important and ambiguous by activists that we interviewed.

The chapter fits into the contemporary broader scholarly debate in citizenship studies (Bellamy *et al*. 2004; Castles and Davidson 2000; Delanty 2007a; Eder and Giesen 2001; Heater 1999; Lister 1997; Miller 2008a). More precisely, it looks at the confrontation and comparison of two of the dominant models of citizenship in the literature, the neo-liberal and the civic republican. Our aim is to discuss the ambiguities inherent to the British and Italian approaches to active citizenship, by arguing that in both cases the political discourses have assumed connotations deriving from these two models, with characteristics that are also often overlapping. The chapter frames the idea of citizenship as a political, social and cultural concept, as it has recently been discussed and criticised by many scholars throughout Europe (Faulks 2000; Ferrera 2004; Isin *et al*. 2008). On this account, it is worth remembering that the emergence of post-national, cosmopolitan or multilevel models of citizenship (Delanty 2000; Shaw 2009) is central in the overall discussion regarding the reframing of the notion of citizenship. We therefore believe that it is important to focus on the ideological connotations of the debate and to unpack the orientation and framework of this concept as they emerge in the two different national contexts.

When we focus on dominant notions of citizenship emerging in different countries, whatever level we are looking at (national or European), it is imperative to reflect upon the relationship between the individual and the political community, as well as on the broader interconnections between individuals and social groups. On this account, while we unpack and discuss the notion of citizenship, we need to focus on the balance between rights and responsibilities (Faulks 1998). Liberal (and neo-liberal) and civic republican models of citizenship have influenced the political setting of different European countries and resulted in different models of balance between these two components, rights and responsibilities, and the overall practices that this status entails. While the neo-liberal perspective of citizenship (Marshall 1950; Heater 1999) accounts for a 'passive citizen' and the rights that are ensured in order to guarantee the expression of certain freedoms, the civic republican perspective accounts for an 'active citizen' and the reciprocal responsibilities that members of a political community have towards each other (Bellamy 2000; Miller 2000, 2008b; Mouffe 1992). This is a key debate that has been taking place in a number of countries in Europe, the UK and Italy included.

On this account, Marinetto (2003) explained the emergence of the debate on active citizenship in the 1980s in the Western world with reference to the existing fragmentation between right-wing and left-wing ideologies: 'Protagonists of the right emphasised the importance of promoting active citizenship to achieve a balance between rights and duties. This was seen as a logical extension of the prevailing political orthodoxy of the time which sought to reduce the burden of state and introduce greater private sector provision of public goods' (Marinetto 2003: 107). Based on neo-liberal roots, the concept of active citizenship put forward by right-wing politicians was aimed at preserving and promoting individual liberty, by enhancing a sense of utilitarian responsibility towards the community. Social democratic viewpoints addressed the emergence of active citizenship from a counter point, looking at the broader civic involvement of the individual in a given community: 'People on the centre left also took up the question of active citizenship for quite different reasons. Their concern was to defend the collective fabric of public life against encroachment by the market' (Marinetto 2003: 107).

The aim of this chapter is to outline the trends that have been driving conceptualisations of citizenship and the practice of active citizenship in Italy and Britain. In the first section, we address the characteristics of the Italian context, by looking first at the debate on public communication that emerged in the 1990s and then by looking at the research agenda on political and civic participation. In the second section, we look at the British case, by overviewing the citizenship reform promoted under the New Right governments of Thatcher and Major and subsequently by New Labour after Blair won the election in 1997. In the third and final section, we outline some general findings based on interviews which we conducted with NGO activists in 2011. The aim of this analysis is to provide insights regarding two of the Discursive Nodal Points that emerged in our overall analysis which we conducted for the PIDOP project, namely 'Political participation' and 'Europeanisation and transnationalisation' (see Bee and Guerrina 2014 and Chapter 20 in this volume). In this regard, the Italian and British discourses on active citizenship provide a valuable evidence base for comparative purposes with the EU's approach to active citizenship.

Explaining the context: active citizenship in Italy

The overall debate regarding active citizenship in Italy is linked to the discussion concerning the enhancement of participatory democracy that started in the 1990s. In a political context marked by political scandals and by growing failure in the public administrative system, the political discourse surrounding active citizenship is enhanced and shaped as a proper policy response to establish better transparency and improve the overall performance of the bureaucratic system. As we will see later, this is a significant contextual factor that signifies an important difference existing between the Italian and British models of active citizenship. In this section, we provide an overview of two interlinked perspectives that have emerged in the academic literature and that describe quite convincingly the debate concerning active citizenship in Italy.

The first perspective looks at the top-down development of institutional models and practices of public communication. As explained below, this emerged in the 1990s and entailed the restructuring of the public administration structures. A second perspective looks at the development of civic activism as a more or less established — and institutionalised — instrument of engagement of civil society. This is a bottom-up process that is well rooted in the Italian socio-political context and can be considered as a micro-verse of the broader instruments, practices and principles that can be defined as political participation.

In one of the many manuals, textbooks and research monographs published on this subject, Grandi defined the 1990s as the decade of public communication (Grandi 2007). This expression emphasises the prominent attention that was devoted to this area in Italy not only by the scientific community but also by political institutions. This is a decade that was shaped by wide reflection on the structures of public communication, which, as was argued by many scholars at the time, was construed as an academic discipline, as an institutional practice, and as a proper field of scientific investigation (Caligiuri 1997; De Marco 2005; Esposito 2000; Gadotti 2001; Griva and Piazza 1996; Mancini 2006; Rovinetti 2000). Overall, scholars' writing at the time shared the argument that public communication was becoming more and more an essential function that public institutions had to perform in order to provide the democratic system with forms of input legitimacy and in order to enhance participation in the cultural, political and social life of the community (Faccioli 2000). The practice of public communication was therefore to be based on the mutual exchange of meanings and behavioural models between institutions and citizens with the scope of shaping citizenship and the sense of belonging.

In terms of broader understanding, it is worth underlining that the Italian debate is linked with the extensive literature on public relations, public management and public communication that emerged in the USA (Grunig and Hunt 1984; Grunig and Grunig 1992) and influenced comparative research in European countries and at the EU level (Fawkes and Moloney 2008; Van Ruler and Verčič 2004). The normative arguments of this literature examine the need to guarantee citizens' right to engagement in public activities through an established set of deliberative practices. Public communication is therefore an institutionally driven activity that entails the establishment of public relations organisations in order to increase and improve dialogue with the general public through specific mechanisms of feedback (Bee 2010; Mancini 2006). These processes are fundamental in the public administration reforms that have taken place all around Europe over recent years and imply a process of transformation from government to governance (Hooghe and Marks 2001). It can therefore be argued that, in terms of principles, the development of institutional communication put into practice the idea of citizens' rights to participate in and strengthen the foundation of participatory democracy within a political community. In terms of practice, it regards the shaping of new modes of governance that entail the development of means and tools that enable citizens to engage with public institutions in the policy process. In their classic work, *Managing Public Relations*, Grunig and Hunt (1984) explained the differences between various models of communication, influencing much of the thinking in this field. The meaning and shaping of public communication as an active process by the public administration has to be understood by looking at the key distinction existing between information and communication. While the first is to be conceived as a top-down process and entails a massive amount of information provided by public institutions on a number of issues (for example, on their activities and political priorities) and can be widely associated with either propaganda or simple public campaigning on public issues, public communication entails a social relation that shapes common understandings regarding public issues (Faccioli 2000: 19). In the bi-directional model of public communication described by Mancini (2006), citizens are active players in the administrative process and key actors in defining, shaping and elaborating the policy cycle.

These assumptions have largely influenced the thinking of the Italian scientific community and followed a specific institutional development that resulted, among other outcomes, in the establishment of Law 150/2000 that regulates public administrations' information and communication activities. The law represents an important development that challenged the typical structures of the Italian public administration, which was put under pressure in order to reorganise its own practices and improve its accessibility, openness and overall performance. The law implied the development of a set of specialised professionals, able to deal with the complexities of communication management and to plan specific strategies in collaboration with the various social actors involved in public policy development.

In terms of overall assessment, this process entailed the widening of responsibilities undertaken by state institutions, the acquisition by citizens of a new form of awareness and consciousness regarding their rights, as well as new responsibilities within a public sphere structure that was under transformation (Rovinetti 2000). Arena (2001) talks directly about a notion of citizenship based on an 'active consensus' that should aim to satisfy the public interest through a process where citizens are *co-administrators* in deciding on public matters. Social problems should therefore be commonly perceived by a number of institutional and non-institutional actors and involve cooperation between citizens and institutions to find the correct policy responses (Arena 2001, 2006). We argue that this form of active citizenship includes civic republican principles, while at the same time integrating a wide number of neo-liberal logics. The active citizen's right to information and communication (Arena 2006) entails her/his transformation into a 'customer' of the public administration (Caligiuri 1997). Therefore, in this process, communicating by focusing on the specific needs of the target audience becomes one of the main 'services' that a public administration should be performing. This overall discussion is parallel to, and for many reasons distinct from, the academic debate that looks at the enhancement of processes of participatory democracy based on a civic republican account of active citizens.

The second broad discussion that takes place in Italy and accounts for active citizenship can be easily linked to the analysis of bottom-up processes and refers to a lively multi-disciplinary debate regarding various models of democracy, namely representative, participative or deliberative democracy (Allegretti 2006; Bobbio 2002, 2007; Ceri 1996; Gelli 2005; Lanzara 2005; Mastropaolo 2001; Morlino 2003; Pelizzoni 2005a).

This is a research agenda (Andretta and Caiani 2005; Bonanni and Penco 2006; Della Porta 2004; Della Porta and Diani 2004; Fedi and Mannarini 2008) that accounts for the growth of political participation, civic activism and civic engagement as constituent parts of the Italian democratic socio-political setting. Pelizzoni (2005b) underlines how Italy, in the present context, has been experiencing a form of revival in citizens' participation in public matters, marred by a growing mistrust towards those who are in charge of controlling resources. It is worth remembering here that thinking on civic activism in Italy is largely influenced by the seminal work of Putnam on *Making Democracy Work* (Putnam *et al.* 1993) that provides an account of the links existing between civil society and Italian public institutions. In his model, high levels of activism are measured by combining factors such as engagement, trust, tolerance and the development of associationism in the country – in other words, by gaining a profound understanding of social capital (see Donati and Tronca 2008; Piselli 1995, 2001).

In this regard, Moro (1998, 2005, 2010) provides a critical account of the bottom-up processes that underlie the dynamics of active citizenship as a new form of political participation and widely discusses the structures, and also the practices, that shape and enable civic activism and participation in Italy. This scholar provides an overview of the forms of participation that are not linked to engagement with institutionalised practices of representative democracy, but rather to broader processes of involvement in the wider 'political public space' (Allegretti 2009) where civil society is acting, contributing and criticising.

Moro criticises the establishment of formalised forms of consultation – which are commonly discussed in the first perspective described above – by arguing that, in a way, they provide evidence of the institutional difficulty of dealing with the complexities represented by civic activism and, more importantly, with civil society in general. He defines civic activism as follows:

> We can define civic activism as an organisational phenomenon which refers to the wide variety of modalities that motivate citizens to get together, to mobilise resources and play an active part in the policy cycle. In this way they undertake powers and responsibilities with the final scope of protecting rights, taking care of the common good and supporting subjects in less advantaged positions. (Moro 2010: 3, our translation)

Moro, in his attempt to define what civil society is, clearly underlines all the difficulties in finding a working definition that can encompass all the varieties and typologies that could be found in reality. In his definition, however, he highlights the centrality that more or less organised interests can assume in the overall policy process, and therefore in shaping the agenda and following the stages of policy formulation and implementation. Moreover, the social function exercised by civic activism is extremely important, as clearly emerged from the analysis that we conducted in the PIDOP project. Social inclusion, social solidarity and integration are some of the key core values that activists point out when they are called to describe the values that orient their action as well as the overall objectives of their policy interventions.

Explaining the context: active citizenship in the UK

The broader political debate on active citizenship in Britain takes a completely different form from the Italian one. It can be argued that, first of all, it has involved an intense discussion of the role of the individual in the community of belonging that started at the end of the 1980s. It is more politically driven than the Italian discussion, and is part of a wider institutional and scientific debate that has been shaped by specific ideological connotations, rooted either in Conservatism or in New Labour's political projects.

At the end of the 1980s (see Brehony 1992), active citizenship was put forward as a possible policy response to a number of social problems emerging in the country. The issues of engagement and participation were at the time politically and socially at the forefront of the Conservative policies of Thatcher and Major. In declaring that 'greater opportunities for active citizens are being offered and taken up […] our action against crime and against drugs relies increasingly on a partnership between statutory agencies, the relevant professions and public-spirited citizens', Hurd (cited in Faulks 1998: 128), Home Secretary at the time, launched the neo-liberal style of active citizenship in Britain, expressing a commitment, which was consequently shaped and renewed in Major's government between 1990 and 1997. The political and social needs at the time were to foster new values and were aimed at favouring a better integration within political communities in Britain (Faulks 1998; Marinetto 2003; Davies 2012). Even though principles evoking the civic republican style of active citizenship were put forward, academic evidence has been rather critical of the association developed by the Conservatives. Research shows that the New Right approach to active citizenship was far from being open and based on participatory means (Faulks 1998; Kearns 1995), being the 'active citizenship campaign' coherent with the neo-liberal politics of the Conservative government at the time and based on the assumption of the need to foster a sense of individual responsibility between members of a community. In interpreting this development, Faulks argues 'the active citizenship campaign was consistent with the Neo-Liberal agenda of Thatcherism, which was concerned more with the development of a citizenship based upon the assertion of the individual and the market, rather than a genuine concern for the promotion of community values' (Faulks 1998: 128).

In order to draw a parallel with the reforms of the public administration in Italy and in Europe, it is worth remembering that this discourse on active citizenship was shaped by another initiative that was taken at the time, the Citizen's Charter which was launched by Major in 1991. The Charter was meant to establish better access of citizens to public services, the need for public services to operate efficiently, and the guarantee of a higher level of choice for citizens based on new market mechanisms. This programme of reforms is to be interpreted in a wider context concerning the reorganisation of public services that includes programmes such as the 1988 and 1993 Education Act, the 1988 House and Local Government Act and the 1990 National Health Service and Community Care Act. All of these, as Faulks explains, were attempts to 'increase personal responsibility and the basic market right of the citizen' (Faulks 1998: 133) by promoting a consumerist culture.

It can thus be argued that a change in the role and functions of the public administration with a growing role given to local authorities was central at the time (Kearns 1995: 159), and implied an opening to the Third Sector, with a more prominent role given to voluntary organisations (Brehony 1992). The New Right style of active citizenship was based on the neo-liberal politics of the Thatcher and Major governments and enhanced social divisions at the community level rather than creating principles and values allowing for conditions of social solidarity to foster the actual exercise of active citizenship. Moreover, it was oriented at the preservation of individual liberty rather than at actual engagement with communitarian life (Faulks 1998: 130) and entailed neither empowerment in the political community nor actual involvement in the public sphere.

The shift in government that led New Labour to emerge as the leading party in Britain was characterised by a renewed commitment to the issue and definition of active citizenship and was based on the political necessity to make 'community a central political theme' (Marinetto 2003: 114). Participatory democracy and civic engagement were thus central in the political discourse of New Labour, especially until the 7/7 events of 2005. During this time, the government put forward a new set of innovative ideas and provided evidence of a 'commitment to extending public involvement in the policy making and democratic process' (Marinetto 2003: 116). In New Labour political discourse, issues such as civic engagement, active citizenship and civil society at the local level were central in order to shape forms of collective action allowing for increased participation in policy making (Giddens 1998, 2000, 2001). The pattern of active citizenship in Britain under New Labour was thus framed by the establishment of a new relationship with public institutions, not merely based on consumerist principles but grounded instead on political and civic patterns (Andrews *et al.* 2008: 225). In line with the Italian case, the key public service reforms driving the New Labour agenda were central in these terms, but at the same time the process entailed openness to civic participation and bottom-up processes of engagement. Andrews *et al.* (2008) shows that this process was similar to that implemented in many Western countries, where policies of active engagement were being put in place in order to shape policy-making. In these terms, under New Labour, a set of initiatives was aimed at improving this relationship, providing evidence of the fact that 'numerous public service providers are now engaged in fostering links with citizens, predicated in part on the instrumental rationale that this will improve service performance' (Andrews *et al.* 2008: 226).

Critics, however, have argued that this approach had many commonalities with neo-liberal principles (Davies 2012). In particular, in comparing the New Labour approach to community and deliberation with the Habermasian ideal model of civic engagement and public participation, Davies identifies a series of critical issues that emerge from a closer analysis of actual policies. Overall, the partnerships developed under New Labour embedded 'the principles of "contributory consensualism" – the duty of citizen activists to mobilise community resources in pursuit of non-negotiable government policies' (Davies 2012: 10). In relation to this, Marinetto argues that New Labour's policies of community involvement 'have not been accompanied by a substantive transfer of executive power from the centre to local institutions and people' (Marinetto 2003: 116). The problem remained that there was an insufficient transfer of power that could be thought of as creating a truly 'citizen-centred government' (Marinetto 2003: 118).

It is worth noticing that, more prominently than in the Italian case, the shaping of active citizenship under New Labour was linked to the emergence of new social problems that resulted in academic and institutional reflection on the reframing of integration policies (see, for example, McGhee 2003, 2006, 2008, 2009). Clashes between communities in Oldham, Burnley and Bradford in 2001, and then the terrorist attack of 7/7 in London in 2005, led to the questioning of a number of policy responses to the fragmentation of British society that had been adopted at the end of the 1990s. This essentially put multiculturalism into question. The emphasis on the lack of integration and separation between communities resulted in a series of policy actions that were taken forward by the New Labour government between 2001 and 2010, which have been characterised as a 'model of civic assimilation based on the idea of forging allegiance to core principles shared by all through the effective engagement of responsible "active citizens" located in "active communities"' (McGhee 2009: 49).

A number of policy documents developed during this time help us to understand the centrality of active citizenship and community cohesion for building a new approach to integration policy in Britain. However, in evaluating these policy responses, Ratcliffe notes that 'the New Labour government remained, at least, somewhat equivocal on the relationship between equality and (community) cohesion' (Ratcliffe 2012: 275). McGhee underlines how these strategies were actually biased by the fact that they were not integrative in the full sense but more closely focused on the adaptation and assimilation of minorities. In his evaluation of New Labour's policies McGhee states that they neglected 'a balanced integration strategy for both potential "host" communities and "new" migrants. At the same time, the strategy of deterrence has had the unintended consequence of legitimizing racism and asylophobia in Britain' (McGhee 2006: 118).

The events of the 7/7 London bombings, and then the shift in government from Blair to Brown, produced a further shift in the policies of active citizenship. The strengthening of the assimilationist approach as well as the shaping of 'Britishness' as a core value for minority groups were expressed through the approach taken towards citizenship after 2005 as represented by the 2008 *Green Paper: The Path to Citizenship*, where the aim was to base integration policies on a journey to citizenship. The three-stage journey (temporary residence, probationary citizenship and British citizenship/permanent residence) proposed in the Green Paper were meant to set a requirement to earn citizenship and the right to stay in the UK. This is marked as a core principle in the section of the Green Paper dedicated to Active Citizenship, where it is stated that:

> We tested the idea of asking newcomers to participate in some kind of community work. For many in the discussions this was an important idea – in particular for the contribution it could make to better integrated communities. It was generally thought to be an idea that should be implemented as early as possible in the migrant's journey into the UK, and it was seen as a positive way in which newcomers could demonstrate a commitment to Britain by making every possible effort to integrate into the local communities where they lived. (Home Office 2008: 16)

It can therefore be argued that the discussion of active citizenship in Britain has been closely linked to a process of closer integration of specific communities in the country. In line with the criticism expressed above and outlined in the literature, it possesses an exclusionary and functional dimension. This is a key factor, we believe, that emerges also from the analysis of our interviews with activists.

Visions of political participation in Italy and in the UK

This section provides an account of the findings of interviews with NGO activists that were conducted in the PIDOP project in 2011. Our aim in conducting the interviews was to unpack the overall discussion of political participation by focusing explicitly on the meanings, definitions and ambiguities that these interviewees associate with the idea of citizenship.

The Italian discourse was linked overall with the need to find a logic to the self-positioning of civil society in the broader institutional context. The portrait of citizenship that emerged from our data was a vision that mirrors all the ambiguities and ambivalences that surround political participation and civic engagement. In relation to this, one of the questions that we asked our interviewees was about the meanings associated with the notion of political participation. Here, various dimensions emerged as relevant and are worth reporting, since our data show evidence of the tension existing between different visions of democracy and rights and also the practices associated with it. The right to vote, typically shaping representative forms of democracy, equilibrates with dimensions concerning opportunities to engage and to have a say in public matters, as expressed in models of participatory or deliberative democracy. In this regard, different layers of political participation were identified and recognised as valid and mutually inclusive, as in the following example:

> Participation should not only be considered as social or cultural associative participation. There are different layers of participation. The first level is economic, then there are social and cultural levels and then the right to vote. (Interview no. 1 in Italy)

In this context, it is important to look at the discussion regarding the actual value assumed by active citizenship and at the actual practices that can lead to engagement and open participation. Among the Italian activists, this was not considered to be prominent and important if it was not linked to full inclusion in the political, economic and social setting. This aspect was found especially in the interviews with activists advocating the integration of migrants. In this regard, the following extract is meaningful, because it unpacks a number of relevant issues. Being excluded from the traditional mechanisms of representative democracy (such as the right to vote or acquire welfare resources) implies a lack of opportunities to play a role in forms of participatory democracy and therefore undermines the significance of active citizenship:

> Citizenship entails the capacity to share public and shared interests, throughout a process that can offer knowledge – that is the capacity to gather different information from different sources, which means free information – and participation in collective moments. We are in a phase where neither of the two is fully guaranteed. In addition, in regard to foreigners, the lack of the right to vote puts them immediately in a condition where they cannot express and therefore participate, even if they are citizens in the full sense [...]. When the weaker layers of society do not have possibilities to be represented, they remain weak. At the least, there must be possibilities for the weaker groups to be represented, at least the rights to have possibilities to have an impact ... (Interview no. 4 in Italy)

Political participation is also conceived as engagement in processes of decision-making. Part of the discussion in this case was focused on the self-perceptions of the role of NGO activists in the policy process. Here we can identify a number of strategies that were envisaged to transform this into a working practice. The following extract reports an example of strategies that should be employed for civil society to have an impact and to become an active player in social change at different levels:

> Lifelong learning, the development of empowerment and the strengthening of possibilities to influence political decisions for organised civil society. Civil society should become a player of social change, capable of positively

influencing political decisions at the local, national and European levels. (Interview no. 3 in Italy)

At this level, there is a wide recognition of the set of instruments that can shape active engagement for NGOs. Providing a stimulus for the emergence of bottom-up processes is seen as a possible solution. However, this cannot happen when political institutions do not acknowledge the importance that non-institutionalised practices of engagement can have for fostering the policy agenda.

This was a matter of discussion also for the British civil society activists, who considered active citizenship as a way to foster democracy and to re-engage citizens with the decision-making process. The New Labour model of citizenship was discussed and recognised because it is based on the fulfilment of responsibilities as part of active participation and the attempt to re-engage citizens with decision-making processes. Participatory democracy and deliberative practices at the community level were seen as the instruments to shape the relationship between public institutions and citizens and therefore to improve decision-making.

According to our analysis, political participation was considered to be a fundamental right that everyone should be entitled to. As shown in the following extract, it was recognised that mechanisms of empowerment are needed in order to provide the actual basis for engagement. When the activist was asked about the meaning associated with political participation, the answer was:

> It means more than consulting and informing (although people are entitled to be informed and consulted) on matters affecting them. Rather, it is about giving them the tools and knowledge to make decisions or challenge decisions affecting their lives. (Interview no. 4 in Britain)

The empowerment of civil society groups dealing with minorities, migrants, women and youth, in particular, was seen as a necessary condition in order to set the basis for participatory democracy and political participation. In this respect, intercultural dialogue was considered to be the specific instrument to develop because of its centrality in bridging between different social groups. Dialogue was also seen as fundamental in building community cohesion and enabling different communities to engage with each other, by favouring the development of positive relationships between minorities and creating opportunities to connect, meet openly and debate everyday life issues and concerns.

Furthermore, participation in community planning and generally in political life at a local level were considered central for the improvement of a communitarian identity and the integration of different social groups. Active citizenship could thus foster community cohesion and the definition of a more integrated society. Our data provide evidence for this, showing that civil society organisations acknowledge – and advocate for – the inclusion of a broader consideration of the principles of difference in the notion of citizenship. This provides evidence that the principles and values of active citizenship put forward by the New Labour government are widely recognised by civil society. There was, however, a widespread criticism of the approach undertaken by New Labour, as it was considered to be based on 'one-sided engagement'. During one interview, for example, an activist declared that active citizenship:

> [...] is very much a one-sided process, where public institutions just ask NGOs to work on issues that interest the national government and there is no partnership in the design or the identification of the important issues. (Interview no. 2 in Britain)

Europeanisation and transnationalisation in Italy and the UK

In order to understand the transformative aspects regarding the status of citizenship as a consequence of the establishment of 'European citizenship', we asked our interviewees a number of questions regarding their idea of European citizenship and, more importantly, their own positioning in the wider European territory. This enables us to compare the different visions of European citizenship emerging in Italy and in the UK.

When looking at the discussions in Italy, we can argue that, overall, a number of key core values were recognised and were considered to be coherent with those promoted at the EU level, such as, for example, social solidarity, social cohesion, lifelong learning and anti-discrimination. The Italian activists, however, appeared to be ambivalent in the evaluation of the Europeanisation process and the status of European citizenship. Indeed, Europeanisation was defined as a top-down process with highly exclusionary dimensions towards weaker groups in society. The following extract is quite meaningful in this sense, because the interviewee clearly addresses this issue by recognising one of the core elements of European citizenship (freedom of movement) as one of the few positive aspects of European integration:

> It is a top-down process, which has a lot of technicalities but without a soul. It is a long process in which we should try to engage more young people. It is, however, worth taking into account that there have been a number of positive effects, for example on the possibility of free movement in the European territory. (Interview no. 5 in Italy)

This is a topic of discussion that was recurrent in our sample. Overall, European citizenship was not seen as a status that could produce actual change, in respect to activating engagement and stimulating political participation. Europeanisation as a process was not perceived as having particular effects on specific target groups, such as for example young people, minorities, migrants and women. In another interview, the interviewee stated that:

> [...] since the process of Europeanisation and the building of a European identity started, what got lost along the way is the capacity of Europe to be

different in the whole international system. Different, in the sense of being the Europe of the people or the Europe of rights. It does not appear to me that we are going in that direction. (Interview no. 2 in Italy)

Therefore, in the Italian sample, and differently from the British one as we will see later, a high sense of dissatisfaction emerged in regard to European integration. As we will argue, this is produced by the lack of existence of processes of participation that can lead to the building of a 'Europe from below' and overall from a lack of political leadership that can promote encompassing European values. On the basis of our argument, this dissatisfaction is not associated with the European project as a whole or with the European idea, but instead is portrayed as an incapacity to foster a social Europe enabling protection for weaker groups. It is also dependent on a perceived lack of concrete opportunities to actively engage and, furthermore, by a persistent failure in the attempt to evaluate and judge the impact of EU programmes on organisations' daily routines. In addition, between the factors that undermine the EU's role, there is a focus on its limited range of action. The lack of impact of European citizenship is therefore mostly explained as being a deficiency produced by the limited powers attributed by member states to the EU, rather than being caused by the EU itself. The lack of possibilities for action by European institutions, i.e. the lack of competences, is thus perceived in the following way:

> In respect to immigration there are still too many restrictions at the national level. It can therefore be argued that the EU still has limited powers. There has been some progress since Lisbon, but the only significant area in which there has been common consensus is regarding border control. The EU, in regard to promoting participation, has not acquired enough competences. (Interview no. 1 in Italy)

It is important to underline that, during the interviews, there was a lack of references to more specific European policies, or a lack of recognition of the supranational instruments that have been designed for fostering active citizenship, such as for example civil dialogue, as well as of a lack of knowledge of the activities of supranational civil society organisations that aim to foster transnational forms of participation. However, dialogue, in its general understanding, was mentioned as a possible instrument and as a policy solution to be employed to foster European citizenship.

> European citizenship has to become concrete throughout a structured dialogue to be established between different civic and social parts. This should be aimed at providing the EU with a better political leadership, a new role as a policy driver. Europe should be able to export certain democratic principles and its values that look at social inclusion. (Interview no. 3 in Italy)

In Britain, according to the interviews that we analysed, there was an open recognition of core EU principles such as social inclusion, integration policy, fundamental rights and citizenship of minorities that should be widely promoted, at both the national and local levels. Contrary to the data that emerged from the analysis of the Italian sample, the EU's approach to civic engagement, which promotes the networking of NGOs in local communities with the scope of challenging ethnic discrimination, was welcomed by a number of NGOs. Local and national NGOs appeared to be committed to 'network building' between different European countries by promoting the understanding of minority issues and positive relations between minority and majority communities across Europe. They also appeared to be aware of different EU programmes, and in terms of policy and political priorities these were convergent with British priorities, especially in the fields of gender equality and equal opportunities.

During the analysis of the interviews, it became clear that a number of organisations were actually welcoming the forms of civil dialogue established in Brussels and the current involvement with supranational organisations such as the European Women's Lobby, the European Youth Forum, the Social Platform and the Policy Migration Group. The process is reviewed regularly and it has developed and matured into an important ongoing feature of the current practices in which organisations are involved. The interviews also highlighted how the participating organisations were able to raise awareness of relevant issues – for example by increasing networking or enhancing communication practices within Europe, as well as with contacts in developing countries – and how this ensured a mechanism for flagging concerns and for maintaining a two-way flow of information.

However, reflecting upon one of the main instruments aimed at fostering civil dialogue in the first Barroso presidency, the *Plan D for Democracy, Dialogue and Debate*, one activist asserted that the implementation of this seemed to show that:

> […] the EU is conscious that it is not effectively engaging with its citizens in general. In the UK that can of course be because of an ambiguity about membership of the EU. However, we are, in general, very positive about engaging with it and look to it for support both financial and legislative. (Interview no. 3 in Britain)

Difficulties encountered in accessing information coming from the EU and coordination between governments and non-state actors were, however, pointed out as some of the factors that undermine NGOs' capabilities to adopt and make the best use of supranational resources. This is an important convergence, we believe, with the Italian discourse. Yet, Europe was seen as a land of opportunities and resources that, however, still seemed to be lacking an impact in providing the bases for enhancing active citizenship.

The prominent issue that was emphasised was the lack of funding and support, especially for small-scale NGOs, since most small voluntary organisations are not able to engage with European funding. The EU was perceived by NGO officials as unable or unavailable to answer questions and give the support that small NGOs from different countries need. This was well expressed in the following passage:

I think one of the really biggest problems coming from an NGO perspective, is that their own house is so, in such disorder about the way they manage their relationships through funding, so the ESF and all that, I mean it's a nightmare, and they can say lots of wonderful things about engagement but when you have an organisation, like Daphne which delivers money as part of its funding in October that has to be spent by the end of December, a year's worth of funding, and then doesn't give it for six months, you know essentially what they are trying to do is kill off NGOs, so, and that's a major problem. (Interview no. 4 in Britain)

During the interviews, the discussion regarding the EU's European Employment Strategy also emerged, as well as the opinion that some Member States have begun to develop a strategy combining measures to promote the integration of disadvantaged groups with those aiming to tackle discriminatory attitudes and practices. However, it was argued that this dual approach could and should be further developed. In particular, emphasis was placed on the growing trend to deal with gender equality alongside measures to combat discrimination set out in Article 13 of the EC Treaty. Indeed, an integrated approach was foreseen in order to respond to situations of multiple discriminations and to develop effective approaches to the promotion of equal treatment.

In terms of perceived policy needs, it was highlighted that the EU should do more to enhance respect for human rights and fundamental freedoms in countries and regions where they are most at risk; furthermore, it should increase its efforts to strengthen the role of civil society in promoting human rights and bring about more democratic reform in support of the peaceful conciliation of group interests and the consolidation of political participation and representation. Within the overall discussion regarding fundamental rights, a specific issue regarding the impact of the EU Gender Roadmap also emerged, which was viewed with general disappointment because of its lack of resources, targets and timelines. On the other hand, it was suggested that the EU could do more to promote the valuable contributions made by migrants to the EU economy and the EU member states. The issue of migration was perceived as having become negatively politicised as a problem, instead of positively promoted as a means of strengthening national economies and promoting cultural diversity. In a similar vein, it was argued that minorities should be supported where they need assistance in regard to services, education, jobs, etc. Overall, it was proposed that the issue of cultural diversity should not be seen as a threat, but as a positive development which should be positively embraced.

Conclusion

The comparison between two different models of active citizenship brings to the fore a number of elements of convergence as well as of differentiation between the Italian and British contexts. In Italy, active citizenship is framed under a set of both institutionalised top-down and non-institutionalised bottom-up practices that do not necessarily complement each other. NGO activists seem to be highly critical of attempts to routinise forms of participation and point at the exclusionary character of the basic forms of engagement, such as the right to vote in elections for migrant groups. In Britain, the discussion is oriented to the evaluation of the top-down mechanisms for the construction of active citizenship that has been taking place since the end of the 1990s. In both cases, we find evidence of the need to establish wider bases for inclusion in policy-making processes and to widen the basis for the representation of interests. Activists could be described as 'conscious active players', ready to participate in the policy process and in search of actual mechanisms that can lead to their own empowerment in the public sphere. This is the first important point to be noted and considers the role and positioning of civil society in fostering social inclusion and social solidarity. This role, at the moment, however, seems to be undermined due to a lack of institutional receptiveness towards these issues in the two countries under consideration.

Discourse regarding the Europeanisation process is where we found more divergences emerging from the interviews. While Italian activists were highly critical of the Europeanisation process, which was portrayed as a top-down construction influenced by member states' interests, the British activists recognised the important role played by the EU in defining and fostering active citizenship through, for example, specific programmes or instruments such as civil dialogue promoted by umbrella organisations. Networking seemed to be key, in this light, to shape the aforementioned bases for social inclusion and social solidarity. The convergence between the two countries lay in the widely perceived difficulties in accessing resources as well as information and opportunities offered at the EU level. This ultimately was viewed as undermining the exercise of active citizenship and participation in EU policies.

In conclusion, we believe that our research sheds light on the dynamics regarding the establishment of active citizenship, in particular concerning tensions between institutional and non-institutional processes. In terms of future research, we believe that this should be oriented at fostering the agenda on the role of interest groups and civil society organisations that currently represent the so-called weak public sphere, in other words migrants, minorities, young people and women, among others. Motivational factors for engagement – or lack of – and outcomes of active citizenship are important dimensions that need to be explored further.

References

Allegretti, U. (2006) 'Basi giuridiche della democrazia partecipativa in Italia: alcuni orientamenti', *Democrazia e Diritto*, 3: 151–63.
Allegretti, U. (2009) *Democrazia partecipativa e processi di democratizzazione*. Paper presented at the conference 'La democrazia partecipativa in Italia e in Europa: esperienze e prospettive', Florence, 3 April.
Andretta, M. and Caiani, M. (2005) 'Social movements in Italy: which kind of Europeanisation?', *Journal of Southern Europe and the Balkans*, 7 (3): 283–98.

Andrews, R., Cowell, R. and Downe, J. (2008) 'Support for active citizenship and public service performance: an empirical analysis of English local authorities', *Policy and Politics*, 36 (2): 225–43.
Arena, G. (ed.) (2001) *La funzione di comunicazione nelle pubbliche amministrazioni*. Rimini: Maggioli.
Arena, G. (2006) *Cittadini attivi*. Rome and Bari: Laterza.
Bee, C. (2010) 'Understanding the EU's institutional communication. Principles and structure of a contested policy', in C. Bee and E. Bozzini (2010) (eds), *Mapping the European Public Sphere: Institutions, Media and Civil Society*. London: Ashgate.
Bee, C. and Guerrina, R. (2014) 'Participation, dialogue, and civic engagement: understanding the role of organized civil society in promoting active citizenship in the European Union', *Journal of Civil Society*, 10 (1): 29–50.
Bellamy, R. (2000) *Rethinking Liberalism*. London: Pinter.
Bellamy, R., Castiglione, D. and Santoro, E. (2004) *Lineages of European Citizenship. Rights, Belonging and Participation in Eleven Nation-States*. Basingstoke: Palgrave Macmillan.
Bobbio, L. (2002) 'Le arene deliberative', *Rivista Italiana di Politiche Pubbliche*, 3: 5–29.
Bobbio, L. (2007) 'Tipi di deliberazione', *Rivista italiana di scienza politica*, 37 (3): 359–83.
Bonanni, M. and Penco, M. (2006) *Preferenze o argomentazioni congelate? Esperienze di democrazia discorsiva*. Milano: FrancoAngeli.
Brehony, K. J. (1992) '"Active citizens": the case of school governors', *International Studies in Sociology of Education*, 2 (2): 199–217.
Burnett, J. (2007) 'Britain's "civilising project": community cohesion and core values', *Policy and Politics*, 35 (2): 353–7.
Caligiuri, M. (1997) *Lineamenti di Comunicazione Pubblica*. Messina: Rubbettino Editore.
Castles, S. and Davidson, A. (2000) *Citizenship and Migration. Globalisation and the Politics of Belonging*. London: Macmillan Press.
Ceri, P. (1996) 'Partecipazione sociale', in *Enciclopedia delle Scienze Sociali*, vol. VI. Rome: Istituto della Enciclopedia Italiana, pp. 508–16.
Davies, J. (2012) "Active citizenship: navigating the conservative heartlands of the New Labour project', *Policy and Politics*, 40 (1): 3–19.
Delanty, G. (2000) *Citizenship in a Global Age*. Buckingham: Open University Press.
Delanty, G. (2007a) 'European citizenship: a critical assessment', *Citizenship Studies*, 11 (1): 63–72.
Delanty, G. (2007b) 'The idea of citizenship: republican roots, cosmopolitan challenges', in *European Citizenship: Theories, Arenas, Levels*. Baden-Baden: Nomos Verlagsgesellschaft.
Della Porta, D. (ed.) (2004) *Comitati di cittadini e democrazia urbana*. Soveria Mannelli (CZ): Rubbettino.
Della Porta, D. and Diani, M. (2004) *Movimenti senza protesta? L'ambientalismo in Italia*. Bologna: Il Mulino.
Donati, P. and Tronca, L. (2008) *Il capitale sociale degli italiani. Le radici familiari, comunitarie e associative del civismo*. Milan: Franco Angeli.
Eder, K. and Giesen, G. (2001) *European Citizenship between National Legacies and Postnational Projects*. Oxford: Oxford University Press.
Esposito, G. (2000) *Elementi di Comunicazione Pubblica*. Naples: Edizioni Giuridiche Simone.
Faccioli, F. (2000) *Comunicazione pubblica e cultura del servizio*. Rome: Carocci.
Faulks, K. (1998) *Citizenship in Modern Britain*. Edinburgh: Edinburgh University Press.
Faulks, K. (2000) *Citizenship*. London: Routledge.
Fawkes, J. and Moloney, K. (2008) 'Does the European Union (EU) need a propaganda watchdog like the US Institute of Propaganda Analysis to strengthen its democratic civil society and free markets?', *Public Relations Review*, 34: 204–17.

Fedi, A. and Mannarini, T. (eds) (2008) *Oltre il Nimby. La dimensione psico-sociale della protesta contro le opere sgradite*. Milan: Franco Angeli.
Ferrera, M. (2004) 'Verso una cittadinanza sociale aperta. I nuovi confini del welfare nell'Unione Europea', *Rivista italiana di scienza politica*, 1: 95–126.
Gadotti, G. (2001) *Pubblicità sociale. Lineamenti, esperienze e nuovi sviluppi*. Milan: Franco Angeli.
Gelli, F. (ed.) (2005) *La democrazia locale tra rappresentanza e partecipazione*. Milan: Franco Angeli.
Giddens, A. (1998) *The Third Way. The Renewal of Social Democracy*. Cambridge: Polity Press.
Giddens, A. (2000) *The Third Way and Its Critics*. Cambridge: Polity Press.
Giddens, A. (ed.) (2001) *The Global Third Way Debate*. Cambridge: Polity Press.
Giddens, A. (2006) 'Positive welfare', in C. Pierson and F. G. Castles (eds), *The Welfare State Reader*. Cambridge: Polity Press, pp. 378–88.
Grandi, R. (2007) *La comunicazione pubblica. Teorie, casi, profili normativi*. Rome: Carocci.
Griva, A. and Piazza, A. (1996) *Guida alla Comunicazione pubblica. Teorie, strumenti esperienze*. Torino: Centro Scientifico Editore.
Grunig, A. and Grunig, J. E. (1992) 'Models of public relations and communication', in J. E. Grunig (ed.), *Excellence in Public Relations and Communication Management*. Hillsdale, NJ: Lawrence Erlbaum Associates, pp. 285–326.
Grunig, J. E. and Hunt, T. (1984) *Managing Public Relations*. New York: Holt, Rinehart & Winston.
Habermas, J. (1994) 'Citizenship and national identity', in B. Van Steenbergen (ed.), *The Condition of Citizenship*. London: Sage, pp. 20–35.
Heater, D. (1999) *What Is Citizenship?* Cambridge: Polity Press.
Home Office (2008) *The Path to Citizenship: Next Steps in Reforming the Immigration System*. Available online at: http://webarchive.nationalarchives.gov.uk/20100422120657/http://www.ukba.homeoffice.gov.uk/sitecontent/documents/aboutus/consultations/pathtocitizenship/pathtocitizenship?view=Binary#page=1&zoom=auto,0,849 (last accessed 30 March 2013).
Hooghe, L. and Marks, G. (2001) *Multilevel Governance and European Integration*. Boulder, CO: Rowman & Littlefield.
Isin, E. F., Nyers, P. and Turner, B. S. (2008) *Citizenship Between Past and Future*. London: Routledge.
Kearns, A. (1995) 'Active citizenship and local governance: political and geographical dimensions', *Political Geography*, 14 (2): 155–75.
Lanzara, G. F. (2005) 'La deliberazione come indagine pubblica', in L. Pellizzoni (ed.), *La deliberazione pubblica*. Rome: Meltem editore, pp. 51–73.
Lister, R. (1997) *Citizenship: Feminist Perspectives*. Basingstoke: Macmillan.
McGhee, D. (2003) 'Moving to "our" common ground – a critical examination of community cohesion discourse in twenty-first century Britain', *Sociological Review*, 51 (3): 376–404.
McGhee, D. (2006) 'Getting "host" communities on board: finding the balance between "managed migration" and "managed settlement" in community cohesion strategies', *Journal of Ethnic and Migration Studies*, 32 (1): 111–27.
McGhee, D. (2008) *The End of Multiculturalism? Terrorism, Integration and Human Rights*. Berkshire: Open University Press.
McGhee, D. (2009) 'The paths to citizenship: a critical examination of immigration policy in Britain since 2001', *Patterns of Prejudice*, 43 (1): 41–64.
Mancini, P. (2006) *Manuale di comunicazione pubblica*. Bari: Laterza.
Marinetto, M. (2003) 'Who wants to be an active citizen? The politics and practice of community involvement', *Sociology*, 37 (1): 103–20.
Marshall, T. H. (1950) *Citizenship and Social Class: And Other Essays*. Cambridge: Cambridge University Press.

Mastropaolo, A. (2001) 'Democrazia, neodemocrazia, postdemocrazia: tre paradigmi a confronto', *Diritto Pubblico Comparato ed Europeo*, IV: 1611–35.
Miller, D. (2000) *Citizenship and National Identity*. Cambridge: Polity Press.
Miller, D. (2008a) 'Immigrants, nations and citizenship', *Journal of Political Philosophy*, 16: 371–90.
Miller, D. (2008b) 'Republican citizenship, nationality and Europe', in C. Laborde and J. Maynor (eds), *Republicanism and Political Theory*. Oxford: Wiley-Blackwell.
Morlino, L. (2003) *Democrazie e democratizzazioni*. Bologna: Il Mulino.
Moro, G. (1998) *Manuale di cittadinanza attiva*. Rome: Carocci.
Moro, G. (2005) *Azione civica. Conoscere e gestire le organizzazioni di cittadinanza attiva*. Rome: Carocci.
Moro, G. (2010) *L'attivismo civico e le pratiche di cittadinanza*. Paper delivered at SISP Conference, Venice, September.
Mouffe, C. (1992) 'Democratic citizenship and the political community', in C. Mouffe (ed.), *Dimensions of Radical Democracy: Pluralism, Citizenship, Community*. London: Verso, pp. 225–39.
Pellizzoni, L. (ed.) (2005a) *La deliberazione pubblica*. Roma: Meltem editore.
Pellizzoni, L. (2005b) 'Cosa significa partecipare', *Rassegna Italiana di Sociologia*, 3: 479–514.
Piselli, F. (1995) *Reti. L'analisi di network nelle scienze sociali*. Rome: Donzelli.
Piselli, F. (2001) 'Capitale sociale: un concetto situazionale e dinamico', in *Il capitale sociale. Istruzioni per l'uso*. Bologna: Il Mulino, pp. 47–75.
Putnam, R., Nanetti, R. and Leonardi, R. (1993) *Making Democracy Work: Civic Traditions in Modern Italy*. Princeton, NJ: Princeton University Press.
Ratcliffe, P. (2012) '"Community cohesion": reflections on a flawed paradigm', *Critical Social Policy*, 32 (2): 262–81.
Rovinetti, A. (2000) *Diritto di parola. Strategie, professioni, tecnologie della comunicazione pubblica*. Milano: Il Sole 24 Ore.
Shaw, J. (2009) 'Political rights and multilevel citizenship in Europe', in S. Carrera and E. Guild (eds), *Illiberal Liberal States: Immigration, Citizenship and Integration in the EU*. Aldershot: Ashgate, pp. 29–49.
Van Ruler, B. and Verčič, D. (eds) (2004) *Public Relations and Communication Management in Europe: A Nation-by-Nation Introduction to Public Relations Theory and Practice*. Berlin and New York: Mouton de Gruyter.

PART V
Reflections and extensions

The volume concludes with three chapters that offer a range of reflections from varying perspectives on political and civic engagement and the issues that have been discussed in this book. These chapters are authored by members of the PIDOP project's International Advisory Board who very generously contributed their expertise to the project in various ways. Between them, these three chapters examine the similarities and differences between the PIDOP project and other major initiatives within this field, draw attention to various ways in which the investigation of political and civic engagement should be pursued in the future, and underline the importance of research in this field for tackling the important challenges that currently face democratic societies.

In Chapter 24, **Judith Torney-Purta and Jo-Ann Amadeo** analyse similarities and differences between what they describe as 'two ground-breaking studies of civic and political engagement taking place within the last ten to fifteen years', namely the PIDOP project and the IEA 1999 Civic Education Study (CIVED) in which 14-year-old school students were tested and surveyed in seven of the nine countries that participated in the PIDOP project. Their reflections on the findings of the PIDOP and CIVED studies are structured around two important issues: (1) the implications of the two projects for understanding individual differences, contexts and processes; and (2) the adequacy of existing results for understanding the relatively understudied topic of political and civic engagement in adolescence and early adulthood. A large part of their chapter is devoted to a detailed analysis of *individual differences, context and process* in relationship to deliberation, discussion and self-expression in school classrooms, a sense of community and collective efficacy, and the participation of women and migrants. The contributions made by individual chapters in the current book are discussed in relation to the findings of the CIVED study, demonstrating the richness of both the PIDOP and the CIVED studies and their complementarity. Numerous questions for further exploration are raised by the authors. These include the role of workplaces and the Internet, the use of person-centred analysis and the analysis of how young adults integrate their attitudes with orientations toward behaviour. Another need for the future is to further contextualise the policy recommendations which are present in several chapters of the current book, especially regarding migrants and even more so regarding women's participation. As the authors argue, all of these questions 'will be of interest to researchers for decades to come'.

In Chapter 25, **Reinhild Otte** analyses the links between the PIDOP project and the Council of Europe (CoE) project on Education for Democratic Citizenship and Human Rights Education (EDC/HRE). She provides a detailed description of the EDC/HRE project. This allows her to identify differences, similarities and interconnections between the PIDOP project and EDC/HRE, underlining some key features such as scope, definition and goals, origin, background and framework, working methods and structure, and target groups, focus and outcomes of both activities. Besides the obvious differences between the two projects, considering their different structures and general goals, what is important are their commonalities. First, both projects were conceived in relationship to *democratic societies* rather than any other type of state or government and are devoted to the promotion of life within democratic societies. A second key feature shared by both projects is an emphasis on *participation and its various forms*. But while in PIDOP the focus is more on the factors influencing participation, the main attention of EDC/HRE is on the role of education in fostering active participation. A third common aspect is the *audiences* to which outcomes and recommendations are aimed. In both projects, there is a wide range of partners, institutions and other stakeholders, among them politicians and decision-makers, educational professionals, media, youth leaders, parents, non-governmental organisations and youth organisations. The chapter concludes that, in spite of the different approaches and perspectives, the two projects are mutually supportive: in particular, PIDOP has provided an empirical evidence base for some of the principles of EDC/HRE. And more importantly, they share a common goal, namely 'to help young people and adults to play an active role in a society based on the values of democracy, human rights and the rule of law'.

Chapter 26 by **Giovanni Moro** raises some extremely important challenges that need to be addressed by future research in this field. Two main topics are discussed: (1) the context in which participation takes place today and the transformation which is currently occurring to democratic regimes and the citizenship paradigm; and (2) the need for a critical assessment of the research toolbox which is used to examine participation in this new context. Moro notes that, in the last few decades, fundamental changes in citizenship have taken place, with the result that the *paradigm of democratic citizenship* has been questioned with regard to some of its basic pillars, namely the state, the territory, national identity, legal status and representation. These changes require a reconsideration of the working of the political system and the way that participation is conceived, which makes research into new forms of participation more relevant but also much more complex and challenging. The second topic addressed concerns the limits and problems of the *research toolbox* on participation, with the discussion focusing on questions related to normative assumptions, conceptualisations (e.g. the distinction between 'conventional' and 'non-conventional' participation, and the distinction between political and civic participation), taken-for-granted correlations, the use of variables, and the sources of data and information. As to the identification of factors and their use as variables to explain and predict different forms of participation, Moro underlines two crucial points: the unclear or contradictory results that have sometimes emerged in relationship to these factors, and the low utility of the information which is sometimes produced. Moreover, he expresses concerns regarding the kind of data collected and the way they are gathered. Moro argues that it is time to renovate our way of thinking and methods of observing political and civic participation.

The three chapters in this final part of this book reveal how the discussions that are to be found within the earlier chapters lock onto other projects and wider debates that are currently taking place about citizen engagement, participation and the changing nature of democratic societies. In reflecting on the discussions contained in this book, the reader is invited to consider this broader context within which they are located.

24
CROSS-NATIONAL POLITICAL AND CIVIC ENGAGEMENT RESEARCH ON EUROPEAN ADOLESCENTS AND YOUNG ADULTS

Considerations at the individual, context, and process levels

Judith Torney-Purta and Jo-Ann Amadeo

The study of civic and political engagement is in a period of expansion. Fifty years ago a small number of researchers became active in political socialization research, studying children as young as seven or eight. The research expanded to cross-national studies in the 1970s and during this period voting was nearly always the focus when adults were surveyed (history reviewed by Torney-Purta in press). In the 1990s researchers returned to the study of adolescents and the favored term became civic engagement. In fact, it was the late-1990s when the term civic engagement appeared to overtake political socialization with more frequent references in the literature. This transition took place for at least two reasons. First, the process was no longer conceived as unidirectional (parents or teachers socializing children). Second, researchers, especially psychologists, wanted to move from narrow concerns with voting and political party membership to include broader concerns with civic activities taking place in schools and communities.

Psychologists, educational researchers, and sociologists recently have investigated in depth by studying the meaning of participation and by looking at an age range between middle adolescence (starting at age 13 or 14) and early adulthood (usually concluding in the mid-to-late 20s). Few studies, however, deal with the full range of this part of the lifespan. There is still an unfortunate tendency by some researchers to treat students who are in compulsory secondary schooling as entirely different from those who are just a few years older and enrolled in higher education or are in the workforce (or seeking work).

The purpose of this chapter is to consider the PIDOP Project (Processes Influencing Democratic Ownership and Participation) together with another project that dealt with a similar age period, the IEA Civic Education Study. PIDOP and CIVED are two ground-breaking studies of civic and political engagement taking place within the last 10-15 years. Some concepts under investigation were the same, others (such as the role of knowledge) were different. From both, important lessons were learned about individual differences, the contexts, and processes. To elaborate on these points, we examined data from a subset of CIVED countries – specifically those that also participated in PIDOP. This is especially appropriate because CIVED and PIDOP tested groups that were from the same age cohort, when they were aged 14 (in 1999) and when they were in their mid-twenties (in 2010–11), respectively. The studies' sampling methods were different, however. Both projects will be described in the next section.

The EU's PIDOP Project and the IEA's CIVED Project

The PIDOP Project was a multi-method, cross-national study funded by the European Union and housed at Surrey University from 2009 to 2012. Policy analysis as well as focus groups and qualitative interviews comprised important parts of the data collection. In addition, the quantitative part of the study used a survey to collect data in nine European countries from 15- to 18-year-olds and 20- to 26-year-olds. Data were collected from the following ethnic minority/migrant groups (as well as from majority group members) in the following European countries:

- England: English, Congolese and Bangladeshi youth
- Belgium: Belgian (French-speaking), Turkish and Moroccan youth
- Czech Republic: Czech, Roma and Ukrainian youth
- Germany: German, German resettlers from Russia and Turkish youth
- Italy: Italian, Albanian and Moroccan youth
- Northern Ireland: Northern Irish, Chinese and Polish youth
- Portugal: Portuguese, Angolan and Brazilian youth
- Sweden: Swedish, Kurds of Turkish origin, Iraqis
- Turkey: Turks, Roma, Turkish resettlers from Bulgaria.

Some of the data collection in 2010–11 took place in schools, but a variety of other sources for recruiting project participants were also employed, especially for the young adults.

The surveys covered a broad range of political participation of a conventional type (voting, party membership) and a non-conventional type (demonstrations, leafleting). In addition, respondents were questioned about their 'civic participation' (volunteering), economic choices with civic consequences (boycotting products for environmental reasons), and civil disobedience, Internet participation with political or civic content, and civic/political interest or attentiveness. The questions covered a variety of specific topics of interest to European psychologists who study young people's relationship to social and political institutions (Azevedo and Menezes 2007; Rubini and Palmonari 2006).

A variety of modes of analysis and publication were used in PIDOP. The Executive Summary (Barrett 2012) is very informative and several publications include enlightening quotations from focus groups and interviews. Presentations reporting theoretical frameworks, qualitative and quantitative findings by country, and policy analyses are contained in a special issue of *Human Affairs* (Zani and Barrett 2012), a special issue of *Journal of Civil Society* (Bee and Guerrina 2014), and in this volume. This project with its breadth of analysis and depth of cross-cultural study of two important groups, women and migrants, is valuable for its up-to-date view of civic and political engagement among European adolescents and young adults. It is welcome in a field that has previously relied on studies conducted in a few countries and focused on conventional participation, especially voting. It reinforces and adds to an ongoing set of studies that focused on civic education and on schools.

The second research project considered here is the *IEA studies of civic and citizenship education* (especially *CIVED* 1999/2000). These studies were conducted under the auspices of the International Association for the Evaluation of Educational Achievement (IEA). In the 1999 study about 90,000 students from nationally representative samples of schools enrolled in the modal grade containing 14-year-olds were tested in 28 countries, 23 from Europe as well as the US, Australia, Hong Kong, Chile, and Colombia (Torney-Purta *et al.* 2001); approximately one year later, pre-university students from 16 counties ranging in age from 16 to 19 and numbering about 50,000 were tested (Amadeo *et al.* 2002).

In both age groups a test of civic knowledge/skills and a survey of participation and attitudes were administered. The participatory activities included expected conventional participation (voting and getting information about candidates before voting, as well as joining political parties), unconventional and civic participation (volunteering), as well as potentially illegal protest. Participation in political communication on the Internet was not a required part of the survey. At the time of testing in 1999 Internet access was limited, especially in the post-Communist and Latin American countries, which together constituted nearly half of the participating nations.

The comparisons between PIDOP and the IEA studies in this chapter will use the CIVED 1999 data. Seven of the nine participating PIDOP countries also tested and surveyed 14-year-old students in CIVED, while only three of these countries participated in a more recent IEA study, the International Civics and Citizenship Study conducted in 2009 (ICCS09).[1]

Similarities and differences between PIDOP and CIVED

These two studies share some common assumptions. First, political and civic participatory behavior is *social behavior* acquired in the context of groups (elaborated by Emler, this volume). It is also behavior that is learned by individuals in contexts that are often non-political (Vráblíková and Císař, this volume) and enacted with particular meaning for each person (Barrett, this volume). A second assumption is that there are several types of participation relevant for fostering a sense of democratic ownership. These include conventional political participation, volunteer participation that is locally based and civic action that takes place through petitions and boycotts often organized online. Of considerable importance is attentiveness to or interest in political and civic matters. Different terms were emphasized in different national settings of the PIDOP project, for example the attentiveness of the 'standby citizen' which was highlighted in the chapter by Amnå and Ekman describing Sweden. They placed observations from the PIDOP study in the context of broader research and theory derived from work in the Nordic countries. Analysis of policy documents in the PIDOP countries also identified several important organizing concepts according to Barrett (2012): 'human rights,' which is important in German policy ambitions; 'active citizenship,' which appeared in Italy and Turkey; and, finally, 'social inclusion and social justice,' which was the description used in Belgium and the UK. Although these terms are complementary, they also show that different constructions of citizenship and participation underlie the policy discourses characterizing different countries (and hence provide different contexts for individuals' development).

A third assumption is that although it is important to examine and interpret differences between adolescents and young adults, it is helpful to avoid making rigid distinctions between these groups. A major context for the former group is their school and for the latter it is their place of higher/continuing education or workplace. However, the completion of secondary education does not suddenly turn the adolescent into a young adult. The process of development is a relatively continuous one. Families, peer groups, and communities (including immigrant organizations) continue to be important contexts for political and civic development. Attaining the age at which one is allowed to vote often prompts the development of new competencies and skills. However, this does not transform all young people's outlook on the political world. To give just one example, substantial proportions of young adults are not eligible to vote in many countries. Future research studies should include both adolescents and young adults and should inquire specifically about workplaces and higher education institutions as settings for political development among the older group.

There are also a number of differences between the two studies. The backgrounds for designing the empirical data collections in PIDOP and CIVED differed. In the CIVED study, a two-year first phase collected extensive and structured case study material on 24 countries' civic education aims and structures. This was essential because in the early 1990s when the project began, very little was known about civic education in areas such as the post-Communist countries. These case studies were published in a book and were informative in preparing a content framework on which the test and survey were built (Torney-Purta et al. 1999).

In early phases of PIDOP, about 15 years later, policy analysis and reviews of theoretical and empirical literature were prominent. Azevedo and Menezes (2007) characterize this period as one when civic participation was 'invading the public and academic discourse' with an intensity that would have seemed impossible a decade or two earlier (paraphrase, p. 96). Both projects involved considerable international collaborative effort by researchers (with continuing benefits, especially for those at early stages of their careers).

The instruments also differed in structure. In the CIVED study, the respondents spent about half of the time answering approximately 40 keyed, multiple-choice questions. The other half was devoted to attitudinal questions (for example, support for women's rights and norms of conventional political participation), questions about intended participation and background information (including measures of the openness of classroom climate and collective efficacy at school).

Although political knowledge received some attention in the literature from which PIDOP measures were drawn, only a minimal measure of knowledge of civic/political topics was included. Interestingly, the Political Engagement Project (a study of university students in the United States) hoped to include knowledge questions, but it was difficult to find appropriate items (Beaumont *et al.* 2006). PIDOP used interviews, focus groups, and a survey of attitudes and participation. Appendices A through C contain the instruments used in PIDOP.

Another important difference between these two projects is the way respondents were chosen and the locales for data collection. In CIVED, a central team of IEA researchers approved sampling plans for schools in each participating country and verified the resulting samples. Controlled testing conditions were employed. In contrast, in PIDOP each country team was responsible for recruiting groups of majority respondents (both male and female) as well as migrants from two cultural backgrounds. One age group was intended to be adolescents (16 to 18) and the other young adults (20 to 26). Interestingly, those who were in the 20–26 age group tested in PIDOP represent the same cohort as the 14-year-olds tested about ten years earlier in CIVED. PIDOP researchers used a variety of locations for the surveys, especially of the adults. This was essential to gain access to groups who are not enrolled in school and may be unemployed.

In summary, although the topics considered in PIDOP and CIVED are quite similar, there are also differences between the projects. Considered together, however, they enhance the picture of political and civic engagement. Findings from the CIVED study provide statistically precise estimates of average responses and country differences and also differences by gender within countries. With this in mind, four tables of country comparisons and gender differences from the CIVED 1999 data collection dealing with topics raised in the PIDOP chapters are provided here. First, however, we introduce the overall framework for the remainder of this chapter.

The individual, context, and processes in the study of political and civic engagement

Our reflections on the findings of the PIDOP and CIVED projects will be structured within the following three categories: the individual, the context, and processes (Table 24.1). In earlier publications we have presented a similar table to categorize research questions that could be answered using particular data sets and to identify cross-cutting themes important in this field (Torney-Purta *et al.* 2010; Torney-Purta and Amadeo 2013). The idea for this table came from a categorization developed by Wentzel (2006), who was studying peer relationships. She suggested a

TABLE 24.1 Conceptual comparison of PIDOP and CIVED projects

Level	PIDOP Project	CIVED Project
Individual	Gender	Gender (support/women's rights)
	Member of minority group (includes immigrant group)	Immigrant status (attitudes/ immigrants' rights)
	Experience in deliberation	Experience of deliberation at school
	Sense of collectivity/ownership/ community	Collective efficacy at school
	Latent participation/trust	Trust/alienation/apathy
Context	Country characteristics: indices of gender equality	Country characteristics: indices of gender equality
	Perceptions of discrimination against migrants	Policies regarding immigrants and citizenship
	Cultures of expression	Economic/educational opportunity
	Community solidarity	Collective efficacy at school
	Social networks (mobilization)	Internet
	Workplaces	
	Internet	
Process	Political action/voting	Intended political activities
	Collective action	Traditional instruction
	Political conversations	Class discuss/deliberation
	Deliberation/discussion	Experience/service learning
	Volunteering	

three-part classification of research questions: those that relate to *person-* or *individual-level variables* (e.g. gender, migrant status), those that relate to *context variables* (e.g. characteristics of a nation or whether the school as a whole comprises one or several socio-economic levels), and *process variables* (e.g. participating in a classroom with open climate or experiencing a sense of belonging at school).

Many studies in this field have dealt with *individual differences*. In our view, however, too few studies have focused on *context*, often resulting in inappropriately generalizing results. The political, economic, and social contexts of a given country as well as the context of the power structure of a community or the cooperative or competitive nature of the school environment are vital in understanding political and civic participation.

Both the PIDOP and the CIVED projects used models that distinguish between macro and micro levels of *context* and attempted to incorporate ideas about processes. However, as Vráblíková and Císař (this volume) point out, assessing macro levels of culture can present something of a puzzle. Simple indices are often not useful, and when more complex indices are sought, it may be difficult to compare across countries. Some useful datasets including country indicators now exist. The use of these indicators will be illustrated later in the chapter when the number of years a country has been a democracy and number of years that a country requires an immigrant to be a resident before applying for citizenship will be discussed as context variables (see also XTXS: A Comprehensive Database of Country-Level, Education-Related Data for Comparative and International Research, online at: http://www.intledstatsdatabase.org/default.aspx).

Relatively few studies have explicitly studied *processes*. Sometimes specific processes are incorporated into the assumptions on which a study is based or serve as constructs in the interpretation of findings. Some interesting examples appear in related literature. Sanchez-Jankowski (1986) considered both processes and contexts. He found in a Hispanic group that older brothers and sisters were especially important as models and coaches for their younger siblings in forming their identities related to activist groups. He also found that the available participation resources and identities for these young people differed between two contexts (different cities in the Southwestern United States). Similarly, Lay (2012) illustrated how the broad context of the community shapes civic socialization processes and outcomes among high-school students (especially immigrant students in the US Midwest).

In subsequent sections we will discuss individual differences, context, and processes with a focus on four topics: (1) deliberation and self-expression; (2) sense of community and collective efficacy; (3) gender; and (4) migrant status. See Table 24.1 for an overall organizer of this discussion. We will discuss the findings from the CIVED study pertaining to the seven PIDOP countries by examining three dimensions – the individual, the context, and the process. Using data from the CIVED study, we will show how the age cohort in these seven PIDOP countries scored in relation to each other in CIVED (when nationally representative samples were tested ten years earlier).

Our overriding questions are as follows:

- What are the implications of these two studies for understanding individual differences, contexts, and processes?
- In what respects are existing results adequate for understanding this relatively understudied content area in the age period that extends beyond adolescence into young adulthood? Which topics deserve further attention?

Understanding individual differences, context, and processes regarding deliberation and self-expression

One aspect that deserves special attention is the character of *democratic contexts*. A number of chapters note that the stability of the democratic process is an important aspect of the country's context and also whether self-expression by individuals is valued. Arguably this feature overarches all of the other aspects of context in a study of democratic ownership and participation.

In a parallel way, in some analyses of CIVED data it proved important to consider how many years a country had been a democracy (distinguishing, for example, between long-standing Western democracies, countries which had overthrown dictators 40–60 years ago, and recent democracies such as the post-Communist countries). The duration of democracy and also a measure of strictness of immigrant policy were important in looking at the meaning of nationalism to young people and its relation to attitudes toward immigrants (Barber *et al.* 2013). This should be considered in terms of the PIDOP findings as well.

Civic education has sometimes been understood in a minimalist way, focusing on rote learning about specific government structures. This may be the reason that some of the respondents in the PIDOP interviews deemed this school subject 'insufficient and perfunctory' (Barrett, 2012: 28). In many countries the content of civic education programs is limited by the desire to avoid partisan messages in classroom instruction. Further, teachers have multiple demands for content coverage and increasingly must prepare students for tests in other subjects. However, many recognize that good civic and political education can have a capacity-building function, and that schools can foster this in non-partisan ways. The process of debate and deliberation that results in seeing different viewpoints on a question is as important in schools as it is in civic organizations.

The importance of an open climate for deliberation in the classroom has been highlighted ever since the first international civic education studies (Torney *et al.* 1975). This can be seen as an element of context and also as an important component of process. In a variety of analyses perception of an open classroom climate and participation in discussion have been associated with cognitive, attitudinal, and participation outcomes (Torney-Purta *et al.* 2001). Classrooms often have some kind of traditional instruction involving textbooks and/or lectures. However, traditional teaching alone in the absence of an interactive process of discussion and deliberation is not optimal for acquiring an understanding of citizenship, or positive participatory attitudes (Torney-Purta and Wilkenfeld 2009).

Table 24.2 shows the extent to which students in each of the seven countries that overlapped in the two studies reported experiences with deliberation and discussion in their classes when they were surveyed in the CIVED Study. Only three of these countries (Germany, Italy, and Sweden) were above the international mean for the 28 countries tested in CIVED. However, on average, girls in all but one of these countries (Belgium) were more likely than boys to find their classrooms open to discussion. This relative lack of deliberation experienced by this age cohort when they were in school in several countries reinforces the value of promoting this process beyond the end of compulsory schooling. The PIDOP project considers discussion or deliberation among late adolescents taking place outside of the school setting to be of particular importance. For example, Emler (this volume) mentions political conversations, while Albanesi, Mazzoni, Cicognani and Zani (this volume) extensively review research on organizations with respect to the opportunities for reflective deliberation they provide.

Understanding individual differences, context, and processes in reference to sense of community and collective efficacy

In the CIVED study, collective efficacy meant the extent to which the 14-year-old respondents in these nationally representative samples agreed with items suggesting

TABLE 24.2 Students' perceptions of the school experience: mean scores from the IEA CIVED study (1999)

Mean	CIVED scales	
	Open classroom climate for deliberation	Sense of collective efficacy at school
10.5–10.8		Portugal
10.1–10.4	Germany* Italy* Sweden*	Sweden*
10.0 International mean	England*	
9.6–9.9	Portugal*	Belgium (French-speaking)* Czech Republic England* Italy
9.2–9.5	Belgium (French-speaking) Czech Republic*	Germany
8.8–9.1		

*Denotes females' mean scores higher than males' mean scores.
Notes: International mean across 28 IEA CIVED99 countries = 10.0, SD = 2.0.
Countries listed participated in both PIDOP (2012) and CIVED99.

that students could get together to make a difference or solve problems in their schools. Table 24.2 shows the country differences in the sense of collective efficacy at school. Portugal and Sweden on average were high, with Germany relatively low. Considering gender differences, females in Belgium, Sweden, and England were more likely than males to experience this sense of collective efficacy at school.

Comparing the two columns in Table 24.2, in Portugal young people experienced collective efficacy in school problem-solving (but not in classroom deliberation), while in Germany the opposite was true with relatively high class deliberation scores and relatively low school efficacy scores. In Belgium and the Czech Republic both deliberation in an open class climate and a sense of cohesion and community at school were low in this age cohort.

The PIDOP project placed emphasis on the sense of community as a part of collective efficacy. The chapters by Zani and her colleagues (this volume) conceptualize the sense of community as more than a simple individual or context variable. This concept has elements of process, one could even call it flow in the sense that it is positively responsive to challenge, self-reinforcing, and perpetuating. It involves both cognitive elements (social representations often shared within a group) and emotional elements (anger against social injustice and also positive emotions such as sense of solidarity and personal investment in action). An internalized sense of civic and political identity is both a dynamic element of the process and an individual characteristic that can be fostered (as Barrett discusses in his chapter).

It forms part of the quality (not merely the quantity) of participation. This is especially true when a range of views is found in discussions and interactions in the community.

In contrast to many conceptualizations of political or civic action, collective efficacy or sense of solidarity often has a focus on the local community and on direct feedback from peers and those with whom one collaborates. The idea of everyday life settings in which one enacts one's beliefs with a connection to values of the community and beliefs of other individuals corresponds to the 'developmental niche' approach to conceptualizing emergent political participation, as we have described elsewhere (Torney-Purta and Amadeo 2011). We will refer to this process at several points in the discussion of specific groups' participation. For example, Noack and Jugert (this volume) have pointed to collective efficacy as especially important for migrants' engagement. Barrett (this volume) points to a number of ways in which this approach could be further elaborated.

Understanding individual differences, context, and processes regarding women's participation

One of the major purposes of the PIDOP study was to understand the extent to which young women have the same opportunities and chances to attain a sense of democratic ownership and participation in society as young men. Although the earlier CIVED study was framed more generally, CIVED researchers examined gender differences within countries for all attitude scales both for 14-year-olds and for pre-university students (Torney-Purta et al. 2001; Amadeo et al. 2002). Gender differences, when they appeared, tended to be consistent across the two age groups.

In addition to the gender differences in school experiences covered in the previous section Table 24.3 shows that support for norms of social movement citizenship on the part of females was higher in three of the seven countries that participated in both the CIVED and PIDOP studies (Italy, Germany, and Sweden). Female students in all seven of these countries also were more likely than males to expect to participate in civic activities at the community level (Table 24.4). In Belgium and Italy, males had higher scores on items referring to expected participation in conventional politics, such as interest in following political news or joining a political party (Table 24.4) and unconventional activities such as protest (similar to Galligan's results from adults, this volume). Across-scale gender differences in the direction of more positive civic participation on the part of females were most characteristic of Italy, Germany, and Sweden. In those countries, females seem to be getting the messages of the importance of citizenship while the males seem to be more alienated.

Portugal stood out for having relatively high scores on scales such as sense of collective efficacy at school, support for social movement citizenship, and expected conventional political and civic activity. However, Portugal was the only country where males were more supportive of conventional norms of political citizenship than were females. One gender difference stood out in the CIVED study. On the

TABLE 24.3 Students' perceptions of norms of participation: mean scores from the IEA CIVED study (1999)

Mean	CIVED scales	
	Support norms of conventional citizenship	Support norms of social-movement citizenship
10.5–10.8		Portugal
10.1–10.4	Italy Portugal+	Italy*
10.0 International Mean		
9.6–9.9	Germany	Germany* Sweden* Czech Republic
9.2–9.5	Belgium (French-speaking) Czech Republic England Sweden	England
8.8–9.1		Belgium (French-speaking)

+Denotes males' mean scores higher than females' mean scores.
*Denotes females' mean scores higher than males' mean scores.
Notes: International mean across 28 IEA CIVED99 countries = 10.0, SD = 2.0.
Countries listed participated in both PIDOP (2012) and CIVED99.

TABLE 24.4 Students' expected civic and political participation: mean scores from the IEA CIVED study (1999)

Mean	CIVED scales	
	Conventional political activity	Civic participation in community
10.5–10.8		Portugal*
10.1–10.4	Portugal	
10.0 International mean		Italy*
9.6–9.9	Belgium (French-speaking)+ Italy+ Sweden England Germany	Belgium (French-speaking)* England* Germany*
9.2–9.5	Czech Republic	Sweden*
8.8–9.1		Czech Republic*

+Denotes males' mean scores higher than females' mean scores.
*Denotes females' mean scores higher than males' mean scores.
Notes: International mean across 28 IEA CIVED99 countries = 10.0, SD = 2.0.
Countries listed participated in both PIDOP (2012) and CIVED99.

scale which measured support for women's political rights, in all countries females had significantly higher mean scores than males (Table 24.5). In some nations these gender differences were nearly a full standard deviation. The highest overall support for women's rights in CIVED was in England and Germany and the lowest in the Czech Republic (Table 24.5). Females were also more supportive of rights for immigrants, although the gender differences were not as large as those regarding rights for women (Table 24.5).

In summary, individual differences by gender were important in both CIVED and PIDOP. The former study measured generalized support for women's rights in a quantitative survey while the latter focused on perceptions of discrimination by young women highlighted in the interviews and focus groups. In both studies we learned about the aspiration of young women for equality in the political, social, and economic spheres. In discussing Belgium, Gavray, Born and Fournier (this volume) review the ways in which males may bring a sense of realistic skepticism to their views of government and promoting social justice. These authors also point to a sense of 'societal vulnerability' and lack of recognition for attempts at engagement experienced by females on an everyday basis. This also could be conceptualized in the developmental niches discussed earlier. This topic has received too little attention in most previous studies.

Turning our attention to context, there are several relevant indices measuring gender equality at the country level (discussed in Galligan, this volume). These indices include the World Economic Forum's Global Gender Gap Index (GGI), an OECD gender indicator, and the EU's Gender Equality Index (where it is part of

TABLE 24.5 Students' support for women's and immigrants' rights: mean scores from the IEA CIVED study (1999)

Mean	CIVED scales	
	Support women's political rights	Support for rights of immigrants
10.5–10.8	England* Germany*	Sweden*
10.1–10.4	Belgium (French-speaking)* Portugal* Sweden*	Portugal
10.0 International mean	Italy*	Belgium (French-speaking)* Czech Republic*
9.6–9.9	Czech Republic*	England* Italy*
9.2–9.5		Germany*
8.8–9.1		

*Denotes females' mean scores higher than males' mean scores.
Notes: International mean across 28 IEA CIVED99 countries = 10.0, SD = 2.0.
Countries listed participated in both PIDOP (2012) and CIVED99.

the Gender Toolkit). The countries near the top of that index (England, Sweden, and Germany) also ranked high on the CIVED women's rights scales. Using indices available a dozen years ago when results from CIVED were released, there was a substantial rank order correlation between the national mean on 'Support for Women's Rights' and the percentage of seats in Parliament held by women. This is an especially fruitful area for exploration with the survey data from PIDOP.

Now we move to the policy analyses in PIDOP. The impression is that although gender discrimination can be identified, the motivation to redress it within Europe is rather moderate. There are many barriers and few specific directions (Ribeiro et al., this volume). Considerably more energy is evident in young women's views about the need for change than in the views of those who might have an impact upon policy.

It is important to consider the school and neighborhood contexts when considering young women's potential participation. Barber and Torney-Purta (2009) used CIVED data to examine perceptions of discrimination on the part of male and female students across 28 countries and how this related to 'Support for Women's Rights' (in which females were higher) and 'Sense of Political Efficacy' (in which males were higher). The most interesting findings in this analysis dealt with processes within the classroom. A multilevel analysis indicated that the gender gap showing female adolescents to be higher in support for women's rights was reduced in classroom contexts characterized by open discussion and deliberation. This was primarily because male students became more supportive of women's rights. Once again the importance of democratic deliberation is suggested.

There is also some evidence that the process of developing collective efficacy and a sense of community is an especially important part of young women's engagement processes (Albanesi et al. this volume). Gavray et al. (this volume), discussing Belgium, report that females felt more willing to participate in social change and to resist discrimination against minorities; they also saw possibilities for collective action in the community. Females also felt more strongly about discrimination and environmental problems but saw barriers to involvement.

Examining these results and projecting to the future several authors recognize that the workplace is an important context for young adults and that it corresponds in some ways to the school as a context for adolescents. There is an important contrast, however. Most school personnel subscribe to equality of educational opportunity for both genders. Furthermore, educational attainment is something that most European parents value for their female as well as their male children, even if some parents may be ambivalent about women's rights more generally. In fact Gavray et al. (this volume) note that many immigrant families place their hopes for social mobility on the achievements of girls. One problem is that once young women leave school, the workplace setting is likely to place them in less empowered positions than young men and to value their contributions less. In fact Galligan (this volume) comments on the importance of labor market participation for women's sense of political belonging but notes that part-time employment and positions with less authority and lower salaries stand in the way of women's empowerment.

Future studies should explore the context of the workplace in greater depth. In particular, one could study what are called 'small democracies,' for example workers deliberating about options and taking action in their places of employment and parents doing something similar in their children's schools (see Kriesi and Westholm 2007; Westholm and von Erlach 2007). These authors found males to be more active than females in the workplace, but fewer gender differences in taking action related to children's schooling (another context for adults that they investigated). Given the importance of strong beliefs about particular issues (such as the quality of local education) in prompting political action (Gavray et al. this volume, and Galligan this volume), more attention should be given to how young parents (especially mothers) may be prompted to political or civic activity. The focus PIDOP places on young adults differs from most cross-cultural studies and the opportunities for democratic action in the workplace, the community, and the school deserve special attention in future research.

Communication using the Internet cannot be neatly categorized under either context or process. Among the most interesting PIDOP findings concerned with the Internet were related to gender. One might expect that young women in certain cultural groups, reinforced by their families' beliefs and values, would experience constraints on expression about social and political issues. In fact there is some evidence in the PIDOP chapters that many females feel free to express themselves in e-communication. Gavray et al. (this volume) comments that this activity can include forwarding links to webpages to friends, participating in online petitions, and consumer boycotts. Even if they are relatively confined at home, females seem to manage to communicate about as freely as males using this medium. However, it is not clear whether they would be willing to place their names on these communications.

Researchers do not know the content of these communications, but the extent to which gender differences were absent (or sometimes favored young women) in responses to PIDOP questions about Internet communication was notable. This kind of communication within the civic sphere can have an educative and capacity-building function with possible extension to conventional political structures where women remain under-represented in the PIDOP countries. This is reinforced by Bozkurt et al. (this volume) and by Gavray et al. (this volume). See also the variety of Internet uses detailed in Anduiza et al. (2012), including attending an in-person event after receiving an online invitation and using a blog or social network site to express an opinion about a social or political issue.

These findings correspond to the report by Livingston (2007) comparing online participation by gender. The group she calls 'civic-minded' (visiting human rights and charity websites) was more likely to be female than the other groups ('interactors' and 'disengaged'). Using CIVED data to predict expectations of social movement and conventional citizenship activities, Amadeo (2007) analyzed the seven CIVED countries where Internet use was included in the questionnaires. She found moderate associations between Internet use and students' expectations for social-movement and conventional citizenship activities in two countries (Denmark and

England) and also found that males were more likely to be active on the Internet than females. However, this analysis was limited because Internet use was a survey item that most countries in CIVED chose not to administer (since it was an international option). Clearly the context has changed as the frequency of opportunities for all kinds of social media and Internet communication has exploded in the 15 years since the CIVED data were collected.

In suggesting the importance of Internet communication for females, we should not ignore the variety of activist organizations in which girls are playing increasing roles. In a volume entitled *Rebel Girls: Youth Activism and Social Change Across the Americas*, Taft (2011) interviewed female activists from three Latin American countries, the US, and Canada. Their activities ranged from rallies against educational privatization to fair trade policies and pointed to the importance of adults taking teenage girls seriously and moving beyond thinking of female activists only in relation to issues with special relevance to their gender.

Understanding individual differences, context and processes regarding migrants' participation

The PIDOP study is a rich source of qualitative information about the discrimination experienced by members of migrant groups. There are interesting differences between groups with varying origins in certain countries; see the Kurdish example cited by Kim and Amnå (this volume) and the Turks and Moroccans studied by Gavray et al. (this volume). The CIVED study has less to contribute here, since we were able to ask only whether respondents were born in the country of the test (that is whether they themselves were immigrants). There was no information about the country from which they had migrated.

The country means on 'Support for Immigrants' Rights' (Table 24.5) in CIVED suggest the least receptive atmosphere in England, Italy, and Germany. The high position of Sweden on this scale should be considered together with findings from the more recent IEA ICCS study (2009). Barber and Torney-Purta (2012) analyzed responses to the individual items in the immigrants' rights scale comparing the 1999 data to data collected from parallel samples in 2009. This ten-year period saw a decline in Swedish adolescents' agreement with two of immigrants' rights items: 'Immigrants should have the right to keep speaking their own language' and 'Immigrants should have the right to retain their own cultural practices.' There was still wide support for immigrants' rights to education and political expression, but the visible aspect of language and culture (experienced in the everyday contexts of school and community) were less likely to be endorsed in Sweden at the later period.

Several of the PIDOP researchers conducted statistical analyses of differences associated with migrant groups in the surveys. In Sweden, for example, the Kurdish group believed that their parents held stronger norms for civic and political engagement, and had higher political interest and a greater sense of political efficacy than did either the Iraqi or Swedish samples (Kim and Amnå, this volume). The Kurdish youth also reported the strongest emotions about discrimination.

Much as the previous section described the possible potential of the Internet for girls' participation and empowerment, online participation may have a similar role to play for migrants, in particular because it has the potential to reduce language barriers or catch young people's interest because of links to issues in the country of origin. The potential of the Internet was noted in areas of both political and economic participation and in relation to prominent issues involving human rights and the environment (Barrett 2012). Another point is that when young people encounter situations where opinions are openly discussed (online or offline), they may subsequently bring up some of these opinions within their families, perhaps influencing their siblings. This function of mediating between home and the broader world may be especially feasible for older adolescents. These points are emphasized by Serek *et al.* (this volume).

At the same time we should not give too positive a picture, since migrants (and others) of low economic means may not have the same access to Internet resources as those from the majority groups, and the meaning of political and civic participation is not yet clearly defined for migrant groups. Studies in this area are indicated, as well as more consideration of the role of both formal education and informal activities organized by NGOs with migrants as members.

In fact, there are several dimensions of the study of migrants' political engagement that deserve additional attention from researchers. Two concern the intersection of categories. How does the socio-economic status of these groups (in particular the educational resources of the family) and the religious orientation influence possibilities for remedying discrimination in the political and civic realm (points emphasized in several chapters of this volume, especially by Fernandes-Jesus *et al.*)? The intersection of gender and status as a migrant was dealt with briefly in the previous section but deserves further attention. And the differences between first- and second-generation immigrants, dealt with briefly by Kim and Amnå (this volume), also should be considered.

Future study of individuals, context, and processes

Each of the three dimensions of interest – individual differences, context (of nation as well as school or community), and processes – has been enriched by the PIDOP study and there are numerous questions raised for further exploration. Enhancing research on workplaces and the Internet holds considerable promise both for documenting barriers and identifying opportunities.

The use of person-centered analysis in several of the chapters (for example, latent class analysis looking at attentiveness and action) has helped to focus attention on subgroups within majority and minority populations. This analysis also indicates how young adults integrate their attitudes with orientations toward behavior. Additional analysis of this type should be considered if the data sets from the different countries can be merged for common analysis (in much the way that the adult survey data was approached by Brunton-Smith and Barrett, this volume).

The analysis of a merged data set would also be a way to explore in young adults the finding from the CIVED data showing Belgium, the Czech Republic, England, Germany, and Sweden to be relatively low on support for citizenship norms (both conventional and social) and on also on the beliefs about expected engagement in conventional or social movement activism.

As is often the case, the policy recommendations are intriguing but difficult to judge for their potential effectiveness. This is true for policy regarding migrants and perhaps even more for policy regarding women's participation. The general fragmentation of policy, rapid changes in European migration patterns and lack of effective ways to leverage action by European institutions is noted in several of the chapters. Each chapter in itself and especially those devoted to policy include some interesting possibilities. In the future it may be helpful to further contextualize these. Certain directions may be more valuable in countries with certain characteristics or with some migrant groups than with others.

This volume makes a distinctive and valuable contribution to understanding European adolescents' and young adults' orientations to political and civic participation with a range of methods of assessing individuals, context (including policy contexts), and processes. The directions it suggests and the questions it raises will be of interest to researchers for decades to come.

Note

1 In all of the IEA's research the two communities of Belgium participate independently. The French-speaking community participated in CIVED99 (corresponding to the group in PIDOP).

References

Amadeo, J. (2007) 'Patterns of internet use and political engagement among youth,' in P. Dahlgren (ed.), *Young Citizens and the New Media: Learning for Democratic Participation*. New York: Routledge, pp. 125–48.

Amadeo, J., Torney-Purta, J., Lehmann, R., Husfeldt, V., and Nikolova, R. (2002) *Civic Knowledge and Engagement Among Upper Secondary Students in Sixteen Countries*. Amsterdam: International Association for the Evaluation of Educational Achievement.

Anduiza, E., Jensen, M., and Jorba, L. (eds) (2012) *Digital Media and Political Engagement Worldwide: A Comparative Study*. Cambridge: Cambridge University Press.

Azevedo, C. and Menezes, I. (2007) 'Learning politics beyond cognition: the role of experience and participation in political development,' in N. Kryger and B. Ravn (eds), *Learning Beyond Cognition*. Copenhagen: Danish University of Education Press, pp. 95–114.

Barber, C. and Torney-Purta, J. (2009, reissued 2012) 'Gender differences in political efficacy and attitudes to women's rights influenced by national and school contexts: analysis for the IEA Civic Education Study,' in D. Baker and A. Wiseman (eds), *Gender Equality and Education from International and Comparative Perspectives*, International Perspectives on Education and Society Series, Vol. 10. Bingley, UK: JAI/Emerald Group Publishing, pp. 357–94.

Barber, C. and Torney-Purta, J. (2012) 'Comparing attitudes in the 1999 and 2009 IEA Civic and Citizenship Education Studies: opportunities and limitations illustrated in five countries,' *Journal of Social Science Education*, 11 (1): 47–74.

Barber, C., Fennelly, K., and Torney-Purta, J. (2013) 'Nationalism and support for immigrants' rights among adolescents in twenty-five countries,' *Applied Developmental Science*, 17 (2): 60–75.

Barrett, M. (2012) *The PIDOP Project: An Overview*. Guildford, Surrey: University of Surrey.

Beaumont, E., Colby, A., Ehrlich, T., and Torney-Purta, J. (2006) 'Promoting political competence and engagement in college students: an empirical study,' *Journal of Political Science Education*, 2: 249–70.

Bee, C. and Guerrina, R. (2014) 'Framing civic engagement, political participation and active citizenship in Europe,' Special issue of *Journal of Civil Society*, 10 (1).

Kriesi, H. and Westholm, A. (2007) 'Small-scale democracy: the determinants of action,' in J. van Deth, J. Montero, and A. Westholm (eds), *Citizenship and Involvement in European Democracies: A Comparative Analysis*. London: Routledge, pp. 255–79.

Lay, J. C. (2012) *A Midwestern Mosaic: Immigration and Political Socialization in Rural America*. Philadelphia, PA: Temple University Press.

Livingstone, S. (2007) 'Interactivity and participation on the internet: young people's response to the civic sphere,' in P. Dahlgren (ed.), *Young Citizens and the New Media: Learning for Democratic Participation*. New York: Routledge, pp. 103–24.

Rubini, M. and Palmonari, A. (2006) 'Adolescents' relationship to institutional order,' in S. Jackson and L. Goossens (eds), *Handbook of Adolescent Development*. Hove: Psychology Press, pp. 264–83.

Sanchez-Jankowski, M. (1986) *City Bound: Urban Life and Political Attitudes Among Chicano Youth*. Albuquerque, NM: University of New Mexico Press.

Taft, J. (2011) *Rebel Girls: Youth Activism and Social Change Across the Americas*. New York: NYU Press.

Torney, J., Oppenheim, A. N., and Farnen, R. (1975) *Civic Education in Ten Countries: An Empirical Study*. Stockholm: Almqvist & Wiksell.

Torney-Purta, J. (in press) 'Political socialization,' in S. Schechter (ed.), *American Governance: An Encyclopedia*. Farmington Hills, MI: Cengage Learning.

Torney-Purta, J. and Amadeo, J. (2011) 'Participatory niches for emergent citizenship in early adolescence,' in F. Earls (ed.), *The Child as Citizen: Annals of the American Academy of Political and Social Science*, 633: 180–200.

Torney-Purta, J. and Amadeo, J. (2013) 'International large-scale assessments: challenges in reporting and potentials for secondary analysis,' *Research in Comparative and International Education*, Special Issue, 8 (3): 248–58.

Torney-Purta, J. and Wilkenfeld, B. (2009) *Paths to 21st Century Competencies Through Civic Education Classrooms: An Analysis of Survey Results from Ninth-Graders*. Chicago: Division for Public Education, American Bar Association.

Torney-Purta, J., Andolina, M., and Amadeo, J. (2010) 'A conceptual framework and a multi-method approach for research in civic engagement and political socialization,' in L. Sherrod, J. Torney-Purta, and C. Flanagan (eds), *Handbook of Research on Civic Engagement in Youth*. Hoboken, NJ: John Wiley, pp. 497–534.

Torney-Purta, J., Schwille, J., and Amadeo, J. (eds) (1999) *Civic Education Across Countries: Twenty-Four Case Studies from the IEA Civic Education Project*. Amsterdam: International Association for the Evaluation of Educational Achievement.

Torney-Purta, J., Lehmann, R., Oswald, H., and Schulz, W. (2001) *Citizenship and Education in Twenty-Eight Countries: Civic Knowledge and Engagement at Age 14*. Amsterdam: International Association for the Evaluation of Educational Achievement.

Wentzel, K. (2006) 'Developing and nurturing interesting and researchable ideas,' in C. Conrad and R. Serlin (eds), *The Sage Handbook for Research in Education: Engaging Ideas and Enriching Inquiry*. Thousand Oaks, CA: Sage, pp. 315–50.

Westholm, A. and von Erlach, E. (2007) 'Small-scale democracy: the consequences of action,' in J. van Deth, J. Montero, and A. Westholm (eds), *Citizenship and Involvement in European Democracies: A Comparative Analysis*. London: Routledge, pp. 280–300.

Zani, B. and Barrett, M. (eds) (2012) 'Engaged citizens? Political participation and social engagement among young people, women, minorities and migrants,' Special Issue of *Human Affairs: Postdisciplinary Humanities and Social Sciences Quarterly*, 22 (3).

25
THE COUNCIL OF EUROPE'S WORK ON 'EDUCATION FOR DEMOCRATIC CITIZENSHIP AND HUMAN RIGHTS EDUCATION' AND ITS LINKS TO THE PIDOP PROJECT

Reinhild Otte

Hearing about PIDOP immediately gives rise to the supposition that there are links to the Council of Europe's (CoE) work in the field of education for democratic citizenship and human rights. To find out more about this relationship, especially its differences, similarities and interconnections, it is necessary to first describe the CoE's work in general and its work on education for democratic citizenship and human rights (EDC/HRE) in particular.

The framework and background to the Council of Europe's work on EDC/HRE

The CoE is the oldest European intergovernmental organisation. Founded in 1949 by the Treaty of London, it currently represents 47 pluralist democracies with more than 800 million citizens and includes the whole of geographical Europe. Its headquarters are located in Strasbourg, France. The CoE is sometimes confused with the European Union (EU) which today has 28 member states. These are two distinct organisations. However, no country has ever joined the EU without first belonging to the CoE.

Formed in the aftermath of the Second World War, the CoE seeks to protect and to promote democracy, human rights and the rule of law. Quite often it is called 'the human rights watchdog' or the 'guardian of human rights, democracy and the rule of law' (or – by a word game – the 'gardener' that cultivates these delicate plants). The CoE believes that these three core values form the necessary basis of a tolerant and civilised society and that they are indispensable in building a stable, functional and cohesive Europe (Council of Europe 2012).

The CoE's most famous achievement is the European Convention on Human Rights (ECHR), adopted in 1950 and entered into force in 1953, and its international enforcement machinery, the European Court of Human Rights, set up in

1959, which allows individuals, groups and governments regardless of nationality to contest alleged breaches of the European Convention on Human Rights (Council of Europe 2009a). The Court's case law and landmark judgments influence national law and policies considerably. Since 1999, there is also an office of the Commissioner for Human Rights, an independent institution with a mandate to promote awareness of and respect for human rights in member states of the CoE.

The work of the CoE covers all major issues facing European societies other than defence. The CoE has worked in the field of education since its foundation and has achieved important results in permanent education (nowadays called lifelong learning), in adult education, in language learning (e.g. the Common European Framework of Reference for Languages and the European Language Portfolio), in history teaching, in intercultural education and in teacher training, to name but a few areas.

In all of these educational activities, democracy and human rights have been well represented. However, a special emphasis was placed on these issues especially from 1992 onwards, which finally led to the activity on 'Education for Democratic Citizenship and Human Rights (EDC/HRE)'. Today, it has developed into a real 'flagship' of the CoE's work (Ólafsdóttir 2011).

This project (which officially started in 1997) cannot be understood without its historical and political background as it forms part of the response of the CoE to the collapse of the communist system and the new challenges in Central, Eastern and South-Eastern Europe which emerged after 1989 (Otte 2013). In 1987, the CoE had started a large project on 'Adult Education and Social Change', in which the elderly and the long-term unemployed were identified as target groups for change. However, in the middle of the project, it became obvious that the most important change was a very different one, namely the political and economic collapse of the communist systems in Europe.

As a consequence of this, the CoE was confronted with a strong demand from the countries in transition to assist them on their path to democracy. For education, this meant that although these countries had a very high level of education, their educational systems were not well equipped for the transition to democracy and human rights. Among the most urgent challenges were:

- how populations could best become acquainted with democracy and human rights inside and outside school;
- who should teach democracy and human rights (certainly not the former teachers of Marxism/Leninism);
- which curricula and textbooks would be needed;
- whether new legislation would be necessary.

The following few examples of the CoE's activities can be seen as milestones which illustrate the developments. The first step was a conference in Belgrade, Yugoslavia, in 1990. Here, for the first time in the history of the CoE, representatives from Western as well as from Central and Eastern European countries (Bulgaria, Czechoslovakia,

Hungary, Poland and Romania) were brought together for a conference on 'Adult Education and Social Change with Special Emphasis on Reducing Unemployment'. Here, not only the need to transform society, the economy and the labour market was mentioned, but also new opportunities for adult education in Europe were envisaged to further mankind's highest values, human rights and freedom, as well as the link between unemployment, social cohesion, education and democracy.

In the field of higher education, in 1991, with the Iron Curtain gone, the CoE set up a special programme to monitor and support the legislative reforms which the transition countries were carrying out to their democratic systems in the field of higher education and research. One of the most urgent questions was how to make the transition from rigid, centralised planning to academic autonomy and research (one has to remember that, under socialism, higher education and research were governed also entirely by a central plan). The CoE's approach was both open and pragmatic, the aim being to help but not to impose particular solutions and above all to give ownership of the results to those affected. It consisted of advisory missions, thematic workshops, multilateral study visits (to give specialists from the East a chance to see democratic systems in action) and a series of publications with pan-European analysis.

The next step was a conference in Stuttgart, Germany, in 1992, jointly organised by the CoE and the Ministry of Education, Youth and Sport Baden-Württemberg on 'Adult Education and Social Change in the Light of New Developments in Europe'. A Recommendation was adopted requesting that a follow-up project of the CoE should focus on adult education as an element of democratisation and economic reform which should pay special attention to developments in the countries of Central and Eastern Europe but also take into account the closer relations among all countries in Europe.

In 1993, this Recommendation found its way into the final conference of the whole 'Adult Education and Social Change' Project, which looked into the socio-economic changes in Europe and existing links between adult education and human rights. There was a consensus among all member states that a new project should focus on strengthening pluralistic democracy and human rights.

The following years from 1993 to 1996 were characterised by an interim phase and a period of intense preparation for a new project to respond to the new challenges and demands. The main questions to answer were:

- How to put together school education, higher education and adult education in the field of EDC/HRE.
- How to combine the different interests of 'new 'and 'old' member states of the CoE.

Many workshops, seminars, study visits, bilateral programmes and pilot projects took place to find out what was really needed for a future project. The goal was to develop the knowledge, skills and attitudes which young people and adults need to become democratic, active citizens who care about and respect human rights.

Two developments during this period gave strong backing to all these efforts: the enlargement of the CoE and political support. By 1995, the CoE had grown from 23 to 35 member states, with most of the new states coming from the former communist system. And 43 states had already signed the European Cultural Convention and therefore were able to participate in all CoE activities in education and culture.

As regards political support, the most important events during this period included the First Summit of Heads of State and Government of the Council of Europe in Vienna, Austria, in 1993, which looked forward to a Europe 'where all countries are committed to pluralist and parliamentary democracy, the indivisibility and universality of human rights, the rule of law and a common heritage enriched by its diversity' (Council of Europe 1994). In addition, in Madrid, Spain, in 1994, the Standing Conference of European Ministers of Education put this in concrete terms and 'asked the Council of Europe to intensify its activities promoting education for democracy, human rights and tolerance ... in school, adult education and teacher training' (Council of Europe 1994).

In Strasbourg, France, in 1996, a broad consultation meeting took place, the result of which was a new project that should look for innovative paths with the following elements:

- Lifelong learning (all age groups)
- Formal, non-formal and informal education
- Holistic approach (all sectors of society)
- Inter-Institutional (close cooperation with other international organisations)
- Pan-European character (new and old member states).

In February 1997, a Steering Group for EDC/HRE was set up. Finally in Strasbourg in October 1997, the Second Summit of Heads of State and Government of the Council of Europe requested in its Action Plan 'the launch of an initiative on Education for Democratic Citizenship and Human Rights' (Council of Europe 1997). This was the official start of the EDC/HRE Project.

The Council of Europe's activity in EDC/HRE

Aims and definition

The EDC/HRE initiative aims to promote the CoE's core values – democracy, human rights and the rule of law – through education, and is 'designed to help young people and adults play an active part in democratic life by equipping them with the knowledge, skills and understanding they need and by developing their attitudes and behaviour to empower them to exercise and defend their democratic rights and responsibilities' (Council of Europe 2010).

Education for Democratic Citizenship (EDC) shows people how to become informed about their rights, responsibilities and duties, and about all matters of community interest; it helps them to realise that they can have an influence, that they can make a difference and play an effective role in their democratic community, be it at the local, national or international level.

'Democratic Citizenship' is both a knowledge and a skill. It is a knowledge because citizens need to know about the functioning of their political system and about their rights. But it is also a skill because democratic citizenship is much more than just voting and being protected by law. It is the capacity – and responsibility – to live in a community according to the principles and values that underlie democracy, most notably openness, tolerance, justice and peaceful conflict resolution. A democratic citizen is both an informed person capable of critical thinking, and an active one practising democracy in his/her daily life in the community (Council of Europe 2005).

For the CoE, democratic citizenship is not confined to the legal status of 'citizen' or the rights derived from the right to vote at national or European Union level or the freedom of movement. Instead, it embraces every aspect of life in a democratic society, emphasising the importance of active participation for the proper functioning of societies founded on respect for human rights and the rule of law.

Main elements

In accordance with these aims and definitions the EDC/HRE activity has the following main elements. First, since democracy is a lifelong activity, Education for Democratic Citizenship is not only for young people (although they have an important role to play); it adopts a *life-long-learning perspective* which involves learning throughout the lifespan from cradle to grave and starting at any age.

Second, it has a *broad multifaceted, holistic approach* which means that it covers all sectors of society. Schools are by no means the only places where democratic citizenship can be acquired: democratic citizens are made in the family, in the playground, in youth clubs, sports organisations, enterprises, at leisure time, in community, even in homes for the elderly, etc.

A third element of EDC/HRE is that it is not limited to formal learning in the school system but covers *all forms of education, including formal, non-formal and informal education* (Council of Europe 2010), where:

- *Formal education* means the structured education and training system that runs from pre-elementary and primary through secondary school and on to university.
- *Non-formal education* means any planned programme designed to improve a range of skills and competencies, outside the formal setting.
- *Informal education* means the lifelong process whereby every individual acquires attitudes, values, skills and knowledge from the educational influences and resources in his or her own environment and from daily experience.

Fourth, EDC/HRE is also an *inter-sectoral project*, which means that it is transversal and touches all sectors of the Council of Europe: education, youth, human rights, social cohesion, political affairs, etc. Representatives of all these Directorates and various bodies (the Parliamentary Assembly of the Council of Europe (PACE), the Congress of Local and Regional Authorities (CLRA), the Conference of International Non-Governmental Organisations (CINGO), etc.) work together with their colleagues from member states in the Steering Committee of the project.

Finally, EDC/HRE is – and also this seems to be unique – *inter-institutional*, which means that all large international governmental (e.g. the United Nations Educational, Scientific and Cultural Organisation (UNESCO), the Office of the High Commissioner for Human Rights (OHCHR), the Organisation for Security and Cooperation in Europe/Office for Democratic Institutions and Human Rights (OSCE/ODIHR) and the EU) and non-governmental organisations work together in a similar way on the Steering Committee. Their cooperation has developed considerably so an 'International Contact Group on Citizenship and Human Rights Education' (see below) has been established.

Phases

After the launch of the EDC/HRE project in 1997 its *first phase (1997–2000)* was conceived as an exploratory project aimed at clarification of concepts and definitions and the development of strategies to promote EDC. The setting up of grassroots initiatives ('Sites of Citizenship') in communities was also supported. The results of this phase were endorsed by the European Ministers of Education at the 20th session of their standing conference in Krakow, Poland, in 2000.

The focus of the *second phase (2001–2004)* was on the development of policies and the dissemination of the results of the first phase through networking and communication activities. Recommendation (2002)12 of the CoE's Committee of Ministers to member states on EDC is one of the main outcomes of this phase. A network of EDC-Coordinators (see below) was developed and became a cornerstone of the project. The 'All-European Study on Policies for EDC' (Birzea 2004) conducted during this phase has become a reference document in this field, as it gave a systematic description of EDC policies in CoE member states and revealed the 'compliance gap' between policy and practice in many countries.

The aim of the very successful 2005 'European Year of Citizenship through Education' with its slogan 'Learning and Living Democracy' was to reach a broader public and to draw attention to the vital role that education plays in fostering citizenship and to the need for citizen participation in any truly democratic society. The 'Year' was marked by many events and activities in various countries and projects and field activities were launched at all levels in member states and by the Council of Europe.

The *third phase (2006–2009)*, which was called 'Learning and Living Democracy for All', was significantly more complex and ambitious than the previous ones, with multiple partnerships being established, and a broad range of activities for various audiences being organised at multilateral, regional and bilateral level. A stronger link between 'Education for Democratic Citizenship' and 'Human Rights

Education' was built up. The main focus was on ensuring that policies and resources developed by the CoE were being put into practice at the country level. The results achieved so far clearly show the added value of the 'Learning and Living Democracy for All' programme to the CoE's mission of both promoting human rights, democracy and the rule of law and as a potent preventative mechanism. The programme was successful in building cooperation networks and strategic partnerships and meeting the needs of education decision-makers, practitioners and civil society organisations.

The main focus of the *fourth phase (2010–2014)* was the consolidation of previous achievements and the development of sustainable mechanisms for future development of citizenship and human rights education. The main objectives are as follows: supporting policy development and implementation; promoting partnerships and networking; and putting CoE instruments into practice. The *Council of Europe Charter on Education for Democratic Citizenship and Human Rights Education* (see below), which was adopted after many years of negotiation, builds on 13 years of intergovernmental cooperation in this field and provides a framework for future action.

Outcomes

During the EDC/HRE Project the CoE has adopted many reference texts, developed political frameworks, produced high-quality materials, and supported networks and partnerships in the area of Education for Democratic Citizenship and Human Rights.

Political framework and legal instruments

Among the legal instruments, the most important is the *Recommendation CM/Rec (2010)7 on the Council of Europe Charter on Education for Democratic Citizenship and Human Rights Education* (Council of Europe 2010). The Charter was adopted by the Committee of Ministers on 11 May 2010 and is a non-binding legal instrument. It is an important reference point for all of Europe and a basis for the Council of Europe's work in this field in the coming years.

As regards the content of the Charter, there are four sections: general provisions, including scope and definitions; objectives and principles; policies; and evaluation and cooperation. The general provisions clarify what the Charter covers and which comprehensive definitions (not only descriptions) are being used for the purpose of the Charter, especially for the key terms 'education for democratic citizenship' and 'human rights education' and the relationship between them. The objectives and principles 'should guide member states in the framing of their policies, legislation and practice'. They are fleshed out in more detail in eight policies which cover formal general and vocational education, higher education, democratic governance, training, NGOs, criteria for evaluation, research, and skills for promoting social cohesion. The final section widens the perspective to evaluation and cooperation in follow-up activities and to international organisations. In a nutshell, the Charter aims to codify best practice and help disseminate it around Europe and beyond. An Explanatory Memorandum explains the background, origins and negotiating history of the Charter.

After the adoption of the Charter, the main priorities have been the dissemination of information about the Charter and the development of an implementation strategy. Among these steps the translation of the Charter into 23 languages (to date) and the production of both a pocket version and a child-friendly version should be mentioned as well as its presentation at many conferences and fora.

To evaluate the implementation of the Charter in member states a questionnaire for governments and for NGOs was sent out in 2012 and an evaluation report on its implementation was prepared and presented in Strasbourg in November 2012 at a conference on 'Human Rights and Democracy in Action – Looking Ahead', which was jointly organised by the CoE, the EU and the European Wergeland Centre (see below). As a follow-up, the CoE and the EU agreed in principle to set up a Pilot Project Scheme on 'Human Rights and Democracy in Action' on specific articles of the Charter which started in 2013.

The child-friendly version of the Charter which is entitled 'Democracy and Human Rights Start with Us: Charter for All' is designed to make the Charter accessible to a wider group of learners, particularly young people. It is accompanied by Guidelines for Educators with many examples of how to use it and a checklist for education for democracy and human rights.

In addition to the Charter, a number of other policy framework texts have also been adopted by the CoE over the years, among them:

- Recommendation (2002) 12 of the Committee of Ministers to Member States on education for democratic citizenship (Council of Europe 2002)
- Declaration and programme on education for democratic citizenship, based on the rights and responsibilities of citizens (adopted by the Committee of Ministers on 7 May 1999) (Council of Europe 1999)
- Recommendation No. R(85)7 of the Committee of Ministers to member states on teaching and learning about human rights in schools (Council of Europe 1985).

Materials

Among the wealth of materials that have been developed, tested and disseminated, the so-called 'EDC-Pack' is one of the most important tools. This consists of a collection of practical manuals and guidelines for education in this area. Each of the tools is intended for various target audiences dealing with EDC/HRE and addresses specific aspects. The tools which form the EDC/Pack are:

- *Strategic support for decision makers – policy tool for EDC/HRE* (tool 1, 2010) which offers strategic support to those making decisions about policy and encourages more effective policy-making in EDC/HRE.

- *Democratic governance of schools* (tool 2, 2007) which describes the importance of the whole-school approach to democracy and human rights. It provides advice and guidance mainly for school directors and teachers, but is also useful for all others interested in school governance.
- *How all teachers can support citizenship and human rights education: a framework for competences* (tool 3, 2009) which sets out the core competences needed by teachers to put democratic citizenship and human rights into practice in the classroom. It is intended for all teachers – not only for specialists but teachers in all subject areas – and teachers' educators and trainers.
- *Tool for quality assurance of education for democratic citizenship in schools* (tool 4, 2005) which addresses the link between quality education and citizenship education. It is addressed primarily to policy-makers, curriculum developers, school inspectors and school directors.
- *School-community-university partnership for a sustainable democracy: education for democratic citizenship in Europe and the United States* (tool 5, 2010) which introduces and critically examines the EDC/HRE partnership model. The guide provides a rationale for partnerships, explores the mechanics of EDC/HRE partnerships and examines partnerships in practice.

These instruments have been negotiated and approved by a large number of experts from all member states, including the EDC-Coordinators (see below), and have been translated into many languages, accompanied by supporting materials (Kerr and Losito 2010).

Another example of materials is the publication *Human Rights Education in the School Systems of Europe, Central Asia and North America: A Compendium of Good Practice* (Council of Europe et al. 2009). Following an OSCE/ODIHR initiative, this document was jointly published by OSCE/ODIHR, CoE, OHCHR and UNESCO. It brings together information on EDC/HRE-related frameworks and guidelines developed by the four partner institutions and provides examples of good practice in member states. As an educational resource book, it collects 101 exemplary practices in human rights education, education for democratic citizenship, and education for mutual respect and understanding from Europe, North America and Central Asia.

In 2010, in Sarajevo, the Council of Europe also launched six manuals for teachers on *Living Democracy* to promote education for democratic citizenship and human rights. The manuals are intended to help countries put into practice the *Council of Europe Charter on Education for Democratic Citizenship and Human Rights*. The manuals were first developed in Bosnia and Herzegovina. They were so successful that it was decided to decontextualise them so that schools throughout Europe and beyond could benefit from their interactive methods and thought-provoking approach to promoting democracy and human rights in schools. They include lesson plans for all levels of education from primary to secondary and high schools. These six manuals provide teachers with high-quality materials which have been tested by educators in several countries and are flexible enough to enable both experienced and trainee teachers to introduce citizenship and human rights education in their schools in a fun, interactive and challenging way.

In the field of youth education, there are specific publications available. One of the most requested documents which has been translated into many languages is *Compass* (new edition 2012), a manual on human rights education with young people, and *Compasito* (2007) for children 7–13 years old. Primarily developed for non-formal education settings, they can also be used in formal education. They familiarise the reader with the key concepts of human rights and children's rights, provide substantial theoretical background to key human rights issues and propose numerous activities.

Networking and partnerships

From the beginning of the EDC/HRE Project, the establishment and promotion of networks and partnerships on a European level as well as in an international (global) context has been an important goal. Numerous forms of cooperation have been fostered, as follows.

- *Multilateral European cooperation.* At the European level, there is a close cooperation among all 47 member states of the CoE. They work together in the network of *EDC/HRE-Coordinators* which plays a key role in the EDC/HRE activity as a whole. The Coordinators are contact persons in each country who are officially nominated by their Ministers of Education, whose main tasks are to ensure that CoE information on EDC/HRE is disseminated in the member states and to keep international partners (the CoE, the network of Coordinators and other international organisations where appropriate) informed about EDC/HRE developments in their own countries. Most of the Coordinators are representatives of Ministries of Education or similar professional bodies responsible for implementation of EDC/HRE in member states. At their meetings (which take place once or twice a year), the Coordinators exchange information on recent developments in their countries, discuss future projects and identify possible solutions to common challenges. They provide feedback on the tools and manuals developed by the CoE and contribute to the organisation of major events. Over the years, the network of EDC/HRE Coordinators has become a fully functional, active and influential community of professionals and decision-makers.
- *Regional and bilateral cooperation in Europe.* The Coordinators also work in smaller groups with common interests on a *regional* basis, for example in the Baltic/Black Sea Network, the Nordic Countries Network and the South East Europe Network. The *bilateral* cooperation of the CoE provides advice, guidance and support to individual countries, particularly newer member states of the CoE, such as Kosovo, Ukraine, Romania, Bosnia and Herzegovina in their reform process to introduce European standards and norms as well as materials (Council of Europe 2009b).

- *Joint programmes of the Council of Europe and the European Union.* Support to specific countries is also provided in the framework of the Joint Programmes between the Council of Europe and the European Commission. Such programmes combine the resources of the CoE and the European Commission and allow good use to be made of the expertise and best practice collected and developed through multilateral cooperation. In the past a large number of Joint Programmes have taken place in South East Europe, especially in states which are in a post-conflict situation. Examples today include the Joint CoE-EU Project 'Democratic Citizenship and Human Rights Education in Turkey' which started in 2011, a three-year project being implemented in partnership with the Turkish Ministry of National Education and its Board of Education, and the Joint CoE-EU Programme 'Supporting Education Policies in Democratic Citizenship and Human Rights Education in Kazakhstan' which was launched in 2013 in cooperation with the Ministry of Education and Science of the Republic of Kazakhstan.
- *International cooperation.* Since the official launch of the EDC/HRE project, the CoE has striven to build synergies with other institutions, and the *inter-institutional* work has been one of the core – perhaps unique – elements of the project. The major organisations working in the field of education for democracy and human rights have regularly been invited to the meetings of the Project Steering Group. In Warsaw, already in 1999, a 'Conference on EDC: Methods, Practices and Strategies' was jointly organised by the CoE, UNESCO and the EU. In all major conferences of the EDC/HRE activity since then, a *Round Table for International Organisations* has been organised. From 2004 to 2011, the CoE hosted and organised *Inter-institutional Meetings on EDC/HRE* at which 20 major international organisations, NGOs and foundations met. The last meeting was organised in November 2011 on 'Strategies for the Implementation of Regional and International Texts on Citizenship and Human Rights Education'. As a follow-up, a 'Letter of Cooperation in view of establishing the *International Contact Group on Citizenship and Human Rights'* was signed by the CoE, UNESCO, OHCHR, OSCE/ODIHR, the EU Fundamental Rights Agency, the Arab League Education, Cultural and Science Organisation (ALESCO), and later on also the OAS (Organisation of American States). The first meeting of the International Contact Group was held in Strasbourg, March 2012, and the second in April 2013. The mission of the Contact Group is to ensure close cooperation among regional and international institutions in the field of citizenship and human rights education in order to avoid overlap and create synergies (Council of Europe 2011).

Close links between the CoE and in particular with UN bodies have also been developed. In 2005–9, the CoE contributed to the *1st Phase of the World Programme for Human Rights Education*, which focused on primary and secondary school systems and consequently took part as the only non-UN organisation – as an observer – in the meetings of the UN Inter-Agency Coordination Committee 'Human Rights

Education in the School System'. In 2007, a *Regional Meeting on the World Programme* was jointly organised in Strasbourg by the CoE, UNESCO, OHCHR and OSCE/ODIHR. At present, the CoE is contributing to the *2nd Phase of the World Programme* (2010–14) through the CoE Programme on 'Learning and Living Democracy for All (2010–14)' (Council of Europe 2008).

Another important international partner is the *Office for Democratic Institutions and Human Rights of the Organisation for Security and Cooperation in Europe (OSCE/ODIHR)* which the CoE works closely together with in the International Contact Group, the organising of conferences and the development of publications (see 'Compendium of Good Practice' and 'Guidelines for Educators and Policy Makers: Combating Intolerance against Muslims through Education').

In addition to the above, contacts have been created with many other international governmental and non-governmental organisations, institutions and foundations, including the Community of Democracies (CoD), the OECD, the International Committee of the Red Cross (ICRC) and HREA (Human Rights Education Associates).

Other important developments

As regards other interesting recent developments there is insufficient space here to provide full detail and names of all of these, but they have included:

- In the field of human rights education, the activity *Learning the key principles and the functioning of the Human Rights Protection System: Explore and Act for Human Rights* which is part of the CoE's Education Programme 2010–14 'Education for Intercultural Understanding, Human Rights and Democratic Culture'.
- The inauguration of the *European Wergeland Centre on Education for Intercultural Understanding, Human Rights and Democratic Citizenship (EWC)* in Oslo in 2009, an independent legal entity according to Norwegian law and financed by the Norwegian government which has been set up in cooperation with the Council of Europe.
- The *Pestalozzi Programme*, which is a transversal project in the CoE's education programme for the training of education professionals.

Links between the Council of Europe's work on EDC/HRE and the PIDOP project

This section will try to identify some links between the PIDOP project and the Council of Europe's work in Education for Democratic Citizenship and Human Rights. The method chosen for this exercise is to mirror the main features of the PIDOP project (for broad overviews of the PIDOP project see Barrett 2012, and Chapter 1 and Appendix D in the present book) in the CoE's EDC/HRE activity to find out differences, similarities and interconnections. In order to get a clear picture about these contacts of PIDOP and EDC/HRE, it seems to be necessary to start by having a look at some key features such as the scope and definition, goals and objectives, origin, background, framework and working methods, structure, target groups, focus and outcomes of both activities.

Scope, definition and goal

Considering the scope, definition and goal, it can be said that PIDOP is a multinational research project funded by the European Commission under the Seventh Framework Programme. Its overall objective is to examine processes which influence political and civic engagement and participation in nine European countries (Belgium, Czech Republic, England, Germany, Italy, Northern Ireland, Portugal, Sweden and Turkey). The project is multidisciplinary, drawing on the disciplines of psychology, politics, sociology, social policy and education.

In contrast to this, EDC/HRE is an intergovernmental cooperation programme of the Council of Europe which aims to promote the CoE core values of pluralist democracy, human rights and the rule of law – through education. The EDC/HRE activity is carried out, supported and implemented in cooperation with all 47 member states of the Council of Europe.

Origin, background and framework

The starting point for the PIDOP project was a decision of the European Commission Seventh Framework Programme, Socioeconomic Sciences and Humanities, after the normal procedures of call for proposals, application, eligibility check, external evaluation and negotiation in Brussels in 2009, to award a grant to 'PIDOP – Processes Influencing Democratic Ownership and Participation' and a grant agreement with the Consortium of nine European universities.

In contrast to this, the official start of the EDC/HRE project was a political decision, namely a request of the Second Summit of Heads of State and Government of the Council of Europe in 1997 for 'the launch of an initiative on education for democratic citizenship with a view to promoting citizens' awareness of their rights and responsibilities in a democratic society' (Council of Europe 1997).

The PIDOP project lifetime was precisely fixed for three years, running from May 2009 to April 2012. Also the EDC/HRE project started as a 'normal' three-year exploratory project (1997–2000). But because of the constant strong political support by Recommendations, Declarations, etc., from the Committee of Ministers and the Parliamentary Assembly of the CoE, Ministerial Conferences and Summits, it developed into a second phase, a 'European Year of Citizenship through Education' in 2005, and then through a third and fourth phase to an enduring theme of the Council of Europe's work which is no longer questioned. In its Steering Committee in 1996, there had already been the far-sighted vision: 'The EDC/HRE project will come to an end in the last year of the 2nd millenium. But in this "fin de siècle" atmosphere it is possible that democratic citizenship will increasingly be a subject of public debate.'

Structure and working methods

As regards structure and working methods, PIDOP has a Consortium of nine partner institutions which are universities in eight European countries, with the University of Surrey, UK, as the coordinating institution. An International Advisory Board of 14 experts concerned with civic and political participation put their expertise at the disposal of the PIDOP project.

The EDC/HRE activity has been carried out under the guidance of an Ad-Hoc Advisory Group on Education for Democratic Citizenship and Human Rights (ED-EDCHR), with the assistance of the network of the EDC/HRE-Coordinators from all 47 member states and in close cooperation with the Directorate for Democratic Citizenship and Participation of the Council of Europe. The responsibility for EDC/HRE as part of the whole education programme lies with the Steering Committee for Education, which has been, since 2011, together with the Steering Committee for Higher Education and Research, replaced by the Steering Committee for Education Policies and Practice, which also oversees the EDC/HRE activity.

Focus, target groups and outcomes

With regard to focus, target groups and outcomes, it can be said that the PIDOP project's focus is on academic research in a specific field, namely processes which influence political and civic participation and engagement. The PIDOP project analysed data from existing surveys and collected new data on political and civic participation among young men and women.

In EDC/HRE, the focus is not on academic research (although there have also been scientific studies conducted), but on intergovernmental cooperation, agreed upon by governments of member states in a very broad field and with a holistic approach, namely to learn to live as responsible citizens in a democratic society. This is much more than a matter of legal and formal rights and responsibilities. It covers also the wide range of possible relations between individuals, groups, associations and communities. EDC/HRE is many sided in its concepts and activities which touch upon the political, legal, social and cultural areas of democratic societies. EDC/HRE encompasses all formal, non-formal and informal learning and is based on an interdisciplinary approach in a life-long learning perspective. It includes the development of legal instruments for the standard setting of EDC/HRE as well as the production of publications targeted at specific audiences (high-level policy-makers, school leaders, teachers, teacher trainers, communities, all levels of schools, universities, etc.). These outcomes, which are developed by specialists on EDC/HRE coming from different countries in Europe and beyond, are based on a regular exchange of information and best practice among the member states and are tested, piloted and evaluated in many countries.

Finally, it should be noted here that, from the beginning of the PIDOP project, one of its main goals was the formulation of policy recommendations which can be used to enhance levels of participation. Similarly, in the EDC/HRE activity, for many years there had been some calls for a framework policy document in this field which finally led to the preparation of a Recommendation of a Council of Europe Charter on EDC/HRE (Council of Europe 2010), which has become one of its most important outcomes. But although the policy recommendations of PIDOP and the Recommendation of a CoE Charter on EDC/HRE are important elements in both activities, they differ considerably as regards origin and development process, form, content and scope, deciding bodies and addressees. Without going into too many details only some examples can be mentioned here.

The PIDOP policy recommendations (see Appendix D to the present book) were

> based in particular on the new findings which emerged from the modelling of existing survey data ... and from the analysis of the new data collected from 16- to 26-year-olds drawn from 27 national and ethnic groups ... The focus groups revealed that these young people often did not participate because they felt they had no voice, were ignored by politicians, and believed they did not have the resources, the competencies or the experience needed to participate ... The recommendations for policy, practice and interventions can be used to enhance levels of participation among youth, women, minorities and migrants ... and are aimed at a wide range of social and institutional actors ...
> (Barrett 2012: passim)

By contrast, in Recommendation CM/Rec(2010)7 of a Council of Europe Charter on Education for Democratic Citizenship and Human Rights Education, the Committee of Ministers of the CoE recommends that the governments of member states implement measures based on the provisions of the CoE Charter on EDEC/HRE as set out in the appendix of this recommendation.

A comparison of the content of the policy recommendations of PIDOP and the provisions of the EDC/HRE Charter reveals that many of the recommendations of PIDOP are already included in the CoE Charter, especially those dealing with educational structures, democratic governance, role of non-governmental organisations, youth organisations, multicultural societies, ethnic groups, diversity, equality, etc. The important difference is that the provisions of the Charter have already been accepted by all 47 governments of the CoE's member states which have committed themselves to take measures for implementation.

Since then, implementation has taken place in member states and there has been an initial evaluation after two years to take stock of the developments and achievements.

After having examined some features which all reveal somehow similarity but at the same time also difference between PIDOP and EDC/HRE, finally a look should be taken at those elements which the two activities indeed have in common and the convictions and reflections that are shared.

The first element – which is perhaps also the most important – is that both activities have been conceived in relationship to *democratic societies* rather than in any other type of state or government. It is not by chance that both activities have the word 'democratic' in their title. This seems so obvious that it might be thought that there is no need to mention it explicitly. However, the contrary is the case. Most of the elements explored in both activities (e.g. citizenship, participation, engagement, empowerment, motivation of youth, education) have been either used or misused in the past and in the present in different parts of the world not only in democratic societies but also in non-democratic totalitarian states. One should not take democracy for granted. It needs to be constantly evaluated, protected and promoted. A democratic culture is not inborn, it needs to be taught and transmitted from one person to another in the family, in the school and in the community and from one generation to the next. Or, as the Deputy Secretary General of the Council of Europe Maud de Boer-Buquicchio (2004) reminded us in her opening speech of the European Year of Citizenship through Education: 'Democracy is precious, and like every precious gift it must be handled and passed on with care to the generations which come after us.' Thus it should not only to be mentioned but highlighted that PIDOP as well as EDC/HRE are devoted to the promotion and advancement of life specifically within democratic societies.

A second key feature that both programmes share is an emphasis on *participation*. In PIDOP, understanding the nature of participation was its key objective. Indeed, by studying not only conventional participation (such as voting and electoral campaigning) but also non-conventional participation (such as protests and demonstrations) and civic participation (such as volunteering and consumer activism), PIDOP construes participation within democratic societies in the broadest sense of the term. Furthermore, PIDOP studied participation not only by those who hold formal legal citizenship of the state but also by migrants who do not hold such formal citizenship. And indeed, the concept of 'good citizenship' concerns the behaviours and attitudes which any member of a democratic society should display towards other members of society, irrespective of their own status within this society.

Perhaps not so obvious at first glance, participation is also a key element in all the endeavours of the EDC/HRE activity which has as its overall objective the empowerment of all people to actively participate in life in democratic societies in a very broad sense as fleshed out in detail in the first part of this chapter. The important role of participation in the CoE's activities may also be seen in the fact that the Directorate of the CoE where the responsibility for EDC/HRE lies is named 'Directorate for Democratic Citizenship and Participation'.

In both projects participation is seen as a crucial element which is restricted neither to the formal, legal sense of electoral processes nor just to citizens of the state. But while in PIDOP the focus is more on the factors that influence participation, the main attention of EDC/HRE is put on how active participation can be fostered by education: how to give people the skills and attitudes that are needed to have an influence and make a difference. Furthermore, both activities have in mind – sometimes perhaps expressed between the lines – how to counteract increasing alienation from politicians and political institutions, to combat xenophobia, racism, social exclusion, violence and the denial of equality and human rights.

A further aspect where there is a close relationship between PIDOP and EDC/HRE is the *audience* at which the messages, findings, outcomes and recommendations are aimed and which actors they involve. In both activities there is a wide range of partners, institutions and other stakeholders, among them politicians and other decision-makers, educational professionals, media, youth leaders, parents, and non-governmental and youth organisations.

In EDC/HRE, many of these stakeholders and actors are mentioned and enumerated in the provisions of the sections 'Objectives and Principles' and 'Policies' of the CoE Charter as well as in the materials targeted at different audiences. PIDOP also explicitly addresses these various stakeholders and user groups in its policy recommendations (see Appendix D to the current book).

Specific attention is also paid in both activities to *youth*. In PIDOP, young people and their needs and wishes regarding participation and engagement are specifically investigated and are emphasised in the policy recommendations. In EDC/HRE, specific reference to young people and youth organisations as important partners is made in several provisions of the Charter, and examples of different faith and ethnic groups in particular are given there in the context of the provisions for 'respect for diversity'. As regards the role of youth in general, in the CoE's activities the youth sector was strongly involved from the very beginning of the EDC/HRE initiative, including the two Council of Europe Youth Centres in Strasbourg and Budapest with their 'educational activities for young people the aim of which is to encourage intercultural dialogue, awareness for human rights and participation in public life among Europe's young citizens' (Council of Europe 2009c).

Conclusion

The various aspects of the Council of Europe's EDC/HRE initiative and the PIDOP project that have been reviewed in this chapter have identified differences but also similarities between the two activities. Many of the findings of PIDOP are well known and already practised in EDC/HRE. But a new aspect in PIDOP is that for some of these findings and recommendations there is an empirical evidence base now for what had been laid down already in EDC/HRE. Thus there is no contradiction between the two activities and, in spite of the different approaches and what may be different perspectives, they are mutually supportive. And – what is more important – they share a common goal, namely to help young people and adults to play an active role in a society based on the values of democracy, human rights and the rule of law.

Acknowledgments

I would like to express my deep gratitude for her ongoing support to Ólöf Ólafsdóttir, Director for Democratic Citizenship and Participation of the Council of Europe, who for many years until her recent retirement was the life and soul of the EDC/HRE initiative. I would also like to thank my colleagues from the

Secretariat of the Council of Europe, in particular Yulia Pererva, Sarah Keating and Villano Qiriazi, and from the Ad Hoc Advisory Group on EDC/HRE for their valuable support and advice throughout many years. My thanks also go to Professor Martyn Barrett, PIDOP Consortium Coordinator, for his understanding, helpful input and manifold support.

References

Barrett, M. (2012) *The PIDOP Project: An Overview*. Guildford: School of Psychology, University of Surrey. Available from: http://epubs.surrey.ac.uk/775796/1/Barrett%20(2012).pdf (date accessed 28 November 2013).

Birzea, C. (ed.) (2004) *All-European Study on Education for Democratic Citizenship Policies*. Strasbourg: Council of Europe Publishing.

Council of Europe (1985) Recommendation No. R(85)7 of the Committee of Ministers to member states on teaching and learning about human rights in schools.

Council of Europe (1993) Declaration of the First Summit of Heads of State and Government of the Council of Europe, Vienna.

Council of Europe (1994) 18th Session of the Council of Europe's Standing Conference of Ministers of Education, Madrid.

Council of Europe (1997) Final Declaration and Action Plan of the Second Summit of Heads of State and Government of the Council of Europe, Strasbourg.

Council of Europe (1999) Declaration and programme on education for democratic citizenship, based on the rights and responsibilities of citizens (adopted by the Committee of Ministers on 7 May 1999).

Council of Europe (2002) Recommendation (2002) 12 of the Committee of Ministers to Member States on education for democratic citizenship.

Council of Europe (2005) *Citizenship through Education – Questions and Answers*. Leaflet produced for the 'European Year of Citizenship through Education'. Strasbourg: Council of Europe Publishing.

Council of Europe (2008) *Education Newsletter*, Special issue on 'World Programme for Human Rights Education', February 2008.

Council of Europe (2009a) *The Council of Europe – 800 million Europeans*. Strasbourg: Council of Europe Directorate of Communication – Public Information Division.

Council of Europe (2009b) *Education Newsletter*, No. 27, Spring–Summer 2009.

Council of Europe (2009c) *Human Rights, Democracy, Rule of Law*. Strasbourg: Council of Europe, Directorate of Communication.

Council of Europe (2010) *Council of Europe Charter on Education for Democratic Citizenship and Human Rights Education*, Recommendation CM/Rec (2010)7. Strasbourg: Council of Europe Publishing.

Council of Europe (2011) *Education Newsletter*, No. 29, Spring 2011.

Council of Europe (2012) *The Council of Europe: An Overview*. Strasbourg: Council of Europe Directorate of Communication – Public Information Division.

Council of Europe, OSCE/ODIHR, UNESCO and OHCHR (2009) *Human Rights Education in the School Systems of Europe, Central Asia and North America: A Compendium of Good Practice*. Warsaw: OSCE.

de Boer-Buquicchio, M. (2004) Speech by Maud De Boer-Buquicchio, Deputy Secretary General of the Council of Europe, presented at the Launching Conference of the European Year of Citizenship through Education, Sofia, Bulgaria, 13–14 December.

Kerr, D. and Losito, B. (2010) *Strategic Support for Decision Makers: Policy Tool for Education for Democratic Citizenship and Human Rights – Drawing upon the Experiences of the Council of Europe's EDC/HRE project*. Strasbourg: Council of Europe Publishing.

Ólafsdóttir, Ó. (2011) *Understanding and Valuing Diversity: Council of Europe Activities in the Field of Intercultural Education*. Speech by Ólöf Thorhildur Ólafsdóttir, Director for Democratic Citizenship and Participation of the Council of Europe, presented at the International Symposium on Interculturalism, Montreal, Canada, 25–27 May. Available from: http://www.theewc.org/news/view/understanding.and.valuing.diversity/ (date accessed 17 January 2014).

Otte, R. (2013) 'The period of transition in Central, Eastern and South-Eastern Europe – the role of the Council of Europe in promoting Education for Democracy and Human Rights', in B. Szlachta, C. Mazur and P. Musiewicz (eds), *Promoting Changes in Time of Transition and Crisis*. Krakow: Jagiellonian University.

26
IN SEARCH OF POLITICAL PARTICIPATION

Giovanni Moro

The research and findings of the PIDOP project offer an important opportunity to reflect on the way participation takes place and can be studied today. The issue is of the utmost importance, because participation is at the centre of the deep and swift changes that the configuration of democracy is currently experiencing. The work of researchers reflects these changes, as well as having the difficult task of analysing them. Studying participation today, indeed, implies dealing with new and in part unexpected social, cultural and political phenomena that call for a general rearrangement of the way in which we think about the relationship between citizens and politics.

My contribution will consist of some reflections inspired by the PIDOP work on two topics. The first concerns the context in which the participation phenomenon takes place today, with reference to changes in the citizenship paradigm and in democratic regimes. The second topic concerns the need for a critical assessment of the research toolbox we use when dealing with participation in this new context.

Participation in turmoil

The citizenship paradigm in question

Usually in political studies, citizens' participation in public life is dealt with as an isolated phenomenon, at best linked to the functioning and accountability of the formal political system, but detached from other social and political phenomena that are, however, of the utmost importance for the study of participation.

This point is of special relevance when participation is considered in relationship to the citizenship-building process. The findings of the PIDOP research show a strong though mostly implicit relationship of participation to citizenship, with two meanings.

First of all, participation is one of the main ways in which citizenship is built, increased and enlarged. It is therefore a process and not only a legal or political status. As a process, citizenship is continuously modified both in its content and scope. And this is due not only to political, institutional or legal decisions, but also to 'citizenship practices', that is the multiplicity of dynamic relations between citizens and the political regime (Wiener 1998). Citizens, therefore, are not only the recipients or targets of changes in citizenship prerogatives, but also actors in these changes. From this perspective, we can consider participation to be one of the citizenship practices, in a sense the most important practice. Participation, thus, is at the same time a fundamental component of citizenship and the factor that makes citizenship an incremental phenomenon. In other words, thanks to participation, the practice of citizenship enriches and enlarges the content and scope of citizenship itself (Bellamy et al. 2006).

Another element that emerges from the PIDOP project is the connection of participation to the other fundamental dimensions of citizenship. The 'return of citizenship' that has taken place after the fall of Berlin Wall in both scientific and political debate has resulted in different approaches, namely the liberal (citizenship as a set of rights), the communitarian (citizenship as belonging to a community) and the neo-republican (citizenship as support of the individual to the republic), that for a long time were dealt with as rivals. In the last decade, however, several scholars have suggested that these approaches are not alternatives, but rather highlight different constituent components of citizenship as a concept and a phenomenon. These components are strictly interrelated: rights cannot be created without the participation of every member of the political community, on an equal basis, to define goals and standards of common life, and cannot be implemented without an engagement of the whole community in promoting and respecting them, this commitment being based on the sharing of strong commonalities (Bellamy 2008; Delanty 2000).

In a normative key, these components can be considered as elements that are necessary to identify citizenship. In a dynamic key, they are the places where changes in citizenship as a process take place and can be observed.

In this framework, the critical point is that in the last few decades the paradigm of democratic citizenship has been put under question with regard to some of the very pillars on which it is based, namely the state, the territory with its boundaries, national identity with its implicit anthropological model, the legal status, and representation (Turner 1994; Isin and Turner 2003; Shafir 1998).

Nation-states are weakened by global risks as well as by claims for recognition of autonomy or independence from regional and local entities, while supranational and international bodies exercise strong powers on matters that were part of the exclusive sphere of competence of nation states. Migrations make state borders more and more porous and vague so that it is much more difficult to define 'who is in' and 'who is out' from the realm of citizenship, this distinction being the very reason for the invention of citizenship itself.

The multicultural configuration of societies makes national identities questioned by a multiplicity of 'national' and group identities that ask to be recognised in terms of diversity and not sameness, putting under discussion the cultural and anthropological model which is the basis of membership. The pluralisation of individual identities and lifestyles – including religion, family, sexual orientation, work, leisure, etc. – play a similar challenging role.

In addition, looking at the legal side of citizenship – intended in this case as a status – several problems can be detected, for example the crisis of welfare systems and their promise of universal access to benefits, or the weakening of justice systems, in a sense the most important shield of citizens' rights, that are dealing with problems that put precisely this prominent role under question, or even the ability of public administrations to manage common problems in an effective (and not only efficient) way.

Many new rights ask to be recognised. They concern both individuals and groups. In the former case, they involve personal conditions, lifestyles, private matters such as family patterns up to the manner of dying. In the latter case, they are group rights, claimed by minorities based on ethnic, gender, sexual orientation, religious or linguistic commonalities. Claims for new rights also include those related to belonging to humanity, such as those concerning the environment or future generations. All of that is far from the classical three generations of rights formalised by Thomas Marshall (1950).

Finally, citizenship is challenged by the weakening of representative relations that had played the role of ensuring the inclusion of people in the political process, at the same time legitimising governments and subjecting them to accountability mechanisms. The decrease in voter turnout, the emergence of anti-politics and 'counter-democracy' and public distrust of politicians are well-known, daily-based, widespread phenomena.

What is the connection between these ongoing changes in the paradigm of democratic citizenship and participation? Various answers are possible, but two of them seem to me the most pertinent here.

The first answer is that participation should be studied taking into account the other two components of citizenship, namely membership and rights. Opportunities and limits of participation are also defined in relation to the basis upon which a political community is built and nurtured, and with the standards of life that individuals who are part of the community can claim for themselves and must assure to others. The PIDOP research findings clearly hint at this multidimensional feature of participation, which is changing together with the whole citizenship machinery. Thus researching participation also means observing citizenship in change.

The second answer is that, in relation to the emerging problems of the democratic citizenship paradigm, a number of evolutionary phenomena in citizenship configuration can be noticed (Moro 2013). They can be considered as anomalies of the paradigm, but at the same time they have an unquestionable relationship to it. Some of these phenomena ('citizenships') are related to places, in the sense that they no longer refer to the territory of the nation state. They are, for example, urban citizenship, based on residing in a city; European citizenship, taking place in a mobile territory not coincident with that of a nation state; and global or 'cosmopolitan' citizenship, claiming the recognition of the same status for all individuals belonging to humanity, independently of their membership of a national political community. Other 'citizenships' are focused on the issue of identity, in the sense that they make a claim for the recognition of diversity: I mean multicultural citizenship, with its 'group rights', but also gender-based citizenship, implying a radical redefinition of the boundary between public and private spheres. Other phenomena concern the economic dimension, often overlooked as a place where citizenship is built but of the utmost importance. Here we can find consumer-related citizenship, focused on the definition of what are luxury and what are essential goods, and corporate citizenship, related to operational responsibilities of private companies in the public sphere.

Last but not least, there are phenomena that concern the realm of participation. Here we can find electronic citizenship, which is linked to the definition of new rights and new forms of civic action through virtual communities, and what I call active citizenship, that is a citizenship practice consisting of the self-organisation and action of citizens in public policy-making for the protection of rights, the caring for common goods and the empowerment of weak people.

These evolutionary phenomena are not at all clear in their nature and development. Nevertheless, all of them, and not only those directly related to the participatory dimension, affect participation. On the other hand, research on participation can shed light on this general transformation process affecting the citizenship paradigm.

The sunset or transformation of democratic regimes

In the public debate ongoing in Europe and abroad, involving primarily but not exclusively the scientific community, the need for an assessment of the state of affairs of contemporary democracy has come to the fore. This assessment is mainly focused on the growing gap between the standards and requirements of democratic regimes and their actual reality. Some emerging issues are the same as those regarding the crisis of the democratic citizenship paradigm mentioned above, but in this case the standpoint is one of democratic regimes and political systems and their consistency with the distinguishing elements of democracy. From this perspective, a number of concerning issues have been noticed (see Mastropaolo 2011).

A first issue is representation. This legitimising mechanism that links a constituency (or a principal) to an agent who speaks and stands for it is questioned more and more. In one way or another, all the mechanisms that found representation – authorisation, protection of interests, accountability, descriptive and symbolic representation – seem to be either no longer pertinent or ineffective, or both.

Another issue is political parties. Their role in modern democracies has been to aggregate (and civilise) the interests of different constituencies and merge them in view of the general interest, as well as acting as mediating actors between society and institutions. This role, however, is less and less relevant, because of the lack of effective relations between parties and their constituencies as well as the weakening of accountability mechanisms. Citizens tend to have direct access to the public arena, so that the shift from a 'democracy of parties' to a 'democracy of the public' has been thematised (Manin 1996).

Related to the weakening of political parties, the dominance of market-oriented forms of both political action and public management has emerged. This can be detected in the conceptualisation of the political arena as a market governed by a logic of supply and demand, where communication is more important than implementation, but also in the priority given to efficiency, productivity and standards that are used to drive public management, increasingly detached from political directions. The growing gap between politics and policies is part of this phenomenon as well.

The shift from government to governance is another issue that is widely discussed, especially with regard to the European Union. It consists of the transfer of governing functions from an institution – the government – to a process, the governance. In this framework, actors not democratically legitimised exercise strong political powers, often without any representative relation, with the risk that vested interests prevail over the needs and concerns of the general public.

The globalisation of politics and the economy means that crucial decisions are taken further and further from citizens and makes democratic life ineffective. What has been happening in Europe since the beginning of the financial crisis is a clear indicator of that. In this case, the role of the ratings agencies (not to mention the 'Eurobureaucrats') in determining the lives of millions of people without any opportunity for them to have a voice is evident.

The weakening or even the disappearance of traditional constituencies is another issue that can be noticed. It concerns especially the working class that shaped the history of democracy in the twentieth century but now seems to have disappeared both as a sociological reality and a political subjectivity, leaving the way clear for neo-liberalism, with the consequence of the weakening of social rights and welfare systems.

Citizens, on their part, distrust politics, political leaderships and public institutions, withdraw from political engagement, and tend to follow populism, antipolitics and counter-democracy. They seem to feel that politics is pointless, and when they engage, they do it in ways that are alternative to traditional politics.

How to assess this situation? According to some points of view, we are witnessing a sunset of democracy (or 'post-democracy': Crouch 2004), since democracy's most important requirements are vanishing. Other interpretations, however, can be plausibly advanced. Let me mention two of them, widely known and recognised in the scientific community and beyond.

One comes from the work of Robert Dahl (1989), who notices an ongoing transformation of democratic regimes, comparable to those that led to city-states in ancient times and to modern national states some centuries ago. The invention of representative democracy did work in the territories of nation-states, but is questioned by the movement of the places where power is exercised far from the *demos*. One of the consequences of this new, ongoing and uncertain situation is that a growing divide and conflict between specialised political elites and common citizens is emerging. How this conflict will end will determine whether polyarchy or a new form of 'government of custodians' will prevail.

Another way to detect the situation is from a position of reflexive modernity, advanced by Ulrich Beck (1992; see also Beck and Grande 2007) and other scholars. What is happening, in this view, is a general reconfiguration of states and societies. Among the features of this new context there is the movement of politics outside the formal political system and the fact that other actors exercise political roles in an autonomous but powerful manner. Beck calls it 'subpolitics' and, with regard to citizens' initiatives, mentions as examples social movements and environmental initiatives. In the reflexive modernisation time, in other words, citizens politically act in an autonomous way, outside the political system.

To sum up the relevant points coming from this consideration of the ongoing changes in participation phenomena in terms of the transformation but not the sunset of democracy, it can be pointed out that the crucial elements of this transformation are: that there has been a redefinition of the relationship between the citizenry and political elites, in which the scope and knowledge resources of the exercise of political power are at stake; that, in relation to the development of democracy, the political sphere has been enlarged and decentralised, so that places and actors that are outside the formal political system acquire a political meaning and role; that among these actors there are citizens who self-organise to advance their values, rights and interests in an autonomous way; and that these ways of participating do not necessarily connect to traditional forms, mechanisms and opportunities of participation, nor do they flow into the representative system.

As a consequence of the 'transformation approach' (defined against the sunset approach), some taken-for-granted elements of the standard view need to be reconsidered, both with regard to the working of the political system and the way that participation is conceived.

In general, I would like to mention three points. The first concerns the definition of politics in terms of taking decisions, something that overlooks the dynamic side of the political process which takes place also before, after, beyond and in spite of the instant cognitive act of deciding. The second point is the demand-answer scheme that overestimates the ability of the political system to answer to societal demands and underestimates the ability of citizens to provide answers by themselves or to cooperate with public institutions to this end. The third point is about the relationship between power and influence, the former usually being recognised in the actors of the formal political system and the latter in those outside; on the contrary, external actors exercise more and more direct political power (for good or ill).

As for participation, political science used to divide it into 'conventional' and 'non-conventional', ascribing a systemic value only to the former. But the transformation of democracy makes visible the political meaning of citizens participating in public policy-making on a daily basis, in the sense that public policies tend to become an autonomous political arena (Fung 2006). What is 'political' and what is not is therefore an open question.

Moreover, when using the 'non-conventional' label, the standard view on democracy does not consider how wide and complex the emerging forms of participation are. The PIDOP research reflects to some extent this new situation, both in the difficulty of using standard definitions and thematisations, and in some of its findings, for example in showing the relevance of 'non-conventional' acts of participation for the studied samples, or in making evident how much distrust towards political elites alters the motivations and purposes of participation, or shedding light on the growing individualised approach to engagement, or in detecting access to the Internet as a factor altering the whole picture, or even in showing the multiple and differentiated relations between participation and belonging to specific target groups, such as youth, women and migrants.

All of that makes research into new forms of participation at the same time more relevant for democracy and citizenship, and more complex and challenging.

Assessing the toolbox of research on participation

The PIDOP research findings, however, shed light not only on the relevance and complexity of the issue of participation in the context of changes in citizenship and democracy, but also on the emerging limits and problems of the research toolbox, so that a rethinking of the way that participation is studied is a necessary step. This further topic is, of course, strictly related to the first one, since it is precisely because of the ongoing changes in reality that the research toolbox shows problems that have to be addressed. Identifying these limits is, in any case, of crucial importance, and PIDOP research development makes it possible to try to do it.

What are the problems of the research apparatus that come from the new context in which participation takes place and that require a close consideration? I will focus on questions related to normative assumptions, conceptualisations, taken-for-granted correlations, the use of variables and the sources of data and information.

Normative assumptions

Research on politics is always based on normative assumptions. Sometimes, however, these assumptions can be misleading if reality does not conform to them and divergences are so wide that they cannot be labelled as pathologies. Research on participation is based on normative assumptions that should be reconsidered. Let me make some cases that can be found in the chapters of this book. Though they are often critically discussed, they nevertheless remain as background to the research.

The first case is the assumption of a continuum, and a necessary relationship, between the various forms of participation, however defined (political, civic, social, community-based, etc.). What is presumed is that all forms of participation go together and reinforce each other, so that taking part in community life will lead to voting, being active in political parties will make one more sensitive to helping neighbours in need, and so on. On the contrary, what is happening tells us that the various forms of participation are increasingly autonomous and independent, if not alternative, in the sense that, for example, taking part in social movements can be practised instead of voting or being active in political parties.

The second case I want to mention is the assumption that a good citizen is an active citizen, and that being active means participating in all forms of common life, that is to say from bowling to voting. According to this assumption, 'standby' or 'monitorial' citizens would not reflect the standard of citizenship. Nor could there be 'good' citizens that support, say, environmental causes but do not vote. Reality, however, is very different.

A last case is the assumption that all people should be engaged in public life, or, put in other terms, that the quantitative benchmark of public participation is the whole electorate. But participation in the protection of consumers' rights does not require the involvement of the whole citizenry. On the contrary, in such a case, a very complicated situation for the everyday life of societies would take place. On the other hand, benchmarking all the forms of participation against voting means overlooking them, since they do not – and could not in absolute terms – accomplish this requirement. Still, they do exist as a growing phenomenon.

A reconsideration of normative assumptions that give shape to research tools and strategies should therefore be taken as a necessary exercise.

Conceptualisations

It was said that participation has become almost 'a theory of everything'. The definitions used in this book confirm this statement, making visible uncertainty, confusion and lack of clarity and consistency of several conceptualisations linked to participation.

The first point, already mentioned but so important that it deserves further attention concerns the distinction between 'conventional' and 'non-conventional' participation, a pillar of political science. As is well known, 'conventional' participation consists of voting and being active in political parties while 'non-conventional' participation means all the rest, especially participating in social movements and, in some cases, contributing to community organising. But this is clearly a residual definition: it is never correct to define something as 'non-something'. And this is more and more relevant in a world in which 'non-conventional' participation grows, while 'conventional' participation decreases (though, as I just stressed, a comparison based on absolute data in this case is not pertinent). The realm of 'non-conventional' participation is a huge world, with a multiplicity of organisational forms, collective identities and operational patterns. It is definitely wider than the world of 'conventional' participation, at least in terms of activism in political parties.

Political science identifies what is 'non-conventional' in terms either of protest, involving social movements, or of interest groups, in this case defined as 'general interest' or 'value-based' or 'for a cause' groups. Again, reality is definitely richer: a lot of citizens' organisations and collective action experiences are not protest-oriented, nor are they aimed at occupying public spaces in order to advance a right or an interest or to make their voices heard; rather, they are often invisible, though not in 'standby' condition. On the other hand, it is very difficult – in my opinion almost impossible – to reconnect citizens' activism in the public arena to traditional corporatist model organisations, such as trade unions: in this case, in fact, neither the constituencies nor the interests that are advanced can be clearly identified. In both cases, participation is conceived as having an exclusive point of reference in the political system, intended as the place where things happen and where 'real' political power is exercised. Political power in this way is reduced to the instantaneous cognitive act of taking decisions, not considering the material side of making things happen. In any case, non-conventional participation remains ancillary to the formal political system.

A second point concerns the distinction between political and civic participation. It is uncertain what precisely these two concepts actually mean. On the one hand, in the realm of political participation there can be found activities, such as protesting in movements, that can also be found in the definitions of the civic component of participation. On the other hand, in the realm of civic participation, a number of activities simply devoted to increasing relations inside communities are included. But these activities do not seem to have a specific political meaning, instead being intended to increase the social capital of communities. The social capital argument is, in my opinion, one of the most confusing factors in discourse on participation. As has been noticed in some of the authors' contributions to the present book, in the social capital approach what is really important is the fact that people get together and build links of trust and reciprocity. For what purpose, in which ways and with what strategies and operational patterns is definitely less important in this approach. On the contrary, these are precisely the factors that make the difference between participation in the public arena and any other form of gathering people together. The social capital approach, therefore, seems to erase the political meaning from the concept of participation.

The various forms of 'civic' participation are often interpreted in terms of 'democracy gymnasiums', that is as activities that are ancillary to 'true' participation which involves taking part in political parties and voting. People's participation in citizens' associations, in other words, would only be a training experience to become good citizens which consists of something else. However, if this can be consistent with non-political activities such as those related to leisure, sport and art clubs, or, in another sense, to religious experiences, it is difficult to say this of initiatives that are aimed at protecting rights, or taking care of common goods, or even empowering citizens and communities, whether in the form of advocacy or service. In these cases, the political meaning of these experiences is intrinsic to them. They are indeed devoted to changing reality and not only to helping other people. And, in a context in which political power is increasingly exercised outside the formal political system, it is difficult to label these experiences as 'pre-politics'.

The main problem, however, in my opinion, is the difficulty of identifying citizens' organisations operating in public policy-making (from the definition to the implementation and evaluation of public policies) as political actors, different both from those of the representative system and the associational forms that nurture social capital but not with public interest purposes. These organisations, characterised by a multiplicity of forms, scope and fields of action, motivations, memberships, strategies and operational patterns, are one of the most relevant phenomena related to political participation of the previous decades, though they are hardly identified in the standard view.

Predictors, variables and correlations

The PIDOP research is based on the identification of factors and their use as variables to explain and predict political participation, either in general or with reference to specific target groups. Several variables are taken into consideration in the research: macro, meso and micro; political, economic, social, cultural, demographic; linked to cognitive and material aspects; related to individuals and to families, communities and other groups; concerning different kinds of associations and organisations; regarding the influence of institutions such as schools or churches or ethnic communities; referring to individual resources such as culture, education, information and wealth; focusing on the opportunities and constraints of institutional, political and electoral systems, and so on.

All these variables are used as explanators or predictors of participation with reference to conceptualisations and theories, such as rational choice, structure of participation opportunities, social capital, modernisation, resource mobilisation, etc., and give place to the definition of explanatory models (the dual path model of protest, the socio-economic status model, the social identity model of collective action, the volunteer process model, the role identity model, the integrative model of the macro and social factors driving political and civic participation and engagement, etc.).

No doubt this methodology is compliant with relevant and diffused requirements. However, when taken and used as variables to predict or explain participation, these factors often produce unclear or contradictory results. Let me give some examples of these results:

- Modernisation can increase participation because it links people to values regarding the quality of life. But it can also decrease participation since people do not feel that it is necessary to act for needs that are already satisfied.
- Economic conditions, whether good or bad, can either favour or hinder participation. If good, they can favour participation because people do not have to attend to their basic needs, or they can hinder it because people do not have a real stake over which to engage. If bad, they can favour participation because they offer motivations that are linked to basic needs, or they can hinder it because poor economic conditions deprive people of the time and resources that are needed to participate.
- Participation in non-political or civic and community initiatives favours the increase of 'conventional' political participation. But these forms of participation are also an alternative to participation in political parties and/or voting because of distrust towards official politics.
- Social capital is a strong predictor of participation because a rich network of links of trust and reciprocity push people to act together for the community.

But it also does not have any detectable effect on participation because engaging in private interest activities with other people does not imply any commitment for the common good.
- Young people are detached from political engagement and participation, being apathetic and focused on individual interests. But they are also engaged in non-conventional forms of participation.
- The Internet favours the engagement of people and is an arena where participation can more easily take place. But it also operates as a disincentive to participate because it favours the detachment of people from reality and limits engagement to 'click-activism'.
- More specifically, the use of the Internet favours offline participation because it multiplies channels of information, contacts and causes to support. But it also hinders participation in the material world, because it brings people into a virtual environment that can be practised in private space.

In all of this, there is no matter of mistakes or the misuse of methodological tools. Nevertheless, a consideration of the productivity of variable-centred research to study a phenomenon so dynamic and multifaceted should be reconsidered.

Moreover, from analysing factors that act as variables operating in samples, several correlations emerge. However, some of them, though not contradictory, sound like truisms. Various examples can be mentioned here: a high sense of community leads to participation in community life or to belonging to community organisations; minority individuals have more positive attitudes towards minority rights and are more active inside their ethnic groups while they are less engaged in general rights and mainstream organisations; the longer democratic traditions have existed in a country, the more public trust there is among youth; engagement in political activities (e.g. in political parties) is less common than voting; young people and minorities are less engaged in voting and more in associational life than the citizenry in general; engagement early in life is a precursor of later participation; electoral rules such as automatic registration, voting by mail or voting at the weekends favour the exercise of voting.

There is no problem with correlations such as those mentioned. But the question is whether they actually contribute to the growth of knowledge about the phenomenon of participation or whether, on the contrary, the information they produce is of low utility.

Sources of information

The final element that should be considered concerns the kind of data collected and the way they are gathered. It is common wisdom in political studies that attitudes are related to behaviours – this is, for example, one of the methodological bases of the analysis of the legitimacy of democratic systems. Moreover, in the case of PIDOP research the analysis is centred precisely on psychological elements related to participation. Nevertheless, one should avoid considering attitudes as a proxy for behaviours, and observing material phenomena related to participation is a very important complement to the analysis of attitudes.

In particular, the study of the organisational forms through which individuals participate in public life is worthwhile, as noted in some of the authors' contributions to this book. The internal deliberative processes, the selection of causes and objectives, the resources mobilised, the strategies and tools adopted, the conflicts raised, the successes and failures, are elements that also provide information about the individual side of participation. Gathering this kind of information can in a sense be more complicated than interviewing individuals, but the lack of it could be misleading.

Moreover, scant attention to participation in and through organisations or collective entities leads to a risk of overestimating purely individual acts, such as signing a petition. This is, of course, easier to detect by simply asking individuals if they did it in the previous year, but this is definitely less relevant for individuals than, say, being engaged in monitoring the accessibility and quality of public services, giving advice to migrants or arranging shelters for victimised women. In sum, the organisational and collective side of participation cannot be ignored, even when studying individuals, and, by the same token, acts and practices cannot be ignored, even when studying feelings, attitudes and intentions.

While more feasible to conduct, interviews managed through quantitative methods, even using large samples, cannot provide data of crucial importance. The problem, here, is not in the way that data are collected, but in the kinds of data that are chosen and the heuristic value that is ascribed to them due to the way in which they are gathered and managed.

Also, generalisations based on global studies such as the World Values Survey should be handled with care, in order to avoid answers to questions being transformed in material reality depending on the way that questions are worded and on the underpinning normative assumptions, as happens with data on people's volunteering. From a Southern European standpoint, one cannot avoid noticing that, in the last few years (just to mention some cases among the most visible), the Spanish *Indignados* movement, the primary elections for the leader of the Italian Democratic Party, the Greek people's reaction against the *Troika* austerity measures and the Italian movement against the privatisation of water supply services took place, with, in addition, leading roles played by women in all of these initiatives. This suggests caution regarding the risk of accepting a knowledge base as taken for granted and simply assuming a 'WASP model' of active citizenship.

Conclusion

Especially nowadays, in the age of public distrust and democratic deficit, the concerns of policy-makers push the scientific community to provide prompt answers or easy formulas capable of reconnecting the citizenry to public institutions, so giving them a new and stronger 'social licence to operate'. In this way, there can be found programmes devoted to the strengthening of the sense of community, the creation of an active citizenship attitude, the inclusion of affected people in discussions (more than deliberations) on issues of common concern, encouragement of people to vote, and so on. It cannot be said that these efforts have produced particularly effective results, while the material reality appears to have moved elsewhere.

Participation both reflects and concurs in producing ongoing changes in the relationship between citizens and democratic regimes. To catch the features and possible outcomes of this change requires, in my opinion, an effort to observe and detect this change rather than trying to put it into a framework of given assumptions, conceptualisations and explanations. Identifying and describing new emerging phenomena is more important today than measuring their compliance with given standards, whether conforming or not to the given paradigms. The PIDOP research is a relevant contribution, since it shows both some emerging new trends and the limits of the existing toolbox. It is therefore a strong call to renovate our way of thinking and methods of observing the phenomenon of participation.

References

Beck, U. (1992) *Risk Society: Towards a New Modernity*. London: Sage.
Beck, U. and Grande, E. (2007) *Cosmopolitan Europe*. Cambridge: Polity.
Bellamy, R. (2008) *Citizenship. A Very Short Introduction* Oxford: Oxford University Press.
Bellamy, R., Castiglione, D. and Shaw, J. (2006) 'Introduction: from national to transnational citizenship', in idem (eds), *Making European Citizens. Civic Inclusion in a Transnational Context*. London: Palgrave Macmillan, pp. 1–28.
Crouch, C. (2004) *Post-Democracy*. Cambridge: Polity.
Dahl, R. (1989) *Democracy and Its Critics*. New Haven, CT: Yale University Press.
Delanty, G. (2000) *Citizenship in the Global Age: Culture, Society and Politics*. Buckingham: Open University Press.
Fung, A. (2006) 'Democratizing the policy process', in M. Moran, M. Rein and R. E. Goodin (eds), *The Oxford Handbook of Public Policy*. Oxford: Oxford University Press, pp. 669–85.
Isin, F. F. and Turner, B. S. (eds) (2003) *Handbook of Citizenship Studies*. London: Sage.
Manin, B. (1996) *The Principles of Representative Government*. Cambridge: Cambridge University Press.
Marshall, T. H. (1950) *Citizenship and Social Class and Other Essays*. Cambridge: Cambridge University Press.
Mastropaolo, A. (2011) *La democrazia è una causa persa? Paradossi di una invenzione imperfetta* [*Is Democracy a Lost Cause? Paradoxes of an Imperfect Invention*]. Turin: Bollati Boringhieri.
Moro, G. (2013) *Cittadinanza attiva e qualità della democrazia* [*Active Citizenship and the Quality of Democracy*]. Rome: Carocci.
Shafir, G. (ed.) (1998) *The Citizenship Debates*. Minneapolis, MN: University of Minnesota Press.
Turner, B. (1994) 'Contemporary problems in the theory of citizenship', in idem (ed.), *Citizenship and Social Theory*. London: Sage, pp. 1–18.
Wiener, A. (1998) *'European' Citizenship Practice. Building Institutions of a Non-State*. Boulder, CO: Westview Press.

Appendix A

THE FOCUS GROUP GUIDE USED IN THE PIDOP PROJECT

The focus group guide was initially drawn up in the English language. Key technical terms were translated into other languages using appropriate back-translation procedures to ensure the cross-linguistic equivalence of the meanings of these terms, but the entire guide was not translated using strict back-translation because the focus groups were only semi-structured and the wordings used in the group discussions needed to be those that were clearest and most conversationally appropriate in the local language. The guide consisted of six main sections, each of which addressed a particular set of issues. Each section contained primary and secondary questions to elicit the required information from the participants. Questions were omitted when the participants had already provided the required information, and moderators elicited additional information by asking appropriate follow-up questions according to the participants' responses.

Section 1: Introduction and ice-breaker

The focus group began with a welcome, an explanation of why the group had been assembled and an explanation of basic ground rules. Participants were then shown photographs depicting young people taking part in various forms of participation about a range of issues (e.g. voting, campaigning, anti-war protests, recycling, etc.) and index cards with an issue written on each of them (e.g. pollution, poverty/starvation, gender violence, immigration, racism, unemployment, etc.).

Primary question

1. What do you think about this photo/issue?

Secondary question

(a) We have shown you photos of issues that some people think are important. Can you think of any other public issues that are important to you?

Section 2: Personal and group experiences of participation
Primary question 1

1. Have you had any personal experiences in relation to those (and other) issues?

Secondary questions 1

(a) Why/why not?
(b) What happened?
(c) How do you characterise these experiences?
(d) Were they positive or negative?
(e) Were they effective or not?
(f) What did you learn from these experiences?

Primary questions 2

1. Are you currently doing anything to deal with these issues?
2. Are you part of a group or are you acting alone?
3. What kind of group (e.g., NGO, scouts, youth groups connected to a religious organisation, student union, voluntary group, etc.)?
4. Why did you join that particular group?

Secondary questions 2

(a) In the past, have you ever tried to deal with these issues as a member of a group/organisation?
(b) What kind of group/organisation was it?
(c) What motivated you to become a member?
(d) Do you think these groups/organisations can generate change?
(e) At what level (local, national or European)?
(f) What opportunities do you feel are open to you to influence the issues that we have been discussing here?
(g) Have you experienced any difficulties when trying to deal with these issues?
(h) Are there options to deal with these issues you have considered but haven't attempted for some reason?

Section 3: Sources of information about participation, and influences on attitudes to participation

Primary question

1. Who/what are your sources of information and influence when you deal with these issues (e.g. family, peer group, school, NGOs, media, Internet, etc.)?

Secondary questions

(a) Are there any people you talk to about environmental issues/human rights?
(b) Have these discussions affected your point of view?
(c) Have your parents/teachers/friends/co-workers talked to you about any of these issues?
(d) What is the importance of media (TV, press) and the Internet as sources of information and influence?
(e) Are your sources of information and influences mainly local, national or European?
(f) Of the people you talk to, whose opinion do you value most?
(g) What do you think these people/groups expect from you?
(h) Which of these sources has impacted on your viewpoints on a particular issue and persuaded you to change them? Can you give examples?
(i) Have you ever tried to persuade anyone else to change their opinion on a particular issue or on how to deal with a particular issue (e.g. through blogs, general discussions, petitions, etc.)?

Section 4: Relevance of participation for young people

Primary question 1

1. Are young people citizens with full rights in our society?

Secondary questions 1

(a) What do you think about young people's participation in public (social/civic/political) issues?
(b) Is it important? Why/why not?
(c) What are the forms of participation that young people usually have to express their views?
(d) Are these mainly at local, national or European level?
(e) What other things do you think could be done?
(f) Have you ever considered protesting through more unconventional ways? For example, in the past people have painted graffiti on government buildings to express a political message or tried to stop the building of roads by chaining themselves to trees, etc. Have you ever done anything like this? Would you consider doing it?

(g) Do you think that young people are properly informed about their rights as citizens?
(h) Are they informed about ways to take a stand?

Primary question 2

1. Do you think young people have opportunities/resources to participate (civic and politically) in our country?

Secondary questions 2

(a) Do you feel that young people are heard and taken seriously?
(b) Do all young people from different groups (e.g. gender, age or immigrant groups) have the same opportunities/resources to participate in our country?
(c) Do you believe that everyone's interests and rights are being properly represented?

Section 5: Perceptions of social exclusion

Primary questions

1. Is participation important for people to be considered members of a community (local, national, European)? Why/why not?
2. Are there any groups of people who are excluded from participation in our country?

Secondary questions

(a) What groups?
(b) Why?/Why not?
(c) What could be done to increase their participation and guarantee their inclusion?

Section 6: Proposals for inclusion

Primary question

1. If you were in charge, what would you do to increase young people's (civic and political) participation [including the participation of the groups that are at risk of exclusion]?

Appendix B

THE INTERVIEW SCHEDULE USED IN THE PIDOP PROJECT

The interview schedule was used to interview individuals who had been identified as influential others by the focus group participants. The schedule was initially drawn up in the English language. Key technical terms were translated into other languages using appropriate back-translation procedures to ensure the cross-linguistic equivalence of the meanings of these terms, but the entire schedule was not translated using strict back-translation because the interviews were only semi-structured and the wordings needed to be those that were clearest and most conversationally appropriate in the local language. The schedule consisted of five sections which targeted different aspects of the interviewees' views. Environmental and human rights issues were explicitly mentioned in some of the questions in order to provide a concrete focus for the interviewees' responses. Questions were omitted when the interviewee had already provided required information, and interviewers elicited additional information by asking appropriate follow-up questions according to the interviewees' responses.

Section 1: Perceptions of young people as citizens

- Do you think that young people in our country are full-rights citizens [or any other expression that might help the interviewee to discuss the issue of young people as citizens]?
- Do you think that young people are properly informed about their rights and responsibilities as citizens?
- Do you think young people have enough opportunities to participate at a social or political level?
- How do these opportunities compare to those enjoyed by other groups?
- Do you think young people are informed about the different ways in which they can participate?

- Do you think there are enough opportunities for them to participate?
- Do you think young people face particular obstacles in their efforts to participate?
- How important do you think it is that young people become involved in social and political issues? Why/why not?
- Do you think it has become easier for young people to participate in social and political issues? If yes, why do you think that is?

Section 2: Views of immigrant youth

- Do you think that what you have just said about young people applies to groups of young immigrants in our country such as [...] and [...], or do you think that they face particular challenges?

Section 3: Expectations of youth

- Do you have any particular expectations about the way and degree to which young people/your children/ pupils/students should participate in social and political issues?
- What are these expectations, especially in relation to environmental and human rights issues?
- What about your expectations of the extent to which immigrant youth should become involved?
- Are there any forms of participation that you explicitly try to dissuade young people/your children/ pupils/students from engaging in?
- Why these particular types of participation?
- In some countries, conscription into the army is compulsory. In a similar vein, do you think it should become mandatory that young people/your children/ pupils/students become involved in social and political issues, especially relating to human rights and environmental issues?

Section 4: Mobilisation efforts

- Is there anything you or your organisation (e.g. school, youth centre, etc.) are currently doing to promote the political participation and engagement of young people, especially in respect to environmental and human rights issues?
- Do you know if any other people in your organisation, or other departments in your organisation, deal with youth participation? If yes, could you tell us a bit more on their activities?
- What about the participation of minority youth?
- What else do you think could be done?
- What factors do you think influenced the level of success (or failure) of these particular ways of promoting participation?

Section 5: Support for youth mobilisation by other agencies

- Do you think that families, schools, media, public institutions, NGOs and political parties have been particularly supportive of young people's participation in social and political processes?
- What about young immigrants?
- In what ways do you think the support they give needs to be improved?

Appendix C

THE QUESTIONNAIRE USED IN THE PIDOP PROJECT

The PIDOP questionnaire was initially drawn up in the English language, and then translated into other languages using back-translation procedures to ensure the cross-linguistic equivalence of meanings. The questions in the core questionnaire were designed to measure the following variables (in the following order):

- Basic demographic information
- Political interest (3 items)
- Political attentiveness (3 items)
- Participation in past 12 months (15 items)
- Effectiveness of participation (15 items)
- Future intentions for participation (15 items)
- Participation and involvement in civic and political organisations (8 items)
- Quality of participation – action (4 items)
- Quality of participation – reflection (4 items)
- Private citizenship (4 items)
- Motivations for participation (6 items)
- Perception of barriers to participation (4 items)
- Internal efficacy (2 items)
- External efficacy (2 items)
- Collective efficacy of youth (2 items)
- Collective efficacy of ethnic group (2 items)
- Collective efficacy of gender group (2 items)
- Political knowledge (3 items)
- Social norms for participation (8 items)
- Trust in institutions (14 items)
- Trust in government and forms of government (6 items)
- Interpersonal trust (1 item)
- Emotions in response to concrete issues (5 items × 2)

- Social well-being (4 items)
- Sense of community (8 items)
- Strength of identification with ethnic group (2 items), religious group (2 items), nationality (2 items), country of origin (2 items), gender (2 items), age (2 items) and being European (2 items)
- Religiosity (3 items)
- Support for minority rights (11 items)
- Socio-economic status
- Family configuration
- Experience of discrimination
- Left–right political orientation (1 item)

In addition, other occasional questions were inserted into the questionnaire in order to assist the flow of questions and to capture further incidental information. All of the scales contained in the core questionnaire were piloted in all locations and included in the final questionnaire because they displayed acceptable internal reliabilities in the piloting. However, after the main data collection with full samples had taken place, it was discovered that not all scales had functioned equivalently with all national and ethnic groups in all locations. For this reason, each research team derived their own scale scores based on the psychometric analysis of their own datasets. Hence, different analyses were conducted by different teams.

In addition to these core measures, all of which are shown in full below, each team included further measures in their own questionnaires according to their own theoretical orientations and the issues which they wished to examine. These additional team-specific items and scales are not included in the copy of the core questionnaire which follows.

The PIDOP Core Questionnaire

1. **How old are you?** _____

2. **Are you a female or a male?** *Tick one box only.*

    Female………. ☐
    Male………….. ☐

3. **Which best describes you?** *Tick one box only.*

    [A] I was born in [country] and so were my parents. ☐
    [B] I was born in [country] but one of my parents was born in another country. ☐
    [C] I was born in [country] but both my parents were born in another country. ☐
    [D] I was born in another country but both my parents were born in [country]. ☐
    [E] I was born in another country but one of my parents was born in [country]. ☐
    [F] I was born in another country and so were my parents. ☐

4. **What is your citizenship?**

   I am a [country] citizen ☐
   I am a [another country] citizen ☐ ......Which country?_____
   I have double citizenship ☐ ......Which countries?_____

5. **If you were not born in [country], how old were you when you came to this country?** *Write in your age at the time.*

   I was _____ years old when I came to [country].

6. **How often do you speak [language of country] at home?** *Tick one box only.*

   Never................................ ☐
   Sometimes........................... ☐
   Always or almost always............. ☐

7. **Please indicate whether you agree or disagree with the following statements by circling the appropriate number next to each item using the scale provided:**

	Not at all				*To a great extent*
(a) I discuss social and political issues with friends and acquaintances.	1	2	3	4	5
(b) I bring political and social issues into discussions with others.	1	2	3	4	5
(c) I am interested in politics.	1	2	3	4	5

	Never				*Almost every day*
(e) I follow what is going on in politics by reading articles in newspapers or magazines.	1	2	3	4	5
(f) I watch television programmes or listen to radio broadcasts that deal with political issues.	1	2	3	4	5
(g) I pay attention to information on the Internet that is about politics.	1	2	3	4	5

8. **Here, we want you to consider a list of activities and then think: Did I do this in the last year? Do I think this is an effective way to change things? and Will I do it in the future?** *Then you should circle the appropriate number. Please note that* **the higher the number, the more you agree** *that you did it, that you think it is effective, and that you are willing to do it in the future.*

	*Have you **done** any of the following during the last 12 months?* *1 never, 2 rarely, 3 sometimes, 4 often, 5 very often*	*To what extent do you think that these actions are **effective for change** (government, social, ...)?* *1 not at all ... 5 very effective*	*How likely are you to take each of these **actions in the future**?* *1 not likely at all ... 5 very likely*
1. Attend a public meeting or demonstration dealing with political or social issues	1 2 3 4 5	1 2 3 4 5	1 2 3 4 5
2. Do volunteer work	1 2 3 4 5	1 2 3 4 5	1 2 3 4 5
3. Wear a bracelet, sign or other symbol to show support for a social or political cause (a badge, a T-shirt with a political message)	1 2 3 4 5	1 2 3 4 5	1 2 3 4 5
4. Distribute leaflets with a political content	1 2 3 4 5	1 2 3 4 5	1 2 3 4 5
5. Donate money to a social or political cause/ organisation	1 2 3 4 5	1 2 3 4 5	1 2 3 4 5
6. Boycott or buy certain products for political, ethical or environmental reasons	1 2 3 4 5	1 2 3 4 5	1 2 3 4 5
7. Write political messages or graffiti on walls	1 2 3 4 5	1 2 3 4 5	1 2 3 4 5
8. Participate in political actions that might be considered illegal (e.g. burning a flag, throwing stones, ...)	1 2 3 4 5	1 2 3 4 5	1 2 3 4 5
9. Take part in concerts or a fund-raising event with a social or political cause	1 2 3 4 5	1 2 3 4 5	1 2 3 4 5
10. Link news or music or videos with a social or political content to my contacts	1 2 3 4 5	1 2 3 4 5	1 2 3 4 5
11. Discuss societal or political questions on the net	1 2 3 4 5	1 2 3 4 5	1 2 3 4 5

12. Visit a website of a political or civic organisation	1 2 3 4 5	1 2 3 4 5	1 2 3 4 5
13. Participate in online based protest or boycotting	1 2 3 4 5	1 2 3 4 5	1 2 3 4 5
14. Vote in elections	1 2 3 4 5	1 2 3 4 5	1 2 3 4 5
15. Connect to a group on Facebook (or similar online social networks) dealing with social or political issues	1 2 3 4 5	1 2 3 4 5	1 2 3 4 5

9. **Have you done any of the above activities in relation to your/your family's country of origin?**

    Yes ☐   No ☐

    9.1 If yes, which ones _____

10. **Are you planning to do any of the above activities in relation to your/your family's country of origin?**

    Yes ☐   No ☐

    10.1 If yes which ones? _____

11. **Have you ever been part of or collaborated with:** *(please tick the appropriate box)*

	Never	Occasionally	Continually for:	
			Less than 6 months	6 months or more
A. Trade unions or student associations?				
B. Political parties or party youth groups?				
C. Volunteering or charity groups?				
D. Youth associations or groups?				
E. Religious associations or groups?				
F. Associations for the protection of human rights (e.g. human rights, racism, peace, etc.)?				
G. Environmental associations or animal rights groups?				
H. Leisure or recreational associations or groups (e.g. music, art, sports, etc.)?				

12. **Thinking of the most important involvement you had in one of those organisations ... which type of organisation or group was it?**
    _____ (please specify the type of organisation using the letter above)

13. **How would you assess your level of involvement?** *Please circle the appropriate number: 1 corresponds to not actively involved and 5 to very actively involved.*

Not actively involved	1	2	3	4	5	Very actively involved

14. **Are you currently involved in this organisation?:** Yes ☐ No ☐

15. **During the time of that experience have you:**

    (a) looked for information, in books, in the media or by asking others, about the issues discussed in the association or group?

No, never	1	2	3	4	5	Very frequently

    (b) participated in activities such as protests, petitions, meetings, assemblies, parties, debates, etc.?

No, never	1	2	3	4	5	Very frequently

    (c) participated in organising activities such as protests, petitions, meetings, assemblies, parties, debates, etc.?

No, never	1	2	3	4	5	Very frequently

    (d) been directly involved in group decision-making?

No, never	1	2	3	4	5	Very frequently

16. **How would you characterise your feelings during that time?** *Please circle the appropriate number.*

    (a) felt that there were a variety of points of view being discussed?

No, never	1	2	3	4	5	Very frequently

    (b) observed conflicting opinions that brought up new ways of perceiving the issues in question?

No, never	1	2	3	4	5	Very frequently

    (c) seen real and/or everyday life problems being the focus of discussion?

No, never	1	2	3	4	5	Very frequently

(d) felt that participating was very important to you as a person?

No, never	1	2	3	4	5	Very frequently

17. **Now, think of your daily life experiences in your family, your school or work context, and your neighbourhood. To what extent do you agree or disagree with the following statements?** *Please circle the appropriate number next to each item.*

	Never				Very often
1. I have decided for myself on my use (or non-use) of contraceptives.	1	2	3	4	5
2. I am able to choose my friends.	1	2	3	4	5
3. I am able to choose my boy/girlfriend.	1	2	3	4	5
4. I am able to make career choices regarding school or work.	1	2	3	4	5

18. **Now think of your personal experience and indicate your agreement with the following statements:**

	Not at all				To a great extent
1. I would participate in a political cause if I felt strongly about an issue.	1	2	3	4	5
2. I would participate in a political cause if I felt I could learn new things.	1	2	3	4	5
3. I would participate in a political cause if I felt I could influence people.	1	2	3	4	5
4. I would participate in a political cause because I like helping other people.	1	2	3	4	5
5. I would participate in a political cause because it's a nice way to meet new people.	1	2	3	4	5
6. I would participate in a political cause because it would help to create a better society.	1	2	3	4	5
7. I don't get involved in political causes because I'm too young.	1	2	3	4	5
8. No one has ever asked me to get involved in an environmental cause.	1	2	3	4	5
9. No one has ever asked me to get involved in a political organisation.	1	2	3	4	5
10. No one has ever tried to persuade me to vote for or against a particular candidate in an election.	1	2	3	4	5

19. **Please indicate your agreement with the following statements using the scale provided, by circling the appropriate number:**

	Not at all				To a great extent
1. I know more about politics than most people of my age.	1	2	3	4	5
2. When political issues or problems are being discussed, I usually have something to say.	1	2	3	4	5
3. The powerful leaders in government care very little about the opinions of people.	1	2	3	4	5
4. In this country, a few individuals have a lot of political power, while the rest of the people have very little power.	1	2	3	4	5
5. I think that by working together, young people can change things for the better.	1	2	3	4	5
6. By working together, young people are able to influence the decisions which are made by government.	1	2	3	4	5
7. I think that by working together, people from my own ethnic group can change things for the better.	1	2	3	4	5
8. By working together, people from my own ethnic group are able to influence the decisions which are made by government.	1	2	3	4	5
9. I think that by working together, people of my own gender can change things for the better.	1	2	3	4	5
10. By working together, people of my own gender are able to influence the decisions which are made by government.	1	2	3	4	5

Now we have a set of questions about current events that we want you to consider. Think carefully and then select the alternative that you think is correct by ticking ONE of the boxes.

20. **A person with conservative/right-wing political beliefs is most likely to support which one of the following?**
    ☐ Higher taxes for wealthy people
    ☐ State control of utilities (like water and electricity)
    ☐ Strong protection of rights of immigrants
    ☐ Lower government spending on welfare

21. **Which of the following countries is not currently a member state of the European Union?**
    ☐ Denmark
    ☐ Latvia

☐ Switzerland
☐ Estonia

22. **Which one of the following is a difference between a democracy and a dictatorship?**

    ☐ in a democracy people have private property rights
    ☐ in a democracy judges make and change laws
    ☐ in a democracy the government is elected by citizens
    ☐ in a democracy people are not allowed to criticise the government

23. **Please indicate your agreement with the following statements using the scale provided by circling the appropriate number**

	Not at all			To a great extent	
1. My friends would approve it if I engaged politically.	1	2	3	4	5
2. My friends are involved in political actions (e.g. by wearing a badge, taking part in a public demonstration, boycotting certain products, signing petitions, etc.).	1	2	3	4	5
3. My friends would agree that the only way to change anything in society is to get involved.	1	2	3	4	5
4. My parents would approve it if I engaged politically.	1	2	3	4	5
5. My parents are involved in political actions (e.g. by wearing a badge, taking part in a public demonstration, boycotting certain products, signing petitions, etc.).	1	2	3	4	5
6. My parents would agree that the only way to change anything in society is to get involved.	1	2	3	4	5

24. **Do you attend a place of worship (e.g. a church, mosque, temple, synagogue, gurdwara, etc.)?**   Yes ☐   No ☐

If yes, please answer the following questions, using the scale provided by circling the appropriate number:

	Not at all			To a great extent	
1. People at my place of worship would approve it if I got involved in social causes.	1	2	3	4	5
2. People at my place of worship would approve it if I engaged politically.	1	2	3	4	5

25. Please indicate how much you trust or distrust each of the following. How much trust do you have in the following institutions?

	Completely distrust				Completely trust
European Union	1	2	3	4	5
National government	1	2	3	4	5
Local council/government	1	2	3	4	5
Schools and colleges/Universities	1	2	3	4	5
Courts	1	2	3	4	5
Police force	1	2	3	4	5
Political parties	1	2	3	4	5
Banks	1	2	3	4	5
Large companies	1	2	3	4	5
Religions	1	2	3	4	5
Newspapers	1	2	3	4	5
The Internet	1	2	3	4	5
Television	1	2	3	4	5
Non-governmental organisations/charities	1	2	3	4	5

26. Please indicate whether you agree or disagree with the following items by circling the appropriate number next to each item

	Strongly disagree				Strongly agree
1. You can generally trust the people who run our government to do what is right.	1	2	3	4	5
2. When government leaders make statements to the people on television or in the newspapers, they are usually telling the truth.	1	2	3	4	5
3. Those we elected to public office usually try to keep the promises they have made during the election.	1	2	3	4	5
4. Most politicians can be trusted to do what is right without our having to constantly check on them.	1	2	3	4	5
5. Whatever its faults may be, the [country] form of government is still the best for us.	1	2	3	4	5
6. I would rather live under the [country] system of government than any other that I can think of.	1	2	3	4	5

27. **Please indicate your agreement with the following statements using the scale provided:**

	Not at all true				Completely true
1. I feel that most people can be trusted.	1	2	3	4	5

Now take into consideration the situation in your country:

	Not at all				To a great extent
28. Do you believe that there are environmental problems in the country where you live?	1	2	3	4	5
29. To what extent do you feel each of the following emotions when you think about environmental problems you face where you live?	Not at all				To a great extent
(a) Anger	1	2	3	4	5
(b) Frustration	1	2	3	4	5
(c) Hope	1	2	3	4	5
(d) Worry	1	2	3	4	5
(e) Shame	1	2	3	4	5

	Not at all				To a great extent
30. Do you believe there are instances of discrimination against any minority groups in the country where you live?	1	2	3	4	5
31. To what extent do you feel each of the following emotions when you think of instances of discrimination against minority groups where you live?	Not at all				To a great extent
a. Anger	1	2	3	4	5
b. Frustration	1	2	3	4	5
c. Hope	1	2	3	4	5
d. Worry	1	2	3	4	5
e. Shame	1	2	3	4	5

32. **In the following situation, how do you react?** *Please circle the appropriate number on the scale provided:*

	Never				Everyday
When someone is unfairly accused, I stand up for him or her.	1	2	3	4	5

33. **For these questions, please circle the number which best fits your opinion using the scale provided:**

In the last month, how much time did you spend feeling that …	Never				Everyday
1. You belonged to a community (e.g. social group, your school, your neighbourhood)?	1	2	3	4	5
2. Our society is becoming a better place?	1	2	3	4	5
3. People are basically good?	1	2	3	4	5
4. The way our society works made sense to you?	1	2	3	4	5

34. **Below you will find some statements that we want you to consider in relation to the place where you live (your neighbourhood). Please indicate your agreement with each statement using the scale provided:**

	Not at all true				Completely true
1. In this neighbourhood, there are enough activities for young people.	1	2	3	4	5
2. In this neighbourhood, there are opportunities to meet other boys and girls.	1	2	3	4	5
3. I think that people who live in this neighbourhood could change things that are not working properly for the community.	1	2	3	4	5
4. In this neighbourhood, there are many events and situations which involve young people like me.	1	2	3	4	5
5. If only we had the opportunity, I think that we could be able to achieve something special for our neighbourhood.	1	2	3	4	5
6. If the people here were to organise themselves better, they would have a good chance of reaching their desired goals.	1	2	3	4	5
7. In this neighbourhood, young people can find many opportunities to have fun.	1	2	3	4	5
8. Honestly, I feel that if we engage more with relevant social and political issues, we would be able to improve things for young people in this neighbourhood.	1	2	3	4	5

35. **For these questions, please circle the number which best fits your opinion using the scale provided:**

	Not at all				Very
1. How proud are you of being your **ethnicity**?	1	2	3	4	5
2. How important is to you that you are your **ethnicity**?	1	2	3	4	5
3. How proud are you of being your **religion**?	1	2	3	4	5
4. How important is to you that you are your **religion**?	1	2	3	4	5
5. How proud are you of being [**nationality**]?	1	2	3	4	5
6. How important is it to you that you are [**nationality**]?	1	2	3	4	5
7. How proud are you of being from your [**country of origin**]?	1	2	3	4	5
8. How important is it to you that you are from your [**country of origin**]?	1	2	3	4	5
9. How proud are you of being your **gender**?	1	2	3	4	5
10. How important is it to you that you are your **gender**?	1	2	3	4	5
11. How proud are you of being your **age**?	1	2	3	4	5
12. How important is it to you that you are your **age**?	1	2	3	4	5
13. How proud are you of being **European**?	1	2	3	4	5
24. How important is it to you that you are **European**?	1	2	3	4	5

36. **Please indicate how often you do each of the following:**

	Never	Occasionally	Monthly	Weekly	Daily
1. How often do you attend a place of religious worship?	1	2	3	4	5
2. How often do you pray?	1	2	3	4	5
3. How often do you read religious texts?	1	2	3	4	5

37. **Please indicate your agreement with the following statements by circling the appropriate number using the scale provided:**

	Not at all				To a great extent
1. Ethnic minority children should have the same opportunities to study as any other person.	1	2	3	4	5
2. Ethnic minority individuals should earn the same wage when doing the same job as any other person.	1	2	3	4	5
3. Ethnic minority individuals should be entitled to the same social benefits (e.g. health care, unemployment benefit, etc.) as [nationality] people.	1	2	3	4	5

4. Ethnic minority individuals should be granted the same rights as any other person.	1	2	3	4	5
5. Ethnic minority individuals should be allowed to preserve their language.	1	2	3	4	5
6. Ethnic minority children should have the right to learn their language in school.	1	2	3	4	5
7. Ethnic minority individuals should have the right to maintain their traditions and cultural heritage.	1	2	3	4	5
8. Ethnic minority individuals should have the right to build a place to worship a different religion from mine.	1	2	3	4	5
9. Ethnic minority individuals should be granted special rights once they are discriminated against.	1	2	3	4	5
10. Ethnic minority individuals should have a representative in the country's parliament because they are a minority.	1	2	3	4	5
11. It should be made easier for ethnic minority children to enter college/university since they have disadvantages in our society.	1	2	3	4	5

38. **When you were under 14 years old, about how many books were there in your home?** *Do not count newspapers, magazines or books for school; tick one box only.*

    None.................... ☐
    1 – 10………………….. ☐
    11 – 50……………….. ☐
    51 – 100……………. ☐
    101 – 200………….. ☐
    More than 200……. ☐

39. **What was the highest level of education which you completed?** *Tick one box only.*

    Elementary school   ☐
    Secondary school   ☐
    College (A-levels) or Vocational training   ☐
    Bachelor degree   ☐
    Masters degree   ☐
    PhD   ☐

40. **Currently, what is your main occupation?** *Tick one box only.*

    Full time student   ☐
    Part time student   ☐
    Looking for my first job   ☐
    Worker (less than 20 hours per week)   ☐

Worker (more than 20 hours per week) ☐
Unemployed ☐

41. What is your situation? *Tick one box only.*

I am single ☐
I am married or have a partner ☐
I am divorced ☐
I am a widow ☐

42. Do you have children?   Yes ☐   No ☐

42.1. If yes, how many? _____

43. How far in school did your mother and father go? *Tick only one box in each column.*

	Mother	Father
Never attended at school	☐	☐
Finished primary school before age 11	☐	☐
Finished primary school at age 11	☐	☐
Finished secondary school at age 16	☐	☐
Finished secondary school at age 18	☐	☐
Some vocational/technical education after secondary school	☐	☐
Some college or university courses	☐	☐
Completed a Bachelor's degree at a college or university	☐	☐

44. When you were under 14 years old, did it happen (or do you feel) that your household or your parents were unable to pay for food or bills (e.g. for housing, electricity, gas, etc.) on time, due to financial difficulties? *Tick one box only.*

Never…………………….. ☐
Sometimes………………… ☐
Often……………………. ☐
I don't really know………. ☐

45. In which configuration of household do you live currently? *Tick one box only.*

With my two parents……………………………………. ☐
With one parent…………………………………………. ☐
In another parental configuration……………………… ☐
Alone……………………………………………………… ☐
In a couple………………………………………………… ☐

With other persons sharing the dwelling............... ☐
With my husband/wife/partner and children....... ☐
With my children... ☐

46. **Does your income cover everything that your family needs?** *Tick one box only.*

Not at all .... ☐
Partly .... ☐
Mostly .... ☐
Fully.................................... ☐

47. **Have you ever felt excluded or discriminated against?** *Please circle the appropriate number.*

No, never	1	2	3	4	5	Very frequently

48. **If yes, why do you think that you were excluded or discriminated against?** *You can choose more than one option.*

Age....................................... ☐
Education............................ ☐
Religion............................... ☐
Gender................................. ☐
Sexual orientation.............. ☐
Economic status................. ☐
Ethnicity.............................. ☐
Other(s) .... ☐

49. **If yes, where did it happen?** *You can choose more than one option.*

School.. ☐
Work.. ☐
Institution (hospital, city hall)..................... ☐
Public place (street, pub, restaurant, …)......... ☐
Other... ☐
Where? _____

50. **In political terms, how would you describe yourself?** *Please circle the appropriate number.*

Extreme left	1	2	3	4	5	6	7	Extreme right

Appendix D

THE RECOMMENDATIONS FOR POLICY, PRACTICE AND INTERVENTION WHICH EMERGED FROM THE PIDOP PROJECT

Martyn Barrett and David Garbin

Introduction

One of the major goals of the PIDOP project was the formulation of a set of evidence-based recommendations concerning the actions which may be taken by political and social actors to enhance levels of participation among youth, women, minorities and migrants. In order to achieve this goal, the PIDOP project focused directly on policy issues from the outset, auditing existing policies on participation in all of the participating countries and at the EU level (for a selection of some of the work undertaken, see Chapters 22 to 25 in the present volume). In addition, the project built up an extensive network of contacts with policy actors and activists from its inception. These included representatives of local community and civil society organisations, governance actors at regional, national and EU levels, and policy development organisations at regional, national and EU levels.

Communications with these external stakeholders were open and bidirectional. The aim was to ensure that the research project addressed issues of concern to the stakeholders and that the recommendations that were to be formulated would meet their needs. Policy stakeholders were kept informed about the progress of the project through a series of newsletters and policy briefing papers that were distributed at regular intervals throughout the lifetime of the project.[1] Some of the stakeholders also input ideas into the PIDOP project and participated in two conferences which took place in the second and third years of the project (held at the University of Bologna, Italy, and the University of Surrey, UK, respectively).[2]

As the project drew to a close, this process culminated in the formulation of a set of detailed policy recommendations, which drew together in a single document all of the recommendations for policy, practice and intervention which had emerged from the project. These recommendations were developed through an audit of the findings that had been obtained in the policy analysis work (see Chapters 20 to 23 in the present volume), the secondary analysis of existing survey data (see Chapter 11), and the focus groups, interviews and survey conducted by all nine research teams in the project (see Chapters 12 to 19 for reports of some of this work).

In drawing up the recommendations, particular attention was paid to common findings that had appeared across many national locations and among many of the ethnic groups under study. These more general findings included young people's cynicism towards politicians, the significance of internal efficacy as a predictor of participation, the importance of organisational membership for participation and the importance of having had previous high-quality experiences of participation. However, the formulation of the recommendations also took into account the variations and differences in political and civic participation (and in the predictors of participation) which the project uncovered across national contexts, age groups, genders and ethnic groups. The project revealed that these variations were pervasive. This in turn implied that policies and interventions to enhance participation may need to be tailored to specific demographic subgroups living in particular countries. The recommendations therefore took due note of both the generalities and the specificities uncovered by the research.

The initial draft of the recommendations was subjected to the scrutiny of the entire PIDOP consortium as well as the scrutiny of an external sounding board comprising of specialist policy experts, activists and academics with substantial expertise in the field of political and civic engagement and in issues concerning participation among youth, women, minorities and migrants.[3] The recommendations underwent considerable revision and refinement as a consequence of this review.

The final set of recommendations that emerged from this process describe the concrete actions that may be taken by politicians, political institutions, media producers, educational professionals, schools and civil society actors to enhance political and civic participation among youth, women, minorities and migrants.

All of the recommendations were based directly on the findings from the project. They were broken down under the following four main headings:

- Recommendations for politicians and political institutions
- Recommendations for media producers and media organisations
- Recommendations for ministries of education, educational professionals and schools
- Recommendations for civil society actors, including youth workers, youth and leisure centres, youth and education NGOs and leaders of ethnic minority communities.

The following presentation of the PIDOP policy recommendations reproduces text from the final policy recommendations document.[4]

Recommendations for politicians and political institutions

1. Our findings show that young people often feel that they are not taken seriously in political terms by politicians and other older adults. This lack of

responsiveness reduces their belief in their own ability to have any influence politically or civically and is experienced as a significant disincentive to engage any further with political issues.

- Young people should be treated more attentively and with greater respect by politicians and other adults. Politicians need to show young people that they do listen and pay attention to their views on civic and political matters, individually and as a group.
- There should be better and more concrete responses by politicians and political institutions to specific forms of youth participation – such as public protests or student demonstrations – so that young people can feel that their voices are being heard.
- At national and European levels, mechanisms should be found to allow a greater involvement of young politicians (through political parties and through appointments to policy-making and decision-making bodies) which could support the identification of young people with leaders of government and with political decision-makers. For example, age quotas are one such mechanism which could be introduced. This is especially important in countries where politics and decision-making are dominated by older generations and younger people are marginalised by political institutions.

2. We also found that young people below the age of 18 years often perceive themselves as excluded from political processes and institutions, and feel disenchanted due to the fact that they are denied fundamental forms of political and civic participation on the grounds of their age.

- In order to encourage greater levels of political and civic engagement among youth aged between 16 and 18 years, national governments should consider lowering the age of voting to 16 years.

3. Our study revealed that young people frequently feel that politicians make little or no attempt to communicate with them, and are not interested in utilising those means of communication which young people themselves use to communicate with each other.

- Politicians and political institutions at all levels (local, national and European) need to engage in better and more effective communication with young people, so that young people can feel that political systems are interested in and concerned with their needs and perspectives on civic and political affairs.
- Such communication between politicians and young people should take advantage of the new social media which are popular among young people themselves (e.g. Facebook, Twitter and YouTube).

4. Our study found that young people are more concerned with civic and non-conventional forms of participation (e.g. charitable activities, consumer activism,

demonstrations and petitions) than with conventional forms of participation (e.g. voting).

- Politicians and policy-makers should view civic and non-conventional forms of participation as equally important as conventional forms of participation, and should address, and provide feedback on, issues which have been raised through these alternative forms of activism.

5. Our study also revealed that membership of organisations is a major predictor of both civic and political participation. Greater involvement in organisations is associated with more interest and attentiveness towards civic and political issues, and with higher levels of civic and political participation among young people.

- National, regional and local governments should ensure that all youth have access to membership of a range of organisations, including youth and leisure centres, sports clubs, cultural centres, local community centres, etc., and should encourage youth to take up membership of these organisations.

Issues relating to ethnic minorities and migrants

6. Our study revealed that young members of ethnic minority and migrant groups often perceive themselves as being excluded and alienated from political processes because of the prejudice and inequity which they commonly experience.

- There should be a more systematic and consistent implementation of EU anti-discrimination laws, which would help to counter the development of feelings of exclusion and alienation among ethnic minority and migrant communities as a consequence of the prejudice and inequity which they experience.
- Political institutions should make more effort to promote equal access to politics for minorities and migrants, for instance by developing more effective links between political parties and ethnic minority and migrant individuals.

7. We found that young members of ethnic minority and migrant groups often feel resentful and disenchanted about being denied fundamental forms of political participation (such as voting) because they do not possess citizenship of the country in which they are living.

- European countries should re-examine the legal framework surrounding the granting of citizenship to permanent residents within their borders, with the view to making citizenship as inclusive as possible.
- Non-nationals and third-country individuals who have been in residence within a country for a specified period of time should be included in the political and civic spheres to a greater extent by granting them voting rights, particularly at the local level.

8. We discovered that young recent immigrants frequently lack knowledge about majority group laws, conventions and regulations pertaining to civic and political participation.

- More information directed specifically at immigrant groups should be disseminated by government institutions through NGOs working with immigrant communities.

Issues relating to women

9. Our study revealed that there are many obstacles that hinder the civic and political participation of women. Female youth often perceived biases against women and in favour of men both in the workplace and in the political sphere. In addition, in some countries, and among some ethnic groups, we found that young women's participation was further hindered by the need to undertake paid employment at an early age, early educational dropout and/or early marriage.

- National governments, political parties and political institutions should promote and implement equal rights and equal access policies more effectively, with the goal of achieving equal access to education, work and politics for women.
- National governments, political parties and political institutions should guarantee gender equity in the political and institutional spheres, not only in fielding candidates for election but also in their own internal administrative and institutional structures.
- Government institutions should use an approach to the monitoring of political, civic and work issues which is sensitive to the interests, approaches and needs of both men and women.

Issues relating to all groups

10. Our research revealed that the participatory experiences of young people are often specific to particular subgroups defined in terms of gender, ethnicity and age (e.g. specific to younger females from an Angolan background, or to older males from a Bangladeshi background).

- Political and civic institutions and policy-makers should give more support to specific groups defined through the intersection of gender, ethnicity and age in order to encourage greater levels of participation by particular groups that have specific needs and concerns.
- Political and civic institutions and policy-makers need to be more aware of the internal diversity which exists within all national and ethnic groups, and alert to the fact that different policies may be required to meet the needs of different subgroups, including those of girls and young women as well as

those of boys and young men. This should occur at all levels in the political and civic systems, but it is especially important that institutions and policy-makers at the local level are aware of this variability and internal diversity.

European citizenship

11. On the specific issue of the European Union, we found that youth often view the EU as an entity which takes decisions following a top-down process. The consequence is that there is a perception of exclusion and distance and thus a very low sense of belonging to a civic EU sphere. In addition, in some countries, there are high levels of Euro-scepticism and a marked lack of knowledge of European political institutions (for instance, about MEPs, the European Parliament, the European Commission, etc.) among youth. These perceptions and lack of knowledge hinder the construction of a European citizenship and restrict the willingness of young people to participate at the European level.

    - The European Commission should take steps to promote greater knowledge of the mechanisms and role of the EU. More information about European politics and institutions should be disseminated by European institutions to schools, to youth or leisure centres, and to NGOs working with youth, in order to challenge pre-conceived ideas, misinformation and lack of knowledge about European institutions.
    - The European Commission should take steps to involve young EU citizens in its activities more directly, for example by mounting a Youth Internship scheme through which young people would be able to gain first-hand experience of working within the Commission and other European institutions.
    - The European Commission should also consider expanding, strengthening and extending the lifetime of the Youth in Action programme, especially those activities within the programme (such as Youth Exchanges, Youth Initiatives, Youth Democracy Projects and European Voluntary Service) that are dedicated to promoting young people's social, cultural, educational, political and voluntary service experience either in their own country or in other countries. These activities provide significant opportunities for youth participation, intercultural exchanges and experiences, and the construction of a European identity through direct personal experience.

12. Additional recommendations addressed specifically to ministries of education are included below under the heading 'Recommendations for ministries of education, educational professionals and schools'.

Recommendations for media producers and media organisations

13. Our research revealed that the mass media and new social media are important for young people, and that TV, radio and the Internet are among the main

sources of influence and points of reference for youth in developing an understanding of other groups within society and for developing opinions on civic and political issues. There is a considerable responsibility on those who produce content for the mass media to represent individuals and groups, and civic and political matters, in a fair and just manner.

- Those who produce content for the mass media should avoid using distorted images and stereotypes of youth, women, ethnic minorities and migrants in their media productions, and should ensure that they do not contribute to the dissemination and perpetuation of myths about these groups.
- Media organisations should set up and effectively publicise communication channels to enable youth, women, ethnic minorities and migrants to have the opportunity to provide feedback on how they have been represented in the media.
- Media organisations should ensure that youth, women, ethnic minorities and migrants have the opportunity to express their own points of view on civic and political matters within media productions.
- Broadcasters, journalists and media organisations should help to establish a higher public awareness of those youth, women, ethnic minorities and migrants who are actively involved in the civic and political spheres, and who may therefore act as positive role models for young people to become involved.
- To address the disinterest towards political issues exhibited by many young people, there should be an incorporation of more engrossing political television productions into the programme scheduling of major national broadcasting networks, which would help to enhance the appeal of the political sphere in the perceptions of young people.

14. Our research also revealed that, when young people engage in acts of political participation, they often feel that the news media fail to represent their participatory actions with fairness and seriousness of purpose, and this is experienced as a significant disincentive to engage any further with political issues.

- The news media should represent the participatory actions of young people – such as participation in protests and demonstrations – with greater fairness, respect and seriousness, so that young people can feel that their arguments and positions are being accurately and impartially represented by the news media.
- The news media should not focus exclusively on the negative, disruptive or anti-social incidents that occur at young people's participation events such as demonstrations, but should instead give equal attention to the positive and well-intentioned character of demonstrations and other social and political participatory efforts by youth.

15. Our research found that young people rely especially on the Internet and new social media (i.e. Facebook, Twitter and YouTube) for obtaining information

about the civic and political spheres. It is therefore important that they learn to recognise the risks and biases which may be encountered in these media.

- Media literacy programmes should be included as a core element in school curricula with the active participation of media organisations, and children and young people should be alerted to the risks and biases which they may encounter on the Internet and on popular web-based social networks.
- Broadcasters, journalists and media organisations should also provide more tools on how to evaluate the credibility of information provided, and they should also encourage critical interaction with young viewers/recipients rather than the passive consumption of media content.

16. As has been noted already, we found that young recent immigrants frequently lack knowledge about majority group laws, conventions and regulations pertaining to civic and political participation.

- More information directed specifically at immigrant groups should be disseminated through those online, print and broadcast media that work with immigrant communities.

Recommendations for ministries of education, schools and educational professionals

The role of schools

17. Our findings reveal that young people frequently feel that they do not know enough about political issues to be able to engage in effective action to influence political, civic and social change. This lack of knowledge is experienced by young people as a significant impediment to their own civic and political participation.

- Ministries of education should ensure that more effective education and information is provided by schools about political and civic issues, and about how to become involved in politics and other voluntary spheres of activity.
- Ministries of education should consider the introduction or the strengthening of civic/citizenship education in the school curriculum.

18. We also found that young people commonly report that they have relatively little experience of civic and political participation, and those experiences which they have had are often viewed negatively and as being of low quality. This is worrying, insofar as we also discovered that the quality of participation is a significant predictor for many types of civic and political participation. Our research further shows that young people often have a pronounced interest in issues at the local (rather than the national) level (including issues of litter, graffiti, local transport, local amenities, etc.) and in broader environmental,

humanitarian and human rights issues at the international or global levels. Their interests in these areas can be harnessed to provide them with high-quality participation experiences.

- Schools should provide a greater range of opportunities for young people to obtain practical experience of active civic and political participation, and should facilitate positive high-quality participation experiences through school projects and volunteering activities that are embedded in the local community in particular.
- Schools should also be more active in raising awareness among young people of campaigns and projects involving environmental, humanitarian and human rights issues at the international or global level, and should encourage young people to obtain participatory experiences by joining these campaigns and projects.
- Because the development of the skills which are required for active citizenship depends not only on the acquisition of knowledge but also on the accumulation of practical experience, students should be given more responsibility in schools through participation in democratic decision-making with teaching staff, so that they learn democracy and participation through their daily practical experience (and not only through formal civic/citizenship education classes).
- All schools should have a school council or parliament, in which elected students may gain experience of representing the concerns of their fellow students and experience of engaging in joint decision-making with teaching staff.
- The implication of the two preceding recommendations is that schools should consider adopting a whole-school approach to the practice of democracy.
- Schools should also disseminate to their students information about local and national youth parliaments and their role.
- Extensive materials on Education for Democratic Citizenship and Human Rights Education have been produced by the Council of Europe. These materials provide an excellent resource which could be used much more widely by teachers and other educational professionals both for teaching about civic and political issues, and for generating positive participation experiences for young people. Ministries of education should set up more effective channels for communicating information concerning the Council of Europe's materials in this area to teachers, teacher trainers and other education professionals within their country.
- The European Commission and/or the Council of Europe, working in collaboration with ministries of education, should consider creating a programme of 'Youth Ambassadors for Democratic Citizenship and Participation', aimed at raising awareness among young people of the value and importance of civic and political participation.

19. In addition, our research revealed that the low engagement of young people civically and politically is often related to lack of time and to involvement in other activities (mainly school work and paid employment).

- Schools should take steps to ensure that their students have sufficient time to undertake civic and political activities, and should consider the attainment of high-quality participatory activity as a formal educational objective.

The psychological predictors of participation

20. Our study examined in detail the various psychological factors that predict the different forms of civic and political participation. We found that opinionation (i.e. having opinions on civic and political issues) can sometimes act as significant predictor of a range of different forms of civic and political participation.

- Schools and universities should identify and implement ways to stimulate opinionation. For example, they should consider:
  - the introduction, or expanding the number, of debating clubs in order to promote political interest and opinionation;
  - hosting public question-and-answer sessions involving politicians to stimulate interest in political matters;
  - organising 'mock elections' in order to encourage young people to form opinions.

21. We also found that the predictors of participation sometimes also include both collective efficacy (i.e. the subjective belief that, working together as a group, citizens can achieve civic and political change) and individual efficacy (i.e. the subjective belief that, as an individual, one is able to understand and to participate in politics effectively).

- Schools should not only develop mechanisms for greater collective opportunities for civic and political participation, but also encourage opportunities for individual participation among students.

22. However, our study also revealed that the psychological determinants of participation can vary according to the specific type of participation concerned.

- Educationalists who are developing interventions aimed at enhancing levels of political and civic participation should be mindful that different forms of intervention may be required to enhance different types of participation.

23. We also found that forms and levels of participation, and influences on participation, can vary according to young people's age, gender and ethnic status.

- Educationalists who are developing interventions aimed at enhancing levels of political and civic participation should be mindful that different forms of intervention may be required for younger vs. older individuals, women vs. men, and minority vs. majority individuals.

24. Overall, however, our research revealed that, irrespective of the specific form of participation and irrespective of people's age, gender and ethnic status, the most consistent psychological predictors of political and civic participation are political interest and internal efficacy (i.e. the subjective belief that, as an individual, one is able to understand and to participate in politics effectively).

- Educationalists who are developing interventions aimed at enhancing levels of political and civic participation should focus on amplifying the political interest and internal efficacy of young people in particular. Thus educational programmes in civic/citizenship education should be aimed primarily at:
    - enabling young people to acquire an interest in political and civic affairs;
    - fostering their knowledge and understanding of political and civic matters;
    - supporting the development of the skills which they require to participate effectively in the political and civic life of their community and country.

Issues relating to gender and minority/migrant status

25. Our research also uncovered some further specific issues concerning the gender gap and minority/migrant individuals which educational institutions need to address.
26. We found that many youth are not aware of the gender gap in many aspects of the civic and political domains.

- To promote a more gender-sensitive culture, schools should provide training and education on gender issues in the civic and political domains.

27. We also found evidence that schools sometimes deal with minority issues in a tokenistic and simplistic manner, which is often resented by minority individuals themselves.

- Schools need to encourage young people from ethnic minority and migrant groups to take part in projects promoting participation and citizenship in an inclusive and non-tokenistic way. Following an inclusive approach to civic engagement and political participation, schools should avoid 'singling out' minority youth for special treatment.
- It is especially important for schools to ensure equal opportunities for minorities and migrants within the education system, and to take active steps to prevent the exclusion of minorities (such as the Roma communities in Europe).

28. There was also evidence in our study that teachers do not always understand the complexities of the subjective identities of minority and migrant youth.

- Schools should recognise the fact that minority and migrant youth may have a fluid sense of their own identities which combines the culture of their parents' homeland, the culture of the country in which they are living and other cultures specific to youth.

Recommendations for civil society actors, including youth workers, youth and leisure centres, youth and education NGOs and leaders of ethnic minority communities

29. Youth workers, youth and leisure centres, youth and education NGOs and leaders of ethnic minority communities often play an important role in relationship to youth, including hard-to-reach and disengaged youth. Their role in shaping youth engagement emerged clearly from our research, and the activities which they provide for youth need to be encouraged.
30. However, our research also found that these actors sometimes need to provide youth with better education about political issues and about how to become involved in politics and other voluntary spheres of social and civic life. There are some specific ways in which the activities of civil society organisations and actors could be channelled more effectively towards enhancing youth participation.

    - Youth workers, youth and leisure centres and youth and education NGOs should strengthen activities requiring shared decision-making between youth and adults in different community contexts, for instance in leisure, sports and volunteering activities. In particular, they should involve young people in decisions concerning the orientation of activities, their organisation and the procedures which will be followed in their pursuit.
    - Youth and leisure centres, and youth and education NGOs, working in collaboration with local government departments, should support schools in providing a greater range of opportunities for young people to obtain practical experience of active civic and political participation, and should facilitate positive high-quality participation experiences embedded in the local community in particular.
    - Youth workers, youth and leisure centres and youth and education NGOs should also disseminate information about programmes designed to promote volunteering in civic issues and participation in campaigns on environmental, humanitarian or human rights issues. This should include disseminating information about volunteering opportunities across national boundaries through programmes such as the European Voluntary Service.
    - Youth and leisure centres and youth and education NGOs should also improve social inclusion processes and guarantee equal opportunities for women, minorities and migrants in order to increase civic engagement and political participation among these subgroups.

- Youth workers, youth and leisure centres and youth and education NGOs should disseminate information about local and national youth parliaments and their role.
- Stronger links should be established between regional or local youth agencies and the European Youth Forum, to enable the youth for whom they provide services to benefit from the activities of the EYF and to give them greater voice, influence and opportunities for participation.

31. Our research also shows the importance of organisational membership for participation. We found that greater involvement in organisations is associated with more interest and attentiveness towards civic and political issues, and with higher levels of civic and political participation by young people.

- Civil society organisations should make greater efforts to attract young people, particularly disengaged youth who are not members of any organisations. Such youth should be offered a wide range of organisational opportunities for participation and the opportunity to obtain high-quality participation experiences within organisations.
- Women's organisations should also make greater efforts to reach out to girls and young women, and to offer them a wide range of organisational opportunities for participation and the opportunity to obtain high-quality participation experiences.

Issues relating to ethnic minorities and migrants

32. We found that ethnic minority and migrant youth are often especially engaged with issues concerning or affecting their own ethnic community. This interest can be built upon to provide these youth with high-quality participation experiences, to develop their participatory skills and to raise their awareness about participation and citizenship through volunteering.

- Ethnic community leaders, youth agencies and NGOs should encourage young people from ethnic minority and migrant groups to take part as volunteers in projects involving their own ethnic community. Such projects might, for example, focus on heritage and cultural issues, promote the role of their own community in a multicultural environment, challenge ethnic stereotypes or promote inclusion.

33. We also found that minority and migrant youth often have a high level of interest in their country of origin or the country of origin of their parents, even when these youth are themselves citizens of the country in which they are living.

- Ethnic community leaders, youth agencies and NGOs should encourage young people to become actively involved in environmental, humanitarian, human rights or governance issues in their families' countries of origin.

Conclusion

Harmonious living within culturally diverse democratic societies requires citizens to participate actively in the life of the societies to which they belong while simultaneously respecting the fundamental principles of democratic processes, human rights and the rule of law. There are many steps which can be taken by a wide range of political and social actors to enhance, encourage and support young people in developing appropriate patterns of civic and political participation. It is hoped that the current set of evidence-based policy recommendations will assist political and social actors to contribute towards this goal.

Notes

1 The newsletters and policy briefing papers may be freely downloaded from the PIDOP project website: http://www.fahs.surrey.ac.uk/pidop/.
2 Details of the two conferences are also available on the PIDOP project website.
3 We would like to express our thanks, in particular, to the following individuals who generously provided extensive commentaries on the draft recommendations: Udo Enwereuzor (COSPE – Co-operation for the Development of Emerging Countries, Florence, Italy), Annette Lawson (National Alliance of Women's Organisations and The Judith Trust, London, UK), Giovanni Moro (Fondaca – Active Citizenship Foundation, Rome, Italy), Reinhild Otte (Education for Democratic Citizenship and Human Rights, Council of Europe, Strasbourg, France), Sylvie Rohanova (PIDOP Project Officer, European Commission, Brussels, Belgium) and Judith Torney-Purta (University of Maryland at College Park, Maryland, USA).
4 This document may be freely downloaded as a pdf file from the PIDOP project website: http://www.fahs.surrey.ac.uk/pidop/

NAME INDEX

Abramson, P. 36
Adler, R. 98, 99, 100
Ajzen, I. 238, 254
Albanesi, C. 137, 191, 468
Albano, R. 270
Almond, G. 37, 97
Amadeo, J. 457, 474
Amnå, E. 29, 55, 63, 65, 66, 157, 191, 252, 464, 475, 476
Amâncio, L. 406
Anderson, M. 136
Andrews, R. 443–4
Anduix, E. 474
Arena, G. 440
Arneson, R. 112
Atkeson, L. 314
Aughey, A. 90
Azevedo, C. 170, 464

Banducci, S. 41
Barber, C. 473, 475
Barnes, S. 67, 100
Baron, R. 278
Barroso, J. 378, 386, 387, 450
Barrett, M. 1, 6, 22, 31, 189, 193, 464, 470, 494
Bar-Tal, D. 90
Beck, U. 504
Bee, C. 22, 373, 374, 375
Beiner, R. 403
Benson, M. 45
Berger, B. 74, 80, 99, 100
Berlusconi, S. 76
Berry, J. 242–3

Blair, T. 438, 445
Bolzendahl, C. 67
Born, M. 22, 191, 472
Bozkurt, S. 374, 474
Brady, D. 165
Brady, H. 101
Braun, V. 356
Briggs, R. 80
Brooks, R. 22
Bronfenbrenner, U. 133, 172
Brown, G. 445
Brunton-Smith, I. 6, 22, 164, 165, 182, 189, 196, 203, 209
Burgess, P. 293
Burns, N. 59

Campbell, A. 87, 88, 89
Campbell, C. 133, 134
Capelos, T. 22
Carpini, M. 99
Chavis, M. 135
Christensen, H. 41, 46, 47
Cicognani, E. 30, 176, 191, 468
Cioni, E. 269
Císař, 27, 466
Claggett, W. 36
Claibourn, M. 60, 64
Clarke, V. 356
Closa C. 379
Cnaan, R. 130
Coffe, H. 67
Çok, F. 374
Collom, E. 238, 255
Converse, P. 150

Name index

Conway, M. 59
Crouch, C. 503
Crystal, D. 171

Dahl, R. 503
Dalton, R. 41, 42, 43, 46, 47
Davies, J. 444
de Boer-Buquicchio, M. 495
de Varennes, F. 75
De Vos, B, 293
Dean, S. 79
DeBell, M. 171
Deutsch, F. 41, 45, 46, 47
Di Gioia R. 270
Diani, M. 36
Diez, T. 385–6
Duverger, M. 54

Eggert, N. 274, 287
Ekman, J. 29, 55, 63, 65, 66, 157, 252, 464
Elff, M. 60
Emler, N. 22, 30, 31, 348, 468
Erdogan, R. 348
Evans, S. 136

Fanning, B. 80
Farthing, R. 312
Faulks, K. 442, 443
Feldman, L. 170
Fennema, M. 80, 312
Fernandes-Jesus, M. 192, 348
Ferreira, P. 374
Finkelstein, A. 132
Florin, P. 135
Follesdal, A. 379
Foucault, M. 403
Fournier, B. 191, 472

Galligan, Y. 22, 28, 473
Garbin, D. 22
Garry, J. 28, 29
Gavray, C. 191, 472, 473, 474, 475
Gerson, K. 158
Geys, B. 86, 166
Ghai, Y. 72, 77
Giugni, M. 274, 287
Glanville, J. 172
Goggin, J. 98, 99–100
Göksel, A. 423
Grandi, R. 439
Granovetter, M. 157
Greenberg, E. 171
Grunig, J. 440
Guerrina, R. 22, 373

Habermas, J. 76, 444
Hajer, M. 410
Hanquinet, L. 271
Hansen, J. 36, 314
Hardy, C. 384
Heidbreder, E. 384
Hendry, L. 270
Hibbing, J. 103, 106
Hobbes, T. 111
Huckfeldt, R. 36
Hughey, J. 137
Hunt, T. 440
Husfeldt, V. 256
Hutton, B. 359

Inglehart, R. 59, 64

Jackman, R. 41
Jacobs, J. 158
Jay-Z 355, 359, 361, 365, 366
Jedwab, J. 75
Jenkins, S. 154, 155
Jennings, M. 168
Joffe, H. 356
Jovchelovitch, S. 133, 134
Jugert, P. 190, 470

Kaase, M. 67, 100
Karp, J. 41
Kaufmann, J. 303
Kenny, D. 278
Keyes, C. 137
Kiliç, K. 422–3
Kim, Y. 191, 475, 476
Kinder, D. 155
Klandermans, B. 125, 127, 128, 178
Knack, S. 152
Knocke, D. 35, 36
Kohler-Koch, B. 382, 384
Kurtaran, Y. 422
Kuzmanovic, D. 422

Laclau, E. 385
Lauckhardt, J. 250
Lay, J. 467
Lazarfeld, P. 37–8
Leach, C. 127
Leahy, P. 293
Leighley, J. 36
Levine, R. 238
Lewis, J. 404
Lijphart, A. 41, 42
Lister, R. 403
Livingstone, S. 474

Lockerbie, B. 36
Lombardo, E. 404
Lovenduski, J. 59
Lyons, E. 22, 255

Macek, P. 22, 190
Maggiotto, M. 89
Magnette, P. 383
Major, J. 154, 438, 442, 443
Malafaia, C. 192, 374
Malcolm X 359
Mallett, R. 128
Mancini, P. 440
Marcelo, K. 312
Marien, S. 46, 330
Marinelli, A. 269
Marinetto, M. 438, 443
Marko, J. 76
Marsh, M. 87, 88
Marshall, T. 501
Mazzoni, D. 191, 468
McAdam, D. 36, 153
McBride, C. 29
McFarland D. 270
McGhee, D. 444
McMillan, W. 135
McPherson, M. 157, 158
Medieros, M. 89
Meehl, P. 152
Melzel, H. 37
Menezes, I. 22, 170, 192, 256, 272, 374, 464
Merkel, A. 76, 386
Messina, A. 73
Miller, D. 128
Montgomery, V. 28
Moro, G. 441, 442, 458, 459, 548
Mouffe, C. 380, 385

Nata, G. 256
Nie, N. 34, 101, 151, 152, 153, 157, 178
Niemi, R. 256
Niemoller, C. 89
Noack, P. 22, 190, 470
Noel, A. 89
Norris, P. 43, 59, 64, 74

O'Keeffe, D. 379
Obst, P. 136
Omoto, A. 131
Otte, R. 458

Pachi, D. 193
Palermo, F. 76

Parry, G. 101
Pascall, G. 404
Pasek, J. 170
Pateman, C. 404
Pattie, C. 238, 254
Paxton, P. 270, 314
Pelizzoni, L. 441
Penner, L. 131, 132, 139
Pereira, P.S. 412, 413
Perkins, D. 135
Petrovičová, Z. 190
Philips, N. 384
Pierson, J. 89
Pitkin, H. 79
Przeworski, A. 37
Putnam, R. 44, 80, 98, 99, 157, 158, 441

Quintelier, E. 272, 284

Randall, V. 59
Rapoport, R. 314
Ratcliffe, P. 444
Ribeiro, N. 192, 374
Richardson, B. 89
Roberts, H. 90
Roche, M. 380, 398
Rochon, T. 45
Rosenstone, S. 35, 314
Rousseau, J-J. 113, 115

Sanchez-Jankowski, M. 467
Santos, M. 406
Sapiro, V. 60, 64
Sarason, S. 135
Schmitt, H. 89
Schudson, M. 97, 103, 105
Schumpeter, J. 97, 110
Şener, T. 22
Šerek, J. 190, 476
Sherrod, L. 250
Shussman, A. 36
Simon, B. 127, 128, 312
Sinha, S. 76
Smith, D. 130–31
Smith, E. 127
Smith, H. 125
Snyder, M. 131
Soule, S. 36
Sprague, J. 36
Stevenson, N. 293
Stoll, M. 312

Taft, J. 475
Tajfel H. 126

Tarrow, S. 153
Taspinar, O. 78
Teney, C. 271
Teorell, J. 36, 101, 103
Teune, H. 37
Thatcher, M. 154, 438, 442, 443
Theiss-Morse, E. 103, 106
Thomas, R. 270
Tillie, J. 80, 312
Torney-Purta, J. 180, 256, 457, 473, 475
Tyler, T. 125

Ugba, A. 72–3
Uhlaner, C. 36

van der Eijk, C. 89
van der Meer, T. 42, 46
van der Stoel, M. 72
van Deth, J. 45, 60
Van Londen, M. 81
van Stekelenberg, J. 125, 128
van Zomeren, M. 125, 127, 128, 178, 256
Verba, S. 34, 36, 37, 46, 74, 97, 100, 101
Verloo, M. 404
Villano, P. 374, 375
Voet, R. 404

Vráblikova, K. 27, 42, 45, 46, 47, 154, 155, 157, 164, 466

Wallström, M. 383
Walther, A. 294
Wandersman, A. 135
Weber, M. 97
Weiler, J. 379
Weisberg, H. 89
Weldon, S. 42
Welzel, D. 41, 45, 46, 47
Wentzel, K. 465
Whiteley, P. 44
Wielhouwer, P. 36
Wiener, A. 380
Woelk, J. 76
Wollheim, R. 114
Wong, J. 312
Wright, S. 125

Yardley, L. 356
Yeich, S. 238
Youniss, J. 271

Zani, B. 1, 22, 30, 178, 191, 468, 469
Zukin, C. 170

SUBJECT INDEX

abstention/abstaining from voting 85–94, 421
adolescents *passim*
agency 7–8, 109–22, 270, 273, 362
Albanians 18, 202, 273–88, 462
Amnesty International 411, 412, 413–14
Angolans 18, 192, 315–30, 462
apathy *see* interest/disinterest, passivity, standby citizens
Arab League Education, Cultural and Science Organisation (ALECSO) 490
associational/organizational membership 4, 5–6, 8, 9, 10, 11, 12, 16, 19, 28, 30, 31, 36, 47, 55, 68, 80–1, 98, 99, 101, 105, 130, 131, 140, 152, 155–6, 157, 159, 162, 165–6, 167, 168, 170, 171–2, 173–5, 177, 178, 179, 190, 191, 195–209, 213–27, 233, 236–43, 249, 268–88, 301, 302, 306, 307, 313, 315, 316, 317, 334, 353, 421, 422, 424, 441, 464, 468, 507, 508, 509, 519; *see also* churches and church youth leaders,
attentiveness, political 6, 12, 19, 30, 65, 150, 153, 176, 177, 178–82, 192, 199, 200, 202, 242, 307, 315, 317–18, 322, 326–7, 328, 329–30, 339, 341, 342, 343, 344–6, 462, 464, 519, 538, 547

Bangladeshis 18, 193, 202, 354–68, 462
barriers to participation 16, 18, 19, 30, 31, 78, 79, 138, 140, 177, 193, 216, 219, 244, 262, 263, 272–3, 301, 303, 307, 337, 339, 341–6, 354, 356, 362–6, 367, 404, 406, 424, 426, 473, 476, 519

Belgium/Belgians 12, 13, 17, 56, 57, 58, 79, 105, 191, 198, 202, 244, 292–306, 462, 464, 468, 469, 470, 471, 472, 473, 477, 492
benefits of participation 7–9, 30, 40, 75, 86, 109, 120, 126, 128, 151–2, 178, 179, 181; *see also* costs of participation
blogging 5, 74, 269, 474
books, household 174, 175, 236, 299, 313, 315, 316, 317, 322–8; *see also* mass media, newspapers, television
books, school textbooks 169, 173, 174, 175, 468, 481
boycotting 5, 6, 35, 67, 101, 147, 169, 195, 217, 236, 278, 317, 462; *see also* buycotting, consumer participation
Brazilians 18, 192, 202, 315–29, 462
Britain/British 60, 74, 77, 90, 148, 202, 436–52; *see also* England/English youth, Northern Ireland
Bulgaria 75, 148, 335–6
Bulgarian resettlers *see* Turkish resettlers from Bulgaria
buycotting 6, 147; *see also* boycotting, consumer participation

Campaign for Diversity against Discrimination 394
campaigning *see* political campaigning
Catholicism/Catholics 18, 64, 89–93, 94, 165
Christianity/Christians 64, 76, 89, 335, 336, 364; *see also* Catholicism/Catholics, Kimbanguism/Kimbanguists, Protestantism/Protestants

554 Subject index

churches and church youth leaders 156, 170, 193, 354–67, 508; *see also* religion
citizen, defined 3–4; *see also* standby citizens
citizenship *passim*
Civic Education Study (CIVED) 21, 165, 170, 254–5, 457, 461–77
civic engagement/participation *passim*; defined: 4–6; *see also* associational/organizational membership, boycotting, buycotting, community service, consumer participation, collective action, donating to charities, fund-raising, volunteering/volunteerism; *see also* conventional political engagement/participation, non-conventional/unconventional political engagement/participation
civil society 3, 20, 22, 43, 45, 56, 64, 65, 100, 105, 264, 315, 377–98, 404, 410–15, 422, 424, 439, 441–2, 443, 445, 446–8, 449, 451, 452, 486, 535, 536, 546–7: *see also* non-governmental organisations (NGOs)
collective action 30, 31, 99, 115, 119, 120, 121, 124–9, 137, 139, 141, 154, 177–83, 303, 312, 347, 359, 362, 367, 422, 443, 466, 473, 506, 508; *see also* marches, protests, rallies
collective efficacy 19, 126, 129, 134, 138, 140, 176–7, 178, 179, 181, 190, 227, 238, 239, 240, 250, 256, 257, 258, 259, 261, 262, 303, 307, 341, 342, 344, 345, 346, 348, 457, 465, 466, 467, 468–70, 473, 519, 544
Commission on Women's Rights and Gender Equality 412, 413
community *passim*; defined 4
community identification/identity 136
Community of Democracies 491
community, sense of *see* sense of community
community service 6, 10, 99, 132, 140, 171, 271, 389, 466, 507, 540, 546
Comparative Study of Electoral Systems (CSES) 17, 38, 148, 189, 197
Conference of International Non-Governmental Organizations (CINGO) 485
Congolese 18, 193, 354–68, 462
Congress of Local and Regional Authorities (CLRA) 485
Conservative Party (UK) 90, 154–5, 442–3
consumer participation 6, 11, 74, 101, 102, 104, 118, 168, 171, 474, 495, 502, 537; *see also* boycotting, buycotting

context *see* macro-level context, meso-level context, micro-level context
Convention on Human Trafficking 413
conventional political engagement/participation 4–6, 9, 11, 17, 20, 22, 27, 31, 65–9, 74, 96–8, 102–6, 148, 150, 154, 155, 162, 164, 165, 167, 180, 182, 195–209, 234, 237–8, 240, 292, 300, 313, 352, 374, 404, 407, 420, 421, 422, 424, 426, 428–9, 431, 459, 462, 463, 465, 470, 471, 474, 477, 495, 504, 506–7, 508; *see also* donating to political causes, electoral participation, letter-writing, political campaigning, political party identification, political party membership, voting; *see also* civic engagement/participation, non-conventional/unconventional political engagement/participation
cost-benefit analysis/calculations *see* benefits of participation, costs of participation
costs of participation 30, 34, 40, 45, 86, 114, 126, 128, 151–2, 178, 179, 181; *see also* benefits of participation
Council of Europe (CoE) 9, 75, 412, 413, 458, 480–96, 543
Council of Europe Charter on Education for Democratic Citizenship and Human Rights Education (2010) 486–7, 488–9
Country Indicators for Foreign Policy (CIFP) 201
Czech Republic/Czechs 12, 13, 14, 17, 56, 57, 58, 60, 64, 190, 202, 213–27, 462, 469, 471, 472, 477, 492

deliberation/deliberative democracy 8, 20, 29–30, 76, 109–22, 271, 373–4, 377–8, 439–40, 444, 445–6, 447, 457, 466, 467–8, 469, 473–4, 510
democracy *passim*; *see also* deliberation/deliberative democracy, direct democracy, electoral democracy, minimalist model of democracy, parliamentary democracy, participatory democracy, representative democracy
democratic ownership 20, 27, 29–30, 109–22, 463, 467, 470
demographic factors 9, 12, 13, 16, 17, 19, 20, 21, 27, 28, 30, 31, 78, 86, 131, 134, 136, 138, 182, 189, 193, 207–8, 287, 508
demonstrations *see* marches, protests, rallies
deprivation, relative 125, 127
determinants of political and civic engagement and participation *see* demographic factors, economic factors,

historical factors, macro level factors, population characteristics, psychological level factors, social level factors
direct democracy 110–11, 113, 116, 171
discrimination 58, 71, 72, 73, 75, 76, 77, 138, 167, 177, 192, 200, 214, 215–16, 224–5, 235, 238, 249, 250, 256, 257, 258, 259, 261, 268, 274, 287, 294, 295–6, 297, 300, 302, 304, 305, 306, 307, 318, 320–2, 328, 329, 330, 337, 347, 348, 354, 358, 389, 390, 391, 393, 394–6, 412, 425, 450, 451, 466, 472, 473, 475, 476, 520, 538; *see also* prejudice, racism
disengagement *passim*; defined 6; *see also* standby citizens
disposition and predisposition for political and civic engagement *see* psychological level factors
distrust 6, 103, 106, 347, 348, 349, 441, 501, 503, 505, 508, 510; *see also* trust
donating to charities 6, 101, 147, 216, 236, 269, 278, 317
donating to political causes 4, 5, 12, 68, 101, 147, 195, 216, 236, 317
dual path model of protest 128, 508

economic factors 11, 13, 16, 27, 31, 34, 39, 41, 42–4, 46, 47, 54, 56–7, 58, 59, 78, 80, 116, 133, 163, 164, 165, 167, 173, 174, 197, 201, 203, 215, 269, 298, 300, 301, 304, 328, 349, 361, 367, 393, 414, 416, 420, 422, 423, 427, 436, 446, 462, 466, 476, 481, 482, 502, 508; *see also* socio-economic status (SES)
Education for Democratic Citizenship/Human Rights Education (EDC/HRE) 458, 480–96, 543
education ministries, recommendations from PIDOP project for 542–6
education professionals, recommendations from PIDOP project for 542–6; *see also* teachers
education 9, 11, 12, 16, 20, 22, 28, 30, 31, 35, 43, 45–6, 54, 56, 57, 58, 59, 62, 66, 74, 77, 78, 130, 138, 140, 149, 150–1, 152, 155, 158, 168, 169–70, 171, 198, 201, 215, 234, 235, 236, 244, 294, 295, 298, 303, 321, 329, 336, 337, 339–40, 363, 364, 367, 378, 379, 383, 388, 389, 396, 397, 405, 407, 411, 415, 422, 423, 424, 427, 428, 430, 451, 457–8, 461, 463, 464, 468, 474, 475, 476, 480–96, 508, 536, 539, 542–6
efficacy *see* collective efficacy, external efficacy, internal efficacy

election turnout *see* voter turnout
elections 4, 5, 55, 58, 65, 67, 85–94, 100, 106, 147, 148, 152, 162, 163, 197–8, 276, 298, 415, 438, 539
electoral campaigning *see* political campaigning
electoral democracy 415
electoral institutions 7, 9, 13, 28–9, 31, 40–1, 60, 61–2, 77, 78–80, 81, 86–7, 163, 167, 171, 174, 197, 234, 508, 509
electoral participation 40, 41, 42, 43, 44–5, 74, 78, 85–94, 99, 100, 101, 104, 148, 151; *see also* voter turnout, voting
emotions 16, 19, 30, 31, 73, 93, 125, 127–8, 129, 135, 136–7, 138, 139, 139, 177, 192, 199, 222, 244, 250, 256, 257, 258, 259, 261, 303, 307, 339, 341, 342, 343, 344, 345, 346, 469, 475, 519; *see also* feelings
employment/unemployment 12, 56, 58, 59, 62, 159, 167, 170, 201, 215, 235, 295, 296, 298, 301, 305, 318, 321, 336, 338, 365, 368, 388, 389, 390–1, 393, 396, 406, 411, 414, 422, 423, 426, 427, 428, 430, 451, 473, 474, 482, 539, 544
empowerment 7, 56, 57, 129, 133, 134, 138, 140, 141, 298, 348–9, 359, 411, 414, 443, 446, 447, 452, 473, 476, 495, 495, 502
England/English 12, 13, 17, 18, 193, 352–68, 436–52, 462, 469, 471, 472, 473, 475, 477, 492; *see also* Britain/British
equality/inequality 8, 37, 45, 46, 112, 116, 117, 125, 158–9, 334, 357, 444, 494, 495; *see also* gender equality/inequality, minority/migrant equality/inequality
ethnic identification/identity 81, 190, 215, 219, 227, 334
ethnic minorities *passim*
Eurobarometer 17, 189, 195, 197
European citizenship 377, 378–84, 390, 436, 437, 448–51, 501, 540
European Convention on Human Rights (1950) 480–1
European Court of Human Rights 81
European Cultural Convention (1954) 483
European Institute of Gender Equality 57, 63
European integration 377–98, 448, 449
European Network against Racism 398
European Roma Rights Center 337
European Social Survey (ESS) 17, 38, 67, 189, 195–209
European Union (EU) 13, 15, 16, 17, 21, 56, 57, 58, 63, 72, 135, 146, 153, 195,

214, 224, 273, 297, 301, 307, 335, 373–4, 375, 377–98, 404, 410, 412–15, 427, 437, 439, 448, 449–52, 462, 480, 484, 485, 487, 490, 503, 535, 538, 540
European Women's Lobby 398, 450
European Year of Equal Opportunities for All 412
European Youth Forum 398, 450
European Youth Week 389
expectations of youth participation held by influential others 352–68
external efficacy 19, 73, 79, 126, 176, 180, 181, 182, 192, 196, 199, 200, 202, 242, 307, 339, 340, 341, 342, 343, 344, 345, 346, 347, 368, 519

factors influencing political and civic engagement and participation *see* demographic factors, economic factors, historical factors, macro level factors, population characteristics, psychological level factors, social level factors
family 4, 13, 16, 31, 54, 55, 56, 87, 131, 135, 138, 140, 158, 168–9, 172, 173, 174, 175, 176, 192, 198, 215, 218, 221, 222, 234, 249, 294, 295, 298, 299, 301, 302, 303, 318, 321, 328, 338, 340, 352, 353, 359, 364, 391, 405, 412, 422, 423, 426–7, 429, 430, 432, 464, 473, 474, 476, 484, 495, 501, 508, 520; *see also* parents
feelings 4, 6, 10, 16, 59, 61, 62, 67, 73, 97, 105, 125, 127, 128, 131, 132, 134, 135, 139, 152, 162, 177, 191, 192, 213, 219, 222, 223, 224, 226, 271, 274, 286, 288, 297, 300, 301, 305, 307, 318, 328, 336, 341, 342, 343, 344, 345, 346, 348, 349, 366, 510, 538; *see also* emotions
females *passim; see also* gender, gender equality/inequality
focus groups/focus group findings in the PIDOP project 18, 190, 193, 217, 219, 222, 233, 235, 237, 273, 274, 275, 294, 296–9, 301, 313, 315–16, 318–22, 330, 337–8, 354, 355, 365, 368, 462, 463, 465, 472, 494, 512–15, 516, 536
focus group guide used in the PIDOP project 512–15
Framework Convention for Protection of National Minorities (EU, 1998) 75
Freedom House Index 41, 46, 47
friends 4, 5, 99, 105, 131, 157, 170–1, 172, 200, 215, 221–2, 238, 243, 301, 303, 304, 317, 338, 474; *see also* peers
Fundamental Rights Agency (EU) 490
fund-raising 5, 6, 170, 278, 317

gender 9, 11, 13, 17, 18, 19, 28, 54–69, 91, 130, 138, 148, 159, 169, 182, 191–2, 204, 205, 234, 238, 254, 269–70, 275, 278, 279, 280, 283, 284, 285, 286, 287, 294, 297, 299, 301–7, 312, 313, 314, 315, 316, 318, 321–2, 323, 325, 326, 329–30, 339, 374, 381, 391–3, 397, 403–16, 423, 424–9, 451, 465, 466, 467, 469, 470–5, 476, 501, 502, 519, 520, 536, 539, 544, 545–6; *see also* gender equality/inequality
Gender Equality Index (GEI, EU) 56, 472
gender equality/inequality 56–8, 63, 64, 191–2, 297, 302, 303, 304, 334, 374, 381, 390–3, 403–16, 424–8, 450, 451, 466, 472–3
Gender Toolkit 473
General Social Survey (GSS) 157
German resettlers from Russia 18, 236, 462
Germany/Germans 12, 13, 14, 18, 38, 56, 57, 58, 60, 63, 78, 190, 202, 232–44, 386, 415, 462, 468, 469, 470, 471, 472, 473, 475, 477, 482, 492
Gezi Park protests (Turkey) 347, 348, 424, 426, 432
Global Gender Gap Index (GGI, World Economic Forum) 56, 57, 472
globalisation 71, 503
goals, personal 139, 177
government *passim; see also* policy, legal institutions, public institutions, recommendations for politicians and political institutions
graffiti 5, 217, 300, 317, 338, 358, 424, 542

Hague Programme (EU) 394
historical factors 9, 16, 31, 58, 76, 135–6, 163, 164–5, 167, 173, 174, 197, 216, 217, 234, 251–2, 304, 305, 314–15, 337, 349, 388, 420, 422, 481, 503
Human Rights Education *see* Education for Democratic Citizenship/Human Rights Education (EDC/HRE)

ICCS *see* International Civics and Citizenship Study
ideology/ideological commitment 30, 46, 149, 150, 154–5, 173, 182, 200, 202, 227, 241, 244, 422, 436, 437, 438, 442
identification/identity *see* community identification/identity, ethnic identification/identity, national identification/identity, religious identification/identity, political party identification/identity, social identification/identity

Subject index 557

illegal forms of participation 5, 67, 68, 102, 125, 149, 178, 179, 181, 195, 217, 317, 358, 366, 463; *see also* graffiti
immigrant youth *passim*
immigrants *passim*
inequality *see* equality/inequality
injustice *see* perceived injustice
institutions *see* electoral institutions, legal institutions, public institutions
instrumentalism 111–12
integration *see* European integration, social/societal integration, theoretical integration
interest/disinterest, political 4, 6, 9, 10, 12, 19, 28, 29, 30, 34, 43, 46, 47, 54, 59–69, 74, 80, 87, 87, 88, 97, 98,101, 103, 104–5, 138, 150, 153, 156, 156, 159, 162, 165, 166, 168, 170, 176, 180, 181, 182, 189, 192, 199, 200, 202, 204, 205, 222, 234, 241–2, 250, 252, 254–5, 257–61, 269, 300, 302, 304, 305, 306, 307, 315, 317, 322, 326–7, 328–30, 339, 341–6, 352, 353, 422, 484, 464, 470, 475, 519, 538, 541, 542–3, 544, 545, 547
internal efficacy 19, 59, 150, 168, 170, 176, 178, 179, 180, 181, 182, 189, 199, 200, 205, 242, 302, 307, 339, 341, 342, 343, 344, 345, 346, 347, 519, 536, 545
International Association for the Evaluation of Educational Achievement (IEA) 463
International Civics and Citizenship Study (ICCS) 463, 475
International Committee of Red Cross (ICRC) 491
International Contact Group on Citizenship and Human Rights 490
International Social Survey Programme (ISSP) 17, 38, 67, 147, 148, 189, 195, 197, 200–6
Internet activism *see* online activism
intervention, recommendations for 3, 9, 14, 19–20, 22, 170, 208, 535–48; *see also* recommendations
interviews/interview findings in the PIDOP project 15, 18, 19, 193, 306, 340, 354–68, 374, 375, 410, 414–16, 436, 437, 438, 445–52, 462, 463, 465, 468, 472, 510, 516–18
interview schedule used in the PIDOP project 516–18
Iraqis 18, 191, 251–65, 462, 475
Islam/Muslims 14, 74, 78, 243, 294–306, 335, 334–49, 491
Italy/Italians 12, 13, 18, 56, 57, 58, 60, 133, 191, 202, 268–88, 373, 374–5, 436–52, 462, 464, 468, 469, 470, 471, 472, 475, 492

Justice and Development Party (JDP) (Turkey) 337, 426, 427, 430, 431, 426

Kimbanguism/Kimbanguists 355
knowledge, political 6, 12, 19, 29, 30, 59, 60, 64, 104, 138, 147, 165, 169, 170, 177, 178, 179, 180, 181, 199, 242, 314, 339, 465, 519
Kurds 18, 191, 251–65, 334, 462, 475

latent class analysis 196, 206–8
leaders of ethnic minority communities, recommendations from PIDOP project for 546–7
Learning and Living Democracy for All Programme 491
legal institutions 31, 163, 164, 165, 173, 174
legitimacy 7, 8, 22, 71, 76, 81, 109, 111–15, 117, 120, 148, 292, 311, 379, 381, 382, 439, 509
letter-writing 5, 170, 180
Lisbon Strategy 412
Lisbon Treaty 415

macro level factors 9, 12, 13, 15–16, 17, 19, 20, 21, 27–9, 30–1, 33–49, 54–69, 71–81, 85–94, 146–8, 153–6, 162, 163–8, 172–6, 182–3, 189, 193, 196, 197, 200–6, 234, 349, 373, 466, 508
marches 4, 5, 98, 338, 357; *see also* collective action, protests, rallies
mass media 16, 31, 168, 171, 173, 174, 175, 540–2; *see also* books, newspapers, television
media organisations, recommendations from PIDOP project for 540–2
media producers, recommendations from PIDOP project for 540–2
membership of associations and organization *see* associational/organizational membership
meso level factors 36–7, 39, 45, 47, 49, 172–3, 176, 508; *see also* social level factors
micro level factors 17, 34–5, 38–9, 45, 172–3, 176, 196, 199, 201, 204, 205, 466, 508; *see also* psychological level factors, social level factors
migrants *passim*
minimalist model of democracy 97, 109, 110–11, 113, 117
ministries of education, recommendations from PIDOP project for 542–6
minorities *passim*

minority/migrant equality/inequality 28, 72–3, 76, 77, 273, 294, 394, 395, 396
mobilisation 11, 16, 27, 30, 34, 36, 37, 38, 39, 41, 43–4, 46, 47, 48, 49, 66, 80, 87, 88, 155, 157, 159, 273, 293, 300, 301, 303, 312, 352, 368, 392, 441, 444, 466, 508, 510, 517, 518
monitorial citizens 97–8, 102, 103, 105, 506; *see also* standby citizens
Moroccans 17, 18, 191, 274, 276–88, 294–307, 462, 475
motivations for participation 10, 13, 16, 18, 19, 30, 31, 34, 35, 127, 131, 138, 139, 153, 154, 169, 170, 172, 174, 175, 177, 178, 179, 181, 182, 183, 191, 199, 215, 216, 219, 238–40, 250, 255, 257, 258, 259, 262, 264, 298, 301, 304, 307, 335, 337, 339, 341, 342, 344, 345, 346, 354, 368, 452, 495, 505, 507, 508, 519
musicians' (hip-hop and rap) expectations for participation 193, 352–68
Muslims *see* Islam/Muslims

national identification/identity 295, 299, 303, 307, 458, 500, 520
neo-liberalism 379, 437–8, 440–1, 442, 443, 444
New Labour (UK) 438, 442–4, 447–8
newspapers 4, 98, 121, 171, 174, 175, 180, 199, 318, 337, 364; *see also* books, mass media, television
NGOs *see* non-governmental organisations
non-conventional/unconventional political engagement/participation 4–5, 11, 17, 20, 27, 31, 69, 74, 139, 147, 148, 162, 164, 182, 195–209, 234, 292, 304, 311, 314, 352, 407, 420, 421, 424, 426, 431, 459, 462, 463, 470, 495, 504–5, 506–7, 538; *see also* blogging, boycotting, buycotting, consumer participation, collective action, donating to charities, fund-raising, graffiti, illegal forms of participation, letter-writing, marches, online activism, protests, rallies; *see also* civic engagement/participation, conventional political engagement/participation
non-governmental organisations (NGOs) 15, 20, 21, 43, 301, 303, 373, 374, 375, 378, 393, 395, 396, 398, 410–17, 422, 424, 438, 445–52, 458, 476, 485, 486, 487, 490, 491, 494
non-governmental organisations, recommendations from PIDOP project for 546–8

non-participation *passim*; *see also* standby citizens
norms for participation 16, 19, 28, 47, 56, 68, 69, 76, 86, 125, 131, 133, 138, 139, 140, 173, 174, 180, 181, 191, 199, 219, 221, 238–40, 243, 250, 251–65, 339, 377, 381, 384, 465, 470, 471, 475, 477, 519
Northern Ireland 12, 13, 14, 18, 29, 76, 79, 85–94, 462, 492

obstacles to participation *see* barriers to participation
Office of High Commission for Human Rights (OHCHR) 485, 490, 491
opinions/opinionation 4, 6, 7, 8, 10, 16, 29, 30, 31, 66, 103, 147, 149, 150, 152, 155, 156, 162, 169, 170, 176, 178, 179, 181, 182, 199, 200, 202, 219, 220, 222, 227, 237, 271, 277, 293, 297, 304, 306, 474, 476, 541, 544
online activism 5, 74, 103, 104, 111, 190, 216–27, 234, 236–9, 251, 255, 264, 269–70, 278, 300, 304, 317, 464, 474, 476, 542; *see also* blogging
Organisation for Economic Cooperation and Development (OECD) 491
Organisation of American States (OSA) 490
Organization for Security and Cooperation in Europe/Office for Democratic Institutions and Human Rights (OSCE/ODIHR) 485, 490, 491
organizational membership *see* associational/organizational membership
ownership, democratic *see* democratic ownership

parents 9, 18, 57, 105, 140, 168–9, 172, 173, 175, 191, 193, 221–2, 236, 238–40, 248–65, 293, 298, 299, 303, 305, 317, 337, 338, 352–3, 352–68, 382, 422, 423, 430, 458, 461, 473, 474, 475, 496
Parliamentary Assembly of Council of Europe (PACE) 485
parliamentary democracy 147, 483
participation *passim*
participatory democracy 7–9, 15, 378, 382, 384, 397, 398, 438, 441, 443, 446, 447
parties, political *see* political parties, political party identification/identity, political party membership
passivity, political and civic 16, 27, 29, 96–106, 213, 250–1, 260, 264; *see also* standby citizens
peers 16, 31, 55, 63, 66, 136–7, 138, 140, 170–1, 173, 174, 175, 176, 198, 221, 224,

234, 238–40, 249, 464, 465, 470, 514; *see also* friends
perceived injustice 10, 120, 125, 126, 127, 128, 129, 139, 177, 178, 179, 181, 224, 226, 295, 305, 354, 358, 469; *see also* social justice
petitions 4, 5, 35, 55, 63, 66, 67, 74, 101, 102, 125, 147, 162, 163, 169, 170, 195, 198, 216, 234, 236, 277, 297, 300, 317, 352, 356, 360, 421, 463, 474, 510, 514, 538
PIDOP *see* Processes Influencing Democratic Ownership and Participation (PIDOP)
Plan D for Democracy, Dialogue and Debate (EU) 382, 283, 450
Policy Migration Group 450
policy recommendations *see* recommendations
policy 1, 3, 4, 9, 13, 14, 15, 19–20, 21, 22, 28, 34, 35, 61, 71, 77, 78, 100, 112, 147, 150, 152, 154, 159, 163, 215, 249, 271, 273, 293, 298, 299, 315, 335, 337, 373–452, 458, 462, 463, 464, 466, 468, 473, 475, 477, 481, 485–96, 502, 503, 504, 507, 510, 535–48
political attentiveness *see* attentiveness, political
political campaigning 4, 5, 10, 12, 55, 68, 101, 152, 162, 163, 171, 180, 195, 196, 495
political engagement/participation *passim*; defined: 4–6
political institutions, recommendations from PIDOP project for 536–40
political institutions *passim*
political interest/disinterest *see* interest/disinterest, political
political knowledge *see* knowledge, political
political opportunity structure (POS) 16, 38, 41, 42, 167, 173, 174, 420
political parties 4, 10, 68, 101, 149, 171, 237, 306, 352, 424; *see also* political party identification/identity, political party membership
political party identification/identity 10, 29, 85–94, 149–50, 352; *see also* political parties, political party membership
political party membership 5, 42, 43, 65, 68, 96, 195, 196, 250, 301, 311, 421, 423, 424, 461, 462, 470; *see also* political parties, political party identification/identity
politicians, recommendations from PIDOP project for 536–40

population characteristics, as factor affecting engagement/participation 28, 31, 86, 88, 93, 166, 167, 173, 174, 197
Portugal/Portuguese 12, 13, 18, 56, 57, 58, 63, 192, 198, 202, 311–30, 374, 403–16, 462, 469, 470, 471, 472, 492
predictors of political and civic engagement and participation *see* demographic factors, economic factors, historical factors, macro level factors, population characteristics, psychological level factors, social level factors
prejudice 71, 215, 222, 224, 226, 295, 320, 395, 538; *see also* discrimination, racism, stereotypes
proceduralism 112–19, 122
Processes Influencing Democratic Ownership and Participation (PIDOP) project: *passim*; *see also* focus groups/focus group findings in the PIDOP project, interviews/interview findings in the PIDOP project, survey/survey findings in the PIDOP project
Protestantism/Protestants 18, 64, 89–93, 165, 197
protests 4, 5, 9, 10, 11, 12, 30, 38, 40, 41, 42, 43, 45, 46, 47, 49, 63, 68, 74, 100, 101–2, 104, 124–9, 137, 147, 152, 168, 169, 192, 195, 217, 277, 278, 292, 312, 314, 317, 318, 338, 347, 348, 374, 421, 424, 426, 429, 431, 432, 463, 470, 495, 506, 507, 508; *see also* collective action, marches, rallies
psychological engagement *passim*; defined 4, 6; *see also* attentiveness, emotions, feelings, ideology/ideological commitment, interest, knowledge, opinions/opinionation, values
psychological level factors *passim*
public institutions 15, 28, 61, 76, 385, 410, 411, 413, 421, 428, 431, 436, 439, 440, 441, 443, 447, 448, 503, 504, 510, 539

quality of participation experience 19, 138, 191, 192, 268, 272, 274–7, 287, 339, 341, 342, 343, 344, 345, 346, 348, 349, 470, 519, 536, 542, 543, 544, 546, 547
questionnaire used in the PIDOP project 519–34

racism 11, 78, 127, 295, 320, 322, 329, 394, 398, 444, 495, 512; *see also* discrimination, prejudice
rallies 98, 128, 147, 234, 358, 475; *see also* collective action, marches, protests

recognition, symbolic 133, 134
recommendations from PIDOP project: for educational professionals 542–6; for leaders of ethnic minority communities 546–7; for media organisations 540–2; for media producers 540–2; for ministries of education 542–6; for political institutions 536–40; for politicians 536–40; for schools 542–6; for youth and education NGOs 546–7; for youth and leisure centres 546–7; for youth workers 546–7
religion 4, 6, 11, 16, 19, 54, 55, 63, 64, 65, 68, 72, 73, 75, 77, 79, 91, 138, 164, 165, 166, 167, 169, 171, 190, 191, 195, 198–9, 233, 236, 237, 238, 240–3, 244, 260, 264, 270, 272, 277, 294, 295, 297–304, 305, 307, 316, 334, 335, 337, 339, 348, 353, 354, 358, 361, 364, 366, 390, 394, 476, 501, 507, 513, 520; *see also* Christianity/Christians, churches and church youth leaders, Islam/Muslims, religious identification/identity
religious identification/identity 299, 335, 339
representative democracy 96, 97, 103, 110, 116, 415, 441, 446, 503
Republican People's Party (RPP) (Turkey) 430
republicanism 380, 383, 390, 437–8, 440–1, 442, 500
resettlers *see* German resettlers from Russia, Turkish resettlers from Bulgaria
resources for participation 16, 27, 28, 30, 30, 31, 34–5, 36, 37, 39, 42, 43, 46, 55, 58, 59, 61, 67, 68, 77, 80, 126, 129, 133, 134, 151, 152–3, 155, 165, 166, 168, 174, 175, 176, 177, 192, 199, 271, 299, 314, 317, 318, 321, 328–9, 373, 406, 467, 476, 484, 494, 508, 510
rights, civil 133, 260
rights, minority 19, 71, 164, 169, 250, 256, 258, 259, 334, 335, 339, 509, 520; *see also* equality/inequality
rights, political 72–3, 75, 147, 149, 201, 216, 425, 472
Roadmap for Equality between Men and Women 412
Roadmap for Gender Equality (EU) 391–2, 392–3, 451
role identity model 131, 132, 508
Roma 17, 18, 190, 192, 213–26, 334–48, 462, 545
Rule of Law Indicator (World Bank) 46, 47

school 6, 10, 20, 47, 135, 139, 140, 169–70, 172, 174, 175, 176, 218, 233, 234, 243, 271, 293, 297, 298, 299, 300, 301, 303, 304, 305, 306, 313, 319, 336, 353, 357, 362–3, 367, 423, 457, 461, 463, 464, 465, 466, 468, 469, 470, 473, 474, 475, 476, 481–96, 508, 540, 542–6; *see also* teachers
schools, recommendations from PIDOP project for 542–6
sense of community 19, 124, 129, 133, 135–7, 138, 140, 191, 268–88, 339, 341, 342, 343, 344–6, 348, 457, 467, 468–70, 473, 509, 510, 520
service/service learning *see* community service
significant others *see* musicians, parents, peers, teachers, youth workers
social cohesion *see* social/societal integration
social identification/identity 16, 30, 31, 120, 125, 126–7, 128, 129, 133, 134, 136, 137, 138, 139–40, 177, 178, 240, 337, 508; *see also* community identification/identity, ethnic identification/identity, national identification/identity, religious identification/identity, political party identification/identity
Social Identity Model of Collective Action (SIMCA) 128–9, 129
social justice 15, 78, 80, 81, 125, 304, 353, 392, 414, 464, 472; *see also* perceived injustice
social level factors *passim*
social movements 35, 36, 38, 40, 41, 43, 49, 68, 125, 140, 163, 178, 179, 181, 272, 381, 470, 474, 477, 504, 505, 506; *see also* collective action, protest
social norms *see* norms for participation
Social Platform (EU) 398, 450
social/societal integration 15, 28, 71–81, 137, 140, 167, 191, 215, 233, 242–3, 244, 249, 263, 273–4, 275, 276, 287, 288, 294–5, 300, 312, 315, 380, 394, 437, 442, 444–5, 446, 447, 451
social well-being *see* well-being
socio-economic status (SES) 9, 10, 12, 13, 16, 19, 28, 31, 34, 35, 36, 38, 39, 46, 59, 72, 73, 134, 138, 168–9, 174, 175, 198, 235, 248, 286, 328, 336, 476, 508, 520; *see also* economic factors
standby citizens 29, 66, 96–106, 157, 252; *see also* monitorial citizens
stereotypes 214–15, 216, 222, 224, 226, 296, 305, 391, 393, 395, 541, 547; *see also* prejudice

Subject index 561

Strategy for Equality between Women and Men (EU) 392
survey questionnaire used in the PIDOP project 519–34
survey/survey findings in the PIDOP project 17, 19, 190–2, 213–349, 461–75, 493, 519–34
Sweden/Swedes 12, 13, 18, 29, 56, 57, 58, 60, 63, 104, 105, 148, 191, 198, 202, 248–65, 462, 464, 468, 469, 470, 471, 472, 473, 475, 477

teachers 18, 170, 173, 174, 175, 193, 198, 298, 306, 352–68, 423, 461, 468, 481, 483, 488–9, 493, 543, 545; *see also* education professionals
teachers, recommendations from PIDOP project for 542–6
television 4, 158, 171, 199, 298, 318, 541; *see also* books, mass media, newspapers
theoretical integration 19, 146–59, 162–183
theory of planned behavior (TPB) 238–9
trade unions 4, 43, 65, 156, 157, 164, 167, 195, 219, 236, 237, 241, 276, 422, 507
transnationalisation 387–92, 395, 438, 448–51
transnationalism 4, 73, 382, 414
Treaty of Amsterdam (1997) 394
Treaty of Lausanne (1923) 335
Treaty of Lisbon (2007) 383
Treaty of London (1949) 480
Treaty of Maastrict (1993) 377
Treaty of Rome (1957) 379
trust 7, 10, 16, 19, 28, 29, 34, 36, 44–5, 47, 61, 67, 69, 87, 98, 99, 137, 138–9, 165, 167, 168, 170, 177, 180, 181, 182, 192, 198, 199, 200, 202, 204, 205, 215, 219, 222, 223, 224–5, 234, 271, 298, 301, 304, 307, 339, 341–6, 347–8, 353, 354, 431, 441, 466, 507, 508, 509, 519; *see also* distrust
Turkey/Turks 12, 13, 14, 17, 18, 56, 57, 58, 60, 61, 66, 190, 191–2, 202, 232–44, 294–307, 334–49, 374, 386, 420–32, 462, 464, 475, 490, 492
Turkish resettlers from Bulgaria 18, 192, 335–6, 339–48, 462
turnout, election *see* voter turnout

Ukrainians 17, 190, 213–27, 462
unconventional political participation, *see* non-conventional/unconventional political participation
unemployment *see* employment/unemployment

UNESCO 485, 490, 491
United Kingdom (UK) 13, 56, 57, 58, 90, 154, 202, 355, 373, 374–5, 436–52, 464; *see also* Britain/British, Northern Ireland
United Nations 335

values 6, 12, 16, 27, 28, 31, 35, 39, 43, 44, 45, 46–7, 56, 74, 75, 76, 100, 130, 131, 132, 133, 134, 139, 149, 170, 173, 174, 176, 191, 303, 304, 305, 306, 353, 357, 364, 381, 382, 405, 416, 423, 430, 432, 442, 443, 447, 448, 449, 458, 470, 474, 480, 482, 483, 484, 492, 496, 504, 508
Voice and Accountability Index 41, 47
volunteer process model (VPM) 131–2, 508
volunteering/volunteerism 6, 9, 10, 12, 30, 31, 55, 57–8, 63–5, 124, 129–32, 135, 139, 141, 162, 168, 169, 170, 177, 178, 179, 180, 181, 182, 183, 233, 236, 237, 241, 269, 271, 272, 274, 276, 278, 287, 312, 317, 352, 462, 463, 466, 495, 510, 543, 546, 547
voter turnout 9, 13, 28–9, 34, 38, 40–1, 43, 44, 65, 67, 73, 74, 79, 80, 85–94, 96, 100, 103, 111, 148, 151, 163, 166, 197–8, 205, 311, 50–1; *see also* electoral participation
voting 4, 5, 7, 9, 10, 11, 12, 13, 17, 20, 22, 27, 29, 31, 33, 35, 40, 41, 43, 44, 45, 54, 55, 65, 67, 73, 74, 78–9, 80, 81, 85–94, 98, 100, 101, 102, 111, 116, 118, 136, 141, 146, 147, 148, 151–2, 154, 162, 163, 164, 165, 166, 167, 169, 170, 171, 177, 178, 179, 180, 181, 182, 183, 195–209, 232, 235, 249, 250, 269, 293, 296, 303, 307, 313, 325, 329, 334, 352, 353, 356, 366, 421, 422, 429, 461, 462, 463, 466, 484, 495, 505, 506, 507, 508, 509, 512, 537, 538

Wallonia 191, 292–307; *see also* Belgium/Belgians
web activism see online activism
well-being 6, 8, 19, 42, 130, 133, 137, 138, 191, 224, 242, 268–88, 300, 302, 306, 339, 357, 358, 520
women *passim*; *see also* gender, gender equality/inequality
work *see* employment/unemployment, workplace
workplace 9, 10, 16, 31, 158, 168, 171, 172, 173, 174, 175, 176, 458, 464, 466, 473, 474, 476, 539
World Economic Forum 56

World Programme for Human Rights Education (2005) 490, 491
World Values Survey (WVS) 17, 59, 60, 62, 66–7, 189, 195, 200–6, 510

youth and education NGOs, recommendations from PIDOP project for 546–7

youth and leisure centres, recommendations from PIDOP project for 546–7
Youth in Action programme 388, 390, 540
youth workers, recommendations from PIDOP project for 546–7
youth workers 18, 20, 193, 352, 354–5, 357–8, 360, 361–4, 367, 536
youth *passim*